CONFLICTING MISSIONS

CONFLICTING MISSIONS

Havana, Washington, Pretoria

Piero Gleijeses

GALAGO

GALAGO BOOKS

Galago Books are published by Galago Publishing (1999) (Pty) Ltd
PO Box 404, Alberton, 1450, Republic South Africa
Web address: www.galago.co.za

Galago Books are distributed by Lemur Books (Pty) Ltd
PO Box 1645, Alberton, 1450, Republic South Africa
Tel: (Int + 2711 – local 011) 907-2029. Fax: 869-0890
Email: lemur@mweb.co.za

First published by The University of North Carolina Press in 2002 as
Conflicting Missions: Havana, Washington and Africa: 1959-1976
by Piero Gleijeses

This South African edition first published by Galago, November 2003 as
Conflicting Missions: Havana, Washington, Pretoria
by Piero Gleijeses

© The University of North Carolina Press
All Rights Reserved
ISBN 1-919-85410-X

Portions of this work were previously published, in somewhat different form, as
Cuba's First Venture in Africa: Algeria, 1961-1965, (Journal of Latin American
Studies 28, February 1996); *The First Ambassadors: Cuba's Contribution to
Guinea-Bissau's War of Independence*, (Journal of Latin American Studies 29,
February 1997); *Flee! The White Giants are Coming! The United States, the
Mercenaries and the Congo, 1964-1965*, (Diplomatic History 18, Spring 1994.
Reprinted here by permission of the publishers.

Set in Berkeley by Keystone Typsetting Inc and by Galago Publishing

Printed and bound by Paarl Print, Paarl, Cape

Front cover designed by Madelain Davies

Cover photograph by the late Captain Connie van Wyk, South African
Special Forces, during Task Force Zulu's advance into Angola, 1975.
By kind permission of Colonel Jan Breytenbach

To Setseko Ono
and
Letterina Gleijses

BOOKS/MONOGRAPHS BY PIERO GLEIJESES

Conflicting Missions: Washington, Havana, Pretoria
Shattered Hopes: The Guatemalan Revolution and the Unit States,
1944-1954
Politics and Culture in Guatemala
Tilting at Windmills: Reagan in Central America
The Dominican Crisis: The 1965 Constitutionalist Revolt and
American Intervention

CONTENTS

ILLUSTRATIONS

MAPS

ACKNOWLEDGEMENTS

Setsuko Ono read this manuscript with insight and care; her comments, ever so insightful, ever so intelligent, stimulated me throughout my journey.

I benefited from the assistance and advice of Isaac Cohen, Jim Hershberg, William LeoGrande, Wayne Smith, Christine Messiant, Peter Kornbluh, Arne Westad, Margaret Crahan, Teresita Múñoz, Sergio Guerra, Jose Abilio Lomba Martins, Lars Rudebeck, Lou Pérez, Joti Kohli, Kathrin Klein, Isabelle de Ruyth, Ben Jones, Jennifer Taylor, and Christopher Leroy. My visits to and from Africa — at a time when my eyesight was very poor — would have been far less restful without the warm hospitality of my friend Elizabeth Faroudja in Paris, and my research in the Belgian archives would have been far less productive without the assistance of Ambassador Jean de Ruyth. Bringing this manuscript to press was eased enormously by the professionalism and grace of Elaine Maisner and her colleagues at the University of North Carolina Press. I am delighted that my book is being published in South Africa and I owe a warm thanks to Peter Stiff, who made it possible.

Every archive I visited had a professional and courteous staff, but I have a particular soft spot for Regina Greenwell at the Johnson Library and Jim Yancey at the Carter Library. At SAIS, where I teach, three superb research librarians — Barbara Prophet, Kathy Picard and Linda Carlson — helped me with great skill and good cheer. At the Central Committee of the Communist Party of Cuba, in Havana, Ivys Silva Jomarrón coordinated the flow of declassified Cuban documents with admirable efficiency, grace and tact. When I began my research, I saw Ivys as a stern guardian; now I consider her a good and esteemed friend.

I suspect I would still be waiting for a visa to do research in Cuba had it not been for my dear friend Gloria León, who was then the head of the U.S. section at the University of Havana. I had broached the idea of this book in Cuba in late 1991 and had received polite expressions of interest, but when I tried to return to Cuba the following spring to begin the research, I was unable to obtain a visa. Gloria began pestering the Cuban authorities on my behalf. She also enlisted the help of her friends, among them Oscar García, dean of the Instituto Superior de Relaciones Internacionales of Havana, who lent his prestige to my quest and invited me to lecture at his institute. Finally, in December 1993, I again set foot in Havana. There I met Jorge Risquet, a Central Committee member who had played an important role in Africa for many years and who had been in Guatemala as a young man. I had written a book about Guatemala. Risquet read it, found it honest (although ideologically weak), and a link was established that led to the authorities' decision to grant me access to the archives. None of this would have been possible without Gloria's relentless efforts and Oscar García's courage in sponsoring a foreigner who not only has contacts with CIA officials as part of his academic research but was rumoured to be a CIA agent himself.

My debt to Gloria has grown over the years. Throughout, she has remained my invaluable adviser. She helps me understand things Cuban. I hate to think how many gaffes and faux pas I would have made during the six years I researched this book had I been unable to count on her advice and guidance.

In Havana, I acquired thousands of pages of documents and also three dear friends who helped me to understand their country: Antonio López López, a lover of history, taciturn, warm, and deeply intelligent; Hedelberto López Blanc, an irreverent and brilliant journalist; and Roberto Gonzáles Gómez, one of Cuba's most insightful intellectuals, who read several drafts of my manuscripts and was unstinting with his penetrating criticism.

Several protagonists graciously read all or part of the manuscript; in the United States, Assistant Secretary Nathaniel Davis, Under Secretary Joseph Sisco, Tom Killoran (the consul general in Luanda in 1975), and Robert Hultslander (the CIA station chief in 1975); in Cuba, Jorge Risquet and Víctor Dreke, Che Guevara's closest aide in Zaire; in Angola, Lúcio Lara, one of the most prominent leaders of the Popular Movement for the Liberation of Angola (MPLA). To them, and to all those who agreed to be interviewed for this book, I give my sincere thanks. And I offer my sincere thanks also to the John D. and Catherine T. MacArthur Foundation for a grant for research and writing and to the Latin America and Africa programmes of the Social Science Research Council: their generous assistance made it far easier for me to do research in Cuba, Africa, and Europe. I also received travel grants from the John F Kennedy Library, the Lyndon B Johnson Library, and the Gerald R Ford Library.

And now I come to the person to whom I owe the greatest intellectual debt, Nancy Mitchell. I have never met anyone who writes as well as Nancy. Whatever literary merits this book might have, they are largely due to her skill. This is my first debt. But Nancy has done more that improve my prose. A superb scholar, she has nudged me and pushed me – she shoved me, at times – forcing me to probe deeper, to avoid easy conclusions that addressed only part of the problem. She has made me search into corners I wanted to overlook, dig deeper when I thought the job was done, and she has driven me to despair with her relentless demands for more intellectual rigour and strong evidence. Not only did Nancy egg me forward, she also helped me find the answers. This is my second debt.

Writing a book can be a lonely endeavour. Nancy was there through my seven years of researching, writing, and rewriting. She read every draft. She helped make it fun. This is my third debt. Ever more, I hope that our collaboration will continue through all my books, and all of hers.

NOTES ON CITATIONS

Cuban archives

The majority of the documents I acquired from Cuban government archives are from the archives of the Centro de Información de las Fuerzas Armadas Revolucionarias, Havana (CID-FAR). Therefore, when a Cuban document is cited, the reader may assume that it is from the CID-FAR, unless otherwise indicated.

I have deposited photocopies of the Cuban documents I cite in the library of the School of Advance International Studies of the Johns Hopkins University in Washington, D.C. (see p.503).

Cuban names

Cubans have two family names but generally use only one (usually, but not always, the first) in everyday life. Throughout the manuscript I follow the common usage, except to distinguish between two people with the same preferred name. The full name is given in the list of interviewees.

Freedom of Information Act

Freedom of Information Act (FOIA) documents that are available through Research Publications are identified by "FOIA" followed by their code number.

FOIA documents that are available through the Department of State Freedom of Information Act Reading Room are identified by "DOS" followed by the microfiche number.

U.S. national archives

Unless otherwise stated, documents from the National Archives are from Record Group 59.

ABBREVIATIONS

AA	Foreign Ministry (of the Federal Republic of Germany and the German Democratic Republic)
ACC	Archives of the Central Committee of the Cuban Communist Party, Havana
AIHC	Archives of the Instituto de Historia de Cuba, Havana
Amcongen	American consul general
Amconsul	American consul
Amembassy	American embassy
ANC	Zairean army (Armée Nationale Congolaise)
ARA	American Republic Area
BOSS	Bureau of State Security, South Africa
CIA	Central Intelligence Agency, United States
CIR	Centro de Instrucción Revolucionaria
CPSU	Communist Party of the Soviet Union
CR	Congressional Record
CSM	*Christian Science Monitor* (Boston)
DCI	Director of Central Intelligence, United States
DCM	Deputy Chief of Mission, United States
DDCI	Deputy Director of Central Intelligence, United States
DDEL	Dwight D. Eisenhower Library, Abilene, Kansas
DGI	General Directorate of Intelligence, Cuba
DI	Directorate of Intelligence, CIA
DIA	Defence Intelligence Agency, United States
DOS	Department of State, United States
EMG	Estado Mayor de Guerra
FAR	Fuerzas Armadas Revolucionarias, Cuba
FLEC	Front for the Libertation of the Enclave of Cabinda
FNLA	National Front for the Liberation of Angola
FO	British Foreign Office
FOIA	Freedom of Information Act
FRG	Federal Republic of Germany
FRG, AA	Foreign Ministry Archives, Federal Republic of Germany
FRUS	Foreign Relations of the United States
GDR	German Democratic Republic
GDR AA	Foreign Ministry Archives, German Democratic Republic
GEI	Grupo Especial de Instrucción
GRFL	Gerald R. Ford Library, Ann Arbor, Michigan
INR	Bureau of Intelligence and Research, DOS
JCS	Joint Chief of Staff
JFKAC	John F. Kennedy Assassination Collection, NA

JFKL	John F. Kennedy Library, Boston
LBJL	Lyndon B. Johnson Library, Austin, Texas
LOC	Library of Congress, Washington, D.C.
MAE	Belgian Foreign Ministry
MAE, (with file number)	Archives of the Foreign Ministry, Brussels, Belgium
Memo Conv	memorandum of conversation
MF	Microfiche
MIECE	Archives of the Ministerio para la Inversión Extranjera y la Colaboración Económica, Havana
MINFAR	Ministerio de las Fuerzas Armadas Revolcionarias, Cuba
MINREX	Archives of the Cuban Foreign Ministry, Havana
MMCA	Cuban Military Mission in Angola
MMCG	Cuban Military Mission in Guinea and Guinea-Bissau
MPLA	Popular Movement for the Liberation of Angola
MWP	Mennen Williams Papers, Lot Files, RG 59, NA
NA	National Archives, College Park, Md.
NIE	National Intelligence Estimate, CIA
NP	Nixon Presidential Materials, NA
NSA	National Security Archive, Washington, D.C.
NSAd	National Security Adviser, GRFL
NSARPF	National Security Adviser, Temporary Parallel File, GRFL
NSC	National Security Council, United States
NSCF	National Security Council Files, NP
NSC Trip Files	National Security Council Files, HAK Trip Files, NP
NSDM	National Security Decision Memorandum
NSF	National Security Files, Presidential Libraries
NSFCF	National Security File Country File, LBJL
NSSM	National Security Study Memorandum
NYT	*New York Times*
OAU	Organization of African Unity
OCI	Office of Current Intelligence, CIA
OH	Oral History
ONE	Office of National Estimates, CIA
PAIGC	Partido Africano da Independência da Guiné e Cabo Verde
PCC	Communist Party of Cuba (Castro era)
PCH	Private Collection, Havana
PDRY	People's Democratic Republic of Yemen
PPS	Policy Planning Council, Policy Planning Staff, Director's Files (Winston Lord) 1969 – 77, Lot Files, RG 59, NA
PRO	Public Record Office, Kew, England
PSP	Communist Party of Cuba (pre-Castro)
RDM	*Rand Daily Mail* (Johannesburg)
SADF	South African Defence Force

Sec State	Secretary of State
SED	Archive of the Political Parties and Mass Organizations of the German Democratic Republic in the "Federal Archive, Berlin
SNF	Subject – Numeric Files: 1963 – 73, RG59, NA
SWAPO	South West Africa People's Organization
Tel Conv	Telephone conversation
Tel. interview	Telephone interview
UM	Unidad militar
Under Sec	Under Secretary
UNITA	National Union for the Total Independence of Angola
USIB	Unites States Intelligence Board, CIA
USUN	U.S. mission of the United Nations
WF	Whitman File, DDEL
WHCF	White House Central File, Presidential Libraries
WHO	White House Office
WP	*Washington Post*
WSJ	*Wall Street Journal* (New York)

PLACE NAMES

The names of numerous Zairean towns changed after Mobutu seized power in 1965. I list here the old and new names of towns mentioned in this book:

Elisabethville:	Lubumbashi
Leopoldville:	Kinshasa
Stanleyville:	Kisangani

The names of many Angolan towns changed after independence in 1975. Listed are the old and new names of those places mentioned in this book:

Carmona:	N'Zeto
Henrique de Carvalho:	Saurimo
Luso:	Luena
Moçãmedes:	Namibe
Nova Lisboa:	Huambo
Novo Redondo:	Sumbe
Pereira de Eça:	N'Giva
Roçadas:	Xangongo
Sá da Bandeira:	Lubango
Salazar:	N'Dalatando
Serpa Pinto:	Menongue
Silva Porto:	Bié
Teixeira de Sousa:	Luau

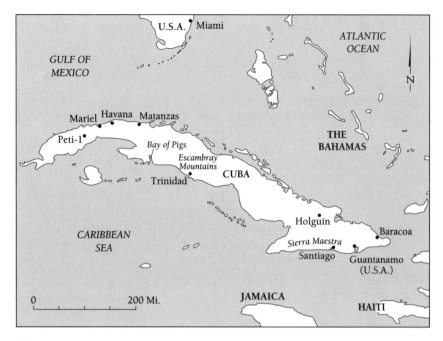

Cuba

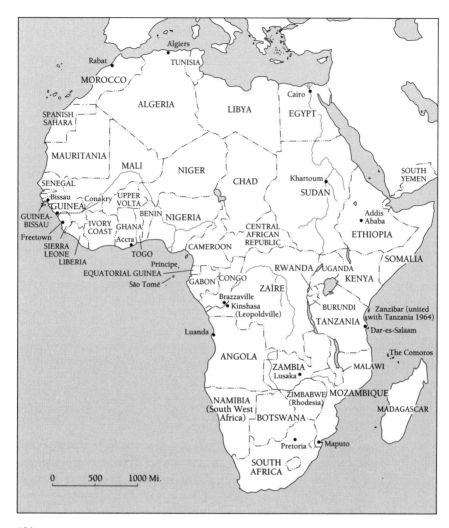

Africa

PROLOGUE

In 1945 virtually all Africa was divided among the Europeans: France and England had the largest shares; tiny Belgium ruled the immense colony of Zaire;[a] Portugal was master of Angola, Mozambique, Guinea-Bissau, and several small islands; Spain held a few fragments; and the fate of the former Italian colonies had yet to be decided. The continent was a backwater, a safe backyard of the Western powers. There was no Soviet threat, no Communist subversion, and no threat to the white man's rule.

Fifteen years later, however, colonial rule was in ruins. The transformation had come without widespread violence, with the major exception of Algeria, and it had come suddenly. In 1957 the first sub-Saharan country, Ghana, gained its independence and became the voice of African nationalism. The following year Charles de Gaulle, who had returned to power in a France fractured by the Algerian war, offered independence to the French possessions in sub-Saharan Africa. They grabbed it. In 1960, the Year of Africa, sixteen European colonies— French, British, and Belgian—became independent.

The swiftness of the Europeans' abdication had many explanations. In a ripple effect, as a colony moved toward independence, expectations swelled in neighboring territories. And when the colonial authorities applied the brakes, the response was not submission but riots. "Africa may become," British prime minister Harold MacMillan warned in August 1959, "no longer a source of pride or profit to the Europeans who have developed it, but a maelstrom of trouble into which all of us would be sucked."[1] By surrendering formal power gracefully, however, the metropole could retain strong political and economic influence over its former colonies. And so Paris and London let their charges go.

As did Brussels, with unseemly haste. In January 1959 riots shattered Zaire's capital, Leopoldville, and shook Brussels from its torpor. A few days later, a sobered Belgian government promised independence "without either baneful delays or ill-conceived precipitousness."[2] No date was set, but Belgian officials speculated that the transition would take fifteen years. As unrest grew and concessions triggered more demands, however, the country seemed headed toward anarchy and radicalization, and Brussels began its headlong retreat. In

a. In colonial times there were two Congos, one ruled by Paris, the other by Brussels. Upon becoming independent in 1960, both retained the name Congo. In October 1971 the former Belgian Congo became Zaire, and in May 1997 it became the Democratic Republic of Congo. To avoid confusion, in the book I always refer to the former French colony as "the Congo" and I always refer to the former Belgian colony as "Zaire." When quoting from a written source in English that uses any other name, I add "Zaire" in brackets when appropriate. When quoting from an interview or when translating from a written source, I consistently refer to the former Belgian colony as "Zaire."

October 1959 the government cut the timetable for independence to four years; three months later it slashed it to six months. On June 30, 1960, Zaire achieved independence, for which it was utterly unprepared.

THE U.S. RESPONSE

The rush to independence took Washington by surprise and stirred deep concerns. Africa had become "a battleground of the first order," Secretary of State Christian Herter told the National Security Council (NSC) in March 1960. One month later, Vice-President Richard Nixon stated that Africa was "potentially the most explosive area in the world." The incoming Kennedy administration agreed. The situation was "potentially unstable," a National Intelligence Estimate noted in August 1961, adding that the new countries' immaturity and the resentment many of their leaders bore toward the West provided opportunities for Moscow and Beijing. "Communist Bloc influence has grown from negligible levels in 1958–1959 to substantial proportions today," it warned. "The Communists probably will enjoy a number of advantages in the competition with the West."[3]

One such advantage was American racism. "Our greatest liability [in Africa] is our failure to live up to some of our ideals," the State Department explained. "[We must] move more quickly to solve our problem of according dignity and equal opportunity to our own African-descended population."[4] The State Department had felt no need for haste when the Africans had been colonial wards, but now that they were sovereign they were pawns in the Cold War, and their views mattered. The founding conference of the Organization of African Unity (OAU) was held in May 1963 while the world's press was saturated with reports of the savage police response to the civil rights marches in Birmingham, Alabama. The assembled African leaders sent President John Kennedy an eloquent message: "The Negroes who, even while the [OAU] Conference was in session, have been subjected to the most inhuman treatment, who have been blasted with fire hoses cranked up to such pressure that the water would strip bark off the trees, at whom the police have deliberately set snarling dogs, are our own kith and kin."[5]

Nevertheless, the United States enjoyed two formidable advantages in the quest for influence in Africa: it could provide far more economic aid than the Soviet bloc, and its European allies retained great influence in their former colonies. It would be U.S. policy to push these Europeans to the fore, to let them carry the burden. "While reserving our right to tender our assistance if necessary, we should put responsibility for assistance to Africa on the U.K. and France," President Dwight Eisenhower told the NSC in March 1960. "A continuing effort must be made by the United States to see that the metropoles face up to their responsibilities in this respect," an NSC paper noted a few weeks later.[6]

America's allies could also be a liability, however. The Portuguese dictatorship balked at even considering independence for its African colonies. As a result, armed struggle began—in Angola in early 1961, in Guinea-Bissau in 1963, and in Mozambique the following year. Kennedy administration officials doubted that Lisbon had the ability to "bear the long and bloody struggle that its present policies seem to ensure"; they feared that the United States, hamstrung by its NATO commitments to Portugal, would watch as the Soviet Union and China strengthened their ties with the rebels and pro-Communist regimes emerged in the liberated colonies.[7]

When these officials thought of Communist subversion in Africa, they pictured Moscow and Beijing, not Havana. They could not imagine that a weak, poor Caribbean island whose only link to Africa was the blood of hundreds of thousands of slaves shipped across the Atlantic to toil in Cuban plantations could play a role on that faraway continent.

THE CUBAN ROLE

Fidel Castro, however, could imagine it. Two years after his victory over Batista, his emissaries crossed the ocean to offer Cuba's help to the Algerian rebels. A few weeks later, in January 1962, a Cuban ship unloaded weapons at Casablanca for the Algerians and returned to Havana with seventy-six wounded guerrillas and twenty children from refugee camps. Cuba's African adventure had begun. "We will never forget how you [Cubans] cared for our orphans and our wounded," Ahmed Ben Bella, prime minister of the fledgling Algerian Republic, said on his arrival in Havana on October 16, 1962.[8]

In December 1964 Che Guevara went to Africa on a three-month trip that signaled Havana's quickening interest in the region. This was the season of the great illusion, when the Cubans, the Americans, and many others believed that revolution might be imminent in Africa. Guerrillas were fighting the Portuguese in Angola, Guinea-Bissau, and Mozambique. In the Congo a new government was loudly proclaiming its revolutionary sympathies. And, above all, there was Zaire, where armed revolt had been spreading with stunning speed since the spring of 1964, threatening the survival of the corrupt pro-American regime that Presidents Eisenhower and Kennedy had labored to put in place. President Lyndon Johnson scrambled for a solution, sending 1,000 white mercenaries from South Africa, Rhodesia, and Western Europe armed and controlled by the CIA to put down the revolt. A few months later, when Che was in Africa, he pledged, on Castro's behalf, Cuban military instructors to the Zairean and the Angolan rebels. In April 1965 a Cuban column led by Che began infiltrating into eastern Zaire through Tanzania. In August a second column arrived in the Congo. Four hundred Cuban soldiers were in Central Africa in the summer of 1965.

But Central Africa was not ready for revolution. By the time the Cubans got to Zaire, Johnson's policy had succeeded: the mercenaries had broken the back of the rebellion. Che withdrew within seven months. Less than two years later, after arming and training hundreds of Angolan rebels, the other Cuban column left the Congo.

While U.S. officials boasted about "Moscow's debacle" in Zaire and concluded that African rebels would be unable to unseat the white regimes on the continent in the foreseeable future, Castro took stock. "Fidel is a little pessimistic about Africa," a senior Cuban official confided in January 1967.[9] Fidel's pessimism, however, did not extend to Guinea-Bissau. Cuban military instructors and doctors joined the rebels there in 1966 and remained through the war's end in 1974. This was the longest Cuban intervention in Africa until the dispatch of troops to Angola in November 1975, and it was the most successful. As the Bissau paper *Nõ Pintcha* declared, "The Cubans' help was decisive."[10]

U.S. officials knew that Cubans were in Africa—in Algeria, Zaire, the Congo, and Guinea-Bissau. But "the State Department was not particularly concerned," the U.S. ambassador in Conakry, the observation post for the war in neighboring Guinea-Bissau, remarked.[11] U.S. officials never dreamed that a handful of Cubans could be effective in distant, alien African countries. Che's failure in Zaire reinforced this complacency. In its overview of Communist activities in Africa, the administrative history of the State Department in the Johnson years did not mention Cuba.[12]

The Nixon administration was confident that the Communist threat in Africa had been defanged. It paid no attention to the continent. "Africa in the 1973 edition of the Key Intelligence Questions hardly rated a mention," the director of Central Intelligence, William Colby, wrote.[13] This would soon change.

In April 1974 an unexpected coup ousted the Portuguese dictatorship and opened the way for the decolonization of Angola, Mozambique, and Guinea-Bissau. In Angola three liberation movements vied for power, and the country slid into civil war. As U.S. policy makers and CIA officials planned a major covert operation there in the spring of 1975, they tried to predict what other foreign powers—African, European, Chinese, and Soviet—might do. Cuba was not mentioned. "Cuba didn't even enter into our calculations," Deputy Assistant Secretary Edward Mulcahy, one of the advocates of the covert operation, recalled. And even when, in late August, the CIA began reporting the presence of a "few Cuban technical advisers" in Angola, Washington paid no heed. A few Cubans would make no difference; U.S. officials were focused on what the Soviet Union might do. They were stunned, therefore, in late 1975 when thousands of Cuban soldiers poured into Angola. "The intervention of Cuban combat forces came as a total surprise," Secretary of State Henry Kissinger wrote in his memoirs.[14] It also came at the precise moment South African troops were racing toward Luanda to crush the Popular Movement for the Liberation of Angola (MPLA), the most leftist of the three Angolan guerrilla groups. By March 1976 the Cubans had pushed the South Africans out of Angola and won the war for the MPLA.

This changed everything. "In Angola Black troops—Cubans and Angolans—have defeated White troops in military exchanges," a South African analyst observed, "and that psychological edge, that advantage the White man has enjoyed and exploited over 300 years of colonialism and empire, is slipping away." Africans celebrated. "Black Africa is riding the crest of a wave generated by the Cuban success in Angola," noted the *World*, South Africa's major black newspaper. "Black Africa is tasting the heady wine of the possibility of realizing the dream of 'total liberation.' "[15]

I was among those stunned by the Cuban intervention in Angola, by this sudden outpouring of thousands of soldiers from a small Caribbean island, which, in 1975, reminded me more of a tropical Bulgaria, a well-behaved Soviet client, than of a fiery revolutionary outpost. I later asked a Cuban official about it and was told, "You can't understand our intervention in Angola without understanding our past."[16] He meant that the Cubans who went to Angola were following in the footsteps of those who had gone to Algeria, Zaire, the Congo, and Guinea-Bissau. But if there was continuity, there were also dramatic differences. Fewer than 2,000 Cubans had gone to Africa between 1961 and 1974, while 30,000 streamed into Angola between October 1975 and April 1976. In the 1960s, the United States had been refusing to consider a modus vivendi with Cuba, and it had been trying to cripple Cuba's economy; Castro had had little to lose by intervening in Africa. In 1975, however, the United States was finally offering Cuba the prospect of normal relations. Why did Castro spurn this unprecedented opportunity? Was he following Moscow's dictates?

For years, I toyed with the idea of tracing the story to its hazy beginnings, of telling the story from Cuba's first steps in Algeria through its massive intervention in Angola in 1975–76. The more I learned, the more my interest grew. Too often, the history of the Cold War is examined from the perspective of the great powers. Here was the opportunity to turn that perspective on its head and to view it from below, from Third World country to Third World country.

Whether as the Soviet Union's Afrika Corps or as an independent actor, the Cuban role in Africa was unprecedented. What other Third World country had ever projected its power beyond its immediate neighborhood? Brazil's mighty generals had gone as far as the Caribbean—sending a small troop to the Dominican Republic in 1965 as the United States' junior partner. In 1980–81, Argentina's generals had reached as far as Nicaragua, to help Anastasio Somoza's defeated cohorts. Extracontinental interventions were the preserve of the superpowers, of a few West European countries, and of China, which sent military instructors and aid to Africa. But China's role in Africa paled in comparison to Cuba's.

To understand Cuba's policy, I had first to discover what it had done, and this meant reading Cuban documents. This was a daunting challenge, because no scholar or writer had had access to the Cuban archives for the post-1959 period.[17]

THE CUBAN ARCHIVES

I started pestering Cuban officials in 1991. My first breakthrough was in late 1993, but it opened the door only a crack. On every subsequent visit to Havana—and there were fourteen such visits, each lasting approximately one month—I had to begin again, and I was rewarded with varying degrees of success.

There was no established declassification process in Cuba when I began my research. Mindful of the fact that the documents I cited would not be readily accessible to my readers, I decided that I would never use a document unless I was given a photocopy of the original. I badgered Cuban officials relentlessly, arguing that in the United States their word has no credibility unless supported by documents. Jorge Risquet, a member of the Central Committee who was assigned the task of dealing with me, understood. His intelligence, sensitivity, and courage made this book possible. We have come a long way since the day in 1994 when I asked him for all the reports written by the chief of the Cuban Military Mission in Angola between August and October 1975 only to be told, "You aren't writing his biography. One will do." Two years later, I received all the others. As my research progressed, the Cubans established a declassification procedure: any document they expected would be declassified they allowed me to read in its entirety, whether in Risquet's office or in the archives themselves. Then the waiting would begin. It could take less than an hour or more than a year for them to give me the photocopies. As I write, there are several hundred pages of documents that I have been allowed to read but have not yet been given.[18]

I have also interviewed eighty-four Cubans who were involved in Africa. I spoke to many of them on several occasions and in relaxed settings. While interviews without documents would be of little use, interviews with documents can be extremely helpful. Furthermore, many of the interviewees gave me letters and journals from their personal collections, and they alerted me to documents in the government archives, which made it possible to be very specific in my requests to Risquet. Some of the interviews took place with the authorization of the Cuban authorities (this was the case for active duty military officers), others through personal contacts I developed in my frequent and lengthy visits to Cuba.

U.S. AND EUROPEAN ARCHIVES

I knew from the outset that U.S. archives would be critical to my pursuit. Not only would they shed light on the U.S.-Cuban relationship, which is part of the texture of my story, but they would give me another perspective on what Cuba was doing in Africa. Furthermore, in writing the history of Cuba in Africa I was also writing the history of U.S. policy toward Africa. My two major case studies—Zaire in 1964–65 and Angola in 1975–76—were also the two major Cold War crises in Africa through 1976. The United States was the main foreign protagonist in Zaire in 1964–65, and it was one of the key players in Angola. It was also present, albeit less centrally, in the other case studies I considered. It was my good fortune that important U.S. documents that shed a fresh light on U.S. policy in Africa, and particularly in Zaire and Angola, have been declassified recently.

I also turned to the West German, British, Belgian, and East German archives to gain more insight into Cuban and U.S. policy. (There are virtually no relevant documents in the declassified material in the Russian archives.)[19] After six years of research, I can confidently state that the best-organized and richest archives that I have examined are those of the United States. Furthermore, I have been highly impressed by the superior quality and objectivity of many of the U.S. reports I have read, particularly those of the CIA.

I was unable to gain access to any archive in Africa. Except for the odd document from private collections, my only African sources are the press of several African countries and interviews that I conducted during a two-month stay in Angola, Guinea, and Guinea-Bissau.

Curiosity about Havana's intervention in Angola sparked this book. In the course of researching and writing it, however, it took, as books always do, many unexpected turns. It became the story of Cuba's halting, self-interested, and idealistic steps in Africa, both at the governmental level and at the individual level, embodied by the thousands of Cubans who doctored, and soldiered, and taught in Africa in the 1960s and 1970s. And it became the story of the emerging U.S. policy in Africa, somnolent and distracted until galvanized by crisis, be it in Zaire or Angola. And it became a parable of the Cold War, in which Washington was blinded by its singular focus on the great powers.

The Cold War has ended with the victory of the United States and its allies, but it is important that amid the din of celebrations, the defeated find a voice. It is important that the history of those years reflect more than the victors' viewpoint and speak also for the defeated, especially those who are poor and weak. This is not a sentimental exercise. If the defeated are silenced, only triumphalism, on the one hand, and resentment, on the other, can result. The story of the defeated is part of the truth and texture of those harried years.

CHAPTER ONE
CASTRO'S CUBA, 1959-1964

The United States did not hesitate to recognize the government established by Fidel Castro. On January 7, 1959, just six days after Fulgencio Batista had fled Cuba, the Eisenhower administration extended the hand of friendship to the victorious guerrillas. To signal its goodwill, the State Department replaced the ambassador to Cuba, Earl Smith, a wealthy political appointee who had been close to Batista, with Philip Bonsal, a career diplomat known to work well with left-of-center governments. Within a year, however, Eisenhower had decided that Castro had to go.

It was not Castro's record on human rights and political democracy that bothered Eisenhower. As historian Stephen Rabe has noted, "During much of the decade [1950s], U.S. officials were busy hugging and bestowing medals on sordid, often ruthless [Latin American] tyrants." U.S. presidents—even Woodrow Wilson, his rhetoric notwithstanding—had consistently maintained good relations with the worst dictators of the hemisphere, so long as they accepted U.S. hegemony.[1]

Castro, however, was not willing to bow to the United States. "He is clearly a strong personality and a born leader of great personal courage and conviction," U.S. officials noted in April 1959. "He is inspired by a messianic sense of mission to aid his people," a National Intelligence Estimate reported two months later. Even though he did not have a clear blueprint of the Cuba he wanted to create, Castro dreamed of a sweeping revolution that would uproot his country's oppressive socioeconomic structure. He dreamed of a Cuba that would be free of the United States.[2]

THE BURDEN OF THE PAST

It was President Thomas Jefferson who first cast his gaze toward Cuba, strategically situated and rich in sugar and slaves. In 1809 he counseled his successor, James Madison, to propose a deal to Napoleon, who had occupied Spain: the United States would give France a free hand in Spanish America, if France would give Cuba to the United States. "That would be a price," he wrote, "and I would immediately erect a column on the southernmost limit of Cuba, and inscribe on it a *ne plus ultra* as to us in that direction."[3]

England, however, had made it clear that it would not tolerate Cuba's annexation to the United States, and the Royal Navy dominated the waves. The United States would have to wait until the fruit was ripe, but time was in America's favor. In John Quincy Adams's words, "there are laws of political as well as of physical gravitation; and if an apple severed by the tempest from its native tree cannot choose but fall to the ground, Cuba, forcibly disjoined from its own unnatural connection with Spain and incapable of self-support, can gravitate only towards the North American Union, which by the same law of nature cannot cast her off from its bosom."[4]

Through the administrations of Jefferson, Madison, Monroe, and Adams, U.S. officials opposed the liberation of Cuba because they feared it would create an opportunity for other powers, particularly England, or lead to a successful slave revolt on the island, or, at a minimum, establish a republic that abolished slavery and promoted equal rights for blacks and whites. The fruit would never have ripened, because such a Cuba would have bitterly resisted annexation to Jeffersonian America, where the blacks were slaves or outcasts.

Cuba became the "ever faithful island"—a rich Spanish colony dotted with great landed estates worked by a mass of black slaves. A ten-year war of independence, which erupted in 1868, failed to dislodge the Spanish. But in 1895 José Martí raised again the standard of revolt. He wanted independence and reform, and he was deeply suspicious of the United States. "What I have done, and shall continue to do," he wrote in May 1895, "is to . . . block with our blood . . . the annexation of the peoples of our America to the turbulent and brutal North that despises them. . . . I lived in the monster [the United States], and know its entrails—and my sling is that of David."[5]

In 1898, as the Cuban revolt entered its fourth year, the United States joined the war, ostensibly to free Cuba. After Spain surrendered, Washington forced the Platt amendment on the Cubans. The amendment granted the United States the right to intervene and to have naval bases on Cuban soil. (Even today, the Platt amendment lives, with the U.S. naval base at Guantanamo.) Cuba became, more than any other Latin American country, in Tad Szulc's words, "an American fiefdom."[6] And when a group of men who were determined to bring about social reform and national independence finally seized power in Cuba in September 1933, President Franklin Delano Roosevelt refused to recognize their new government and urged the Cuban army to seize power. And so it did, and the era of Batista began.

When Fidel Castro began fighting against Batista in 1956, the United States supplied arms to the dictator. Castro took note. In a letter of June 5, 1958, he wrote: "The Americans are going to pay dearly for what they're doing. When this war is over, I'll start a much longer and bigger war of my own: the war I'm going to fight against them. That will be my true destiny."[7]

Many of the opponents of Batista's regime wanted to accommodate the United States, either because they admired its culture or had a fatalistic respect for its power. Castro, on the other hand, represented the views of those anti-Batista youths who were repulsed by Washington's domination and paternalism. This, however, baffled Eisenhower and most Americans, who believed that America had always been the Cubans' truest friend, fighting Spain in 1898 to give them their independence. "Here is a country that you would believe, on the basis of our history, would be one of our real friends," Eisenhower marveled. As American historian Nancy Mitchell has pointed out, "Our selective recall not only serves a purpose; it also has repercussions. It creates a chasm between us and the Cubans: we share a past, but we have no shared memories."[8]

THE BREAK

In 1959 Castro might have been willing to accept a modus vivendi with Washington that promised Cuba complete independence in domestic politics, while setting some limits on its foreign policy. History, after all, taught that no government could survive in the region against the will of the United States, and Castro had no assurances whatsoever that the Soviet Union would befriend Cuba, a fragile outpost in the American backyard. On the other hand, it is likely that very influential members of Castro's entourage—including his brother Raúl and Che Guevara—were not only deeply skeptical that such an accommodation would be possible but also ideologically inclined to move Cuba toward the socialist bloc. Furthermore, given the youthful pride of the Cuban leadership, even a hint of bullying from Washington was bound to radicalize rather than intimidate.

The Eisenhower administration wanted a modus vivendi with Castro, sincerely but on its own terms: Cuba must remain within the U.S. sphere of influence. The U.S. press and the Congress, Republicans and Democrats, agreed.

If Castro accepted these parameters, he could stay. Otherwise he would be overthrown. The Eisenhower administration began to plot his ouster six months after he had seized power. At an NSC meeting on January 14, 1960, Under Secretary Livingston Merchant noted that "our present objective was to adjust all our actions in such a way as to accelerate the development of an opposition in Cuba which would bring about . . . a new government favorable to U.S. interests." He then asked the assistant secretary for inter-American affairs, Roy Rubottom, to summarize the evolution of U.S.-Cuban relations since January 1959:

> The period from January to March might be characterized as the honeymoon period of the Castro government. In April a downward trend in U.S.-Cuban relations had been evident. . . . In June we had reached the decision that it was not possible to achieve our objectives with Castro in power and had agreed to undertake the program referred to by Mr. Merchant. In July and August we had been busy drawing up a program to replace Castro. However some U.S. companies reported to us during this time that they were making some progress in negotiations, a factor that caused us to slow the implementation of our program. The hope expressed by these companies did not materialize. October was a period of clarification. . . . On October 31, in agreement with CIA, the Department had recommended to the President approval of a program along the lines referred to by Mr. Merchant. The approved program autho-

rized us to support elements in Cuba opposed to the Castro government while making Castro's downfall seem to be the result of his own mistakes.[9]

It was probably as part of this program that Cuban exiles mounted seaborne raids against Cuba from U.S. territory and that unidentified planes attacked economic targets on the island, leading the U.S. embassy to warn Washington that the population was "becoming aroused" against the United States.[10] And in January 1960, when Director of Central Intelligence Allen Dulles "presented an Agency proposal [to Eisenhower] for sabotage of sugar refineries of Cuba," the president replied that "he didn't object to such an undertaking and, indeed, thought something like this was timely. However, he felt that any program should be much more ambitious, and it was probably now the time to move against Castro in a positive and aggressive way which went beyond pure harassment. He asked Mr. Dulles to come back with an enlarged program."[11] This enlarged program, which Dulles presented to the president in March 1960, led to Kennedy's Bay of Pigs, in which some 1,300 CIA-trained Cuban exiles stormed a Cuban beach in April 1961, only to surrender three days later.[12]

MONGOOSE

Flush with his victory at the Bay of Pigs, Castro tendered an olive branch to the United States. On August 17, 1961, at an inter-American conference at Punta del Este, Che Guevara arranged a meeting with Kennedy's close aide Richard Goodwin. "He [Che] seemed very ill at ease when we began to talk, but soon became relaxed and spoke freely," Goodwin reported to Kennedy. "Although he left no doubt of his personal and intense devotion to Communism, his conversation was free of propaganda and bombast. He spoke calmly, in a straightforward manner, and with the appearance of detachment and objectivity. He left no doubt, at any time, that he felt completely free to speak for his government and rarely distinguished between his personal observations and the official position of the Cuban government. I had the definite impression that he had thought out his remarks very carefully—they were extremely well organized."

The Cubans, Che told Goodwin, "didn't want an understanding with the U.S., because they knew that was impossible. They would like a *modus vivendi*—at least an interim *modus vivendi*. . . . He said they could discuss no formula that would mean giving up the type of society to which they were dedicated." But they were willing to accept limits on their foreign policy: "they could agree not to make any political alliance with the East—although this would not affect their natural sympathies." And he indicated, "very obliquely and with evident reluctance because of the company in which we were talking [a Brazilian and an Argentine diplomat were acting as interpreters], that they could also discuss the activities of the Cuban revolution in other countries." According to Goodwin, therefore, Guevara was hinting at a tropical Finlandization: complete freedom at home and some limits on foreign policy.[13]

When Che and Goodwin met, Cuba's support for revolutionary movements in Latin America was just beginning to gather momentum. "At present time, there is no hard evidence of an actual supply of arms or armed men going from Cuba to other countries to assist indigenous revolutionary movements," the CIA had noted three months earlier. "There has been some movement of individual armed agents into other countries and some Cuban effort to train the revolutionaries of other countries. The export of physical aid to revolutionary movements, while important, is much less significant than the threat posed by Castro's example and general stimulus of these movements."[14]

This threat haunted Kennedy. "Latin America is ripe for revolution in one form or another," a National Intelligence Estimate noted in 1962. Looking back thirty years later, Kennedy's national security adviser, McGeorge Bundy, explained, "That was a real fear! People [in Washington] were really nervous that somewhere, somehow they [the Castroites] would pull it off again. The fear in Washington was really intense. There was the idea that the situation was potentially very explosive and could spread."[15]

Castro was hurling a two-pronged assault against the United States. He was leading his island into the Soviet embrace, and he was fomenting revolution throughout the hemisphere. Kennedy was not interested in exploring a modus vivendi. He would defang the threat in Latin America by launching the Alliance for Progress—an unprecedented program of social reform and economic growth—and by strengthening democratic institutions and the military in the region.[16]

As for the rebel island, John Kennedy knew only one answer, the one Eisenhower had given in 1954 to Guatemala's president, Jacobo Arbenz: the upstart must be removed. It was the answer that was consistent with the imperial tradition of the United States in the Caribbean and that was endorsed by the overwhelming majority of Americans. Defeat at the Bay of Pigs added an element of personal venom to Kennedy's crusade.

Kennedy rejected Castro's overture and instead " 'chewed out' " CIA deputy director for plans Richard Bissell for " 'sitting on his ass and not doing anything about getting rid of Castro and the Castro regime.' "[17] He asked his brother, Attorney General Robert Kennedy, to lead the top-level interagency group that oversaw Operation Mongoose, a program of paramilitary operations, economic warfare, and sabotage he launched in late 1961 to visit the "terrors of the earth" on Fidel Castro and, more prosaically, to topple him. "Robert Kennedy's involvement in organizing and directing Mongoose became so intense that he might as well have been deputy director for plans for the operation," Bissell recalled. "Because of the failure of the Bay of Pigs," Bissell's successor, Richard Helms, observed, "Jack Kennedy and Bob Kennedy were absolutely like demons—to get rid of Castro. Jack Kennedy wanted it done. He didn't want any arguments against it. If you went to Robert Kennedy and told him: 'This can't be done,' he'd tell you: 'Hell, then we'll get someone who can do it.' "[18] Bypassing the CIA, discredited in the president's eyes by the Bay of Pigs, the Kennedy brothers placed a man they trusted, General Edward Lansdale, in charge of Mongoose. "There will be no acceptable alibi [for failure]," Lansdale told his senior aides in January 1962. "It is our job to put the American genius to work on this project, quickly and effectively." Lansdale's plan was to provoke a popular revolt by early October 1962 through a combination of paramilitary operations, sabotage, and economic strangulation. His robust optimism contrasted with the more sober assessment of a November 1961 National Intelligence Estimate, which noted that "The Castro regime has sufficient popular support and repressive capabilities to cope with any internal threat likely to develop within the foreseeable future."[19]

While the United States succeeded in forcing third countries to curtail trade with Cuba, the paramilitary effort failed. Successful operations were "few and far between . . . and none of the big ones really succeeded." A National Intelligence Estimate noted in March 1962 that "Fidel Castro and the Revolution retain the positive support of a substantial proportion of the Cuban people. There are substantial numbers of Cubans who care nothing for ideology, but are still under the spell of Fidel Castro's magnetic personal leadership . . . who feel a surge of nationalistic pride in revolutionary Cuba, and who attribute all present short-comings to the implacable malevolence of Yankee imperialism." At an October 4 meeting of the Mongoose interagency group, Robert Kennedy complained forcefully about "the meager results, especially in the sabotage field," and warned that "higher authority" was concerned about the lack of progress and felt that "more priority should be given to trying to mount sabotage operations." Duly chastened, Lansdale promised that "another attempt will be made against the major target [the Matahambre copper mine] which has been the object of three unsuccessful missions, and that approximately six new ones are in the planning stage." On October 16, Robert Kennedy again expressed the "'general dissatisfaction of the president'" with Mongoose. "He spoke of the weekly meetings of top officials on this problem and again noted the small accomplishments despite the fact that Secretaries Rusk and McNamara, General Taylor, McGeorge Bundy, and he personally had all been charged by the President to find a solution. . . . The Attorney General stated that in view of this lack of progress, he was going to give Operation Mongoose more personal attention." He would hold a meeting every morning with Mongoose's senior staff.[20]

That same day, October 16, President Kennedy was informed that there were Soviet missiles in Cuba.

THE CUBAN-SOVIET MINUET

The Cubans were the suitors. Some, like Raúl Castro and Che Guevara, were motivated by ideology. As a young man in Batista's Cuba, Raúl had been a member of the Cuban Communist Party (PSP) youth group and Che, who had never belonged to any political party, considered himself a Marxist-Leninist by the time he joined Castro. "I belong to those who believe that the solution of the world's problems lies behind the so-called iron curtain," he wrote in December 1957.[21]

Fidel Castro was different. He was not a Marxist-Leninist when he came to power. "I always thought of Fidel as an authentic leader of the leftist bourgeoisie," Che wrote in the same December 1957 letter.[22] It was in self-defense that Fidel sought the Soviet embrace. Only strong Soviet support could protect his regime from the United States. The fate of Jacobo Arbenz in Guatemala was a bitter reminder of what befell errant presidents in the U.S. sphere of influence.

When he came to power, Castro did not have a clear idea of the kind of relationship he would seek with the Kremlin. There were too many uncertainties—how far relations with the United States would deteriorate, how the Soviets would respond to his overtures, how the situation in Cuba would evolve. The Soviet leaders were equally uncertain. They knew very little about Castro, except that he was not a Communist and his country was in the heart of the American empire.

For several months, Havana's only contacts with Moscow were through PSP leaders who visited Moscow and vouched for the revolutionary credentials of the new government. It was as if the Cubans and Soviets were eyeing each other from a distance before deciding on the first move. This was, on both sides, an incremental process that can only be imperfectly retraced—because of its own tentative nature and because of the lack of documentation.[23]

In October 1959 a KGB official, Aleksandr Alekseev, arrived in Havana, establishing the first direct link between the Kremlin and the new Cuban leadership. At Castro's request, transmitted through Alekseev, Soviet deputy premier Anastas Mikoyan, who was touring Latin America as the head of a Soviet technical and cultural exhibition, arrived in Havana in February 1960. He was authorized to offer the Cubans a limited package of economic aid. The visit went well. Castro impressed Mikoyan as " 'a genuine revolutionary, completely like us. I felt as though I had returned to my childhood.' "[24] Suddenly, the tempo accelerated. The following month, Castro asked Alekseev for Soviet bloc weapons. He was convinced, he explained, that the United States was preparing to attack Cuba. Within a few days, Moscow approved the request. The arms would be provided free of charge. That same month, March 1960, a handful of Spanish officers, members of the Spanish Communist Party who had emigrated to the Soviet Union after Franco's victory, arrived in the island to help organize the Cuban armed forces.[25] Diplomatic relations between Cuba and the Soviet Union were established on May 8. Over the next year the relationship grew close and ebullient as Soviet bloc arms and economic aid began to arrive. Castro was charismatic, he seemed steadfast, he worked well with the Communist Party, and he humbled the United States at the Bay of Pigs. The Soviet Union would transform the island into a socialist showcase in Latin America. The Soviets' enthusiasm was all the greater because they greatly underestimated the economic cost. It was the Missile Crisis that brought this honeymoon to an abrupt end.

In a December 1963 analysis, Tom Hughes, director of the State Department's Bureau of Intelligence and Research (INR), assessed why the Cubans and Soviets had placed missiles in Cuba. "We have no doubt that Castro, and probably the Soviets too, were increasingly worried in the late winter and spring of 1962 about the possibility of a new US invasion attempt," he wrote. "Castro, as the more directly involved party, may well have placed an ominous interpretation on President Kennedy's remarks to [Khrushchev's son-in-law Alexei] Adzhubei (January 30, 1962) regarding the parallelism between the Soviet attitude toward Hungary and ours toward Cuba." Kennedy had "pointed out that the USSR would have the same reaction if a hostile group arose in the vicinity of its borders. In this connection, the president referred to the Soviet reaction to the [1956] Hungarian uprising." Kennedy's words were made particularly ominous by the background chorus: influential Americans demanding military action against Cuba, the administration's paramilitary operations and acts of sabotage, its efforts to cripple Cuban trade, its successful drive to expel Cuba from the Organization of American States, and U.S. military maneuvers in the Caribbean. In Hughes's words, the spring of 1962, when the decision to install the missiles was made, "was a time of heightened Cuban concern about invasion."[26] Looking back, thirty years later, Kennedy's defense secretary Robert McNamara concluded, "I want to state quite frankly with hindsight, if I had been a Cuban leader [in the summer of 1962], I think I might have expected a U.S. invasion. . . . And I should say, as well, if I had been a Soviet leader at the time, I might have come to the same conclusion." As Hughes and McNamara suggested, and recent scholarship confirms, Castro was motivated by a legitimate concern for his country's security. The Soviets added to this concern the desire to close the "missile gap"—America's well-publicized overwhelming superiority in strategic weapons.[27]

The Cubans and Soviets would have been even more alarmed had they been privy to the secrets of Operation Mongoose. Lansdale's plan was based on two assumptions: "(1) The United States will make maximum use of Cuban resources, but recognizes that final success will require decisive U.S. military intervention; and (2) the development of Cuban resources will be for the purpose of facilitating and supporting this intervention and to provide a preparation and justification for it." The president was not asked to "make a policy decision at this time, but simply to note the assumption." A U.S. invasion of Cuba was the heart of Mongoose, and Kennedy knew it.[28]

Kennedy learned that there were Soviet missiles in Cuba on October 16. On October 24 the U.S. Navy quarantined the island. Four days later, Khrushchev agreed to remove the missiles. He did not consult Castro. "We realized that we had become some type of game token," Castro later said. He had expressed his feelings equally bluntly at the time: "I do not see how you can say that we were consulted in the decision you took," he wrote Khrushchev. Crowds in Havana chanted: "Nikita you fairy, what you give you can't take back."[29]

Arguably, however, Castro gained something from the crisis: in his October 27 letter to Khrushchev, Kennedy pledged that if the Soviet Union removed the missiles from the island "under appropriate United Nations observation and supervision" and provided "suitable safeguards" against the introduction of offensive weapons in the future, the United States would "give assurances against an invasion of Cuba."[30] In a stimulating essay, John Lewis Gaddis writes, "whatever the prospect of an American attack on Cuba before the missile crisis, there was never a serious one after it."[31] While the point is true, it must be qualified. Kennedy had hedged his pledge with conditions that the Cubans rejected. Castro had refused to allow on-site UN supervision of the missiles' removal or any future on-ground verification that no missiles had been installed, and Kennedy had consequently rebuffed Khrushchev's repeated requests to sign a document formalizing the noninvasion pledge. At his November 20 press conference Kennedy gave himself more wiggle room. After noting that his conditions for a U.S. noninvasion guarantee had not been met, he said, "If all offensive weapons are removed from Cuba and kept out of the hemisphere in the future . . . and if Cuba is not used for the export of aggressive Communist purposes, there will be peace in the Caribbean."[32] This new condition was elastic. If Kennedy or Johnson had wanted to invade, he could have argued that Castro's support for armed struggle in Latin America had rendered the noninvasion pledge invalid.

The fact that the United States did not invade Cuba has given Kennedy's pledge more weight than it deserves. The documents that have been declassified suggest that the prospect of an invasion was "shunned"[33] because of its potential cost—the toll in American lives, the risk of a confrontation with the Soviet Union spiraling into global war, the negative impact on the allies and on public opinion worldwide—rather than scruples pursuant to the purported noninvasion pledge. Furthermore, Cuba would soon be overshadowed by Vietnam.

Not surprisingly, the noninvasion pledge offered no comfort to the Cubans. They had lost a real guarantee—the presence of the missiles—for a hollow promise. They had no reason to believe an American president's assurances, particularly when qualified with conditions they would not meet. Castro put it plainly, "We don't believe in Kennedy's words. Moreover Kennedy has given no pledge and, if he did give it, he has already taken it back."[34] The Missile Crisis did not affect Castro's prestige at home. ("On the contrary," the CIA remarked, "the way in which Castro stood up to the Soviets and the US and got away with it probably bolstered his position at home.") But it increased the Cubans' insecurity by making clear, as historian Nicola Miller put it, "that at any critical juncture the USSR would subordinate its ties with Cuba to its relationship with the United States."[35] For the Cubans, this was chilling.

The Missile Crisis was followed by an improvement in relations between the United States and the Soviet Union. On June 10, 1963, in a commencement address at American University, Kennedy urged, "Let us reexamine our attitude toward the Soviet Union" and work together toward peace. "As Americans, we find communism profoundly repugnant. . . . But we can still hail the Russian people for their many achievements—in science and space, in economic and industrial growth, in culture and acts of courage." It was, Khrushchev said, "the best speech by any President since Roosevelt."[36] Six weeks later, in Moscow, American, British, and Soviet officials initialed the test ban treaty, "the most important arms-control accord since the start of the Cold War."[37]

This incipient détente did not extend to Cuba. A senior CIA official noted that during the first months of 1963 Castro had made "tentative overtures for normalizing relations" and had been rebuffed. The paramilitary raids, the sabotage operations, and the efforts "to tighten the noose around the Cuban economy" continued.[38] So did the attempts to assassinate Castro.

On June 19, nine days after his speech at American University, Kennedy approved an "Integrated Covert Action Program" that aimed "at maintaining all feasible pressures on Cuba and at creating and exploiting situations in Cuba calculated to stimulate dissident elements within the regime, particularly in the armed forces, to carry out a coup." The program contemplated sabotage operations against "four major segments of the Cuban economy: (a) electric power; (b) petroleum refineries and storage facilities; (c) railroad and highway transportation; and (d) production and manufacturing." Paramilitary operations and efforts to cripple Cuban trade with third countries would be intensified. This program was more realistic than Mongoose in that it no longer set a deadline for Castro's fall or even proclaimed it as inevitable.[39] Hope had replaced certitude. Cuba was still a burning issue in the United States, and Kennedy's mind was on the 1964 presidential elections. "You'd pay a political price if you didn't do all you could to overthrow Castro; you wouldn't pay a political price if you did everything you could to overthrow him," McGeorge Bundy recalled. Furthermore, American pressure might keep Castro on the defensive and make it more difficult for him to support subversion in the hemisphere. Above all, the CIA was confident that its program would undermine the Cuban economy and offer the Latin American people a salutary object lesson. "Cuba was the key to all of Latin America," DCI John McCone had told President Kennedy and his top aides in an August 1962 meeting. "If Cuba succeeds, we can expect most of Latin America to fall."[40]

CASTRO'S GUERRILLA OFFENSIVE, 1961–1964

While Kennedy was promoting subversion in Cuba, Castro was promoting revolution in Latin America. Self-defense and idealism motivated the Cubans. "His [Castro's] desire to promote other Cubas," a senior U.S. intelligence official remarked, "was probably . . . related to his quest for internal consolidation—had another country gone the way of Cuba, Castro's situation might have been easier—and perhaps to his fear that the US might move against him. The US might threaten or create difficulty for one Cuba standing alone, but—Castro may have thought—the presence of two or more revolutionary regimes would force an American accommodation to the new reality." The United States "will not be able to hurt us," Castro explained, "if all of Latin America is in flames."[41]

Revolution in Latin America, however, was not only in Cuba's interest. It was also, Cubans believed, in the interest of the people. Only through armed struggle could the Latin Americans attain social justice and national sovereignty.

Cuban leaders and U.S. officials agreed on one key point: the objective conditions that gave rise to revolution—misery, ignorance, and exploitation—were present in Latin America. As INR director Hughes pointed out, the Cubans viewed Latin America "as a tinder box to which one merely had to apply a spark . . . to set off the revolutionary explosion."[42] This spark would be provided by what the Castroites termed "the foco," the small guerrilla vanguard that would launch armed struggle in the countryside.

Castro wanted the armed struggle to start immediately. "The struggle must come first," he explained. "In the course of the struggle the revolutionary conscience [the people's awareness that they could and should fight back] will surge forth." The war against Batista had shown that the foco could create this awareness and set the forest ablaze. One of Che Guevara's close aides recalled: "We were absolutely convinced that we had discovered an infallible method to free the people." Because the objective conditions were present, a handful of dedicated revolutionaries could triumph against impossible odds. "We have demonstrated," Che wrote, "that a small group of men who are determined, supported by the people, and not afraid of death . . . can overcome a regular army." This was the lesson of the Cuban revolution.[43]

It echoed throughout Latin America. "The Cuban revolution . . . was like a continental detonator," a member of the Central Committee of the Venezuelan Communist Party remarked. "It justified revolutionary impatience, and it ended the old discussion about geographic fatalism—the belief that no revolution in Latin America could ever succeed because it was in the backyard of the U.S. empire. In one fell swoop, the Cuban revolution swept away that old ghost." Fired by the Cubans' example, and by Castro's call to the true revolutionaries to fight, guerrillas became active in Venezuela, Guatemala, Nicaragua, Honduras, the Dominican Republic, Peru, and Argentina.[44]

Castro argued that "the virus of revolution is not carried in submarines or in ships. It is wafted instead on ethereal waves of ideas. . . . The power of Cuba is the power of its revolutionary ideas, the power of its example." The CIA agreed: "The extensive influence of 'Castroism' is not a function of Cuban power," it noted in mid-1961. "Castro's shadow looms large because social and economic conditions throughout Latin America invite opposition to ruling authority and encourage agitation for radical change." Cuba, however, did not just rely on the power of its example. "By 1961–1962, Cuban support began taking many forms," a CIA study noted, "ranging from inspiration and training to such tangibles as financing and communications support as well as some military assistance."[45]

Under Castro's overall direction, Che Guevara orchestrated Cuban assistance to insurgencies in Latin America. He was assisted by the General Directorate of

Intelligence (DGI), which was established in 1961 within the Ministry of the Interior and was headed by Manuel Piñeiro.

The most significant aid was military training in Cuba. U.S. intelligence estimated that between 1961 and 1964 "at least" 1,500 to 2,000 Latin Americans received "either guerrilla warfare training or political indoctrination in Cuba."[46] Very few Cubans, however, joined the guerrillas in Latin America. Havana's revolutionary fervor was tempered by self-preservation. While a conflagration would stay Washington's hand, igniting the blaze was dangerous. Cuba did not want to give the United States a pretext for intervention, and the export of Cuban guerrillas would be far more provocative than the import of hundreds of Latin Americans to train on the island. As a result, between 1961 and 1964 only two Cubans fought in Latin America (both in Argentina).[47]

The same caution governed the dispatch of weapons. Cuba, the CIA noted in 1964, "generally has avoided sending arms directly to other Latin American countries."[48] In November 1963, however, a three-ton cache of arms and ammunition was discovered on a Venezuelan beach, and some could be directly traced to Cuba. Furthermore, the motor on a small boat found nearby had been shipped from Canada to Cuba one month earlier. This was, the CIA pointed out, "The first certain instance of major Cuban involvement in the supply of arms to subversive elements in Latin American countries."[49] The Cubans had thrown caution to the wind in this case because the stakes appeared high and the need urgent: the weapons were an indispensable part of the "Caracas Plan," a series of major military attacks that the Venezuelan guerrillas intended to launch in the capital to disrupt the December 1963 presidential elections and trigger a popular insurrection.[50]

From 1961 to 1964, the degree of Cuban involvement in the guerrilla wars of Latin America varied. At one extreme was Argentina, where the Cubans prepared the 1963–64 insurgency and selected its leader; at the other, the 1963 guerrilla uprising in the Dominican Republic, where Cuban involvement was virtually nonexistent.[51] In every case, however, Cuba helped those who were willing to fight, even if they did not belong to the local Communist Party. For Castro, the foco was the nucleus of the authentic revolutionary party.

TILTING AT A MODUS VIVENDI

While supporting the guerrillas in Latin America, Castro also explored the possibility of some form of accommodation with the United States.

A new chapter began on September 18, 1963, when William Attwood, a Kennedy political appointee who was attached to the U.S. mission to the United Nations after serving as ambassador to Guinea, wrote a memorandum on Cuba. "This memorandum proposes a course of action which, if successful, could remove the Cuban issue from the 1964 [U.S. presidential] campaign," was the catchy beginning.

It does not propose offering Castro a "deal"—which could be more dangerous politically than doing nothing. It does propose a discreet inquiry into the possibility of neutralizing Cuba on our terms. . . .

Since we do not intend to overthrow the Castro regime by military force, is there anything else we can do which might advance U.S. interests without risking charges of appeasement?

According to neutral diplomats and others I have talked to at the U.N. and in Guinea, there is reason to believe that Castro is unhappy about his present dependence on the Soviet bloc; that he does not enjoy being in effect a satellite; that the trade embargo is hurting him—though not enough to endanger his position; and that he would like to establish some official contact with the U.S. and go to some length to obtain normalization of relations with us—even though this would not be welcomed by most of his hard-core Communist entourage, such as Che Guevara.

All of this may or may not be true. But it would seem that we have something to gain and nothing to lose by finding out whether in fact Castro does want to talk and what concessions he would be prepared to make. . . .

For the moment, all I would like is the authority to make contact with [Carlos] Lechuga [Cuba's chief delegate at the UN]. We'll see what happens then.[52]

Attwood's proposal went to Robert Kennedy and McGeorge Bundy and then to the president. Attwood "obtained the president's approval . . . to make discreet contact with Dr. Lechuga," and Lechuga "hinted that Castro was indeed in a mood to talk."[53]

After several weeks of discreet and intermittent contacts, on October 31 René Vallejo, Castro's personal physician and confidant, informed Attwood that Castro wanted to see him or any other U.S. envoy, "anytime and appreciated the importance of discretion to all concerned. . . . he wanted to do the talking himself." On November 11, Vallejo sent a second message. "He emphasized that only Castro and himself would be present at the talks and that no one else—he specifically mentioned Guevara—would be involved," Attwood told Gordon Chase, an NSC aide who was Bundy's point man on Cuba. "Vallejo also reiterated Castro's desire for this talk and hoped to hear our answer soon."[54]

The next day Bundy told Attwood that the White House had decided to first hold preliminary talks with Cuban officials at the United Nations to find out what concessions the Cubans were willing to offer, "stressing the fact that, since we are responding to their invitation and are not soliciting a meeting, we would like to know more about what is on Castro's mind before committing ourselves to further talks in Cuba." On November 18, Attwood reported, "Vallejo informed me by telephone that instructions were being sent to the Cuban representative, Dr. Lechuga, to discuss an agenda with me."[55] Three days later, in Havana, a prominent French journalist, Jean Daniel, had a lengthy conversation with Castro. "Jean Daniel is regarded by INR analysts as a reliable journalist who reports accurately what he hears," INR director Hughes wrote. According to Daniel, Castro had told him that " 'Kennedy . . . has the possibility of becoming . . . the leader who may at last understand that there can be coexistence between capitalists and socialists, even in the Americas.' "[56]

Perhaps, but the emphasis must be placed on "the possibility of becoming." What had taken place was only, as Bundy said, a "very tenuous, sensitive, and marginal" beginning,[57] and at the same time, the paramilitary program against Castro was continuing. On November 12, Kennedy approved a CIA plan for "autonomous anti-Castro groups" to operate against Cuba from Nicaragua and Costa Rica, and "destruction operations . . . against a large oil refinery and storage facilities, a large electric plant, sugar refineries, railroad bridges, harbor facilities, and underwater demolition of docks and ships."[58]

Ten days later, Kennedy was assassinated. ("It is likely," the CIA inspector general wrote, "that at the very moment President Kennedy was shot a CIA officer was meeting with a Cuban agent in Paris and giving him an assassination device for use against Castro.")[59] Gordon Chase, the White House point man on Cuba, noted, "Basically, the events of November 22 would appear to make accommodation with Castro an even more doubtful issue than it was. While I think that President Kennedy could have accommodated with Castro and gotten away with it with a minimum of domestic heat, I'm not sure about President Johnson. For one thing, a new president who has no background of being successfully nasty to Castro and the Communists (e.g. President Kennedy in October, 1962) would probably run a greater risk of being accused, by the American people, of 'going soft.' "[60] On December 2, Lechuga told Attwood that "he had received a letter from Castro authorizing him to talk with me about certain problems 'in a general way,' " and inquired whether, in view of Kennedy's death, "we still wished to have such a talk. I told him I would let him know."[61]

The new administration was not interested. "We never picked up . . . the message which Castro sent to Lechuga for us in November 1963," Chase remarked the following April.[62] President Johnson was more interested in figuring out how, as he said, "to pinch their nuts more than we're doing." Reflecting the consensus of U.S. intelligence, McGeorge Bundy pointed out at a February 1964 White House meeting that "the chances are very good that we will still be living with Castro some time from now and that we might just as well get used to the idea. At the same time, we should probably continue our present nasty course; among other things, it makes life a little tougher for Castro and raises slightly the poor odds that he will come apart and be overthrown."[63] Johnson stayed the course, continuing the paramilitary operations and the efforts to cripple the Cuban economy. "We want to make the industrial situation in Cuba grind to a halt," Dean Rusk told the British prime minister.[64] Washington rejected renewed Cuban feelers in mid-1964.[65]

An analysis written in early 1964 by the State Department's Policy Planning Council offers insight into the administration's state of mind. If Castro were to promise to desist from exporting revolution in the hemisphere, the document asked, "where would this leave us?" Assume, for example, that he went as far as to

> abandon identifiable activities such as the training of nationals of other countries, the dissemination of insurrection propaganda, and insurrection inciting broadcasts. But could we have any assurance that once he had formally complied with our wishes and we had eased the pressures mounted against him, he would not quickly resume his previous course? . . . The problem is not alone that Communists in a situation like this literally and as a matter of principle on their part cannot be trusted. There is the added difficulty of the peculiar character of Castro and certain of his closest associates. Evidently revolution is their *raison d'etre* as political beings. We have every reason to believe that they no more could give up their revolutionary agitations and activities than they could stop breathing.

And this was not even the greatest threat, the document warned. "Perhaps of even greater moment is that the primary danger we face in Castro is not what he does in the way of distributing arms, disseminating propaganda, training subversives, and dispatching agents, but in the impact the very existence of his regime has upon the leftist movement in many Latin American countries." Presume, for example, that Castro did abandon all his efforts to export revolution. "Would this lead to an improvement of the situation in Venezuela? The simple fact is that Castro represents a successful defiance of the US, a negation of our whole hemispheric policy of almost a century and a half. Until Castro did it, no Latin American could be sure of getting away with a communist-type revolution and a tie-in with the Soviet Union. As long as Castro endures, Communists in other Latin American countries can, to use Stalin's words, 'struggle with good heart.' "[66]

Would Castro have been willing to abandon support for armed struggle in Latin America? In early February 1964 he told Lisa Howard, an ABC correspondent who had played a significant role in the Attwood conversations: "Tell the President [Johnson] (and I cannot stress this too strongly) that I seriously hope that Cuba and the United States can eventually sit down in an atmosphere of goodwill and of mutual respect and negotiate our differences. I believe that there are no areas of contention between us that cannot be discussed and settled within a climate of mutual understanding. But first, of course, it is necessary to discuss our *differences*. I now believe that this hostility between Cuba and the United States is both unnatural and unnecessary—and it can be eliminated."[67]

The next month a CIA report quoted a high-ranking Cuban official close to Foreign Minister Raúl Roa, a member of Castro's inner circle, saying that Roa had said, "Castro sincerely desires to enter negotiations with the United States with the aim of reducing tensions between the two countries" and that the Soviets were urging him in that direction. Furthermore, Castro "and leading Fidelistas" had concluded that "despite Soviet good will, Cuba cannot again achieve a state of prosperity with Soviet economic aid alone."[68]

In August 1964 the British ambassador in Havana told the Foreign Office that he believed that Castro was "ready to give up subversion and lessen appreciably his dependence on the Communist world," provided that the United States would "in return call off the subversive measures taken against him" and cease its efforts to cripple Cuba's trade with third countries. Castro was not thinking "of cordial ties" with the United States and U.S. aid. "Even diplomatic relations may not be possible at the first stage." He would "pay the price of giving up subversion, in return for an attitude by the United States administration which he would call 'cold but correct.' "[69]

It is impossible to know what Castro's intentions were because the United States consistently rebuffed his overtures. A modus vivendi with the United States would have lowered his international profile and curtailed his activism. It would have run counter to his sense of mission and his deep hostility to the United States. It would have satisfied, however, a deep longing. Tad Szulc, Castro's foremost biographer, stresses "the obsession of Fidel Castro to do away with human, social and economic underdevelopment in Cuba. . . . To eradicate underdevelopment . . . was, indeed, Castro's magnificent obsession from the beginning."[70] INR's director Hughes wrote insightfully in the spring of 1964:

> The combined weight of economic troubles, revolutionary failures, and Soviet pressures has created a difficult problem for Cuba's leaders. On the one hand, they are still dedicated revolutionaries, utterly convinced that they can and must bring radical change to Latin America some day. Many would rather be remembered as revolutionary martyrs than economic planners. Yet on the other hand these same men are aware that the current pressing problems demand amelioration that can only be brought by muting the call to revolution, by attempting to reach live and let live arrangements with the US, and by widening trade and diplomatic contacts with the free world.
>
> Tension between the two paths, between peaceful coexistence and the call for violent revolution, will continue to exist within the Cuban hierarchy, both within and between individuals, for the foreseeable future.[a,71]

It would be fascinating to have Cuban sources to help assess whether this was, indeed, a missed opportunity, but, unfortunately, the Cubans have said nothing about their attempts to develop a modus vivendi with the United States in the 1960s, except for a very shallow and inaccurate account by Lechuga, and they have not declassified any of the relevant documents.[72]

---

a. Four months later, a National Intelligence Estimate made virtually the same point: "We believe that Castro has a serious interest in improving relations with the US. . . . His interest in stabilizing relations with the US wars with elements in Castro's temperament, with his strong revolutionary bent, and with his recurring conviction that the US price for normalization would be nothing less than his own disappearance. . . . Nevertheless, he has made various overtures toward the US from time to time." (NIE, "Situation and Prospects in Cuba," Aug. 5, 1964, p. 20, NSFCF, box 24.)

Spurned by the United States, Castro continued to support armed struggle in Latin America. But by 1964 he faced a string of setbacks. The most notable was the spectacular failure of the guerrillas in Venezuela to disrupt the country's December 1963 presidential elections. Guerrilla uprisings in Peru, Argentina, Nicaragua, and the Dominican Republic had been swiftly crushed. Castro's belief that a small guerrilla nucleus could set the forest ablaze had been wrong.[b] The security forces of the various Latin American countries were strong enough to annihilate the handful of guerrillas, and the modest aid Cuba could afford—a few weapons, a little money, some training—paled in comparison with the massive aid Kennedy gave to Latin American military and security forces. Bent on crushing the Castroite challenge, the Kennedy administration paid unprecedented attention to Latin America. It rewarded those Latin leaders it judged reliable allies in the anti-Communist crusade, be they democrats or autocrats, with economic aid and political support; and it undermined constitutional government whenever necessary to uphold pro-American stability—in Argentina, in Brazil, in British Guyana, in Guatemala. "The Kennedy administration . . . did not readily distinguish between political radicals loyal to Moscow and Havana and nationalist reformers," writes Stephen Rabe, author of the best study of Kennedy's Latin American policy. "Like Dwight Eisenhower and John Foster Dulles, the president and his advisers opted for the short-term security that anti-Communist elites, especially military officers, could provide over the benefits of long-term political and social democracy."[73]

The Soviets understood the power of the army in Latin America. For a moment, they had been intrigued by the prospect of revolution in Latin America. In 1961–62 "Moscow was ambivalent about the merits of Castro's regional offensive," write two scholars who had access to the Soviet archives,[74] but by 1964 this ambivalence was gone. As reciprocal disappointment set in, relations between Cuba and the Soviet Union grew strained. The Cubans found the industrial equipment and raw materials provided by the Soviets to be of poor quality, and Soviet technicians and bureaucrats arrogant; they resented Moscow's growing antipathy for armed struggle in Latin America and its interest in courting better relations with Washington even though the Americans were continuing their assault against Cuba.

The Soviets were also disappointed. Cuba was proving to be a far greater economic burden than they had anticipated, and Castro's foolhardy support for guerrilla warfare in Latin America complicated their relations with the United

---

b. The Fidelistas' belief that the Cuban example could be replicated throughout Latin America rested on their mistaken overemphasis on the role of Castro's guerrillas in the overthrow of Batista. When, in the late 1970s, guerrilla movements did finally threaten the existing order in Latin America (Nicaragua, Guatemala, and El Salvador), they did so using methods that had very little in common with the foco theory.

States. Furthermore, most Latin American Communist parties, Moscow's loyal followers, had come to resent Havana's encouragement of armed struggle in the hemisphere, irrespective of their wishes. Several of these parties, the CIA wrote, "made strong demarches to Moscow protesting Cuba's interference in revolutionary affairs of their own countries." With Soviet encouragement, Castro approved the convocation of "a highly secret extraordinary conference" of Latin American Communist parties in Havana in November 1964.[75] The CIA reported that at the conference "the Soviets helped to work out a secret compromise agreement which called for support to insurgency efforts in a few Latin American countries, but specified that in all cases the local Communist party should determine whether violent or nonviolent means were to be pursued."[76] A report from the GDR embassy in Havana confirms the CIA's assessment:

> We have learned from reliable sources that Comrade Fidel Castro initially accused several Latin American parties of not being sufficiently aggressive: They should make the revolution, not wait for it. . . .
>
> Several representatives of the Latin American parties answered vehemently that Cuba's harsh criticism was unjustified and that Cuban interference in their internal affairs, and the aid given by the Cuban leadership to radical, sectarian groups, had led, at times, to tragic consequences. . . . Revolutions could not be generated according to one's wishes, but had to be prepared with the greatest care and attention to all the circumstances. Each respective party should determine, without outside interference, the form the struggle should take at any given time.
>
> Comrade Fidel Castro listened to all this in silence and accepted all the criticism. By stressing the areas of agreement, the well-known and certainly positive results of the conference were achieved.
>
> Even a hasty analysis of Fidel Castro's speech of January 2, 1965, shows that the Cubans have adopted a new stance toward Latin America. Except for a brief reference to the liberation wars in Venezuela and Guatemala, [Castro] referred to the underdeveloped countries only in generalities, stressing instead the liberation struggle in Asia and Africa. This is the first time that in a speech of this importance Latin American problems were not accorded special treatment. . . .
>
> Since the Latin American party conference, Cuba has kept some distance from the Latin American liberation struggle. . . . For now it seems as if Cuba will try to compensate for this through a strong focus on Africa (including Asia).[77]

The East German assessment was right: Castro's focus had shifted to Africa.

CHAPTER TWO
CUBA'S FIRST VENTURE
IN AFRICA: ALGERIA

When Castro came to power in January 1959, Cuba had only one diplomatic link with Africa: a legation in Cairo. Guevara's trip to Egypt that June was the first visit by a high-ranking Cuban official to the continent. Raúl Castro followed in July 1960. Two months later, Fidel Castro delivered a speech at the United Nations dealing forcefully with African issues. Cordial relations were established with Egypt, Ghana, and Guinea. In October 1961 fifteen students from Guinea arrived in Havana to attend university or technical institutes, with Cuba paying all expenses, including the students' stipends; they were the first of many African students to go to Cuba on scholarships provided by the Cuban government.[1] A small number of Africans also arrived in Havana for military training.[2]

Through 1964 the Cubans' interest in Africa was modest, as they focused on promoting revolution in Latin America. With the single exception of Algeria, there was no Cuban military presence anywhere in Africa, not even in Ghana, reports to the contrary notwithstanding. The DGI had no African Department, and there were no DGI operatives based in any African country except Algeria. By 1964, Cuba had embassies in the five radical countries of Africa (Algeria, Egypt, Ghana, Guinea, and Mali) as well as in Morocco and Tanzania.[3] The State Department eyed Cuban activities on the continent warily. In November 1963, when a rumor circulated about an impending Cuban goodwill mission to West Africa, Washington responded with unsubtle blackmail, instructing its embassies in the region to tell the host governments that receiving the mission—not to mention allowing the Cubans to open an embassy—would jeopardize U.S. aid. With dignity, the Nigerian foreign minister replied "in friendly but firm tones . . . [that] we must accept Nigeria's independence." U.S. officials, however, had no reason to fret—the mission never materialized.[4]

U.S. intelligence knew that Africans were going to Cuba for military training. A May 1965 CIA report noted that between 1961 and early 1965, 100 to 200 Africans had been trained there. The British embassy in Havana, which acted as the eyes and ears of the United States after the January 1961 rupture in diplomatic relations between Washington and Havana, also reported that several scores of Africans had been trained in Cuba.[5] But U.S. officials were not concerned. INR noted in April 1964 that, although the Cubans vigorously pursued armed struggle in Latin America, in Africa they sought "peaceful coexistence." Until late 1964 U.S. officials saw only two exceptions to this tranquil pattern: in

Zanzibar, for a brief moment in early 1964, and more persistently in Algeria, which, the same report noted, was "viewed by the Cubans as having a fraternal regime."[6]

FIRST ENCOUNTERS

In late October 1961 a young Argentine journalist, Jorge Ricardo Masetti, traveled to Tunis carrying a message from Fidel Castro. Masetti had gone to Cuba in early 1958 to write about Castro's struggle against Batista, and during the weeks he had spent with the guerrillas he had developed a deep admiration for their cause and become friends with Che Guevara. A few days after the fall of Batista, Guevara invited Masetti to Havana to found and direct the Cuban news agency, Prensa Latina. In early 1961 he began working full time for the fledgling Cuban intelligence service.[7]

It was in this capacity that he was in Tunis. Castro's message was an offer of help to the National Liberation Front of Algeria (FLN), which had been fighting against French rule since 1954. Masetti met the rebel leaders and, as recorded by one of his aides, "it was agreed that Cuba would send weapons." In December a Cuban ship, the *Bahía de Nipe*, left Havana with 1,500 rifles, more than thirty machine guns, four U.S.-made 81-mm mortars, and a large quantity of mortar rounds, also of U.S. manufacture. (Masetti followed, by plane, to supervise the operation.) The weapons were unloaded at Casablanca and transported in January 1962 to the FLN camp near Oujda, near the Algerian border.[8] This was the first military aid Cuba sent to Africa. It included what was, for Cuba, a significant amount of weapons, but no volunteers; it was a tangible token of the Cubans' sympathy with the Algerian cause. (The episode, which was a well-kept secret, was not without irony: Cuba was supplying the FLN with U.S. weapons.)

The *Bahía de Nipe* returned to Havana with seventy-six wounded Algerian fighters, "invited by our government," the Cuban daily *Revolución* reported, "to rest and recuperate in Cuba." With them came twenty children from refugee camps, most of whom were war orphans. "The children," explained *Revolución*, "will study and grow up here . . . and one day become productive citizens of a free Algeria."[9]

The aid Cuba gave Algeria in 1961–62 had nothing to do with the East-West conflict. Its roots predated Castro's victory in 1959 and lay in the Cubans' widespread identification with the struggle of the Algerian people. As Roberto González, a Cuban intellectual, remarked, "A very close bond, a kind of spontaneous 'brotherhood,' developed between the Cuban revolution and the Algerian revolution even before 1959, because they were evolving along parallel paths. The Cuban people identified with the Algerian struggle to an extent that would not be repeated until, perhaps, the Nicaraguan revolution. The anti-Batista papers, like [the weekly] *Bohemia*, fostered this. Since it was not always possible to attack Batista's regime directly, they covered the revolutionary struggle in

Algeria instead—emphasizing the military successes of the FLN and the perfidy of the French."[10]

It was risky for Cuba to assist the FLN, because it meant clashing with French president Charles de Gaulle, who was willing to have normal relations with Cuba, in part to spite the United States. But Cuban officials, from Fidel Castro down, forcefully proclaimed their country's support for the Algerian cause, and Cuba embraced that cause at the United Nations. Alone in the Western Hemisphere, Cuba recognized the Algerian government in exile on June 27, 1961.[11] "We knew we would incur de Gaulle's hostility, and we were ready to pay that price," observed a senior Cuban official. "Fortunately, the reaction wasn't too violent: we had problems with France, but there was no break."[12]

Algeria gained its independence from France on July 3, 1962. On September 26, the National Assembly elected Ahmed Ben Bella prime minister. Two weeks later, Ben Bella left Algiers for New York to attend the ceremony marking his country's admission to the United Nations. He then flew to Washington, where President Kennedy received him cordially on October 15. Only one cloud marred the visit: Ben Bella was going to Cuba.

On October 16, he boarded a Cuban plane in New York for a two-day visit to the island. It was a trip that made a deep impression on him and contrasted sharply with his visit to the United States. In his own words,

> What I missed most in the United States was the warmth of human companionship. America is a wall . . . a wall that separates people. What is lacking is communication among people. . . . I was struck by the absence of that human warmth that is, for us Algerians, an essential element of life, without which we cannot breathe.
>
> With what delight we immersed ourselves, as soon as we had boarded the plane, in the warmth of the Cubans. We had just sat down when they served us an excellent *cafecito*, very strong, very sweet, very fragrant, which was a welcome change from the pale brew they call coffee in the United States. We began talking at once—I don't know in what language because they didn't speak Arabic and I only knew a little Spanish. . . . But friendship overcame everything. . . . Between Cubans and Algerians the communication proved to be immediate and deep.

At the airport, Castro was waiting. And so were the Algerian children, the war orphans who were the guests of Cuba. "I was terribly moved when I saw them there," remembered Ben Bella. "We were only in Cuba for thirty-six hours—but what a celebration it was! I don't know who prepared the schedule, but Fidel paid no attention to it. Protocol was forgotten and we talked, talked. . . . The two youngest revolutions of the world met, compared notes and together envisioned the future. . . . Never had thirty-six hours seemed so short!"[13]

Cubans and Algerians felt that there was a parallel between the struggle of the

In October 1962 Ahmed Ben Bella, prime minister of the fledgling Algerian republic, visited the United States to attend the ceremony marking his country's admission to the United Nations. President Kennedy received him cordially. But the next day, Ben Bella flew to Cuba. Americans were outraged and Kennedy himself "was perplexed," an aide recalled, "by what seemed either hopeless naïveté or calculated insult." The *Christian Science Monitor* was unusual in pointing out that Ben Bella might have had honorable reasons for going to Havana: "gratitude for Cuba's moral support of the Algerian independence movement, and for the care given by Cubans to Algerian war orphans, many of whom are still receiving treatment in Cuba." The paper did not know that Cuba had also sent military aid to the Algerian rebels. This had been Castro's first covert operation in Africa. (This cartoon by Fischetti, captioned "Let me take you to the Casbah," originally appeared in the *New York Herald Tribune* and was reprinted in the *Washington Post*, October 18, 1962.)

Cuban revolution and that of the Algerian revolution. And this created a sense of community. Castro welcomed Ben Bella, saying:

> The peoples of Algeria and Cuba have faced huge obstacles and fought hard, beautiful battles for their independence and self-determination. Both revolutions are irreversible. We greet you and your delegation as the representatives of a people that has freed itself from the shame of colonialism, and spared no sacrifice. We greet the brave guerrillas who for seven years fought gloriously against a powerful army equipped with all the latest weapons. We greet all those who suffered persecution, torture, imprisonment and exile during those seven tragic years. We greet those who represent the indomitable spirit of the National Liberation Front.[14]

Ben Bella responded: "In prison, I followed the heroic struggle of the Rebel Army and its victorious advance from the Pico Turquino [in the Sierra Maestra] all the way to Havana. . . . We Algerians applauded the feats of the bearded Cuban fighters. We celebrated the victory of the Bay of Pigs as though it were our own." He expressed his country's gratitude. "I know that the Cuban guerrillas felt the suffering of their Algerian brothers as if it had been their own. . . . Just as Cuba

In October 1962 Castro urged Cuban doctors to volunteer to serve in the newly independent Algeria. "Most of the doctors in Algeria were French, and many have left the country," he explained. "There are four million more Algerians than Cubans, but they have only a third—or even less—of the doctors we have. . . . Their situation is truly tragic." Among those who responded was Sara Perelló (second from left), who was then a young doctor and a new bride. "When Fidel spoke, we were moved," she recalled. She left in May 1963 with the first Cuban medical mission that went to Algeria. This was the beginning of Cuba's technical assistance program abroad. "It was like a beggar offering his help, but we knew that the Algerian people needed it even more than we did and that they deserved it," Cuba's minister of public health said.

stood with Algeria at every moment," he pledged, "so Algeria is and will be with Cuba. These are not just words, because among combatants words are of secondary importance." In the final communiqué, Ben Bella endorsed Castro's demand that the United States return the naval base at Guantanamo Bay to Cuba.[15]

American citizens sent irate telegrams to President Kennedy venting their indignation. "What goes on that our Government gives millions in aid to Ben Bella," a typical correspondent inquired, "when he brazenly applauds Castro's communist build-up in defiance of [the] U.S.?"[16]

Reactions in the U.S. press and among American political leaders ranged from anger to irritation. (Kennedy, writes an aide, "was perplexed by what seemed either hopeless naïveté or calculated insult.")[17] The *Christian Science Monitor* was unusual in pointing out that Ben Bella might have had honorable reasons for going to Havana: "gratitude for Cuba's moral support of the Algerian independence movement, and for the care given by Cubans to Algerian war orphans, many of whom are still receiving treatment in Cuba. Several of the orphan children presented greeting flowers to the Algerian Premier."[18]

In the Kennedy administration, after momentary choler, cooler tempers prevailed. "There is no visible alternative to the Ben Bella government at this time," a State Department memorandum noted, "and no other combination inherently more promising from our viewpoint."[19]

For the Cubans, Ben Bella's visit was a noble gesture. In Fidel's words,

> To visit Cuba when the powerful and rich Yankee empire is redoubling its hostility and hatred toward us and trying through threats and blackmail and bribery to impose a criminal economic and commercial blockade on us in the hope of crushing the revolution with hunger; to visit Cuba when the Yankee imperialists are also threatening to attack our country at any moment and to drown the creative work of our people in blood is, on your part, Mr. Prime Minister, an act of valor and resoluteness that defines your character; it is a gesture of friendship that we shall never forget. It is also an act that honors the Algerian nation before the peoples of the world.[20]

THE MEDICAL MISSION

It was during Ben Bella's visit that Fidel Castro thought of a way to continue his country's aid to the Algerian revolution. A few hours after the prime minister's departure, Castro delivered a speech at the opening of a medical school:

> Most of the doctors in Algeria were French, and many have left the country. There are four million more Algerians than Cubans and they have been left a great many diseases by colonialism, but they have only a third—or even less— of the doctors we have. In terms of health care, their situation is truly tragic.
>
> This is why I told the students that we need fifty doctors to volunteer to go to Algeria.
>
> I am sure that there will be no lack of volunteers. . . . Today we can send only fifty, but in eight or ten years who knows how many, and we will be helping our brothers . . . because the revolution has the right to reap the fruits that it has sown.[21]

There was indeed no lack of volunteers. They were motivated by a spirit of adventure and, above all, by the desire to respond to Fidel's appeal. "When Fidel spoke, we were moved," remarked Sara Perelló, who was then a young doctor. "My mother told me: 'We must help this muchacho [young man]' (my mother called Fidel muchacho) 'and those people.'" Perelló wrote a letter volunteering and handed it to the director of the hospital where she worked. A few days later she received a telegram telling her to see the minister of public health. She went and was accepted.[22]

Time passed and nothing happened. "Then, all of a sudden, we were told that the medical mission had to leave for Algeria at once," Dr. Manuel Cedeño recalls. Fidel had gone to the Soviet Union and he was going to stop in Algeria on his way back to Havana; the mission had to be there by then. The volunteers left on May 23, 1963, on a special flight of Cubana de Aviación. "None of us had a passport; we just had a sheet of paper from the Foreign Ministry," remembers Dr. Angela Morejón. "We didn't even know how long we were going to stay," adds Perelló, "or where [in Algeria] we were going, or anything at all." Cuban officials knew little more. The two countries had not yet signed an agreement, and many important points (such as the duration of the mission) had yet to be decided. This uncertainty was reflected in newspaper articles about the departure of the mission: the volunteers, said *Revolución*, had agreed to remain in Algeria for no less than one year, and some for two or three years.[23]

The minister of public health, José Ramón Machado Ventura, led the group, which included twenty-nine doctors, three dentists, fifteen nurses, and eight medical technicians. (There were forty-five men and ten women.)[24] "The majority," wrote a journalist, "had only a hazy idea of what Algeria was like. They thought of deserts and palm trees; of beduins and the Foreign Legion; of French terrorists and Arab guerrillas; of Ahmed Ben Bella and [French General Jacques] Massu; of bombs and Arab dances. . . . But they were all agreed on one thing: it was a heroic country that had won its independence with its own blood. It was like Cuba. And Fidel Castro had said it needed their help."[25]

With the arrival of this medical mission in Algeria on May 24, Cuba's technical assistance abroad began. It was an unusual gesture: an underdeveloped country tendering free aid to another in even more dire straits. It was offered at a time when the exodus of doctors from Cuba following the revolution had forced the government to stretch its resources while launching its domestic programs to increase mass access to health care. "It was like a beggar offering his help, but we knew that the Algerian people needed it even more than we did and that they deserved it," Machado Ventura remarked.[26] It was an act of solidarity that brought no tangible benefit and came at real material cost.

"It was a special moment," a member of the mission mused thirty years later, "because it was when this process of internationalist aid began. . . . Nowadays when you say that you have been on a mission people understand what you mean; there is a history, a tradition. Back then there wasn't any. We were taking a first step; we were launching out into the unknown."[27]

How truly unknown it was is described by Dr. Cedeño. "Before we left Cuba," he recalls,

They gave us a lecture about Algeria at the Foreign Ministry; the speaker was the official in charge of North Africa. We wanted to know about the climate, about what kind of clothes to pack. He told us that Algeria was a tropical country and that we should take short-sleeved shirts. This was the full extent of our preparation! When we arrived in Algeria it was very cold. We were freezing; no one had brought an overcoat. Machado Ventura had to buy them for all of us.

When we arrived we didn't know whether Algeria was a desert, or if we were going to examine our patients under a tent. We didn't have the foggiest idea. Our vision of Algeria was straight out of American movies![28]

After a week in Algiers, the volunteers were divided up and sent to several towns. Cedeño went to Sétif with two other doctors, two male nurses, and two medical technicians. They worked in the local hospital and lived in an apartment in it. Sara Perelló went with another group to Sidi Bel Abbès. They, too, worked in the local hospital. At the beginning they lived in an apartment in the hospital; later, in small apartments nearby.[29]

Before leaving Cuba, the volunteers had specified whether the Cuban government should pay their salary, which was exactly the same as they would have earned in Cuba, to their families or deposit it in a bank until their return. They would receive a stipend in Algeria to cover their living expenses, and it would be the same for all, irrespective of their qualifications.[30] In fact, they were not paid any money whatsoever for the first weeks because the Algerians thought that Cuba would pay the stipend and the Cubans thought Algeria would. In the meantime, the members of the mission were penniless.[31]

"We ate in the hospital," recalls Cedeño. "The food in Cuban hospitals was usually bad, but in Sétif it was dreadful. Machado Ventura had given us each fifty dollars cash in Algiers, but no bank in Sétif would change it (they said that we had to go to Algiers); and so we were stuck with $50 in our pockets and hungry! We smoked each butt three times!"[32]

Fortunately, Che Guevara arrived in Algeria in July for the celebration of the first anniversary of independence. "He came to Sétif; he asked us if we had any problems; we told him about the money. He immediately ordered the embassy to give us a loan while the matter was settled between the two governments."[33] Finally it was decided that Cuba would pay their stipend in dinars. The members of the mission were "totally taken care of by their own government," Le Peuple of Algiers pointed out. "The Algerians only provided our lodging, in the hospitals or in nearby apartments," observes a Cuban doctor, "and in some cases offered us meals in the hospitals. But whenever possible we cooked our own meals with the money that Cuba gave us."[34]

The stipend was not always paid on time. "It was very irregular," Perelló remembers. Indeed, after visiting the Cuban medical staff in Tebessa, a Cuban journalist wrote that "they didn't even have the money to buy a postage stamp."[35]

The French and Algerian doctors looked at these strange newcomers from across the Atlantic with some suspicion. "They couldn't understand why we weren't charging for our services—it puzzled the Algerians, and the French even more," Perelló remarked. "And we were doing a lot of things that the doctors there [in Algeria] didn't do. The men [in our group] did their own washing and ironing. We didn't have any money, and we didn't have a car—so we walked everywhere! But the French and Algerian doctors drove their cars. And to make matters worse, we wanted to put in longer days than they did."[36]

The Cubans also found things that unsettled them. Coming from a society that had established free health care, some were shocked that in Algeria, the revolution notwithstanding, patients had to pay for examinations and drugs. And while machismo certainly existed in Cuba, many of the Cubans who went to Algeria were deeply troubled by the treatment of women there. The medical missions always included women (ten in the first: four doctors, five nurses, and one medical technician), and some of them had difficulties dealing with Algerian men. Others were more fortunate. "They didn't give me a hard time," Sara Perelló mused. "I didn't go out alone; I didn't smoke; as a pediatrician I worked with children."[37]

The first medical mission remained in Algeria for a little over a year, until a second arrived in June 1964 with twenty-four doctors, four dentists, twenty-four nurses, and nine medical technicians. (The mission included twenty-seven women: three doctors, twenty-one nurses, and three technicians.)[38] Other missions followed and by the late 1960s many of the problems had been ironed out: the stipend, for instance, was paid regularly; the housing had improved. The first mission, however, retains a special aura. Looking back some thirty years later, one member remarked:

> Our work there was extremely difficult in emotional terms. First, I found a country with habits and customs completely different from mine; an Arab country, Muslim, very different from our culture. Second, the different language—Arabic and some French. There were some unbelievable situations, like when we had to form a chain of translators just to understand what the patient was saying. For many of us our time in Algeria was an extraordinary learning experience; it was the first time that we had left Cuba, and we faced a world very different from our own. . . . There aren't many things in life that you remember thirty years later with a feeling of pride and warmth. Now, with more than sixty years under my belt, I still remember my stay in Algeria as something good, something that helped me, something that made me the man I am today.[39]

THE DESERT WAR

When the Cuban medical mission arrived in Algiers in May 1963, Ben Bella was in Addis Ababa at the founding conference of the Organization of African Unity

(OAU). There, he electrified the assembly with his call for the liberation of Africa. A French journalist captured the moment:

> Pushing his notes aside, pounding the podium with both hands, very pale, the Algerian leader made an impassioned appeal in a breathless voice for aid to the Angolan rebels, reminding the assembly that Algeria's experience showed that only shared sacrifice would force open the gates of freedom. His homage to the Tunisians, Moroccans, and Egyptians who had died for Algeria provoked an emotional response that kept growing for the rest of the speech. . . . I do not think that I have ever had such a profound sense of African unity as when I listened to Ben Bella, tears in his eyes, visibly moved, urge his listeners to rush to the assistance of the men dying south of the equator.[40]

No African leader—not Egypt's Gamal Abdel Nasser, or Ghana's Kwame Nkrumah—had moved the assembly like Ben Bella did; none had found such passionate and sincere tones. Ben Bella, the Arab, "won approval of subsaharans," the U.S. State Department noted dryly. He left Addis Ababa as one of the leaders of the Third World struggle.[41]

He returned home to a far grimmer situation. Ben Bella's honesty, his commitment, his austere life-style were not at issue. Even unsympathetic U.S. officials acknowledged his "passionate desire for drastic social change, for economic progress," and noted that he had adopted "a regimen of austerity in both his personal and his public life."[42] But despite massive French economic aid, his country, ravaged by seven years of war and hit by the departure of 800,000 skilled French settlers, was mired in a severe economic crisis. Unemployment and grinding poverty contrasted sharply with the hopes raised during the war and bred discontentment even though his personal popularity remained high. Meanwhile internal power struggles alienated many in the revolutionary elite and aggravated unrest in the turbulent Kabylia region.[43]

From neighboring Morocco a new threat arose. In the spring and summer of 1963, Morocco's young king, Hassan II, veered sharply toward repression in the face of growing economic, social, and political tensions. "Hassan," a U.S. report noted, "appears obsessed with the preservation of his power, rather than with its application toward the resolution of Morocco's multiplying domestic problems."[44] He flaunted his nationalism by demanding a greater Morocco. In addition to territories still in Spanish hands, he claimed Mauritania (a member in good standing of the OAU), a corner of Mali, and a broad strip of Algeria along the ill-defined border.[45]

Through the late summer of 1963 tension between Morocco and Algeria grew. The border dispute was deepened by the growing ideological rift between the two governments. Hassan was well aware that many in the Moroccan opposition looked with admiration to Algeria, while the Algerian authorities believed that Hassan was stirring the troubles in Kabylia, where, by the end of September, armed revolt began.

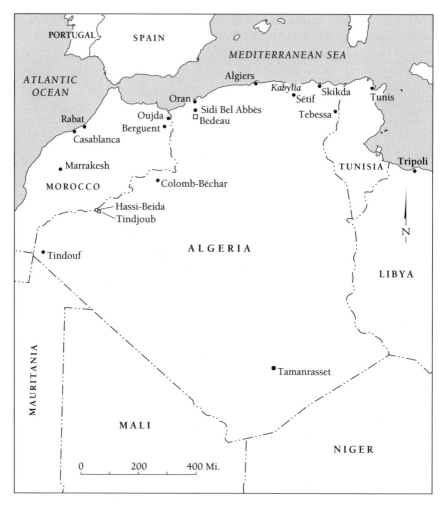

Algeria

Hassan sought to take advantage of the unrest in Kabylia to press his territorial claims. On September 25, following weeks of border incidents, Moroccan troops occupied the Algerian border posts of Hassi-Beida and Tindjoub. "The problem of our borders . . . cannot wait any longer," Rabat warned ominously on October 1. Four days later, representatives of the two governments met at Oujda to try to hammer out a solution. But the Moroccans wanted to change the border, and the Algerians considered it sacrosanct. The meeting, the semiofficial *Le Petit Marocain* pointed out, could not be considered a success: "the Moroccans came to Oujda weighed down with documents and maps of the border. . . . The border incidents," it added, "are the inevitable consequence of the lack of an agreed border between the two countries."[46]

But "if [the] Algerians underestimated Moroccan intentions to force talks on frontiers," the *New York Times* observed, "the Moroccans appeared to have overestimated the threat to Mr. Ben Bella of the dissidence in the Kabylia region."[47] Hassan failed, in any case, to take Ben Bella's determination to maintain his country's territorial integrity into account. On October 8, the Algerians struck back, retaking Hassi-Beida and Tindjoub in a bloody clash. The War of the Desert had begun.[48]

Algeria was at a disadvantage. Its army had neither modern equipment nor training in conventional warfare. These "ragtag forces," as the CIA deemed them, were armed with a "motley salad" of French, German, Czech, and American weapons.[49] "The Algerians really reminded us of ourselves in 1959," mused a Cuban volunteer. "One had a rifle, another had a shotgun, another a machine gun and so on. It was as if we were back in the days of our own Rebel Army in 1959."[50]

The Moroccan army, though slightly smaller than the Algerian, was better equipped and trained. It had forty heavy tanks bought from the Soviet Union in 1962 while the Algerians had only a dozen French-built light tanks and a few others for mine clearing sent by the Soviets. "Those were supplied," the London *Times* noted, "mostly without turrets and armaments." The Algerians were also short of trucks, aircraft, and jeeps.[51]

Taking advantage of this military superiority, and their shorter logistical lines, the Moroccan troops scored several successes along the disputed border in the next three weeks, while Moroccan officials kept insisting that any discussion that did not address the recovery of the Moroccan territories in Algerian hands would be "a dialogue of the deaf."[52]

Cuba identified with Algeria. "Of all the countries in Africa," wrote the Cuban weekly *Verde Olivo*, "it is Algeria that takes the lead in helping the movements of national liberation. . . . It is a model that inspires other Africans who are still marching along the slow road to national independence. The Algerian republic is a beacon for millions and millions of people throughout Africa."[53]

Furthermore, Cuba saw more than greed behind Morocco's aggression: it saw the hand of the United States. "Hassan has become a trained bear against the Algerian revolution, and for this he receives dollars and guns," a high-ranking Cuban official observed. The Cubans believed that the United States hoped that the Desert War would unseat Ben Bella, whose crimes included his loyalty to Cuba. "We will never forget the visit of President Ben Bella to our country one day before the Caribbean crisis [the Cuban Missile Crisis] exploded," Jorge Serguera, Cuba's ambassador in Algiers, asserted. "Nor will we ever forget Algeria's solidarity with our struggle."[54]

According to Serguera, a few days after the Moroccans had seized Hassi-Beida and Tindjoub, Ben Bella asked him if Cuba could send military aid. "I told him, 'If you want I'll call Fidel and explain the situation.' . . . He said, 'OK, go ahead: call Fidel; call Cuba.' "[55]

Serguera went straight to his residence and from there called Piñeiro, the head of Cuban intelligence. "He spoke to him in a language that was not foreign—the words were Spanish—but it was in a code only the two of them could understand," recalled the director of the Cuban news agency, Prensa Latina, in Algeria, Gabriel Molina, a close confidant of the ambassador who was with him that morning.[56] Serguera remembers that he reminded Piñeiro of a battle in which they both had participated against Batista's troops in late 1958. "I talked about that tank coming up from behind on the day they killed Eduardito Mesa and Raúl Perozo.[57] Piñeiro understood what I meant. Then I said, 'Well, we need some of Pedrito's nurses here' (Pedrito Miret was the head of the artillery in Cuba), 'and they should come in jeeps to vaccinate the people, because it's getting bad, and he must take precautions so that everything will work out well and the epidemic that is spreading here is eradicated.' Piñeiro . . . called me back within an hour and a half and said that Fidel had said yes, . . . they were coming."[a,58]

Rabat had just signed a three-year contract with Havana to buy a million tons of Cuban sugar for $184 million, a considerable amount of hard currency at a time when the United States was trying to cripple Cuba's foreign trade.[59] Nevertheless, as soon as it received Ben Bella's request, the Cuban government began forming the Grupo Especial de Instrucción (GEI), the special force that would be sent to Algeria, even though this jeopardized the sugar contract and even though Cuba was, itself, in the middle of a terrible disaster: beginning on October 4, for five harrowing days, Hurricane Flora battered the eastern half of the island, killing 1,400 people. It was "the worst hurricane ever to hit Cuba," the CIA noted.[60]

Lieutenant Pedro Labrador Pino, who would soon fly to Algiers, was near Guantanamo, "right in the middle of the hurricane," when he was ordered to report to the Ministry of the Armed Forces in Havana at once. There, the army chief of staff, Sergio del Valle, addressed him and seven other officers. He said

that we had been chosen for a mission to a sister country that had just asked for our help and that we should tell our families, if we agreed to go—because the mission was absolutely voluntary—that we were going to the Soviet Union to study. (We discussed this for a while—what, exactly, we should tell our families.) Sergio del Valle said again that we should think about it, that the mission was voluntary and if we didn't want to go we should say so. . . .

a. Serguera could have contacted Havana by secure telex, but the telephone was faster. "Furthermore," claims Serguera, "I never trusted coded messages" (interview with Serguera). In fact, in the days that followed, Serguera began sending indiscreet cables, earning a reprimand from Raúl Castro: "Our ambassador must report all matters pertaining to the Grupo Especial de Instrucción only to the Ministry of the Armed Forces. . . . I will then relay all the relevant information to our Minister of Foreign Affairs [Raúl Roa]. While we have full confidence in Roa, we do not know how many hands reports sent to the Foreign Ministry pass through. In one of Serguera's last reports to Roa, he spoke of the 'aid,' of the 'cars' we were going to send, etc. This is improper. It must not happen again" (Raúl Castro to Flavio Bravo and Jorge Serguera, Havana, Oct. 20, 1963, p. 3).

When the meeting was over, I left with [Captain] Ulises [Rosales del Toro]. We talked about it; we wondered where we would be going; there were guerrilla activities in some Latin American countries, and we thought it could be Venezuela, or somewhere else in Latin America. We never even considered Algeria.

The men went to see their families and prepare for the trip. Two days later, they met again at the house of the minister of the armed forces, Raúl Castro. "He received us early; it must have been 6 A.M. . . . . He asked us again whether we were sure we wanted to go. We all said yes. Then he explained our mission— that President Ben Bella had asked Fidel . . . for Cuban fighters. . . . [Raúl] spoke at great length. Then we went straight to the airport of Boyeros; he came to see us off." The leader of the group was Flavio Bravo, a member of the inner circle of the Cuban government.[61]

They flew "under false names, on false passports," on a commercial flight of Cubana de Aviación bound for Madrid. "The plane was full of *gusanos* [exiles] who were leaving the country," Labrador Pino recalled. The plane landed in Algiers, and "we got off, and some of the *gusanos* said, 'Look, they let us out of one communist country only to take us to another!'" Serguera and Algerian officials were waiting for them at the airport. "The first thing we did was to go see Ben Bella to tell him that the weapons were coming," Aldo Santamaría, the commander of Cuba's tiny armored forces, recalled. Then they drove straight to Oran to prepare for the arrival of the Cuban ships bringing the GEI.[62]

On their way to Oran they discovered, to their surprise, that the French army was still in Algeria. "We ran into convoys of French troops and saw French barracks and military camps, and above a hill that dominated the port [of Oran] there was an immense French fort [Mers-el-Kébir] with a commanding view."[63] In their haste, no one in Havana had mentioned that the 1962 independence agreements had allowed the French to keep 80,000 troops in the country for three years and to lease military installations such as Mers-el-Kébir.

THE GEI

Meanwhile, in Cuba, some 350 soldiers were congregating at the military camp of Managuaco (near the town of San José de las Lajas, eighteen miles east of Havana). "We were all asking each other," one of the soldiers recalled, "'Well, where are we going? What will our mission be?'"[64]

In the afternoon of October 9, Raúl Castro came and spoke to them. "He told us that the mission was absolutely voluntary, that a sister country was under attack from reactionary, imperialist forces and that it had asked for our help," one of them recalled. "He said that we could choose not to go, that anyone who did not wish to go should say so." And a handful did. One said, "'Minister, my wife is sick.' Another said: 'My mother is sick.' A third, 'My mother broke her leg.'" They were sent to another barracks (and later returned to their units) while Raúl addressed the rest. Again he stressed "that even though we were members of the armed forces . . . and this was a military mission, participation was absolutely voluntary. . . . For security reasons," he added, "he was not going to tell us where the mission would be." A few hours later, in the early hours of October 10, the volunteers boarded the Cuban merchant vessel *Aracelio Iglesias*, which was also carrying the GEI's tank complement and other heavy weapons, and left Cuba.[65]

"The crossing was terrible because none of us was used to the sea and, in the wake of Flora, the swell was terrible," the head of medical services of the GEI recalled. Furthermore, most of the regular crew had been replaced by men who were politically trustworthy but less familiar with the sea. "Some of them were as green as we were. This was their first day at sea and they were as seasick as we were and they threw up as much as we did. That . . . was an avalanche of vomit! There was no way to control it. And what made it worse (this is a mistake that our medical services will never repeat) was that we had given the volunteers their smallpox vaccine just a few hours before we left and the reaction to it hit us while we were at sea, along with the seasickness, the vomit, and the tension."[66]

While the *Aracelio Iglesias* steamed toward Algeria, more members of the GEI were assembling. They, too, did not know where they were going. ("During all these long hours of waiting," one wrote in his diary, "we have been wondering what our mission is going to be. Maybe we'll be sent to Oriente province, which was so devastated by Flora. Or maybe we'll go abroad to help people who are fighting for their freedom.") On October 16 Raúl Castro came to visit them and, as he had with the previous group, he asked if they were willing "to fight side by side with a brotherly people for their independence" and emphasized that the mission was strictly voluntary. As before, only a handful chose not to go, and the rest were urged to tell their families that they were going to the Soviet Union for several months. A few hours later, at 1 A.M. on October 17, they left Cuba aboard the *Andrés González Lines*. As the coast of Cuba disappeared in the distance, they were told of their destination—Algeria.[67]

The *Aracelio Iglesias* and the *González Lines* were carrying a tank battalion with twenty-two T-34s; an artillery group with eighteen 122-mm guns; eighteen 120-mm mortars; antiaircraft artillery with eighteen guns; a battery of 57-mm recoilless rifles. The entire force had 686 men, including 170 who left Havana on October 21 on two special flights of Cubana de Aviación.[68] (The *González Lines* carried also 4,744 tons of sugar that Cuba was giving the Algerian people.)[69]

The commander of the GEI was Efigenio Ameijeiras, a highly respected officer who presided over the GEI's five-member Military Council. "The orders I had from Fidel," Ameijeiras recalled, "were to place myself at their [the Algerians'] complete disposal, to go wherever they wanted, whenever they wanted."[70]

From Havana, Raúl Castro issued firm instructions to the Military Council. These included a strict code of conduct: no alcoholic beverages of "any type whatsoever, at any time . . . no intimate relationship, of any kind, with women . . . a complete and absolute respect" for Algerian customs and religion. "Do not boast about our Revolution, or our ideology," Raúl went on. "Be modest at all times, share the little we know and never act like experts." The members of the Military Council "should enforce these instructions, above all, by dint of their own example. . . . The orders of the Commander in Chief are," Raúl concluded, " 'Train and Fight; Fight and Train.' "

Raúl Castro included a warning: "Do not be tempted to do more than has been planned, and never volunteer for tasks that are beyond our capabilities." And he explained, "This is the first time our Revolutionary Armed Forces have gone on a mission like this, and we expect the most exemplary behavior from you. . . . We have sent you good men, who are, moreover, volunteers. . . . You will be able to accomplish any task with them, and you must exercise the greatest possible concern for their welfare."[71]

While Raúl Castro was supervising the dispatch of Cuban troops to Algeria, Che Guevara was supervising Cuba's guerrilla offensive in Latin America. Two operations in which Havana set great hope were under way: a group was preparing to start an armed struggle in Argentina, and the DGI was sending weapons to help the Venezuelan guerrillas trigger a popular uprising that would bring down President Betancourt. At the same time Fidel Castro had sent out feelers in New York to explore a modus vivendi with the United States.

In the early hours of October 22, the *Aracelio Iglesias* reached Oran. The first men disembarked dressed in Algerian uniforms, "but then we ran out of uniforms and the rest [of us] wore civilian clothes." They began unloading. "We worked fast, but daylight caught us off guard," Labrador Pino recalled. "Imagine the racket in Oran," Ameijeiras remarked, "lowering those tanks with cranes, and then driving them through the city to the railroad station where they were loaded on trains to Sidi Bel Abbès in broad daylight! Mers-el-Kébir towered above us and we drove past armored personnel carriers with French paratroopers. There was no way to keep our arrival secret."[72]

Within days, the world press announced that a Cuban ship loaded with tanks and military equipment had docked at Oran. The reports were repeated when the *González Lines* arrived a week later. The Cubans would have preferred their presence to have remained a secret, but speed was their first priority. In Ameijeiras's words, "The most important thing was to get there as fast as possible."[73] The American consul in Oran wrote the State Department: "every day persons . . . came to the Consulate to report shipment of tanks, cannon and personnel." The French, the British, and the Canadians also informed Washington, which, in turn, harassed the Algerians. "Highest levels US Government acutely concerned at shipment Cuban arms to Algeria, and potential effect this could have on USG [U.S. government] ability maintain friendly relations with Algeria," Under Secretary George Ball cabled the American embassy in Algeria.

So Embassy should make clear to GOA [Government of Algeria] US aware shipments taking place and keep emphasizing at all appropriate levels GOA that this aid likely further affect image of Algeria in US. We particularly concerned that Cuban personnel and arms may be more difficult for Algeria [to] control in delicate situation than aid from other sources. Aid from a regime so closely tied to USSR will also make Algeria appear to be moving closer to Communist world and hurt GOA image in Africa as unaligned African State. Algerians must be made to understand that the closer GOA-Cuban ties become, the more US-GOA relations will inevitably be affected.[74]

The Algerians, however, had more pressing concerns—namely, their country's territorial integrity, which the Cubans had come to help defend.

In 1997 Ben Bella denied that he had asked Cuba for military aid. "A ship flying the Cuban flag arrived at Oran," he wrote. "To our surprise, tanks and hundreds of Cuban soldiers who were coming to help us were aboard, and I received a brief message from Raúl Castro—written on a page torn from an exercise book—informing me of this act of solidarity."[75]

The evidence indicates otherwise. First, Raúl Castro's October 20 letter to Flavio Bravo, telling the GEI to "train and fight, fight and train," makes it clear that Bravo was in Algeria specifically to prepare for the arrival of the GEI, and to do so required Algerian assistance. Furthermore, on October 21 Flavio Bravo wrote Raúl Castro, describing the Algerians' response to Cuba's offer of aid. "My dear Raúl," Bravo wrote from Algiers, "Yesterday we got the news that Efigenio and 170 compañeros are arriving tomorrow at 3:00 in two planes and that, finally!, the ship is going to arrive today. . . . Everything is ready for them. . . . After our conversation with Ben Bella, Eslimán [Algerian Commander Sliman Hoffman] talked to us about some ideas they have about how to put us to best use: the GEI will begin training at once and, meanwhile, we'll go with him to the front to evaluate, on the ground, plans they have for a counterattack in which we will participate."[76] This indicates that Ben Bella's dramatic tale sheds light on his feelings toward Cuba in 1997, not on the facts.

There is no controversy, however, about what occurred after the Cubans disembarked in Oran. The volunteers went immediately to Bedeau, a former French Foreign Legion camp, near Sidi Bel Abbès. "There are only a few trees around here; no one knows when it last rained; there are dust clouds every-where," wrote a Cuban officer. Bedeau "had been evacuated by the French troops and was in very poor condition," another remembered.[77]

The Cubans prepared to fight. "We met [Defense Minister Houari] Boumedienne in Colomb-Béchar. He has decided to use us, with Algerian troops, in an attack against enemy territory," Flavio Bravo wrote to Raúl Castro. Operation Dignidad, as the Cubans called it, proposed a joint assault across the border on the Moroccan town of Berguent. The Cuban contingent with its twenty-two tanks would spearhead the attack. On the evening of October 28, the commander of the tank battalion, Melquiades González, informed Ameijeiras that his tanks were ready to move. Ameijeiras told him to wait until he heard from Serguera, who was meeting Ben Bella. "At about 1:00 A.M.," González remembered, "Papito [Serguera] called and told him [Ameijeiras] that Ben Bella had decided to suspend the attack . . . because there was the possibility that negotiations could resolve the dispute peacefully, that things could be put right and I don't know what else. Well, Efigenio [Ameijeiras] was furious. . . . He was fuming." Ameijeiras wanted to fight. "He was saying 'But we don't need to talk to anyone! We can kick those people out of there!' " Ameijeiras himself remembers, "It had never occurred to me that it [the War of the Desert] could be settled without our having to fight. I'd assumed that we'd fight and that's why I'd volunteered to lead the GEI. It had never crossed my mind that we wouldn't fight."[78]

On October 29, Ben Bella and Hassan met at Bamako, Mali; they signed a cease-fire the following day. (This was followed, in February 1964, by the return to the status quo ante.)[79]

Press interest in what the Cubans were doing in Algeria immediately faded. As for the U.S. government, the available reports indicate that while U.S. officials were surprised by the Cuban intervention, the focus of their concern was not a small Cuban force in faraway Algeria but the possibility that the war with Morocco might lead the Algerians to deepen their military ties with Moscow and open their country to Soviet military instructors and Soviet weapons.[80]

The Cubans believe that an important consideration in Morocco's decision to negotiate was the arrival of their troops. "We were disembarking in Oran with tanks and artillery," says Ameijeiras. "What must have gone through the Moroccans' minds! It must have given them pause!"[81]

Certainly other factors influenced Hassan. In Algeria, the population rallied in a blaze of patriotism against the aggression, and even the rebels in Kabylia offered their services in defense of the nation. Internationally, Morocco was isolated and there was "a growing Arab inclination to side with Algeria," as the London *Times* wrote on October 22. Egypt, Algeria's closest friend in the region, began sending men and matériel in late October. In Africa, even moderate governments that were Morocco's natural allies were wary of Rabat's territorial ambitions. "Morocco," noted the State Department, "has generally been regarded as a violator of one of the OAU's key precepts—the sanctity of pre-independence national frontiers."[82]

Moreover, Morocco's Western friends failed to offer support. "Paris has maintained sympathetic neutrality and favors a peaceful solution," the Algerian foreign minister observed.[83] Washington, too, disappointed Hassan. Contrary to Cuban suspicions, the Kennedy administration had not instigated the Moroccan aggression. While willing to provide limited assistance, U.S. officials were not eager to satisfy Hassan's "increasingly pressing appeals" for large-scale military aid. "A significantly large injection of U.S. arms . . . would create grave problems both for the king and for us," Assistant Secretary Mennen Williams told the U.S. ambassador in Morocco on October 25. The conflict "could become polarized and would escalate," providing the Soviet Union an opportunity to intervene on Algeria's behalf. "We certainly do not wish to enhance Ben Bella's prestige or otherwise contribute to his influence," Williams explained, but "in our view mediation affords the only useful course now, difficult as that will be."[84]

Nevertheless, the Cuban intervention may have tipped the balance. Morocco's military superiority over Algeria rested on the strength of its hardware— its forty tanks, its heavy guns—and, in a sudden and unexpected move, Castro was sending Algiers both heavy weapons and men trained to use them. "Morocco must have been shocked," Ameijeiras argues. "Until we arrived, they had superiority—the Algerians had only infantry battalions. But all of a sudden, at the hottest moment of the war, tanks and artillery roll off at a port [Oran] very close to the Moroccan border."[85] Furthermore, Morocco seems to have overestimated the number of tanks and the amount of equipment Cuba sent. Certainly press reports and diplomatic cables did. The Cuban ships had unloaded "more than forty Soviet tanks" as well as "crates understood to contain MIG fighters in parts," the London *Times* stated, announcing what became accepted wisdom.[86] Without the personnel to use them, the weapons were of limited significance, but the Moroccans knew that an undetermined number of Cubans had disembarked with the military equipment.

A few weeks later, Boumedienne expressed the "warm thanks of the Algerian people and the Algerian army for the help the Revolutionary Armed Forces [of Cuba] gave us in these critical times."[87]

Looking back, Ameijeiras remarked, "As a soldier I would have liked to have fought, but what happened [the Bamako agreement] was for the best." After Bamako, "we began training the Algerians. We transformed them into tank crews, gunners; we taught them as much as we could in such a short time. We created an Algerian brigade that could perform a number of different tasks. We told the Algerian high command that we were willing to stay longer, and that more time was needed to perfect the training, but they were in a hurry to take over the unit. When we handed it over to them it was the most powerful unit in the Algerian army." Even so, the chief of staff of the GEI wrote in his report to Raúl Castro, "We trained only 926 Algerian compañeros. . . . We could have trained three or four times that number, but the Algerian high command never sent enough men. . . . We could have done more for the Algerian armed forces if they had taken better advantage of our presence."[88]

While the training was under way, the medical services of the GEI provided free health care to the population. "Once they realized that we would examine them for free and that, on top of that, we also gave them medicine for free, they came en masse," the head of medical services of the GEI explained. "We were soon providing medical care to our troops, to the Algerian troops with us at Bedeau, and to a multitude of civilians. We were overwhelmed by the demand for medicine. . . . We tried to stretch our scarce resources as far as possible. . . . Still, sometimes we ran out, and Serguera had to send us supplies as fast as he could." Occasionally, Sara Perelló and other members of the medical mission who were in nearby Sidi Bel Abbès came to help. Their endurance and their commitment impressed the Cuban troops. "The Cuban doctors have faced as many hardships as we have," a young officer wrote in his diary. "They cook for themselves; they have managed for two or three months without receiving their stipend; they live in an area that looks like a graveyard."[89]

Bedeau was not a pleasant place. With their scarce resources, the GEI's political instructors were busy devising ways to occupy the troops during their free time. Pedro Rodríguez Delgado's diary describes how he and his fellow instructors prepared lectures on Algerian history and other unfamiliar subjects. Angelito Martínez, the Spanish colonel who had fought against Franco and had become a member of the Military Council of the GEI, lectured to his heart's content on the Spanish civil war. Enrique, a Venezuelan guerrilla who was living in Algiers, lectured about his country. There were also movies, sports, and, on occasion, excursions. "Our plan was that every Sunday a third of the troops would leave Bedeau to visit historic and scenic places in the region," Rodríguez Delgado wrote.[90]

On December 8, the first shipment of mail finally arrived. "This caused an explosion of happiness. Some compañeros received ten or twelve letters. Many did not sleep at all that night: some were too happy and too busy reading all the letters they had received; others were too upset because they hadn't gotten any."[91] Adopting a system that would be later followed in the Congo and Guinea-Bissau, the families in Cuba were told to send their letters—purportedly bound for Moscow—to an address in Havana, from whence they were routed to Algeria. The system did not work well. "We only got mail four times in the six months we were there," the chief of staff of the GEI told Raúl Castro.[92]

On March 11, 1964, the Cubans officially handed the fully equipped and trained unit over to the Algerians. "By the time the border crisis had subsided in early November 1963, large quantities of Egyptian and Cuban material . . . had entered Algeria," a U.S. intelligence report noted. "The Cubans have withdrawn many of their training personnel and technicians, but unlike the Egyptians they apparently have left most of the military equipment which was sent in October and November 1963." Ameijeiras explained, "We left them all the equipment without charging them anything, not one cent."[93] After the ceremony, each member of the GEI received a small cash bonus from the Cuban government. Throughout the next day, small groups of Cubans shuttled back and forth from Bedeau to nearby towns so that they could all buy small presents for their families. Finally, on March 17, half of the GEI left Algeria aboard the *Aracelio Iglesias*. On March 29 at 4 P.M. they saw the Cuban coastline, and forty-five minutes later they saw, in the distance, a warship steaming toward them. Assuming that it was a U.S. ship, "they sounded the alarm and all the troops went below deck"—seeking to hide from the inquisitive Americans, while preparing to fight, if need be. "A few minutes later, the captain announced that it was a Cuban warship that was going to accompany us to Havana. We were thrilled." They docked the next day. On April 1, Raúl Castro visited them at the military camp of La Cabaña, where they were resting. He praised them, "and spoke of how well we had fulfilled our mission. Then he said that the officers would be given twenty days of vacation and the noncommissioned officers and soldiers one month. . . . He also said that each of us would receive thirty pesos and transportation back home."[94] Two weeks later, the rest of the force returned to a similar reception. After six long months, the GEI had come home. The Cuban press was as silent about its return as it had been about its departure.

COVERT OPERATIONS

This first expedition of Cuban troops to Africa had been a success. There had been no casualties. At one moment it had seemed that Morocco, which had just signed a contract to buy 1 million tons of Cuban sugar, would retaliate: on October 31, 1963, due to "the dispatch of Cuban weapons and volunteers to Algeria," Rabat broke diplomatic relations with Havana and began searching for another supplier. Eager to deprive Cuba of a market, U.S. officials wanted to help but could not find any sugar producer willing to match Cuba's price (8.4 cents per pound against a world price of 10.3). And so Morocco resumed relations with Cuba on January 13, 1964, and honored the contract, despite the objections of U.S. officials.[95]

Cuba's act of solidarity impressed the Algerians. In a postmortem on the war a U.S. intelligence report noted that Cuba's aid "probably reinforced Ben Bella's feeling that natural ties exist between Algeria and Cuba. . . . Ben Bella's attitudes on Cuba are a peculiar admixture of emotional identification with a nation which supported the Algerian independence struggle, admiration for Castro's radical zeal, and intuitive certainty that the US wishes to extinguish Latin America's leading revolutionary light."[96]

Ben Bella expressed his feelings toward, as he called it, "the heroic Cuba"[97] in a speech in honor of visiting Cuban president Osvaldo Dorticós in October 1964:

> If today Algeria feels so close to Cuba, if we have always felt so close to Cuba, it is because . . . there have never been, since the world began, two other countries that have triumphed over the problems we both have faced.
>
> If our country feels so close to Cuba it is because we have endured the same trials, faced the same obstacles, and accepted the same enormous sacrifices. It is also because we have nurtured and still nurture the same generous dreams. . . .
>
> If we feel so close to our Cuban brothers it is because they too refuse to bend. It is because given the choice—to bend or to stand firm—they, like us, have chosen to stand firm against the aggressor.[98]

Ben Bella "has an emotional attachment for Castro, and apparently admires the Cuban social revolution," concluded the CIA, while a State Department intelligence report lamented: "Algeria has literally become a congenial second home for traveling Cubans, and an all-important base for extending Cuban influence in Africa."[99]

Indeed, Algeria was Cuba's headquarters in Africa. Until 1964, Havana's involvement with the rest of the continent was limited and the ambassadors Cuba sent to Africa were men of the second rank. This was true even for Ghana and Egypt, which were, after Algeria, Cuba's closest friends on the continent. But to Algiers Havana sent thirty-year-old Jorge Serguera, a man who had fought against Batista in the Sierra Maestra, rising to comandante, the highest rank in the rebel army, and had then occupied a series of key posts, including attorney general and chief of an army corps. He was a close friend of Fidel and Raúl Castro, and of Che Guevara. He was, in short, "an ambassador of substance."[100]

Until 1965 Cuban intelligence did not have any operatives in Africa, except in Algeria. "When I arrived there [in January 1963] as our embassy's third secretary," Darío Urra remarked, "I was already working full time for [DGI chief] Piñeiro." Other members of the embassy also worked for the DGI. And it was above all in Algeria that Cuba began developing contacts with African guerrilla movements, particularly from the Portuguese colonies. "The first time I saw Amílcar Cabral [the leader of the insurgency in Guinea-Bissau] was in Nourredine Bakhti's house," Urra recalled. Bakhti, who was a captain in the Algerian Defense Ministry, "was one of our key contacts for intelligence operations."[b,101]

Algeria was more than Cuba's window on the continent. The close collaboration between the Cuban and the Algerian intelligence services went beyond Africa. "They did many of the things that we couldn't do for ourselves in Latin America," notes Ulises Estrada, who was a senior DGI officer.[102] "During one of his visits to Algeria," Ben Bella explained, "Che Guevara relayed a request to me from Fidel. Since Cuba was being closely watched, it was virtually impossible to send arms and military cadres who had been trained in Cuba to Latin America. Could Algeria help? . . . My answer was, of course, a spontaneous 'yes.' "[103] The Algerians were motivated both by their desire to help Cuba and by their belief in the community of interests between Africa and Latin America. The close relationship with Cuba, Defense Minister Boumedienne told Le Peuple upon returning from a trip to Havana, "will help us achieve one of our major goals: that Latin America and Africa help one another in their common struggle."[104]

The Algerians "served as a bridge for us with Latin America," observes Urra. Ben Bella's Algeria established diplomatic relations with a number of Latin American countries, such as Argentina, Brazil, and Venezuela, that had broken diplomatic relations with Havana. Furthermore, several Latin American guerrilla movements had representatives in Algiers, and Algeria was "cooperating

b. If Algeria was to be Cuba's headquarters in Africa, then the choice of Serguera as ambassador was unfortunate. Intelligent and physically brave, the mercurial Serguera lacked both the sensitivity to understand Africa and the humility to realize how much he needed to learn. His advice during Che Guevara's visit to Africa in early 1965 contributed to Havana's overestimation of the revolutionary potential of the region.

with Cuba in training and materially supporting some Latin American revolutionaries," as the CIA reported. "Our relations with the Algerians were really close," Serguera explained. "We were more than an embassy."[105]

Algerian assistance was particularly useful for Cuba's efforts to help the guerrillas in Argentina and Venezuela. In the fall of 1962 Jorge Masetti, the young Argentine who had brought Castro's offer of support to the FLN in late 1961 and had been selected to lead the guerrilla uprising in Argentina, left Cuba for Algeria, where he was joined by four or five members of his group. They underwent training in urban guerrilla warfare, which was, as Urra said, "a specialty of the Algerians." In the spring of 1963 Algeria provided Masetti and his companions diplomatic passports and, disguised as members of an Algerian commercial delegation, they flew to Brazil and then to Bolivia.[106]

Of the other Latin American guerrilla movements, it was the Venezuelans who had the most established presence in Algeria, where they had two safe houses. Small groups of Venezuelans who had trained in Cuba returned home via Algiers, with the assistance of the Algerian intelligence services.[107]

The U.S. State Department's INR reported, correctly, "The Algerians have also been tied in to elaborate and unlikely plots to ship arms to the Venezuelan FALN [Fuerzas Armadas de Liberación Nacional] by hiding them in food shipments." Estrada recalled, "We sent weapons to Venezuela through Algeria." Urra added that "we wrapped the guns in plastic bags and put them in barrels of olive oil." The deputy chief of mission remembered, "They were gigantic barrels!"[108]

In December 1964 Che Guevara's first stop on his three-month tour of Africa was Algiers, to speak with Ben Bella, and he returned twice before flying back to Havana in March. "One result of Guevara's trip was to bring Cuba and Algeria even closer together than before," a senior U.S. official remarked.[109]

Among the topics that Guevara discussed with Ben Bella were Cuba's assistance to the Venezuelan rebels. A Cuban ship, the *Uvero*, was going to dock in the Algerian port of Skikda with weapons for the Venezuelans. On June 19, 1965, the *Uvero* reached Skikda, but it left immediately without unloading the weapons. A few hours earlier, Ben Bella had been overthrown.[110]

THE FALL OF BEN BELLA

"United States diplomats in Algiers were openly exultant with the downfall of Ben Bella," two journalists noted. The uneasiness that U.S. officials had felt toward his administration during the Desert War had hardened into hostility. "B.B. is playing into the hands of the Soviets," National Security Adviser McGeorge Bundy told President Johnson in January 1965, "not because he is a communist, but because of his own fanatical emotions."[111] Ben Bella had told *Le Monde*, "If necessary, I am ready to sacrifice myself for Cuba. If the Cuban revolution were crushed or stifled, it would be cause for despair, because it would mean that there is no place for justice, for dignity in this world."[112]

Satisfaction in Washington was matched by grief in Havana. "It is widely believed," the *New York Times* reported from Cuba, "that Premier Castro regards Mr. Ben Bella's fall as a personal loss. Few events pleased and heartened Mr. Castro so much as the visit Mr. Ben Bella made here in October 1962 in defiance of the United States during the missile crisis."[113]

On June 27 Fidel Castro expressed his feelings with passion, eloquence, and bitterness. "I will not speak in the language of a diplomat; I will speak as a revolutionary," he announced. And so he did. He assailed the military coup that had ousted his friend, had bitter words for its leader, Houari Boumedienne, and for Foreign Minister Abdelaziz Bouteflika, who had been one of its prime movers. ("I don't remember if his name is Butterfly or Butterflyka," he quipped.) He praised Ben Bella's "idealism and generosity of spirit." He stressed Cuba's gratitude to him who, "with nothing to gain—and no hope of any material benefit—had come to Cuba braving the imperialists' wrath in those fateful days" of October 1962. And he told, for the first time, the story of Cuba's aid to Algeria in October 1963: "Men and weapons from our country crossed the Atlantic in record time to fight alongside the Algerian revolutionaries. . . . Distance did not prevent us from being the first to arrive. . . . We, a small country relentlessly threatened by the imperialists, sent some of our best weapons to the Algerian people. Sadly, it is possible—even likely—that these weapons that left our shores in a moment of glorious and beautiful solidarity to defend the Algerian revolution and the Algerian people may have been used now in this moment of shame, in this fratricidal act, against the government and the people of Algeria."[c,114]

Serguera, who had been in Brazzaville when Ben Bella fell, returned to his post; "he remained twenty-four hours in Algiers and was recalled at once to Havana." He was replaced by a chargé.[115] After Castro's speech, Boumedienne closed the Algiers office of Prensa Latina,[116] the Algerian ambassador left Havana, and relations between the two governments "shrank to their present nominal condition," as the British ambassador in Havana reported the following April.[117] In the late 1960s, Cuba's relations with Algeria began to improve, but they never recovered the extraordinary warmth of those first few years.

The story of Cuba and Algeria is now almost forgotten, and yet it was not only Cuba's first major contact with Africa, but also a foretaste of Cuban policy toward the continent. The military aid to a national liberation movement—the Algerian FLN—was repeated, on a larger scale, with aid to the liberation movements of the Portuguese colonies. The military aid to an independent African government (Algeria, in October 1963) was repeated with aid to other governments, beginning with the Congo in 1965. And it was in Algeria that the saga of

c. Until this speech, the only public references in Cuba to Cuban aid to Algeria in the Desert War had been an article mentioning that the members of the medical mission had volunteered to fight and another that stated that Cuba had sent 4,744 tons of sugar to Algeria. (*Revolución*, Oct. 17, 1963, p. 1, and Nov. 5, p. 1.)

Cuba's civilian internationalism began. The doctors who went to Algeria in 1963 were followed by others who went to independent countries in Africa and by the *médicos guerrilleros*—those doctors who went to Zaire with Che and to the guerrilla-held areas of Guinea-Bissau.

Above all, the Algerian episode illustrates aspects of Cuban foreign policy that are usually forgotten in the daily polemics against the Castro regime. One may argue that helping Algeria was in Cuba's interest, because Cuba needed friends in the Third World, but one cannot deny that in helping those whom they considered victims of aggression, the Cubans risked tangible interests: the relationship with de Gaulle and an important contract with Morocco. If Cuba's foreign policy were based solely on realpolitik, Cuba would not have helped Algeria. Its assistance reflects a degree of idealism that is unusual in the foreign affairs of great or small powers.

Although none of the Cuban documents I have seen refers to any Soviet demand or suggestion about Algeria, some might nevertheless argue that Cuba was acting in Algeria as a Soviet proxy. The documents that bear on the question, however, suggest otherwise: the oral histories of Ambassador Serguera and, less important, of Molina, the director of Prensa Latina in Algeria, are adamant that the request for military aid in October 1963 originated with Ben Bella and that the Cuban response was immediate—so fast that there would have been no time to consult with the Soviet Union even had Fidel been so inclined. Furthermore, the one available Cuban document that refers to the Soviets does so only to lament their lack of involvement. On October 21 Flavio Bravo, the deputy commander of the GEI, wrote to Raúl Castro from Algiers:

> The situation demands that the entire socialist camp send aid. Unfortunately, however, our friends here are not receiving this aid: promises and more promises, but the weapons never arrive. Meanwhile, Hassan has a battalion of Soviet tanks, MIGs, and other Soviet weapons. And so we are going to face the bizarre situation of having to go to war against Soviet weapons! Some of the Algerian officers are not only worried . . . but indignant. They ask, and rightly so, how can the Soviet comrades help feudal kings like Hassan and not understand that a real revolution, like Cuba's, is taking place here. . . .
>
> As for the socialist countries of Eastern Europe, the less said the better. According to compañeros here, "They have behaved like greedy shopkeepers who want to be paid in dollars (and at higher prices than the Yankees) for the help the Algerian people need." . . .
>
> If you consider it useful, I think you should share these impressions of mine with our good friend Alejandro [Aleksandr Alekseev, the Soviet ambassador to Cuba]. I know that this is not the first time that the Algerian problem has been raised. I believe that Fidel discussed it there [in the Soviet Union], but there is no harm in raising it again. Our Algerian friends have their own customs and their pride. They don't like asking for help, and they say that they would rather fight with knives than ask again. They say that

they have already explained the problem, which in any case is not difficult to understand.[118]

Eventually Soviet weapons did arrive, in great quantity, and by 1964 the Soviet Union had embarked on a major program to strengthen the Algerian armed forces.[119] What the evidence suggests, however, is that the Cubans were in the forefront and, if anyone influenced anyone, it was they who urged on the Soviet Union, not vice versa.

The evidence also reveals the extraordinary warmth of the relationship between Cuba and Algeria, a relationship that explains Cuban policy without any need to refer to the Soviet Union. Havana's decision to provide weapons to the FLN in late 1961 and to receive Algerian wounded and war orphans in Cuba elicited an Algerian response—Ben Bella's visit to Cuba in October 1962—that further strengthened ties between the two countries. No one has argued that this trip was made at the behest of the Soviet Union, and no one has questioned the extraordinary impression that it made on Fidel Castro. It contributed both to his decision to send a medical mission to Algeria and to his undiplomatic speech in 1965 in the aftermath of Ben Bella's overthrow. The medical mission may have been conceived, in part, to build the friendship, to develop ties, but it was above all a way to say thank you for what the besieged Cubans considered an exceptionally brave gesture. It is this web of ties, the closeness of this relationship, that explains the Cubans' unprecedented decision to send troops in October 1963. Two decades later, an Algerian officer recalled, "[Those were] difficult moments for our army, which lacked the necessary war matériel, like tanks and planes. Those were difficult moments for Cuba, which was suffering through Hurricane Flora, one of the worst natural disasters in decades. And yet our Cuban comrades did not hesitate, not even for one minute, to send their brave fighters and their tanks to Algeria to become our brothers in war."[120]

The Cubans rushed to Algeria in Cuban ships and Cuban planes. They brought Soviet weapons—but what other modern weapons did Cuba have at the time?

The closeness of the ties between Algeria and Cuba, and their shared objectives, led to the collaboration between their secret services. Support for Masetti and the Venezuelan guerrillas served Cuban goals in Latin America, which, by 1963–64, the Soviet Union clearly did not share.

It is unlikely, however, that Moscow knew about this collaboration. As Cuban intelligence officers stress, in the 1960s they kept the Soviets in the dark about a great many of their operations.[121] This is understandable because the Soviets strongly opposed Cuba's support of armed struggle in Latin America, a policy the Cubans doggedly and defiantly pursued.

For U.S. officials, Algeria's ties with Cuba had been a major item in their bill of indictment against Ben Bella. It was a wound that had opened in early October 1962, when Ambassador William Porter had warned the Algerian foreign minister that the U.S. government was "deeply disturbed" by press reports that Ben Bella was planning to visit Havana after being received by President Kennedy at the White House. "I said we hoped for prompt denial that visit would occur. Khemisti [the Algerian foreign minister] said there would be no denial, that sensible attitude for US Government would be that it has friendly relations with Algerians who are free to go where they like."[122] This dialogue of the deaf set the pattern for the next two and half years. Unlike the United States, Cuba had sided with the Algerians in their war of independence, and Cuba's generosity had deeply impressed Ben Bella. Once again, their "selective recall" led the Americans astray.[d] Unable to grasp that Ben Bella had a debt of gratitude toward Cuba, they could explain his behavior only as immature, irresponsible, and peevish. They even berated him for receiving Cuban military aid when his country was attacked by Morocco—as if this elementary act of self-defense was an act of hostility against the United States. Hubris led the United States astray.

d. I borrow this expression from Nancy Mitchell, "Remember the Myth," *News and Observer* (Raleigh), Nov. 1, 1998, G5.

CHAPTER THREE
FLEE! THE WHITE
GIANTS ARE COMING!

The anxiety U.S. officials felt about Cuba's ties with Algeria was slight compared with their sudden panic when Zanzibar exploded. This tiny island state of 300,000 people off the coast of Tanganyika had been a sleepy British protectorate until becoming independent on December 10, 1963. One month later, on January 12, 1964, an unexpected and bloody revolt overthrew the Arab ruling elite and established a provisional government that was led by the immensely popular Shaykh Abeid Karume and included a few radicals, notably Foreign Minister Babu, who was sympathetic to China. On the day after the revolt, INR director Hughes wrote a report dramatically titled "The Communist Specter Looms in Zanzibar."[1] The Johnson administration, in office less than two months at the time, saw two red hands stretching over the island: China's and Cuba's.

These fears were based, in part, on CIA reports of Cuban involvement. "A three-man office of the Zanzibar Nationalist Party opened in Havana in September 1961," the CIA noted in January 1964. "In mid-1962 eleven Zanzibaris left for military training in Cuba and returned from there during late 1962 and early 1963. In April 1963 . . . 20 Zanzibaris were still in Cuba. This December, a Tanganyikan official met 3 new arrivals from Cuba; as many as 20 Cuban-trained nationals reportedly arrived home this month. John Okello, 'Field-Marshal' of the new regime, is believed to have returned to Zanzibar after more than 18 months of training in Cuba."[2] U.S. fears were magnified by ignorance. Washington knew very little about Havana's contacts with the Zanzibaris and even less about the revolution that had swept Zanzibar. "We had no information, no knowledge [of the situation there], no CIA presence," recalled Larry Devlin, who was the branch chief for East Africa in the CIA Deputy Directorate for Plans and became the agency's point man for Zanzibar.[3] Vague rumors about Cuban, Soviet, or Chinese intrigue acquired disproportionate significance.

In Dar-es-Salaam, capital of nearby Tanganyika, U.S. ambassador William Leonhart worried that the non-Communist leaders of the new Zanzibari government would be manipulated "by subversive Communist elements." The danger loomed that "pro-Chinese and pro-Cuban leaders," assisted by "revolutionary technicians trained in Communist China and Cuba," would transform Zanzibar into a Communist state. "A Communist Zanzibar," Leonhart cabled,

> would serve them as base for subversive and insurgency operations against mainland from Kenya to the Cape. . . . It would permit Chicoms and Cubans

to move their training sites to African location and export "African model" of their revolutionary tactics. It would serve as propaganda example for all southern Africa of "African Socialist state" where majority has eradicated unpopular racial and economic minority which in past governed country with support of West. It would probably lead to Communist takeover of leadership of southern African liberation movements. It would bring [outbreak of] war in Mozambique much nearer, further reduce chance of avoiding violence in Southern Rhodesia . . . and advance Communism in South Africa. It would afford Communist lodgement on western reaches of Indian Ocean.[4]

Washington's alarm intensified when, on January 20, the tiny Tanganyikan army mutinied, followed by similar uprisings in neighboring Kenya and Uganda, which, like Tanganyika, had just become independent from Britain (Tanganyika in 1961, Uganda in 1962, and Kenya in 1963). The three East African governments turned to Britain to help them put down the mutinies. Within a week the British had sent more than 3,000 troops and restored order. "British response was superb," Leonhart cabled. "Rapid, effective, precise and economical." In Dar-es-Salaam, on January 27, President Julius Nyerere cautioned, "There is no evidence whatever to suggest that Communists were responsible for the events of last week." The CIA agreed; nor did it suspect Communist involvement in the mutinies in Kenya and Uganda. But Zanzibar was different. "The crux of the Zanzibar matter," President Johnson was told, "is to prevent takeover by the Communists."[5]

U.S. officials—from Assistant Secretary Williams all the way to Lyndon Johnson—urged the British to send troops to Zanzibar. As the former colonial power, they had "primary responsibility for handling the problem," Secretary Rusk cabled Ambassador David Bruce in London. The United States would stand squarely behind them but would not provide military support. "We have already informed the British," Williams told Under Secretary Averell Harriman, "of our agreement to give US support publicly, diplomatically and in the United Nations." To the Americans' dismay, the British refused. "The British simply are not putting their minds on this problem," National Security Adviser Bundy told Johnson in early February. In fact, Whitehall believed that the Communist threat in Zanzibar could be defused by working with Karume and Nyerere, who, at Karume's request, had sent 300 Tanganyikan policemen to Zanzibar to help maintain order. The Americans disagreed. "We are extremely concerned over what appears as UKG [United Kingdom government] complacency with Zanzibar situation," Rusk lamented in late March, while Deputy Assistant Secretary Wayne Fredericks confided to the South African chargé in Washington that Zanzibar "had become a real pawn of the Communists."[6]

For the first, and only, time until Cuban troops intervened in Angola in November 1975, the U.S. press saw a Cuban threat to sub-Saharan Africa. "United States refugees arrived from Zanzibar today," the *New York Times* reported on page one on January 15. "They said that they had seen Spanish-speaking soldiers wearing Cuban-type uniforms in the ranks of the rebels who overturned the island's government." Four days later it warned, "Zanzibar is on the verge of becoming the Cuba of Africa, Cuban-trained guerrillas planned and carried out the uprising to establish a communist regime in Zanzibar, long a starting point for penetration of the heart of the African continent."[7] The Zanzibar revolution, the *New York Times* affirmed, had been hatched in Cuba and was part of a Cuban master plan that went well beyond the island:

> Preparations for last week's pro-Communist revolution in Zanzibar began quietly in Cuba late in 1961, when a Zanzibar political office was established in Havana. They reached their peak with the arrival six weeks ago of a Cuban chargé d'affaires in Dar es Salaam. . . . Several hundred African "students" are being trained in Cuba. The training is said to include guerrilla warfare tactics. The students are divided into four main groups. Special emphasis is being placed on the first group, trainees from South Africa, and on the second group, trainees from . . . Kenya, Tanganyika and Zanzibar. This is believed to indicate that Cuba, working with the Soviet Union and possibly Communist China, is centering her attention and activities on South Africa and the east coast of Africa. . . . The Cuban embassy there [in Dar-es-Salaam], which began functioning suddenly last month, might be one of the key elements in this effort.[8]

The truth was far less exciting: Cuban involvement in Zanzibar was modest. CIA reports that a few Zanzibaris had been manning the Havana office of the Zanzibar Nationalist Party since early 1962 and that another small group had come to Cuba for military training were accurate, but that was all there was to it. As DGI officer Estrada recalled, "There were just a few of them" and, as another DGI officer explained, "After they left Cuba, we lost contact with them. We had no idea what they were doing, and the revolt took us completely by surprise."[9] Cuba and Zanzibar did not have diplomatic relations. The only Cuban presence in all East Africa was a small embassy in Dar-es-Salaam, which had opened in late 1963 and had no representative from the DGI; relations between Tanganyika and Cuba were courteous but distant. As for the rumor that there were "Spanish-speaking soldiers" among the rebels, Zanzibaris who had been in Cuba "commonly wore a Castro-like beard and uniform," a well-informed scholar writes, "and . . . some even used the Cuban victory cry *venceremos* ('we shall conquer') as a political slogan." (The same explanation was provided by President Nyerere to the U.S. ambassador.) By late January even the U.S. State Department had concluded that "There were . . . no Cubans in Zanzibar" during the revolt.[10]

Jorge Serguera, the Cuban ambassador to Algeria, flew to Zanzibar immediately after the revolt to assess the situation. A few days later he flew to Moscow to join Fidel Castro, who was visiting the Soviet Union from January 13 to 23. Castro was completely surprised by the revolt. "Fidel asked me," Serguera recalls, "'Is is true that they [the revolutionary leaders in Zanzibar] speak Spanish?' I said: 'It is true, Fidel.' Then he asked: 'Is it true that they say "Patria o muerte. Venceremos!"' I said: 'It is true, Fidel.' Then he asked: 'Is it true that we trained them?' I said: 'It is true, Fidel.' And he said: 'And I thought it was CIA propaganda!'"[11]

Serguera's trip to the island was the high point of Havana's involvement in Zanzibar. On January 15, Cuba recognized the new government and established diplomatic relations with it but did not open an embassy.[12] Beyond the infrequent visits of the Cuban chargé in Dar-es-Salaam, there was no Cuban presence in Zanzibar.

The truth was gradually accepted by U.S. officials and the American press. By February, neither mentioned a Cuban threat. Instead, they focused on how the Soviets, the Chinese, and the East Germans had descended on Zanzibar like the Three Kings, bearing gifts of economic and military aid and opening embassies. From Zanzibar, U.S. chargé Frank Carlucci sent a message of gloom: "Zanzibar is well along road toward becoming communist state and the rest of distance will undoubtedly be covered rapidly." In a hard-hitting memorandum on April 15, INR's director Hughes echoed him: "Barring unforeseen (and unlikely) ruptures in its growing web of relations with the East, Zanzibar in six months could be Africa's first communist-aligned state."[13]

Two days later, the British informed Washington that Nyerere and Karume had agreed to establish a federation. Tanganyika, the British explained, would smother Zanzibar's revolutionary embers in its embrace. The next day, Under Secretary Ball cabled the U.S. embassy in Dar-es-Salaam, "Dept prepared give blessing and support Tanganyikan initiative . . . this . . . appears to be best and perhaps only possibility reversing present critical situation Zanzibar."[14] On April 26, the United Republic of Tanganyika and Zanzibar (Tanzania) was born, and Africa faded once again from Washington's concerns.

THE REVOLT OF THE SIMBAS

In the spring of 1964, President Johnson was preoccupied with the war on poverty, the civil rights bill, and, above all, winning the presidential election in November. He worried that his stance on civil rights would cost him votes, and he feared that any foreign policy mishap would expose him to charges that he was either soft on communism or a warmonger. The conversations he secretly recorded in 1964 seep insecurity, and ambition.[15]

After the stormy Kennedy years, the foreign front seemed quiet: no crisis with the Soviet Union, no major East-West tension in Europe, and the guerrillas were losing ground in Latin America. Vietnam was not yet in the spotlight, but it haunted Johnson. He was determined not to lose Vietnam: the prestige of the United States was at stake, as was his own. Withdrawal would cost him votes, and so would a land war. It was prudent to postpone any action until after the November election, if he could. "I don't think the people of the country know much about Vietnam and I think they care a hell of a lot less," he complained to his friend, Senator Richard Russell (D.-Ga.). "It just worries the hell out of me," he told National Security Adviser Bundy.[16]

Johnson's top foreign policy aides spent more and more of their time on Vietnam. The Soviet Union, Europe, and Latin America lagged behind. Africa was the booby prize, given to Under Secretary Averell Harriman, whose close ties to Robert Kennedy undermined him in Johnson's eyes. Harriman complained that he had been "exiled to Africa."[17] The continent was a backwater as long as there was no imminent Red threat. The guerrillas fighting against the Portuguese in Angola and Guinea-Bissau had not made much headway. Nasser of Egypt, Ben Bella of Algeria, and Nkrumah of Ghana were irritants, but they were not leading their countries into the Communist orbit. U.S. officials knew that guerrilla war was likely in Mozambique, and they were concerned about the intransigence of Rhodesia's white minority, but these were distant rumbles, unworthy of the attention of the top policy makers. The same seemed true of Zaire.

Zaire had become independent from Belgium on June 30, 1960. Unprepared for self-government, it had descended into anarchy a few days later. Belgium immediately sent troops to protect its citizens and economic interests. On July 11 the richest of the country's six provinces, Katanga, whose mines were owned and operated by a Belgian company, seceded, fully supported by Brussels. Belgian military officers—soon to be joined by white mercenaries—supervised and trained the Katangan gendarmerie. In despair, the Zairean government turned to the United Nations, but the arrival of thousands of UN troops in July neither restored Zaire's unity nor saved it from the vortex of the Cold War. Through the next year, the Communist bloc sent money and weapons to Zaire, but its interference was paltry compared with that of the United States, both on its own and through the United Nations, over which it exercised an extraordinary degree of influence. In the summer of 1960 the Eisenhower administration concluded that Patrice Lumumba, Zaire's first prime minister, was an African Castro, a Soviet instrument, and threw its support behind Lumumba's rival, President Joseph Kasavubu. (Scholars now agree that Lumumba was in fact "a genuine nationalist, fanatical in his opposition to foreign control of the Congo [Zaire].") For the Americans, he was an enemy of the most dangerous type—charismatic. He would have to be eliminated.[18] In August 1960 CIA scientists, who had just begun working on a project to poison Castro's cigars, began searching for a way to poison Lumumba. But the CIA was beaten to the gate. On December 1, Lumumba was captured by Zairean soldiers loyal to Chief of Staff Joseph Mobutu, an ally of Kasavubu and a CIA asset. On January 17, 1961, Lumumba and two of his aides were flown to secessionist Katanga on the orders of Kasavubu and Mobutu and delivered into the hands of Katanga's prime minister, Moise Tshombe, whose hatred of Lumumba was legendary. At the airport of Elisabethville, Katanga's capital, the three prisoners were brutally beaten. "'It was sickening,'" an eyewitness told the New York Times. "'Lumumba and the other two fell to the ground where they were clubbed, hit in the face with rifle butts, and kicked and pummeled. The [Katangan] police let them lie awhile and then resumed the beating.'" Belgian officers stood watching. Eyewitnesses said that the three prisoners "had groaned as they were beaten, but that they had not protested or begged for mercy." After the beating, they were thrown into a jeep, pushed to the floor, "and sat on by four policemen." This was the last image of Lumumba alive. A few hours later, he was dead, and a martyr.[19]

President Kennedy inherited a raging crisis as Lumumba's followers prepared to avenge their leader's death. Kennedy said that he wanted the Zaireans to chart their own course and expressed his preference for a coalition government that would even include Lumumbists. But in mid-1961 when the Zairean Parliament seemed ready to elect a Lumumbist as prime minister, Kennedy's response was not very different from what Eisenhower's would have been: U.S. officials proffered bribes, plotted a military coup, and succeeded in having their candidate, the lackluster Cyril Adoula, elected prime minister in a contest that would otherwise have been won by the Lumumbist. Washington would soon forget this and consider Adoula the true and legal expression of the Parliament's will.

Adoula's election did not resolve the Katangan crisis. The province's prime minister, the dynamic, brave, and corrupt Tshombe, who had ordered the murder of Lumumba, enjoyed the sympathy of many Americans, including members of Congress. The CIA warned that "resentment is growing" against Adoula for his failure to unify the country and that the government's survival was threatened "if a solution is not found to the Katanga problem very rapidly."[20] Turmoil would offer opportunities to the Soviets. Therefore, after much hesitation, in December 1962 Kennedy approved the use of UN troops to quash the Katangan rebellion. Confronted by a determined UN offensive, Tshombe's white mercenaries and Katangan gendarmes fled after offering little resistance. By late January 1963 the rebellion had collapsed.

With the reintegration of Katanga, Zaire settled into corrupt, oppressive, pro-American stability resting on two pillars: thousands of UN troops and the Zairean army (ANC), led by General Mobutu, the CIA asset who had been involved in the murder of Lumumba. "The ANC relied on brutality to control the country," U.S. Army major Thomas Odom wrote in a well-researched study. "Untrained and poorly led, the ANC was also a disaster in the field. Its cruelty toward unarmed civilians was infamous." U.S. officials, however, appreciated its virtues: this was the army that had defeated Lumumba, with some assistance from the United States and the United Nations. "General," a grateful Kennedy addressed Mobutu in the White House in May 1963, "if it hadn't been for you . . . the Communists would have taken over."[21]

Beneath the surface, however, danger lurked in Zaire. The UN troops were scheduled to leave by the end of June 1964, and the Adoula government was weak and unpopular. "Like Spanish moss, it has its roots in the air, not in the Congolese [Zairean] hinterland," the CIA remarked. Rebellion flared up in the western province of Kwilu at the end of 1963. The rebels were poorly armed, but the ANC proved singularly inept in quelling them. The CIA intervened, hiring several Cuban exile pilots (green-card holders, not U.S. citizens) and providing them with a few Italian planes to strafe and bomb the rebels. When Belgian officials proved less than discreet about the CIA role, Under Secretary Ball fired off a furious cable demanding that the U.S. embassy in Brussels read them the riot act and make them "refrain from further dissemination any rumors or suggestions that would indicate USG [U.S. government] connection with these Cuban pilots."[22]

By mid-February the rebellion seemed to have "run out of steam," as the British ambassador, Edward Rose, reported, and U.S. officials were confident that Zaire was once again stable. After a fact-finding mission, Harriman told the congressional leaders in early April that "real progress had been made toward restoring economic health" and that the Belgians were moving ahead with a program of military and economic aid "responsive to the responsibilities they have in the Congo [Zaire]." Harriman was satisfied that "the tasks in Africa were being divided and carried by many [Western] countries rather than the U.S. alone." In mid-May, General Mobutu promised a sympathetic audience in Brussels: "We will be able to maintain order [in Zaire] after June 30, 1964" (when the last UN troops would leave the country). The crowd broke into warm applause.[23]

As he spoke, new troubles were breaking out in the vast eastern province of Kivu. Leading the revolt were the fractious followers of Lumumba, whose vague ideology was couched in Marxist jargon. "Despite the revolutionary slogans which its leaders mouthed . . . the rebels have to all intents and purposes no political programme," Ambassador Rose reported. "It's definitely an African and a Congolese [Zairean] movement but all very confused," explained the U.S. consul in Stanleyville. Ethnic rivalries, old feuds, and the fear of witchcraft added to the brew that bubbled up through the thin crust of the Pax Americana.[24]

The revolt spread "like a forest fire,"[25] taking the Johnson administration by surprise. In mid-June 1964, the U.S. ambassador in Leopoldville, McMurtrie Godley, had assured Assistant Secretary Williams, "all of us here share your optimism that the economic and political progress that has been made in the Congo [Zaire] during the past four years will . . . continue." A few weeks later the ANC had virtually collapsed. "Everywhere the soldiers of Mr. Mobutu, armed with machine guns, flee from rebels who usually have only bows, arrows, and bicycle chains," Le Monde reported. As they advanced, the Simbas ("lions"), as the rebels were called, seized the weapons abandoned by fleeing troops. For the ANC, this was "almost accepted practice," the West German embassy reported.[26]

The ANC's collapse was due, in part, to the troops' belief that the rebels were using witchcraft. As the foremost student of the revolt put it, "The mere announcement of their [the Simbas'] arrival terrorized the soldiers of the Zairean army, convinced as they were that their [ANC's] bullets would turn into water or fly back to strike them." In the words of one eyewitness, an African journalist, "This superstition has had a powerful effect on Congolese [Zairean]

National Army troops. In many places they lay down their arms and run when the rebels advance." This was what Zairean businessman Charles Badjoko explained to Ambassador Rose. "I was very struck by Badjoko's account of the techniques of what I suppose we must call psychological warfare, employed by the rebels," Rose reported. "Since we are all on the alert for signs of Communist, particularly Chinese, training, I was particularly interested to note that the rebels seem to be inspired more by primitive African superstition than by Comrade Mao's experiences and directives. For example, one of the most potent weapons in the rebels' armoury appears to be the assertion that Lumumba is not dead: not only is he not dead, but he is waxing bigger and fatter and waiting for a propitious moment to return."[27]

More than magic, however, explained the Simbas' successes, as the U.S. consul in Elisabethville made clear:

> There is in this and contiguous areas strong, nearly universal feeling of dissatisfaction at present GOC [government of Zaire]. . . . All levels population this area are thoroughly disgusted with first four years of Congolese [Zairean] independence, whose corruption, inefficiency, public violence and economic decline are in crass contrast with their original exaggerated expectations. . . . These disaffected views shared also by ANC troops here. The main reason for their failure to fight is not so much lack of military capacity and superstitious fear of rebels, which of course are important factors, but that they do not want to fight.[28]

Not only were the troops unwilling to fight, they also helped the rebel cause by their "acts of brutality and pillage." The U.S. embassy noted that "indiscriminate killing, looting and raping" were "normal pursuits" for the ANC, and the CIA was equally blunt: "The ANC is . . . hated and feared. Now it is near collapse as an organized force. [It is] woefully lacking in leadership, prone to mutiny, and manned by soldiers who tend to regard their rifles as meal tickets." Therefore, Godley pointed out, the population usually welcomed the rebels, "who treat them better than ANC in most cases." Rose agreed: the Simbas, he wrote, "were received with open arms" by the population.[29]

On June 26, four days before the last UN troops left the country, the erstwhile leader of Katanga, Moise Tshombe, returned to Zaire from self-imposed exile in Spain. Frightened by the rebels, the country's leaders turned to him, their former nemesis, who towered over them in vigor, courage, and charisma. The United States welcomed his return. "Lumumba was probably the only Congolese [Zairean] who exceeded Tshombe in what is known as the charismatic quality of leadership," noted a U.S. intelligence report. "We are all for . . . giving Tshombe important post in gvt," Godley cabled.[30]

But neither he nor any other U.S. official expected what happened next: on July 6, in a move that testified "to the extent of the desperation felt by President Kasavubu and General Mobutu," Tshombe was appointed prime minister. "It all happened so fast," observed the embassy's deputy chief of mission (DCM).

Rebel Areas in Zaire, August 1964

"Before we knew it the decision had been made. It was very much a Zairean decision." Reserved at first, the U.S. reaction soon turned into warm endorsement. "Prime Minister Tshombe has brought zest and dynamism to his job," Assistant Secretary Williams said.[31]

African leaders were less impressed. Despised by many of them as "a walking museum of colonialism"[32] because of his past collusion with South Africans, Portuguese, and Belgians and his attempt to divide Zaire, Tshombe was also fingered as the moving force behind Lumumba's murder. "How could anyone imagine," the king of Morocco asked in a broadcast to his nation, "that I, the representative of my country's national conscience, could sit at a conference table or at a banquet with the man who personifies secession? How could anyone even begin to imagine that I, Hassan II . . . could observe a minute of silence in memory of our African heroes when one of their murderers is seated among us?"[33]

In the weeks that followed, the United States increased its military aid to Zaire, but it could not stem the revolt. By late July frantic cables were reaching Washington from Leopoldville: the rebels were winning, the ANC was collapsing, well-trained, foreign soldiers were necessary. On August 5, 1964, Stanleyville, Zaire's third-largest city, fell to the Simbas, while in Washington a National Intelligence Estimate on Zaire predicted "a total breakdown in governmental authority."[34]

U.S. intelligence reports indicated that the revolt was "largely tribal," that the rebels were receiving very little outside assistance, that no Communist country other than China was involved, and that its role was incidental. "While the Chicoms may have contributed an element of sophistication to insurgent activity, the eastern Congo [Zaire] fundamentally collapsed from within. In comparison with indigenous causes of dissidence, the Chicom contribution to the collapse of central government authority probably has nowhere been more than marginal."[35] Furthermore, there was no indication that the Simbas were Communists. An intelligence appraisal noted that "while at this point it is impossible to make firm judgments about the orientation of a rebel government, it would certainly seek close links with the East and there is a good chance that it would make the position of the West in the Congo [Zaire] increasingly difficult. (On the other hand, given the enormous reliance of the Congo [Zaire] on the West and the inability of the East to duplicate Western assistance, we do not believe the position of the West would become untenable—at least not in the short run.)"[36]

President Johnson and his aides were not interested, however, in the subtleties of U.S. intelligence reports. For them, a rebel victory meant the end of Zaire's pro-American stance that had taken four years and two U.S. administrations to establish. The loss of Zaire ("the richest country and the richest prize in Africa")[37] could have cost Johnson votes in the presidential race. The revolt had to be crushed.

Washington turned to Europe. Disregarding their own intelligence reports, U.S. officials argued that Zaire was threatened by a Communist takeover. Just as they had urged the British to send troops to Zanzibar a few months earlier, so now they badgered the Belgians. The most effective measure, Ambassador Godley informed Washington, would be the "use of Belgian paratroop battalions to come in rapidly, clean up [the] situation and then withdraw as soon as possible."[38]

Secretary of State Rusk and Under Secretaries Harriman and Ball agreed.[a] On August 4, Harriman cabled the U.S. ambassador in Brussels, Douglas

a. Initially Harriman was the administration's point man on Zaire, but he was eventually edged out by Ball, who recalled: "Rusk left it to me, but there was considerable interference from Harriman." Ball warned McGeorge Bundy that Harriman considered

MacArthur, to ask: "Under what conditions would [the] GOB [government of Belgium] be willing to provide troops?" On August 6, Rusk cabled the Belgian foreign minister, Paul-Henri Spaak: "Events in the Congo [Zaire] have reached so critical a point that you and we and all our European friends must move immediately and vigorously to prevent total collapse. . . . We must concert urgently on tangible, specific measures to save the Congo [Zaire]."[39]

The next day Harriman arrived in Brussels "for a final effort" to convince the Belgians to take "primary responsibility."[40] The United States would provide the hardware; Belgium, the men. "I will tell you, but you must keep it to yourselves," Spaak later told a group of Belgian ambassadors, "that they [the Americans] asked me if Belgium was willing to send troops. And when Mr. Harriman came, that is what we talked about." The Belgians balked: they agreed to put more military advisers in Zaire, but no Belgian would be authorized to engage directly or indirectly in combat.[41]

The Americans were also rebuffed on a second proposal: that Belgium "take the lead in the organization . . . [of] a joint military force of the Six [European Community countries], or some of its member nations." As Harriman prepared to fly to Brussels, MacArthur had cabled Rusk, "He [Spaak] did not want to mislead us, and among other things he did not r[e]p[ea]t not see the slightest chance of getting any of the 'Six' to intervene militarily in Congo [Zaire]. Luxembourg had no military forces and he was certain France, Germany and Netherlands would refuse participate in any military intervention." Further attempts in the next few days, including a direct appeal to Bonn to send a battalion of troops to Zaire, proved futile. The Europeans "had no stomach for it," Ball observed.[42]

Not only did the "gutless Belgians" fail to respond with the requisite zeal, but they also seemed to be flirting with the enemy. Washington worried about the "apparent Belgian preference to try to do business with the rebels, even if Communist, rather than facing up to putting down the rebellion."[43] In fact, the Belgians were simply being practical. Spaak told Ambassador MacArthur that if Belgium intervened "and Belgians civilians"—hundreds of whom were stranded in rebel-held territory—"were executed by rebels [in retaliation], Belgian parliamentary and public opinion would react violently against present govt, which would no repeat no longer be able to muster majority support."[44] Because the Belgians believed that no other Western country would send troops, that the ANC would be unable to defeat the revolt, and that the Simbas were not Communists, they were prepared to let events in Zaire run their course and to establish a modus vivendi with the rebels if they won. The Belgians, Ambassador Rose reported from Leopoldville, "laugh at the Americans for seeing a

---

himself the "Prince of Africa." (Quotations from tel. interview with George Ball and from TelConv, Bundy and Ball, Aug. 26, 1964, 3:55 P.M., Ball Papers, box 2/3, LBJL. See also Abramson, *Spanning the Century*, pp. 633–35.)

Communist behind every bush." In Brussels, the day before Harriman arrived, Spaak told Ambassador MacArthur that "top Belgian industrialists having most extensive interests in Congo [Zaire] . . . agreed that they could do business with . . . rebel leaders since latter realized Belgian economic and technical presence and assistance was essential to economic life of Congo [Zaire]." A few days later Spaak told a group of Belgian ambassadors, "My assessment of the situation . . . differs markedly from that of the Americans. People always say that I do everything the Americans want, that I always agree with them, but in this affair of Zaire that is not true at all. Neither my assessment of the situation nor my solutions were similar to theirs."[45]

U.S. officials also worried about France. "The French always have three positions," the DCM in Leopoldville remarked: "the official position, the one that is almost the opposite, and the fall back—way back—position. We were picking up things about the French preparing to switch sides." The French thought the Americans were overreacting. François Poncet, a senior Foreign Ministry official, told his staff that "the French government believes there is . . . no reason for the West to be alarmed. Even if the Communists try to use the rebels for their own ends, this revolt is not fomented from the outside. . . . There is no evidence that foreign weapons have been delivered to the rebels. . . . There is no reason for the West to overdramatize the situation." The French ambassador made the same point more gently to Rusk: "perhaps the United States had overresponded to African crises, which in turn has encouraged a greater Communist response resulting in cold war confrontations. . . . it was particularly useless to try to interfere in the Congolese [Zairean] imbroglio, where tribal conflicts are bound to keep the country in a state of uproar for an indefinite period." The British also deemed American fears "apocalyptic" and thought Washington attached "much more importance to the element of Communist inspiration in the rebellion than we would be inclined to do."[46]

Rusk did not mince words. He told the Belgian ambassador that he was "bitter that the European governments had refused to intervene in Zaire, even though the African continent was above all their responsibility. He added," the ambassador reported, "that if Zaire were to be lost because of the Europeans' failure to act, it would have a profound impact on US-European relations."[47]

Washington, unlike Brussels, was not interested in a modus vivendi with the Simbas. Failure to act, an August 6 memo warned Johnson, would "let chaos run its course, hoping the Congolese [Zaireans] will work out an adjustment without serious Communist intrusion; and rely on Congo's [Zaire's] need for our aid and support for influence with the eventual government. This would be hard to explain politically in US, but it is essentially what Belgians and Europeans are doing."[48]

These were ominous words for a president who was consumed by the desire to win big in the November presidential elections. On August 7, Congress approved the Tonkin Gulf resolution with virtually no debate, giving Johnson a reasonable hope to keep Vietnam under wraps until November. But another storm was brewing at home. The Democratic convention, which would be held in Atlantic City in late August, faced an insurgency of angry and politically savvy African Americans from Mississippi who were demanding that their mostly black delegation be seated instead of the all-white regular state delegation. George Wallace's powerful campaign, winning about one-third of the votes cast in the Democratic primaries in Wisconsin, Indiana, and Maryland, made Johnson fear a white backlash if the convention seated the black delegates. "The only thing that can really screw us good is to seat that group of challengers from Mississippi," he told United Auto Workers president Walter Reuther on August 9.[49]

On August 11, Johnson and his key advisers met in a hastily called session of the National Security Council (NSC) to discuss Zaire. This was the first NSC meeting about the revolt. The mood was somber. DCI John McCone stated that "Western troops would be necessary." Harriman concurred. The ANC "in most cases has proven useless. . . . the people in government are demoralized and Leopoldville in danger."[50]

No one challenged the basic premise: the rebels had to be defeated, and the ANC alone could not do it. Direct U.S. military involvement was considered only as "an extreme last resort," as Treasury Secretary Douglas Dillon argued. "The President said emphatically that we all share this view." Therefore African and European troops had to be found. Harriman suggested France, Great Britain, Germany, the Netherlands, Italy, and Canada. "The job . . . should be put squarely to the Europeans as their responsibility," Rusk asserted. "We should urge them immediately to put troops into Leopoldville, using Presidential pressure if necessary." Lyndon Johnson agreed. "Time is running out and the Congo [Zaire] must be saved."[51]

The discussion had a surreal aspect because no European government was willing to send its troops, and Washington already knew it. In addition to the Europeans, the administration had already been rebuffed by Ethiopia, Nigeria, and Senegal, and, in any case, African troops would not have been welcome in Zaire: Mobutu and Tshombe trusted neither them nor their governments. "Despite our efforts, the Congolese [Zairean] Government has not so far asked any other African country for military forces save South Africa which fortunately refused," noted a U.S. official.[52]

Much more realistic, however, was an item that is only cursorily mentioned in the minutes of the NSC meeting: Harriman briefed the assembled dignitaries about the agreement he had reached with Spaak in Brussels on "mercenary forces" for Zaire. The minutes do not elaborate, and the entire issue rates less than one line. And yet "special volunteers" (the "new euphemism for mercenaries," Godley noted)[53] were the obvious answer to the Zairean problem.

The United States preferred a "clean solution" (European or African troops) but would rely on mercenaries if necessary. This had been its two-track approach from the outset. A cable from Godley on August 5 had posed the problem crisply. "There are only three places," he wrote, the Zairean government

(GOC) could turn: "a) GOC can seek direct Belgian military intervention; b) it can attempt to recruit white mercenary brigade; c) it can ask for US troops. . . . If Belgian Government refuses to accept risks of intervention . . . mercenary brigade is second best alternative. . . . From US standpoint [the] employment of mercenaries would carry advantage of being done on GOC responsibility and would reduce overt western (i.e. Belgian or US) involvement. . . . It would place burden of responsibility on GOC and not on ourselves or Belgians."[54]

Washington concurred. "Tshombe and GOC should proceed soonest to establish effective gendarmerie-mercenary unit," Rusk had cabled Leopoldville on August 6, as Harriman was about to leave for Brussels. "US prepared to assist with transport, communications and other reasonable requirements."[55] Tshombe was an old hand at the mercenary game: they had helped him when he had been the leader of secessionist Katanga, and he was happy to use them again.

In Brussels, on August 7, Spaak told Harriman unequivocally that neither Belgium nor any other European country would send troops. That same day Rusk approved a proposal by Mennen Williams for an "immediate effort . . . to concert with Belgians to help Tshombe to raise mercenary force," and he cabled Harriman urging "Belgian help on mercenary problem including recruitment of Belgians." Washington and Brussels would supply the money to pay the mercenaries and the weapons to arm them; Washington alone would provide the planes to fly them. Bowing to U.S. pressure, the Belgians embraced the mercenary option. " In fact, mercenaries were the only possible solution," concluded Colonel Frédéric Vandewalle, who would head the Belgian military mission in Zaire and was briefed by Spaak on the talks with Harriman. "In private, both Washington and Brussels admitted it." And so the United States embarked on a dual policy in Zaire: it openly provided military aid to Tshombe while it covertly financed, armed, and oversaw the mercenaries. "The Americans," a British official wrote, "regard white mercenaries as the essential cutting edge of the Central Government's forces."[56]

THE WHITE GIANTS

The mercenaries flowed into Zaire. Most came from South Africa and Rhodesia. "Hundreds in queue for Congo [Zaire] army," reported the *Cape Times* from Salisbury. "They will be formed into all-White commandos." The weekly *Jeune Afrique* noted that "at Johannesburg they are lining up in front of the recruitment center. All you need to be is white, able to shoot, and ready to help Mr. Tshombe, 'the good friend of Whites and foe of the Red Chinese.' . . . *Air Congo* planes fly the South African mercenaries to Leopoldville. There, they are met by instructors who hand them machine guns (American), and then they are flown in planes (American) toward Stanleyville or Bukavu to crush the rebels." South African prime minister Hendrik Verwoerd, who initially said that his government "did not intend to interfere" in the recruitment, soon became concerned about the stampede. "The extent of recruiting must not get out of hand," he warned. "There is a manpower shortage [in South Africa]." Ambassador Godley, who would have liked the operation to be as discreet as possible, was frustrated. "It now public knowledge that substantial number of white mercenaries have arrived Congo [Zaire]. . . . These mercenaries are everywhere evident, talk frequently to press and anybody who will listen to them," he cabled Washington on August 26. The arrival of the mercenaries "is the talk of the town," wrote a Leopoldville daily two days later.[57]

Mobutu and Tshombe denied everything: "We don't need any foreign troops, white or black," Tshombe said. "The mercenaries in Leopoldville have not been recruited by the Zairean government," Mobutu declared. The government's successes on the battlefield, he explained the following October, were due to the prowess of his regular troops. By then, there were, by CIA estimates, "over a thousand" mercenaries in Zaire.[58]

The U.S. embassy kept the mercenaries at arm's length—in public. In private the CIA, the military attachés, and the military mission were in close contact with them. The army attaché, Colonel Knut Raudstein ("a salty character," according to Secretary Rusk),[59] was an admirer of their leader, Mike Hoare. "Tshombe's supporters most fortunate in having man of Hoare's temperament, character and capability in his position," Raudstein cabled. "He . . . conducts self as typical upper class Briton proud of Irish extraction. Avows disagreement with some SA [South African] political concepts calling himself a moderate."[60]

Hoare's "moderate" views on race were reflected in his comment to a fellow mercenary: "I believe . . . we have a great mission here. The Africans have gotten used to the idea that they can do what they like to us whites, that they can trample on us and spit on us."[61] And they were reflected in his response to a South African black who wanted to enlist: "We only engage white mercenaries."[62]

Why did men volunteer? "For money, first of all," five freshly arrived French mercenaries told a journalist over drinks in Leopoldville. But there were loftier reasons: "Because we're ashamed of France. . . . We've lost Indochina; *le grand Charles* has tossed Algeria aside. The *fellouzes* will not get Zaire."[63]

The year 1963, a philosophical mercenary mused, "was the heyday of African unity, of the dream of African grandeur and of the expulsion of the white man from the continent." The year 1964 would be the year of the White Giants—"tall, vigorous Boers from South Africa; long-legged, slim and muscular Englishmen from Rhodesia"—who would restore, in Zaire, the white man to his proper place. "How often was I to hear the muffled drumming in the night, through forests and savannahs, 'Flee, the White Giants are coming!' "[64]

The U.S. ambassador was less romantic. The mercenaries were, he thought, "an uncontrolled lot of toughs . . . who consider looting or safe-cracking fully within their prerogatives." Their "serious excesses," the CIA reported, included "robbery, rape, murder and beatings."[65]

They were also boastful and naive. Once in Zaire, they tended to trust every

In 1964 the Johnson administration raised an army of white mercenaries to defeat a revolt that threatened to topple the pro-American government of Zaire. In the photograph above, a mercenary leads two captured rebels to be hanged. In the photograph opposite, "smiling mercenaries" fight for the privilege of doing the "stringing up" (as the British newspaper the *Observer* wrote). With the exception of *Muhammad Speaks*, an African American weekly, the U.S. press ignored these photographs. (The *Observer* [London], August 29, 1965.)

white face, even that of a journalist. "These mercenaries are everywhere evident, talk frequently to the press and anybody who will listen to them," Godley complained. They talked openly, for instance, to an Italian journalist, who subsequently described their entry into the town of Boende in late October 1964. "Occupying the town," he wrote, "meant blowing out the doors with rounds of bazooka fire, going into the shops and taking anything they wanted that was movable. . . . After the looting came the killing. The shooting lasted for three days. Three days of executions, of lynchings, of tortures, of screams, and of terror."[66]

Just as tourists send postcards home, so the mercenaries sent photos of their exploits. Several found their way into the British weekly, the *Observer*. The first showed two almost naked black men, their hands tied behind their backs, ropes around their necks, being led by a white mercenary to their hanging. In the second, "smiling mercenaries" fought for the privilege of doing the "stringing up." A photograph of the swinging corpses was described but not printed. "The

pictures," the *Observer* noted, "show how mercenaries not only shoot and hang their prisoners after torturing them, but use them for target practice and gamble over the number of shots needed to kill them."[67]

In a two-part article in the *Cape Times*, a returning South African mercenary wrote of the mercenaries' "senseless, coldblooded killings," of their rule of never taking prisoners ("except for the odd one for questioning, after which they were executed"), of their thievery. He pleaded with his government "not to allow decent young South Africans" to enlist and become "senseless killers." In an off-the-record conversation with British journalist Colin Legum, Mike Hoare described his men as "appalling thugs."[68]

Appalling and efficient. They advanced along the paths of Zaire in mobile columns. "Lightly armored Belgian jeeps mounting some automatic weapons and, for heavier work, British Ferrets [armored cars] have been backbone of counterinsurgency military effort," Godley reported. Four U.S. C-130s with American crews transported the mercenaries and their equipment across Zaire's immense expanses. "Nothing went by road, rail or boat—all was supplied by the C-130s," the *New York Times* journalist who covered the campaign explained.[69]

When they met resistance, the mercenaries called on the Zairean air force, which included not one Zairean. It consisted of the "21st Squadron" (seven T-6s from Italy piloted by South African and European mercenaries) and several T-28s and B-26s supplied by the United States. The State Department's official line was that no U.S. citizens would be "called upon by the Congo [Zaire] government to engage in operational missions in the police action," and none therefore would fly the planes. The pilots and crews of the T-28s and B-26s were Cuban exiles who, as Under Secretary Ball reassured the U.S. mission at the United Nations, were not U.S. citizens. "Guiding them into action," the *New York Times* reported after the operation had ended, "were American 'diplomats' and other officials in apparently civilian positions. The sponsor, paymaster and director of all of them, however, was the Central Intelligence Agency. . . . Its rapid and effective provision of an 'instant air force' in the Congo [Zaire] was the climax of the agency's deep involvement there."[70] It was an impressive air force, particularly against an enemy without planes or antiaircraft guns. "The pattern," notes a careful study, "was always the same: [exile] Cuban-piloted T-28s and B-26s bombing and strafing in front of ground columns; Simbas either scattering in panic or being slaughtered by the more accurate and lethal fire-power of the mercenaries." The planes, the CIA stated in November 1964, "operate over insurgent territory with impunity." This remained true throughout the war.[71] Only one plane was hit by enemy fire.[b] The Simbas responded by taking Americans and Belgians hostage, the majority of whom were in Stanleyville, the rebel capital.

A mercenary ground offensive against Stanleyville got under way on November 1, 1964. A mercenary column, accompanied by truckloads of ANC troops and led by Ferret armored cars, advanced from the south. The CIA air force "terrified the Simbas," a U.S. military officer writes.[72] One by one, the rebel towns were recaptured and the mercenaries closed in on Stanleyville. Then, on

---

b. The pilot, John Merriman, was a U.S. citizen and a CIA contract officer who oversaw the exile Cuban wing of the "Zairean" air force. He was badly wounded when his plane crash-landed and died a few days later. The CIA went to extraordinary lengths to hide this fact, and his family did not learn the real circumstances of his death until 1996. (Gup, *Book*, pp. 133–62.)

The exile Cubans lost one plane. A *Life* reporter, who spent a day or two with them, reported that it had been shot down by the rebels, but Hoare asserts that it crashed on take-off. The pilot was the only fatality of the exile Cuban wing of the "Zairean" air force. The "21st Squadron" also suffered casualties: in late 1965, the squadron's commander writes, a pilot "had gone on a practice run with napalm bombs, a donation from our generous CIA mentors," when he lost control and the plane slipped into a nosedive. Two other pilots died in another accident. (Quotations are from "Red Arsenals Arm the Simbas," *Life*, Feb. 12, 1965, p. 32, and Puren, *Mercenary Commander*, pp. 199–200. See also Hoare, *Congo Mercenary*, p. 245; Mendez, "Fausto Gómez.")

November 24, as the mercenary column was approaching, Belgian paratroopers in U.S. planes raided the city, freeing the hostages, whose number, with the passing of time, has swelled to 1,500 or even 3,000.[73] According to Colonel Vandewalle, who headed the Belgian military mission in Zaire, "There were about 300 hostages in Stanleyville, not 1,500. It is already a grim story, why make it worse?" Militarily, the operation was not necessary, because the mercenaries were closing in and resistance was slight. Whether the raid saved lives—or the opposite (about 60 hostages were killed)—remains an open question. "The analysis of the facts and the examination of the documents," Vandewalle writes, "justify well-founded doubts."[74] This raid and that on nearby Paulis two days later were the only operations in which Belgian troops intervened directly in the war.

MOSCOW RESPONDS

Until Stanleyville, African support for the rebels had been "mainly moral and concealed," as the British ambassador reported, and the Simbas had received no assistance from the Communist countries, with the possible exception of some limited Chinese aid.[75] The raid provoked an uproar in Africa and many public pledges to help the Simbas. "We help the rebels. It is our duty," Ben Bella proclaimed defiantly, while Nyerere lashed out: "In an action reminiscent of Pearl Harbour, foreign troops were flown into Zaire at the very moment that negotiations were taking place to secure the safety of all who lived in the Stanleyville area."[76]

The raid also galvanized the Soviet Union. East German reports indicate that before Stanleyville the Soviets had been reluctant to help a revolt about which they knew virtually nothing. "Our Soviet comrades do not yet have a clear idea of the present situation of the liberation movement in Zaire," the GDR embassy reported from Moscow in mid-September 1964. "They only know that . . . the leaders . . . are engaged in a power struggle that is about personal ambition, not politics." Right up until the raid on Stanleyville, the constant, petty infighting among the rebel leaders gave the Soviets pause. A GDR official wrote, "When I asked about the possibility of our Soviet comrades providing the patriotic forces in Zaire material aid in the future, comrade K replied: 'This is extraordinarily problematic, because there is no cohesive leadership and no acknowledged leader, only rival groups. Which one should we support?' "[77]

A few days after the raid on Stanleyville, however, the GDR was informed that the Soviet Union would provide military aid to the rebels. By the end of December, the GDR itself followed suit.[78]

After Stanleyville, therefore, the rebels began receiving small amounts of military aid from African countries, and larger amounts of weapons from the Soviet Union and China.[79] The weapons were, however, of little significance, because the Simbas did not know how to use them. "We're not worried too much about the rebels getting small arms and ammunition," a Western military attaché in Leopoldville told the *New York Times* in December 1964. "We're not even worried about their getting heavier equipment, like mortars and bazookas, which they don't know how to handle any better than the Congolese [Zairean] army. But if they get some guerrilla veterans from outside, the war could change overnight." The CIA agreed: "The appearance in the Congo [Zaire] of combat 'volunteers' from the radical African states . . . [would create] a new, more ugly and dangerous situation." The radical African states, however, sent no volunteers. "The African governments that opposed Tshombe were a worthless bunch," according to Ambassador Godley. "They did nothing effective, nothing that I'm aware of."[80] As for the Chinese military advisers in eastern Zaire reported by some newspapers, they turned out to be a myth.[81]

Only Cuba sent men—led by Che Guevara.

CHAPTER FOUR
CASTRO TURNS TO
CENTRAL AFRICA

The Cuban press followed the crisis in Zaire closely, and Cuban leaders drew bitter lessons from Lumumba's fate. Nevertheless, until 1964 Cuba was merely a concerned spectator. "Lumumba," Che Guevara said, "was murdered by the imperialists, but he was also the victim of his own mistakes." He had trusted international law, the United Nations, and even the United States. He had not understood that violence, not reason, was necessary to defeat the imperialists. "He . . . thought he could defeat all the inherited evils of the system—everything we also fight against—with truth as his only weapon."[1]

For the Cubans there was no doubt: the United States had destroyed Lumumba just as it was trying to destroy the Cuban revolution. In Africa and in Latin America the enemy was one and the same.

In the summer of 1964, the Cuban press welcomed the resurgence of rebellion in Zaire. "When they buried Lumumba they thought they had dug the grave so deep that no one would ever find his bones and raise them as their battle flag," *Verde Olivo* wrote. "The struggle has just begun; these are its first flames. . . . It will, no doubt, be a long struggle . . . but what matters is that a powerful guerrilla movement has taken root in Zaire."[2] The Cuban press celebrated the Simbas' victories, and, as the summer turned to the fall, it remarked caustically on the growing U.S. intervention in Zaire. Then came Stanleyville.

On December 9, 1964, the front page of *Revolución* carried an unexpected announcement: "Today, . . . Comandante Ernesto Che Guevara will fly to New York . . . to address the General Assembly of the United Nations."[3] Two days later, at the General Assembly, Che lashed out at U.S. aggression against Cuba—the CIA-sponsored exile raids, the U-2 overflights, and the attempt to cripple the economy. Responding to Ambassador Adlai Stevenson's claim that the United States was not involved in the exile attacks on Cuba, Che dripped sarcasm.

We come now to Mr. Stevenson, who, unfortunately, is not here. We understand perfectly why Mr. Stevenson is not here.

We have once again listened to his weighty pronouncements, worthy of an intellectual of his calibre. Similar emphatic, weighty and serious statements were made [by Mr. Stevenson] to the First Committee [of the General Assembly] on April 15, 1961, on the very day that North American pirate airplanes with Cuban markings . . . bombed Cuban airports [at the onset of the Bay of Pigs operation]. . . .

Once again Mr. Stevenson claims that there has been no violation of the law, that no aircraft, and no ship, have left these shores for Cuba; that the pirate attacks come from nothingness, that everything comes from nothingness. He is using the same tone of voice, the same confident demeanor, the same intellectual bearing that he used in 1961 when he so emphatically declared that the Cuban planes had come from Cuban territory and were flown by political exiles, until, that is, the lie was exposed.

So of course I understand why my distinguished colleague, Mr. Stevenson, has, once again, chosen to absent himself from this Assembly.

But it was with unadulterated fury that Che went on to speak about the "tragic case of the Congo [Zaire] . . . which shows how the rights of a people can be flouted with absolute impunity and the most insolent cynicism." He spoke of the martyred Lumumba and of his murderer, Tshombe. He spoke of the role that the Western powers had played in Zaire in 1960–61 and of the role they were now playing, and he cried out: "All the free men of the world must prepare to avenge the crime of the Congo!"[4]

CHE'S TRIP TO AFRICA

Six days later, on December 17, 1964, Che left New York for Algiers. It was the beginning of a three-month tour that took him to eight African countries and to China. It was the first time that a top Cuban leader had visited sub-Saharan Africa. The U.S. government followed his trip closely. "Department most interested in Guevara's movements in Africa," Rusk cabled all the U.S. embassies in the continent, "and would appreciate . . . full reporting on his activities."[5]

Che remained in Algiers until December 26. Then he spent four weeks visiting the four radical states of sub-Saharan Africa—Mali, the Congo, Guinea, and Ghana—accompanied by Jorge Serguera, Cuba's ambassador at Algiers. His next stop, Dahomey (now Benin), a small country with a moderate government, was an odd choice. "Che Guevara arrived . . . unexpectedly yesterday by road from Accra [Ghana]," U.S. ambassador Clinton Knox reported from Cotonou, Dahomey's capital. The State Department went into a tailspin after Che announced at a press conference that Cuba "keenly" wished to establish diplomatic relations with Dahomey. The United States "would have difficulty understanding [Dahomey's] recognition [of] Cuba," Knox warned top Dahomean officials. Brushing aside their argument that it was Dahomey's practice to establish diplomatic relations with any country that so desired, he stressed that this "would make most unfortunate impression on US public opinion . . . [and] would be regarded as putting . . . [Dahomey] in same category as . . . radical African countries."[6] (Cotonou listened, and Dahomey and Cuba did not establish diplomatic relations until February 1, 1974.)

After four days in Dahomey, Che returned to Algiers. On the day he arrived,

January 25, two senior Cuban officials, Osmany Cienfuegos and Emilio Aragonés, flew in from Havana. Che was waiting for them at the airport. On January 29, they all flew to Paris. Two days later, Che, Aragonés, and Osmany left Paris for Beijing.[7] Relations between China and Cuba had deteriorated during the previous months. "The meeting of Latin American Communist leaders in Havana last November [1964] seems to have been a kind of watershed," the CIA reported. Not only had the Chinese not been invited—unlike the Soviets— but, in a clear rebuke to Beijing, the conference had "categorically" condemned "all factional activities [within the Latin American Communist parties], whatever their character or sources." This was the first time, the GDR embassy in Havana observed, that Cuba had officially taken a position on the Sino-Soviet conflict that reflected "the views of . . . our [Soviet bloc] parties." Cuba had also agreed to attend the March 1965 Consultative Meeting of Communist Parties in Moscow, which the Chinese were boycotting.[8] The Chinese were furious, the CIA remarked, and Che's trip to Beijing was "an attempt to smooth matters over." Beijing, however, was "in no mood for reconciliation."[9]

After leaving Beijing on February 9, Che spent a week in Dar-es-Salaam. He stopped in Cairo on February 19, and on February 20 he returned to Algiers to attend the Second Economic Seminar of the Organization of Afro-Asian Solidarity. Cuba had been invited "as an observer and as the only representative from Latin America."[10] It was at this meeting, on February 24, that Che delivered a speech "that provoked," a GDR official noted, "the justified indignation of the majority of our fellow socialist parties."[11]

Addressing the gathering as the representative of "an underdeveloped country that was building socialism," Che focused on relations with the Third World. Instead of praising the Soviet Union, he took it to task. The socialist countries were, "to a certain extent, accomplices to the imperialist exploitation" of the Third World. Like the West, they relied on trade agreements that were based on exploitative terms of trade. "The socialist countries," Che warned, "have the moral duty to liquidate their tacit complicity with the exploiting countries of the West."[12]

On March 2, Che flew from Algiers to Cairo, where he spent ten days. On March 14, he was back in Havana.

U.S. officials were unsure what the real objectives of Che's trip had been. They noted that it appeared to have been organized at the last moment, and they also betrayed respect for Che. Ambassador Porter reported from Algiers that Che's speech had been the "most interesting intervention" at the Afro-Asian seminar. "Guevara's address gives further impetus to the independent leadership role that Cuba is attempting to develop," Tom Hughes, the head of the Bureau of Intelligence and Research of the State Department (INR), opined. "The speech clearly acknowledges that Cuba belongs to the socialist world, yet dares to stand off and both criticize and exhort the socialist powers. Thus Cuba by means of the example of its revolution, and its intellectual leadership, hopes to cast a far larger shadow in the 'national liberation' struggle than its small size would otherwise permit."[13]

A few weeks later, Hughes wrote a report that reflected the assessment of the U.S. intelligence community of Che's trip:

Che Guevara's three-month African trip was part of an important new Cuban strategy. Cuba's immediate goal is the development of a close and useful relationship with the revolutionary African states. Ultimately the Cubans hope to encourage the creation of a vaguely defined third world force in which Cuba would play an important role, and from which Cuba would draw significant political and psychological advantages.

A prime motive of Cuba's new interest in Africa is the continuing failure of its subversive policy in Latin America. . . . The Cubans appear to believe that conditions in Africa . . . are currently more susceptible to Cuban exploitation–manipulation than in Latin America. Ultimately the Cubans want to develop an African position that will aid in their fight for Latin America. . . . Cuba's strategy is designed to provide new political leverage against the United States and the socialist bloc. . . . The Cubans want to develop political support (including Afro-Asian votes at the United Nations) that can force an easing of US policy toward Cuba. . . .

The Cubans doubtless hope that their African ties will increase Cuba's stature in the nonaligned world and help to force the major socialist powers to tolerate a considerable measure of Cuban independence and criticism. . . . It is noteworthy that Guevara warned the Africans privately and publicly of the dangers that can arise from extensive Soviet or Chicom involvement in their countries. Fidel Castro has backed Guevara's statements by speeches and remarks critical of the communist world.

Cuba is employing a variety of techniques to win African interest and support. It offers intellectual leadership and the Cuban example, extends limited aid and propaganda support, encourages exchange of persons, provides scholarships for African students, and gives some guerrilla and terrorist training and arms aid. The Cuban regime's most important weapon in Africa appears to be its example and intellectual leadership. . . .

Guevara's African venture must be judged a modest success. He succeeded in conveying Cuba's message in meetings with high level officials, in speeches, and in interviews. . . . Guevara's demands for socialist aid for developing countries, his sharp criticism of the great powers, and the very idea of small Cuba's revolutionary audacity personified in the person of Guevara undoubtedly proved attractive to many audiences.[14]

This is a judicious report, but it, like all the other U.S. reports on the trip I have seen, misses the key point. Che's trip was not a public relations blitz. Che was in Africa to hammer out specific agreements with African governments and liberation movements. Che, a senior Cuban official recalled, "carried instructions from Fidel to meet with the liberation movements to see how we could help them."[15] His trip had two key moments: Brazzaville and Dar-es-Salaam.

BRAZZAVILLE

The Congo had gained its independence from France in 1960, along with the rest of French West and Equatorial Africa. Its economy, however, remained in French hands, and its security was assured by a defense treaty with Paris and the presence of several hundred French troops and a French military mission.[16]

The broad expanse of the Congo River separated Brazzaville, the capital of the Congo, from Leopoldville, the capital of Zaire. Just as Brazzaville was dwarfed by the city across the river, so the Congo was dwarfed by its neighbor—in size, in natural resources, and in population (less than 1 million versus 15 million). This did not matter, however, so long as the flamboyant and defrocked priest, Fulbert Youlou, ruled the Congo. He was on good terms with Zairean president Kasavubu and the other conservative, and corrupt, leaders in Leopoldville. "The conspicuous consumption, sensuous venality and scandalous affairs of Youlou and most of his ministers . . . starkly contrasted with the poverty of Brazzaville's unemployed," a careful scholar writes. Youlou was also a fierce anti-Communist, winning him high marks from the U.S. embassy, which in June 1963 praised him as "an extremely competent local politician, if not international."[17] Less than two months later, Brazzaville was rocked by three days of street demonstrations led by trade unionists and students, who were fed up with the government's corruption and incompetence. "When the French army . . . received instructions from de Gaulle not to obey Youlou's order to fire on the crowd," and the tiny Congolese army refused to defend the government any longer, Youlou resigned.[18] The Congolese revolution, such as it was, had begun. The new president was Alphonse Massamba-Débat, a former school-teacher and a man whom the CIA deemed "one of the most intelligent and capable leaders in the Congo. . . . Energetic, quick, vigorous and hard-working, he was one of the few who [had] dared to speak out against the Youlou government."[19] He formed a government of teachers and university students who had studied in France and been impressed with the revolutionary rhetoric of the European left. From mid-1964 on, the regime adopted strident leftist rhetoric—while pursuing a moderate economic policy—and began establishing relations with the socialist countries. Its foreign policy became more assertive. "One manifestation of Brazzaville's militant radicalism," the CIA argued in May 1965, "is its apparent willingness to permit the Congo to be used as a base, staging area, and transit point for African revolutionary movements against colonial regimes and moderate African states. One faction of the Leopoldville rebels has maintained its headquarters in Brazzaville for well over a year. Also, the Communist-supported and armed MPLA [Popular Movement for the Liberation of Angola], which has had its headquarters in Brazzaville for some time, has apparently now established a base for training and forays against the Portuguese territory of Cabinda."[20]

This "accelerating leftward slippage," the CIA conceded, was fueled by "fear and hatred" of Prime Minister Tshombe in neighboring Zaire. The Congolese army had only 700 men. "In view of the imbalance of forces," Congolese prime minister Pascal Lissouba recalled, "we lived in constant fear of an invasion: the Zaireans had only to cross the Congo River to be in the heart of Brazzaville."[21]

Cuba had established diplomatic relations with the Congo in May 1964,[22] but when Che and Serguera arrived in Brazzaville on January 1, 1965, the Cuban embassy had not yet opened.

The U.S. embassy reported that Che "had at least three lengthy meetings with President Massamba-Débat," as well as with other top officials, but it did not know that the Congolese had asked Cuba for military instructors to train the militia they intended to create.[23] Although his visit to the headquarters of the MPLA was public knowledge, the United States did not know what had been discussed there.

The MPLA had been founded by a group of Marxist Angolan intellectuals in the late 1950s. It began armed struggle in 1961, but it was soon crippled by the lack of a friendly rear guard. Until October 1964, when Zambia became independent, the Congo and Zaire were the only independent countries that shared a border with Angola. President Youlou was keen in maintaining good relations with Portugal. The Zairean authorities considered the MPLA too leftist, jailed its militants, and refused to allow it to organize in their country. As a result, the MPLA lay prostrate, torn by internal divisions that grew more bitter as it became weaker.

The August 1963 revolution in the Congo saved the MPLA. The Massamba-Débat government invited it to move its headquarters to Brazzaville, to open training camps, and to use Radio Brazzaville. "One year ago," *Révolution Africaine* reported in March 1964, "the MPLA, condemned to nomadism, seemed moribund. Today Brazzaville gives it a new lease on life." The MPLA soon began to engage in low-level guerrilla activities in Angola.[24]

Through 1964 Cuba's main contacts with the MPLA had been in Algiers and Dar-es-Salaam. Relations were friendly, but distant. Occasional requests from MPLA leaders—for military instructors, weapons, and the dispatch of a Cuban officer to assess the situation inside Angola—received a sympathetic hearing but no concrete response. "We had not received any material aid from Cuba," recalls the MPLA leader Lúcio Lara, except for six scholarships granted to Angolan university students who had fled Portugal. The first of the six arrived in Cuba in late 1962. While studying agricultural engineering at the University of Havana, he became one of the island's best soccer players and was a member of the Cuban national team in the Central American games in Puerto Rico in 1966 and the Pan American games in Winnipeg in 1967. The other five Angolans arrived in 1963 and 1964.[25]

Che's visit to Brazzaville, in January 1965, opened a new chapter in Cuba's

In December 1964 Che Guevara went on a three-month trip to Africa that signaled Havana's quickening interest in the continent. Che "carried instructions from Fidel," a senior Cuban official recalled, "to meet with the liberation movements to see how we could help them." Here Che is meeting in Brazzaville with the leaders of the Popular Movement for the Liberation of Angola (MPLA). A few months later, the first Cubans joined the MPLA guerrillas fighting against the Portuguese in Angola.

relations with the MPLA. It was the first meeting between MPLA leaders and a member of the Cuban inner circle. "We talked, we debated," recalls Lara, who was one of the three MPLA leaders present (the other two, President Agostinho Neto and Foreign Secretary Luís de Azevedo, died in 1979 and 1995 respectively, leaving no known account of the encounter). "We wanted only one thing from the Cubans: instructors. The war was getting difficult, and we were inexperienced. We wanted Cuban instructors because of the prestige of the Cuban revolution and because their theory of guerrilla warfare was very close to our own. We were also impressed with the guerrilla tactics of the Chinese, but Beijing was too far away, and we wanted instructors who could adapt to our way of living. We also asked the Algerians to send instructors, but they didn't."[26]

The conversations were awkward, at least at the beginning. "They were not very happy after speaking with Che," the irrepressible Ruth, Lúcio Lara's wife, said of the first encounter. Guevara knew little about the MPLA, and his mind was focused on the revolt in Zaire. He told them that Cuban instructors would soon go to the liberated areas of Zaire to train the Simbas. The MPLA should send its men there to be taught by the Cubans. Neto, Lara, and Azevedo held their ground, and Che relented. Cuba would send the instructors to the Congo.[27]

While Che was talking to the three MPLA leaders, Serguera visited the move-ment's training center. There the MPLA played the same trick on him that Castro had played on a *New York Times* journalist in the Sierra Maestra: rows of armed men marched before the visitor, who did not realize that they were, in fact, a recirculating loop. Fooled by the ruse, Serguera returned to Brazzaville very impressed with the military strength of the MPLA.[28] Che left Brazzaville on January 7 full of optimism. He had been favorably impressed by the Congolese leaders and by the leaders of the MPLA.[29]

After visiting several more African countries and China, Che landed at Dar-es-Salaam on February 11. "Judging by recent Tanzanian interest in Cuba, he should get a good reception," the CIA had predicted a few weeks earlier. President Nyerere, the Tanzanian vice-president, and the foreign minister had attended the January 2 National Day reception at the Cuban embassy. This "unprece-dented appearance [of] more than one of Tanzanian Big Three . . . may represent only [an] inexpensive revolutionary zig," Ambassador Leonhart cabled from Dar-es-Salaam, "but there are rumors of more bothersome zags, among them reports of early Guevara visit."[30] A few days later, an editorial in Tanzania's government newspaper added another zig—or even a zag. "Cuba today," it said, "is a unique example of a little state that has refused to be bullied by any major world power. How was it that a little state such as Cuba . . . has been able to resist powerful external influences and has survived in a hostile hemisphere without flinching one inch from the path it has set before itself? That is what interests us. And perhaps a look at the Cuba scene should provide a guide, if one is needed at all, to the young independent African states to assert their true independence without being used as pawns in present world power politics."[31]

DAR-ES-SALAAM

During the Zanzibar crisis the previous year, U.S. officials had regarded Nyerere with approval, but a few months later their goodwill had evaporated. Dar-es-Salaam "has become a haven for exiles from the rest of Africa," the CIA la-mented in September 1964. "It is full of frustrated revolutionaries, plotting the overthrow of African governments, both black and white." President Nyerere, the report complained, "was long esteemed the most moderate, able, and pro-Western of all African nationalist leaders. . . . It seems that Nyerere's strength of character and qualities of leadership, as well as the firmness of his pro-Western inclinations, have been overrated."[32]

The CIA acknowledged, however, that Nyerere was still "a man of great prin-ciple." Principle made Nyerere recoil in horror at Tshombe's return to power in Zaire and his use of white mercenaries. Principle made Nyerere demand an end to white-ruled regimes in Africa. He had hoped, the CIA admitted, that this could be achieved by "peaceful procedures," and he had urged the West-ern powers to apply pressure on these white governments—their friends and allies—to resolve the situation. "The political solutions he occasionally pro- poses to Western leaders for the dismissal of . . . Tshombe or for the termination of Portuguese rule in Africa may seem naive and idealistic, but they are none the less sincere."[33] As time passed, Nyerere had become increasingly disillusioned and convinced that armed struggle was, regrettably, necessary. Of all the African leaders who proclaimed their support for the liberation struggle in Africa— Nkrumah, Nasser, Ben Bella, Sékou Touré—he was the most committed. And by the second half of 1964, spurred by events in Zaire and the obvious failure of peaceful attempts to end white rule in southern Africa, this commitment, and his disappointment with the Western powers, was increasingly evident.

By the time Che arrived, Dar-es-Salaam had become the Mecca of African liberation movements. In September 1964, Frelimo, the movement against Por- tuguese rule in Mozambique, had launched the opening salvo of its guerrilla war from bases in southern Tanzania, its only rear guard. Following Stanley- ville, Nyerere had thrown his full support to the Simbas, and Tanzania had become their main rear guard and the major conduit of Soviet and Chinese weapons for them. It was also the seat of the Liberation Committee of the OAU. The head offices of Frelimo and a host of other movements struggling against the white regimes in South Africa, Namibia, and Rhodesia were in Dar-es- Salaam.[34]

The Cuban embassy there was, the CIA reported accurately in March 1965, "the largest Cuban diplomatic station in sub-Saharan Africa."[35] The ambas- sador, Captain Pablo Rivalta, was a close friend of Che Guevara.

In early 1964 Rivalta had been the commander of the Libertad air force base near Havana. "One day," he told me, "Che arrived and said, 'Listen, Fidel wants to send you to Tanzania.' He told me I had to establish good relations with the liberation movements there. So they sent me to the Foreign Ministry to learn about Africa, and especially about Tanzania."[36]

Rivalta arrived in Dar-es-Salaam on February 25, 1964, with four trusted aides from Libertad: his driver, Rogelio Oliva; his secretary; the cook; and a man who spoke English. None had any experience in intelligence. "Before leaving . . . Piñeiro's people taught us the rudiments," Oliva recalled.[37]

The selection of Rivalta, with his close ties to Cuba's inner circle, was a sign of Havana's awakening interest in the region. This interest grew as the revolt in Zaire gathered momentum in the second half of 1964. Time and again, during his Africa trip, Che stressed the significance of the struggle under way in Zaire: "If the imperialists succeed in tightening their grip over Zaire and use it as a base of operations, many progressive governments in Africa will be imperiled," he said in January 1965, a few weeks after Stanleyville.[38] Zaire was not just an African problem, he wrote in his memoir of his African sojourn. "We considered the situation in Zaire to be a problem that concerned all mankind." This was his refrain when he met the leaders of the liberation movements in Tanzania. "I decided to try to get a sense of the freedom fighters' state of mind," he wrote.

I had intended to do it in separate meetings, in friendly conversations, but because of a mix-up at the embassy, there was a big "monster" meeting with at least fifty people representing different movements, each divided into two or three factions, of at least ten countries. I addressed them and discussed the requests for financial aid or training that almost all of them had made of us; I explained the cost of training a man in Cuba—the amount of money and time that it took—and the uncertainty that it would prove useful to the movement. I described our experience in the Sierra Maestra, where, for every five recruits we trained, we ended up, on average, with only one soldier and only one in five of these was really good. I argued as vehemently as I could in front of the exasperated freedom fighters that the money invested in training would be largely wasted; one cannot make a soldier in an academy, much less a revolutionary soldier. This has to be done on the battlefield.[a,39]

Che urged instead that the guerrillas be trained where they would fight—in Africa—and he promised that Cuban instructors would train them and fight alongside them. This was the most effective way to teach, he declared; this was the Cuban way. But instead of scattering Cuban instructors in different countries, Che continued, there should be a centralized training center, and it should be in Zaire. Moreover, before the guerrillas returned to their homelands, they should help to free Zaire.

In Che's words,

I explained why we considered the liberation of Zaire to be of fundamental importance: victory there would have repercussions throughout the continent, as would defeat. The reaction [of the assembled Africans] was more than cold; even though most refrained from comment, a few reproached me bitterly. They stated that their people, exploited and abused by the imperialists, would object to suffering more to free another country. I tried to make them understand that the real issue was not the liberation of any given state,

a. There are several copies of Che's 140-page manuscript, "Pasajes de la guerra revolucionaria (Congo)," in private collections in Havana. In 1994, I was given a copy. At roughly the same time three other scholars received copies from other private collections. (See Castañeda, Compañero; Anderson, Che; Taibo, Ernesto Guevara.) In 1999 Che's widow, Aleyda March, oversaw the publication of a slightly revised edition of the manuscript: Ernesto Che Guevara, Pasajes de la guerra revolucionaria: Congo. Its differences with the copy in my possession are mostly stylistic and, according to March, were made by Che when he was in Cuba in mid-1966. I have decided to use my copy of the manuscript, rather than March's published version, for two reasons: it is the version that Che wrote immediately after leaving Zaire, and I am unable to verify whether all the changes in the book version were made by Che.

No researcher, myself included, has seen Che's 1965 diary, on which "Pasajes" is based. According to María del Carmen Ariet of the Archivo Personal del Che Guevara and Aleyda March, Fidel Castro has the only copy. (Author's conversation with Ariet and March, Havana, January 18, 1999.)

but a common war against the common master, who was one and the same in Mozambique and in Malawi, in Rhodesia and in South Africa, in Zaire and in Angola. Not one of them agreed. Their goodbyes were polite, but frosty.[40]

In the days that followed, Che met separately with each liberation movement. He was not impressed. The majority of African rebel leaders in Dar-es-Salaam, he wrote, "live comfortably in hotels and have turned rebellion into a profession, at times lucrative and almost always comfortable. . . . Almost all asked for military training in Cuba and economic aid. This was the constant refrain."[41]

From Cuba's vantage point, the most important liberation movements in Dar-es-Salaam were Zaire's Simbas and Mozambique's Frelimo. Che's encounter with the leaders of Frelimo was stormy. Fidel Castro still remembered it twelve years later when talking to the East German leader Erich Honecker. "The differences we [Cubans] had with Frelimo go back to the time when . . . Che Guevara met [Eduardo] Mondlane [Frelimo's top leader]."[42] Mondlane's irritation with Che's insistence that Frelimo send its guerrillas to train in Zaire was heightened by a personal clash with Che. Like other liberation movements, Frelimo greatly exaggerated its military prowess,[43] a temptation Castro had shunned during the war with Batista. According to a Cuban official, Colman Ferrer, Che, who was not the most tactful of diplomats, expressed skepticism about Frelimo's claims in a way that offended Mondlane. The conversation became acrimonious, and they parted at odds.[44]

This is indirectly confirmed by a Frelimo leader, Marcelino dos Santos, who attended the meeting. He addressed the issue discreetly. "We told Che," he said, "about our situation, about the armed struggle that had just begun, and questions were raised about our facts. Some of these facts struck Che as rather extraordinary. We told him about the battles we'd fought against the Portuguese, of how we'd prepared for the struggle. These facts seem to have surprised Che a little. As for Che's view of the struggle in Africa: the Cubans believed that it was very important to focus on Zaire. It was one point of view. We explained that Frelimo had a different point of view."[45]

Were the Cubans, then, trying to "impose ideas and leadership on the war in Mozambique," as some historians have asserted?[46] "We were not trying to impose our views," Ferrer argues, "but we had the right to say what we thought, because we were offering to risk our lives with them."[47] More to the point, the Cubans agreed to train Frelimo guerrillas in Cuba, and the Cuban ship *Uvero* left Cuba in April 1965 carrying weapons, food, and uniforms for the movement.[48] In his report to the second Congress of Frelimo in July 1968, Mondlane stated that Cuba was helping "us materially and technically, sending us war material [sic] and training some of our [military] cadres."[49]

But the most important aspect of Che's stay in Dar-es-Salaam was his three meetings with the Zairean rebels, who were also eager for money and training. "He said that Cuba could not give us financial aid—they had economic problems—but could send us cadres to train our fighters," one of these rebels,

Godefroid Tschamlesso, remembered. Che was very impressed, he added, by Laurent Kabila, the twenty-six-year-old university student from northern Katanga who had become a Simba leader.[50]

Kabila told Che that he had just returned from rebel-held territory—a claim bound to impress Che, who despised revolutionaries who led the struggle from hotels and conference rooms abroad. "Kabila's presentation was clear, concrete, and firm," Che wrote. "He understood that the real enemy was US imperialism and declared that he was ready to fight against it to the end. I was very favorably impressed with his analysis and his confidence. . . . I offered him, on behalf of our government, about thirty instructors and all the weapons we could spare, and he accepted with delight. He urged us to hurry, as did Soumialot [another Simba leader] in the course of another conversation. Soumialot also asked that the instructors be black."[51]

This was, therefore, a mutually satisfactory encounter. Kabila and Soumialot were confident that the Cuban instructors would come, even though no date was set. (They never imagined, however, that Che would lead the instructors.)[52] Che left Dar-es-Salaam filled with "the joy of having found people ready to fight to the finish. Our next task," he wrote, "was to select a group of black Cubans— all volunteers—to join the struggle in Zaire."[53]

Actually, the volunteers were already training. Che arrived in Dar-es-Salaam on February 11, and the internal history of the Cuban column that went to Zaire states that "Between January 29 and February 2, 1965, groups of officers, non-commissioned officers and soldiers from the three regional commands of the Revolutionary Armed Forces arrived . . . at the military camp called Peti-1. . . . On February 2, 1965, the column was officially constituted . . . [and] its commanding officer, Comandante Víctor Dreke, addressed his men for the first time."[54]

THE FIRST COLUMN

Meeting Víctor Dreke thirty years later, it is difficult not to be impressed by the charisma, integrity, and intelligence of this taciturn man. He is one of the heroes of Cuba's African story, in Zaire and, later, in Guinea-Bissau. Che paid Dreke unusual praise. "He was, throughout our stay, one of the pillars on which I relied," he wrote after seven months in Zaire. "The only reason I am not recommending that he be promoted is that he already holds the highest rank."[55]

A veteran of the war against Batista, Dreke had been a captain in the rebel army when the dictator had fled. In July 1962 he became commander of a unit of the elite antiguerrilla force. The following December, at age twenty-five, he was promoted to the rank of comandante.

"In January 1965," Dreke remembers, "the commander of the Central Army, Comandante Calixto García, sent for me. He told me that he had just returned from Havana, and our Commander in Chief [Fidel Castro] had a mission for me, a secret, dangerous mission, and that I could choose to go or to stay. I answered, 'I'm ready. When am I going?' (I assumed that I'd be a guerrilla in Latin America—something I had dreamt of. Africa never crossed my mind.) The army commander offered me coffee . . . and after a while he said, 'You have to choose a platoon of men who have shown their mettle, who are all volunteers and who are dark-skinned blacks.' At that moment I got it: I was going to Africa."[56]

In great secrecy, Dreke, who is black, selected thirty or thirty-five men (soldiers, noncommissioned officers, and lieutenants) from the central army, while two other officers, Lieutenant Manuel Agramonte and Captain Santiago Terry, chose others from the western and eastern armies, respectively.[57]

In Havana, the minister of public health, Machado Ventura, began choosing the doctors who would accompany the column. "Machado told me that he had an important mission abroad for me," recalled Rafael Zerquera, who had just graduated from medical school and was an intern in the Sierra Maestra. "He didn't tell me what it was or where I would go. He only said that it was dangerous and that I'd go with a group of very brave compañeros who needed a doctor and that I was free to decide whether or not I wanted to go."[58]

While Machado was selecting the doctors, the men chosen by Dreke, Agramonte, and Terry were taken to Peti-1.[59] They were in for a shock. All the column's 113 members were black, including all the officers. "It was the first time that I had seen so many blacks together," Lieutenant Rafael Moracén remarks. "Blacks, only blacks, we were all blacks. It baffled me. I wondered, 'Shit! What's going on?' "[60]

Both the Simba leaders and the DGI thought that it would be easier for black Cubans to pass incognito. DGI officers wanted the men to be not only black, but "dark-skinned blacks," the history of the column recorded, and they almost drummed out one of the men, Lieutenant Catalino Olachea, because, they said, he was too white. (Olachea is a dark-skinned mulatto.) Dreke had to appeal all the way to Fidel Castro. "Later we realized that there are mulattoes in Africa," Dreke told me, "so in Guinea-Bissau we were less strict. But Zaire was our first experience."[61]

Castro visited the column several times. "He told us that we were going on an internationalist mission, that it was voluntary, and that if any of us didn't want to go, there was no problem," one of the volunteers, Lieutenant Erasmo Vidiaux, recalls. They were not told, however, where they were going or for how long. "Most of us assumed it would be Africa (because all of us were black), but we weren't sure," Vidiaux adds.[62]

They trained for almost two months in the Petis. For security reasons, they were cut off from the world. "We were worried about our families," Olachea recalls. "They didn't even know where we were. We hadn't been in touch with them since we'd been selected. We appealed to Dreke, and he asked Fidel to give us home leave. Fidel said, 'If you promise not to breathe a word of this to your families, I'll give you five days of leave.' He also made sure that we got some pocket money." The volunteers were told to tell their families that they were going to the Soviet Union for training. "Our security people in the Petis were not very happy about the leave," Dreke mused, "but all the compañeros were back on time, and they were all really discreet—or, if they weren't, their families were, because there were no leaks."[63]

I was skeptical when I first heard this story; it seemed to be an embellishment. I was intrigued when it was repeated by several other participants. And I was convinced when I read the internal history of the column, which recorded: "Very strict security measures were in place during the training. . . . Toward the end of the training, however, the Commander in Chief met with the men and . . . after explaining how important the mission was, granted them a week's home leave, asking them to maintain absolute secrecy about the mission. All the compañeros returned on time, including those who lived far away."[b,64]

At the end of March, the men were driven in small groups to safe houses in Havana, where they remained until they left Cuba.[65]

DECISION MAKING IN HAVANA: PROTAGONISTS

The analysis of Cuba's decision to send the column to Zaire must be tentative. I have not been able to interview the men who made it, nor have I had access to the documents that could explain it, beyond Che's memoir of the seven months he spent in Zaire.[66]

The timing of the decision is problematic: the column was created on February 2, but Che did not arrive at Dar-es-Salaam until February 11, and the Simba leaders did not agree to receive Cuban instructors in Zaire until some days later—that is, almost two weeks after the column had been created.

It is likely that when Che left Cuba in December 1964 one of his goals was to convince the Simbas to accept Cuban instructors. He was so confident he would succeed that in Brazzaville, one month before he set foot in Dar-es-Salaam, he urged the MPLA leaders to send their men to Zaire, where the Cubans would train them.

"Our ardent desire to help the Simbas," a senior official explained, "and the MPLA's and Brazzaville's requests for instructors in early January led us to be-

---

b. These are some accounts by participants: "Fidel visited us several times in the Petis. Once he announced: 'You're going on home leave and you'll each get 100 pesos. Tell your families that you're going to the USSR'" (interview with Hernández Betancourt). "Fidel gave us time off to see our families and he told Dreke to give us 100 pesos" (interview with Veitía). "Fidel said that if we didn't tell our families what we were doing, we'd get a seventy-two-hour home leave; they took care of the transportation; they even used airplanes" (interview with Moracén). "Fidel gave us leave to visit our families. Since we were from all over the place, he told Osmany [Cienfuegos] to organize ground and air transportation to take us to our homes. For example, I was from Santiago. A special plane took us there, and at the airport ground transportation was waiting to take each of us home. When it was time to return [to the camp], a car came and took me to the airport, where a special plane was waiting" (Interview with Chaveco).

gin preparing a column of black Cubans for Brazzaville, but their destination was still flexible. If the Simbas accepted our proposal, then they would go to Zaire."[67]

Cuban decision making at the time was ad hoc. The circle that approved covert operations was very small. Serguera makes a good point in discussing Che's trip to Africa when he writes, "I do not want to offend or belittle anyone, but one must not confuse participation in the discussion of a problem . . . with making policy."[68] It is likely that no more than three men made the decision to send Cubans to Zaire: Fidel, Che, and Raúl Castro, the country's most prominent leader after Fidel. Raúl was focused, however, on creating a powerful military, not on Cuba's wars of national liberation. He was never mentioned in the recollections of the members of the column I interviewed, in Che's "Pasajes," or in any of the other documents I have seen.

Two men played key roles in implementing the decision: Piñeiro and, above all, Osmany Cienfuegos. On the face of it, Osmany was an unlikely choice. An architect, in 1965 he was the minister of public works. Intelligent, canny, a man of action, he was the brother of the late Camilo Cienfuegos, a hero of the revolution and, many believe, Fidel's closest friend. Initially overshadowed by his late brother, Osmany was appointed—to the surprise of many—president of the Foreign Affairs Committee of the Central Committee of the new Cuban Communist Party (PCC) in October 1965. Until 1967 Osmany was Castro's point man in Africa. During the Zairean operation he was the top aide. He pops up in the most unlikely places—in Dar-es-Salaam, in eastern Zaire, in the Congo.

Two African presidents—Nyerere and, to a lesser extent, Nasser—actively assisted Cuba in Zaire. Tanzania was the rear guard through which everything had to pass. Without Nyerere's cooperation, it would have been impossible for the Cubans to get to Zaire. Almost all the Cubans who went to Tanzania and most of their weapons passed through the Cairo airport, where they were assisted by Egyptian officials. In Ferrer's words, "Cairo was the hub."[69]

The timing and the circumstances of Cuba's agreements with Tanzania and Egypt are unclear. Who approached whom? And when? In Tanzania's case there is one piece of written evidence, a letter from Che indicating that it was the Cubans who approached Nyerere, after Che had spoken with the Simba leaders. "Cuba offered aid [to the Simbas] on condition that Tanzania approve," Che wrote in October 1965. "It did, so we went ahead." Rivalta confirms this account.[70]

Che was in Cairo for one day on February 19, and again from March 2 to 12. He had several conversations with Nasser without any witnesses.[71] There is only one published account of these conversations, written by Nasser's confidant Mohamed Heikal, who tells a riveting tale of how Che told Nasser that he had been in Zaire visiting two battalions of black Cubans fighting there, and that he was thinking of taking over their command. Nasser was, according to Heikal, stunned. "'You want to become another Tarzan, a white man coming among black men, leading them,'" he told Che. "'It can't be done.'" Over the next few days, Heikal writes, the two men talked late into the night at Nasser's house. "'You must forget all about this idea of going to the Congo [Zaire],'" Nasser told Che. "'It won't succeed.'"[72]

One problem with Heikal's story is that Che did not set foot in Zaire until April 24; another is that the only Cubans there before that were the exiles working for the CIA in the Zairean air force. And even if Che had already decided to lead the Cubans who would go to Zaire, it is not credible that he would bare his soul to a foreign leader (whom he had met only a few times) before discussing his decision with Castro in Havana.

In a recent article, Ben Bella implies that Che also confided in him about his plans to go to Zaire.[73] Ambassador Rivalta—Che's trusted companion—seems to have been the only one not in the loop. He was with Che during his conversations with the Simbas, and before leaving Dar-es-Salaam Che asked him to suggest a commander for the column, but, with uncharacteristic (if one believes Heikal and Ben Bella) discretion, Che never mentioned that he intended to be that man.[74]

Rivalta and others who were at the Cuban embassy in Dar-es-Salaam assert that Algeria, Ghana, Mali, and China knew of the operation, but they do not know when.[75] Che's biographer Jorge Castañeda believes that China was told as early as February 1965, when Che visited Beijing. Che "realized," Castañeda writes, "that any Cuban initiative in Africa, at least in the Congo [Zaire] and Tanzania, could not dispense with Mao's approval. . . . Nyerere possessed an enduring affection for China's leaders. . . . Pierre Mulele, the most strongly rooted among the Congolese [Zairean] leaders, was also a sinophile. So without a green light from China, there could be no African expedition—either for Cuba or for Che."[76] On this point, however, Castañeda is not persuasive. Mulele was in western Zaire, cut off from all outside help, and the Cubans were planning to go to eastern Zaire, where there was a completely different set of leaders who sought assistance from all possible sources and were beholden to none. Furthermore, there is no indication in the limited evidence that is available (Che's "Pasajes" and GDR documents) that the Chinese provided more assistance than did the Soviets. Finally, Nyerere was fiercely independent. He would not have sacrificed precious Cuban help for the Simbas in order to please Beijing. (Similarly, in 1965 he risked a break in diplomatic relations with Bonn, an important aid donor, rather than renege on his promise to allow the GDR to open a general consulate in Dar-es-Salaam.)[77] The Cubans did not need a green light from China, or, for that matter, from the Soviet Union, and there is no indication that they asked for anyone's but Nyerere's approval before going to Zaire.

According to Aleksandr Alekseev, the Soviet ambassador in Cuba, it was on April 18 or 19, 1965, that Castro told him that a Cuban column, led by Che, was going to Zaire. This was the first, he says, that the Soviet government heard of the operation.[78] By then, Che and some members of the column had left for Dar-es-Salaam. The available evidence indicates that the Soviets provided no assistance in the preparation of the operation and thus supports Alekseev's recollection.[79] As to the degree of Soviet-Cuban cooperation once the column reached Zaire, no documents illuminate the issue.[80] I have only clues, from Che's "Pasajes" and from the testimonies of men who were not in Fidel's inner circle. It is better, then, to let the story unfold, present the clues as they occur, and then offer a tentative answer.

DECISION MAKING IN HAVANA: MOTIVATIONS

One can be far less tentative when it comes to explaining why Havana sent the column to Zaire. Altruism, self-defense, and ignorance went hand in hand.

Cuba's sense of isolation and vulnerability had deepened in 1963 and 1964. The defeats suffered by the guerrilla movements in Latin America—most notably in Argentina, Peru, and Venezuela—and the failure of Salvador Allende in the September 1964 Chilean presidential elections meant that, for the foreseeable future, Cuba was alone in the hemisphere.

Its isolation had been formalized in the OAS (from which Cuba had been expelled in January 1962). Following the discovery in November 1963 that Cuba had sent arms to the Venezuelan guerrillas, Caracas called for OAS sanctions against Havana. The five OAS members that still had diplomatic relations with Cuba—Brazil, Mexico, Uruguay, Chile, and Bolivia—resisted Venezuela's bid. "They seem determined," the CIA noted, and "present this position as a facet of their 'independent' foreign policies." The U.S. National Security Council concluded in early March 1964 that as long as Mexico and Brazil opposed sanctions, "It would . . . be very difficult to obtain a politically desirable majority [in favor]."[81] Less than a month later, a military coup supported by the United States brought down Brazil's left-leaning president, João Goulart, and replaced him with a rabidly anti-Communist government. "The overthrow of Goulart has dealt a severe blow to Cuba's foreign policy in Latin America," the *New York Times* explained. "Cuban diplomats who several weeks ago were scornful of suggestions that the OAS might take effective measures against the Castro regime are taking a new look at the situation."[82]

On July 26, by a 14-1-4 vote, the OAS imposed mandatory sanctions against Cuba: the severance of diplomatic and consular relations and the cessation of trade and shipping with the island. (Argentina abstained; Mexico, Chile, Bolivia, and Uruguay voted against; Venezuela did not vote.) Castro denounced the vote, "pointing out, with justification," a British historian remarks, "that the kind of aggressive acts for which he had been condemned had for long been committed on a much larger scale by the United States against himself."[83] Be that as it may, Chile, Bolivia, and Uruguay soon buckled under U.S. pressure and broke relations with Cuba. Only Mexico held out.[84] When Chile hinted that "for purely domestic purposes" it might have to make occasional noises about the need to approach the Cuban problem on a different basis, the U.S. embassy was blunt: "Nothing could hurt US-Chilean relations more than to re-open the Cuban question."[85] Meanwhile, as the Johnson administration bullied its allies

The threat of a U.S. military attack on Cuba haunted Havana's leaders throughout the 1960s. In October 1964 Jorge Risquet, a senior Cuban official, went to Moscow, where he had two tense meetings with Khrushchev. "Our talks did not go well," he recalled. "We were convinced that the United States was planning to attack Cuba; this was what I had come to tell him." But Khrushchev was not receptive. "The tone was bitter." Khrushchev's fall, in mid-October, brought no improvement in the strained relationship between Havana and Moscow. Risquet is shown here in uniform behind Khrushchev. To his left is the Cuban ambassador to the Soviet Union, Carlos Olivares.

and clients throughout the world to join the crusade to cripple the Cuban economy, CIA-sponsored exile groups continued to launch armed raids against the island.

We know with hindsight that even though influential voices in the United States clamored for a military strike against Cuba, Johnson had no intention of mounting one; he only sought to inflict pain. Cuba's bitter experience, however, and the cacophony of snarls and threats emanating from the United States made it reasonable for Havana to fear the worst.[86]

Furthermore, Cuba's relations with the Soviet Union had grown testy. In October Jorge Risquet, a senior Cuban official who was in Moscow to prepare for the forthcoming visit of President Dorticós, had two tense meetings with Khrushchev. "Our talks did not go well," he recalled.

We were convinced that the United States was planning to attack Cuba; this was what I had come to tell him, but Khrushchev said it wasn't so. But we were convinced, and so I asked him for three things. First, an increase in the size of the Soviet brigade in Cuba—as a symbolic gesture of support. Khrushchev said no. Second, an increase in military aid. Khrushchev said no. And third, membership in the Warsaw Pact. Khrushchev said no. (We weren't really serious about joining the pact, and we knew Khrushchev would say no, but we thought it would give us leverage for the first two items.) The tone was bitter. Khrushchev spent almost all the time talking about the Chinese. He was fixated on them.[87]

After the fall of Khrushchev on October 14, relations with the Soviets improved, but several fundamental problems remained, particularly the Soviet leaders' opposition to Havana's support for guerrilla movements in Latin America. At the November 1964 Havana conference of Latin American Communist parties, Fidel Castro had deferred to the Soviet position on armed struggle, but this had been no surrender. As the CIA reported, "the meeting represented an armistice which could not last either as a beginning or as the end of a process."[88] Castro's feelings were clearly expressed in a speech on January 2, 1965, in which, as the CIA remarked, he "went out of his way to assert his regime's autonomy within the 'socialist camp.'" Castro was referring to the Soviet Union, the CIA explained, when he said, "'We do not need the brains of other people.'" East European Communists confirmed the CIA's assessment: the Soviet bloc embassies "have noted with concern . . . the part of his speech that . . . mentions Soviet aid . . . in what seems to be a dismissive manner. . . . Castro reduced this selfless aid, which has virtually been Cuba's lifeblood for years, to arms deliveries and sugar purchases. Moreover, he mentioned the Soviet Union and the People's Republic of China in the same breath."[89]

Khrushchev's departure did not assuage the Cuban leaders' doubts about Soviet steadfastness in the defense of Cuba. "The Cubans do not know where they stand with the Soviets," the CIA reported in early December. "After what happened with the missiles—with Nikita [Khrushchev] or without Nikita—there were always doubts," Risquet explained. Castro expressed these doubts forcefully in a 1968 conversation with high-ranking GDR officials. "You are members of the Warsaw Pact," he began,

so you have a guarantee against imperialist aggression. You have a lot of Soviet divisions nearby which are ready to fight on your side. This is not the case in Cuba. We have no guarantee against imperialist aggression. We don't have twenty divisions to protect us. You can sleep peacefully, even though the West German imperialists are on your border. They will not attack you because if they do, there will be war. . . . We cannot have even a moment's peace. . . . No one could guarantee to help us in case of US aggression. We have no common border with the Soviet Union. The US fleet is more powerful than the Soviet Navy. You have every guarantee; we have none. I say it clearly: ideologically we are part of the socialist community, in our aims, in our way of thinking, in our feelings. But when it comes to our ability to withstand this enemy that can attack us at any time, we are not part of the socialist community. . . . The Soviet Union has given us weapons. We are and will be forever thankful . . . but if the imperialists attack Cuba, we can count only on ourselves.[90]

For the wary Cubans, the United States was on a rampage in Latin America and throughout the world, ever more arrogant, ever more threatening. The August 1964 Gulf of Tonkin resolution had given Johnson a blank check in Vietnam, and in February 1965 the sustained bombing began, without eliciting a powerful Soviet response. Week after week, as U.S. planes bombed North Vietnam, the CIA's "Weekly Cuban Summary" gave eloquent testimony of the Cuban reaction:

> The US air strikes in North Vietnam are particularly relevant to Cuba. The Cubans recognize that they themselves could well be subject to such US action in retaliation for the downing of a US aircraft over Cuba or to active Cuban participation in armed subversion elsewhere in Latin America. (Mar. 3)

> Cuban officials see a great deal of similarity between developments in Vietnam and Cuba's international situation. . . . The Cubans reportedly feel that a lack of aid to North Vietnam by the USSR and Communist China could indicate a similar disinclination to assist Cuba if it were subjected to some type of direct US action. (Mar. 10)

> Western observers in Havana . . . report Cuban officials are apprehensive that the "lack of backbone" exhibited by Soviet and Communist Chinese reactions to the US air strikes against North Vietnam are indications that Havana could not count on World Communist support in the event of similar raids against Cuba. (Mar. 17)

> Havana's relations with Moscow are by no means smooth. Raul Castro, who led the Cuban delegation to the Moscow meeting [of Communist parties] early this month, [sanitized] caused considerable discord by his intransigent insistence upon the need to send material assistance to North Vietnam as the first step toward achieving world Communist unity. . . . Cuban officials fear that a lack of Soviet "backbone" in Vietnam might indicate a similar lack of willingness to assist Cuba if it were subject to future US actions. (Mar. 31)

> For the past two weeks, Havana propaganda media have been engaging in a flamboyant agitational effort . . . to dramatize the Cuban view of the "duty" of all bloc states to assist a "brother socialist country"—North Vietnam today but, by clear implication, Cuba itself in some possible future situation. . . . [Cuba] has made plain the concern that Vietnam today could be Cuba tomorrow. . . . [sanitized] a discussion of the possible repercussions of the Vietnam situation was one of the principal reasons for Raul Castro's visit to the USSR to attend the 1 March international Communist meeting. Reportedly, Raul asked for a definition of the Soviet Union's potential stand in the event of any possible US "aggression" against Cuba, ranging from a preventive blockade of Cuba to isolated attacks against Cuban military objectives. (Apr. 7)[91]

As the CIA pointed out, Raúl Castro's trip to Moscow was not proof of Havana's obeisance to Soviet demands. Instead, Raúl had been outspoken and "intransigent." Vietnam was, for Cuba, a test case. If the Soviets failed to respond forcefully to the American bombings there, what reason was there to hope that they would behave differently when Cuba was the target?[92]

In April 1965 U.S. troops invaded the Dominican Republic. While U.S. policy makers debated the extent of the Castro-Communist threat in Santo Domingo (it was nonexistent),[93] Cuban officials prepared to defend their country against a U.S. attack. "Beginning on 30 April, Cuban air defense, naval, and some ground units were placed on alert in response to the situation in the Dominican Republic," the CIA noted. "The alert was subsequently extended to all military units, including paramilitary anti-insurgency units. Cuban extra sensitivity regarding foreign aircraft was noted during the night of 1 May when two Cuban MIGs were scrambled to reconnoiter a US peripheral reconnaissance mission." A few days later the British ambassador in Havana reported that "United States intervention in Santo Domingo has really disturbed Castro government. . . . Main reaction is one of alarm that United States should be able to act in this way with impunity and apprehension as to what next American move may be."[94]

Meanwhile, the CIA mercenary army was slaughtering Simbas. The Cuban exiles among the mercenaries, manning the planes for Tshombe, were getting, one of them boasted, "target practice for Fidel Castro." Their contract stipulated, he explained, that "all will be released as soon as conditions favourable for action against Castro present themselves."[95]

Havana had tried to defuse the tension with Washington—in August 1961, when Che had approached Goodwin, and again in late 1963 and in mid-1964. Washington had rebuffed all these efforts and had continued its economic strangulation and paramilitary operations.[96]

Che expressed the Cuban response eloquently on *Face the Nation* in December 1964: "We are aware of the overwhelming power of the United States. We don't delude ourselves about it. But the US government wants us to pay a very high price for the non-peaceful coexistence that exists between us at present, and we refuse to compromise our dignity in any way. If we have to kowtow to the Americans to be left alone, then they will have to kill us first."[97]

Perhaps some would have counseled Castro to be quiet and humble to avoid exciting the aggressive neighbor, but this was not the approach of the proud Cuban revolutionaries—leaders and followers alike. Castro's "success has been based, to a large extent, on his activism and willingness to run risks," the chair of the CIA's National Board of Estimates had noted. "When put under strong pressure, he has always been prone to counteract."[98] If the United States refused to negotiate, then Cuba would gird itself for the struggle. "It was almost a reflex," Dreke remarks. "Cuba defends itself by attacking its aggressor. This was our philosophy. The Yankees were attacking us from every side, so we had to challenge them everywhere, along all the paths of the world. We had to divide their forces, so that they wouldn't be able to descend on us (or on any other country) with all their might. Our response had to be bold."[99]

The Cubans, however, were not suicidal. "Fidel has stopped short of any actions that might bring him into conflict with the US," the CIA wrote in 1966.[100] They complained vehemently about the U-2 overflights but never fired at the U.S. planes violating their airspace.[101] They gave moral support to radical African American groups, but were careful not to provide them any material assistance, and certainly not military training.[102] The Cubans tried to avoid the lion's jaw. They responded to the U.S. challenge, instead, in the Third World.

In the years immediately after the revolution, Cuba focused on aiding rebels in Latin America. By 1965, however, its attention had shifted to Africa. In an insightful report, INR director Hughes went a long way toward explaining Cuba's motivations. The Cubans now considered Africa ready for revolution, he wrote in April 1965, more ready than Latin America. "Ultimately the Cubans want to develop an African position that will aid in their fight for Latin America. . . . Cuba's strategy is designed to provide new political leverage against the United States and the socialist bloc. . . . The Cubans want to develop political support (including Afro-Asian votes at the United Nations) that can force an easing of US policy toward Cuba. . . . The Cubans doubtless hope that their African ties will increase Cuba's stature in the nonaligned world and help to force the major socialist powers to tolerate a considerable measure of Cuban independence and criticism."[103]

As insightful as Hughes was, even he failed to imagine that Castro would send an armed column to fight alongside the Simbas.

Pragmatism and idealism led Cuba to choose Zaire as the battlefield. The atrocities of the mercenaries, the brazen U.S.-Belgian raid on Stanleyville, and the memory of Lumumba demanded a response in the name of justice. This response was possible because of the revolutionary ferment in Zaire and, indeed, throughout sub-Saharan Africa. Zaire would become the center from which revolution would spread to the neighboring countries, especially the Portuguese colonies. This is why the Cubans were particularly eager to help the MPLA and Frelimo. "Africa is rising from the ruins," *Verde Olivo* wrote in December 1964. "The fire of national liberation is burning in Angola. The Zairean patriots are raising the flag of independence on the points of their guns. Rebels are fighting heroically in Mozambique. The people of southern Rhodesia are rejecting false independence that would only perpetuate the rule of the racist minority."[104]

This was Cuba's perception of what was happening in Africa, but it was not reality. Beyond pragmatism and idealism, a third element governed Cuba's African strategy in 1965: overestimation of the revolutionary potential in Africa in general, and in Zaire in particular. "We knew very little about the Simbas or about Zaire," Dreke observed. "And what we knew included so much exaggeration—tales of battles that had never been fought, of heroes who never existed!"[105] Che's trip through Africa exemplifies the problem. He had never been to sub-Saharan Africa before, and the "expert" who accompanied him, Serguera, had been there only once, for twenty-four hours. Che's most important commitments were undertaken at Brazzaville and Dar-es-Salaam. There was no Cuban embassy in Brazzaville and that in Dar-es-Salaam had a new team that had arrived only a few months earlier and knew little about the country. "I am still having problems with the language [English]," Ambassador Rivalta had written in late June 1964 in a letter that suggests how ill suited he was for the job, "and so I only understand fragments of the reports about what is going on here." Two members of Rivalta's small staff spoke English (one, Oliva, even became fluent in Swahili), but none had any experience in diplomacy or in intelligence. Indeed the Cuban intelligence service, the DGI, had no presence in sub-Saharan Africa until early 1965. As Ulises Estrada, a senior DGI officer, remarked, "Bear in mind that when Che was going to Africa with scores of Cubans, here [in Havana] we didn't have an organization. We created it on the go in 1965."[106]

STEAMING TO AFRICA

On April 26, 1965, the *Uvero*, the largest ship of the Cuban merchant navy, left Matanzas to carry out "Operation Triángulo," the DGI's first venture in sub-Saharan Africa. Two days later, U.S. marines landed in Santo Domingo. While U.S. warships patrolled the waters of the Dominican Republic, the *Uvero* steamed ahead with its important cargo hidden in large crates marked "sugar" and "rice": weapons and supplies for the rebels of Guinea-Bissau (fulfilling the promise Che had made to their leader in Conakry); weapons and supplies for Frelimo; and weapons for the Venezuelan guerrillas. Nine Cuban military instructors were also aboard; they were the vanguard of the column destined for the Congo. Ulises Estrada was in charge.[107]

This was Estrada's first contact with Africa. "When Piñeiro told me about this mission, I said, 'Piñeiro, don't get me involved in this; I don't know anything about Africa, and I like what I'm doing [working on Latin America].' He told me, 'Compadre, you'll learn fast, and it won't take so long. Before you know it, you'll be back home!' Well, it took seven months! Seven months I'll never forget!"[108]

When the *Uvero* arrived in Conakry, "nothing was ready. No one was there waiting for us," Estrada recalled. Serguera, who was supposed to have made all the necessary arrangements with the government of Guinea, was still in Algiers; the Cuban embassy in Conakry knew nothing about the *Uvero*. "We had to wait a couple of days outside the port, with our crates of weapons," Estrada continued, "until Serguera finally showed up." At last, on May 14, the *Uvero* entered the port. "A ship without a manifest has unloaded 315 crates for our national defense," the customs form stated.[109]

The nine instructors disembarked in Conakry; they would continue to Brazzaville by plane. Estrada remained aboard. Steaming north, the *Uvero* hugged the western coast of Africa, entered the Mediterranean, and reached the Algerian port of Skikda, where the arms for the Venezuelan guerrillas should have been unloaded, but were not, because Ben Bella had been overthrown.[110] With the weapons still on board, the *Uvero* proceeded eastward to the Suez Canal and from there to Tanzania. On June 29, it crossed the Equator.[111] That same day, Che Guevara's men fought their first battle in Zaire.

CHAPTER FIVE
CHE IN ZAIRE

Toward the end of March, when the training of the First Column was almost completed, a senior DGI officer, Luis Delgado, visited Dreke at Peti-1 with several photographs of a man called Ramón. "He asked me whether I recognized him," Dreke recalled. "I said I didn't. Delgado insisted: 'Look, he says he knows you, that you are friends.'" Dreke was categorical: "I don't know him. I have never laid eyes on him."[1]

About a week later, on March 30, Osmany Cienfuegos drove Dreke to a house on the outskirts of Havana. While driving, he told him: "It has been decided that Ramón will be in command of the column, not you." Dreke silently wondered: "And this Ramón, where does he come from?" When they arrived at the house, Osmany said, "'Listen, Ramón is here.' He went upstairs and came back with Ramón. I still didn't recognize him, but Osmany insisted: 'Don't you know him?' I said, 'No.' Ramón was looking at me, but he didn't speak. I was getting annoyed. Then he spoke, and I knew immediately who he was."[2]

It was Che Guevara in disguise. Che would lead the column. "I myself suggested the idea to Che," Fidel Castro explained. "He had time on his hands; he had to wait. And he wanted to train cadres, to get experience."[3]

CHE'S CHOICE

More than anyone else, Che was the theoretician of the foco theory and the man who, on Fidel's behalf, had orchestrated Cuba's support for the wars of liberation in Latin America. Spurred by his example, and the example of the Cuban revolution, men had risked death in search of a better future. "Once again, youthful blood has fertilized the fields of America to make freedom possible," Che wrote as he mourned the death of a dear friend in Guatemala in 1962. "Another battle has been lost; we must make time to weep for our fallen comrades while we sharpen our machetes."[4]

Che dreamed of returning to South America to lead a guerrilla war in Argentina, his native land. In 1962 he had begun preparing Operation Segundo Sombra and had selected his close friend Jorge Masetti to lead the vanguard of the guerrilla group until he joined him and assumed the leadership of the movement. In mid-1963 Masetti and his men had entered Argentina clandestinely and begun reconnoitering the northern province of Salta. But early in 1964 the Argentine gendarmerie realized that they were there and in March and April it closed in, killing or capturing the entire group of some thirty guerrillas. Che was still in Cuba. The disaster upset him deeply: another friend had died on the battlefield while he waited in Havana. "Che had a very big complex about Masetti's death," Estrada remarked.[5]

Che explored the possibility of joining the Venezuelan guerrillas, but the Venezuelan Communist Party (PCV) was not responsive. "It was our problem, a Venezuelan problem," PCV leader Pompeyo Márquez argued. "A movement led by Che Guevara would not have been a Venezuelan movement." In any case, Piñeiro adds, Che preferred to lead his own guerrilla movement, and, "above all," he wanted to operate in the Southern Cone, "particularly in Argentina."[6] Masetti's debacle, coming just a few months after a similar failure in Peru, meant, however, that if Che wanted to lead armed struggle in Argentina, he would have to start organizing from scratch.[7]

Therefore, as Fidel said, Che "had time on his hands." He was also increasingly uncomfortable in Cuba, according to American journalist Jon Lee Anderson and Mexican professor Jorge Castañeda, whose recent biographies of Guevara, based on extensive research, are the new standards. "Cuba's political atmosphere was becoming claustrophobic; he had new enemies at home and abroad," Anderson writes, and Castañeda concurs.[8]

Both agree that Che's economic policy had become increasingly controversial. Since early 1961 Che had been in charge of the Cuban economy, and his emphasis on moral incentives and centralization were increasingly under fire. By late 1964 Castro himself was leaning toward the views of Che's critics. More important were foreign policy disputes: Che did not hide his increasingly critical opinion of the Soviet Union. He was dismayed by the corruption and inefficiency he had discovered in Soviet society, and he was wary of Moscow's foreign policy: its growing opposition to armed struggle in Latin America; its lack of generosity in dealing with Third World countries; and its attempts to influence the Cuban revolution. The Soviets, in turn, began to consider Che their most dangerous opponent in Cuba and branded him as pro-Chinese—a poisonous accusation in the mid-1960s. "The suspicion had cast a pall over his work in Cuba and his dealings with even some of his closest comrades, such as Raúl Castro, who had developed strong links with the Soviet military and its party leadership," Anderson writes. "As Che's relations with Moscow soured, Raúl had become increasingly pro-Soviet and was reportedly given to cracking jokes about Che's being 'China's man' in Cuba."[9]

Castañeda and Anderson differ, however, in their analysis of Che's relationship with Fidel. Castañeda sees more tension and deeper differences than does Anderson. It is difficult to speak with authority on this subject: no written sources are available, and the people who know the truth remain silent, while others speak with great confidence. It is easy to go astray. Castañeda relies on accounts that are indeed eloquent. He was so impressed, for example, by what the prominent Cuban exile Carlos Franqui told him about Che's relationship with Fidel that he based his analysis of Che's decision to go to Zaire on it. Franqui's story takes place in July 1963, when Che, who had just spent three weeks in Algeria, stopped in Paris on his way back to Cuba. There he met

Franqui, the former editor of the Cuban daily *Revolución*, "who had been living in intermittent exile in Algeria and Europe for some time. Relations between them were strained," Castañeda writes.

They had clashed several times in Cuba over a number of issues, but had just celebrated a virtual reconciliation in Algiers, where Franqui had interviewed Ben Bella and mounted an exhibit of Cuban art he had brought from Paris. According to Franqui's memoirs, the two now discovered many affinities: "We were both friends of Ben Bella, [Che] was seeking another path. . . . It was one of our best meetings."

Che put an arm around Franqui's shoulders and the two went walking along a deserted boulevard in the Paris summer. . . . Guevara tried to persuade the journalist to return to Cuba, without denying the problems there and his own frictions with Castro. It was then, in the heart of the Latin Quarter, that Che gave vent to a feeling that would soon lead him away from his closest friend and dearest companion in arms: "With Fidel, I want neither marriage nor divorce."[10]

It is a powerful account, detailed, poetic, poignant. It does not, however, ring true. One of the most consistent aspects of Che's character was that he was discreet, even secretive. Few would disagree with the comment of Oscar Fernández Mell, one of Che's closest friends: "Che told you only what you needed to know."[11] Che was also fiercely loyal. Anything is possible, of course, but it is difficult to imagine Che confiding very personal thoughts about his alleged frictions with Fidel, thoughts that verged on state secrets, to a man who was not a close friend (he kept secrets even from them) and who was a semidissident.

Castañeda's Che was growing increasingly critical of the Soviet Union while Fidel Castro was surrendering his independence to Moscow, and this purportedly pulled the two friends apart. Relying on the word of Guevara's aide Benigno, who claimed to be relaying what he had been told by one of Che's bodyguards, Castañeda writes that Che "spent forty hours talking with Fidel, Raúl and several others" immediately after his return to Cuba from Africa on March 14, 1965. In the course of these discussions a "heated dispute" erupted between Che and Raúl. Raúl accused Che of being a Trotskyite. Che "got up very violent [sic], as if he were about to jump on Raúl," Benigno told Castañeda, "and said to Raúl: 'You're an idiot, you're an idiot.' . . . Then he looked over at Fidel . . . and Fidel did not respond. When Che saw that attitude, he left very upset, he slammed the door and left." Castañeda concludes that "the fact that Castro had not sided with him, and had allowed Raúl's accusations to stand, left Guevara with little choice. It was time to leave."[12]

Castañeda's portrait is dramatic, but misleading. Raúl was not in Cuba. On this point the Cuban press and the CIA agree. Raúl arrived in Moscow on February 26 to attend the meeting of world Communist parties. He returned to Cuba on April 6, after visiting Poland, Hungary, and Bulgaria.[13] Che, however, was only in Cuba between March 14 and April 1, when he left again for Zaire.

Therefore Raúl Castro and Che were never in the same country from December 1964 (when Che left Havana for New York) until mid-1966, when Che returned to Cuba.[14]

Furthermore, Castañeda mischaracterizes Fidel's relationship with the Soviet Union. He may have been a less harsh critic than Che, but he was no devotee. As noted, his support for armed struggle in Latin America continued despite the concessions he had made at the Havana conference, and although he was indeed moving increasingly away from Beijing, he was also, at the same time, keeping Moscow at a distance.

Revolución, which reprinted Che's February 1965 speech in Algiers that was openly critical of the Soviet Union, commented that this "very important" speech had been very well received and clearly expressed the Cuban position. "Cuba has again broadcast its position to the world," it blared.[15] On March 13, just one day before Che returned to Cuba, Castro delivered a major speech critical of the Soviet Union. "We're no one's satellite and never will be," he exclaimed. "Castro's latest speech," INR director Hughes remarked, "is in line with other recent developments indicating that Cuba wants to establish an independent and highly critical position within the socialist world." A month later Hughes noted, "Fidel Castro has backed Guevara's statements by speeches and remarks critical of the communist world."[16]

It would seem, therefore, that there was little disagreement between Che and Fidel Castro on relations with the Soviet Union. Yet there was a clash. The archives of the East German Communist Party include several reports from GDR officials in Havana that after Che's return from Africa there were "arguments and angry exchanges" between him and Fidel; "the root of the matter," the reports state, was "Guevara's speech in Algeria."[17] It is difficult to dismiss these reports: there are too many, and the GDR embassy was usually well informed. Perhaps the Soviet DCM in Havana provided a key to Fidel Castro's attitude when he said in 1965, "Whether Fidel Castro rejects the criticism of the socialist countries expressed by Guevara in Algiers or merely considers it wrong to express it in public remains unclear."[18] While some Cuban leaders, including Raúl Castro, disagreed in principle with Guevara's attack on the Soviet Union and his emphasis on armed struggle, others, like Fidel, agreed in principle but disagreed with the form—with the vehemence and bluntness of Guevara's words. Fidel Castro also criticized Moscow in his speeches, but he did so indirectly, without ever naming it. As Risquet said, "The problem was not just whether Che was right. It was also whether it was wise to say these things in public. The disagreement was not about the substance of his [Algiers] speech, but there are truths that should not be said."[19]

Castañeda uses his interview with Che's close friend, Emilio Aragonés, to highlight the extent of the disagreement between Che and Fidel. Aragonés and Osmany Cienfuegos had flown to Algiers in January 1965 to accompany Che to Beijing. Aragonés told Castañeda that "After waiting for him [Che] in vain for more than a month in Algiers, where Piñeiro's team presumed him to be, . . . [they] traveled to Paris; there they finally hooked up with the errant Argentine." Castañeda remarks that "Aragonés's quip that Piñeiro did not really know where Che was or when he was due to arrive in Algiers confirms that Che organized his African trip very much on his own, with only Serguera's help, informing Havana as little as possible of his movements and his actions."[20] The problem is that Piñeiro could have easily kept track of Che by reading *Revolución*, which regularly reported his movements. Furthermore, the Algerian daily *Le Peuple* noted that Che went to the Algiers airport on January 25 to meet Aragonés and Cienfuegos and that the three men then flew to Paris.[21] Aragonés's quip only indicates how faulty memory can be. Che's Africa trip was not the quixotic perambulations of the rebuffed, but the expression of the policy of the Cuban government. Che went as Castro's personal emissary and as one of Cuba's foremost leaders, with wide powers to offer aid to the liberation movements and make agreements with African governments.

Piñeiro told Anderson that it was Fidel who, upon Che's return, first suggested that Che lead the column to Zaire. "It would be for only a couple of years, and in the meantime, they [Fidel and Piñeiro] promised him, Piñeiro's people would continue building the guerrilla infrastructure in Latin America until conditions were right for him to transfer there. The Congo [Zaire] war would be an invaluable toughening-up exercise for Che's fighters and would provide a useful screening process for those who would go with him afterward to South America. As Piñeiro recalled it, Che didn't need much convincing."[22]

According to Anderson, Castro also urged Che to go to Zaire to remove a major source of friction with the Soviet Union.[23] Whether this is true or not, it is a distraction. It must not obscure the essential point: the Zairean operation was Cuba's most daring move yet in the Third World; more Cubans fought in Zaire than in all of Latin America through the first two decades of the Castro regime. Given the importance that Cuba attributed to Zaire, the stakes were extremely high, and it made eminent sense to put one of Cuba's foremost leaders, and one of Castro's closest companions, in command. Irrespective of any tensions with Fidel, Che was eager to see action; he was tired of exhorting guerrillas from a desk in Havana. His heart was in the Southern Cone of Latin America, but he deeply believed in the international nature of the struggle against capitalism and imperialism, and in the community among Latin America, Africa, and Asia. His trip through sub-Saharan Africa had inspired him. "I have found here in Africa . . . entire populations that are, if you'll allow me this image, like water on the verge of boiling," he told a journalist shortly before returning to Cuba. "I have found leaders who understand the importance of the struggle against colonialism and neocolonialism."[24] The Zairean operation was a key initiative of Cuba's foreign policy; it was not Che's personal escape.

Che spent the day before his departure for Zaire in a safe house near Havana "writing and then tearing up the paper, speaking to no one," Dreke, who was with him, remembered. That night Fidel arrived to say good-bye, and Che gave him a farewell letter that Fidel made public the following October.[25] The letter read:

Fidel,

Right now my mind is flooded with memories: of when I [first] met you in María Antonia's house [in Mexico City in 1955], of when you suggested that I join you [to fight against Batista in Cuba], of all the tensions involved in the preparations. . . .

I feel that I have fulfilled the part of my duty that tied me to the Cuban revolution in its own territory, and I say farewell to you, to the compañeros, to your people who are now also my people.

I formally resign my positions in the leadership of the party, my post as minister, my rank of commander, and my Cuban citizenship. I no longer have any legal tie to Cuba, only a bond of an altogether different nature that, unlike titles, can never be renounced.

Looking back on my life, I believe I have worked with sufficient integrity and dedication to consolidate the triumph of the revolution. My only serious failing was not having had more confidence in you from the first moments in the Sierra Maestra and not appreciating your qualities as a leader and a revolutionary quickly enough.[26] I have lived magnificent days, and at your side I felt proud of belonging to our people in the brilliant yet sad days of the Caribbean [missile] crisis. Seldom has a statesman shone more brightly than you did in those days. . . .

Other nations of the world now call for my modest efforts. I can do what is denied you because of your responsibility at the helm of Cuba, and the time has come for us to part. . . .

I carry to new battlefields the faith that you taught me, the revolutionary spirit of my people, the conviction that I am fulfilling the most sacred of duties: to fight against imperialism wherever it may be. This comforts me and more than heals the deepest wounds.

I reiterate that I am freeing Cuba from any responsibility for me, except that the power of its example is my inspiration. If my final hour finds me under other skies, my last thoughts will be of the Cuban people and especially of you. I thank you for all I have learned from you and for your example, to which I will try to be faithful until my last breath. . . .

I could say many things to you and to our people, but I feel that it is unnecessary, that words cannot express what I want to say, and that it would only waste paper to try.[27]

The letter formally freed Cuba from any responsibility for Che's actions in Zaire, but informally it also expressed Guevara's profound affection for Fidel. His heartfelt avowals make it difficult to believe that the two men were estranged. A Cuban intellectual put it very well: in his farewell letter, "Che's admiration for

Fidel is obvious, and Che was a man who could not have expressed this if he had not felt it. He was a straight shooter."[28]

RETURN TO DAR-ES-SALAAM

On April 1, Che flew from Cuba to Prague, on the first leg of his journey to Africa. "I left behind almost eleven years of work for the Cuban revolution at Fidel's side, a happy home (if one can ever call the house of a revolutionary who is dedicated to his work a home), and a bunch of kids who had barely known my love."[29] He was accompanied by Dreke and a DGI officer, José María Martínez Tamayo (Papi), who was one of his closest aides. Under Che's supervision, Papi had worked closely with the Guatemalan guerrillas in 1962 and had helped Masetti in Bolivia the following year. As Dreke explained, "Che included Papi in the column, even though he was white, because he was one of the cadres who would accompany him to Latin America when the time came. Zaire would be his training ground."[30]

The rest of the column left Cuba over the next few weeks. The Cuban airline, Cubana de Aviación, did not fly to Africa, and it would have attracted too much attention if a Cuban plane had suddenly landed at Dar-es-Salaam. Therefore the volunteers flew in groups of three to six on regularly scheduled commercial flights. They claimed to be athletes, agronomists, engineers, musicians. The DGI had not handled every detail with the hand of a master: all the volunteers wore identical suits and carried identical suitcases. For security reasons, they traveled by different, circuitous routes, "but at one point two groups ended up waiting for the same flight in an Italian airport. They were the only blacks around," Dreke recalled. "Six blacks sitting at the same gate area, all wearing the same suit, looking at each other, and not saying one word in case they said something wrong!"[31]

Meanwhile in Dar-es-Salaam Ambassador Rivalta had created a "support group" in the Cuban embassy—trusted men who worked full time on the Zairean operation. Initially the group was just the four aides he had brought from Havana; during the spring half a dozen more joined them.[32]

When the volunteers arrived at Dar-es-Salaam, they were whisked from the airport to a small farm on the outskirts of the city that Rivalta had bought for the purpose. The first group—Che, Dreke, and Papi—arrived on April 6 or 7. "We played the same trick on Rivalta that they had played on me in Cuba," Dreke explained. "'Don't you know Ramón?' I asked him. 'No,' he said. 'Of course you do.' 'I know I've never seen this man before!' Finally Che, with that voice of his, asked him: 'Are you the same shit-head as always?'—and Rivalta understood." (Once, when he was in Che's column during the war against Batista, Rivalta had lost a knapsack with documents in it and Che had called him a shit-head.)[33] They waited in the farm for the arrival of other groups. Che was anxious, because he had not told the Simba leaders that he would be leading the column.

In his memoir, he explained his reasoning at length: "In my first conversation with [the Simba leader] Kabila [in February] I hadn't been able to [tell them my plans] because nothing had been decided yet, and after the plan was approved it would have been dangerous for it to have been known before I got to my destination because there was a lot of hostile territory to cross. I decided, therefore, to present [the Simbas with] a fait accompli and to see how they responded. I was aware that a negative response would put me in a difficult position, because I couldn't go back now, but I figured it would be difficult for them to refuse me. The fact that I was already there would give me leverage."[34]

There was, however, an unexpected development. The Simbas had not known that the column was arriving: "after Che had left Dar-es-Salaam [the previous February], we hadn't heard a word from them," recalls Godefroid Tschamlesso, a Kabila aide whom Che had met during his Africa trip.[35] When Che, Dreke, and Papi arrived in Tanzania, the Simba leaders were in Cairo "trying," as the CIA reported, "to sort out their differences. They . . . managed only to fight among themselves."[36] The most senior rebel official left in Dar-es-Salaam was Tschamlesso. Che, who had been apprehensive that the Simbas might fear that his presence, if detected, would provoke a very strong U.S. reaction, and that therefore "some of the Zaireans, or even the friendly [Tanzanian] government, would ask me not to join the fray," decided that he would keep his identity secret until he met Kabila. Therefore he had Rivalta tell Tschamlesso that Dreke was the column's commander and that more than 100 instructors (all black, like the Simbas had asked) would soon arrive. "In order to explain the presence of two whites," Dreke recalls, "I said that Ramón [Che] was a doctor and interpreter (Che spoke French) and that Papi was a nurse." Tschamlesso sent word to Kabila, who was unfazed and sent back word that he had decided to stay in Cairo for at least two more weeks. "To be honest," Che wrote, "I wasn't too upset." Kabila's absence helped him postpone the day of reckoning. He conveniently decided that it would not be appropriate for him to inform Nyerere of his presence before he told Kabila. Therefore, he would get into Zaire before anyone knew his true identity.[37] It was a decision that would continue to haunt him throughout his stay in Africa.

Having decided to enter Zaire without asking anyone's approval, Che was suddenly in a hurry, fearful that his hosts—Tanzanians or Simbas—might find out who he was. At first he had intended to wait until enough volunteers had gathered at the farm before driving to Kigoma, the Tanzanian town on the shore of Lake Tanganyika that was the last stop before Zaire, but now he was impatient. "'Listen,'" he told Rivalta, "'if some more compañeros [members of the column] don't arrive very soon, the three of us [Che, Dreke, and Papi] will go to Zaire alone.' I thought," Dreke recalled, "'Now we're screwed!' Fortunately, more compañeros arrived."[38]

Among them were Torres and Dr. Zerquera. "Che told us who he was and why Cuba had decided to help the Simbas," Torres recalls. "He said that our mission would last five years. If any of us didn't want to participate, we could still withdraw." This was the first time that they had been told how long the mission might last and where they would go. "Che said that we had to learn the language [Swahili]," Zerquera adds, "that we had to share everything with the natives, that we had to set an example, and that he demanded strict discipline: we could disagree with him and say so, but once he had made a decision we had to obey."[39]

With the help of a dictionary, Che gave everyone a nom de guerre in Swahili. "To simplify matters," he writes, "we decided to use numbers according to the order in which we had arrived." Dreke became Moja (1), Papi was Mbili (2), Che was Tatu (3). Torres became Nane (8) and Zerquera, Kumy (10).[40]

"We had been told that all the necessary equipment for the men had been bought," Dreke recalled, "but when we arrived at Dar-es-Salaam we discovered that a lot of things, like boots, were missing." Che was in such a hurry that he left for Kigoma anyway, taking thirteen volunteers, a Tanzanian police officer, two Tanzanian drivers, and Tschamlesso, and leaving four volunteers behind to wait for boots. "I still wonder how we all fit in that truck," Torres mused.[41]

Two days later, on April 22, after driving more than 900 miles on unpaved roads, they reached Kigoma. There they received their arms—light weapons that DGI officers had brought in suitcases to Dar-es-Salaam between March and May.[42] They planned to cross the 30-mile-wide lake to Kibamba, a tiny rebel village on the Zairean shore, but the boats were not ready and they had to wait in Kigoma. "The Tanzanian provincial governor," Che writes, "received us immediately and gave us lodging." Finally, in the early hours of April 24, the crossing began. Armed and in uniform, the Cubans headed for Zaire. Tschamlesso accompanied them. The Simba crew sang, Dreke recalls, "in that language of theirs that was so foreign to us. Che kept telling them to be quiet, but they paid no attention." It was the Cubans' first brush with the alien culture. "They [Simbas] sang to chase away their fear," Tschamlesso explained, "and that's why they broke the security rules."[43]

A few hours later, the fourteen Cubans landed on the Zairean shore. Eighteen followed on May 8, thirty-four on May 22, and nine more the next day. A final group of thirty-nine reached Kibamba on June 22 or 23. A few more volunteers arrived during the summer.[44]

THE FIZI-BARAKA

Kibamba was the gateway to the Fizi-Baraka pocket, the only important rebel zone left in Zaire. Virtually cut off from the world, the Kwilu rebellion in the west had never developed into a major threat. By the spring of 1965, the rebels there had been reduced to small, famished bands confined to their forest hideouts.[45]

It was the eastern rebellion that had gathered momentum in mid-1964 and forced Washington to intervene. At its peak, the revolt had encompassed one-third of Zaire. But by April 1965 the mercenary leader, Mike Hoare, had suc-

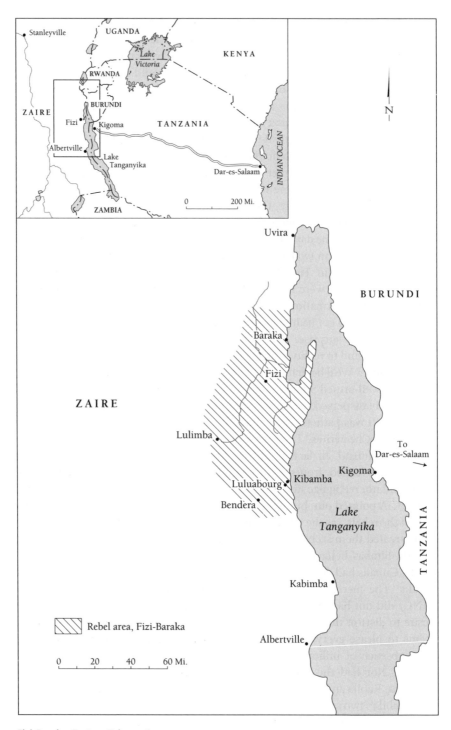

Fizi-Baraka, Eastern Zaire, 1965

cessfully concluded a series of military sweeps in the northeast, cutting off the Simbas from the Sudanese and Ugandan borders. The rebellion in the northeast "appears to be crumbling," the CIA remarked two weeks before Che's arrival.[46] Except for isolated pockets that the mercenaries would mop up over the next few weeks, all that was left of the eastern rebellion was the Fizi-Baraka, which stretched for about 100 miles along the western shore of Lake Tanganyika and about 50 miles inland. "It was a land of sudden escarpments, rushing rivers and twisting tracks," Hoare wrote. It included two small towns, a few villages, and a sparse population of subsistence farmers and hunter-gatherers.[47]

Rivalta had sent his former driver, Oliva, who spoke Swahili fluently, to explore the rebel zone before the column had arrived. "I was [told] to go to Kigoma and cross into Zaire, together with Tschamlesso, to study that area," Oliva recalled. "We left [Kigoma] at approximately 9 A.M. . . . and we were back [in Kigoma] that same day." Those few hours—crossing the lake both ways must have taken more than twelve hours—were the extent of the embassy's exploration of the rebel zone. Therefore the reports that Rivalta sent Havana between February and April were not based on firsthand observation. "We relied," he explained, "on information from the Simba leaders and the Tanzanian government," which also got its information from the Simbas.[48]

"It was a bad surprise," Dreke recalled. "The reports [from the embassy] didn't correspond to reality. Che got to Zaire expecting to find one thing, and he found another. We'd been misled." Che had been told that he would find several thousand well-armed Simbas, eager to fight. There were, in fact, some 1,000 to 1,500 widely dispersed rebels, who had no idea how to maintain their modern weapons. "It was pathetic to see how they wasted the resources of the friendly countries," Che writes. They were also poorly organized, and they lacked a unified command. In fact, there was little coordination among the different rebel groups (called "fronts"). Although Kabila was the paramount leader, some fronts did not recognize his authority.[49] The Simbas did enjoy popular support, as the CIA pointed out, but if the local inhabitants were "almost entirely on the side of the rebels," as the West German embassy reported,[50] this was because the army treated them so badly. Che's memoir, "Pasajes," makes it clear, however, that the Simbas' behavior also left much to be desired.

The Cubans had definitely not expected the eerie calm they found in the Fizi-Baraka. The mercenaries were busy in the northeast and the Zairean army (ANC) did not have the stomach to attack without them. The Simbas had no desire to disrupt this armed truce that gave them a safe haven. "This situation seems to please everybody," a Belgian official remarked. Except the Cubans: "The absence of military activity in those days was almost complete," Che wrote.[51] Nor had the Cubans expected the cool reception they received at Kibamba. Kabila and Soumialot, who had asked them to come, were far away, as were Kabila's two senior military aides. No one came forward to welcome them. "From the very moment we arrived," Paulu, the column's diarist, wrote, "we could feel a kind of chill from the guerrillas, and we wondered: 'Is it because there are a few whites among us? Is it because we are foreigners?'" Fourteen Cubans were stranded on the shore of Lake Tanganyika, in a world that was utterly foreign. "This was the beginning of a difficult time," Zerquera remembered. "We had to figure out what we could do."[52]

A few hours after their arrival, Dreke and his interpreter, Ramón, had a desultory conversation with the local Simba leaders, who seemed surprised to see them and did not know what to do with them. Tschamlesso, who had escorted them in, was almost a stranger—a midlevel cadre who lived in Dar-es-Salaam and visited Kibamba only occasionally.[53]

Che's response was to act quickly. "We had left [Havana] thinking that we had plenty of time," Dreke recalls. "We thought it would take us five years to win in Zaire. It was a long-term commitment, and we were in no hurry. We were not interested in getting drawn into big battles for the first few months, and we wanted to postpone the day that the enemy figured out we were there." Che had thought that they would first familiarize themselves with the region, and then start training groups of guerrillas, organized in columns of 80 to 100 men each. After approximately three months' training, a column would go to the front with its Cuban instructors and engage in small-scale attacks against the enemy. Eventually, the instructors would return to the base—the big training school that Che intended to create—and begin training another column. Throughout these first months, the Cubans would remain at their base except for those teams that accompanied the Simbas in the field.[54]

After their reception at Kibamba, Che's confidence that they had plenty of time evaporated. From that point onward, his manuscript exudes the sense that time was running out.

WAITING FOR KABILA

"The day after we got to Kibamba," Tschamlesso recalled, "Che told me who he was. It made me feel like the world was falling in on me. Che said that I had to go to tell Kabila and ask him to come so that they could prepare a plan of action at once." Che's "Pasajes" confirms Tschamlesso's account: "I told . . . [Tschamlesso] who I was; he was thunderstruck. He kept repeating 'international scandal' and 'no one must know, please, no one must know.' It was like he had been struck by lightning on a clear day." That night Tschamlesso left for Cairo to inform Kabila.[55]

According to Tschamlesso, Kabila was "stunned" to learn that Che was in Zaire. "I think he thought, 'Now I've got to go there and direct the war from within.'"[56] Nevertheless, he did not rush to Kibamba. Instead, he flew to Dar-es-Salaam, where he denied rumors that the Cairo meeting had failed to unite the rebel factions, and on May 5 he left, as a Tanzanian daily said, "for an undisclosed destination," probably Khartoum, where the rebels held yet another unsuccessful meeting in mid-May.[57]

The days went by very slowly for Che. The fourteen Cubans were stuck at

Kibamba for two weeks. Eager to do something, Che proposed to the local Simba commanders that he and his men start training rebels right away and accompany them on small-scale military operations, but there were no takers. "They asked me to put my proposal in writing," Che noted. "I did, but I never heard anything more about it."[58]

Stymied on that front, Che proposed that he start exploring the region. His hosts agreed in principle but told him to wait. "And so the days dragged on," Che writes. "Whenever I repeated my request (and I did so with irritating regularity) there was always a new pretext. Even now [seven months later], I don't quite understand why." Unable to train, unable to fight, unable to explore, Che, who had been a doctor before joining the revolution, began practicing medicine and put Dr. Zerquera to work as well. "Che gave me a textbook on contagious illnesses," Zerquera remembered, "and said, 'Find out which ones are here.'" Zerquera, who had just finished his medical studies, thought: "Hell, he's out of his mind. I'm sunk: There won't be anyone I can ask for a second opinion, and my patients are going to die." As the news spread that two doctors were in Kibamba, peasants from the surrounding area flocked in. "We had brought only a small supply of medicine," Che wrote, "but we were saved because the Soviets had sent some [for the rebel army]."[59]

Meanwhile Che waited—for the rest of the column and for Kabila or, at least, one of his senior aides. Finally, on May 8, a boat brought eighteen Cubans and Kabila's chief of staff, Léonard Mitoudidi. Che was "pleasantly impressed" by Mitoudidi: "he seemed to be confident, serious and a gifted organizer." Mitoudidi told Che that Kabila wanted him to keep his identity secret, and Che complied. ("I continued in disguise, carrying out my apparent duties as a doctor and an interpreter.") With Mitoudidi's assent, the Cubans moved up to the Luluabourg ridge, some three miles away. "The canopy of the immense trees blocks the sunlight," a Cuban wrote, "so it is very humid and very cold." Nearby was a rebel camp with "twenty bored, lonely and freezing Zaireans," Che wrote.[60]

There were now thirty-two Cubans and no rebels to train. "We had to do something to avoid absolute idleness," Che wrote. "Our morale was still high, but the compañeros were beginning to grumble because they saw the days go by wasted." And so he put them to study—French, Swahili, Spanish, mathematics. The teaching was not impressive, he admitted, "but at least the classes passed the time, and this was what mattered." Kahama's diary gives a sense of their life in those first weeks. "At 9 A.M. we began our Swahili classes," he jotted down on May 12. (He had arrived on May 8.) "In the afternoon we studied French. . . . Tatu [Che] was our professor." On May 23, he wrote: "Very little has changed. . . . We have continued our Swahili and French classes. . . . Tatu told us that we have to learn both languages in three months." On June 1, "Still no change, except that a lot of us have gotten sick." Malaria, which had been eliminated in Cuba, struck them. "Our poor doctor [Zerquera] was going crazy," Dreke recalled, "because he didn't know what to do." Che, too, fell ill with malaria, complicated by a violent flare-up of his asthma.[61]

On May 22, an unexpected visitor appeared: Osmany Cienfuegos, the Cuban minister of public works who was Castro's point man for Africa. "After the hugs, the explanations," Che wrote. "Osmany had come to speak with the Tanzanian leaders and had asked permission to visit us in Zaire." The Tanzanians had initially refused, fearing that all the other Cuban cabinet members would want to go to Fizi-Baraka, "but in the end they relented. . . . Osmany told me that the government of Tanzania was not yet aware I was here."[62]

In late May, with Mitoudidi's permission, three small teams of Simbas and Cubans left to explore the region. Che and Mitoudidi had also planned to go, but "Kabila had sent word that he was on his way, and we had to wait for him, day after day, without result." The scouting teams were gone several days. They brought back grim reports from the fronts they had visited: local commanders who spent their time drinking, idle rebels who expected the population to feed them but did not know how to use their firearms and showed no inclination to attack or to prepare to defend themselves. Everywhere chaos, disorganization, and lack of discipline. "I informed Mitoudidi of these reports," Che wrote, and "he told me they were accurate."[63]

Yet Che was optimistic. In his analysis of May, he noted, "Until Mitoudidi came, the time had been wasted," but now things were improving. His men had begun reconnoitering the area; Mitoudidi seemed receptive to his suggestions and had promised to send a group of Simbas to be trained. "It is almost certain," Che wrote, "that in June we will be able to . . . start fighting."[64]

On June 1, the training began. One of the instructors remembered, "Che told us, 'Take two months. I want them to be well prepared when they leave.'" The problem was that there were more instructors than recruits. Only twenty-five rebels had bothered to make the trek to the Cuban camp to be trained. And so most of the Cubans continued studying. Che had divided them into three groups, "according to how much schooling we'd had," Kahama writes, "so we wouldn't waste our time while we were on standby." Occasionally, a few Cubans left with Simbas to explore the area. Che was frustrated: "Days full of anguish," he wrote. "Mitoudidi, despite his goodwill, has not put us to good use." He was probably waiting, Che surmised, for Kabila; everything was on hold until then. "Every day we would hear the same refrain: Kabila didn't come today, he will come tomorrow for sure, or the day after tomorrow."[65]

On June 7 tragedy struck: Mitoudidi's boat capsized on Lake Tanganyika and he drowned; the Cubans lost their best ally. "We mourned," Paulu wrote, "because we could tell that he had been trying to find answers for all the problems and . . . because he had understood that we wanted to get the rebels ready to fight against the men who had exploited, betrayed, and murdered his people."[66]

Shortly after Mitoudidi's death, Che wrote a blunt letter to Kabila about the lack of a central command, the lack of discipline within the rebel units, and the rebels' inability to use their weapons. "These are problems that every revolution must face," he added diplomatically, "and they must not discourage us. Nevertheless, we have to develop a strategy to remedy them." He then made his request: he wanted the Cubans and the Simbas to fight together in mixed units, initially under Cuban commanders and against small targets.[67]

He got an answer on June 18, when a rebel commander, Mundandi, arrived at Luluabourg with a letter from Kabila, who was in Dar-es-Salaam. After assuring Che that he had "read and reread" his report, Kabila came to the point. He wanted Che to place fifty Cubans under Mundandi's orders to participate in an attack against one of the ANC's strongest positions in the region, the military garrison and hydroelectric plant at Bendera, on June 25. Kabila insisted, however, that Che wait for him at Luluabourg. "You are a revolutionary," he lectured Che. "You must endure every hardship. I will arrive soon."[68]

The Cubans, Paulu writes, resented Kabila's order that "Tatu . . . stay at the base to wait for his arrival, which had already been announced a million times, . . . but we also saw that we were finally going to get to do something, and we had been beginning to think that they were going to tell us to go back to Cuba."[69]

Lacking confidence in Mundandi's military skills, Che feared for the safety of his men in an attack against an enemy stronghold, but he also worried that if he hesitated the Simbas would conclude the Cubans were cowards. He did not want to send his men out without him, but he also did not want to defy Kabila. And so, he wrote again to Kabila. The letter was, for Che, a model of diplomacy. "My dear comrade," it began,

> Thank you for your letter. Let me assure you that if I am impatient it is because I am a man of action, and it in no way implies any criticism. I can empathize with you because I have lived through similar circumstances.
>
> I, too, am eagerly awaiting your arrival, because I consider you an old friend and I owe you an explanation [for my being here]. . . .
>
> As you ordered, the Cubans are leaving tomorrow for Front de Force [Bendera]; many of my men are ill and a few less than you have requested will go (40). . . .
>
> I am writing to ask you for a favor: please allow me to go to Front de Force, with no title other than that of "Political Commissar" of my comrades, completely under the orders of Comrade Mundandi. I have just spoken with him and he supports my suggestion.[70]

Mundandi had indeed agreed, but only on the condition that the Cuban contingent leave with him while Che waited for Kabila's reply. And so, at dawn on June 20, Che bid Godspeed to his men as they left for battle, and he gave their commander, Dreke, "a box of cigars, saying that they should not smoke them until the victory celebration." A few days later, Che received Kabila's answer which was, "as usual, evasive. I wrote him yet another letter, urging him to tell me frankly yes or no, . . . but he never answered, and so I never went to the Front de Force."[71]

Four days after Dreke's troop had left for Bendera, the last group of thirty-nine Cubans arrived at Luluabourg. "Che spoke to us," remembers Vidiaux, who led the group. "He told us how little he had been able to accomplish so far. He said that our mission could last three to five years. He said that those who wanted to leave could still do so." Che wrote, "I was very explicit about what we faced, not just hunger, bullets, suffering of all kinds, but also . . . the possibility of being killed by one of our own [Simba] comrades who didn't have a clue how to shoot properly; the struggle would be very difficult and long. I forewarned them like this because they still had a chance to express their misgivings and go back to Cuba if they wanted; later this would not be possible. My tone was harsh. Not one of them showed any sign of wavering."[72]

BENDERA

At 5 A.M., on June 29, 1965, 160 Simbas and 40 Cubans attacked Bendera. "The compañeros say that when the battle began, the Simbas fled in panic and left the Cubans facing the enemy alone," Kahama, who had remained in Luluabourg, jotted down in his diary. The attack failed, and four Cubans and approximately twenty Simbas lost their lives. "We were unable to retrieve our dead compañeros," one of the Cubans recollected.[73]

This tipped off the CIA. In early July, the agency concluded that "two of four foreigners found among rebel dead . . . appear to have been Cubans. Partial diary written in Spanish on pages Russian memo book recovered from one body . . . indicated bearer had departed from Cuba in early April 1965." This was, the British defense adviser in Leopoldville noted, "the first indication of any Cuban presence with the rebels." The dead Cubans, however, attracted little attention in the international press. When people thought of the Red threat in Africa, they thought of Moscow or Beijing. A few Cubans, stranded so far away from their natural habitat in Latin America, merited only a few lines. The CIA was not unduly concerned. It did not expect to find a significant number of Cubans among the rebels, because this would have been "a sharp departure from Havana's customary practice—both in Africa and in Latin America—where Cuban participation has been basically limited to propaganda, training in Cuba, and the provision of arms and money."[74]

The rout at Bendera demoralized many of the Cubans and stirred distrust of the Simbas. One of the Cubans who had participated in the attack wrote a few days later, " 'The Simbas fled the minute they heard a shot; our brothers who died, died because of them. . . . I wish I were back in Cuba, and a lot of the others who were in the battle feel the same way.' "[75]

After the news of the debacle reached Luluabourg, Che addressed his men. "He gave us a tongue lashing because of the remarks that several compañeros had made," Kahama wrote, "and he stressed: 'Our struggle has just begun. What happened at Front de Force [Bendera] is nothing. We'll find ourselves in much more difficult situations than that. We cannot expect Zaire to be like home. . . . Anyone who wants to abandon this struggle is a traitor to the Revolution and to his own word. . . . To return home you will have to have crushed an arm or a leg. . . . We will celebrate together in Leopoldville, unless our bones lie buried along the road.'"[76]

KABILA

Che had been somber and anxious even before he received news of the defeat. In his diary, on June 30, he had written: "'The balance sheet [of this month] is the worst yet. Just when everything seemed to indicate we were entering a new era, Mitoudidi died, and the uncertainties have multiplied. . . . Again and again Kabila has said he is about to arrive, but he hasn't come yet; the disorganization is complete." One question plagued him: "What will Kabila's attitude be toward us, and especially toward me? . . . There are serious signs that he is not at all pleased that I'm here. But is this due to fear, or jealousy, or wounded pride because of the way I arrived?"[77]

Che kept trying to establish contact with Kabila in Tanzania: "I sent . . . [him] a short letter, explaining that I was needed at the front more and more every day. . . . I asked for a rapid reply, and received nothing. I sent another letter . . . insisting, once again, that I was needed at the front." Again, no answer. "I was feeling very pessimistic," Che writes, "but on July 7 I was told that Kabila had arrived in Kibamba, and I went to meet him with happy relief. At last the Jefe was in the field of operations!"[78]

It was not a meeting between equals. Che, the legendary commander who had come to risk his life for another people's cause, was eager for the approval of Kabila, the petty chieftain who directed the war from Dar-es-Salaam. Kabila was "cordial but evasive," Che wrote. When Che suggested that they inform Nyerere of his presence, Kabila said that the time was not right, but he did not explain why not. When Che stated once again how eager he was to go to the front, Kabila changed the subject.[79]

But Kabila did take Che on a tour of the rebel zone, and Che was impressed with what he saw. Kabila was quick, he could be witty, he knew how to speak to the people, he let them express their feelings, and he gave answers that satisfied them. "His energy was intense, and he seemed eager to make up for the lost time." And so Che dared to hope, but on July 11, five days after his arrival, Kabila told Che that he was leaving for Kigoma that night. Simba leader Soumialot, who was the president of the Zairean rebel government and a Kabila rival, was there, and they had important matters to settle. He promised that he would return in two days. Che never saw him again.[80]

When Dreke first told me, in 1993, that "our column, including Tatu, was completely dependent on Kabila," and that "we couldn't make any decisions on our own," I was skeptical. It certainly was at odds with what happened in Bolivia less than two years later—when Che brushed aside Mario Monje, the secretary general of the Bolivian Communist Party.[81] Yet Che's "Pasajes" and Paulu's diary confirm Dreke's assertion and help to explain Che's behavior in Zaire.

Throughout his stay in Fizi-Baraka, Che was haunted by the fear that the Simbas would ask him to leave. In part this was due to the haphazard and secretive way the mission had been planned. In Dar-es-Salaam, the previous February, Kabila and Soumialot had agreed only to receive 30 Cuban instructors. "When I told Tschamlesso that 130 Cubans were coming," Dreke recalls, "I did so with much trepidation; they might say that they didn't want so many instructors, and then what would we do? The compañeros were already leaving Havana; it would have been a mess. And we said nothing about Che." Che smuggled himself into Zaire. The Simbas never openly, formally, accepted him. He was tolerated. "This was the cloud that hung over Che all the time: he had entered Zaire without getting Kabila's or Tanzania's approval," Fernández Mell explained.[82]

Che's sense of insecurity was heightened by the feeling that he did not belong: he was a Latin American, not an African. He was white; they were black. He was in a world he did not know—not the language, not the customs, and not the way of thinking. He was utterly dependent on Kabila's goodwill. In Bolivia, in late 1966, Che could defy Monje because he could rely on other Bolivian leaders, because his color did not set him apart, because he knew the language, the customs, and the country. He was not an interloper. In Bolivia his name meant a great deal, but it meant very little in Zaire. Most Simbas had never heard of him. Their leaders had, but in the Fizi-Baraka it was a muffled echo that carried little weight, only a whiff of danger—he might want to take over, he might spell trouble. His presence might lead the Americans to redouble their efforts to quash the rebellion.[83]

Che could have defied Kabila only if he had been supported by the rebel commanders in Fizi-Baraka. This is why Mitoudidi's death was such a blow. Afterward, because Che saw no alternative to Kabila, he treated him and his lieutenants with utmost care, "as if they were made of glass," Dreke explains. "He was afraid that they would turn around and say, 'Who asked you to come?'"[84]

SMALL TRIUMPHS

And so Che stayed in Luluabourg for over a month after Kabila had left, waiting for his permission to go to a front. He tried to keep busy teaching mathematics and French to a dwindling number of Cubans, many of whom were leaving for the front. Several Simba commanders had asked "that we send instructors to them," Dreke explains, "and we felt we couldn't refuse. We had planned to keep the column intact, but what good was a column of Cubans stuck in a camp? So we sent our men forward in groups of no less than ten, so that they could have some impact." They began training the rebels at the different fronts, and they urged them to mount a series of ambushes. There were "small triumphs," Che writes. One ambush "was particularly successful," the British defense adviser in Leopoldville observed: on August 16, a group led by Papi attacked a small enemy convoy, destroying one jeep and an armored car, and killing three mercenaries and four Belgian military advisers.[85]

At last, on August 18—thirty-eight days after Kabila had left—Che could no longer bear "begging for permission" to leave, and he went to the front. "I felt a little like a criminal on the lam," he writes, "but I was determined not to return to the base for a long time. . . . 'My vacation is over,' " he jotted in his diary. " 'The world looks a little brighter, at least for today.' "[86]

By September, press reports and diplomatic dispatches noted the "sudden rebel recrudescence" in the Fizi-Baraka pocket. A Belgian official explained the situation to *Le Soir*: "We have proof," he said, "that thirty Chinese have been brought from Kigoma . . . to the rebel headquarters [on the Zairean shore of the lake]." Ambassador Godley knew better. There were Cuban instructors among the rebels, he told Washington in mid-September, and their "impact on [the] military situation [was] inarguable."[87]

By then, the Cuban column had grown to about 120 men, including seven instructors who had landed in Dar-es-Salaam in August to train Frelimo guerrillas at the request of the Tanzanian government, which had not told Frelimo that the Cubans were coming. The Frelimo leader, Mondlane, had refused to accept them and Rivalta had sent them to Che.[88]

In late August three high-ranking Cuban officials, Oscar Fernández Mell, Emilio Aragonés, and Aldo Margolles, joined the column. Like his close friend Che, Fernández Mell was a doctor who had not often practiced. In 1965 he was the chief of staff of the Western Army. "At the beginning of August I was at the beach with my family," he wrote, "when I got a call from Piñeiro." The next day he was back in Havana, where Piñeiro told him that Che was in Zaire and that he had asked Fidel to send him, "to strengthen the senior staff [of the column]."[89]

But while Che had been expecting Fernández Mell, he was surprised by the arrival of Aragonés, who was one of Cuba's most prominent leaders. For a moment, he even worried that Aragonés might be bringing a message from Fidel asking that he return to Cuba, "because it didn't make any sense for the secretary of organization of the party to leave his post to come to Zaire," Che wrote, "particularly in a situation like this where everything was up in the air." The truth, however, was that Aragonés had asked to join Che, and Fidel had agreed. (Margolles, who was a deputy minister of the interior, had in turn asked to accompany his very close friend Aragonés.) Fernández Mell, Aragonés, and Margolles had told the Simbas that they were doctors, fearing that otherwise they would not be allowed to remain in Zaire, because they were white. Che baptized them with noms de guerre in Swahili: "Compañero Aragonés, because of his size, became Tembo (elephant) and compañero Fernández Mell, because of his character, became Siki (vinegar)."[90] For the introverted Che, this dubious honor was a sign of affection.

The column included seven full-time doctors (and at times Che and Fernández Mell pitched in). Because there were still very few black doctors in Cuba, four of the doctors and the column's only nurse were white. One of the doctors was the only foreigner in the group, a Haitian who had been in Cuba training to fight against the Haitian dictator, Papa Doc Duvalier. In Zaire he worked more as a doctor than as a guerrilla; he would have preferred it the other way around, but Che did not allow it.[91] All the other members of the column were black, except Che, Papi, Fernández Mell, Aragonés, and Margolles. There were no women.

OVERCONFIDENCE

While Fernández Mell, Aragonés, and Margolles were making their way to Fizi-Baraka, a group of 250 Cubans led by Jorge Risquet was arriving in the Congo. Castro had sent them to protect the Brazzaville government from Tshombe's mercenaries, to help the MPLA spread revolution in Angola, and to train Zairean rebels in the Congo, hoping that one day the training would take place in Zaire itself.[92]

This dream was built on quicksand—misjudgment of the revolutionary potential of the Brazzaville government, overestimation of the strength of the MPLA, and a profound misreading of reality in Zaire. By the time Risquet's column left Cuba in early August, Che had been in the Fizi-Baraka for more than three months, but Havana remained unaware of his travails. "We didn't know what was happening in Zaire," Risquet, who was briefed by Fidel at the end of July, remembered. "We thought that even though it was slow, everything was still on the right track."[93]

This misperception was due, in part, to a gross oversight by the DGI. "Later, Cuban intelligence would be considered, correctly, highly professional," General Markus Wolf, head of East German intelligence, who flew to Havana in January 1965 to advise the DGI "on how to build an efficient intelligence service," wrote in his memoirs. "But in the mid-1960s they were as wet behind the ears as my own service had been ten years earlier."[94] In preparing the Zaire operation, these novices had overlooked the need to establish safe and reliable communication links between Che and Havana.

When Che arrived in Zaire, the Cuban embassy in Dar-es-Salaam had no secure line with Havana. Dispatches were encoded and either hand-carried to Havana or sent by encrypted cable from the commercial telegraph office in Dar-es-Salaam. Nor was there any radio communication between the embassy and Che. "We communicated by courier," Ferrer, a member of the support group, explained. Oliva would travel back and forth from Dar-es-Salaam to Luluabourg carrying messages. And once Che left Luluabourg, communication became even more difficult. He had ordered Rivalta to send a courier every fifteen days, but this order, Che wrote, "was never carried out."[95]

On August 27, five black Cuban communication specialists boarded a plane in Havana carrying the radio equipment that was needed in Fizi-Baraka. Oscar Fernández Padilla, a deputy minister of the interior, flew with them. He would replace Rivalta as head of the support group.[96]

They landed in Moscow en route to Africa under false names and without the required Soviet permit for the radio equipment. "Piñeiro's people had goofed," Fernández Padilla recalls. "Back then, we made a lot of mistakes like that because we were so disorganized." The equipment aroused the suspicions of Soviet immigration officials. "They kept us for a long time in an office at the airport. I didn't tell them that I was a deputy minister, only that we were going to Cairo. They let us call our embassy." The DGI, however, had forgotten to inform the embassy of their arrival. Finally, "someone from the embassy came. They [the KGB] let us sleep in a hotel near the airport, but they kept our passports."[97]

The next day, Fernández Padilla was taken to the office of a senior KGB official.

We began by shouting at each other. (We used to believe that socialist countries were obliged to assist our operations without asking questions.) The KGB guy was yelling that we should have asked for the permits [for the equipment] and that we should have coordinated [our mission] with them. I was not authorized to say anything about our operation. I kept saying that we were going to Cairo on a special mission. Finally I told him that I was a deputy minister of the interior and I complained that they had treated us like enemies, and that they had taken our passports. He had them with him, and he gave them back to me. We wanted to continue on our trip and I'm sure that they wanted us to leave. So we settled the matter over a bottle of vodka.[98]

A few days later, Fernández Padilla and his companions flew to Cairo, where there were no difficulties. They reached Dar-es-Salaam on September 7.[99]

In order to establish radio contact between Che and Havana, the five specialists had to install equipment in the embassy and in Kigoma. "When I got through to Havana," the lead engineer recalled, "Che said, 'You're the first efficient thing I've seen since I got here.' " Che noted his pleasure in his memoir. "They accomplished their task with flying colors," he wrote. "From October 22, when the transmissions began, to November 20, when we left Zaire, we sent 110 encoded messages and received 60."[100]

Before October 22, however, Che had barely communicated with Cuba. This contributed to Havana's failure to understand what was happening in Zaire. "I was briefed by Piñeiro," Fernández Padilla remarked. "He didn't have a clue that the situation was critical." Fernández Mell had a similar experience: "Havana didn't know what was going on," he recalled. "When Fernández Mell arrived," Dreke remembered, "he was full of optimism. He lost it within five days."[101]

Communication problems were only part of the explanation. Unwittingly, Che misled Havana. He was grasping at straws; he was ready to face death but not reality. He could not accept that the undertaking was hopeless, that he had been wrong, that Fidel had been wrong. He could not admit it—not to himself, not to his men, and not to Fidel. The monthly analytical summaries in his diary reveal an optimism that had little basis in reality. This "blind optimism," as Che later called it,[102] must have colored his reports to Fidel.

Che's optimism was surpassed by the even more unrealistic optimism in Havana. "I had already gotten the impression from Tembo [Aragonés] that Cuba thought I was being very pessimistic," Che wrote in early October. "Then this was reinforced by a personal message from Fidel in which he counseled me not to despair, urged me to remember the first stage of the struggle [against Batista], and noted that bumps along the road are inevitable."[103]

The leaders' optimism influenced the embassy's reporting. If Fidel and Che saw reality in Zaire through rose-tinted glasses, no one in the embassy was going to challenge them. No one wanted to be accused of the terrible sin of pessimism; no one wanted to be called a defeatist. "Ours was a revolution that did not know retreat," Ferrer remembered, "that had the triumph of the Sierra Maestra, the victorious march from the Moncada to Havana, as its point of reference."[104]

Havana's optimism was further inflated by the arrival of a Simba delegation led by Soumialot, the peripatetic president of the Zairean rebel government, in Cuba at the end of August. "Soumialot and his group were given red carpet treatment during their almost two week stay in Cuba," U.S. under secretary Ball noted.[105] In his lengthy conversations with Fidel, Soumialot "painted an idyllic picture" of the military situation in Zaire, with rebel units "everywhere . . . [and] intense fighting," Che later learned. And the Simba leader extracted "a large sum of money" from Castro and the promise that Cuba would send fifty doctors to the rebel zone.[106] The fact that Castro would even consider sending fifty doctors to Fizi-Baraka indicates how little he understood the situation there.

Machado Ventura, Cuba's minister of public health, left for Zaire to prepare for the doctors and to bring a letter from Fidel to Che. "I hid it under my undershirt for almost a month," Machado told me. After following a circuitous route—from Havana to Madrid, Rome, Paris, and Dar-es-Salaam—he "wasted a week in the Tanzanian capital because our ambassador suggested a meeting with [Vice-President Rashidi] Kawawa that never materialized." He then went to Kigoma escorted by Ulises Estrada, the DGI officer who had left Cuba the previous April aboard the *Uvero* and had joined the support group in Dar-es-Salaam. Estrada accompanied Machado through Tanzania, finally reaching Kibamba in late September. But Che was no longer at Luluabourg and they had to walk for several days before they found him, on October 4. It is easy to remember the date of their encounter, Machado Ventura explained. The day before, in Havana, Fidel had released Che's farewell letter.[107]

For months, the wildest rumors had flown throughout the world about Che's fate: he was in a psychiatric ward in Cuba; he had been killed by Castro; he had died fighting in Santo Domingo; and so on. As Castro said, "Our enemies have spread many rumors; at times they were confused, at other times they wanted to spread confusion: . . . whether he is here, whether he is there, whether he is alive, whether he is dead."[108] On October 1, Fidel announced the members of the Political Bureau, the Secretariat, and Central Committee of the new Communist Party of Cuba, and Che was not among them. If Castro said nothing about his fate, even those who sympathized with the Cuban revolution would begin to wonder. It was time, therefore, for Castro to speak up.[109]

Not so, according to Che. He was listening to a small radio with other members of the column when Fidel began to read the letter. "Che was near me," one of the volunteers recalled. "He became very serious, he lowered his head and began to smoke." The fact that Fidel had made his letter public bothered Che a lot, Dreke explained. "I think Che knew that things in Zaire were going badly, and once Fidel had read the farewell letter, he felt like it would be awkward to return to Cuba."[110]

After a few days in Fizi-Baraka, Machado returned to Havana a much wiser man. "Machado and I agreed," Che writes, "that it was impossible to have fifty doctors there. . . . He agreed with me that the situation was truly alarming. . . . With all this new information and his new appreciation of reality, Machado began his trip home."[111] Before he left, Che gave him a letter for Fidel. "Dear Fidel," he wrote, "It worries me personally that . . . you could think I suffer from the terrible malady of undue pessimism. . . . I'll just tell you that, according to those around me, I'm no longer considered an objective observer because I've stayed optimistic in spite of the facts." And he proceeded to lay out these facts, lucidly, before concluding, "I've tried to be explicit and objective, concise and truthful. Do you believe me?"[112]

Machado also carried a letter from Fernández Mell to Guillermo García, the commander of the Western Army, saying that while he wanted to be optimistic, "because I know how high everyone's hopes are for this [operation]," the grim facts were that Soumialot "is a clown"; that Kabila had refused to join his men; and that the Simbas had treated Che in a disgraceful manner. "No one has paid any attention to him. They have simply ignored him, and he himself thinks that on two or three occasions they have been on the verge of throwing him out." The mercenaries had begun a new offensive, Fernández Mell wrote, and "I believe that these next three or four months will determine whether this operation has any chance of success or not. We are devoting all our heart and soul to it."[113]

CHAPTER SIX
A SUCCESSFUL COVERT OPERATION

Thee mercenaries' offensive against the Fizi-Baraka was the final act of one of the most successful covert operations undertaken by the United States during the Cold War. By deftly managing public opinion at home and foreign governments abroad, Washington kept the costs of the operation risibly low while the benefit seemed large: a pro-American regime ensconced in the heart of Africa.

The mercenaries saved Johnson from having to make a choice between sending U.S. troops or accepting a rebel victory. British, Belgian, and U.S. officials all agreed that, as Belgian foreign minister Spaak said, Zaire's "safety" depended "almost entirely on the mercenaries' presence." The ANC was "an incompetent, undisciplined and cowardly rabble," British ambassador Rose wrote in January 1965. CIA reports, by far the best source on the campaign, concurred: the "regular Congo [Zaire] army troops, with a few exceptions, are no better than they ever were," a July 1965 analysis said. Ambassador Godley cabled that the "cardinal resource of [the] GDRC [government of Zaire] is [the] mercenary force." Even General Mobutu, proud commander of the Zairean army, told Godley: "mercenaries indispensable in Congo [Zaire] until rebel pockets eliminated."[1]

For President Johnson, the mercenaries were also indispensable. Throughout 1964, he had been preoccupied with Vietnam. He had delayed a major escalation there until 1965, when he opened the floodgates. Approximately 80,000 U.S. troops were in Vietnam by late June. By year's end there were 175,000. It would have been practically impossible for him under these circumstances to have ordered U.S. troops to Africa.

OF TSHOMBE AND MERCENARIES

Victory would be Pyrrhic, however, if it caused a backlash in Africa or at home. American officials were painfully aware that the United States was vulnerable to African charges of racism despite the sincere efforts of the Johnson administration to strengthen civil rights legislation, and relying on white mercenaries was a potential public relations disaster. As long as Africans had been colonial wards, controlled by their white European masters, their views had hardly mattered, but now they were pawns in the Cold War.

"I cannot underline too strongly the need for progress in the elimination of discrimination in our country as an essential to the development of full friendship and confidence between our country and the new African states," Averell Harriman had written John Kennedy in September 1960, after visiting eight African countries. In somber tones, Dean Rusk warned three years later that discrimination at home "deeply affects the conduct of our foreign policy relations. . . . Our voice is muted, our friends are embarrassed, our enemies are gleeful." American racism was crippling American foreign policy, he said. "We are running this race with one of our legs in a cast." Looking back at those years, Assistant Secretary Williams commented, "I think you could make a barometric chart of how civil rights were going through the relationships you had with many Africans."[2] In the summer of 1964, as the Zairean operation began, the United States was alone, with South Africa, in depriving millions of its citizens of the right to vote because of their color; intermarriage was a crime in nineteen U.S. states; segregation was institutionalized; and violence against blacks was apparent to anyone who glanced at a newspaper or turned on a television. In mid-July, the second summit meeting of the OAU convened in Cairo while police attacked blacks in Mississippi and race riots in New York reminded Africans that racial hatred was not limited to the Deep South. The assembled African leaders unanimously approved a resolution condemning "continuing manifestations of racial bigotry and oppression against Negroes in the United States."[a,3]

This background of racist violence at home made it imperative that the Johnson administration escape all association with the thuggish white mercenaries in Zaire. "I believe that there are some things that we can do to make our actions in the Congo [Zaire] more palatable internationally and to make ourselves less vulnerable to Communist propaganda," Carl Rowan, the prominent black journalist who headed the United States Information Agency (USIA), told Johnson.[4] This meant polishing Tshombe's image. And it meant making the use of mercenaries as anodyne as possible, while transforming the United States from their patron into a concerned onlooker.

Through reams of documents, we see senior U.S. officials trying to get Tshombe to utter the right noises and make the right gestures; they worked directly with him, and they worked through his advisers and public relations people. It was a thankless task, Ambassador Godley and his Belgian and British colleagues concluded, as they swapped stories of Tshombe's stubbornness. The man's survival depended on the United States, but he knew that his patrons also needed him. "We all agreed that dire threats should never be made unless we

a. A systematic reading of the *Tanganyika Standard*, the *Daily Nation* (Nairobi), the *Egyptian Gazette* (Cairo), the *Nationalist* (Dar-es-Salaam), and *Le Peuple* (Algiers) reveals their interest in U.S. race relations. In late July 1964, they devoted substantial articles daily to the New York riots. Through the rest of the year they included on average three to four articles a month on racial problems in the United States. The coverage became more intense in early 1965, as the situation in Alabama grew increasingly tense. Then, in the month that followed "Bloody Sunday" in Selma on March 7, 1965, every issue of these five dailies included at least one article on racial violence in the United States.

prepared accept consequences and have tangible alternative in mind," Godley cabled in December 1964. "For moment, we can see no satisfactory person replace Tshombe."[5]

Mindful of Tshombe's well-deserved reputation as the friend of Portuguese colonialism, U.S. officials sought to drape him in anticolonialist veils. Tshombe did not oblige. Within days of assuming the premiership, he let the U.S. embassy know, "in no uncertain terms," that he intended to reverse his predecessor's policy of providing assistance to the National Front for the Liberation of Angola (FNLA), a liberation movement based in Zaire that was fighting against Portuguese rule. True to his word, he began harassing the FNLA. "Rebel activity on the northern border of Angola decreased and morale collapsed in the terrorist camps across the border," the Portuguese foreign minister wrote.[6]

"I indicated [to Tshombe that] there are many rumors around Leo[poldville] that he is giving [FNLA leader] Holden Roberto and his Angolans a rough time," Godley cabled in March 1965. "He again referred to fact that from his limited resources he gave Holden $800. . . . I suggested he let this be known to African leaders and that he not conceal his pro-Holden tendencies." A few days later the U.S. ambassador in Dar-es-Salaam chimed in: Zaire should make a "special [financial] contribution" to Roberto at the next meeting of the Liberation Committee of the OAU. The contribution would be "more symbolic than substantial and explicable [to the] Portuguese in these terms if [the] closed session leaked."[7]

The suggestions fell on deaf ears. "Holden complains bitterly," *Jeune Afrique* reported two months later. "Tshombe is making his life tough." Tshombe, U.S. officials groused, had an "incredibly poor sense of public relations."[8]

The previous August, U.S. efforts at remaking Tshombe's image had faced a far deadlier threat. Unbeknownst to Washington, Tshombe had asked Pretoria for weapons as well as "white officers and white enlisted men." While sympathetic to Tshombe, the South Africans had hesitated. They told U.S. officials that they were worried that any evidence of their military involvement would be "grist for the mill" for Tshombe's enemies and would complicate American efforts to aid Zaire. Washington agreed heartily: the South African connection would be a "continuing magnet for cold war in form of greater sovbloc, chicom, and radical African interest." Pretoria held back. It sent Tshombe a few military supplies—the arrival on August 22, 1964, of a South African C-130 "with what is obviously military equipment" was immediately reported in the press.[9] And it sent, according to the CIA, some military personnel under cover: "many of the mercenaries arriving at [the Zairean base of] Kamina are actually South African Army regulars placed on leave status for six months." There were a few dozen such soldiers, sent to perform specialized tasks and "probably . . . to gather intelligence," Lawrence Devlin, the CIA station chief in Leopoldville, observed.[10] Fortunately for Washington, this operation remained a secret.

U.S. officials would have preferred that both the South African government and the South African mercenaries stay out of Zaire, a point that Under Secretary Ball made forcefully: Zaire "cannot expect its friends, such as Nigeria, Senegal, the Ivory Coast and others, to be effective in promoting its interests against strong opposition of radical African states if Congo [Zaire] does not take parallel actions which will make it more acceptable to Africa." Among such actions, Ball stressed, was the "replacement of at least the South Africans and Rhodesians among the mercenary contingents in the Congo [Zaire] ASAP." In their stead should be Europeans. "Such a shift," Harriman told Spaak during a three-hour luncheon in New York, "would not in itself overcome African opposition to Tshombe but would make it easier for moderate African countries to support GDRC [government of Zaire]."[11]

The Belgians agreed. "The attitude of the [Belgian] Ministry of Foreign Affairs to the mercenary question," the British embassy reported from Brussels in April 1965, "could probably be best summed up as follows: the ANC is at present incapable of carrying out serious operations without some form of backing by mercenaries; Tshombe is therefore forced to recruit mercenaries; but it would be much more convenient if he could avoid recruiting South Africans and Rhodesians; recruits from anywhere else in the world would be on the whole acceptable."[12]

Initially—in July and August 1964—Spaak had refused to let Belgians serve as mercenaries; he had even threatened to withdraw military assistance "if Belgian white mercenaries enter the Congo [Zaire]."[13] With American prodding, these reservations soon dissipated. Honored as one of the fathers of European unity, Spaak appears here in less distinguished garb. He looked aside while the Zairean military attaché supervised the recruitment of mercenaries in Belgium. "Several recruitment centers, of which we know the addresses, exist in Brussels and in the provinces," Spaak cabled Belgian ambassador Charles de Kerchove in Leopoldville. "We know [of] about ten recruiters as well as the names of about thirty-five mercenary candidates." On his behalf, Kerchove urged Tshombe to try to be "as discreet as possible" when recruiting in Belgium, but no one was fooled. "All this was public knowledge," remarks Colonel Vandewalle, who headed the Belgian military mission in Zaire. It was also in frank violation of a 1936 Belgian law that outlawed the recruitment of mercenaries on Belgian soil, and of Spaak's own public and categorical pledges that recruiters of mercenaries would be prosecuted.[14]

Nevertheless, fewer than 200 Belgians signed up and even fewer Frenchmen; the number of Italians and Germans could be counted on one hand; 46 Spaniards (under an active duty officer on unpaid leave from the Spanish army) arrived in late 1965, when the fighting was virtually over. The Americans knew that with so few Europeans volunteering, the white South Africans and Rhodesians would have to stay. In fact, for the duration of the war they constituted well over half the total. Godley was philosophical: while a shift to Europeans might "alleviate political unacceptability mercenaries . . . none of us [the Belgian and British ambassadors and Godley] believe this would appreciably modify situation." Moreover, he added, "the English-speaking mercenaries . . . have proven themselves more able than the Belgian and other heterogeneous French-speaking mercenaries."[15]

Since little could be done to change the mercenaries' nationality, U.S. officials did what they could to package the unsavory product better. Why not call them "military technical assistance volunteers," the U.S. ambassador in Belgium asked. (Others preferred "special volunteers.")[16] Well-meaning, repetitive suggestions rained on Godley. Rusk told him to "play down to extent possible role mercenaries." USIA director Rowan urged "more emphasis on Congolese [Zaireans] and less on mercenaries," and Ball insisted that he take "measures to avoid publicity such as keeping mercenaries out of Leo[poldville and] impressing upon [mercenary leader] Hoare necessity keep quiet."[17] Not an easy task: "Hoare can never resist the temptation to say the wrong thing to the press," the British embassy in Leopoldville remarked. He told the Durban *Sunday Tribune*, "I can see a stable Congo [Zaire] as the buffer between White and Black Africa, but siding with the white democratic nations"—South Africa, Rhodesia, and Portugal. Zaire "will need white troops for many years to come," he told *Le Figaro Littéraire*. "The work we have started has to be completed, and the only way to complete it is to kill all the rebels." The British embassy noted dryly that statements like that "cannot fail to arouse the most acute fear and suspicion on the part of Tshombe's critics."[18]

The United States stayed in the background and built "a few fires under [the] Belgians"; as the former colonizers, they could dirty their hands. "We had to press them, cajole, yell at them," recalled a U.S. official. The Belgians were "small in resources and small in imagination," observed another.[19] The Americans wanted the Belgians to take the lead in Zaire—the lead, that is, in executing Washington's policy. The Belgians cooperated: by early 1965—before Che had even set foot in Dar-es-Salaam to offer Cuba's help to the Simbas—their military mission in Zaire had swelled to almost 450 people, and Belgian officers were placed "in de facto command of most major Congo [Zaire] Army detachments."[20] Furthermore, it was the Belgian military advisers who openly maintained the daily contact with the mercenaries. "Overtly at least," Godley recommended, "US Rep[resentative]s should keep as far away from mercenaries as possible."[21] The United States wanted the mercenaries to be seen as the responsibility of the Zairean government and of Brussels. To make this unequivocally clear, "in accordance with the wishes of the American government," the mercenaries would not include U.S. citizens.[22]

A PATRIOTIC PRESS

The figleaf was transparent, but as long as the policy was successful, the U.S. press, riveted on Vietnam, was not inclined to scrutinize the mercenaries' behavior or the role of the Johnson administration in masterminding the operation. On August 7, 1964, Congress had approved the Tonkin Gulf resolution, which, as McNamara remarked, "brought home the possibility of U.S. involvement in the war as never before."[23] When, a few days later, Johnson sent four C-130 transport planes with American crews and fifty-six paratroopers to guard them to Zaire to provide logistical support to the Zairean army, the *New York Times* warned, "The United States is getting itself militarily involved in still another conflict. . . . [It] is starting with only enough arms, men and matériel to put out a little bonfire . . . but as Southeast Asia showed, bonfires can grow into great conflagrations." These fears were echoed by several members of Congress. "Today we are providing transport service," Senator John Stennis (D.-Miss.) remarked. "I cannot but wonder whether the next step will be the function of advising and training the Government forces, in the style followed in South Vietnam so that ultimately our men will be fighting and dying in combat."[24]

The administration was eager to dispel these fears. The C-130s were "mostly for evacuation purposes," Under Secretary Ball assured the prominent columnist Walter Lippmann. "We have no intention of getting . . . bogged down in the African swamp." And upon learning that the *New York Times* was "thinking of writing some editorials on the Congo [Zaire] situation," Ball called editorial page editor John Ochs and volunteered to send Deputy Assistant Secretary Wayne Fredericks "to N.Y. and have him talk to Ochs and [his] colleagues."[25]

It was not Ball's or Fredericks's eloquence but the mercenaries' successes that quelled the fear that the United States might be "drawn ever deeper into the Congolese [Zairean] jungle."[26] In the following months, the U.S. press reported the obvious: "It has been the white mercenary force . . . that has contained and rolled back the insurgents." Led by the "intelligent, poetry-reading Colonel Mike Hoare," as the *Washington Post* called him, the mercenaries squared the circle: Zaire would be saved, and American soldiers would not die.[27]

Nor were the mercenaries such bad chaps either, according to the U.S. press. "They resemble rough-hewn college boys," a *Life* reporter wrote. The *New York Times*, which provided more intensive coverage of the Zairean crisis than any other U.S. newspaper, made only one attempt to inform the American people about who the mercenaries were. It did so by devoting two articles to Lieutenant Gary Wilson, "a lean, 25-year old South African" who had enlisted, he confided, "because he believed Premier Moise Tshombe was sincerely trying to establish a multiracial society in the Congo [Zaire]. 'I thought that if I could help in this creation, the Congo [Zaire] might offer some hope, some symbol in contrast to the segregation in my own country.' "[28] We hear Wilson's distress at what he witnesses in Zaire. "It's a weird war," he muses, "frightening, brutal, sometimes comic, utterly unreal." We hear him talk about performing acts of great bravery. "He recalled the time two weeks ago when he captured Lisala with 15 men [white mercenaries] against more than 400. . . . 'The rebs have one thing in common with our own Congolese [Zaireans],' he added. 'They don't take aim. They think that noise kills.' "[29] We hear his reaction to the cruelty of the Zaireans—on both sides. " 'It's mass murder, it's mass murder,' " he muttered. Moreover, we learn that "his words summed up the feelings of most of his compatriots here."[30]

Perhaps Wilson was indeed the sensitive, idealistic man described by the *New York Times*. If so, he was the exception. More typical was Wally Harper, a fellow South African fighting in Zaire. When asked, "How do you feel when you're out there fighting? How do you feel about killing anyone?" Harper replied, "Well, I've done a lot of cattle farming, you know, and killing a lot of beasts it's just like, you know, cattle farming, and just seeing dead beasts all over the place. It didn't worry me at all." Harper's words appeared in *Africa Today*, a scholarly magazine read by very few Americans, not in the *New York Times*.[31]

In its eighteen-month coverage of the war the *New York Times* reported the mercenaries' successes time and again; only rarely did it mention—and then ever so briefly—their transgressions. On December 2, 1964, a few days after Hoare's men had reconquered Stanleyville, columnist C. L. Sulzberger abruptly referred to "atrocities committed by white mercenaries in the Congo [Zaire]," but he provided no details; three weeks later he called the mercenaries "unsavory." On December 6, the *Times* wrote that they "stalked through" the African section of Stanleyville, "looting and shooting. There seemed to be no end to the killing; any African man or woman was considered a rebel and shot on sight." In January, the *Times* quoted a UN official in Zaire saying that the mercenaries "loot everywhere they can," and it noted in passing that "the mercenaries habitually loot the towns they take."[32] This was the extent of the indictment. No photos like those published in the *Observer* (see chapter 3) appeared in the *Times*. Its readers learned instead of the mercenaries' efforts to protect the Zaireans from both the rebels and the army.

The *New Republic* and the *Christian Science Monitor* mentioned the mercenaries' crimes once. The former reported that at Stanleyville the mercenaries shot "at anything that moved that was black"; the latter noted, with uncommon sensitivity, that "the African nations have been . . . appalled by the cruelties of the white mercenaries toward Africans." *Newsweek* regularly referred to the atrocities perpetrated by both the Simbas and the ANC, and to the mercenaries' revulsion at them. (After witnessing an atrocity by a government soldier, one mercenary, "his face wrinkled in disgust, snapped out: 'They are all the same. Take the uniform off that one [pointing to the soldier] and put it on that one [pointing to a dead rebel] and what's the difference?'") Only once did *Newsweek* mention a crime committed by the mercenaries: in Stanleyville they "divided their time between mopping up the remnants of rebel resistance and pillaging."[33] *Life*, *Time*, and *U.S. News & World Report* constantly assailed the rebels' atrocities and occasionally mentioned those of the army, but none uttered a single word of criticism of the mercenaries. They stressed instead how the mercenaries were saving Zaire from communism. The closest the *Washington Post* came to mentioning mercenaries' crimes was an isolated reference to "the wholesale looting, killing and burning of villages . . . in areas captured by mercenary-led forces in the northwest Congo [Zaire]."[34] There were no such references in the *Wall Street Journal* or in the *Nation*.

Perhaps the American journalists who went to Zaire were silent about the atrocities the mercenaries committed because they were dependent on the U.S. embassy for information and transportation.[35] Perhaps it was because the mercenaries were doing America's work and saving American boys' lives. Perhaps it was because the mercenaries, like the journalists, were white and they killed only blacks, while they saved the lives of white hostages (including some Americans). *Le Monde* put it well: "Western public opinion is more sensitive, one must acknowledge, to the death of one European than to the deaths of twenty blacks."[36]

AFRICAN AMERICANS AND ZAIRE

Given the press's selective reporting, it is not surprising that very few white Americans expressed any qualms about their country's policy in Zaire. African Americans were less placid. Malcolm X and the Black Muslims lashed out at President Johnson, his "hireling Tshombe," and the "hordes of white Nazi-type mercenaries" descending on Zaire. In the petition he addressed to the second summit of the OAU in Cairo in July 1964, and until his death in February 1965, Malcolm X called on African Americans and Africans to join together against their common enemy—in Alabama and in Zaire alike.[37]

Martin Luther King's wing of the civil rights movement was more cautious. The Call Committee of the American Negro Leadership Conference on Africa (a group of civil rights leaders that met occasionally to discuss African issues) repeatedly expressed unhappiness with U.S. policy in Zaire, called for a withdrawal of "mercenaries and other external forces," and asked that the problem be resolved by negotiations.[38] But these leaders and their constituencies were absorbed in the civil rights struggle raging in the United States. They had no desire to quarrel with a president whose help they needed. Insofar as they paid attention to foreign policy, they focused on issues that directly affected African Americans—Vietnam, above all, where black soldiers were dying. "To them, Africa was distant, far off," remarked Congressman Charles Diggs (D.-Mich.).[39] Their interest in the Zairean drama was limited; their complaints, somewhat perfunctory. Nevertheless, even their mild criticism provoked hostility. "Insofar as the civil rights leaders allow their movements to become hostage to the uncertain and confused events in Africa, they can provide heedless comfort to their enemies," the *Washington Post* lectured in an editorial. "There ought to be the utmost caution in statements that can enable bigots to assert that race is a stronger bond than citizenship."[40]

After the U.S.-Belgian raid on Stanleyville, the leaders of the American Negro Leadership Conference on Africa asked for a meeting with Johnson, who handed them over to Secretary Rusk. "What the President hopes is that you might find a way of making the point that we do not think it is a good thing at all to encourage a separate Negro view of foreign policy," National Security Adviser Bundy told Rusk. "I get loud and clear that the President wants to discourage emergence of any special Negro pressure group (a la the Zionists) which might limit his freedom of maneuver," noted an NSC official.[41] In March 1965, Rusk met with King and other representatives of the Negro Leadership Conference. The meeting "was quiet and friendly. Concerning the Congo [Zaire], the Secretary and the Negro Leadership group agreed on the necessity . . . for Tshombe to get rid of the white mercenaries. . . . The meeting was given minimal press coverage and is not likely to give rise to any undesirable repercussions."[42]

Even the black press gave the meeting short shrift. With the notable exceptions of the Black Muslim paper, *Muhammad Speaks*, and the Baltimore *Afro-American*, it paid very little attention to Africa, and even less to Zaire. During the eighteen months that the crisis raged, the influential *Amsterdam News* published only three articles that mentioned it, and the *Crisis*, the monthly organ of the NAACP, printed not one word on the subject.[43]

Two U.S. newspapers, both African American, roundly denounced the U.S. role "in the raising and paying of white mercenaries." The *Afro-American* wrote: "We hire the hated anti-Castro mercenary pilots. . . . If we must fight the Congolese [Zairean] people, why don't we openly send in our army, our navy and our airforce instead of hiring thugs to do our dirty work for us." *Muhammad Speaks* was equally outspoken, asking: "If it is wrong for a rich individual to hire a thug to kill his enemy, does it become right for a rich country to hire killers to slaughter people of another country? . . . Or is it forgiven because the killers we hire are just 'killing niggers?' "[44]

The white press was more understanding. It mentioned that Cuban exiles were piloting the T-28s and B-26s provided by the United States, but it did not ask how these Miami Cubans had found their way to Leopoldville. In fact, the only references to any connection between the United States and the mercenaries were a phrase in the *Nation* that Cuban exiles were flying the planes "on CIA contracts," another phrase in *Life* about Cuban exiles having been "recruited by the United States" to fly the planes, and three short sentences buried in a full-page article in the *Washington Post*: "The United States is flying mercenaries to the front. Better still, the United States is in effect underwriting the cost of the entire force of 'operational technicians,' as they are known in official circles. The monthly payroll: $300,000." One might have expected other newspapers to pick up the story, or the *Nation*, *Life*, and the *Washington Post* to elaborate on it. In fact, nothing happened. The CIA station chief in Leopoldville ventured an explanation: "Most of them [the U.S. journalists in Zaire] knew very well or guessed if they didn't know; but they didn't want to embarrass the U.S. government."[45]

This reticence was not new. It had been present in 1954, at the time of the CIA covert operation in Guatemala, in 1957–58, during the covert operation against Indonesia, and in 1961, in the weeks before the Bay of Pigs. "If the leaders of the U.S. government decide that all the risks and perils of a major covert operation are required . . . it is not the business of individual newspapermen to put professional gain over that of country," the prominent columnist, Joseph Alsop, explained.[46]

The Africans were less cooperative. African leaders despised Tshombe, abhorred the mercenaries, and fully understood that the United States—not Tshombe or the Belgians—was behind the operation. American involvement in Zaire "has resulted in a considerable strain in United States relations with a number of African countries," the British ambassador in Washington remarked. "The United States seems to have lost, in African eyes, that reputation for innocence which it once enjoyed because of its lack of colonial connection with the African continent."[47]

The appointment of Tshombe to the premiership of Zaire and the arrival of the white mercenaries had enraged many African governments. The U.S.-Belgian raid on Stanleyville on November 24, 1964, hardened that fury into resolve. "The almost universal hatred and distrust of Tshombe outside of the Congo [Zaire] . . . has driven many moderate African countries into support for the rebels," the British Foreign Office noted. Determined to bring Tshombe down, the governments of Algeria, Egypt, the Sudan, Guinea, Ghana, the Congo, Tanzania, Kenya, Uganda, and Burundi provided money or weapons to the Simbas or allowed aid to pass through their territory.[48]

Pragmatism, however, soon muted their rage. With the exception of the Congo, all these governments relied on U.S. economic aid (or, in the case of Burundi, Belgian)—a fact that U.S. officials did not let them forget. (Nasser, for example, had been a strong rebel supporter but, a White House aide noted, "his hope that we would resume shipments [of wheat to Egypt] led him to pull back.")[49] Moreover, from the outset England used its clout with African governments to rally support for U.S. policy, and in early 1965 the French joined in.[50] Finally, the mercenaries' victories could not be overlooked. By April 1965 rebel resistance in the northeast had crumbled, and the only important rebel area left was the Fizi-Baraka. "My personal relations with [President Jomo] Kenyatta healed slowly," the U.S. ambassador in Kenya writes. "But on May 5 [1965] he called me over [to] the State House, held out his hand and said, 'The Congo [Zaire] is finished. Now we can be friends again.'"[51]

Sudan, which had allowed aid for the rebels to pass through its territory, was subjected to more direct pressure. In April 1965 mercenary leader Hoare led his men to the Sudanese border. On April 28, the CIA reported that "South African mercenaries sallied across the frontier." As one mercenary recalled more poetically, "in the heart of Africa, at Aba on the border between Zaire and Sudan, South African soldiers sang the Boers' folksong in the tropical night." It was an ominous humiliation for the Sudanese; they ended their support for the rebels and toned down their criticism of the United States.[52] The Congo, also fearful of a "US-backed attack" by Tshombe's mercenaries, as the CIA observed, did "little to aid the insurgents."[53]

At times, sheer luck helped the Americans. Algiers had been providing some aid to the Simbas ever since the raid on Stanleyville. Relations between Algeria and the United States were strained, and in April 1965 Dean Rusk told the Algerian ambassador that "bilateral relations could not usefully be discussed as long as Algerian policies on Vietnam and the Congo [Zaire] were at such variance with those of the US."[54] But Ben Bella's overthrow at Boumedienne's hands in June 1965 broke the impasse. Boumedienne, the CIA noted, "has been warm, open, and attentive with US officials." He promised that no further aid would be given to the Simbas.[55]

The storm was subsiding. Ghana's hostility was unchanged, but in material terms, as the CIA station chief in Leopoldville observed, "Nkrumah did not play a role in Zaire in 1964–65, or a very limited one at most." Egypt, Burundi, Kenya, Uganda, and Guinea were "adopting a more pro-Western stance," the senior White House aide in charge of Africa told Johnson, and he added: "The back of the Congo [Zaire] rebellion has been broken."[56] This was on June 16, less than two weeks before the Cubans' first attack in Zaire at Bendera. Only Tanzania remained firm in its support for the Simbas—defiant in its revulsion for the "traitor" Tshombe and his mercenaries.[57] Tanzania, Rusk told the Portuguese foreign minister in June, "was now the only [African] country that had not pulled out from supporting the Congolese [Zairean] rebels." Tanzania, a senior Soviet official agreed, "is basically the only country that allows arms shipments and other assistance [for the Simbas] to pass through its borders without difficulty."[58]

THE CIA'S NAVAL PATROL

By the summer of 1965, the rebels' last remaining link with the external world was Lake Tanganyika, separating Zaire and Tanzania, across which arms and supplies from the Soviet Union and China were shipped. The Simbas could cross the lake virtually unopposed. "They even went to spend the weekend at Kigoma, using small boats," Paulu, the diarist of the Cuban column, wrote in late June. The previous month, Che had noted, "If the Yankees have learned the lesson of other revolutions, this is the moment they will strike hard and . . . neutralize the lake; they will do everything they can to cut off our major supply route."[59]

And so they did. While Che was writing, the CIA was busy creating a naval patrol on Lake Tanganyika. It consisted of eight heavily armed fast patrol boats and several older vessels. "It was a very successful operation against great odds," DCM Robert Blake recalled. "It was a big job," Devlin agreed. "First, the [patrol] boats were flown in in pieces. We had to put them together in Albertville [a port on Lake Tanganyika]. Then it wasn't easy to find people to man the boats." Some came from the ranks of Hoare's mercenaries. "They lacked experience; we had to train them." Others were anti-Castro Cubans: a CIA operation that specialized in Cuban exiles' raids against Cuba from Nicaragua had just folded. "Some of the people who served with me in Nicaragua volunteered to fight in Africa too," a Cuban exile recalled. A twenty-six-year-old Navy Seal lieutenant, James Hawes, was brought from Vietnam and placed in charge of the naval patrol. He was the only U.S. citizen openly involved with the operation, and he reported directly to Devlin in Leopoldville. His task, in this phase of the war, was to prevent Simba traffic on the lake. Later, when the offensive against Fizi-Baraka began, he would also provide support for amphibious and offshore operations.[60]

The Simbas had several motorboats, courtesy of the Soviet bloc, but they did not know how to maintain them. Che had sent one of his men, Changa, to Kigoma, to supervise lake traffic for the column. Changa soon gained the respect of the Simba crews. (Che, who rarely praised his men, called him "the ineffable Admiral Changa, master and Lord of the lake.")[61] But Changa was only one person, and he was neither a trained sailor nor a mechanic.

"I have been asking for two motor mechanics for a long time to fix this graveyard of boats that once was the pier of Kigoma," Che wrote Fidel on October 5. "Three brand-new Soviet launches arrived a little over a month ago, and two are already useless and the third . . . leaks all over the place. The three Italian launches will suffer the same fate unless they have a Cuban crew."[62]

As the Simbas' boats gathered rust, the CIA naval patrol became increasingly effective, making it dangerous for the Simbas to cross the lake. "I remember one occasion," a CIA officer told me. "We were not supposed to have CIA men on those boats. A machine gun starts firing at the mercenaries while they're in the water and starts killing them. One of our CIA men fires back with a recoiless rifle and kills the Simbas. There were two American cameramen—they got it on tape. Can you imagine the scandal this would have created! I convinced them to hand the film over to me."[63]

THE CIA'S ONLY FAILURE

In only one respect was the CIA derelict in the Zaire operation: it was very slow to discover that the Cubans were there. This intelligence failure baffled Che and his men.

"Our operation was impossible to hide," argues Colman Ferrer, who was a member of the support group. "The compañeros arrived at the Dar-es-Salaam airport on commercial flights and then they disappeared! Besides, a Cuban ship [the Uvero] loaded with weapons docked at Dar-es-Salaam." Che, too, was incredulous: "The purchase of articles in unusually large quantities, such as backpacks, plastic sheeting, knives, blankets, and so on in Dar-es-Salaam should have attracted attention."[64]

Kigoma was more than 900 miles from Dar-es-Salaam. "It took forty hours, and we were in a hurry," Ferrer points out. "So we had to drive day and night. We drove through several important towns. When there weren't too many of us, we went in embassy cars or in Tanzanian police land rovers; when there were a lot of us we would go in Tanzanian army trucks. I'd disappear from Dar-es-Salaam for four or five days at a time."[65] This activity, too, should have been obvious to U.S. officials in Dar-es-Salaam.

It is true that the Cubans were extremely secretive. "Even I," Tschamlesso remembers, "and I was very close to them, never got to know their real names." But the Simbas, as Dreke explains, "were totally undisciplined. They came and went as they pleased. It was amazing." And until the CIA flotilla made it dangerous, the rebels crossed the lake in droves to enjoy the whorehouses of Kigoma, to Che's dismay.[66] And they knew that the strangers in their midst were Cuban. "Therefore," Ferrer concludes, "we kept wondering why the United States didn't create an international scandal. The CIA should have known what was going on."[67]

It didn't. A July 1 Intelligence Memorandum noted that the rebels "are reportedly being trained by a small number—five have been reported—of Chinese Communists," but it mentioned no Cubans (and the information about the Chinese was wrong).[68]

The CIA found two Cubans among the rebel dead of Bendera, but in the weeks that followed it seemed unconcerned. The rebels, a CIA memorandum noted in late August, were "probably accompanied by a few Cuban and Chinese advisors." The Americans had "been looking for whites and their eyes have passed over Cuban blacks or mulattos," the British defense adviser in Leopoldville remarked with hindsight.[69] It was not until five months after the Cubans had arrived that the CIA finally realized that a large number of Cubans were in Zaire. Ambassador Godley cabled on September 21 that credible reports indicated that more than 100 Cubans were with the rebels. Later in the day he sent another cable, which expressed alarm:

> Country team wishes to call urgent attention to report contained in our tel 523 . . . which is first reasonably hard information we have re number of African mercenaries on rebel side in Fizi-Baraka. . . . We have number intelligence reports which were difficult [to] confirm indicating travel of Cuban, Chinese and other Commie advisers into DAR [Dar-es-Salaam], Kigoma, and thence across Lake Tanganyika to Congo [Zaire]. Implications of arrival substantial number commie mercenaries in Fizi pocket are, in our view, most serious. Believe it safe to predict that Congolese [Zairean] rebellion will soon pass into totally new period unless something done in next few months to eliminate Fizi pocket and Commie technicians.[70]

Godley's concern was not shared in Washington. "For some time there was disbelief that the Cubans were really involved," Devlin recalled. "No one really believed that Che was there. Then a fellow called Tatu showed up. No one could identify him from the photos we had of Che. It was confusing: we made different pictures of Che, with a beard, without a beard, with a moustache and so on. I decided that Che was Tatu, but no one really believed it in Washington. They thought I was smoking the wrong kind of hemp. Why in the hell would Che be fighting in Africa?"[71]

CHAPTER SEVEN
AMERICAN VICTORY

Less than a week after Ambassador Godley reported that there were over 100 Cubans in the Fizi-Baraka, the offensive against the rebel pocket began. About 3,000 soldiers, spearheaded by 350 mercenaries, were supported by the CIA flotilla and by the CIA air force. "We expect the campaign to take about a month, but we still don't know how tough it will be," the NSC point man on Africa, Robert Komer, told President Johnson on September 27, as he announced that the offensive had "finally been launched."[1]

Despite the attackers' superiority in the air, on the lake, and on the ground, the rebels held their own. "Mercenaries advancing . . . have met stiff resistance and are bringing up reinforcements before pushing ahead," Komer noted on October 4. The Simbas were showing "signs of greater tactical ability and determination," the British embassy reported from Leopoldville, and Godley cabled, "The Fizi-Baraka situation certainly differs considerably from the rebellion we have known up to now. It is quite apparent that here we are faced with considerable rebel resolution well supported not only with foreign arms but also with foreign technical advisors." The White House was concerned. "We've impressed on Godley that we can't afford any setback that would give the rebels an image of having a new lease on life," Komer assured President Johnson.[2]

He need not have worried. Within two weeks, the Simbas' resistance crumbled. It is impossible to reconstruct exactly what happened. There are no scholarly accounts of the offensive, the press was not allowed to cover it, the Simbas have not told their own story, very few U.S. or Belgian documents bearing on the subject have been declassified, and the two key Cuban sources, Che's "Pasajes" and Paulu's "Diario de campaña," focus on the column's increasingly tense relations with the rebels and on the decision to withdraw, rather than on the military aspects of the offensive.[3] Still, some broad lines emerge from the confusion. First, it is clear that the Cubans had had neither the time nor the authority to improve significantly the Simbas' organization and training. Despite Che's repeated pleading, training had begun in earnest only after the battle of Bendera, in July. It had been episodic and haphazard, involving only those Simbas who wanted to be trained and occurring only when they wanted. Given the rebels' poor fighting skills and low morale, this was not enough. Overwhelmed by the mercenaries' blows and the roaring of the CIA planes ("this small air force terrorizes our Zairean comrades," Che wrote),[4] the Simbas collapsed. On October 30, Godley reported the "surprisingly swift conclusion of

Phase I [the occupation of a number of key points] of military clean-up operation [in] Fizi-Baraka area." Che agreed: "The demoralization of the people [Simbas] is terrible, and they all want to flee to the lake." October, he added, had been a "month of unmitigated disaster."[5]

The question that haunted the Cubans was whether they should continue to fight even if the Simbas gave up. Che was not inclined to discuss this with his lieutenants. He did not want to hear the unthinkable; he did not even want to articulate the idea that his column might have to leave Zaire. So he kept it bottled up inside. Finally he turned to Dreke, who, unlike his closer friends, Fernández Mell and Aragonés, had never expressed any doubts about the outcome of the struggle or wondered aloud about whether the Cubans should remain in Fizi-Baraka. On the morning of October 28, Paulu writes, "Tatu [Che] went to Moya [Dreke], who was lying down, because he had a fever and a headache . . . [and] asked him how he was feeling and said that in the last couple of days he had seemed worried, and was it because of the situation? Moya answered that it might have been because he wasn't feeling well, although he was also a little worried. . . . Tatu said . . . that the situation was indeed very grave . . . and was getting worse . . . [and when he asked] what he thought they should do about it, Moya replied that he would stay [in Zaire] as long as necessary, as many years as it took."[6]

Che and Dreke prepared a list of fifteen or twenty Cubans who were in the best physical condition and whose morale seemed highest. If the mercenaries overran the Fizi-Baraka, this group would join Mulele, the leader of the Kwilu revolt. "We don't know anything about Mulele, since we haven't had any contact with him," Fernández Mell told Guillermo García, "but the fact that he stays in his guerrilla zone and doesn't travel abroad speaks well of him." They didn't even know, however, where Mulele was, except that he was somewhere near Leopoldville. "We had to face the fact that there was a continent between us," Dreke recalled. The plan was abandoned, but the idea that a select group would remain no matter what happened comforted Che as the situation deteriorated.[7]

Just as the Simbas were falling apart on the battlefield, so they were sinking fast on the diplomatic front. For several months they had offered their foreign friends only the desolate spectacle of their petty, bitter infighting.[8] Then, in October, on the eve of the OAU summit in Accra, a political crisis in Leopoldville sealed their isolation: on October 13 President Kasavubu dismissed Prime Minister Tshombe.

Relations between these two intensely ambitious men had been strained for months, worrying Washington, which wanted stability in Leopoldville. "We've

---

Víctor Dreke was Che's closest aide in Zaire. "He was . . . one of the pillars on which I relied," Che wrote in the secret "Evaluation of the Personnel under My Command" that he prepared for Fidel Castro after seven months in Zaire. "The only reason I am not recommending that he be promoted is that he already holds the highest rank."

turned ourselves inside out to keep Kasavubu from firing Tshombe and to keep Tshombe from trying to take the presidency from Kasavubu," National Security Adviser Bundy wrote Johnson in August 1965. And when Kasavubu finally fired Tshombe, a frustrated White House aide lamented: "So, just when the mercenaries are mopping up the last organized rebel remnants, we have a real political mess on our hands."[9] It was, however, a blessing in disguise. The removal of Tshombe—Lumumba's murderer and the leader of the Katangan secession—made it easier for African leaders to accept the mercenaries' victory in Zaire. At the OAU summit (October 21–26) the African governments pledged that they would not tolerate "any subversion originating in our countries against another member state of the Organization of African Unity." It was well understood that "subversion" meant the Simbas and "member state" meant Zaire. Tanzania joined in the unanimous vote in favor. Nyerere told a press conference that the demise of Tshombe meant that Zaire "was now on a course which could lead to its being regarded as 'an ordinary African country.'"[10] This was immediately reflected in a change in Tanzania's policy. On October 31, the U.S. ambassador in Dar-es-Salaam informed Washington, Nyerere "has disengaged from support [of] Congolese [Zairean] rebels." The head of the Cuban support group in Dar-es-Salaam, Fernández Padilla, wrote Che at the same time: "Compañero Tatu, this morning Pablo [Rivalta (the Cuban ambassador)] was called by the [Tanzanian] government and told that in view of the [OAU] agreements . . . on noninterference, they and the other governments which had been aiding the Liberation Movement of Zaire [the Simbas] will have to change the nature of this assistance. Therefore, they are asking us to withdraw. . . . We have informed Havana. Let us know your views."[11] This was, Che noted, "the coup de grâce for a moribund revolution."[12] To Fidel, he wrote:

Here are my suggestions. A high-level Cuban delegation and/or Tembo [Aragonés, the senior Cuban official who had joined Che the previous August] must go to Tanzania and say more or less the following: Cuba had offered its aid [to the Simbas in February 1965] subject to Tanzania's approval. Tanzania had approved, and the aid program had been implemented. It had been given without conditions or time limit. We understand Tanzania's present difficulties, but we do not agree with its solution. Cuba does not renege on its commitments, and it cannot be party to a shameful retreat that would leave its unfortunate [Simba] brothers to the mercy of the mercenaries. We will abandon the struggle only if, for well-founded reasons or force majeure, the Simbas themselves ask us to, but we will do our utmost to see that this does not happen. . . . Against the imperialists neither retreat nor appeasement is possible. They understand only force. . . .

We must ask Tanzania to allow us: to maintain our cable station; to ship food [across the lake to the rebels] at least once or twice a week; to keep two speedboats [on the lake]; to bring some of the weapons that have been stored [in Tanzania] into Zaire; and to send couriers [through Tanzania] once every 15 days.[13]

That same day, November 4, Che received a cable from Fernández Padilla:

I am sending you, via courier, a letter from Fidel. Its key points are:
  1. We must do everything except that which is foolhardy.
  2. If Tatu [Che] believes that our presence has become either unjustifiable or pointless, we have to consider withdrawing.
  3. If he thinks we should remain we will try to send as many men and as much matériel as he considers necessary.
  4. We are worried that you may wrongly fear that your decision might be considered defeatist or pessimistic.
  5. If Tatu decides to leave [Zaire], he can return here or go somewhere else [while waiting for a new internationalist mission].
  6. We will support whatever decision [Tatu makes].
  7. Avoid annihilation.[14]

Castro was hinting gently that it was time to withdraw from Zaire, but he made it very clear that the decision was Che's and that Cuba would support whatever decision he made.

Nyerere had said that he would not inform the Simba leaders that he wanted the Cubans to withdraw until the Cubans had told him that they were ready to leave, and he kept his word. On November 9, Fernández Padilla wrote to Che, "The government here has said nothing more. I think they are giving us time to make our decision." But while he waited, Nyerere began tightening the screws. On November 9, Fernández Padilla told Rivalta that the Tanzanians had become noticeably less cooperative. Nyerere had begun restricting the flow of weapons, medicine, and other supplies to the Fizi-Baraka from Dar-es-Salaam. He was also preparing to stop supplies for the Simbas from entering his country. "The president of Tanzania," a Soviet official observed in early November, "had already declared that he was going to close the borders of Tanzania for such transports."[15]

Aware that it would be a terrible blow to the rebels' faltering morale, Che postponed telling them about Tanzania's decision, "waiting to see what would happen in the next few days," hoping against hope that something would happen—that Nyerere would reconsider, that successes on the battlefield would strengthen the Simbas' resolve. Hinting to Masengo, who had replaced the late Mitoudidi as Kabila's senior aide in the Fizi-Baraka, that Tanzania might withdraw its support as a result of the OAU conference, Che urged him "to develop a strategy that would free them from dependence on the lake [i.e., Tanzania]." Only in mid-November did he tell Masengo the truth, "because I didn't think it was right to keep him in the dark any longer."[16]

On November 14, Che received a note from Fernández Padilla: "I think that we should immediately begin to lay the groundwork to enable us to continue fighting [without the support of Tanzania]. What do you think? What do you want me to do?"[17] Che replied at once: "We must prepare a clandestine base that includes the following: a small grocery store . . . to keep most of the food we will need without attracting attention; a small house near one of the lake's natural harbors and at some distance from Kigoma; a fallback location for the transmitter; one or two . . . [Cubans? one word is illegible] who can live there without arousing suspicion." Che also asked for "a few small things: multivitamins, because illnesses due to malnutrition are already occurring, a good quantity of plastic sheeting," and something that revealed his dreams: "a 1966 diary."[18]

Che was determined to continue the struggle, but events forced his hand. Not Fidel, not Beijing, not Moscow. Not even Tanzania. Paulu's diary and Che's own manuscript give a vivid sense of what happened as the mercenaries closed in on Luluabourg and Kibamba.

The Simbas wanted to abandon the struggle, and they resented the Cubans for urging them on. Azima, the Cuban commander of a group of nine Cubans at one of the fronts, sent a note to Fernández Mell (who relayed it to Che). "Compañero," Azima wrote, "I have only fourteen Zaireans [Simbas] left . . . and our position gives us absolutely no protection from the air. The Zaireans have said they want to leave, that they no longer want to fight, that I am holding them here at gunpoint, and that as soon as the enemy attacks they will flee. I'm telling you all this because the situation is bad. Forgive me for saying it but I think I have lost my will. We're forcing men to fight who do not want to, and I don't think this makes any sense. Honestly, I don't think we have the right to force them. I do not have much education, but this seems wrong to me."[19]

Che was appalled. He wanted to replace Azima, but before he could, Azima sent him "a personal message, swearing that he would defend his position as if it were Cuban soil." This did not, however, solve the fundamental problem. Papi, one of Che's closest aides, who was at another front, also reported that the Simbas no longer wanted to fight and that their commanders were saying that "'we were bad . . . and that when the enemy arrived they would withdraw and they would shoot at us.'" On November 18, Tschamlesso delivered the final blow: he told Che that all the Simba commanders had agreed to end the war.[20]

Che's manuscript shows how tempted he was to continue fighting without the Simbas. "From the perspective of a combatant's self-respect it was the right thing to do." This was his frame of mind when, on November 19, he received a cable from Fernández Padilla in Dar-es-Salaam describing the embassy's efforts to make Nyerere reconsider. He and Ambassador Rivalta had spoken with Vice-President Kawawa and Foreign Minister Oscar Kambona, the two Tanzanian officials who oversaw the Zairean operation on Nyerere's behalf, and they were also trying to enlist the help of friendly embassies. "We spoke with the Russians and the Chinese," he cabled. "We intend to speak with the ambassadors of the United Arab Republic [Egypt], Ghana, and Mali. . . . Kabila is speaking with

[Tanzanian] government leaders . . . and also with the Chinese and the Russians." Che, who had previously embraced any glimmer of hope, replied soberly: "I believe that these efforts are too late." He told Fernández Padilla that he had decided that the bulk of the column would leave Zaire, but he would remain "with a small group as a symbol of Cuban honor. Inform Havana."[21]

The next day, Che changed his mind and decided that the entire column, himself included, would leave Zaire. He radioed Changa, the Cuban who was in charge of the boats in Kigoma, asking him to bring the boats to the Zairean shore that same night to evacuate the column: "The enemy has not yet reached the coast. . . . Masengo has decided to abandon the struggle and it is best for us to leave as soon as possible."[22]

Why did Che reverse himself? We only have the guesses of those who were with him, and a few tormented pages in "Pasajes"—pained musings rather than explanations. Che's own words, and the recollections of Dreke and Fernández Mell, suggest that he understood that remaining meant courting almost certain death and that, while he was very tempted to remain, he hesitated to sentence others to this same fate. He would have done so, and gladly, had he believed that the sacrifice would have helped the rebel cause, but, even though he refused to acknowledge it, he understood that for the present the cause was lost.

Fernández Mell and Dreke recall that when Che had told some of his senior aides that the time had come for them to leave and that he would stay behind with a few men to continue the struggle, they had refused to leave without him. Aragonés, who was in poor health, was one; another was Captain Santiago Terry. "Terry told Che: 'Tatu, if you remain, I too will remain.' "[23]

Concern for the lives of his men and the grim awareness that those who were ready to die with him believed that their sacrifice would be senseless haunted Che in those dark hours. "I could be reasonably sure that six or eight would stay with me without the slightest grumbling," he wrote. "The others, however, would do it out of a sense of duty—to me, or to the [Cuban] Revolution, and I would therefore be leading men to their deaths who would not be able to fight with enthusiasm." Even so, he hesitated. "The minute we leave, all the naysayers will descend upon us with their lies, in Zaire and elsewhere." But if he stayed? "All the [Simba] commanders were leaving, [and] the population was increasingly hostile to us. And yet the idea of . . . abandoning defenseless peasants and men who had weapons but were defenseless nonetheless because they didn't know how to fight, men who had been defeated and would feel that we had betrayed them, this pained me deeply. . . . The truth is that even up to the last minute the idea of staying behind kept running through my mind, and perhaps in the end I made no decision, I just joined in the flight. . . . This is how I spent my last hours [in Zaire], lonely and hesitant."

At 2:00 A.M. on November 21 Changa arrived with two boats to take the column of Cubans back to Tanzania. "First the sick climbed aboard, then Masengo's staff . . . then all the Cubans," Che wrote. "It was a painful scene without

After seven months of hardship and frustration, Che's column left Zaire on two boats in the early hours of November 21, 1965. "I believe more than ever in guerrilla warfare, but we have failed," Che wrote Fidel. "My responsibility is great. I will forget neither our defeat, nor its precious lessons."

glory: I had to turn men [Simbas] away who begged us to take them with us; there was not one shred of glory in our retreat, not one spark of defiance."[24]

THE STORY OF BENIGNO

There is another account of Che's last moments in Zaire. According to Benigno (Dariel Alarcón), a Cuban who knew Che well, who fought with him in Bolivia, and is one of the three Cubans to have survived that ordeal, Che was reluctant to embark as the boats pulled up on the Zairean shore; he was hesitant, postponing the irrevocable decision, arguing that the women and children who were assembled on the shore should board first, until finally Changa cut him short, saying that "he had precise orders from Fidel that Che absolutely had to leave. They began arguing, but Lawton [Changa] refused to listen and told him, 'If I have to tie you up, I will. You must be the first to leave, and I'll just toss all these blacks [Africans] into the water.'"[25]

Benigno's account has received much attention, in part because of his ties to Che, and in part because Benigno, of all the Cubans who have written or spoken about their experiences in Zaire, is the only one to have left Cuba and therefore he alone cannot be accused of toeing the official line. Unwilling to endure life under Castro, he sought political asylum in France in January 1996 and wrote his memoirs, which include a few pages on the months he spent in Zaire as one of Che's most trusted aides. This is particularly welcome because no other Cubans have written of their experiences in Fizi-Baraka, except in a few newspaper articles. Benigno's integrity has been vouched for by the prominent French intellectual Régis Debray and Che's biographer Jorge Castañeda.[26] His numerous mistakes in dates and names can easily be attributed to the blurring of time, and an all-too-human desire for self-aggrandizement can explain why he records some glorious feats of derring-do that no one else mentions. These warts do not diminish the interest of his story.

Benigno explains that he was already in Tanzania when Che arrived. "When Che found me there," he writes, "he asked me to join him, and he appointed me commander of a company of the avant-guarde. This is how I began fighting in Zaire." Dreke gave him the nom de guerre "Katanga." "Since a black compañero, who was a very good friend of mine, was also called Katanga, Dreke decided to call me Katanga I and the other Katanga II."[27] His brief account of the war adds important insights on Che and on relations between the Simbas and the Cubans. The Simbas, he writes, refused to take orders from the black Cubans. "They said that the whites had to be in command. Since I am white, they obeyed me without hesitation. I could have done anything—beaten them up, hit them in the face—they would have just crossed their arms and lowered their heads." As for Che, Benigno writes, his command was harsh and uncompromising. He decreed that any Cuban who had sexual relations with an African woman would have to marry her, even if he was already married. A volunteer who had a wife and two children in Cuba was forced to marry a Zairean woman, Benigno writes, and, when they were all leaving Zaire, Che ordered him to bring his new bride to Cuba. "The man shot himself in the head. It was a sordid story, we were devastated, but Che bawled us out, saying that we lacked discipline, and that only extreme severity could avert a complete breakdown of discipline. Che even considered our burying our comrade to be an act of defiance."[28] This story casts a startling light on Che Guevara. It is also new: none of the Cubans I interviewed ever mentioned it—perhaps out of shame, or perhaps because they, unlike Benigno, are still in Cuba.

Or perhaps because it never took place. Che's manuscript never mentions the incident, or indeed any policy on sexual relations. Nor is the incident or the policy mentioned in Paulu's "Diario de campaña." Furthermore, both "Pasajes" and "Diario de campaña" record all the Cuban deaths in Zaire and the circumstances in which they occurred. Six Cubans died; none in the circumstances described by Benigno.[29] Did Che and Paulu lie because they were ashamed of what had happened? Or to hide the truth from Fidel?

There are other problems with Benigno's account. He writes that the Simbas obeyed all his orders because he was white. But Che's "Pasajes" is a tale of woes—of how the Simbas disregarded his advice and ignored him—and he was white. Is Che, then, lying? Or did the Simbas obey only Benigno?

Before reading Benigno's memoirs, I had never heard of his being in Zaire. Not one of the twenty-two participants I interviewed about the operation ever mentioned him, not even, for example, when I was assiduously compiling the list of whites in the column.[30] He is never mentioned in "Pasajes" or in Paulu's diary. And he himself said not one word about his being in Zaire in a January 1995 article in which he described his relationship with Che, mentioning his stint as head of Che's personal guard in the early 1960s and his participation in the Bolivian guerrilla war in 1966–67.[31] It could be argued, of course, that he censored himself because of orders from on high, but it is difficult to understand why. Several members of the column had already spoken or written about their participation in the Zairean operation.[32]

When I asked Dreke, after the publication of Benigno's memoirs, his answer was categorical: Benigno, he said, had never been in the column. He had not been with them in Zaire, or even in the Petis during the training. This assertion is backed up by three key Cuban documents about the campaign in Zaire, which I received before Benigno defected, that is, before there would have been any reason to alter them.

The first, Che's highly secret "Evaluación del personal a mis ordenes," is a ten-page document Che dictated in the Cuban embassy in Dar-es-Salaam, in December 1965 or early 1966, and in which he briefly evaluated the performance of each member of the column, excluding Che himself. The document lists the 6 Cubans who died in Zaire as well as the 3 members of the column who were sent back to Cuba because of illness or wounds. It lists, in all, 125 names in Swahili and 2 in Spanish. Benigno's name is nowhere to be found. There is no Dariel Alarcón, there is no Benigno, there is no Katanga I, and there is no Katanga II.[33]

The second document, Che's "Relación nominal," lists both the real names and the noms de guerre of all the members of the column (again minus Che). Che dictated it using the pocket diary in which he had jotted down the personal data of each member of the column in order of arrival. Benigno's name is not included.[34]

Nor can one find Benigno's name in "Columna 'Patricio Lumumba': Planilla de control," which includes eighty-nine questionnaires filled out between June and October 1985 by the members of the column who were still alive and in Cuba.[35]

To be more specific, there is no Benigno, there is no Dariel Alarcón, and there are no Katangas. He was not there.

Therefore, the only reasonable explanation is that Benigno decided to enrich his memoirs with a description of life with Che in Zaire that is based on what he had heard over the years from men who really had been there, and he spiced it up with anecdotes to please his readers. To be fair, he limited his Zairean reminiscences to a dozen pages, while devoting about seventy to the Bolivian guerrilla war, in which he did participate, but his creativity casts a shadow over the credibility of his entire book.[36]

This helps clear up a puzzle that troubled Castañeda: why did the CIA fleet fail to attack the Cubans as they withdrew from the Fizi-Baraka "in their leaking and overcrowded vessels"? Benigno expressed his astonishment to Castañeda: "'We passed between two [enemy] sloops. . . . I at least expected them to start shooting at us any second. It was humanly impossible for them not to see us.'" Since Benigno was not there, it would have been humanly impossible for the

At dawn on November 21, 1965, as the Cubans withdrew from Zaire, Che (center, standing) addressed his men for the last time. "I must leave you," he said. "Perhaps we will meet again, in Cuba or in another part of the world."

men in the sloops to have seen him. What happened, as told by Paulu, who was there, is less dramatic: "We saw and heard an enemy launch in the distance, but it went its own way."[37] Castañeda, who sets great confidence in Benigno, speculates that there was a secret last-minute agreement between Washington and Havana to let the Cubans withdraw from Zaire, but as Castañeda himself notes, CIA station chief Devlin categorically asserts that he had received no instructions to spare the Cubans. "I had [exile] Cubans with me [the CIA pilots] and they were very eager to interrogate Che," he recalled wistfully when I interviewed him on this matter. Jim Hawes, the Navy Seal lieutenant in charge of the patrol, was equally firm: "I never received any order to let the Cubans pass," he told me. "No, absolutely not." Devlin and Hawes attribute the failure to intercept the Cubans to human error and to the fact that, as Hawes said, "we [the naval patrol] were a deterrent, but we were not impenetrable."[38] Furthermore, the Cubans were not aboard leaking boats. Two Soviet motorboats had arrived at Dar-es-Salaam at the end of October. A few days later, seven specialists from the Ministry of the Interior who could maintain the boats had finally arrived from Cuba. At 3:00 A.M., on November 21, Che's column left the Zairean shore aboard the two new motorboats manned by a Cuban crew.[39]

Four days after the Cubans had left Zaire, the ANC commander, General Mobutu, shoved Kasavubu aside and seized power in Leopoldville in a bloodless coup. Mobutu had worked with the CIA since 1960. The agency agreed with Belgian foreign minister Spaak: Mobutu's coup was "the best thing that could possibly have happened."[40] It sealed the American victory in Zaire.

While the Americans celebrated, the Cubans spent a few grim days in Kigoma. On November 27, Tanzanian army trucks drove them to Dar-es-Salaam. On December 6, they boarded two Aeroflot IL-18s, which had been sent for them, flew to Moscow and from there to Cuba.[41]

Che Guevara was not among them. He had left the column as it had approached Kigoma. Paulu's diary records the moment. "At 7:30 A.M., when we were near Kigoma, Tatu gave the order to stop the two boats and to bring them close together." After boarding a small launch that had come to take him to Kigoma, he addressed his men. His farewell was not gracious. "I must leave you," he said. "I hope that despite all the difficulties we have endured, if Fidel someday offers you another mission like this, a few of you will say yes. I also hope that if you're home in time for the 24th [of December], that when you're eating the roast pork some of you longed for so much that you will remember these unfortunate people and the dead compañeros we left in Zaire. Only those who are willing to forgo every comfort to fight for another country can call themselves revolutionaries. Perhaps we will meet again, in Cuba or in another part of the world."[42]

Che left aboard the launch; he was accompanied by three aides (Papi, Pombo, and Tuma, who would go with him to Bolivia). Ferrer was waiting in Kigoma and drove them to Dar-es-Salaam. "I'd never gotten there so fast," Ferrer recalls. "Che wouldn't let me stop; we only paused, as briefly as possible, for gas."[43]

Osmany Cienfuegos, who was Castro's point man for Africa, and Tony Pérez (the head of the Political Bureau of the Cuban armed forces) were waiting for Che in Dar-es-Salaam. They had left Cuba before Castro had learned that Che would leave Zaire. "Fidel had sent us," Pérez recalls, "to talk with Che and discuss the situation, and get his opinion of it. The idea that he would remain in Zaire with a small group was considered extremely risky and almost suicidal. Our task was to convince him to leave, but we had to do it skillfully, carefully, and respectfully. Our marching orders were that it was Che's decision and that if he decided to remain, Cuba would give him everything he needed."[44]

Upon arriving in Dar-es-Salaam, they learned that Che had decided to leave with the entire column. "Our mission had been successful!" Pérez joked. "We had worried a lot about what we would say to Che, about how we could be persuasive and yet delicate, about which arguments to use. And now we didn't have to!"

Their meeting with Che, however, was not pleasant. "He was tense, his legs were swollen. (He had developed beri beri due to malnutrition.) He didn't want to talk. He only wanted to write. And he was in a very bad mood. We stayed in Dar-es-Salaam for several days; he spent his time writing and playing chess with Rivalta."

Che lived in a small apartment in the embassy in Dar-es-Salaam for more than three months, and due to security concerns he never went out. In this apartment, he wrote two documents for Fidel: "Pasajes de la guerra revolucionaria (Congo)" and "Evaluación del personal a mis ordenes."[45]

Che considered his Zairean adventure, as a former DGI officer has written, an "odyssey of frustration,"[46] but he was not dwelling on the past. "Che's polestar was the liberation of Argentina," Dreke pointed out. "He had gone to Zaire thinking that he would return to Latin America and Argentina afterward." He had included four aides whom he wanted to take to Latin America in the column; Zaire would be their training ground. "The few times we talked about it," Dreke recalled, "Che told me, 'After this [Zaire], some of the compañeros will go to Latin America.' And it's possible that, if the war had gained momentum, Che would have told us: 'I'm leaving you here to continue fighting. I'm going [to Argentina].' "[47]

Things had turned out differently, and Che was not leaving Zaire of his own free will. He had suffered a defeat, but he was not defeated. "One of the things that persuaded Che to get out was that he had already decided that he would go to South America," Fernández Mell observes. First, however, he had to analyze his odyssey of frustrations, so that Cuba could learn from his experience. "I believe more than ever in guerrilla warfare, but we have failed," he wrote. "My responsibility is great. I will forget neither our defeat nor its precious lessons."[48]

The Cubans did, indeed, make egregious mistakes. At times Osmany Cienfuegos, Piñeiro, and Fidel Castro himself behaved like rank amateurs. The lack of communications between Che and Havana was a serious oversight, and the failure to send a Cuban crew for the boats until October—despite Che's repeated requests—was a blunder. The selection of Rivalta was unfortunate. Rivalta, an honorable man who had distinguished himself in the struggle against Batista, went to Dar-es-Salaam with a very difficult task. He had to perform two jobs at once: ambassador to Tanzania and chief of the support group. Moreover, he was given little time to familiarize himself with the country and the region. As he points out, he did not have enough aides to help him perform such an important and demanding mission.[49] More to the point, these aides—all chosen by Rivalta—were not up to the task.

When Che arrived in April, the embassy in Dar-es-Salaam was still uninformed about the political and military situation in the rebel area. As Rivalta acknowledges, "Che was the first one to reconnoiter the area. We [the embassy] couldn't do it; we didn't have enough people."[50]

As time passed, and new personnel arrived, the performance of the support group improved. In September, Fernández Padilla replaced Rivalta as head of the group. He was far more adept at intelligence work but, as in the case of the communications and the crews for the boats, the improvement came very late.[51]

But even if the Cubans had made no mistakes, there was nothing they could have done to stave off defeat. By the time the column arrived, the patient was in his death throes. One thousand mercenaries, armed and transported by the

United States and assisted by the CIA air force, had broken the back of the rebellion; and the eastern revolt, which in August 1964 had controlled more than one-third of Zaire, was now confined to isolated patches in the northeast and the Fizi-Baraka. Che's column had no planes or armored cars and only 120 foot soldiers. While the mercenary leaders and the Belgian officers could conduct the war without interference from the Zairean government, the Cubans were dependent on the goodwill of the local chieftains and on the whims of the elusive Kabila. "My first experience of guerrilla warfare was [against] Batista. Our leaders fought with us," Torres remarks. "But in Zaire the leaders weren't with their men. This was our first shock."[52]

The second shock was that the Simbas had lost their will to fight. All they wanted was to be left alone in their liberated zone, and so the Cubans, with their insistence on fighting, annoyed them. Che bothered them, for example, when he told a rebel commander "that he had to move closer to the enemy positions so that he could harass them without respite and harden his men."[53] The history of the column noted that many Simbas

responded badly to the Cubans, saying that everything had been alright and that no one had been bothering them until the Cubans arrived. Then things got bad. Others, even more ignorant, claimed that the Cubans had come to seek gold. . . . The worst part, however, was that none of the Simba leaders who could and should have put an end to these lies was there, because they weren't living in their own country.

These accusations shocked many Cubans, particularly since they had been told that the Simbas were very good and very brave. Furthermore, we couldn't understand how the leaders of the revolution could live abroad, in Egypt, France, and other countries, and travel around the world, while their people were fighting and dying there [in the Fizi-Baraka], and no one was there to tell them why.[54]

Che tried desperately to counter the negative attitudes of both Cubans and Simbas. "I kept insisting on what I believed to be fundamental. . . . We had to integrate ourselves more and more into the [Zairean] liberation movement, and we had to become, in the eyes of the Simbas, just like them." Therefore he wanted the Cubans to live with the rebels, eat what they ate, share everything. When their boots fell apart, they should go barefoot, unless there were also boots for the Simbas; and when they lacked medicine they should go without unless there was enough for the Simbas. It did not work. "I changed my policy about the supplies, because it proved wrong," Che wrote. "We had arrived with the idea of . . . sharing all the hardships of the Zaireans and showing them, through our spirit of sacrifice, how to become revolutionary soldiers, but the result was that our men were starving, barefoot, and almost naked, while the Zaireans divided up the boots and uniforms that they got from other sources among themselves. All we had done was to provoke discontent among the Cubans."[55]

"Compañeros," Che wrote on August 12 in a message to his men, "some of us have already been here for almost four months. . . . We cannot say that the situation is good." The rebel leaders were spending "most of their time away from the territory" and the Simbas' morale was low and their fighting skills were poor, but, he insisted, this should only spur the Cubans to greater sacrifice:

Our mission is to help [them] win the war. . . . We must be eager to teach, but . . . we must not look down on those who are uninformed; on the contrary, we must let them feel our human warmth. . . . We must have the modesty of true revolutionaries . . . and a spirit of sacrifice that will be an example not only for our Zairean compañeros but also for the weakest among us. We must never worry whether our position is more dangerous than that of others or whether more is demanded of us; one must demand more of a true revolutionary because he has more to give. Let's not forget that we know only a fraction of what we should know; we must learn about Zaire in order to grow closer to our Zairean compañeros. . . .

One disrespectful action can spoil forty positive deeds. . . . Our main task is to prepare men for the war—not just how to kill but especially how to endure the hardship of a long struggle—and we can only do this if we truly grow close to them. . . . You must not forget this, compañeros, just as you must not forget that if a veteran of our war of liberation [against Batista] says that he never ran away, you can tell him to his face that he is lying. We all ran away, and we all went through dark times when the shadows frightened us.[56]

What Che was asking of his men was almost superhuman. He acknowledged as much himself: "I don't need good men," he wrote to Fidel on October 5. "Here, we need supermen."[57] And he succeeded, in part: there are no reports of the Cubans—unlike the mercenaries, the ANC, and the Simbas—perpetrating any crimes or acts of violence against the population in Zaire.[58]

But there were the "rajados" (quitters), those who asked to be sent back to Cuba. This has been a deep, painful secret for the Cubans. I heard of it for the first time only after months of interviews, so shameful was the memory. Suddenly, one day, one member of the column said simply, "Of course, there were the rajados." But he refused to give details. I then pressed the point with others. "Yes," they conceded, "it's true, but there were only a few, and, in the end, all of them asked to fight again." Fernández Mell was curt, and emphatic. "They told Che that they wanted to go back to Cuba, and he took their weapons away. That's the worst thing you can do to a guerrilla. Che made them do domestic chores: cook, search for wood. During our last days [in the Fizi-Baraka], they all asked for their weapons back, and they fought again. One by one, they all rejoined the ranks. But," he stressed, "there were only a few of them."[59]

I was skeptical. If there were really so few, why the wall of silence? Then I read "Pasajes."

Yes, the rajados existed and, yes, there were just a few. Che carefully recorded what was for him, obviously, a horrible cross to bear. It began, suddenly, after the battle of Bendera. "To my surprise," he writes,

> three of the men who had participated in the attack . . . announced they wanted to go home. To make matters worse, one of them was a member of the [Communist] party. . . . I chastised them and warned them that I would request the strongest sanctions against them. . . .
>
> As if to increase my surprise and my pain, compañero Sitaini, who had been with me since the war [against Batista] and had been my aide for six years, said that he wanted to go back to Cuba. What made it even more painful was that he pretended not to have heard what I had warned everyone about—that the war would last at least three years and with bad luck five. . . . I told him that he couldn't leave because it would discredit all of us.[60]

Over the next two weeks four more members of the column asked to leave. In early August, three more asked to return to Cuba. "I was extremely harsh with them, refusing categorically to consider their requests."[61]

Che referred to the rajados in his August 12 message to the column. "You all know," he said,

> that a group of compañeros have not honored their commitment as revolutionaries and have betrayed the trust placed in each of them and have asked to abandon the struggle. This cannot be justified, and I will demand the most severe moral sanctions against these compañeros. Nevertheless, we must not forget that they are not traitors; they must not be treated with open contempt. Understand me well: their action is the most contemptible possible for a revolutionary, but it is only contemptible if done by a revolutionary. Otherwise it would be simple cowardice. . . . They must still spend months here; if we empathize with the shame they must certainly feel . . . we may save some of them and persuade them to remain and share our fate, which, whatever it may be, is one thousand times better than that of a quitter. Without forgetting their faults, let's give them some human warmth.[62]

At first, there were 11 rajados, including 3 doctors, out of 128 men, but in August, Che writes, "three of the compañeros who had said they wanted to leave the war asked to be reintegrated."[63]

I met one of the rajados, a doctor, Chumi, an articulate, sensitive man. It was clear that the experience still troubled him, deeply. "Hindi [another doctor] and I told Che that the war was pointless." Che refused to let them leave, and they continued to work as doctors, as before, at the front.[64]

Chumi impressed me. After our conversation, I went back to Che's evaluation of his men, which he wrote in the Cuban embassy in Dar-es-Salaam. Chumi, Che wrote, "was one of the first who asked to abandon the struggle." Che ordered him to stay—"and he accepted reluctantly." Nonetheless, "he was a good doctor and toward the end he said that he was once again ready to fight."

Hindi had "made the same request," received the same answer, and, thereafter, "he maintained a good attitude and demonstrated courage."[65] It is interesting to note that after the column had returned to Cuba, Chumi was asked whether he was willing to serve as a doctor among the guerrillas in Guinea-Bissau, and he went in 1967.[66]

This, then, is the story of the rajados, Cuba's bitter secret. Eleven men tried to abandon the struggle. Not one surrendered to the enemy; not one deserted. And yet, I believe, the Cuban authorities' sense of shame about this predictable occurrence is one of the reasons they kept Che's manuscript secret for so long.

"I must now undertake the most difficult analysis, my self-criticism," Che wrote in the concluding pages of "Pasajes."

> Plumbing my depths, I have come to the following conclusions: I was unable to overcome the problems that my somewhat unusual way of entering Zaire caused in my relations with the Simba leaders. . . . I did not learn Swahili fast enough and deeply enough. This was a failure due, primarily, to my knowledge of French, which allowed me to communicate with the [Simba] leaders but distanced me from the rank and file. I lacked the willpower to make the necessary effort.
>
> In my contact with my men, I believe I showed enough self-sacrifice to prevent anyone from impugning me (my two fundamental weaknesses, however, were satisfied: cigars . . . and books). . . . The discomfort of having damaged boots or only one change of dirty clothes, or eating the same slop as the troops and living in the same conditions, for me this is not a sacrifice. But my habit of retiring to read, escaping the daily problems, did tend to distance me from the men, without mentioning that there are aspects of my character that make intimacy difficult. I was exacting, but I don't believe excessively so. . . . I tried to make my men see the situation from my point of view and I failed; they could not look optimistically into a future that had to be imagined through a gloomy present.[67]

These last few lines touched on Che's greatest mistake in Zaire: his excessive optimism led him to condemn the realism of others as weakness.[68] He became increasingly harsh, relying more and more on diatribes to spur his men, and he became more unapproachable. Far more than his reading separated him from his men. Searching for an explanation of this growing distance, he wrote in the last pages of "Pasajes" that "my relations with the column were affected by my farewell letter to Fidel [which Fidel made public on October 3]—I could sense this very clearly, although it is completely subjective. This made my men see me, like many years ago . . . in the Sierra, as a foreigner; then as one who had just arrived, now as one who was preparing to leave. There were some things we no longer shared, some common desires I had silently or explicitly renounced and which are the most sacred to every individual: his family, his country, his surroundings. The letter . . . created a gulf between me and my men."[69]

Perhaps. But Che underestimated another reason for the distance he felt from his men. The pages of "Pasajes"—as Che relates those last, harrowing weeks in the Fizi-Baraka—indicate that many of his men had begun to doubt the common sense of his leadership; they had begun to fear that he was pushing them toward a sacrifice that was pointless. For Che, the simple fact that his men were glad when the boats appeared in the early hours of November 21 to take them away from certain and, to them, meaningless death proved their weakness. It is not surprising, then, that distance grew between Che and some (or many) of these men. And yet, with the exception of the handful of rajados, they kept fighting even though they believed that their effort was doomed. When Che, in October, called a meeting of all the Communist Party members at his front (possibly half of the thirty-five Cubans who were with him) and asked who among them still believed in the possibility of victory, only Dreke, Papi, and two doctors raised their hands and Che wondered whether they might just be showing their support of him. When Che asked the party members whether they were ready to keep on fighting until death, "they all raised their hands."[70]

Che's optimism distanced him from his men, but his willingness to endure any sacrifice and share any hardship commanded respect and admiration. He never asked more of them than he demanded of himself. He lashed out at those he felt deserved it, but he also lashed out at himself, in front of his men, when he felt he was at fault. He believed, for example, that his leadership had been inadequate during a clash with the mercenaries in which a young volunteer had been mortally wounded. On the morning of October 26, as they buried their comrade, Che addressed his men. "In a monologue heavy with self-reproach, I acknowledged my mistakes and told them . . . that I was responsible for this death. I told them that I would do everything I could to make atonement; I would work harder and with more vigor than ever."[71]

Unlike his men, Che left Zaire confident that the Simbas would ultimately emerge victorious. This victory would not be easy. "What will our contribution be?" he asked.

> Perhaps we will send some cadres . . . weapons . . . perhaps money. But we must change one of the precepts that has guided our revolutionary strategy until now. . . . We must . . . tie our aid to the behavior of the movements and their leaders. . . .
>
> Finally, if I were asked whether there is a leader in Zaire whom I consider capable of becoming a national leader, I could not answer affirmatively, leaving aside Mulele, whom I do not know. The only man who has the charisma to lead the masses is, I think, Kabila. . . . However, he has not yet developed an ideology or displayed the seriousness and spirit of sacrifice necessary to be the leader of a revolution. . . . He is young and may change, but I . . . have very great doubts that he will be able to overcome his deficiencies.[72]

These were the last lines of "Pasajes." As Che had hoped, Zaire served as a learning experience. In 1966, the Cubans began an operation in Guinea-Bissau in which they avoided many of the mistakes made in Zaire, and in which Dreke, who had been at Che's side in Zaire, was the most important commander.

For Cuba, the cost of failure in Zaire was primarily psychological. The operation had not been costly in human lives—six volunteers had been killed, none captured. The column's presence (and its retreat) had not been made public, and the episode did not have a negative effect on Cuba's interests elsewhere in Africa. Furthermore, whereas Cuba's support for armed struggle in Latin America generated friction with the Soviet Union, there is no indication that this occurred in Zaire. Fernández Padilla and Rivalta assert that they were in contact with Soviet and Chinese officials in Dar-es-Salaam while the column was in the Fizi-Baraka, and that these officials were supportive.[73] Their recollection is corroborated by the only available document that bears on the subject: a letter from Fernández Padilla to Che on November 18 describing how he and Rivalta had asked Soviet and Chinese officials in Dar-es-Salaam to help them persuade Nyerere to reconsider his request that the column leave Zaire.[74] They would not have turned to the Soviets and Chinese had Moscow and Beijing opposed the column's mission.

Actually it would have been surprising if Moscow (or Beijing) had opposed the Cuban operation. Cubans, Soviets, and Chinese were all supporting the rebels in the Fizi-Baraka. We know from "Pasajes" that Moscow and Beijing were the major source of outside aid to the Simbas, and an East German report of November 1965 indicates that the Kremlin intended to continue sending them aid even though, a Soviet official noted, "one must quite frankly acknowledge that at present there is no hope of success."[75]

Aleksandr Alekseev, the Soviet ambassador in Cuba, has asserted that Moscow did not know that Castro was sending a column to Zaire until the column was on its way to Tanzania. The operation was certainly mounted without Soviet help: the volunteers flew on commercial flights to Dar-es-Salaam and DGI officers brought their weapons to Dar-es-Salaam on commercial flights, even though Soviet ships and planes stopped there regularly.[76] There is no indication that the Soviets helped the Cubans once they were in the Fizi-Baraka, and their help was not necessary. It is clear from "Pasajes" that Che's problems were not caused by any lack of assistance from the Soviets. Take, for example, his need for Cuban crews for the boats—the answer was in Havana, not Moscow. The same is true for the lack of radio communications. On one occasion, however, the Cubans turned to the Soviet Union for help, and Moscow delivered: two Aeroflot planes arrived at Dar-es-Salaam to take the column back to Havana.

It is Tanzania, not the Soviet Union, that deserves special mention in a discussion of the Cuban operation in Zaire. Nyerere supported the column wholeheartedly. "He had told his minister of the interior to help us," Fernández Padilla recalled. "We [the support group] also met frequently with [Vice-President] Kawawa and [Foreign Minister] Kambona. They were very helpful. Everything was very well organized, very well structured. When we had to, we went all the way to Nyerere."[77]

Reeling from the shock of Tanzania's demand that the Cubans withdraw, Che was bitter, calling it "the coup de grâce."[78] This was unfair. The rebel cause was irrevocably lost, and Nyerere knew it. Tanzania was overexposed: its support of Frelimo invited reprisals from the Portuguese, and its support of the Simbas could have provoked incursions from the mercenaries. It had virtually no army, and it was estranged from those Western countries that could have restrained Tshombe and Lisbon: the United States was exasperated by its support of the Simbas, and England was irritated by its stance on Rhodesia, where the whites were moving toward a unilateral declaration of independence (UDI) in order to block majority rule.[a]

If Che had persisted in a doomed cause, he would have sacrificed his men; had Nyerere persisted, he would have endangered his country. When the president withdrew Tanzania from the war, he did so with dignity, and he treated the Cubans with respect as they waited in Dar-es-Salaam to leave for Havana. "Nyerere handled our [the column's] departure admirably," Rivalta remarked. "He placed a stadium and several dignitaries' houses at our disposal, and then he let us organize our departure ourselves."[79]

Throughout their joint endeavor, Tanzania had been Cuba's ally, not its client. When Osmany Cienfuegos arrived at Dar-es-Salaam in May 1965, he had to get Tanzania's permission before he could visit the column in Zaire. And Havana had to seek Tanzania's permission to station a few Cubans in Kigoma to help maintain and operate the boats.[80] The Cubans were guests in Tanzania and, with one exception, they behaved as such.

The exception was that Che had entered Zaire in April without informing Nyerere. Toward the end of June, he wrote Rivalta asking him to tell the Tanzanian authorities of his whereabouts and "to apologize to them for the way [he had entered Zaire]." However, he instructed the bearer of the letter to stop first in Kigoma "to ask Kabila's opinion. When Kabila learned what I intended to do, he categorically objected to informing the Tanzanians and said that he would explain why when he got to Zaire."[81] Che raised the issue when Kabila came to Luluabourg in July, but to no avail.

a. Nyerere wanted British prime minister Harold Wilson to send troops to prevent UDI, but Wilson decided to follow British public opinion, which was, the CIA noted, "firmly opposed to the use of force against 'kith and kin.'" After UDI on November 11, Tanzania was one of the sponsors of an OAU resolution pledging the member states to break diplomatic relations with London if the Rhodesian rebellion had not been crushed by December 15. On December 15 Tanzania was the first of nine OAU members to do so. (CIA, OCI, "The Rhodesian Situation: African Pressure and British Dilemma," Dec. 11, 1965, p. 7 quoted, NSFCF, box 97; CIA, OCI, "African Response to the Rhodesian Rebellion," Jan. 3, 1966, ibid.; Niblock, "Aid," pp. 289–313.)

One wonders, however, whether Che and Havana remained silent for all those months simply in deference to Kabila's wishes. It is more likely that they were relieved to have an excuse, or, at least, that they were ambivalent about it. "We were worried that they [the Tanzanians] might get scared," Ferrer remarked, "that they would worry that Che's presence would provoke the United States." Rivalta informed Nyerere only after Che had left Tanzania in early 1966, explaining that the silence had been due to security considerations. The Tanzanians were angry, but the column had left, and their relations with Cuba remained friendly.[82]

Meanwhile, across Lake Tanganyika, Mobutu was tightening his grip over a cowed population. He was "the latest in a series of disastrous Congolese [Zairean] leaders," the NSC Africa specialist wrote with refreshing candor,[83] but he was solidly pro-American and Washington was forbearing—even when, in October 1966, he asked for the recall of Ambassador Godley.

When Godley and CIA station chief Devlin had directed the war against the Simbas in 1964–65, Mobutu had been a cog, the commander of an army that was utterly dependent on the mercenaries and Washington. Times had changed. The Simbas had been crushed, and Mobutu was the president of Zaire. Unlike Devlin, Godley found it difficult to make the transition and treat the dictator with the respect he craved. And so Mobutu sent him packing. Washington was unfazed. It wanted a client in Zaire who could be an influential player in Africa, not a puppet despised by the African leaders. "Our bilateral relations with the Congo [Zaire] receded—healthily, I think—from a pro-consul status to something more approaching a standard relation between independent foreign powers," the NSC Africa staffer wrote two months after Godley had left Zaire.[84]

Eager to "gain respect in African councils," Mobutu broke diplomatic relations with Portugal, and began, "occasionally if reluctantly, to promote the cult of the 'martyred' Patrice Lumumba," in whose murder he had connived. And he proceeded to ease the mercenaries out of Zaire. Having crushed the Simbas, they were no longer needed; they had become "an embarrassment," the *New York Times* explained.[85]

By May 1967 some 230 mercenaries remained in Zaire, down from 1,000 when Mobutu had seized power in November 1965. They knew that they too would soon be asked to leave and so, on July 5, 1967, they rebelled, dragging with them about 1,000 Zairean soldiers. U.S. government reports explain what followed. "Mesmerized by supposed mercenary invulnerability," the ANC responded to the uprising with customary cowardice, compensating for its "dismal failure" to engage the mercenaries by indulging in savage violence against the population. Mobutu turned to Washington, asking Johnson for three C-130 transport planes with U.S. crews to ferry Zairean troops and military supplies. "I am acutely aware of difficult moral, human and public relations position in which US gvt has been placed over Congolese [Zairean] C-130 request because of [ANC's] repulsive brutality," Ambassador Robert McBride cabled on July 8, as he endorsed Mobutu's request. The Johnson administration stood by its man. "We must keep Mobutu in power because there is no acceptable alternative to him," Under Secretary of State Nicholas Katzenbach told a July 13 NSC meeting. No one disagreed.[86] The administration made its views clear to Brussels and Lisbon, where there was some sympathy for the mercenaries. It sent the three C-130s with U.S. crews as well as Cuban exiles to fly Mobutu's T-28s, which were grounded because Mobutu no longer trusted his own pilots.[87] This time no African government criticized Washington's actions—none wanted a mercenary victory.

Totally isolated, the mercenaries, who had holed up in the eastern town of Bukavu, were able to hold out for five months only because of the staggering ineptness of the ANC. "At no time did the ANC penetrate the thinly held mercenary perimeter or otherwise seriously challenge the military integrity of the rebel force," the U.S. Defense Intelligence Agency noted. Finally, on November 5, when their ammunition "was virtually expended," the mercenaries withdrew to Rwanda, unopposed. Mobutu wanted them returned to Zaire to stand trial. But the mercenaries were white, and in 1964–65 they had done the West's job against the Simbas, saving in the process "innocent lives—mostly white lives," the *New York Times* explained. Their trial, and likely execution, would have offended Western sensibilities. And it could have led to embarrassing revelations about their contacts with the CIA. "We believe best interests of everyone including Congolese [Zaireans] would be served if mercs were allowed to leave Africa," Rusk cabled Ambassador McBride in Kinshasa, Leopold-ville's new name. Mobutu understood, and in April 1968 the mercenaries were flown to Europe in two planes chartered by the International Red Cross. (Their Zairean auxiliaries, who were not white and had nowhere to go, were handed over to Mobutu with the promise of amnesty and were slaughtered.)[88]

"Mr. President, . . . A stormy chapter has quietly closed in the Congo [Zaire]," National Security Adviser Walt Rostow told Johnson the day after the two planes with the mercenaries had reached Europe. The administration had reason to celebrate. The Simbas had been crushed, the mercenaries were gone, Mobutu was firmly in the saddle, he was poised to become a major player in sub-Saharan Africa, and he knew to whom he owed his success. "President Mobutu clearly regards the United States as the Congo's [Zaire's] best friend," Vice-President Hubert Humphrey told Johnson after visiting Kinshasa in January 1968. Relations were "excellent," a State Department study concluded at the end of the Johnson administration.[89]

U.S. officials boasted about "Moscow's debacle" in Zaire and the Chinese "humiliating" defeat there. But they virtually ignored the Cubans, even though Cuba alone had sent men to Zaire to help the rebels. The concern expressed by Godley in a September 1965 cable about the presence of a large group of Cubans in Fizi-Baraka had been fleeting; two months later, the Simbas had been crushed and the Cubans were gone. Soon, the memory that the Cubans had been in

Zaire faded away. In late 1967 a CIA memorandum provided an overview of Communist subversion in Africa over the past few years. It mentioned that "some" Cubans had fought alongside the Simbas and noted that the Cuban presence in the continent was "not large," but that on one occasion "Havana was able to make a major contribution to maintaining a radical, anti-western regime in power."[90] This had been in the Congo, Zaire's neighbor, where a Cuban column had arrived in the summer 1965.

CHAPTER EIGHT
CUBANS IN THE CONGO

Brazzaville, the capital of the Congo, had been one of Che's most important stops during his three-month trip to Africa in early 1965. While there, he had promised a troop of Cuban soldiers to the Congolese government and Cuban military instructors to the leaders of the MPLA, the leftist Angolan rebel movement. In all likelihood, the column that assembled at Peti-1 on February 2 and went to Zaire had originally been intended for the Congo. Havana's commitment to send a column to the Congo, however, remained.

The vanguard of this column—nine military instructors—left Mariel aboard the *Uvero* on April 26, 1965, two days after Che had entered the Fizi-Baraka with thirteen men. "We were the first explorers," the leader of the group, Manuel Agramonte, explained. "We were going to uncharted lands." They disembarked in Conakry and flew to Accra, where there was still no news about Darío Urra, the intelligence officer who was meant to open the Cuban embassy in Brazzaville. "Entralgo [the Cuban ambassador to Ghana] phoned the Congolese Foreign Ministry to ask whether Urra had arrived," Agramonte remembered. "They said he had, and they told us where he was staying." The nine Cubans flew to Brazzaville on May 20. No one met them at the airport. They went straight to the hotel where Urra and the five members of his staff were staying. "They looked as lost as we did. We all stayed in the same hotel, and the Cuban embassy was also there for a few weeks," Urra explained. "We were all blacks," he added.[1]

The fall of Ben Bella one month later deprived Cuba of its closest friend in Africa and increased the importance of Brazzaville, which became, with Dar-es-Salaam, a center of Cuban activities on the continent. Serguera was reassigned from Algeria to the Congo as resident ambassador. Then, in late July, Castro summoned Jorge Risquet.

THE SECOND COLUMN

During Batista's dictatorship, Risquet had been second in command of the youth wing of the outlawed Cuban Communist Party (PSP). An intelligent and forceful man, he is an intellectual with a good dose of common sense and, occasionally, a sense of humor. After working in the party's urban underground and spending five months in jail, where he was tortured, he joined Castro's guerrillas in the Sierra Maestra in mid-1958. After the overthrow of Batista, Risquet occupied a series of senior positions in the army and government. In 1965 he was secretary of organization of the fledgling Cuban Communist Party

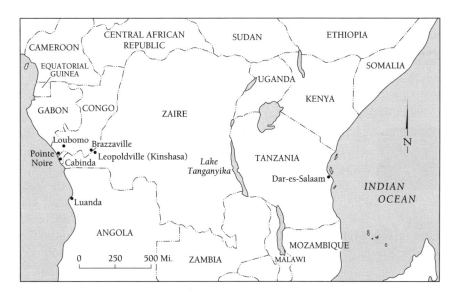

Central Africa

(PCC) in the province of Oriente when, "out of the blue, Fidel sent for me. I wondered," Risquet recalled, " 'What have I done wrong?' "[2]

Castro briefed him on Che's column in Zaire, and then, Risquet remarked, "without pausing for breath, he told me about his plans for the Congo." Cuba was preparing to send an armed column of approximately 250 men there. "Fidel was worried about the safety of the two columns [one in Zaire, the other planned for the Congo], which involved almost 400 Cubans, and had decided to strengthen the command structure," Risquet explained diplomatically. In fact, Castro had reason to be worried. Serguera was bold, brave, and lacking in common sense; he was the right man to storm an enemy position, but not to preside over a major covert operation. His latest exploit had been his arrival in Brazzaville with a French woman, Elizabeth Lagache, whom he had met in Algeria and would later marry. It was a romantic tale—and a gross breach of security. Therefore Castro created an unusual structure: in the Congo there would be a military commander of the Cuban troops (Rolando Kindelán), an ambassador (Serguera), and, above both, Risquet, who would lead the column.[3]

Castro told Risquet that his job "was to help the MPLA wage its guerrilla war, to defend the Congo . . . against aggression from Zaire, and to help the Congolese government . . . form a militia to strengthen the country's ability to counter foreign aggression, to keep reactionary army cliques in check and, if necessary, to defeat a military coup." (The Congolese leaders did not trust the tiny Congolese army: it had been created by the French before independence and its officers had graduated from French military schools.) The column also had a more tentative task: "It was . . . a reserve force for Che's troop in Zaire, which it would join if the opportunity presented itself."[4]

In 1965, 400 Cuban soldiers left their homeland to stoke the flames of revolution in Africa. One column, led by Che Guevara, went to Zaire. The other, led by Jorge Risquet, went to the Congo. Castro told Risquet that his column must train and assist the Angolan rebels based in the Congo and defend the government there. They should also be prepared to provide "a reserve force for Che's troop in Zaire, which it would join if the opportunity presented itself." Aboard the Soviet liner that took the Cuban column to the Congo, Risquet (right) and the Soviet captain of the ship shake hands, having swapped uniforms in a friendly jest.

During the spring of 1965, the column had trained in the Petis. "We were preparing for our mission, but we didn't know what it was going to be," Kindelán recalled. They left Mariel on August 6 aboard the Soviet liner *Felix Dzerzhinskii*. "We rented the *Dzerzhinskii*," Risquet explained. "Since we were going at the request of a government [rather than an insurgent group], the Soviet Union didn't have any problem with it. And it was safer for us." The Cubans, who were always haunted by the prospect of a U.S. attack, thought that there was little danger that the Americans would interfere with a Soviet ship.[5]

The *Dzerzhinskii* reached Pointe Noire, the Congo's only seaport, on August 21. Like the members of Guevara's column, almost all of Risquet's men were black. This confused Western officials. "One hundred fifty Cubans have disembarked at Brazzaville [sic]," de Gaulle's point man on Africa, Jacques Foccart, noted. "When I say one hundred fifty Cubans, I mean that thirty are real Cubans; the others are Africans who have been trained in Cuba." The West German embassy reported the arrival of "one hundred twenty Africans . . . from Mozambique and Angola," while British ambassador Terry Empson cabled that "a dozen or so Cubans plus about fifty Africans" had landed at Pointe Noire. "They then disappeared and I have no reliable information as to where they are now, but it seems quite possible that the Africans are M.P.L.A.-trainees returning and the Cubans are instructors for the M.P.L.A. camps. The Cuban embassy here," Empson added, "has grown considerably over the past month and now includes a Military Attaché who, in reply to my disingenuous question as to what he would find to do here, replied simply, 'Don't be naive!' "[6]

From Pointe Noire, most of the Cubans went to Madibou, a camp some six miles southwest of Brazzaville. Smaller groups stayed in Pointe Noire or went to Loubomo, the country's third-largest city. "The oral agreement [with the Congolese government] was that our troops would remain in the Congo for one year, that is, until August 21, 1966," Risquet writes. It was understood that they might stay longer, if both governments deemed it useful.[7]

A VERBAL REVOLUTION

Risquet and his men had never been in Africa. They knew nothing of the Congo, but they had been told they would find a revolutionary government there determined to uproot the neocolonial structures left by the French and to spread revolution abroad. They were in for a shock. The strident leftist rhetoric of the Congolese leaders bore little relationship to their policies. The Congolese revolution was, notes a scholar, "a verbal revolution, a salon revolution." The rhetoric masked opportunism, personal feuding, and ethnic polarization.[8]

On one point, however, the Congolese leaders were in agreement: they all feared and loathed Tshombe. They were "very conscious," in the British ambassador's words, "of their inability to stop the A.N.C. [Zairean army] striking where and how it would, if it wanted to." Behind Tshombe loomed the United States. "We are particularly concerned about the possibility that the American imperialists will act through their puppet Tshombe," Prime Minister Pascal Lissouba told an East German official in February 1965. "Although the strong anti-US attitudes of the Brazzaville government are to be expected as a matter of course from the extremists who dominate the regime," the CIA noted three months later, "they also have specific anxieties stemming chiefly from the important US involvement in the affairs of Congo (Leopoldville) [Zaire]."[9]

These anxieties were exacerbated by the Americans in their midst. "The Americans in Brazzaville have been very heavy-handed," the West German ambassador, Jakob Hasslacher, wrote. "Their unusually large embassy—they have, for example, three military attachés alone—was bound to arouse fears of subversion and interference in the internal affairs of the Congo." For their part, the Americans were at a loss to understand what was going on in Brazzaville. "It was like something out of a Graham Greene novel," a political officer at the U.S. embassy recalled, "what with the Russians, and the Chinese, and the Cubans!"[10] They did not have long to figure it out: in August 1965, following three incidents in which U.S. diplomats alleged that they had been harassed, Washington closed its embassy in Brazzaville, over the strong objections of its own ambassador, who argued that "our case isn't all that airtight." Brazzaville responded by closing its embassy in Washington. (The embassies were not reopened until 1977.)[11]

The departure of the Americans barely affected the West's position in the Congo: France remained the dominant foreign presence. "The French continue to run virtually all the modern sector [of the economy]," the CIA noted. "Our economic, financial, cultural, and political ties with France are in many ways as strong as they were when we were a colony," President Massamba-Débat stated in January 1965. "We're like an old married couple that no longer has the passion of newlyweds (which so often leads to arguments, or even divorce), but who love each other with that delicate, serene, and strong affection that gradually makes their reflexes, their attitudes, and their tastes strangely similar." The acting foreign minister of the Congo put it less poetically: "France has us in a stranglehold."[12]

As the regime "veered sharply to the left" in 1964, in the CIA's words, its rhetoric hardened. By the time Risquet's column arrived, the Congolese leaders were proclaiming their Marxist-Leninist leanings, but they were also keenly aware of their dependence on foreign aid, as they demonstrated in their handling of the German question. West Germany was the second-largest donor after France. Relations between Bonn and Brazzaville were "excellent," the Belgian embassy noted. Bonn was "extraordinarily important" to the Congo's economy, an East German official pointed out. Therefore, their rhetoric notwithstanding, the Congolese leaders consistently rebuffed the entreaties of the German Democratic Republic (GDR) to establish relations between Brazzaville and East Berlin. Ambassador Hasslacher noted proudly that "Alone among the progressive capitals of Africa, Brazzaville still has no official or unofficial representative of the Soviet Occupation Zone [GDR]."[13]

Except when it came to the GDR, however, the Congolese leaders were eager to develop ties with the socialist countries and proclaimed the virtues of nonalignment. "The policy of nonalignment opens new vistas and brings new friendships, and therefore enhances our prospects for international aid," Massamba-Débat explained. By early 1965 the socialist countries—the "new friends," as Massamba-Débat called them—were present in force: North Korea, North Vietnam, Yugoslavia, Czechoslovakia, the Soviet Union, and the People's Republic of China had opened embassies. Wisely, Brazzaville cultivated good relations with both Moscow and Beijing, and both gave economic aid.[14]

The CIA was convinced that Chinese instructors were training the Congolese army. This claim was, however, pure fantasy. "Despite its many efforts, the People's Republic of China has been unable to gain any influence whatsoever in the army," Ambassador Hasslacher reported in July 1966. There were only two Chinese military instructors in the Congo, he added, "one of them—with the help of an interpreter—teaches the history of the Chinese Revolutionary Army." Half a dozen Egyptians were training the paratroop battalion, a few Russians were training the army's artillery unit, and a French military mission was training the gendarmerie.[15] And there were Cubans.

The Cubans had by far the strongest military presence in the country, and they were the government's most trusted foreign partner. The Congolese leaders, Hasslacher wrote, "see Cuba as the communist country that has most in common with the Congo; the Cubans have Congolese blood in their veins; their country is in the tropics and was also exploited as a colony; Cuba is not a great power that could threaten the Congo, but a small country that is itself threatened by the superpowers, above all the United States."[16]

The Cubans lived in spartan conditions like the Chinese, but, unlike the Chinese, they made friends with the Congolese and partied with them. Their shared love of dance and music strengthened the bond. (One of the most popular bands in the Congo, Aragonés, was Cuban.) French officials warned that their " 'Latin temperament' " made the Cubans "more influential and therefore more dangerous than the Chinese." The Belgian chargé agreed. "The Cubans are really very popular," he remarked.[17] "Beards and cigars are becoming fads," the New York Times reported from Brazzaville in March 1966. "What strikes the visitor," it noted,

is not the revolutionary fervor of Brazzaville but the bourgeois comforts it offers. President Massamba Debat's Cuban aides, if they were so inclined, could be far more self-indulgent than the Belgian military officers who advise President Joseph Mobutu in the other Congo [Zaire]. The stores and restaurants here are an epicure's delight with shipments arriving by air from Paris. It is a strange feeling to be sitting at the terrace of the Hotel Relais, reading about "the second phase of the revolution" and deciding whether to have chateaubriand or lobster. . . .

But it is neither the Cubans nor the Chinese . . . who enjoy the delicacies.

Those are here for the French officials who still play a vital role in public administration, and for businessmen passing through.[18]

The Cubans were on a tight budget. Their salary was deposited in Cuba, and they received only a modest monthly stipend in local currency, roughly $15 for the soldiers and $30 for the officers.[19] As in Algeria, the host country was not expected to pay anything. Western embassies confirmed that the Cubans were "paid exclusively by the Cuban government," but they were unable to ascertain how many Cubans were in the Congo. "Their number is impossible to estimate, and they are difficult to pick out because they are all colored," the Belgian ambassador noted. Estimates varied from 100 to 800.[20]

The 1,350-man Congolese army had welcomed the Cubans as a shield against Tshombe's mercenaries, but its welcome faded when they began training the militia, which had been established in June 1965 to be a counterweight to it. The army's resentment grew as the need for the Cuban shield lessened after the ouster of Tshombe in October 1965. For the civilian leaders of the Congo, however, the shield remained as necessary as ever, as a series of military coups in Africa—including those against Ben Bella in June 1965 and Nkrumah in February 1966—demonstrated how dangerous an army could be. The weekly *Dipanda*, which was very close to the youth branch of the ruling Mouvement National de la Révolution (MNR), called for civilian control of the army and a strong militia: "We must never forget that power flows from the barrel of the gun," it warned in February 1966.[21] A military coup seemed to be a distinct possibility. Fearing that military rebels might blow up or seize the bridge spanning the Djoué River that separated Madibou from Brazzaville, Risquet moved his force in early 1966 to the camp of the Bosque, on the outskirts of the capital, in order to be ready to intervene at once, if necessary.[22]

THE CUBAN DOCTORS

The Cuban column included a small medical brigade: five doctors, a dentist, two nurses, and two nurse's aides.[23] All were volunteers, but three of them—Manuel Jacas, a surgeon; Rodrigo Álvarez Cambras, an orthopedist; and Julián Álvarez, a clinician—had volunteered to go to Vietnam, not the Congo.

"We all graduated at the same time," Julián Álvarez recalled, "and we were doing our social service (new doctors were sent to rural areas) when we bumped into each other in the Ministry of Public Health. It was early 1965. Álvarez Cambras asked me, 'Would you be willing to go to Vietnam?' 'Of course,' I said. (The United States had recently begun bombing North Vietnam and people were eager to help Hanoi.)"[24] About one month later all three were called back to Havana, where the minister of public health, Machado Ventura, told them: "'Stay in Havana; we'll pay for your hotel. Eat in restaurants. Bring us the receipts, and we'll pay.' We were stunned: Machado was known to be very stingy, a real tightwad. We looked at each other in disbelief." And so they

When the Cubans arrived in the Congo in 1965, nine foreign doctors served the entire civilian population of 850,000 people. Two of these doctors had been sent by the North Vietnamese government. In 1967 the two doctors (far left and far right) visited Manuel Agramonte, Cuba's ambassador to the Congo, and Agramonte's wife. It was Agramonte's first diplomatic assignment, but he was already well versed in Congolese affairs: he had been a senior officer in the Cuban military mission in the Congo since 1965.

remained in Havana, eating in restaurants and sending the check to Machado Ventura. "We got used to the good life!"

The days went by. They were taken to a safe house, then to the Petis. "There were blacks, blacks, blacks!" (The three doctors are white.) They heard people talking about two columns, and they assumed that one column was for Vietnam and the other for Africa and that by mistake they had been assigned to the Africa column. They went to see Machado Ventura. "'We're worried,'" they told him. "'They've put us in the wrong column.' Machado started laughing: 'You're not going to Vietnam; you're going to Africa.'" A few days later, they boarded the *Dzerzhinskii* for Brazzaville.

Before the Cubans arrived, there were only nine doctors—two Congolese, three French, two North Vietnamese, one Angolan, and one Zairean—treating the entire civilian population of the Congo, a country of some 850,000 people. (A few Egyptian doctors staffed the military hospital.)[25] "It was depressing," Dr. Rodolfo Puente Ferro, who was in charge of the Cuban medical brigade, remarked. To address the problem, the Cubans offered full scholarships to 210 Congolese teenagers to attend secondary school and, eventually, nursing, agronomy, or, ideally, medical school in Cuba. Unfortunately, the Congolese government selected many of the teens on the basis of personal connections (or bribes), and quite a few had almost no schooling. Nevertheless, on January 24, 1966, 254 young Congolese left for Havana aboard the Cuban ship *Luis Arcos Bergnes*.[26] Cuba bore all the expenses: transportation, board, lodging, clothing, and a small monthly stipend. This was the first time a significant number of foreign scholarship students were in Cuba, and there were misunderstandings. Some of the Congolese, including some who were virtually illiterate, expected to enter the university right away and become doctors. They felt cheated, and there were some incidents, even the beginning of a riot. By late 1967 more than 100 students had returned to the Congo, some at their own request, some not. "Cuba is obviously not in a position to handle a large number of foreign students," the West German embassy in Brazzaville remarked. "Furthermore, it seems that the Congolese who were selected were not exactly the most disciplined or hardworking."[27] However, in 1969, 41 Congolese were studying in technical schools and 24 were at the university, and by 1978, 25 had earned their medical degrees. "What Cuba did for us was immense," one of the Congolese students recalled. "What Cuba did—a small, poor country like that—no other country did as much."[28]

Meanwhile, in Brazzaville the Cuban doctors organized the Congo's first vaccination campaign against polio. "The dreaded poliomyelitis has struck many victims in the Congo," *La Semaine* reported. "In Brazzaville, more than one thousand children are afflicted by it." Therefore, remarked Álvarez Cambras, "a vaccination campaign was the best gift we could give the country."[29]

Risquet wrote Machado Ventura for help with the campaign, and Machado sent Cuba's director of epidemiology, Dr. Helenio Ferrer, to Moscow to get the vaccines. Three days later, on April 27, 1966, Ferrer flew to Brazzaville with good news: "They [the Soviets] have agreed to send 200,000 units at a cost of approximately $4,000 to Brazzaville. (I think we might be able to get them for free.)"[30]

The Congolese authorities approved the Cuban plan to vaccinate all children under five in the three major cities, adding only that they could not bear any of the cost. Badgered by the Cubans, the Soviets agreed to send the vaccine for free.[31]

"The dreaded poliomyelitis" struck many Congolese children. In Brazzaville alone, a Congolese paper reported, "more than one thousand are afflicted by it." In 1966 the Cubans organized the Congo's first vaccination campaign. "It was the best gift we could give the country," a Cuban doctor recalled. Because there were not enough nurses in the Congo, fifty Cuban military instructors were drafted to administer the vaccine.

There were not enough doctors and nurses to administer the vaccine, but since it was in a caramel, the Cuban doctors trained 270 young militia members to do it. "The kids are smart and quick, and they have a revolutionary conscience," Ferrer wrote. "They know that the vaccine will be beneficial, and they are enthusiastic about Cuba's help." Fifty Cuban military instructors were also drafted to administer the vaccine. "Congolese, it is your urgent national duty to make sure that your children . . . are inoculated," a government leaflet urged on June 11. The next day, the campaign began. Three days later, 61,000 children had been vaccinated.[32]

The campaign had just ended when, on June 22, the Congolese National Assembly approved a bill that tightened the MNR's control over the army. The intention was to create, *Dipanda* boasted, "an army as tied to the people as a belt is to a pair of pants."[33] The plan, however, backfired.

TEN DAYS THAT SHOOK BRAZZAVILLE

On June 27, while President Massamba-Débat was in Madagascar, the revolt began. It was sparked by the demotion of a popular captain, Marien Ngouabi, for insubordination. Ngouabi, a northerner, was the commander of the 250-man-strong paratroop battalion, the elite force of the puny Congolese army. The paratroopers went on a rampage. In Poto-poto, a district of Brazzaville with a predominantly northern population, there were pro-rebel demonstrations. On the rebels' orders, the ferry service between Brazzaville and Kinshasa (formerly Leopoldville) was interrupted, as were telecommunications. Brazzaville was cut off from the world.

Press reports and later accounts of the next few days are vague, and they are particularly confused about whether the Cubans intervened to put down the revolt. After the collapse of the Simba rebellion in Zaire, press interest in central Africa had subsided and foreign journalists visited the Congo only occasionally; once the airport was closed and the ferry service interrupted, none could arrive. Recently declassified West German and Belgian reports, and Cuban documents, however, shed light on the crisis and bring the Cuban response into sharp focus.[34]

"We must act quickly," Risquet noted upon receiving news of the revolt. Determined to make sure that the government radio station "The Voice of the Revolution" did not "suddenly turn into the Voice of the 'Counterrevolution,'" he immediately told Dr. Álvarez Cambras to lead a platoon of twenty-five Cubans to occupy the station, which was located in a building about 500 yards from the Cuban camp. "Risquet told me, 'Forget the medicine and defend the radio,'" Álvarez Cambras recalled. Risquet chose a doctor to lead the operation because he wanted to rely on diplomatic, rather than military, skill. "He said I must do everything I could to avoid bloodshed, Cuban and Congolese."[35]

Threatened by the rebellious paratroopers and unsure of the loyalty of the rest of the army, the members of the cabinet and of the MNR's Political Bureau sought protection in the Cuban camp. Risquet decided to house them in the stadium, which was less than 100 yards from the camp. "I invited them to make themselves at home in the locker room," he writes, "which had electricity and where . . . [we] had put camp beds."[36] The Congolese government slept there, protected by the Cubans, until the end of the crisis.

Paratroopers and gendarmes repeatedly tried to break into the radio station. "There was a lot of commotion," Álvarez Cambras explained. "We yelled at each other; I don't know whether they understood what we were saying. We used a mixture of Spanish, French, and a lot of swear words. We threatened them, and they withdrew."[37] Unable to seize the station or the government, the insurgents negotiated. On June 28, rebel officers talked with government officials at the Cuban camp. "We purposely kept our distance," Risquet wrote. "It was already awkward that they were meeting in our camp. If we had been there, it would have looked like the height of interference. All I did was send them coffee." The rebels' demands included not only the restoration of Ngouabi to his rank and his post but also the dissolution of the militia and the departure of the Cuban instructors.[38]

The Cubans would have been eager to put down the revolt if the Congolese government had been willing to take the lead. They would not act in place of the government. The Congolese had to rouse themselves and rally their supporters and the militia. "Keep demanding that the government act with more decision," Castro cabled Risquet on June 29.[a] He cabled again on July 3, "We entirely approve your program: to demand categorically that they adopt a revolutionary stance, refusing all concessions, or we will withdraw our men and weapons, except those which were sent for the militia. There is a Cuban ship in Conakry awaiting instructions."[39]

Despite Castro's words, the Cubans were cornered. They would not abandon the government while the mutiny was on, and they would not act in its stead. They remained in their camp, ready to intervene if the government roused itself.

An eerie calm descended. The paratroopers did not dare attack because, the Belgian chargé explained, "they did not want a test of strength with the Cubans." The rest of the military and the gendarmerie, while officially neutral, sympathized with the rebels. The capital was divided along ethnic lines, but there were no riots. "Brazzaville has been outwardly completely calm since yesterday," the West German embassy reported on June 30. On the same day, Le Monde stated, "The people are going about their daily chores, the shops are open, and all the government offices are functioning." The government remained in the Cuban camp, and the rebel officers went there to talk, threaten, and cajole. "They keep saying that it's all among brothers," a baffled Moracén noted in his diary.[40]

On the evening of June 28 the Soviet ambassador, Ivan Spitzki, had gone to the Cuban camp to speak with Risquet. "We talked for about two hours," Risquet wrote, "but not about anything important. The ambassador was cautious; he didn't want to express any opinion but just wanted to learn about the situation and show solidarity with the beleaguered government." The next day, Risquet met the Soviet military instructors who had been teaching the army's artillery unit. "The Soviet instructors told us that although the army's artillerymen had never fired a shot (they had only observed the Soviet instructors), they knew how to calculate and fire, and how to maintain the weapons. Ten months ago," Risquet mused, he and other Cuban officials "had talked to these same instructors in the ambassador's presence. We had told them that they should delay the training of the artillerymen as long as possible because, given the reactionary nature of the army, which had been created by the French in colonial times, once they knew how to use those heavy guns they would pose a danger to the Revolution. . . . The Soviets replied with some banalities, and we cut the conversation short. . . . Now we have to face the fact that the mutinous army has a battery of four 120-mm mortars, another of four 122-mm antiaircraft artillery pieces, another of four 100-mm guns, and another of four 57-mm guns."[41]

a. On the same day the Cuban government made public that it had sent "weapons and instructors" to Brazzaville in response to a Congolese request. (Granma: June 29, 1966, p. 12 quoted; July 2, p. 12; July 4, p. 4.)

Risquet reckoned that there were about 1,100 Congolese soldiers in the capital. There were also some 600 gendarmes. There were only 220 Cubans, but it was very unlikely, Risquet concluded philosophically, "that all these units would . . . coordinate a joint attack against us."[42]

He was right. The army was intimidated by the Cubans' "determination and actions," the Belgian embassy reported.[43] Furthermore, the militia, which had vanished during the initial days, began tentatively patrolling the streets of the capital again and, on July 3, President Massamba-Débat finally returned from Madagascar. For the occasion, the cabinet left the Cuban camp and went to the airport "in the battle dress of the militia and armed with submachine guns" to receive him. "No army unit was there to render military honors," Le Monde noted, but "several thousand Congolese received him triumphantly." Massamba-Débat remarked dryly, "Today we have broken with the foreign custom that an arriving chief of state be greeted by the army. Instead, I've found the people."[44]

For the next two days the protagonists eyed one another warily. On July 6, the uprising suddenly ended. The insurgents returned to their barracks and proclaimed their loyalty to the government, while Ngouabi's demotion was rescinded. Only one Congolese had been killed.[45]

"The situation had been saved only by the approximately two hundred Cuban soldiers," said a Soviet official. The Americans, West Germans, French, and Belgians agreed. "Certainly the Cubans have played the decisive role in the defense of the present regime," echoed Ambassador Hasslacher. The army "has recoiled before the bayonets of the Cubans . . . who saved the regime," the Belgian chargé reported, while the French ambassador concluded that the Cubans had "fulfilled their role perfectly in maintaining the fragile equilibrium" in the country. From Kinshasa U.S. ambassador Godley joined the chorus: the government had survived "because of the indispensable support of Cuban armed forces."[46]

Risquet, however, was dispirited. "As he had bid us Godspeed, that memorable night of August 6, 1965 . . . Fidel had ordered us . . . 'to organize, arm and train the people without delay; to be ready to fight with them against any aggression from the imperialist camp, against any aggression from Tshombe, against any military coup.'" But a year later, only the Cubans had been ready to fight. Le Monde put it very well: "When the army rose up, the militia responded with complete disarray. . . . Their Cuban instructors were expecting more."[47]

THE CUBANS PREPARE TO LEAVE

In the wake of the uprising, the government assured the Cubans that it would reduce the size of the army and the gendarmerie, but it failed to act. "They haven't done anything, and they're not going to do anything," Risquet groused in an August 15 report to the head of Cuban intelligence, Piñeiro. What the government did was to ask all foreign military instructors but the Cubans to leave forthwith: Russians, Egyptians, Chinese, and French. The first to leave were the two Chinese, who said "they would 'set the example,'" reported the U.S. defense attaché in Cameroon, who suspected that the dismissal of the instructors was a devious Chinese ploy to tighten their hold over the country. Risquet knew better: the government was trying to weaken the army without directly confronting it. "They were right in terminating the foreign military training of the artillery, the paratroopers, and the gendarmerie," he told Piñeiro, but it would not be enough because the army remained intact. And so he vented his frustration. "The way these bureaucrats handled the situation was utterly stupid," he wrote, "both regarding the Egyptian, Soviet, and Chinese friends, whose instructors were virtually ordered to leave the country . . . and also regarding the French, who, though not a friend, have to be handled with some sensitivity."[48]

In the oral agreement between the two governments, Cuba had promised to keep the column in the Congo for one year—that is, until August 21, 1966. The Congolese government was vocal in its desire that the Cubans extend their stay. "We give heartfelt thanks to our Cuban friends," Prime Minister Ambroise Noumazalaye declared at a July 8 rally. "They will continue to train our people."[49] The Cubans, however, had other plans.

In his January 1965 visit to Brazzaville, Che Guevara had been very favorably impressed with the country's leaders and its revolutionary potential, but once in the Congo, the Cubans realized that the Massamba-Débat government's commitment to socialism was only rhetorical. Its foreign policy was pragmatic and ideologically inconsistent. It was not a government of hardy revolutionaries, but rather, as a historian has written, a "cauldron of ambitious personalities and ill-defined ideological factions." One can appreciate Risquet's dismay as he surveyed the political scene after the mutiny: "The political leanings of the government are not clear. . . . Everything gets mixed up, these different ideas, the tribal questions and the personal ambitions." As the Cuban chargé, Darío Urra, remarked, "Even the Cuban volunteers would ask us, 'What are we doing here?'"[50]

One of the column's tasks had been to protect the Congo against Tshombe's mercenaries, but by late 1966 Tshombe was in exile and relations between the Congo and Zaire, if not cordial, were at least correct. "The government of General Mobutu is a progressive regime . . . [which] defends the interests of the Congolese [Zairean] people," Massamba-Débat stated, pragmatically, in August 1966.[51]

The only reason, then, for the Cubans to stay in the Congo was to protect the government from its own army. Had the Cubans been convinced of the revolutionary fervor of the government, or had they believed that their presence would have helped spread revolution throughout the region, they might have stayed. But by 1966 it was clear that the neighboring countries were not ready for revolution. When Che had visited Brazzaville in 1965, two insurgent groups had had their seat there: the MPLA and the Union des Populations du Cameroun (UPC). A large group of refugees from Zaire, including many who proclaimed their eagerness to return home to fight, was also in the Congo. Ser-guera, who had arrived as ambassador in July 1965, had been enthusiastic about the possibility of spreading revolution from Brazzaville. "He outlined a plan of Napoleonic proportions," a DGI officer remembered. "He wanted to open guer-rilla fronts in almost every country of Africa."[52] But by mid-1966, the ebullient Serguera was back in Havana,[b] and the Cubans in the Congo were beginning to understand that the UPC was in disarray, that the refugees from Zaire had no intention of fighting, and that the MPLA did not need a Cuban column in the Congo. In letters to Piñeiro in the weeks following the uprising, and again when he returned to Havana in October for consultations, Risquet recommended that the column leave the Congo.[53]

Castro agreed. He told the Congolese foreign minister, who visited Cuba in late October, that the column would leave in December. A smaller force, about 100 men, would remain to train the militia, assist the rebel movements, pri-marily the MPLA, and defend the Congo in the unlikely event of foreign aggres-sion. They would not, however, intervene to protect the government from an internal attack.[54]

In early November, Risquet stopped in Moscow on his way back to Brazza-ville. He wanted to rent a Soviet liner that would take the column back to Havana. The Cuban ambassador at Moscow reported to Castro: "Risquet and I spoke with Soviet officials about the ship for our instructors. With great respect and circumspection, they urged us to consider extending the column's stay in the Congo. . . . They believe that the departure of the Cubans will leave a dangerous vacuum, and this worries them. Risquet replied that it was your decision and it is final. Nonetheless . . . he asked that I inform you of the request. The Soviet comrades will give their final answer about the ship within two days, but they have already said in principle that their response will be positive."[55]

The Soviets must have feared that the Cubans' withdrawal would destabilize the country and provide the Chinese an opportunity to increase their influence. Castro, however, disregarded their request and on December 15 the Soviet liner *Nadezhda Krupskaya* left Pointe Noire with 182 Cubans aboard.[56]

THE MPLA

The departure of the column did not end the importance of the Congo to the Cubans. While they shed their hopes for the Massamba-Débat govern-ment, they continued to work with the MPLA, which had its headquarters in Brazzaville.

b. Serguera, who had become increasingly marginal after Risquet's arrival, left Brazza-ville in December 1965, and Urra, a more practical man, became chargé. In his memoirs, Serguera wrote, "It was my decision to leave the Congo," without explaining why. His brief account of his stay in the Congo is marred by inaccuracies and self-aggrandizement. (See Serguera, *Caminos*, pp. 306–13, p. 312 quoted.)

In 1965, when the Cubans arrived in the Congo, the MPLA had two guerrilla fronts. The older of the two (the "First Region") was in Dembos and Nambuangongo, a mountainous, densely forested area some sixty miles northeast of Luanda. In order to reach the First Region from the Congo, MPLA reinforcements had to traverse Zaire, which supported the rival FNLA and whose army harassed, disarmed, or jailed them. In the words of MPLA's leader Lúcio Lara, "Zaire was always our Great Barrier."[57]

Those guerrillas who managed to get through Zaire into northern Angola were exposed to both the Portuguese army and the FNLA. The MPLA had tried twice, in late 1961 and early 1963, to run the gauntlet. Of the twenty-one men in the first attempt twenty had been killed; all thirty in the second were killed.[58] The leader of the FNLA, Holden Roberto, acknowledged that his organization was responsible in an interview with an Algerian journalist.

"People say that you gave the order to destroy any MPLA column entering Angola."

Holden Roberto looked at me and said: "It's true." . . .

"Could you tell us why you've been so harsh?"

"These columns were trying to go through territory we control, and they hadn't asked for our permission."

"And if these Angolans had asked for permission, would you have given it?"

"No."[59]

The MPLA did not send any more reinforcements to Dembos and Nambuangongo. "We were cut off from the First Region," recalled Lara. "We didn't even know what was going on there. We only knew that they needed everything."[60] The MPLA concentrated instead on the Second Region, which was located in the 2,900-square-mile enclave of Cabinda, the only part of Angola that bordered the Congo. In 1964 the MPLA had begun military operations there, with little success: "Our operations were hit-and-run raids with a handful of guerrillas," MPLA commander Kiluanji explained.[61]

CABINDA

Six of the nine Cuban instructors who arrived in Brazzaville in May 1965 went to the Second Region. They assumed new identities as Angolans who had grown up on the island of Fernando Po, in Spanish Equatorial Guinea. "We had been serving in the Spanish army there and had heard about the MPLA's struggle for the independence of Angola on the radio and had decided to help," one of the six, Rafael Moracén recalled. They would be military advisers to the guerrilla commanders, MPLA president Neto had told them when he had first met them in May. They would train the guerrillas and, of course, participate in the fighting. The guerrilla commanders were told that they were Cubans, but the rank and file were told they were from Equatorial Guinea. They did their best to live

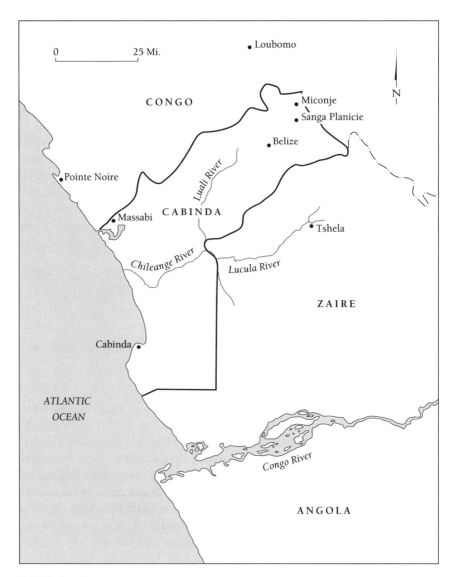

Cabinda, Angola

like Angolans and avoid doing anything that might betray their identity, but it was hopeless. "No one was fooled for very long," Moracén remarked.[62]

Over the next weeks, there were some skirmishes, many marches through the tropical forest, and military instruction in the guerrilla camps. There were moments of frustration for the instructors who had learned their trade in the exacting school of Fidel Castro's rebel army and who found themselves in a completely alien culture with a very different conception of discipline, but there were also warm moments of humanity in that inhospitable forest. "I looked at them all," Moracén wrote after delivering a particularly severe lecture to the MPLA guerrillas, "and I was moved, I felt love for them. . . . They had so much dignity I believed it was worth dying with them if I had to." Ten years later, Moracén pestered Raúl Castro to be allowed to return to fight in Angola. "I am an Angolan," he pleaded.[63]

In the fall of 1965, the Cubans and Angolans began planning an operation against the Portuguese fort of Sanga Planicie, in the northeastern corner of Cabinda. The MPLA's aims were modest. "We only wanted to harass the fort with a few artillery pieces we had just gotten from the Cubans," Lara explained. But Risquet proposed a much more ambitious operation: a column would attack Sanga Planicie, while another would lie in ambush and decimate the Portuguese troops that came to rescue the garrison. "We were very hesitant," Lara remarked. "The Cubans were talking about at least 100 men, and we didn't have many men, and we weren't used to operating in a big group. We were used to groups of 20 to 30 men at most."[64]

The Cubans insisted. "They argued that the circumstances were propitious and that we should take advantage of them," Lara recalled. Furthermore, a Cuban officer remarked, the Tricontinental Conference would open in Havana in January 1966 and "we wanted to inflict a heavy blow on the enemy so that when the conference began everyone would know that the guerrillas were fighting in Cabinda." Finally, the MPLA leaders agreed. Operation Macaco was on.[65]

"We had never mounted an operation like that one, so big, with heavy weapons," Lara said. (The arms included four 75-mm artillery pieces provided by the Cubans, and machine guns.) One hundred Angolans were assigned to the operation—an impressive number, given that the total strength of the MPLA, in Cabinda and the Congo, was about 300 guerrillas. They were joined by about 40 Cubans. "By then we all knew that we had Cuban advisers," Gato remarked. (Even the Portuguese knew it, but they did not know how many Cubans there were or whether they were helping out in Cabinda, "since many of the Cubans are quite dark and of the same general appearance as the MPLA forces.")[66]

On December 25, the rebel force entered Cabinda. "The march was slow and difficult," Captain Fernando Galindo, who was in command of the Cubans, reported. The guerrillas didn't know the area, and their guides, who had been hired for the operation, were not much better. On December 27, when they were about one mile from Sanga Planicie, the rebels were ambushed by the Portuguese. "There was tremendous confusion in our column," Galindo wrote. "I had never seen such a stampede; it was an absolute rout. Fear, panic not only gripped the Angolan ranks, but ours as well." They withdrew in haste, leaving the artillery pieces behind. (Three days later, on Galindo's orders, the same Cubans who had abandoned the guns sneaked back to recover them.) By year's end the column was back in the Congo.[67]

The failure of the operation reinforced the MPLA's feeling that Cabinda was not a promising region for guerrilla warfare due to its small size and, above all, to the apathy of the population. Most of the guerrillas in the Second Region were not from Cabinda, and the population's "indifference, even hostility, to the nationalist project" affected their morale. "They [the MPLA guerrillas] don't want to do anything because they don't consider Cabinda their own country," Kindelán wrote to Piñeiro.[68]

Therefore the MPLA decided to devote its meager forces to two more alluring projects. First, Zambia, which had become independent in October 1964, had offered the MPLA a rearguard base for a new front (the "Third Region") in eastern Angola, an immense area the Portuguese would have difficulty controlling. Second, the Cubans in the Congo could help the MPLA to send reinforcements to the first region (Dembos and Nambuangongo), which remained cut off. "This was Neto's great obsession," Risquet remarked. Shortly after Operation Macaco, most of the MPLA forces and all the Cubans left the Second Region. Cabinda became a backwater. While a group of MPLA guerrillas went to Zambia to begin the war in the Third Region, the MPLA leaders began the preparations for the dispatch of a column to the First Region. "All their [MPLA's] hopes" were now fixed on the First and Third Regions, Kindelán wrote to Piñeiro in June 1966. "As you know, there is tremendous enthusiasm about them. I believe that it is true that the MPLA's future depends on these two fronts."[69]

THE MPLA COLUMNS

In Havana, in early May 1966, Moracén received an unexpected visit from Risquet, who was in Cuba for consultations. Risquet invited him to lunch at a Chinese restaurant. "Let's go to the Mandarín, my friend. Have you ever had Chinese food?"

> I thought: "Gee, Risquet's become very friendly." (In the Congo I'd just thought of him as my boss.) He took me to the Mandarín, he gave me egg rolls, he kept offering me more food, and I kept eating. He gave me soy sauce—I'd never had Chinese food before. While I was eating, he said: "You know, we need you back in the Congo." I wasn't very eager to go back; I had been disappointed with the government of Massamba-Débat. Risquet insisted: "Please, chico, consider it." I said, "OK, I'll think about it." We kept eating. Then he told me that I had to decide right now. I said, "OK, I'll go." Risquet didn't say anything. I asked: "When am I going?" I thought he'd say in a few days, but he said: "Tomorrow. I already have your ticket." Even my passport was ready.

On May 8, Moracén left Havana. Five days later, he was in Brazzaville. The Cubans had begun training the column for the First Region, and Risquet wanted Moracén as head of the instructors because, as he said, "Moracén knew how to relate to the Angolans."[70]

While the Cubans were training the column, the MPLA was figuring out how to get it through Zaire. Brazzaville and Kinshasa faced each other across the

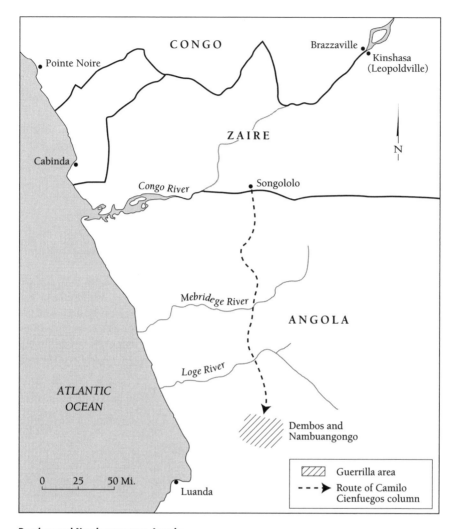

Dembos and Nambuangongo, Angola

broad expanse of the Congo River. The ferry traffic between the two cities, which had been stopped for almost two years, had resumed on November 6, 1965, the day the two countries had reestablished diplomatic relations. When the MPLA had left Kinshasa for Brazzaville in 1963, a small underground had remained behind. "We began preparing hideouts for the weapons and ammunition," Lara said. "We bribed members of the government . . . and officials who provided us with the documents we needed to travel in the country."[71]

Then they began moving the weapons. "We [Cubans and MPLA] have already smuggled seventy-five SKS [semiautomatic rifles] and P.M. (P.P.CH) [submachine guns used by the Red Army in the Second World War] and 25,000 bullets," Kindelán wrote to Piñeiro in early June. "We will keep transporting

"Soon I will go into the interior of my country to offer my contribution, even my life, if necessary," one of the six Angolan guerrillas shown here in the Congo jotted in her diary. A few days later five of these women (the sixth fell ill) left to join a guerrilla column of the Popular Movement for the Liberation of Angola (MPLA) that had been armed and trained by the Cubans. But they never reached their destination, an MPLA guerrilla area in northern Angola. They were murdered by the rival National Front for the Liberation of Angola. The woman wearing a white blouse (center) is Nancy, a Cuban intelligence officer.

P.M. and ammunition, until we have reached a total of 150 weapons, each with 1,000 bullets." Most of the weapons had been provided by the Cubans; some came from the Soviet Union. They were gradually transported in cars or minivans to Songololo, a Zairean town thirteen miles from the Angolan border, where many Angolan refugees lived and where the MPLA had an underground network.[72]

After the weapons, the men. The column trained for over two months—"tough, rigorous training." The members of the column, which the MPLA named after the Cuban hero Camilo Cienfuegos, left the Congo in July 1966, crossing the river in small groups, with false documents. Some had Congolese ID cards (courtesy of the Brazzaville government), others laissez-passer as Angolan refugees. "I crossed as a tourist, with a camera," Tiro recalled. "I crossed with an Angolan ID card," said Kiluanji. With the help of the underground in Kinshasa, they made their way to Songololo by train, in small groups, over several days. They waited there until August 16, when the column—about 100 men—entered Angola.[73]

As the crow flies, there are some 190 miles from the Zairean border to the First Region. The column's commander, Monstro Imortal, wrote in his report to Brazzaville, "Our march must be considered one of the luckiest accomplishments of the revolution. We never encountered the enemy. . . . There was no way to escape hunger and sickness, but all the difficulties, the rivers, the mountains, and many other obstacles, were overcome as if they did not exist. Everything went well and on September 23 the column entered Ngalama [in the First Region] triumphantly."[74]

For the first time in six years, MPLA reinforcements had reached the First Region. There were no Cubans in the column, but their role had been decisive. As Lara explained, they had "made it possible to give our men a level of training we couldn't have provided ourselves," and they had provided the weapons.[75]

Monstro Imortal had ended his report with a plea for immediate reinforcements and supplies.[76] The MPLA, fired by this first success, decided to send a second column as soon as possible. It proceeded to organize the "Kamy": 127 guerrillas, trained and armed by the Cubans. "I pledge allegiance to the flag of the Kamy," one of the five women in the column jotted in her diary on November 20. "This is an important day in my life when we vow in unison to fight to overthrow Portuguese colonialism. Soon I will go into the interior of my country to offer my contribution, even my life, if necessary." They made their way to Songololo. "Several days before the members of the column arrived, the arms, the ammunition, and the other equipment had been carefully hidden near the border," a Cuban historian noted.[77]

In mid-January 1967 the Kamy entered Angola. It pushed forward, searching for deserted paths, in order to escape the notice of the Portuguese, who had tightened their control of the area after the successful infiltration of the Cienfuegos. "We got lost, even though we had two guides," one of the Kamy's officers, Ludy Kissassunda, remembered. "It was the rainy season, and the rain was very heavy and there were a lot of wide rivers, with raging currents, and the ropes we had brought weren't for crossing rivers. On the fourth day we were ambushed by the FNLA; we lost three or four compañeros. We had no contact of any kind with Brazzaville or with the First Region. We were beginning to get hungry, and hunger makes discipline more difficult." Finally they reached the Loge River. "The current was very strong, and crossing it would be very dangerous, and a lot of us were already in bad shape." Therefore, the column's commander decided that those in poor physical condition—a total of forty-seven—should return to the Congo, choosing Ludy to lead them.[78]

Of the seventy-odd guerrillas who continued toward the First Region, only twenty-one arrived; the others died fighting against the Portuguese and the FNLA, or of hunger or accident. Only fifteen of those who had turned back made it to the Zairean border; among them were Ludy and the only five women. "When we reached the border," Ludy recalled, "we hid the weapons." At dawn on March 2 they began walking toward Songololo. As they approached the town, they were captured by the FNLA. "The terrorists are liquidating one another," a Portuguese newspaper applauded. Eventually most were freed through the good offices of the OAU, but the five women never returned. The FNLA killed them in early 1968.[79]

Upon learning of the fate of the Kamy, the MPLA leaders in Brazzaville decided to send one more column to the First Region. This column, the Bomboko, included ninety-eight Angolans who had gone to Cuba in late 1966 for military training. In May 1967 a Cuban ship brought them back to the Congo, where other guerrillas, who had been trained by Moracén and his men, were waiting for them.[80]

The Bomboko was the most powerful of the three columns the MPLA sent to the First Region. Not only was it the largest—about 180 men—and the best armed, but it also carried extra weapons. "The idea," one of its officers explained, "was that each of us would carry two weapons: one for himself, the other for a fighter already in the First Region."[81]

In June 1967 the Bomboko left the Congo for Kinshasa. "We crossed the Congo River by ferry in small groups, wearing just normal clothes as workers," one of the guerrillas, Rui de Matos, recalled. Gato, the commander of the Bomboko, left Kinshasa for Songololo ahead of his men, escorting a truck loaded with weapons. With him were three or four of his officers and his wife, Yovita, a young Angolan who lived in Kinshasa and belonged to the underground. The rest of the column traveled by train. They did not leave, however, on different days, in small groups, as their predecessors of the Cienfuegos and the Kamy had done. "We all boarded the train for Songololo at the same time. It was a mistake!" Rui de Matos said. João Gonçalves Benedito, the able leader of the underground in Kinshasa, had been arrested the previous November with some of his men and the underground was in disarray. "There were many leaks," Gato remarks.[82]

As on the previous occasions, officials had been bribed, and false papers bought. But as they approached Songololo, Gato, his companions, and the truck with the weapons were detained by Zairean soldiers. And when the train with the others reached Songololo, a member of the column recalled, "we found three armored cars and a tank waiting for us and the station surrounded by Zairean troops." They did not try to resist. "We were taken to the prison. When we got there, what a shock! Our commander [Gato]—beaten to a bloody pulp! His wife—beaten up! One of his officers—beaten up! Another—dead!" After several weeks of captivity, they were sent back to Brazzaville. Mobutu, however, kept the weapons. "And with this adventure we ended our attempts to cross through Zaire," Lara concluded. "We would have tried again, but we didn't have any more weapons, and it had become too difficult—there were spies everywhere and too many checkpoints."[83]

Instead, the MPLA decided to send the reconstituted Bomboko to the Third Region in eastern Angola. It took almost a year to get there. After waiting for planes provided by the Soviet Union, delays in Tanzania, and a long trek through Zambia, in July 1968 the Bomboko finally got to the Third Region.[84]

The Cubans' work with the MPLA had ended with the departure of the Bomboko for the First Region in June 1967, and the following month Moracén and his men returned to Cuba. Only a handful of instructors—perhaps forty— stayed behind to continue training the Congolese militia.[85]

On September 4, 1968, after days of bloody clashes, Massamba-Débat stepped down. An army captain, Alfred Raoul, presided over a provisional government, but the real power was Ngouabi, the paratroop officer whose bid for power the Cubans had stopped in 1966. On September 22, the last Cuban instructors left the Congo. "Brazzaville's new regime has veered slightly to the right by quietly diminishing its ties with Cuba," INR director Hughes reported in December 1968.[86] Four weeks later Ngouabi became president of the Congo.

LOOKING BACK

The dispatch of Risquet's column to the Congo had been part of the same dream that had inspired Che's column in Zaire. Reality had been cruelly different. The Cubans were fortunate that the Congolese government chose not to use force to put down the revolt in June 1966, because if it had, they would have supported it, risking both Cuban and Congolese lives for a cause they were increasingly questioning. The departure of all the non-Cuban foreign military instructors the following month increased the Cubans' relative importance and could have tempted them to remain. But to what end? To be the praetorian guard of a government they did not respect? To Risquet's credit, he was able to understand that the best thing the Cubans could do was get out—and make Havana understand why. "We should hasten our departure," he wrote Piñeiro in September 1966. "He got us out at the right moment," Risquet's second-in-command, Kindelán, remarked. "Our major achievement was to get out of the Congo in time," Galindo agreed. "Our men didn't understand what we were doing there. We were disappointed—about the Congo and about the MPLA as well."[87]

The Cubans had intended to use the Congo as a base to spread revolution in Central Africa. They had hoped, in Raúl Castro's words, that Risquet's men would serve as a "reserve force for Che's column," at first training the Simbas in the Congo and then, perhaps, accompanying them to western Zaire. In fact, the two columns had no contact in the few months in which they were both in Africa, and Risquet's men never set foot in Zaire. By the time they arrived in the Congo, western Zaire had been pacified, except for remote hideouts in Kwilu, and the Zairean refugees in the Congo, as the Belgian embassy reported, had lost "all confidence in the future . . . and only wanted to go home."[88] The Cubans trained and armed the handful who wanted to fight, Thomas Mukwidi and his group of twenty men. In June 1967 this little troop entered Zaire and disappeared in the tropical forest, not to be heard from for two decades when, after the fall of Mobutu, a few survivors surfaced in Kinshasa. Several of their companions, including Mukwidi, had died fighting Mobutu's soldiers, they explained, and they had abandoned the struggle.[89]

The Cubans' efforts in favor of the Cameroonian guerrillas, the UPC, were equally futile. The group of twenty to twenty-five UPC guerrillas whom they had trained entered Cameroon in the spring of 1967. "It was a disaster!" Enrique

Montero, the DGI officer in charge of the operation, recalled. Within a few days the Cameroonian army had killed or captured every member of the column. Whereas the Mukwidi operation had been carried out with the approval of Massamba-Débat, in the case of the UPC, the Cubans had acted with the support of some high Congolese officials, but without informing Massamba-Débat.[c,90]

Finally, the Cubans used the Congo as a base to deliver aid to the MPLA. There were clouds in the relationship. The Cuban insistence on Operation Macaco caused some resentment. Furthermore, the Cubans were disappointed in the military performance of the MPLA and critical of the failure of its leaders to join the guerrillas in the field. Their disappointment was heightened by the fact that their expectations had been so inflated. In 1966–67 many Cubans, including Fidel Castro, were less than discreet in expressing their frustration, and this too bred resentment.[91]

Nevertheless, the Cubans did help the MPLA. The Cienfuegos reached its destination intact and brought crucial assistance to the First Region. In fact, the Cienfuegos and the remnants of the Kamy were the only large groups to make it to the region during the war of independence.[92]

Following Moracén's return to Cuba, in 1967, relations between Cuba and the MPLA became distant, as the MPLA's efforts shifted to the Third Region, and Cuba's focus in Africa shifted to a far more successful guerrilla movement, the Partido Africano da Independência da Guiné e Cabo Verde (PAIGC), that was fighting the Portuguese for the independence of Guinea-Bissau. Cuba's early aid to the MPLA, however, established a bond that would be dramatically rekindled a decade later.

c. The Cubans also helped the minuscule Movimiento Nacionalista de Guinea Ecuatorial, which was based in the Congo. "We gave them some economic aid and military training—more precisely, we trained three of them." (Interviews with Urra [quoted], Risquet, and Moracén.)

CHAPTER NINE
GUERRILLAS IN GUINEA-BISSAU

"**F**idel is a little pessimistic about Africa," a senior aide told top Cuban officials on January 18, 1967, during a postmortem on the Congo. This pessimism, however, did not extend to Guinea-Bissau.[1] The Partido Africano da Independência da Guiné e Cabo Verde (PAIGC) was, the Cubans believed, the strongest guerrilla movement in the Portuguese colonies. The Americans agreed. U.S. reports stressed time and again that the PAIGC was "Africa's most successful liberation movement."[2] Beginning armed struggle in January 1963 after three years of thorough political work in the countryside, the PAIGC guerrillas controlled a third of Guinea-Bissau by 1965 and posed a significant challenge to the 20,000 Portuguese troops. "Guinea-Bissau is our strategic priority in Africa," Piñeiro announced at the January meeting.[3]

THE PAIGC

Guinea-Bissau was an unlikely place for the most successful guerrilla movement of Portuguese Africa. It is a tiny country (14,000 square miles) wedged between Senegal to the north and Guinea to the east and the south, with a population estimated at 540,000 in 1960. Like Angola and Mozambique, it was inhabited by diverse and frequently hostile ethnic groups. The war's foremost scholar, Patrick Chabal, concludes that the PAIGC was the most adept of the rebel movements in the Portuguese colonies "in achieving nationalist unity, in carrying out political mobilisation and in establishing new political structures in the liberated areas." Its leaders were outstanding, above all Amílcar Cabral, the secretary-general. "Amílcar Cabral is a very unusual breed of political exile: everyone respects him," the Cuban ambassador in Ghana wrote in 1963. "One of the more surprising impressions gained during the visit [of an embassy official to Guinea-Bissau]," the U.S. ambassador wrote from Senegal six years later, "was the regard in which Amilcar Cabral is held. There were Portuguese who said that he was a Communist, others who said he was a leftist nationalist, and others, a moderate nationalist who would cooperate with the Portuguese. However, in most cases, there was also an expression of respect for him, not only for the organizational and military success of his guerrilla campaign, but also for him as a person."[4] While Cabral was influenced by Marxism, he was not a Marxist. "He came to view Marxism as a methodology rather than an ideology," Chabal remarks. "When useful in analyzing

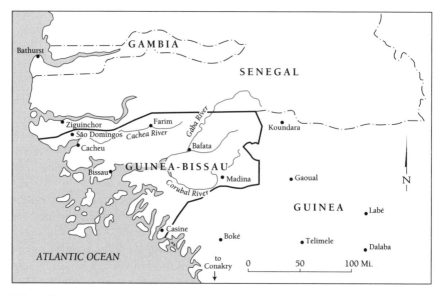

Guinea-Bissau

Guinean[a] society it was relied upon. When it was no longer relevant, it was amended or even abandoned."[5] Cabral "was no Communist," a Cuban intelligence officer who knew him well agreed. "He was a progressive leader with piercing insight into Africa's problems." He was also, as Chabal writes, "the undisputed commander and tactician of the war and, crucially, he kept an unusual degree of control over its conduct. . . . He kept in constant touch with his military commanders in the interior and he was directly responsible for all important decisions concerning the organisation of the armed forces, their deployment and the coordination of operations being carried out."[6]

EARLY CONTACTS WITH CUBA

The PAIGC directed the war from Conakry, the capital of Guinea, whose president, Ahmed Sékou Touré, offered essential haven to the guerrilla movement. Amílcar Cabral and other top PAIGC leaders had their headquarters in Conakry. By early 1963 they had established contact with the Cuban embassies in Algeria, Guinea, and Ghana. The following August, the PAIGC asked whether five of its members could receive "military and political instruction in Cuba for five or six months," the Cuban chargé in Conakry reported. Havana said yes, but did nothing. "The PAIGC is still waiting for us to make good on our promise to train its members," the Cuban ambassador in Accra complained the following De-

a. In English, the word "Guinean" refers to natives of both Guinea and Guinea-Bissau. To avoid confusion, throughout this book I use it to refer only to natives of Guinea-Bissau.

cember. "If we don't help them now, we won't be able to complain later."[7] But it is unclear whether the five PAIGC members ever went to Cuba, and throughout 1964 Cuba did nothing else to help the PAIGC.

It was Che Guevara's three-month trip to Africa in December 1964 that forged the link between the PAIGC and Havana. "While in Conakry," the Bissau newspaper *Nô Pintcha* reported, "Che Guevara asked to meet our leaders, and he even delayed his departure from Guinea to see our secretary-general." On January 12, 1965, he met Amílcar Cabral.[8]

In mid-May, the *Uvero* brought food, arms, and medicine to the PAIGC in Conakry, fulfilling Che's promise to Amílcar Cabral. "Cuban military aid is reaching the Portuguese Guinean rebels, probably as a result of 'Che' Guevara's visit to Guinea last January," the U.S. naval attaché reported a few days later. "Some sixty cases of arms for the Guinea-based 'African Party for the Independence of Guinea and Cape Verde' were unloaded at night from the freighter Uvero, which was in Conakry last week. Guinean [from Guinea] soldiers maintained tight security while the operation was in progress."[9]

In July a handful of Cape Verdeans who had been studying in Europe left Algiers for Havana aboard a Cuban ship to undergo military training. The PAIGC was also fighting for the independence of the Cape Verde Islands, some 430 miles west of Guinea-Bissau. It expected that the group of students, which would grow to thirty-one, would "then return home to start guerrilla warfare in the Cape Verde Islands," and that several of their Cuban instructors would accompany them.[10]

In January 1966, Cabral made his first trip to Cuba when he led the PAIGC delegation to the Tricontinental Conference in Havana. He was "the most impressive African in attendance," U.S. intelligence reported, and he made a powerful impression on his Cuban hosts. "His address to the Tricontinental was brilliant," Risquet remembered. "Everyone was struck by his great intelligence and personality. Fidel was very impressed by him."[11]

After the speech, Cabral and Castro spoke at great length. They were alone, except for Oscar Oramas, a Foreign Ministry official who took notes.[12] "Amílcar explained the history of our independence struggle," wrote Luís Cabral, Amílcar's half brother and close aide. "Fidel became increasingly aware of . . . the problems we faced. When Amílcar spoke of our need for artillery, Fidel understood that we would also need instructors; when Amílcar spoke of life in the liberated regions . . . the Cuban leader understood that we had to have doctors. And he understood that our armed forces needed better transportation to be more effective: Cuba would send us both the vehicles and the men to teach our fighters how to drive and maintain them." And so Castro pledged doctors, military instructors, and mechanics to the PAIGC. "Everything was simple in Amílcar's talks with the top Cuban leader," Luís Cabral explained.[13] At the end of the conversation, "Fidel said to Amílcar, 'Come with me. I'll take you to the Escambray [mountains].'" He asked Oramas to accompany them. A car took them from Havana to Trinidad; from there they proceeded by jeep and, in some places, on foot. The trip lasted three days. During it, Amílcar Cabral asked Castro to appoint a new ambassador to Conakry who would serve as a liaison with the PAIGC.[14] (Cabral "has a low opinion of our chargé in Conakry," a Cuban intelligence officer had remarked a few months earlier.) At Cabral's request, Castro appointed Oramas.[15]

Amílcar Cabral returned to Conakry, where he informed President Sékou Touré of his conversations with Castro. In Conakry, two Cuban intelligence officers hammered out the details of the aid that Castro had promised. "We met with Amílcar Cabral," one of them wrote in his report to Havana, "and we gave him the revolvers and the money that Alejandro [Fidel Castro] had sent." Cabral asked

> that we send him three mechanics . . . and ten mortar experts . . . and that they be blacks or dark mulattoes so that they would blend in with his people. They should instruct his men . . . and participate in the fighting. The PAIGC needs them very urgently because they are planning to take the . . . [fortified camp] of [Madina de] Boé. . . . Amílcar asked if we could send these instructors by plane, because the operation is on hold until they get there.
>
> There should be nine doctors, as was agreed there [in Havana]. He told us that he does not have any doctors. He urgently needs three (one clinician, one surgeon, and one orthopedist) for the hospital [in Guinea] near the border [with Guinea-Bissau]. He would like us to send these three by plane. The other six will go to Guinea-Bissau . . . and can come by ship.

Cabral also provided a detailed list of supplies he needed: tobacco, cotton cloth, 500 tons of sugar, uniforms, twelve trucks with spare parts, ammunition, and other military supplies.[16]

In March 1966 Oramas flew to Conakry to deliver a message from Castro to Touré, "informing him that Cuba had decided to give the PAIGC a substantial amount of aid and wanted his go-ahead."[17]

At the beginning of the 1960s, Guinea and Cuba had seemed destined to become close friends. The former faced the hostility of France (in 1958 Touré had defied de Gaulle, which had precipitated French efforts to wreck the country's economy and to overthrow Touré) and the latter of the United States; both spoke eloquently in favor of African liberation; as a Cuban daily stated, "Our revolutions are like sisters." On October 14–16, 1960, Touré was the first African chief of state to visit Cuba.[18]

But a strong friendship did not develop, in part, perhaps, because Cuba was not yet concerned with sub-Saharan Africa, and also because Touré developed cordial relations with the Kennedy administration and refused to let the Soviet planes flying to Cuba during the Missile Crisis [of October 1962] refuel in Conakry. From 1963 on Cuba had only a chargé in Guinea. Relations were "cool," Guinea's ambassador told Secretary Rusk in November 1964.[19] It was Cuba's decision to help the PAIGC that breathed new life into the relationship. Touré responded favorably to Castro's message, and Oramas presented his credentials as ambassador on April 29, 1966.[20]

Meanwhile, a group of Cuban volunteers had been undergoing intensive military training for the mission. Among them was Lieutenant Armando Galarza, a veteran of the Sierra Maestra. "I had frequently told my superiors that if we ever sent men to fight for the liberation of other peoples, I wanted to go. And so in 1966 when they asked me whether I was willing to go on an internationalist mission, I immediately said yes." He was told to inform his family that he would be attending a course in Kiev, and he was not told how long the mission would last.[21]

At the PAIGC's insistence, two artillerymen and three doctors flew ahead of the group, arriving in Conakry on May 8. Then, on May 21, the merchant ship *Lidia Doce* left Cuba, reaching Conakry on June 6. "The first Cuban technicians had arrived," Luís Cabral writes, "and with them came the important aid that had been promised: cigars, the dark sugar that would become so popular with our people, olive green uniforms and other equipment for our armed forces, vehicles, etc. Fidel's promises to Amílcar had been rigorously honored."[22]

There were thirty-one volunteers in all: eleven artillery specialists, eight drivers, one mechanic, ten doctors (seven surgeons and three clinicians), and an intelligence officer, Lieutenant Aurelio Ricard (Artemio), who was the group's leader.[23]

Amílcar Cabral wanted the fact that Cubans were there to remain a secret. That was why, writes his brother, "he asked Fidel that the technicians be blacks. . . . But it soon became public knowledge that the men who were driving the PAIGC trucks were Cubans; they were the only people in Conakry who smoked cigars!" It wasn't only the cigars that gave away the secret. One of the Cubans wrote in his diary that Amílcar Cabral himself had revealed their identity to a group of PAIGC combatants. "'Meet the Cubans,' Cabral had said before he asked us to introduce ourselves. He then explained that we had come from a distant country, a revolutionary country, that we would play a very important role in their struggle, and that we had foregone the advantages of the Cuban revolution to join them."[24] Furthermore, on several occasions the PAIGC captured Portuguese soldiers, held them in camps in which there were Cubans, and later freed them. And, as Galarza points out, "our ships docked openly in Conakry with supplies and combatants. There was no way people wouldn't see every Cuban ship."[25]

Accordingly, in February 1967, Portuguese military communiqués began mentioning that Cuban advisers were operating with the guerrillas, and a month later the CIA wrote that "At least 60 Cubans . . . are reportedly engaged in PAIGC training at the present time." Even though the secret was out, however, U.S. officials did not respond. As Robinson McIlvaine, the U.S. ambassador at Conakry from October 1966 through August 1969, remarked, "the State Department was not particularly concerned about the Cuban presence. It wasn't a big worry." This complacency stemmed from Washington's confidence that a handful of Cubans could not be effective in distant, alien African countries, and it had been reinforced by the failure of Guevara's column in Zaire.[26]

The Cuban Military Mission in Guinea and Guinea-Bissau (MMCG), which handled Cuban assistance to the PAIGC, had its headquarters in Conakry, in a house provided by Sékou Touré, and it reported directly to Cuban intelligence (DGI) in Havana, and in particular to Ulises Estrada, the head of the DGI's Dirección 5, which covered Africa and Asia.[b] The head of the mission, Artemio, was its major weakness. He was respected by neither the Cubans who served under him nor the PAIGC. "Artemio was not up to the job," one of the Cubans, Pina, said diplomatically. He was "arrogant and impulsive," a PAIGC commander observed. "He was a poor choice," Oramas concluded.[27]

Artemio defended himself in a letter to his successor, Víctor Dreke. He stressed "how difficult my task was: I had been placed at the head of a complex and important mission without ever having been in combat myself. . . . I was a junior officer and I had to lead a group that included at least twenty officers of my rank, or just one rank below." Dreke answered sternly: "One's authority, particularly in time of war, does not depend on rank, but on one's conduct."[28]

On November 11, 1966, 350 PAIGC combatants attacked the important fortified camp of Madina de Boé and suffered a serious setback: the PAIGC failed to take the camp and took heavy casualties. Among the dead was its senior military commander, Domingos Ramos. "Ramos's death was a heavy blow," a PAIGC leader remembered.[29] This spurred Castro into action. He "suggested that we do more to help," Oramas recalled, "and Amílcar accepted our offer to increase our aid with great pleasure."[30]

Castro sent for Dreke, who, since returning from Zaire, had headed the bureau that trained Cubans going on military missions abroad and foreigners coming to Cuba (the UM, or Military Unit, 1546). "Fidel told me: 'You have to take charge of the military mission in Guinea.'" He also urged Dreke to take some of the men who had been with him in Zaire, "the best."[31] A few days later, Dreke called on one of them, Erasmo Vidiaux, who was in charge of the UM 1546 training camp in Baracoa. "'How are you doing?' Dreke asked me," Vidiaux recalled. "'Fine,' I answered. [Dreke:] 'And your mother?' [Vidiaux:] 'Fine too.' [Dreke:] 'We've got a little mission for you; you've got to get ready.'"[32]

The next day Vidiaux flew to Santiago to say goodbye to his mother. "I told her I was going to take another course in the Soviet Union." (He had said the same when he had gone to Zaire.) "Our families were used to sudden departures."[33]

In February 1967 he flew to Conakry with Dreke, Pablito Mena (another

---

b. Until 1972, the DGI was in charge of the MMCG. In 1972, a special task force within the FAR, the Décima Dirección, took charge of all Cuban military missions abroad. (Quesada González, El MINFAR, p. 44.) Initially, this meant only the MMCG; by 1973 it also included missions in Sierra Leone, Equatorial Guinea, and South Yemen.

veteran of Zaire), and Reynaldo Batista, a member of the UM 1546 and Dreke's driver.[34]

Unlike Artemio, Dreke was a comandante, a member of the Central Committee, and a man who knew Africa and guerrilla warfare. Moreover, he inspired enormous confidence and respect. "Dreke has always been a role model," Batista recalls. "Very simple, very austere." The power of his example and his quiet charisma were evident when I interviewed the Cubans who had served under him, thirty years earlier, in Zaire and Guinea-Bissau. And they were evident when I went to Bissau. Time and again, I heard the same words of respect, warmth, and admiration for him. "We learned a great deal from Moya [Dreke's nom de guerre]," remarked Arafam Mané, a PAIGC commander. "Moya was an exceptional leader," the president of Guinea-Bissau, Nino, who had been a senior PAIGC military commander during the war, told me. For their part, the Cubans were impressed with the commitment and the discipline of the PAIGC. "We had had a really bitter experience in Zaire, and we encountered something completely different in Guinea-Bissau," Dreke observed.[35]

By April 1967 there were almost sixty Cubans in Guinea-Bissau, including several who had been in Zaire with Che Guevara. Dreke himself spent half his time in Conakry and half at the front.[36] He was in Conakry when, in October 1967, Guevara was killed in Bolivia. "My dear brother in the struggle," Dreke wrote to Estrada, "with this letter comes a strong embrace. . . . I imagine how you and all the others must be feeling about Che's death. . . . This has been a very heavy blow for all of us here, but we all know that tears and acts of desperation will achieve nothing and my advice to all the compañeros has been to remain calm and to redouble their efforts. You know what Che means for all of us. . . . But I know that right now we need to be calm and resolute, because every one of us is needed to continue the work that Che began."[37]

PORTUGAL STRIKES BACK

Dreke headed the MMCG for one more year. By the time he returned to Cuba in late 1968, the PAIGC's position in Guinea-Bissau had improved significantly. In January 1969, U.S. ambassador Dean Brown reported from Dakar:

> The war in Portuguese Guinea . . . has gone from bad to worse for the Portuguese during the past three years. During this period, despite an increase in Portuguese troop strength from 20,000 to 25,000, the Portuguese have lost increasing areas of the hinterland to rebel control. There is only one major road still open. . . . Other main roads cannot be used because of the twin dangers of mines and ambushes. The rebel PAIGC forces control large areas of the country, perhaps 60%, or at least deny access to them to the Portuguese. This situation applies, however, only to the countryside. . . .
> The Portuguese are correct when they assert that they control most of the

population and that there is no area of the country in which they do not continue to hold all major towns. On the other hand, the rebels are not too far from the truth when they claim . . . that two-thirds of the country is theirs, and that in these regions they have set up their own administration. . . . The areas of rebel control, like inkblots, spread over the country and ever closer to the Bissau region itself.[38]

Portuguese general Arnaldo Schultz, who had arrived in Bissau in 1964 predicting "the war in Portuguese Guinea would be over within six months," was "sadly disillusioned" when he left four years later.[39] A highly respected officer, General António de Spínola, replaced him as governor and commander in chief in May 1968, a time when "the military situation for the Portuguese was clearly deteriorating."[40]

Spínola promised "the greatest generosity toward those who repent and surrender their weapons . . . and the greatest severity toward those who persist in their criminal rebellion."[41] Reinforced from Portugal, he engaged in "a vigorous military campaign" that stressed helicopter-borne attacks on the liberated areas where his troops "were free to destroy villages and crops, to kill civilians and generally to terrorize the population."[42] At the same time, he set in motion a massive political, social, economic, and psychological campaign to gain the support of the population. "He wanted to deprive the fish of water," a PAIGC commander remarked. "Whether Cuban aid, supported by Conakry, will be sufficient to hold off the increased Portuguese offensive, remains to be seen," Ambassador Brown warned from Dakar. In fact, Spínola's policy of "smiles and blood," as Cabral called it, was able only to bring about a stalemate with the rebels, who "effectively" controlled, U.S. intelligence noted in 1970, "almost half of the country."[43] In a desperate attempt to break the impasse, Spínola launched a commando attack on Conakry on November 22, 1970, to bring down Touré, thereby cutting off the PAIGC's rear guard. (It was expected "that Sékou Touré and Amílcar Cabral would be killed," a senior Portuguese officer explained.) "We face a watershed in the life of this province," Spínola told the Portuguese prime minister a few days before the attack. "Either we use all the means at our disposal to eradicate the enemy's sanctuaries or we lose Guinea[-Bissau] irrevocably."[44]

The operation was a fiasco. After a few hours of fighting, the attackers withdrew in haste, having failed to kill either Touré or Cabral, who was out of the country. "This ill-considered affair has thoroughly aroused Africans of all political persuasions and has . . . strengthened Sekou Toure's regime," the U.S. ambassador to the United Nations, Charles Yost, noted.[45] Nevertheless, the United States abstained as the UN Security Council condemned Portugal for the invasion, even though Yost conceded that the United States had "no reason to question" the UN report that placed responsibility for the attack on Portugal.[46]

The war dragged on, dashing Spínola's hopes and giving the PAIGC time to hone its skills. PAIGC training, guerrilla tactics, and arms were "first class," a

Portuguese colonel told a visiting South African journalist in April 1971. "There are times when I sincerely wish I had some of their young leaders with me in the field," he added. The PAIGC, a captain told the same journalist, " 'was in a class of its own.' . . . Their tenacity impressed the Portuguese captain. It frightened his men at times." The rebels also impressed U.S. officials. The PAIGC "has been increasingly ready to stand and fight when engaged by the Portuguese, reflecting improved leadership and troop discipline," the U.S. ambassador in Lisbon noted in October 1971. A State Department study concluded two months later that the PAIGC had "around 7,000 well-armed, well-trained effectives," that it received "extensive Soviet support," and that the Cubans were "involved in PAIGC insurgency activities."[47]

STOKELY CARMICHAEL AND THE PAIGC

As the most successful guerrilla movement in Africa, the PAIGC became a symbol of pride for some African Americans, and for a moment it seemed that this admiration might evolve into something more tangible. Exasperated by the escalation of the war in Vietnam—where a disproportionate number of African Americans served and died—and by the pervasive reality of discrimination and police brutality at home, many African Americans turned away from Martin Luther King's message of nonviolence. On August 11, 1965, less than a week after Johnson had signed the Voting Rights Act, the most destructive race riot in more than two decades erupted in Watts, sparking "a succession of 'long, hot summers' " in the country's urban centers.[48] Dismissing King's credo as naive and irrelevant, young black militants wanted "Black Power." This new mood, born out of rage and despair, found its political expression in the Black Panther Party, an overtly revolutionary, paramilitary organization that advocated a black-led, socialist-inspired insurrection.

In June 1967, while Tampa and Cincinnati were convulsed by riots, Black Panther leader Stokely Carmichael went to Cuba, where he was treated "like a movie star." He told his Cuban hosts that he wanted African Americans to fight alongside the PAIGC in Guinea-Bissau to stress their solidarity with Africa and to atone for their participation in the war of aggression against Vietnam. In late September, Ulises Estrada and another DGI officer accompanied Carmichael to Conakry, where he presented his plan to Amílcar Cabral. Cabral was wary. He preferred to avoid having foreigners fighting in Guinea-Bissau, and he feared repercussions with Washington, but he finally relented, agreeing to accept twenty or thirty African Americans. His only condition was that they had to be trained in guerrilla warfare in another country.[49]

"We couldn't train them here in Cuba: the United States would have clobbered us," Estrada told me. Therefore, two DGI officers accompanied Carmichael to Tanzania to ask Nyerere to allow the training there. Nyerere agreed. Carmichael returned to Conakry in November to inform Cabral and to make further arrangements. Then he met the South African singer Miriam Makeba, and his plans changed. "He dropped us!" Dreke remarked. He married Makeba, became a citizen of Guinea, and settled down.

THREE U.S. ADMINISTRATIONS AND THE PAIGC

Those few white Americans who followed African affairs generally felt some sympathy and respect for the PAIGC. U.S. officials were impressed by Amílcar Cabral. They appreciated "his combination of modesty and quiet confidence" and his "rational, non-ideological, common-sense approach." After a two-hour unofficial conversation with him, the U.S. deputy assistant secretary for African affairs reported: "Cabral made his points calmly and politely, and listened well, apparently willing to consider others' views even when he did not agree with them." After Cabral's death, a former U.S. ambassador to Guinea wrote, "I came to know Amílcar Cabral . . . as a passionate fighter for the rights of his people but also as a reasonable man with no animosity toward the American people." His words were echoed by Terence Todman, who was the U.S. ambassador in Conakry in 1972–74. "I was very favorably impressed with Amílcar Cabral," he said. "He wanted independence, but there was no negativism. He was sensible, reasonable."[50]

This did not, however, affect U.S. policy. "We attempt to straddle the fence by distinguishing between Portugal (Europe) and Portugal (Africa)," the U.S. ambassador in Lisbon wrote in 1968.[51] From the Kennedy through the Nixon administrations, U.S. officials firmly proclaimed that their policy was that the United States gave weapons to Portugal only on condition that they not be used in Africa. How the United States should respond to Portuguese violations of this policy was settled in mid-1963 during a sharp debate within the Kennedy administration about Portugal's use of U.S. planes in Guinea-Bissau. Adlai Stevenson, the ambassador to the United Nations, was the most forceful spokesperson for the minority view. "I am greatly concerned," he cabled Secretary of State Rusk, "with the presence and use of eight US-supplied F-86 aircraft in Portuguese Guinea. . . . I have previously known nothing about this and have always understood that nothing of this sort had gone to any African territory. Presence of these aircraft in Guinea and their use for military purposes cannot remain unknown indefinitely. . . . We have repeatedly stated here at UN that equipment we supply Portugal is for defense of Europe and not for use in Portuguese African territories. We have said we oppose such use and take measures to insure that such equipment has not been diverted to Africa."

After listing a litany of statements by the Kennedy administration to that effect, Stevenson concluded:

> Now I learn that Portugal has had eight F-86s in Guinea [Bissau] since "at least September 1961," that this was reported at time of original transfer . . . and that they are currently used in combat role. . . . If attention of the [UN] SC [Security Council] or GA [General Assembly] is drawn to uncorrected

presence of US-furnished aircraft in Portuguese Guinea, as no doubt in time it will be, this revelation will greatly reduce, if not completely destroy, the credibility of US claims of being able to keep a check on US-furnished equipment as well as credibility of "assurances" from Portuguese government. . . . And if, finally, this diversion having been revealed, we are not in position to honestly state that every effort has been made to have Portuguese government withdraw aircraft from use in Portuguese territories, sincerity of US position on entire question of Portuguese territories will be shattered.

The Kennedy administration complained to Lisbon, but not too harshly, for Portugal was a valued ally, and the planes stayed in Guinea-Bissau.[52] "Portugal's diversion and continued use of vast amounts of U.S. MAP [Military Assistance Program] equipment in Portuguese Africa are embarrassing to us in our relations in Africa and at the UN," Assistant Secretary Mennen Williams lamented, as the F-86s continued to be used in combat in Guinea-Bissau. From Conakry, the U.S. ambassador added: "Our position is indefensible."[53] Stevenson had written Kennedy in June 1963 that the Africans wanted to know whether the United States stood "for self-determination and human rights" or whether "we will give our Azores base . . . priority." Despite Kennedy's uneasiness and the strong opposition of a few U.S. officials, the administration's policy was clear: the base in the Azores was more important than self-determination in Africa. In the final analysis, as a German scholar concludes, "What worried the [Kennedy] administration was not Portugal's use of the arms in Africa, but the danger that it might become public. In fact the administration . . . continued to deliver weapons to Portugal."[54]

Subsequent administrations followed Kennedy's lead, claiming that the Portuguese were using the weapons supplied by the United States only in Europe. But, as Tanzanian officials pointed out, "US and other arms given Portugal under NATO arrangements, however restricted, at the very least free other military and economic resources for use by Portugal in Africa," and, moreover, the Portuguese continued to divert the weapons to their African territories. "We would have been fools not to have done so," a Portuguese general who had been in command in Mozambique and Angola remarked. "Now and then the Americans would grumble," he added. "It was all for show."[55] Under President Richard Nixon, U.S. policy developed an even more pronounced pro-Portuguese bent, consistent with the administration's support for white-ruled Africa. The most notorious manifestation was the December 1971 executive agreement that gave Portugal $436 million in credits for the use of the Azores base until February 1974. It was, noted the *New York Times*, "one of the largest economic assistance packages negotiated in many years in exchange for foreign base rights," and it would "prop up the Lisbon Government's floundering economy," exhausted by a decade of colonial wars.[56] As Amílcar Cabral told the UN Security Council in Addis Ababa the following February, "Portugal would not be in a position to carry out three wars against Africans without the aid of her allies."[57]

By the time of the Azores agreement, however, the PAIGC had fully recovered from the initial setbacks inflicted by Spínola and the best the latter could hope for was an uneasy stalemate. That the PAIGC fought so well was due primarily to Amílcar Cabral, his commanders in the field, the guerrilla troops, and the Cubans.

"We want no volunteers," Cabral told a British journalist in 1967. "Foreign military advisers or commanders, or any other foreign personnel, are the last thing we shall accept. They would rob my people of their one chance of achieving a historical meaning for themselves: of reasserting their own history, of recapturing their own identity."[58] Cabral was being disingenuous: the Cubans were already in his country, at his request. What he said, however, did reflect his deepest convictions. This was the Guineans' war, and it offered them the opportunity to forge a nation out of separate ethnic groups. ("Ten years ago we were Fulas, Manjacos, Mandingas, Balantas, Papéis, and others. Now we are a nation of Guineans," he told a group of visiting African Americans in 1972.) "Amílcar didn't want foreign fighters to join us," a PAIGC commander observed. "He used to say: 'We have to free our own country.' But we needed specialists who knew how to use long-range weapons."[59]

Cabral limited foreign participation in two ways. First, he turned only to the Cubans. Throughout the war, they were the only foreigners who fought in Guinea-Bissau.[60] Second, he limited their number to the minimum. When Risquet offered in late August 1966, for example, to ask Fidel if his men in the Congo, who would soon be returning to Cuba, could go instead to Guinea-Bissau, Cabral refused.[61] The following year he rejected Dreke's suggestion that Cuba send 200 to 300 men to help attack Portuguese strongholds.[62] On average, there were only 50 to 60 Cubans assigned to the MMCG.[63]

And yet, despite their small numbers, their military contribution was, as President Nino said, "of the utmost importance." There was, first of all, "the boost to our morale," a PAIGC commander remarked. "Here were men who had crossed the ocean to come to our aid; they lived with us; they shared in our sacrifices." The Cubans, said another, "were brave; they endured everything; they ate what we ate; we did everything together."[64]

Amílcar Cabral had invited the Cubans because, as Nino recalled, "we needed training in the use of mortars and other types of artillery."[65] As the war progressed, the weapons that the PAIGC received from the Soviet Union grew more sophisticated. The gunners had to shoot targets they could not see in the dense forest. This required a degree of knowledge that very few PAIGC fighters even approached having. Battery chiefs, for example, needed to know calculus. In Cuba, battery chiefs were sergeants or second lieutenants and all had completed at least high school. Almost all of the volunteers who went to Guinea-Bissau were artillerymen who were officers and sergeants.[66] In 1966 they were both battery chiefs and gunners. As time went by, the PAIGC combatants took over the role of gunners, but the battery chiefs—those who made the calculations and directed the gunners—were, to the end, almost always Cubans.

There was one exception to this rule: many of the Cape Verdean students who had been sent to Cuba in 1965 ended up in Guinea-Bissau. In the fall of 1967 Amílcar Cabral had decided that a guerrilla war in Cape Verde would not succeed: there was almost no water, there were no natural hideouts, no animals to eat, and the population was not ready. "We disagreed, but we did what Amílcar wanted," Dreke remarked. "When I finally went to Cape Verde several years later I realized that Amílcar had been right and that a guerrilla war there would have been a disaster!" And so the thirty-one Cape Verdeans arrived in Conakry in late 1967 and assumed a variety of specialized positions in the PAIGC. In the words of one of them, "some of us joined the [PAIGC] navy, most joined the guerrillas on land, others were assigned to political and diplomatic tasks, etc." Several fought with distinction in the artillery.[67]

The Cuban contribution was also critical to military planning both in Conakry, where Amílcar Cabral developed the strategy, and on the ground. The PAIGC had divided the country into three fronts (south, east, and north). "The leader of the Cubans in each front was told to stay glued to the PAIGC chief and to be his adviser," Dreke explained. "Therefore, the MMCG tried hard to put their best men in charge of the Cubans at every front."[68]

The Cubans were also the specialists in laying land mines and using sophisticated infantry weapons that the PAIGC was receiving from the Soviet Union. "This was very important," a PAIGC commander remarked. "They trained us on the spot. We called our first bazookas 'Cubans.' They were made in the United States, but it was the Cubans who gave them to us and taught us how to use them."[69]

Amílcar Cabral's style "was not necessarily our own," Enrique Montero, who headed the MMCG in 1969–70, commented.[70] While Cabral kept a tight rein on military strategy, he spent most of his time out of the country—in Conakry or traveling in search of foreign support. This support was critical to the success of the movement. Cabral was the key protagonist in a diplomatic campaign to gather everything, from weapons to medical supplies, doctors, scholarships, books, and humanitarian aid. "Amílcar was a great diplomat," a PAIGC official remembers. "If people throughout the world were aware of our existence, it was due to him. We would go to international conferences with maps of Guinea-Bissau: 'You see,' we would say, 'This is Guinea-Bissau!' No one knew anything about it. Amílcar kept telling me: 'We must be everywhere, we must listen even if we don't want to, we must laugh even when we don't feel like it.' "[71] Cabral's diplomatic activities, however, kept him from the front. He did not direct the military operations in person. "This concerned us," Dreke explained. "Our training and our experience taught us that the leader had to be at the front." Furthermore, Amílcar Cabral waged a war of attrition. He was not interested in big operations in which the PAIGC might suffer heavy casualties or a defeat, and he remembered "the bloody and bitter lesson" of the November 1966 attack

Amílcar Cabral, the leader of the independence movement of Guinea-Bissau, asked the Cubans to send instructors to train his guerrillas and to fight alongside them. "Cuba made no demands; it gave us unconditional aid," another guerrilla leader recalled. In August 1966 Cabral visited the Cuban military camp in Brazzaville. "I don't believe there is life after death," he told the Cuban soldiers, "but if there is, we can be sure that the souls of our forefathers who were taken away to America to be slaves are rejoicing today to see their children reunited and working together to help us be independent and free."

against Madina de Boé.[72] He believed that the Portuguese would be unable to withstand the strain of a long war and would be forced to negotiate. "We would have preferred a more aggressive strategy, but we adapted," Dreke recalled. "It was their country and their war. I would make suggestions to Amílcar; he would listen without saying yes or no, and eventually he made his own decision. Sometimes he followed my advice; sometimes he didn't."[73]

On more than one occasion, Cabral asked the Cubans to help with an operation, only to cancel it at the last moment. In 1967, for example, he asked Cuba to send a group of explosives experts to blow up the bridge of Ensalma which connected Bissau with the interior. "I told him, 'Amílcar, we're ready. We only need the [PAIGC] guide,'" Dreke recalls. "Amílcar said: 'Wait two or three days.' Two or three days went by, and then two or three more, and two or three more and two or three more. Finally Amílcar told me: 'We're not going to blow up the bridge. If we do, Bissau will be isolated but when the war is over we'll have to wait until we get help from the Soviet Union or Cuba or someone else before we'll be able to rebuild it.' The operation was canceled."[74]

Some Cubans grumbled, but virtually all, from Fidel Castro to the successive chiefs of the MMCG and their subordinates, accepted their role: this was Amílcar's war; they were there to help, to offer advice, and to follow the PAIGC's lead. Had the Cubans behaved with less humility, the proud PAIGC commanders who talked to me about Cuba's contribution would, I suspect, have expressed their gratitude with less warmth. Back in 1965–66, Amílcar Cabral had decided that Cuba alone should send its fighters to Guinea-Bissau. He chose Cuba in part because he felt some cultural and ethnic affinity with the Cubans and, above all, because he respected the Cuban revolution. "I remember that when I was in Cuba, Fidel told me that Cuba is also Africa," he told a group of Cubans in August 1966. "I don't believe there is life after death, but if there is, we can be sure that the souls of our forefathers who were taken away to America to be slaves are rejoicing today to see their children reunited and working together to help us be independent and free." Thirty years later, other PAIGC leaders echoed his words. "We greatly admired the struggle of the Cuban people. The Cubans were a special case because we knew that they, more than anyone else, were the champions of internationalism," one recalled. "Cuba made no demands, it gave us unconditional aid," said another.[75]

This help was not merely military; it was also medical.

THE CUBAN DOCTORS

"The medical care of our combatants and of the people in the liberated zones reached a completely new level with the arrival of the first Cuban doctors in 1966," Luís Cabral writes. There were no native doctors. "The colonial administration had trained some good nurses and nurses' aides in Bissau, but being a nurse was quite a prominent position . . . so very few of them left their jobs in the colonial administration to join the freedom fighters." Therefore the arrival of the Cuban doctors "was, without any doubt, of utmost importance for our struggle, not just because of the lives they saved, but even more because of the boost they gave us." Once the Cubans came, explains Nino, the guerrillas "knew that their wounds need not be fatal and that their injuries could be healed."[76]

A veteran of the struggle against Batista, Luis Peraza, a doctor in the UM 1546, was one of the first to go to Guinea-Bissau. "If you're interested in volunteering to help a national liberation movement," the head of medical services in the UM 1546 told him in early 1966, "go to army headquarters." Like the others, he was told to tell his family that he was going to study in the Soviet Union. "But I told my wife, 'I'm going on an internationalist mission. Don't tell anyone. I don't

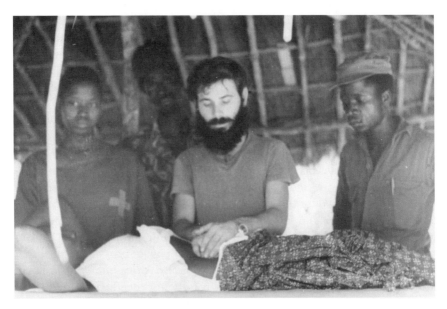

During Guinea-Bissau's war of independence (1963–74), all but one of the foreign doctors in the liberated zones were Cubans. Enrique Romero, shown in this makeshift hospital in a rebel zone, was one of them. "The Cuban doctors really performed a miracle," a rebel official recalled many years later. "Not only did they save lives, but they put their own lives at risk. They were truly selfless."

know where I'm going or how long I'll be away, but I'll stay in touch.'" A few days before leaving, he was told that he was going to Guinea-Bissau, but he still did not know how long the mission would last. "All I knew about Africa was the Tarzan movies," Peraza remarked.[77]

He left aboard the *Lidia Doce* in May 1966. "We didn't bring any food with us because we expected to eat whatever the guerrillas ate. Once we got there we discovered that there was almost no food in the jungle; I lost forty pounds in three months." His group included ten doctors but no nurses; the first nurses (all of whom were male) arrived in December 1967 with the second group of doctors. "Havana learned from our experience," Peraza recalled. "They decided to send an equal number of doctors and nurses, working as a team, and to send food from Cuba."[78]

When heavy fighting was expected, the doctors accompanied the combatants. Otherwise they stayed behind in makeshift hospitals of two or three huts: one hut would be an operating room, the others were for patients.[79] "Whether they were with our guerrilla units at the front, or in our field hospitals, the Cuban doctors . . . won the hearts of our fighters and our people," Luís Cabral writes. "They taught our health care workers, who had received minimal training abroad, how to serve our people better. The Cuban doctors and nurses . . . fulfilled all our hopes."[80]

To be sure, there were a few glitches. In late 1973, Dr. Enrique Romero went to a makeshift hospital in the southern front to replace another Cuban doctor, who had been rejected by the population because he had failed to show respect for their customs. "I looked like my predecessor," Romero recalled, "and initially everyone snubbed me. Sure, they fed me, and protected me, and let me be their doctor, but they didn't talk to me." It took a month to convince them that he was different.[81]

Throughout the war, all but one of the foreign doctors in the liberated zones of Guinea-Bissau were Cubans. The exception was a young Panamanian, Hugo Spadafora, who had become impressed with the PAIGC while living in Cairo and started to write to Amílcar Cabral volunteering his services. "He wrote so many letters that Amílcar finally decided to let him come," PAIGC leader Fidelis Cabral recalled. "At that time we didn't have any doctors." Spadafora arrived in Conakry on February 10, 1966, and was sent to the village of Boké, in Guinea near the border with Guinea-Bissau, where the PAIGC had recently opened a hospital staffed only by a few nurses. "With my limited experience I had a hard time running the hospital," Spadafora wrote. Within a few weeks, however, the first Cuban doctors arrived, bringing a "large supply of medicine, surgical and medical equipment, and supplies . . . [and] the quality of the hospital's care increased exponentially." Spadafora left Boké in July for Guinea-Bissau, where he worked for nine months. In May 1967 he returned to Panama. "Had other foreign doctors volunteered to come to Guinea-Bissau, Amílcar would have allowed it," Fidelis Cabral surmised.[82] It is impossible to say, based on the available evidence, whether others did volunteer. What is certain, however, is that during the war Spadafora and the Cubans were the only foreign doctors in the liberated areas of Guinea-Bissau.[83]

In Guinea, on the other hand, there were non-Cuban doctors at the two PAIGC hospitals in Boké and Koundara, a village near the border with Guinea-Bissau. At Boké, there were only Cubans until 1969, when a new, well-equipped hospital, built with Yugoslav money, became the flagship of the PAIGC medical services. Its staff included one or two Cuban doctors, one Yugoslav (Ivan Mihajlovic, a surgeon who was the hospital's director), and three or four Yugoslav medical technicians.[84] The smaller hospital at Koundara was staffed for several years by Dr. Binh, a Vietnamese professor from the University of Hanoi. "Only a great people like the Vietnamese would have offered us a doctor when they themselves were enduring one of the longest and cruelest wars," Luís Cabral writes. PAIGC health personnel who worked at Koundara remember Binh with great warmth. "He was an extremely intelligent man, a great surgeon. I learned a lot from him," said Ernesto Lopes Moreira, who was then a physician's assistant. "And he was also very simple; he didn't mind living in very poor conditions, sharing our sacrifices."[85]

The PAIGC also had a small hospital in southern Senegal, in the town of Ziguinchor, just ten miles north of the border. It was staffed by only one doctor, at various times Portuguese, French, Angolan, or Dutch. If a surgeon was needed, Luís Cabral writes, "the [Cuban] surgeon Mariano Sixto or another Cuban doctor would come across the border at night." This was tricky because the Dakar government barred all Cubans from entering Senegal. "I myself went to get them," Luís Cabral continues, "and they accepted the risk of entering Senegal just like they accepted all the other risks of the war. . . . I would take them back to the border very early in the morning."[86]

Between 1966 and 1974 there were, on average, fifteen to twenty Cuban doctors and nurses in Guinea-Bissau and Boké. Overall, more than forty Cuban doctors, most of whom were in the military, served in Guinea-Bissau and at Boké.[87] The significance of this contribution is highlighted by the fact that throughout the war only eight to twelve non-Cuban foreign doctors served in the PAIGC's medical services at Boké, Koundara, and Ziguinchor and none, with the exception of Spadafora, served in Guinea-Bissau.[88]

During the war, the PAIGC understated the role of the Cuban doctors (just as it denied the presence of Cuban military personnel). Its official publications stressed that by 1972 there were eighteen Guinean doctors and twenty-three foreign doctors in the liberated areas of Guinea-Bissau, an assertion that scholars have accepted as fact.[89] To set the record straight, and to assess accurately the importance of the forty Cuban doctors' contribution, it is important to ascertain how many Guinean doctors the PAIGC really had, and how many were in Guinea-Bissau. I therefore decided to interview the protagonists themselves.

Early one Sunday morning, I went to the house of Dr. Paulo Medina, a Guinean who had been a doctor during the war. I hoped, through him, to learn how many native doctors there had been in the PAIGC, when they had completed their training and started practicing, and where they had worked. This would help me assess the relative importance of the Cuban role.

Dr. Medina was candid and did not try to embellish his role. He had graduated in 1969 from Moscow's Patrice Lumumba University, he explained, and the PAIGC had sent him to Boké, not to Guinea-Bissau, where he worked with Cubans and Yugoslavs until 1972. He then went to Belgrade to further his medical training, and he was there when the war ended in 1974.

Medina told me that during the war eight Guineans (including himself) had received their medical degrees, all from Patrice Lumumba University; there were also, he added, four physician's assistants and one dentist. Three of the doctors and one of the physician's assistants had died, but the others were living in Bissau.

By the time I left Bissau, I had interviewed two of the doctors, the dentist, and two of the physician's assistants. They were impressive, unassuming, pleasant (with one exception), and, like Medina, disinclined to embellish their past. Three told me flatly that they had not practiced in Guinea-Bissau during the war; two said they had, and these assertions were confirmed by the others. With one major difference—that there were five, not four, physician's assistants—they all corroborated Medina's account.[90]

They said that the PAIGC had no native doctors until 1968, when the first two qualified. Two more received their degrees the following year, one in 1970, two in 1971, and one in 1972. Upon graduating, they all returned to PAIGC headquarters in Conakry.

The PAIGC was in no hurry to send them to Guinea-Bissau. "At the beginning of the war, we had no doctors, so we sent our people abroad to become doctors," a senior PAIGC official explained. "When they returned we thought that they should first gain some experience in good conditions—in Boké, in Koundara."[91] Accordingly, only one of the first four doctors to graduate was sent to Guinea-Bissau; the other three went to Boké. In January 1972 they were all sent to Europe to pursue their specializations and all four were in Europe when the war ended. Of the remaining four doctors, all of whom qualified between 1970 and 1972, two went straight to Guinea-Bissau upon graduating; the other two and the dentist went to Boké and Koundara. The experience of the physician's assistants was similar. After graduating in 1968–70 from institutes in Kiev and Sofia, they were sent to Boké and Koundara. Later, two went to Guinea-Bissau and two returned to Europe to pursue their medical studies.[92]

To sum up, before 1968 there were no native Guinean doctors; between 1968 and 1974 eight doctors, five physician's assistants, and one dentist received their degrees in the Soviet Union or Bulgaria. Of these fourteen, only five went to Guinea-Bissau (for varying lengths of time), and five went to Europe for further training.[93] This was PAIGC policy: Amílcar Cabral was planning for the future, when the war would be over. Such farsightedness was possible only because, year after year, Cuban doctors bore the brunt of the effort in Guinea-Bissau. "Many of our comrades are alive today only because of the Cuban medical assistance," Francisca Pereira, a senior PAIGC official, observed. "The Cuban doctors really performed a miracle. I am eternally grateful to them: not only did they save lives, but they put their own lives at risk. They were truly selfless."[94]

THE VOLUNTEERS

All the members of the MMCG—doctors and soldiers—were volunteers, like their predecessors in Algeria, Zaire, and the Congo.[c,95] Until 1972 the DGI, in collaboration with the armed forces, chose who would be asked; thereafter the armed forces made the selection. The overwhelming majority of those who were chosen—both the rank and file and the leaders—were dark-skinned blacks.[d] Some critics have detected a racist tinge to this policy, but not the CIA.

c. In Algeria the volunteer principle was less carefully observed. The 686 men chosen for the mission were hastily assembled, and those who did not want to go were asked to say so in front of the entire group. Nevertheless, some did withdraw.

While this section focuses on the volunteers in Guinea-Bissau, much of what it says is relevant for the previous missions.

d. This was particularly true for the mission in Zaire. After realizing that there were many mulatto as well as white Cape Verdeans in Guinea-Bissau, the Cubans relaxed the policy somewhat.

"These Cubans are evidently selected, in part, for darkness of skin so that they may be less conspicuous and more assimilable during their sojourn in the host countries."[96] Moreover, what the CIA did not know was that the Simba leader Soumialot and Amílcar Cabral had specifically requested that the instructors be black for just that reason.

Many of the volunteers had previously expressed their eagerness to participate in an internationalist mission. "Some of us who worked in the armed forces and the Ministry of Interior," remarks Montero, "would learn of operations that were being planned or were already under way, and we would try to find a way to join." Others did not know about specific operations, but had friends who were in the thick of things. "People who knew I worked with Piñeiro," recalls Osvaldo Cárdenas, who for many years was in charge of West Africa within the DGI, "kept telling me, 'Please, if you hear anything, if you get a chance, get me in.' Some bugged me for years." Others, who had no such contacts, wrote letters to Fidel or Raúl Castro. "Compañero Raúl," said one, "I am writing to tell you about my desire to fight against the imperialists anywhere in the world." Another wrote, "Compañero Fidel, I want to let you know that I am eager to fight anywhere in the world, anywhere a liberation movement may need me. I want to help those who are now fighting against the common enemy of all mankind: imperialism."[97]

What motivated them? There was the mystique of guerrilla war. "We dreamed of revolution," muses Estrada. "We wanted to be part of it, to feel that we were fighting for it. We were young, and the children of a revolution." There was altruism; there was a spirit of adventure; there was the desire to help Cuba. Fighting abroad, they would defend the revolution at home. "In all those years we believed that at any moment they [the United States] were going to strike us," Cárdenas remarked in 1993, "and for us it was better to wage the war abroad than in our own country. This was the strategy of 'Two or Three Vietnams'; that is, distracting and dividing the enemy's forces. I never imagined then that I would be sitting here [in a living room in Havana] talking about it now—we all assumed we were going to die young."[98]

The volunteers received no public praise in Cuba. They left "knowing that their story would remain a secret."[99] They won no medals or material rewards. Once back they could not boast about their deeds, because they were bound to secrecy.

Among the Cubans who went to Guinea-Bissau was one woman, Concepción Dumois (Conchita), who spent four or five months there in 1967. Conchita, who worked in the DGI with Ulises Estrada, was haunted by the death of her companion, Jorge Masetti, who had been killed in 1964 leading the guerrillas in Argentina. "She kept asking to be allowed to join a guerrilla war; she kept insisting." As soon as Dreke became the head of the MMCG, Estrada asked him if Conchita could go to Guinea-Bissau. "I knew Conchita and I respected her," Dreke remembers. "I said yes."[100] She was the first Cuban woman to fight in Africa.

Women participated in Cuba's technical assistance program in Africa from its beginnings in 1963, when twenty-three joined the first Cuban medical mission to Algeria. But until Cuba's intervention in Angola in 1975–76, only one woman had joined a Cuban military mission in Africa: Conchita Dubois, an intelligence officer shown here in 1967 with Víctor Dreke, the head of the Cuban military mission in Guinea and Guinea-Bissau. "I respected her," Dreke remembers.

The volunteers were instructed to tell their families that they were going to the Soviet Union to attend courses. "There were about 7,000 to 10,000 Cubans on various forms of scholarships in the USSR," Dr. Milton Hechavarría explained. "So there was nothing strange if someone said he was going to study there."[101]

Mail was routed through a special zip code in Havana which in theory led, via diplomatic pouch, to the Soviet Union, but in fact led to the DGI and then to

Africa. (The system had been inaugurated in Algeria in 1963 and was also used in the Congo.) "We get mail, but with a three- to four-month delay," wrote Vidiaux in Guinea-Bissau.[102] DGI officers in Havana screened the letters from the volunteers. "If there was anything that could give away where they were or what they were doing, we would hold onto them," Estrada recalled. Some volunteers pretended that they were in the USSR. "Sometimes we'd get together and someone who had been in the Soviet Union would help us put in authentic touches."[103] Others never mentioned where they were or what they were doing.

Back home many believed that they were in the Soviet Union; others knew better. "My dear Moya," Conchita wrote to Dreke upon returning from Guinea-Bissau, "Tell all the compañeros . . . that the first Sunday after my return to Havana I had lunch with all their wives and children and we laughed a lot, always saying that you're in the USSR, but I don't think that even Sobeida [Dreke's four-year-old daughter] believes it. But they are all very discreet, and no one asks any questions."[104] While some may have wanted to avoid problems with the authorities, most seem to have shared the values of those who had gone and respected the need for secrecy.

The volunteers' life in Guinea-Bissau was spartan. Cuban ships brought canned food, rice, sugar, beans, oil, and coffee, and the MMCG had a little money to buy fresh food. "Comrade Vera," the acting chief of the mission wrote to Vidiaux, who was in charge of the Cubans on the southern front, "along with this note I am sending you 24,700 [Guinea] francs so that you can buy the necessary food [in Boké]. You must guard these francs with the greatest care; in a few days we will send you the supplies from the ship; therefore you will be able to keep the money in reserve for unforeseen circumstances."[105] But when the food arrived, it was never enough because the Cubans shared it with their PAIGC comrades. "Once," a Cuban volunteer remembers, "I had a can of beef. I didn't want to share it. The PAIGC fighters near me were Moslems, so I told them it was pork. 'It doesn't matter,' they said, 'Allah doesn't see through these thick trees.' So I gave them the meat."[106]

Although the volunteers who went to Guinea-Bissau in 1966 had been told that they might be gone at least five years, in 1967 Dreke proposed that their tours of duty last only one year. "I decided that we shouldn't keep people there indefinitely when it was possible to replace them relatively easily. I proposed one year because the climate was very harsh, parasites and malaria were endemic, and food was scarce."[107]

The recommendation was informally accepted and, on average, the volunteers remained in Guinea-Bissau about eighteen months.[108] The head of the MMCG was expected to safeguard the psychological and physical well-being of his men. "If they were suffering from malaria, we treated them in country," Montero remarked. "If it was something severe, we sent them back in one of the Aeroflot flights from Conakry through Prague or Moscow."[109]

There was no provision for "rest and relaxation" for the Cubans in Guinea-Bissau, but those in the southern and the eastern regions would occasionally go to Boké "to breathe a little."[110] Boké was then a small village of 2,000 to 3,000 people, not the bustling town I visited in 1996. "At night it was lit by a few streetlights, but for those of us coming from Guinea-Bissau it seemed like Paris!" Montero remembered. He arrived one night, by truck, after a long trek from eastern Guinea-Bissau. "In the distance we could see some small lights. For us, on the truck, it was as if we were looking at the Champs-Elysées!"[111] Things were more difficult for the Cubans in the north: for them the rear guard was Senegal, where no Cubans were allowed to go.

Following the system that had been established in Algeria in 1963, the volunteers signed a document before leaving Cuba specifying whether the Cuban government should pay their salary to their families or deposit it in a bank until their return. The amount was exactly the same as if they had remained in Cuba. They also received a monthly stipend of $30 for the officers and $20 for the others. The stipend was kept for them at headquarters in Conakry because money was not used in the liberated areas of Guinea-Bissau.[e] When the time for their return to Cuba approached (they were withdrawn in large groups by boat or plane), the volunteers were told to write a list of things they wanted to buy; "people wanted to get small presents for their wives, their children, themselves." Headquarters then appointed two or three people to drive to Freetown in Sierra Leone to buy the presents because the prices were lower there and the selection much broader.[112] "It was a disaster to be on one of those committees," Melesio Martínez Vaillant explained. "It was impossible to please everyone. People would criticize you no matter what you bought. They'd say: 'Buy me a pair of pants!' but they wouldn't tell you the size! There were always complaints! No one was satisfied."[113]

When they returned to Cuba, the volunteers were told to say that they had been in the Soviet Union. This could be awkward. "Why aren't any of the presents from there?" Pina's wife asked him. There were other problems, too. "I lost sixty pounds in Guinea-Bissau," Dr. Hechavarría recalls. "My family was amazed. 'Where were you? Why did you lose so much weight?'"[114]

Some, like Hechavarría, maintained the cover story. (Only after the dispatch of Cuban troops to Angola in 1975 did he tell his family that he had been in Guinea-Bissau.) Others told a few family members and close friends, "but not the entire neighborhood!" In any case, people "were discreet in these matters— they didn't ask many questions."[115]

Why did the Cubans keep secret a role of which they were proud? Portugal was in no position to retaliate. Most African governments would have welcomed the news that Cuban instructors and doctors were assisting African guerrillas fighting against colonial rule. It would not have affected Cuba's relations with the Latin American and European governments, which were improv-

e. The Cubans in Guinea received their stipend every month from the outset, but those in Guinea-Bissau got no monthly stipend until 1971; instead, when their mission was over they received presents worth $50 to $60.

ing in the early 1970s, or even with the United States, which knew that Cubans "worked as advisers with the guerrillas"[116] and was untroubled.

Therefore, the explanation for the Cuban silence must be sought elsewhere. It was PAIGC policy to deny that foreigners were fighting with the guerrillas in Guinea-Bissau, and Cuban policy to honor the wishes of the PAIGC.

The story of Captain Pedro Rodríguez Peralta, the only Cuban volunteer captured in Africa before November 1975, illustrates this point. Peralta, who headed the Cubans in the southern region, was wounded and taken prisoner by Portuguese paratroopers on November 18, 1969.[117] "We know that these things happen in war, but we never expect them to happen to us," the chief of the MMCG wrote to his predecessor a few weeks later.[118]

The Portuguese hailed Rodríguez Peralta's capture as proof that Cubans were fighting alongside the PAIGC, but Amílcar Cabral told an inquiring American congressman, "Sir, we have Cuban doctors helping us in our country. And this man came . . . to visit his colleagues there, the doctors. . . . He is not our Lafayette, and we have no Cuban people fighting in our country." Rodríguez Peralta was tried and sentenced to ten years. "The prosecutor was unable to prove that the defendant . . . had been sent to Portuguese Guinea on orders from the Cuban authorities," the *New York Times* wrote.[119] His capture was not made public in Cuba; only his family was told. "We had to explain to them why he had been in Africa and stress that it was a state secret," a DGI officer recalled.[120] In March 1971 Havana offered to free Kirby Lunt, a U.S. citizen imprisoned in Cuba for espionage, in exchange for Peralta, but despite gentle U.S. pressure, Lisbon refused to free Peralta until Havana acknowledged its aid to the PAIGC and promised, as the U.S. DCM in Lisbon explained, "not to send 'more Peraltas.'"[121] And so Rodríguez Peralta remained in jail, his sister spent several months in Portugal to be able to visit him, all expenses paid by the Cuban government,[122] and the Cuban press remained silent.

CASTRO VISITS CONAKRY

Guinea-Bissau was the only place in the world where Cubans were fighting in May 1972 when Castro visited Africa for the first time. It was also the only place in Africa where a guerrilla movement was successfully challenging a white regime. In Angola the rebels were losing ground, in Mozambique their progress was slow, and in Namibia, Rhodesia, and South Africa armed struggle was virtually paralyzed. "Provided that substantial assistance is forthcoming," U.S. intelligence noted, "the PAIGC might become in the relatively near future the first sub-Saharan liberation movement facing a white regime to win its war." The PAIGC's "traditional supporters—the Soviet Union, Cuba, and Guinea—all seem disposed to increase the pressure on the Portuguese."[123]

Castro stopped in Guinea and Algeria on his way to Eastern Europe and the Soviet Union. "Guinea and Algeria were two key countries for us," Risquet explains. "Algeria was very important in Africa and in the Third World, and we wanted to reestablish the very close ties that had existed before the overthrow of Ben Bella." Guinea was desperately poor, and by 1972 it enjoyed little prestige abroad, but it was the PAIGC's indispensable rear guard. Not only were the rebels steadily gaining ground, but the war in Guinea-Bissau could have an impact far beyond its borders. As early as 1963, a U.S. official had observed that "whatever Portugal does in Portuguese Guinea will directly affect its capacity to maintain its position in the much more valuable territories of Angola and Mozambique. . . . Portuguese withdrawal under fire would give a boost to African morale and determination. It would also be a severe psychological blow to the Portuguese." This was precisely the Cuban view. "I believe that Guinea can play an important role in Africa," Castro told GDR leader Erich Honecker after his African journey. "Guinea can be a launching pad against colonialism throughout Africa."[124]

Castro visited Guinea on May 3–8, 1972, bearing gifts: economic and military aid. "They have . . . lots of fish . . . but no fishing boats," he told Honecker. "I thought about our [Cuban] fleet, and how we could send them a ship . . . so that they could learn how to catch fish." Cuba sent four fishing boats, manned by Cubans who trained local crews and gave the catch to Guinea. "There was not even a hint that our country should repay the Cubans," a Conakry official wrote. "Guinea occupied a strategic location from which Cuba could lend valuable aid to African National Liberation Movements," that is, to the PAIGC.[125] Cuba also granted a large number of scholarships to students from Guinea. In August 1972, 133 students left for Havana on a Cuban ship; two other groups, each of slightly more than 100, left in 1973 and 1974.[f]

Cuba also extended military aid, because it believed that the Portuguese, as their fortunes in Guinea-Bissau deteriorated, might be tempted to strike again at Guinea to deprive the PAIGC of its safe havens.[126] Guinea had a few MIGs, but no pilots trained to fly them in combat; furthermore it had only one airport (at Conakry), so its air force was vulnerable. Following Castro's visit, Cuba sent several pilots for the MIGs and construction workers to build airports near the towns of Kankan and Labé and to make improvements to the Conakry airport, including building special hangars for the MIGs.[127]

PORTUGAL STUMBLES

Meanwhile the PAIGC was gaining ground internationally. One month before Castro arrived in Conakry, a special mission of the UN Decolonization Commit-

---

f. The pattern was the same for the three groups: after spending an academic year at the language school of Siboney, in Havana, most went to the university, a few to technical schools. Cuba bore all the expenses: transportation, board, lodging, clothing, and a monthly stipend. (Interviews with Aboubacar Sidiki and Safayo Ba [who went in 1972], Moussa Beavogui and Mamoudou Diallo [who went in 1973], and Mohamed Sadialiou Sow and Sékou Sylla [who went in 1974].)

tee had visited liberated areas of Guinea-Bissau. Its report condemned "the devastation and misery caused by Portugal's actions, particularly the widespread and indiscriminate bombing of villages and the use of napalm to destroy crops"; it stated that "Portugal no longer exercises any effective administrative control in large areas of Guinea (Bissau)" and stressed that "the population of the liberated areas unreservedly supports the policies and activities of [the] PAIGC."[128] From late August to mid-October 1972, the PAIGC organized elections for a Popular National Assembly in the areas it controlled. On November 14, the UN General Assembly recognized the PAIGC as the sole legitimate representative of the people of Guinea-Bissau and Cape Verde by 98 votes to 6, with 8 abstentions. (The negative votes were cast by Portugal, the United States, England, Spain, South Africa, and Brazil.)[129]

On January 20, 1973, Amílcar Cabral was murdered by disgruntled members of the PAIGC who had been urged on by the Portuguese secret police.[130] But the war in Guinea-Bissau continued with, if anything, even more vigor. Cabral's fifteen-year effort had paid off. The PAIGC had "developed into a disciplined and well-run political and military force," U.S. intelligence remarked. It enjoyed international support and had become "a lean, close-to-the-people party."[131] Furthermore, a few weeks after Cabral's death, the PAIGC was decisively strengthened by the delivery of surface-to-air missiles from the Soviet Union. Until then, the rebels had not had an effective defense against Portuguese air power, but in late 1972, Luís Cabral recounts, "we learned about a Soviet antiaircraft weapon that was light and very efficient. Amílcar made a special trip to Moscow to explain our needs to the Soviet authorities and to urge them to give us that precious weapon." The mission, in December 1972, proved successful. In March 1973 the Portuguese prime minister wrote, "surface-to-air missiles unexpectedly appeared in the enemy's hands in Guinea[-Bissau] and within a few days five of our planes had been shot down." This meant that "our unchallenged air superiority, which had been our trump card and the basis of our entire military policy . . . had suddenly evaporated."[132] It became very dangerous for the Portuguese to fly. "The situation deteriorated dramatically. . . . The arrival of the missiles opened, without any doubt, a new phase of the war," Spínola explained. A Portuguese officer who was in Bissau wrote: "That easy and constant cruising of the air space by our . . . [planes] to gather intelligence, to transport His Excellency [Spínola] and other dignitaries, to provide air cover for our troops, to bomb [the enemy areas], to transport troops and supplies—all this had suddenly become very dangerous. The psychological shock suffered by our pilots was spectacular."[133]

In May 1973 the rebels, who were, by that point, about 8,000 strong and in control of nearly two-thirds of the country and half of the population, launched Operation Amílcar Cabral in the south. Forty-one Cubans participated and were in charge of the artillery, including the SAMs. On May 25 the Portuguese abandoned Guiledje, an immense fort that was the key to the southern defense.

"We knew that Guiledje had fallen," a Portuguese officer writes. "We knew that the captain there . . . after repeatedly asking Spínola for help and receiving only negative replies . . . decided to save himself and his men and abandoned Guiledje on foot, taking only the weapons that his demoralized and defeated men could carry through the jungle." The offensive continued for one month, inflicting heavy casualties on the Portuguese and downing four of their planes. "We are getting ever closer to military collapse," Spínola informed Lisbon. "The operation was a complete success," the Cubans concluded. U.S. intelligence agreed and called the PAIGC "Africa's best-led, -equipped, and -trained liberation movement."[134] On September 24, 1973, the Popular National Assembly proclaimed the independent state of Guinea-Bissau.

On November 2, 1973, with the war still raging, the young republic achieved what *Nõ Pintcha* called "our greatest diplomatic victory"[135] when the UN General Assembly approved a resolution condemning the "illegal occupation by Portuguese military forces of certain sectors of the Republic of Guinea-Bissau and acts of aggression committed by them against the people of the Republic." As the Dutch representative pointed out, an affirmative vote meant de facto recognition of Guinea-Bissau. The resolution passed by 93 votes to 7, with 30 abstentions. The 7 negative votes were cast by Portugal, the military dictatorships of Brazil and Greece, Franco's Spain, South Africa, England, and the United States.[136] "Taking our votes on Portuguese issues together, we note growing feeling among Africans that US is in Portuguese pocket," the U.S. ambassador to the United Nations told Kissinger. In Western Europe public opinion was increasingly critical of Portugal's colonial wars, and the West German government—long one of Portugal's most steadfast friends—was instituting "fundamental changes" in its policy on Portuguese Africa. "The United States is increasingly isolated with Portugal and South Africa and, occasionally, Britain and France on issues relating to those [liberation] movements [in the Portuguese colonies]," Assistant Secretary for African Affairs David Newsom lamented.[137]

In early 1974 a Cuban military analysis concluded: "We believe that the Portuguese in Guinea-Bissau could not resist a sustained PAIGC offensive for more than a year, and that such an offensive would liberate the country."[138]

It took less than a year. On April 25, 1974, war-weary Portuguese officers overthrew the dictatorship and brought their country's imperial folly to an end. On September 10, Portugal recognized the Republic of Guinea-Bissau. That same day, Rodríguez Peralta's name first appeared in the Cuban press, when *Granma* mentioned, out of the blue, that Lisbon had announced that he would soon be freed. (Another article, six days later, mentioned that he had been captured in 1969 in Guinea-Bissau.) Rodríguez Peralta returned to Cuba on September 16, 1974. In a front-page three-column article, *Granma* described his arrival at the airport where Fidel Castro and top Cuban officials were waiting for him; it described Rodríguez Peralta's suffering at the hands of his captors, but it said not one word about Cuba's aid to the PAIGC.[139]

Many countries had helped the PAIGC in its struggle. Guinea had provided the rear guard. In the West, Sweden had sent economic aid as early as October 1969. "Sweden . . . is giving us more than a number of socialist countries put together," Amílcar Cabral told high-ranking GDR officials in 1972. In 1972–73, Norway, Denmark, and the Netherlands followed suit.[140] It was the Soviet bloc, however, whose help was decisive. It provided arms, educational opportunities, and other material and political support. The Soviet Union was, by far, the major source of weapons. Cuba, too, gave material help, in the form of supplies, military training in Cuba, and scholarships.[141] This was a considerable and generous effort for a poor country. But Cuba did much more, and its role was unique. Only Cubans fought in Guinea Bissau alongside the guerrilla fighters of the PAIGC. As *Nõ Pintcha* said, "In the most difficult moments of our war of liberation, some of the finest children of the Cuban nation stood at the side of our freedom fighters, enduring every sacrifice to win our country's freedom and independence."[142] This aid was given despite the fact that the PAIGC was not a Marxist movement and its leaders wanted Guinea-Bissau to be among the nonaligned.

The Soviet Union began giving aid to the PAIGC in 1962, well before Cuba did. The Cuban military presence from 1966 on complemented and enhanced the Soviet role, because the Cubans were in charge of the increasingly sophisticated weapons provided by the USSR.[143] While there is a frustrating lack of documentary evidence about any Soviet-Cuban dialogue on Guinea-Bissau, the easy and comfortable supposition that the Cubans were the Soviets' cannon fodder is belied by the evidence that does exist. In Guinea-Bissau, Cuba was following its own policy.

The origins of Cuba's relationship with the PAIGC had nothing to do with the Soviet Union; they were rooted in Guevara's trip to Africa and Cuba's budding interest in sub-Saharan Africa. Neither the trip nor the policy responded to Soviet instructions. When Guevara went to Africa, he focused on Zaire and, to a lesser degree, the MPLA and the government of the Congo. The PAIGC was just one movement among others, and not the most important. But the Cubans had overestimated the revolutionary situation in Africa in 1965: the revolt in Zaire was crushed and Che's column withdrew in November 1965; the government of the Congo was a disappointment, and the Cubans wisely withdrew in December 1966; the MPLA proved less strong than the Cubans had hoped. The PAIGC, on the other hand, was not a disappointment. The relationship that had begun in 1965 grew in mutual appreciation. For Cuba, realpolitik and altruism went hand in hand. The independence of the Portuguese colonies would weaken the West and bring Cuba new friends. The cause was morally compelling: a people fighting with impressive courage against colonial rule. And Cuba could afford the costs, both financial and human: between 1966 and 1974, nine Cubans died in Guinea-Bissau, and only one was captured.[144] There is no reason to see a Soviet hand.

Cuba's role in Guinea-Bissau, as elsewhere in Africa, was defined both by policy determined by a handful of men in Havana and by the bravery of the volunteers in the field. Just as Havana was not bowing to Soviet pressure in helping the PAIGC, so too did individual Cubans volunteer of their own free will. And just as the valor of the PAIGC influenced Havana's decisions, so too did it influence the volunteers. "I fell in love with Guinea-Bissau," remarks Torres, who had earlier been with Che in Zaire. "They [the PAIGC] fought, and we would see the tangible results of our efforts. They were committed. And there was warmth, gratitude toward us; we were like brothers. It was so different from Zaire." Several of those who went to Guinea-Bissau, Torres among them, returned a second time. "When I got back to Cuba, I couldn't forget Guinea-Bissau," said Dr. Hechavarría. "I had endured a lot, faced a lot of problems, but I could see how useful my work was, and I kept thinking about the people I had met, about the patients who so desperately needed a doctor." He returned to Guinea-Bissau in 1970, twenty months after he had left.[145]

It was fitting that Cuba's first ambassador to Guinea-Bissau (1975–80) was Alfonso Pérez Morales (Pina). "The comrade ambassador," President Luís Cabral said, "is an old friend of ours; he lived with us in the jungle; he shared our hardships."[146] Pina had arrived in Guinea-Bissau in June 1966 and had remained until January 1968. In June 1972 he returned, at Amílcar Cabral's request, and he did not leave until April 1974. On both occasions he served as chief of the Cubans on the northern front. Pina was "a wonderful comrade, very active, exemplary, for us he is a brother," a PAIGC commander remarked. He learned to speak like a native, "and on several occasions our people believed that he was a Guinean," writes Luís Cabral. "I came to this country as ambassador with first-hand knowledge of the difficult and glorious struggle that you waged against Portuguese colonialism," Pina said in his farewell speech as ambassador in June 1980. "My relationship with you . . . did not begin with my appointment as ambassador. . . . It was forged on the battlefield. And so I don't consider myself Cuba's first ambassador to Guinea-Bissau. The first ambassadors were those Cubans who volunteered to come here to make their modest contribution to your liberation struggle."[147]

CHAPTER TEN
CASTRO'S CUBA, 1965-1975

After the departure of Che's column from Zaire in November 1965 and of Risquet's column from the Congo thirteen months later, Cuba's major activity in Africa was its assistance to the PAIGC. The presence of Cubans in Guinea-Bissau was virtually ignored by the Western press and by U.S. officials. Suddenly, in 1975 Castro stunned the world by dispatching thousands of troops to Luanda.

The question of whether Havana was acting as a Soviet client in Angola is at the heart of the investigation of why it intervened on this unprecedented scale. Before examining the Angolan war, therefore, it is necessary to set the stage. First, one must explain the relationship between Havana and Moscow in the years before 1975, a relationship affected by Cuba's policy in Latin America. Cuba's relations with the United States, which had moved from frank hostility to tentative dialogue, are also relevant, as are its relations with Western Europe and the Middle East. Thus Cuba's international position in 1975 must be clarified before plunging into the Angola story.[1]

STOKING THE FLAMES IN THE WESTERN HEMISPHERE

Castro's guerrilla offensive in Latin America in the late 1960s can be traced by following Che's footsteps from the Cuban embassy in Dar-es-Salaam to Bolivia.

After Che left Zaire, his first task had been to write an analysis of the campaign and an assessment of the men who had served under him. Writing these reports in Dar-es-Salaam gave him time to decide what to do next. He knew he would return to Latin America to lead a guerrilla war, but he had to decide where to go and he had to prepare the operation.[2]

Che's plans dovetailed perfectly with Cuban foreign policy. Although the Cubans had accepted restrictions on their freedom of action in Latin America at the Havana conference of Latin American Communist parties in late 1964 and had shifted their focus to Africa, they had never stopped supporting armed struggle in the hemisphere. "The Cubans began chipping away at the edges of the [Havana conference] agreement with the Soviets during 1965," the CIA wrote. In some cases—Venezuela, Colombia, Peru, and Guatemala—it is likely that there was no slackening whatsoever in Havana's support for the guerrillas, even though the rhetoric was toned down.[3] In a major speech on July 26, 1965, Castro dropped this restraint. "At several points," the GDR embassy wrote, "Comrade Castro exhorted the revolutionaries of Latin America to follow the Cuban example. [He said that] Cuba shows the power of revolution to the peoples of Latin America and that no threats, dangers, or risks could hold her back. With great emphasis, he stressed the importance of guerrilla war as a powerful, revolutionary weapon against exploitation, colonialism, and imperialism. In this way Comrade Castro abandoned the moderate approach . . . that he had voiced since the conference of the Latin America Communist parties in December [sic] 1964, and stressed again that the Cuban way was an example for all."[4]

In early January 1966 Juan Carretero, head of the Latin America division of the DGI, arrived in Dar-es-Salaam accompanying Che's wife, Aleyda, who was joining her husband for a few precious weeks. Carretero gave Che a detailed briefing on the prospects for armed struggle in each of the countries of Latin America. He told Che that Castro hoped he would return to Cuba "to prepare for the guerrilla war that he would undertake, and that he [Castro] hoped Che would choose Bolivia," but that the choice was Che's to make.[5]

"The long-range objectives underlying Cuba's strategic plan for continental revolution largely explain the selection of Bolivia as a logical initial target," the CIA observed in a 1968 retrospective.

Cuba's design—to advance the proletarian hemispheric uprising—was not limited to overthrowing an "oligarchic" puppet regime and substituting one of pro-Cuban socialist style in any one country. The target was to serve primarily as a seedbed for the spread of guerrilla warfare to many areas of South America in accordance with the thesis of establishing the "second, third, and fourth Vietnams" on the continent. Bolivia was to be a practical training ground of guerrilla warfare for Latin American revolutionary cadres under experienced and indispensable Cuban direction. . . . Once the guerrilla movement was secure in Bolivia, Havana would then compile its list of other national targets. Both Peru and Argentina were relatively high in priority.

The CIA pointed out that Bolivia, with its long borders "providing relatively easy access to five neighboring countries . . . and a rugged and broken topography ideally suited for guerrilla operations . . . might well have been selected on the geographic criterion alone." In fact, it noted, there were also other considerations: Bolivia—"a land of chronic political and economic instability" with a combative labor movement and security forces notorious for their inefficiency—"seemed to present an ideal background for a liberating guerrilla movement." Given the strategic design "of Cuba's subversive plan . . . almost any other part of the area [South America] would have posed more serious obstacles and higher risks than Bolivia."[6]

For Che, Bolivia was the back door to Argentina. "His plan was to go to Argentina and the choice of Bolivia was very much in function of that," Carretero explained. Che told another DGI officer, "I cannot die until I've got at least one foot in Argentina."[7]

He chose Bolivia, but he refused to return to Cuba. Pride held him back. The previous October, Castro had made public the farewell letter in which Che had announced that he was leaving Cuba to go "to new battlefields," but now he had abandoned the first battlefield. Che, "with his particular character, didn't want to return to Cuba," Castro said, "because it would have been an embarrassment to come back after the publication of the letter." He finally accepted a compromise: he would go to Prague, where the DGI had several safe houses. "It would be a secure place to wait while the preparations were under way," Carretero explains.[8]

Before leaving Dar-es-Salaam, Che was visited by a senior DGI officer, Luis Carlos García Gutiérrez (Fisín), who was one of Cuba's foremost experts in the art of disguise. Among other things, he fitted Che with a prosthesis. (He was also a dentist.) "It made him look sort of half-witted, like someone stupid, uncultivated," Fisín recalled. "Che didn't like it," Estrada, who had accompanied Fisín to Dar-es-Salaam, remarked; "he looked like an animal, he could barely speak. While Fisín worked on Che's prosthesis they kept arguing, because Fisín is very stubborn, and Che even more so."[9]

In late February or early March, Che and Estrada flew to Prague, where Che remained for approximately three months. "Che read a lot; I slept a lot," Estrada remembered. "It was so boring. Che taught me how to play chess; he'd let me win so I'd start liking it. Eventually I refused to play."[10]

While Che was in Czechoslovakia, the DGI was laying the groundwork for the guerrilla war in Bolivia, and Castro kept urging Che to return to Cuba. Finally, Che relented. "He saw that the work we were doing in Bolivia was very serious," Carretero, who visited him in Prague, recalled, "and so there was no danger that he would be stuck in Cuba." In June or July 1966, Che flew back to Havana and immediately went to the place where the Cubans who were going to Bolivia were training.[11]

Che was eager to get going. Three years earlier, he had waited in Havana while Masetti had been killed leading the vanguard in northern Argentina. Che was not going to let this happen again. "He wanted to go there [to Bolivia] almost at the very beginning," Castro recalled. "We managed to hold him until at least some preliminary work had been carried out, so he could go there with a little more safety." In October, he left for Bolivia.[12] Fidel Castro and Che Guevara would never meet again.

Speculation about Che's relationship with Fidel when he left for Bolivia has increased over the years. The Cuban government has not opened its archives, and the testimony of those Cubans who are still on the island is considered automatically suspect. Outside of Cuba, some writers argue that Castro willfully sent Guevara on an impossible mission in Bolivia hoping that he would die. Therefore, it is worth pausing over the words of Régis Debray, the prominent French intellectual who in 1966 was a trusted aide of Fidel Castro and has since become a fervent critic. In 1996 Debray wrote: "It happened that I was the last link between the two companions in arms. [Before leaving for Bolivia] I listened to Fidel, the two of us alone, talk for an entire night about Che, with that mixture of tact, pride, and concern that an older brother might feel for his youngest brother who is setting off on an adventure, knowing his faults all too well, and loving him for them. [Then, in Bolivia] I heard Che, before I left for . . . my return trip to Havana . . . speak to me of Fidel . . . with unquestioning devotion."[13]

One fact seems incontrovertible: Che's departure for Bolivia was not the desperate gesture of a lonely leader who had nowhere to go, but the linchpin of an extremely ambitious plan hatched in Havana. The setback in Zaire had pushed Latin America back to the foreground with a vengeance. In 1966 and 1967 Cuba made its strongest attempt to promote armed struggle in the hemisphere. "Cuban propaganda returned to the more strident pitch noted in 1963," the CIA observed. "The operational emphasis, however, in comparison with the earlier years, changed to the selected list of target countries—Venezuela, Guatemala, Colombia and Bolivia." In the pursuit of this offensive, Havana initiated, a U.S. official remarked, "a new strategy of sending special teams to selected countries to serve as cadres for the development of guerrilla movements."[14] Four Cuban officers landed in Venezuela in July 1966; more followed in May 1967.[15] (These were the first Cubans to fight in Latin America since the failed operation in Argentina in early 1964.) And sixteen Cubans went to Bolivia with Che. Cuba had put its "first team" there, the CIA wrote.[16]

There were moments, from late 1966 through the summer of 1967, when U.S. officials feared that Latin America might be facing a serious guerrilla threat. The rebels seemed to be on the offensive in Bolivia; there was "a marked increase" in the level of insurgent activity in Venezuela and Colombia; and in Guatemala, the CIA reported, the guerrillas were "the most disciplined and best trained organization in the country."[17]

The Cubans agreed, with more fervor. "A revolution is seething on this continent," Castro thundered in August 1967. "The victory of the people is inevitable."[18] These were not empty words. As the CIA wrote one year later, "The record shows that 'export of the revolution' has been a dominant ambition of Castro next to maintaining his own firm grip on power at home. Indeed, the Cuban leader is a 'compulsive revolutionary': a man who sees himself as another Simon Bolivar, destined to bring a new 'freedom and unity' to Latin America. Castro has been consistent in this dream, although he has pursued it with varying degrees of intensity since 1959. . . . The evidence is overwhelming that Cuba made special adventuristic efforts in 1967 to establish 'other Cubas and Vietnams' in Latin America."[19]

TENSIONS WITH MOSCOW

Cuba's renewed focus on armed struggle in Latin America created strains with the Soviet Union. Moscow was trying to expand its commercial and diplomatic ties with the Latin American governments—those same governments that Castro was hoping to overthrow. Castro was blunt. "It is absurd," he said, referring to Soviet offers of aid to Colombia, "loans in dollars to an oligarchical government that is . . . persecuting and murdering guerrillas. . . . This is absurd."[20] The Soviet ambassador in Havana warned his senior aides that when Castro gave a speech, "one had to be prepared for the worst." Castro also deemed Soviet aid to North Vietnam woefully inadequate, and the Soviet response to the Israeli attack on Egypt, Syria, and Jordan in June 1967 spineless. And even though Cuba was dependent on Soviet aid, Castro did not hesitate to criticize even Soviet domestic policies, such as the reliance on material rather than moral incentives for Soviet workers. "We don't believe that you can form a Communist by appealing to his ambition, his individualism, his egotism," he said, and everyone knew he was referring to the Soviet Union.[21]

Relations with Moscow reached their nadir in the aftermath of Che's death. That moment was captured with brio by the Board of National Estimates of the CIA, a group not known for its wit, in a November 1967 report. "Brezhnev thinks that Castro is some kind of idiot, and Castro probably isn't very fond of Brezhnev either," the analysis began.

> The Soviets may now be close to losing their patience, and the Castroites never had very much to begin with. . . . The mixed blessings of alliance with Castro's Cuba have never been so dramatically demonstrated as during the events surrounding the USSR's 50th anniversary celebrations [November 7]. For one thing, the Cubans directly affronted the Soviets by appointing a member of Castro's third team [Minister of Health Machado Ventura] to head the Cuban delegation to the Moscow festivities after the Soviets had officially announced the planned attendance of Cuban president Dorticos. For another . . . this worthy did not even deliver the customary congratulatory address to his Soviet hosts. Next, the Cubans compounded the insult by boycotting the traditional diplomatic reception in Moscow presided over by Soviet chief of state Podgorny. And finally, lest anyone miss the point, the Cubans were the first to leave Moscow after the celebrations were over (presumably racing the Rumanians to the airport for the honor).
>
> The Soviets for their part demonstrated little of the restraint that has heretofore characterized the public handling of their recalcitrant Cuban ally. Just prior to the anniversary gathering in Moscow, Soviet publications carried obituaries of Che Guevara, and also articles . . . that seemed to challenge the value of Castro's revolutionary philosophy and to convey—concerning Guevara's death—more of a smug "we told you so" than an expression of sympathy to the bereaved. . . .
>
> Clearly, a low point has been reached in the relationship of the two communist partners. . . . Castro has at times displayed some sensitivity to Soviet views on one issue or another, but Moscow's official positions are rarely an overriding consideration in his pursuit of causes either at home or abroad. Indeed, the modest Cubans have specifically criticized the USSR's manage-

ment of its own affairs, its interference in Cuban affairs, its handling of the Vietnam war and the Middle East crisis, its aid to Latin American governments, and its attitude toward revolutionary tactics in the Third World.

Examining the Soviet leaders' options vis-à-vis their obstreperous protégé, the report pointed out that they still saw advantages in the alliance with Cuba. "Surely, they are pleased to point to their sponsorship of a socialist 'beacon' in the Western Hemisphere, and they are well aware that Cuba stands as a symbol of Soviet willingness and ability to provide support even to remote allies." They also appreciated Cuba's value "as a propaganda device with which to taunt the US. They are also happy at times with Castro's nuisance value vis-a-vis the US." However, the Soviets were also "painfully aware" that in economic aid alone Cuba had cost them roughly $300 million annually since 1961. Moscow's relationship with Castro, the report concluded, provided a continuing demonstration that small allies could be extremely expensive. "But . . . how could the Soviets pull out of Cuba and look at the world or themselves in the morning?"[22]

On January 2, 1968, Castro announced that gasoline was going to be rationed because of the "limited capacity" of the Soviet oil deliveries to meet the growing demands of the Cuban economy. "Cuban officials," GDR intelligence reported, "assert that . . . Cuba would receive more oil if it was willing to surrender its 'dignity' and its 'principles,' that is, 'her political independence.'" Castro, however, was obdurate. Over the next few weeks, the Cubans accused Soviet officials of interfering in Cuba's domestic affairs and announced that the Cuban Communist Party (PCC) would not attend the forthcoming Budapest meeting of Communist parties sponsored by the Soviet Union in opposition to China. "At present . . . there is, unfortunately, absolutely no contact whatsoever at a high level between the PCUS [Communist Party of the Soviet Union] and the Cuban party," a senior Soviet official told the GDR leaders in July.[23]

Having reached the brink, Castro drew back. "Beginning in May," an American intellectual who worked in Cuba wrote, "a significant decline in public manifestations of Cuban-Soviet irascibility could be observed. . . . Even more remarkable was the new and unexpected warmth in Cuban–East German relations." Havana had earlier accused the GDR, one of Moscow's most loyal allies and a major aid donor to Cuba, of interference in its internal affairs. In April 1968, however, Castro invited the East German Communist Party (SED) to send a high-level delegation to Havana. In the following weeks, a SED document noted, "the Cuban leaders' effort to downplay contentious issues with the SED . . . became obvious." The East Germans concluded that Castro was turning to them as a first, tentative step toward building a bridge with the Soviet Union. Castro may have been motivated by the desire not to jeopardize Soviet aid at a moment when he was trying desperately to improve the Cuban economy. Above all, the approach of the November 1968 U.S. presidential elections heightened what a State Department analyst called his "deep and continuing concern for defense against the US." Richard Nixon, whose personal animosity toward him was notorious, was pledging that if elected he would inaugurate a tougher Cuban policy. From Havana's perspective, the timing was particularly inopportune: relations with Moscow were tense, relations with Beijing were no longer friendly, the attempt to open a new front in Africa had failed, and the guerrilla offensive in Latin America had been defeated. If Nixon won, Castro told the Soviet chargé d'affaires that October, "[U.S.] military actions [against Cuba] could not be excluded. . . . The time had come," he added, "for an improvement of the friendly relations between the USSR and Cuba."[24]

The Soviet invasion of Czechoslovakia provided the opportunity. On August 23, two days after Soviet tanks had entered the Czech capital to stifle the "Prague Spring," Castro addressed the Cuban nation. Many, in Cuba and abroad, expected him to condemn the Soviet Union. As a prominent journalist recalled, Castro was the leader of "a nation with a maximum concern for national independence, for the sovereignty of small countries."[25] Instead, however, Castro almost endorsed the invasion. The Soviet action was a "flagrant" violation of Czech sovereignty, but, he added significantly, it had been absolutely necessary: Czech prime minister Alexander Dubček "was heading toward capitalism and was inexorably heading toward imperialism."[26]

This struck many observers as an abject surrender to Soviet economic pressure.[27] Castro, however, had his own reasons to welcome the invasion. "The worst thing that could have happened," he later said, "was chaos in the Socialist camp."[28] Dubček had allowed political freedoms—free speech, a free press, independent trade unions—that were bound to lead to free elections, the defeat of the Czechoslovak Communist Party, and the rupture of the Warsaw Pact. If the Soviet Union had been willing to accept the loss of such a key country, how much easier it would have been, someday, to abandon Cuba, a distant, obstreperous forward-base and drain on the Soviet economy.

Therefore, if there were Soviet pressures to endorse the invasion, they were not necessary. Castro saw in Dubček not the champion of a small socialist nation's sovereignty but an irresponsible demagogue who was wrenching his country from the socialist camp and, in the process, establishing a precedent that could destroy Cuba.

On November 5, Nixon was elected president of the United States. A few days later, a high-level SED delegation arrived in Havana. "Our Cuban comrades," it reported, "stressed repeatedly that Nixon's election . . . means an acceleration of US aggression against Cuba. . . . Comrade Castro repeatedly pointed to its implications for Cuba's security" and was forthright about his desire to improve relations with the Soviet Union.[29] By 1969 public criticism of the Soviet Union had ceased.

RETREAT IN LATIN AMERICA

This improvement in relations with Moscow was made easier by a shift in Cuba's policy in Latin America. The guerrillas had been crushed in Bolivia in

October 1967, they had been virtually wiped out in Guatemala by 1968, and they had suffered cruel setbacks in Colombia and Venezuela. There were no other insurgent groups active in the hemisphere. These defeats and, above all, Che's death forced Castro to question the foco theory. He finally accepted that a handful of brave men were insufficient to ignite armed struggle in Latin America. "By 1970 Cuban assistance to guerrilla groups and other efforts to export revolution had been cut back to very low levels," U.S. officials remarked.[30]

The ordeal of Francisco Caamaño, the military leader of a revolt in the Dominican Republic in 1965, illustrates this new maturity. The DGI had worked hard to persuade Caamaño to come to Cuba to prepare for armed struggle in his country. He had arrived in Havana in November 1967, one month after Che's death, and he stayed for over five years, and never lost his confidence in the foco theory. The Cubans, however, did. They urged Caamaño to wait. "He kept insisting that he wanted to go," a knowledgeable journalist has written, "and the Cubans kept trying to convince him that it was not possible," that conditions in the Dominican Republic were not yet ripe. Finally they relented; "Caamaño was not willing to stay in Cuba any longer," a member of his group explained. With arms and money provided by the DGI and a yacht bought in Antigua, Caamaño and eight followers landed in the Dominican Republic in early February 1973. Within two weeks the Dominican armed forces had murdered him and crushed his little band.[31] The Cuban press, which would have vehemently supported the guerrillas in the 1960s, refrained from comment. When Castro evoked Caamaño's memory later that year, he referred to him only as the leader of the 1965 Dominican revolt.[32]

The point is not that Castro no longer supported armed struggle. In those same years Cuba helped the Tupamaros in Uruguay and the armed wing of the Peronist movement (the future Montoneros) in Argentina. This support, however, was far more discriminating and discreet than it had been in the 1960s. Castro no longer launched fiery appeals for revolution throughout Latin America. Instead, in February 1970 Cuba signed a trade agreement with the Christian Democratic government of Chile, and the following August, one month before the Chilean presidential elections, Castro announced, "It is possible to arrive at Socialism through the polls."[33]

The Chilean election was won by Castro's good friend Salvador Allende, who headed a coalition that included the Communist and the Socialist parties, but not the Movimiento de la Izquierda Revolucionaria (MIR), the country's Castroite group. This put Castro in a complicated situation. Miguel Henríquez, the leader of the MIR and a man for whom Castro had great respect, argued that the country's conservative forces would try to overthrow Allende, and he asked Cuba for arms. Even though he believed Henríquez was right, Castro refused to arm the MIR without Allende's permission, which never arrived. In the meantime, Castro urged Allende to allow Cuba to arm the government parties. "We kept insisting that the situation required it and that Unidad Popular [the government coalition] had to be ready," he told GDR leader Honecker in 1974.

Finally, a few months before the September 1973 coup, Allende gave Castro the green light to give weapons to the members of the government coalition.

First he [Allende] gave us permission to give weapons to the Communist Party. . . . He had great confidence in the Communist Party. . . . The socialist party is more heterogeneous and he was afraid that they would one day take to the streets with machine guns. Ultimately he also gave us permission to arm the socialists and the other parties of Unidad Popular. . . . However . . . they were not ready. They took a few weapons, but far fewer than we wanted to give them. . . .

When the coup took place, there were enough weapons for a battalion in our embassy, automatic weapons, antitank weapons. . . . Most were for the Communist Party. We had asked them to come and take them a few weeks before the coup, but they never did.[34]

Cuba's new approach to armed struggle in Latin America—more subtle, more discriminating, and, in the case of Chile, respectful of Allende's wishes—eliminated a major source of tension with the Soviet Union.

THE REVOLUTIONARY OFFENSIVE AT HOME

Cuban domestic policies, on the other hand, became more radical. It seemed as though Castro was trying to compensate for his foreign policy setbacks by increasing the revolutionary tempo at home. On March 13, 1968, he suddenly nationalized the 55,000 nonagricultural businesses still in private hands, from auto repair shops to small stores, cafés, and street vendors. It was a costly error that further destabilized the economy. The absolute reliance on moral incentives to stimulate workers was accompanied by increased demands on the population for voluntary labor, in a vain attempt to compensate for low productivity and gross mismanagement. These internal problems were aggravated by the U.S. economic strangulation of the island. "As long as the US successfully maintains its present economic pressures, the prospect for much significant improvement in Cuba's drab economic performance is remote," a senior INR specialist concluded in late 1967. ("Furthermore," he wrote, "the fear of potential US aggression impels the regime to divert disproportionate resources to military preparedness.")[35]

A 1968 State Department study noted that "Castro retains his magnetism and political skill. . . . He still has great appeal for important elements of society, especially among the youth. . . . His personal popularity as a revolutionary caudillo have [sic] proved durable."[36] He used his charisma to urge a tired population forward, promising a better future with just one more effort. Staking the "honor of this revolution"[37] on a grandiose goal, he pledged that in 1970 Cuba would reap the largest sugar harvest in history—10 million tons, almost double the 1968 harvest. Mobilizing the nation as if for war, he diverted scarce resources to attain the impossible goal. In the end, he failed dismally: the harvest fell short of the target and the economy went into free fall. On May 20, 1970, Fidel Castro spoke to the nation. "The Battle of the Ten Million [tons of sugar] was not lost by the people. We lost it. We, the administrative bureaucracy of the revolution, we, the leaders of the revolution, lost this battle." And on July 26, 1970, he acknowledged, "Our apprenticeship as leaders of this revolution has cost too much."[38]

The gamble had failed, and Castro drew the lesson. Cuba adopted the Soviet economic model. It was inefficient and wasteful, yet it was a dramatic improvement.

A WISER CUBA

The next few years saw an impressive turnaround in the country's economy. "The Cubans are on the verge of making their system work—that is to say, of constructing a socialist show case in the Western Hemisphere," Pat Holt, the chief of staff of the Senate Foreign Relations Committee, reported after visiting the island in June 1974. This improvement was due to massive Soviet aid, which had increased from $400 million a year in the late 1960s to $600 million a year in 1972–74, more rational economic management, high sugar and nickel prices, and the diminishing effects of the U.S. embargo.[39]

For U.S. officials, Vietnam had become the all-consuming preoccupation. Cuba's offensive in Africa in 1965–66 had gone almost unnoticed, and Washington had been comforted by the repeated defeats of the guerrillas in Latin America. In 1965 the Johnson administration had curtailed the paramilitary program against Cuba "because of the decision that the damage to our broad interests, especially our relations with the USSR and the Vietnamese situation, would be disproportionate to the benefits which we might obtain in terms of our Cuban policy. . . . [sanitized] moreover, there were, in practice, very limited benefits." Some paramilitary operations against economic objectives continued through the end of the Johnson administration, and the program was briefly expanded under Nixon.[40] Whether U.S. attempts to assassinate Castro continued after 1965 is unclear.[41]

The United States did continue to try to stifle Cuba's foreign trade, and it continued to forbid subsidiaries of U.S. companies to do business with Cuba. These efforts bore fruit, and resentment. "The stiletto with which we endeavor to prick our enemies can, if we are not careful, wound us grievously," the U.S. ambassador to Canada wrote in early 1965.[42] Three years later, a major U.S. study on policy toward Cuba added another note of caution. "Continuance of present policy," it stated, "is probably the easiest course for the U.S. to follow at this time, since it requires no basic change. The capacity of the U.S. to isolate Cuba, exert pressure on Castro and exploit vulnerabilities is declining, however . . . as Castro continues to replace American capital stock and consolidates other trade and supply patterns. The political cost to the U.S. of discouraging other nations from trading with Cuba is increasing. . . . The ability of the U.S. to keep Cuba isolated, even with respect to Latin America, is also unlikely to remain constant, and the prospects are that it too will be eroded in time."[43]

The report was prescient. By the early 1970s, Cuba's isolation in the Western Hemisphere was steadily decreasing. This was due, U.S. officials told the *New York Times*, to "factors entirely outside Washington's influence: the determination of a growing number of Latin-American governments to decide their own foreign policies . . . [and] the Castro Government's decision to conduct its hemispheric relations in traditional diplomatic channels rather than by encouraging revolution."[44] In 1972 and 1973 Peru, Argentina, and four newly independent Caribbean countries established diplomatic relations with Cuba. "Several former strong supporters of sanctions (including notably Colombia and Venezuela) now see the policy as a relic," the State Department noted in August 1974.[45] At the same time, several foreign governments—particularly Argentina, Mexico, and Canada—grew increasingly resentful of the extension of U.S. law to subsidiaries of U.S. companies based in their countries, perceiving this to be a direct challenge to national sovereignty. "U.S. subsidiaries operating in Argentina are caught in a crossfire between the Argentine Government's insistence that they trade with Cuba and our own Cuban denial regulations," Kissinger told Nixon in December 1973. "If they comply, the companies stand in violation of our Cuban control regulations. If they do not comply, they run the risk of serious GOA [government of Argentina] retaliation that could put them out of business." U.S. officials granted a few export licenses (when the host country "exerted heavy pressure on us") but the problem would not go away. "The future political cost of such enforcement can be expected to exceed any lingering benefit," Deputy Secretary of State Robert Ingersoll warned President Gerald Ford fourteen months later.[46]

Cuba's new respectability in Latin America and its growing economy also helped improve its relations with Western Europe. In mid-January 1975 Cuban deputy prime minister Carlos Rafael Rodríguez visited France. It was the first official visit of a high-ranking Cuban since 1959. Paris extended a $350 million line of credit to Cuba for 1975–76. In May, Rodríguez led a delegation to London, where he concluded "a massive £250 [$550] million credit deal."[47] On June 28 Swedish prime minister Olaf Palme arrived in Havana on a four-day official visit.[48] Even Japan, Washington's model ally, broke ranks, becoming Cuba's largest non-Communist trading partner, as exports swelled from $51 million in 1972 to $438 million by 1975.[49]

KISSINGER'S OLIVE BRANCH

Washington noticed. In June 1974 Kissinger sent Castro a message suggesting secret discussions between the two governments. Kissinger had "something . . . dramatic in mind," a Cuban official recalled, "the full normalization of relations." Kissinger and his aides had concluded that the existing policy had become counterproductive. Several key Latin American countries were "quietly going AWOL from the 1964 sanctions—and use our evident intransigence on Cuba to play to their domestic left," Assistant Secretary of State for Inter-American Affairs William Rogers told Kissinger. "In most of these countries, US movement on Cuba would be a considerable plus in our relationship." In the United States, a growing number of members of Congress, opinion makers, and corporate leaders were demanding a change in a policy they deemed anachronistic and self-defeating. A March 1975 State Department paper noted that it was in the administration's interest to get "Cuba off the domestic and inter-American agendas by extracting the symbolism from an intrinsically trivial issue. . . . Our interest is in getting the Cuba issue behind us."[50]

The conversations proceeded slowly. Whereas in 1961 Guevara had suggested, on Castro's behalf, something akin to a "Finlandization" of Cuba, by 1974 Cuba was more secure—economically and militarily. "We would foresee no substantial Cuban concessions, political or otherwise," a State Department analysis had warned in 1974.[51] In a secret meeting on July 9, 1975, Cuban and U.S. representatives discussed what Assistant Secretary Rogers described as "a series of ideas for a reciprocal, across-the-board improvement of relations" leading to full bilateral ties.

Two weeks later, the United States voted with the majority in the OAS to lift the organization's 1964 sanctions against Cuba. (The motion passed sixteen to three—Chile, Paraguay, and Uruguay—with two abstentions.) Kissinger knew that if the resolution had failed, many Latin American countries would have reestablished relations with Cuba anyway, transforming the sanctions, and the OAS, into an empty shell. The same enlightened self-interest spurred the administration to loosen the regulations that prohibited foreign subsidiaries of U.S. companies from trading with Cuba, "thus averting growing problems with Canada, Mexico, and Argentina."[52]

A SOVIET CLIENT?

It is paradoxical that while the United States was softening its stance on Cuba, it was also increasingly viewing it as a client of the Soviet Union. A new Cuban-Soviet relationship had developed on the ruins of the Fidelista economic policy and the guerrilla offensive in Latin America. Castro no longer publicly criticized Moscow. When Brezhnev warmly received Nixon in Moscow in May 1972 while U.S. planes were pummeling Hanoi and Haiphong, not a peep was heard from Havana.[53] Castro acknowledged the leading role of the Soviet Union in the socialist family; the Cuban armed forces now called the Soviets, in a phrase heavy with symbolism, their "older brothers." In December 1972 Castro signed five new economic agreements with Brezhnev, telling the Cuban people that the Soviet Union was giving "extraordinary" economic aid to Cuba and that Cuban-Soviet relations were "a model of truly fraternal, internationalist, and revolutionary relations."[54]

Had Cuba become a well-behaved Soviet client, a tropical Bulgaria? Would the Cubans now carry out policies that Moscow told them to, even if they disagreed with them? Cuba's foreign policy in the years between the collapse of the guerrilla offensive in Latin America and its intervention in Angola sheds little light on this question, because Havana and Moscow agreed on most international issues.

Soviet and Cuban policies were certainly very close in the Middle East. In the spring of 1973, Cuba played an active role in the region for the first time with the dispatch of about 100 instructors to Aden to train the militia of the ardently pro-Communist regime of South Yemen (the People's Democratic Republic of Yemen, or PDRY). The PDRY supported insurgent movements in North Yemen and Oman; in return, North Yemen and Saudi Arabia plotted against it. The PDRY leaders turned to the Soviet bloc for help. The Soviet Union helped the army, East Germany the security services, and Cuba the militia.[55]

On October 28, 1973, a few months after the arrival of the first Cuban instructors in Aden, 110 Cuban soldiers arrived in Syria, which had just been defeated, again, by Israel. President Hafez al-Asad had asked Castro for tank crews to replace those lost during the war. By mid-November about 1,000 Cubans, enough to man three tank battalions, had arrived.[56]

From November 1973 through May 1974, Israel and Syria fought a war of attrition in the Golan. Small Cuban tank units manning Soviet T-54 tanks engaged in artillery duels with the Israelis. On May 31, 1974, the fighting ended as Syria and Israel agreed to a demilitarized zone. The Cubans returned home in February 1975.

Cuba had never before sent so many soldiers abroad. In a careful study, Department of Defense analyst William Durch asked why Cuba sent troops to an army that already had been bolstered by Moroccans, Jordanians, and Saudis. The answer, he wrote,

> would seem to lie partly in revolutionary Cuba's concept of its "international duty"—something that figures in all Cuban missions—and partly in Fidel Castro's own actions just before the war.
>
> In his speech to the Nonaligned Conference in Algeria in September 1973, Castro emphasized the need for Third World solidarity with "progressive" states and national liberation movements. He vigorously denounced Israel. A few days later, Cuba severed relations with Israel. When the [October] war broke out, it was up to Castro to make good his rhetoric and to show at least as much solidarity with the beleaguered Syrians as the "reactionary" Saudis had done. Thus the Cuban response was in part a matter of principle and in part a matter of face.[57]

There is no indication that Cuba had acted at Moscow's request. Nevertheless, Castro's decision dovetailed with Soviet policy: Moscow was giving Asad the hardware, and the Cubans helped him to put it to good use.

Compared with the Middle East, Africa was a backwater. The U.S. victory in Zaire in 1965 was followed in February 1966 by the overthrow of Ghana's Nkrumah, one of Africa's most radical leaders. "The lusty confidence and assurance that marked African politics in the wake of independence has eroded," the CIA observed in May. "Right now, reactionaries have the upper hand in Africa," a Soviet official remarked in August.[58] The trend intensified as Mobutu consolidated his rule in Zaire and Modibo Keita of Mali, another of the dwindling band of radical leaders, was overthrown in 1968. Sustained armed struggle was limited to Eritrea, fighting against Ethiopian rule, and to three Portuguese colonies: Guinea-Bissau, Mozambique, and Angola.

Cuba's role in Africa in the late 1960s and early 1970s was modest. Some Africans, notably Mozambicans, Zimbabweans, Eritreans, and a handful of South Africans and Namibians, received military training in Cuba,[59] but in Africa itself the only significant Cuban military presence after Risquet's column left the Congo was in Guinea-Bissau. Havana would have liked to do more to help Mozambique's Frelimo, the strongest guerrilla movement in Africa after the PAIGC, but neither Havana nor Frelimo had fully recovered from the bad feelings generated by Che's 1965 clash with Mondlane, the movement's leader, in Dar-es-Salaam, in which Che had deemed Mondlane unreliable and Mondlane had found Che disrespectful. Against this backdrop, Mondlane's determined efforts "to seek aid from West and East to maintain a balance," as the CIA wrote, made Havana wary.[60]

Nevertheless, Cuba offered to send instructors to Frelimo's camps in Tanzania or directly into Mozambique, but Frelimo turned down the offer. "We sent guerrillas for training to several countries, including Cuba," Frelimo leader Marcelino dos Santos explained, "but the only foreign instructors we allowed in Tanzania were Chinese, and we didn't let any foreign instructors into Mozambique." An American authority on Frelimo noted, "Apart from a modest but unknown number of Mozambican trainees, Havana did little else but carry a half dozen FRELIMO speeches or articles in its bulletin *Tricontinental*." Risquet agreed: "Our contribution to the independence of Mozambique was not very important."[61]

The Cubans did send instructors to Sierra Leone to help organize and train the militia that President Siaka Stevens wanted to create as a counterweight to his army. It was an opportunistic move to please Guinea's Sékou Touré, a key partner in the struggle for the liberation of Guinea-Bissau.[a] The twenty-

a. While visiting Guinea, Castro flew to Freetown, Sierra Leone, on May 7, 1972, for a few hours. (*Daily Mail* [Freetown]: May 5, 1972, p. 1; May 8, p. 1; May 9, p. 8; *Granma*, May 8, 1972, p. 1, and May 13, p. 5.) For him, Sierra Leone was terra incognita. The only, fleeting, Cuban presence in the country had been those Cubans who went to buy gifts for the members of the military mission in Guinea and Guinea-Bissau.

man military mission was, however, short-lived. The opposition press in Sierra Leone protested the presence of the Cuban "mercenaries," and the instructors, who had arrived in late 1972, were withdrawn two years later.[62] In 1974, Cuba sent a handful of military instructors to train the local militia in Somalia, which had embarked on a self-styled socialist revolution. As in South Yemen, the Soviets were training the army.[63]

Havana also sent military instructors to Equatorial Guinea in 1973 to prop up the regime of one of Africa's worst despots, Macías Nguema. In 1974 it added forty-one technical assistants, including doctors and forestry experts. Havana's motivation is unclear. Perhaps, as a Cuban official has suggested, it was swayed by the fact that Equatorial Guinea was Spanish-speaking and that hundreds of Cuban patriots had been deported there in the late nineteenth century. But this is just grasping at straws: while there is no evidence that the Cubans participated in the government's repression, their aid to Nguema is puzzling.[64]

Cuba also sent several hundred doctors, nurses, and other experts to a handful of African countries. The medical mission in Algeria continued without interruption, although the size fluctuated from about thirty to sixty.[65] Guinea, the Congo, Tanzania, Mali, and Somalia also received technical assistance. In all cases, the aid was free.

This was Cuba's peace corps. It was the most expedient form of aid for a country that was poor but making great strides in education. The experts were volunteers and included many highly qualified personnel. Irrespective of their qualifications, they all lived in modest circumstances. "Unlike some other countries, we do not use material incentives in our internationalist missions," a senior Cuban official explained. "We merely pay our expert his full salary in Cuba, the same amount he was receiving before leaving for the mission. We give everyone the same lodging, food, and stipend, whether he is a highly qualified specialist or a skilled worker."[66]

Through the first fifteen years of the Cuban revolution Havana's foreign aid went almost exclusively to Africa (and to North Vietnam); Cuba was cut off from Latin America. The amount was modest, consistent with Cuba's poverty, yet it increased as Cuba's economic situation improved. Aid to the Congo, which had ended in 1968, resumed in 1972 on a larger scale. In 1974 Cuba agreed to a massive increase in its assistance to Tanzania, including aid for development projects.[67]

The growth in Cuban aid was also evident in the increasing numbers of Africans studying there. The first foreign scholarship students in Castro's Cuba were from Guinea in 1961. Over the next fifteen years, small numbers of African students continued to arrive in Cuba. In 1969, for example, there were 65 from the Congo, 29 from Guinea, and 36 from Guinea-Bissau. The numbers increased dramatically when, in 1972–74, Guinea sent 400 university students to Havana.[68]

Few Western observers thought of Africa, however, when they assessed Cuban foreign policy in 1974. They were struck instead by the maturation of

Havana's relations with the United States, Western Europe, Latin America, and, above all, the Soviet Union. Cuba seemed to have abandoned its guerrilla diplomacy of the 1960s for more traditional forms of diplomatic intercourse. The Cuban military presence in Syria and South Yemen provoked little concern, and not even U.S. officials worried much about what happened in tiny Guinea-Bissau.

They were wrong. It was the war in Guinea-Bissau, far more than Angola or Mozambique, that convinced a group of Portuguese officers to overthrow the regime of Prime Minister Marcello Caetano. On April 25, 1974, they made their move, setting in motion a process that would lead to the dispatch of thousands of Cuban soldiers to Africa.

CHAPTER ELEVEN
THE COLLAPSE OF THE PORTUGUESE EMPIRE

The Portuguese officers staged their coup against Caetano while the United States was negotiating the renewal of its military facilities at Lajes air base in the Azores. Lajes's importance had been brought into sharp relief during the October 1973 war in the Middle East, when it had been critical to Washington's massive arms airlift to Israel. "All our NATO allies," Kissinger wrote, "except Portugal, the Netherlands, and the Federal Republic of Germany (for a time) either directly or indirectly dissociated from the airlift and banned our overflights of their territories."[1]

The Portuguese wanted their reward: weapons. Haunted by the growing strength of the PAIGC in Guinea-Bissau and confident of the U.S. government's gratitude, they arrived in Washington for the negotiations on the Azores with a long shopping list, which included some very advanced weapon systems, like the RedEye antiaircraft missiles.[2]

The U.S. negotiating team, led by Under Secretary William Porter, understood that the Portuguese wanted, in fact, much more. They wanted the United States to reverse publicly its policy that Portugal could not use any weapons in Africa received from the United States. "They were pressing us hard to publicly break off our embargo on weapons for their colonies," Willard DePree, the State Department's Policy Planning Staff (PPS) Africa specialist, recalled. "We offered them economic aid instead, but they wanted weapons." PPS director Winston Lord was blunt: "I don't think there is any question that everyone [on Kissinger's senior staff] would love the option . . . of not breaking the embargo," he told Kissinger, "perhaps even stretching it a little bit, and giving them an awful lot in other fields. That is not what they want. They want the symbolic political impact, obviously. . . . They are pretty much alone in the world. . . . That is why they would like us to break the embargo—for that reason, as well as for military reasons." A change in the official U.S. position would send a powerful signal at a time when Portugal was increasingly isolated in Europe with even loyal friends like the British and West German governments drifting away amid the outcry aroused by revelations of Portuguese massacres in Mozambique.[3]

Kissinger was sympathetic to the Portuguese demands, and he brandished a very powerful weapon. "You heard the president yesterday," he told Porter on October 19, the day after the negotiations had begun. "What we have also to keep in mind is that there has been a presidential conversation with the Portuguese ambassador in which the president told him he would be very forthcoming."[4]

Kissinger agreed with Nixon. "Without them [the Portuguese] we could not do the airlift into the Mideast," he told his staff on October 15. "They are running a hell of a risk for it that none of our NATO allies would have run in similar circumstances." As his frustration with the Europeans grew, his resolve to help Portugal hardened. At issue was more than fairness. It was, above all, an object lesson: the United States must show the world that it rewards its friends. "If we are going to be tough to those who don't cooperate, we have to be helpful to those who do," he explained. "I do want the Portuguese to be rewarded for having been the only European country to help us in the Middle East." Furthermore, he stressed, it was futile to court Portuguese goodwill with economic aid alone: first, because they wanted weapons; and, second, because, "contrary to what my colleagues at Harvard have been teaching for 10 years, history shows you get much more influence with military sales than with economic aid." Philosophically, too, Kissinger was sympathetic to the Portuguese position. "You know, it is not self-evident that the Soviets have a right to introduce advanced arms into rebel . . . sides [in Africa], and we don't on the other."[5]

The transcripts of Kissinger's staff meetings indicate that several aides, including Under Secretaries Porter and Joseph Sisco, worried about the political cost of openly breaching the embargo, but they were even more wary of opposing the Nixon-Kissinger juggernaut. A few others (the State Department's counselor Helmut Sonnenfeldt and INR director William Hyland foremost) were vocal in their support of Kissinger's position. Only two aides—Assistant Secretary for African Affairs Donald Easum and PPS Africa specialist DePree—were forthright in their criticism.

Easum warned about the African reaction: "Anything that looks as if it punctures the embargo will be viewed as extremely inimical to the Africans," he argued. "This is the one action the U.S. could take that would be most damaging in terms of U.S. interests in Africa," DePree added. Kissinger brushed their objections aside. The Africans had no means of retaliating, and their opinions did not matter: "I recognize that the Africans won't like any of it," he said. "But, you know, we don't like some of the things that the Africans are doing either."[6] And when Easum tried another tack—"Sir, we have not talked about the United Nations costs. It is not for me to judge those, but there are some repercussions there"—Kissinger's loyalists shot him down. "We tend to get over-excited. The French have no problems at all selling weapons to South Africa of any kind whatsoever," said one. "They have no problems with adverse United Nations votes either," another chimed in. And when Easum raised the African reaction again, Kissinger cut him off: "There is no sense looking at it only from the African point of view. . . . This is not done to promote our African policy." And he waved his presidential club. "Is my impression correct that there is not complete unanimity in support of what the President has already promised?"[7]

The most serious roadblock, however, was the U.S. Congress. "We have not talked about Congress very much," Under Secretary Sisco said, "and I know that it is in the back of all our minds." Kissinger, however, was confident. "The

Congressional reaction will be heavily influenced by the Israel situation," he explained. "Everything we do should be handled by—should be discussed with those who tend to vote the Israeli line or are sympathetic to Israel." He would warn these members that another war between Israel and its neighbors was a distinct possibility and that the United States would need Lajes. He would enlist the Israeli government's help to sway Congress. "The Israelis will support us, I am sure."[8]

It is difficult to know whether Kissinger really believed that the increasingly isolated Portuguese would refuse a future U.S. request to use Lajes if Washington did not change its policy on arms for Africa. The threat of Portuguese retaliation provided him with good ammunition to promote a policy that would show that the United States knew how to reward a loyal ally, that was consistent with his conception of U.S. prestige, and that could be accomplished at little cost: the unhappiness of a bunch of Africans and the self-righteous indignation of a few minor NATO allies, like Denmark, Norway, and the Netherlands, which were openly sympathetic to Portugal's African rebels.

At his January 28 staff meeting, Kissinger said that he was willing to explore the possibility of using "a plausible third country supplier" for the weapons the Portuguese wanted, but then went on to explain that this was not likely to be a viable option because it would be difficult to find a third country and it would be hard to keep it a secret if one were found. "I think when that hits Congress, we are worse off than if we face it head on." He also added that the Defense Department was eager to accommodate the Portuguese. "They want to do the whole package," he said. "Defense wants to do everything."[9]

While the negotiations were proceeding toward accepting the Portuguese demands, embassy officials were reporting the increasing tension in Lisbon. "Pressures are beginning to build up," the director of the State Department's Office of Iberian Affairs told a House subcommittee in mid-March. Richard Post, who was the DCM in Lisbon, was astounded when he learned years later about Kissinger's attempt to change U.S. policy on arms in Portuguese Africa. "We were reporting that things were falling apart and Kissinger wanted to get weapons for Portugal for its African wars!" As he read the reports from Lisbon "on the tense and changing situation in Portugal," the U.S. ambassador to Guinea, Terence Todman, wrote Easum: "For us to decide to provide any military assistance to Portugal for use in its African territories at this time would surely not be . . . in the best long-term interest of anyone."[10]

Kissinger knew that the internal situation in Portugal was very shaky, DePree recalled, "but we moved ahead nonetheless. There was tremendous pressure from the White House, according to Kissinger, to do it."[11] On April 25, Kissinger was saved by the coup. The coup, he wrote Nixon, "could possibly provide some near-term benefits for the United States—for example, a possible lessening or end to Portuguese pressure for U.S. weapons to use in the African territories."[12]

The military junta that replaced Caetano moved quickly toward decolonization. In September 1974 it recognized Guinea-Bissau's independence, and it signed an agreement with Frelimo granting Mozambique's independence the following June.[13]

Demographic, economic, and political circumstances combined to make Angola "the most difficult case," in the words of a senior Portuguese officer.[14] It was the richest of the Portuguese colonies. Almost twice the size of Texas, it was the fourth-largest coffee producer in the world, the sixth-largest diamond producer, an important exporter of iron ore, and sub-Saharan Africa's third-largest oil producer. It was also the Portuguese colony with the largest white population and the weakest insurgency. Moreover, the rebels in Angola were divided, unlike those in Guinea-Bissau and Mozambique. The three Angolan guerrilla movements had fought one another as bitterly as they had the Portuguese. They had never been able to exercise effective control over more than a tiny percentage of the population for any extended period of time, they had never penetrated any of the most densely populated and developed areas of the country, and they had never developed an urban underground. The war, which had begun in 1961, did not slow the colony's economic development. On the contrary, the U.S. consul general in Luanda noted in 1970, "The wheeze about building a monument to the terrorists for the stimulus their activity has given to economic and social development in the province [Angola] is now hoary with age but not lacking in validity. Road and other infrastructural development, stimulated to a considerable degree by strategic considerations, has gone forward at an accelerated pace since 1961, as has the building of schools and hospitals." The demands of the war made the Portuguese overcome their suspicion of foreigners and open the country to foreign investment, which brought much-needed financial resources and technical expertise. In the words of Christine Messiant, one of the foremost authorities on modern Angola, "Late colonial society was greatly transformed in its last fourteen years, with spectacular development in infrastructure, roads, towns, modern agriculture, and a surge of industries."[15] This transformation was accompanied by a dramatic increase of the white population, almost doubling between 1960 and 1974. The guerrillas were but a distant rumble.

Portuguese statistics were notoriously unreliable, but in 1974 Angola's population was probably around 6.4 million, including 320,000 whites. There was only one large city, Luanda, with over 550,000 residents. (The second-largest city, Lobito, had a population of 60,000.) A quarter of Luanda's residents were whites, and about 8 percent were mulattoes.[16]

Angola's mulattoes—estimates range from 60,000 to 100,000—were not a homogeneous social group. They made up the great majority of Angola's non-white elite, but they were also found among the most destitute. For most black

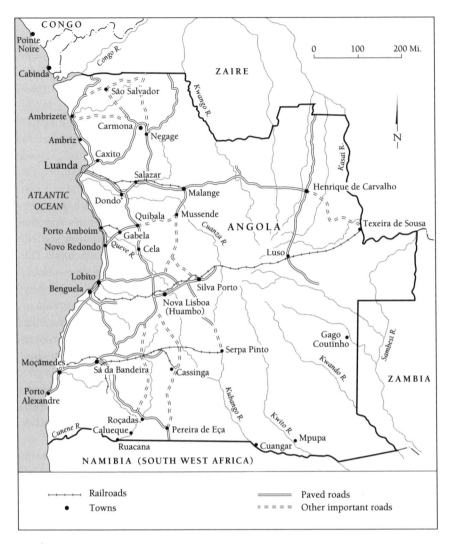

Angola

Angolans, however, the mulattoes were the willing auxiliaries of the Portuguese, ready to serve the white man and betray the African. As John Marcum, one of Angola's keenest observers, pointed out, "a legacy of mistrust between mulatto and African" had developed over the centuries.[17]

At the bottom of Angola's society were the blacks, more than 90 percent of the population. Until 1961, when legal discrimination was abolished, they had been divided between a handful of *assimilados*—who were legally Portuguese citizens—and the rest, who were subject to forced labor. They were the unlucky charges of Europe's most backward colonial power.

Seventy-five percent of Angola's black population belonged to the country's three major ethnic groups: the 2 million strong Ovimbundu in the central highlands; the 1.3 million Mbundu in the north-central region; and the 400,000 Bakongo in the northwest.[18] Angola's ethnic and racial complexity helps explain the divisions among its rebel movements. Each was based on one of the three major ethnic groups: the MPLA on the Mbundu, the FNLA on the Bakongo, and UNITA (National Union for the Total Independence of Angola) on the Ovimbundu. But only the FNLA, which was active in the Bakongo northwest, fought in its ethnic area. UNITA and the MPLA operated in eastern Angola, among populations that were neither Ovimbundu nor Mbundu.[19]

THE REBELS

Our knowledge of the three movements is meager. John Marcum's *Angolan Revolution*, published two decades ago, remains the most authoritative source, but he did not have access to any of the insurgents' internal documents.[20] The only researcher who has used any of these documents is a Congolese scholar, Jean Michel Mabeko Tali. In the late 1960s, he had been unofficially adopted by MPLA leader Lúcio Lara and his wife in Brazzaville. Mabeko Tali continued to live with the Laras, who had three other children, when they moved to Luanda in the mid-1970s. Over the years, he gathered documents and spoke extensively with members of the MPLA. To the dismay of many, he used the documents and his recollections in a doctoral dissertation that is strikingly nonpartisan. While based on only a limited number of documents, it is a major step forward.[21] Nothing comparable exists for UNITA and the FNLA. The important biography of the leader of UNITA, Jonas Savimbi, by British journalist Fred Bridgland is interesting but undermined by its pervasive pro-Savimbi bias.[22]

Each of the three movements was led by an authoritarian leader. All three leaders were black. However, unlike their rivals, the MPLA leaders, some of whom were mulatto, thought in terms of class rather than race. The top military aide to MPLA president Agostinho Neto, Iko Carreira, was a light-skinned mulatto, as was Lúcio Lara, Neto's closest aide. "Its [the MPLA's] largely Mulatto character helps it to transcend tribal division and to render its appeal multiracial," the British consul in Luanda remarked in 1965. The movement also included whites. Both Neto and Lara were married to white women. "Let's not reject people who can help us just because they're white," Neto urged. "All that matters is that they're progressive and honest." This attitude caused the rank and file to grumble, and it deepened the rift between the MPLA and its rivals. The leaders of both the FNLA and UNITA were suspicious of mulattoes and antagonistic toward whites, and they accused the MPLA of selling out to the exploiters of Angola's black population.[23]

Whereas the top echelons of the FNLA had no more than a secondary education, many UNITA leaders had university degrees. None, however, had attained the intellectual prominence of the MPLA leadership. President Neto and several of his colleagues were, the CIA noted, "distinguished intellectuals who have studied in Europe." Neto was a "well-known doctor and poet. . . . Brilliant student; led his class at the university of Lisbon," INR director Hughes wrote. "As a distinguished intellectual," Hughes's predecessor stated, "Neto commands widespread admiration from politically aware Africans and mulattoes in Angola."[24] He was a deeply honest man, who asked little for himself in the way of material comforts. After his visit to East Berlin in May 1963, GDR officials remarked that "Dr. Neto was modest and unassuming. He asked for no special treatment of any kind." A sympathetic journalist wrote that he was "a strong character, built stronger by adversity, little given to words, often finding words a waste of time (even when they might not have been), a privileged *assimilado* who had measured himself against the test of assimilation and academic acceptance but had risen beyond their limits, a poet and a scholar who had made himself into a revolutionary. Uninspiring as a public speaker . . . though witty and persuasive in private talk, a man whose mildness of manner concealed a tough, unyielding stubbornness, Neto combined an unbending devotion to his cause with a corresponding moral power."[25]

This omits the fact that Neto was an authoritarian leader, acting at times, as one of his aides wrote, "without even informing his closest aides." He could be vengeful, and he was not a brilliant politician. A senior Portuguese officer who admired Neto's "generous ideas" and "history of struggles against fascism and colonialism" expressed doubt "that he had the ability to lead the country through such a complex process [as the transition to independence]."[26]

Neto, Lara, and several other MPLA leaders espoused an eclectic interpretation of Marxism. A few intellectuals, none in a senior position, supported orthodox socialism oriented toward the Soviet Union. The great majority of the military commanders had no ideological compass beyond a vague belief that independence should be followed by deep changes in Angolan society. However murky the MPLA's ideological commitment may have been, it set it apart: the leaders of the FNLA and UNITA espoused no political doctrine.[a]

None of the three rebel movements developed an effective fighting force, unlike the PAIGC in Guinea-Bissau and Frelimo in Mozambique. The MPLA almost succeeded, for a while. After uncertain beginnings in Cabinda in 1964–65, it shifted its military efforts to the vast, thinly populated areas of eastern

---

a. During the war some U.S. officials suspected that Savimbi was a Maoist; more soberly, INR noted that he was "an intelligent and ambitious political maneuverer" who sought aid from the Chinese but was not "ideologically committed to them." Given the dearth of reliable information about Savimbi in those years, it is impossible to be categorical. By 1975 he had changed his tune so dramatically that U.S. officials considered him "basically moderate," which suggests that his "Maoism" had been opportunistic. Edward Fugit, who served in the U.S. consulate in Luanda in 1973–75, put it well: "He wasn't any more Maoist than I am." (Quotations from INR, "Africa: Prospects for Liberation from White Minority Regimes," Sept. 22, 1971, p. 45, Pol 13 Afr, SNF, NA; Mulcahy to Kissinger, May 16, 1975, p. 1, NSA; tel. interview with Fugit.)

Angola. The existence of a friendly rear guard—Zambia—allowed it to receive aid and maintain links with the outside world, even though landlocked Zambia's support was tempered by its dependence on Angola's Benguela railroad, which carried half of its exports to the Atlantic.[27] "Portugal's problems in Angola have dramatically increased," the West German consul reported in September 1966, a few months after the MPLA had begun the war in the east. Through the early 1970s, the Portuguese considered the MPLA their "most dangerous foe [in Angola]," the U.S. consul in Luanda called it "the single most significant threat for the future," and INR concluded that it was "the best disciplined and most effective" of the three rebel groups. "We were at our peak," Lara recalled, in 1970 and early 1971.[28] After that a series of Portuguese offensives battered the eastern front. "Raining napalm and defoliants in a 'scorched earth' assault on nationalist villages," Marcum wrote, "they inflicted serious defeats on MPLA forces." Many MPLA military commanders blamed the movement's political leadership, which had been unable to supply them adequately, for their reverses. The debacle also inflamed latent ethnic tensions between, on the one hand, the local population (Chokwe, Luena, Luchazi, Bunda) and the rank-and-file guerrillas drawn from it and, on the other, those MPLA commanders who were Mbundu or mulattoes. This led to a serious challenge to Neto's leadership. Daniel Chipenda, a charismatic Ovimbundu, led an "Eastern Revolt" against the intellectuals, mulattoes, whites, and northerners in the MPLA and expelled Neto's supporters from the areas he controlled on the eastern front. In November 1973 the U.S. consul general in Luanda reported, "the terrorist presence in the eastern Military Zone is the lowest it has been since the outbreak of warfare in 1967." Zambia's president, Kenneth Kaunda, sided with Chipenda. "The [Zambian] government is more and more openly hostile to the movement [MPLA] and especially to me," Neto wrote in March 1974.[29]

By April 1974, when Caetano fell, the MPLA had come full circle militarily; it was, once again, weak and ineffective. Nevertheless, it "remained the most important movement in Angola," as the chief of the general staff of the Portuguese armed forces remarked. Over the years, the MPLA's shortwave broadcasts had kept its name alive for hundreds of thousands of Angolans who had never seen an MPLA fighter or read an MPLA tract. The movement's emphasis on class rather than ethnicity had gained it supporters throughout Angola's urban centers and had made it, in the words of U.S. consul general Everett Briggs (1972–74), "the only Angolan [rebel] organization that had any national representativeness, that could be considered an Angolan-wide organization." Furthermore, as the State Department noted in 1975, the MPLA commanded "the allegiance of most of the best educated and skilled people in Angola." It was, Briggs's successor Tom Killoran explained, "head and shoulders above the other two groups in terms of skills, education, and knowing what to do and how to do it."[30]

The FNLA, on the other hand, Killoran observed, "was totally disorganized, totally corrupt." Robert Hultslander, who was the CIA station chief in Luanda in 1975, agreed. "This organization," he wrote, "was led by corrupt, unprincipled men who represented the very worst of radical black African racism."[31]

Throughout the war, the FNLA's greatest asset was the support of Zaire, where it was based and where half a million Angolan Bakongo had settled. The relationship with Zaire, however, was also a liability. Mobutu was playing a complicated game. While loudly proclaiming his support for the FNLA, he was also discreetly cultivating good relations with Portugal because, like Zambia, Zaire depended on access to the Benguela railroad, which carried more than half of its foreign trade. Furthermore, he did not want to provoke Lisbon into unleashing against him the Katangan gendarmes—a well-trained force of a few thousand Zairean exiles under Portuguese command fighting the Angolan rebels. Mobutu therefore kept tight control over the FNLA's activities in Zaire. He gave the FNLA sufficient political and material support to allow it to retain some international credibility and to give Zaire a stake in Angola in the event of decolonization.[32]

The leader of the FNLA, Holden Roberto, was more interested in personal power than in the war. He was, U.S. intelligence noted, "subservient" to Mobutu, and Mobutu protected him from any challenges to his leadership. "The FNLA is Holden Roberto and Holden Roberto belongs to Mobutu, to whom he is connected by an umbilical cord," the Portuguese weekly *Expresso* noted in 1974.[33] It was a squalid spectacle: a corrupt leader dancing to the tune of a foreign master. With the fall of Caetano, however, the tune changed. Mobutu increased his assistance to the FNLA.[34]

The Chinese joined the fray. After a hiatus in the late 1960s—when the Cultural Revolution was raging in China—Beijing had begun focusing again on Africa in 1970, but its approach had changed. It was "deemphasizing subversion in the interest of establishing diplomatic relations with existing governments," Assistant Secretary for African Affairs David Newsom explained. Its diplomatic offensive was bolstered by economic aid to friendly governments, irrespective of their domestic politics. Roughly half of Chinese foreign economic aid went to Africa. "Peking's current image in Africa," INR noted in late 1972, "is that of a substantial and diligent aid donor, eschewing intervention in internal affairs." Following the example of Ethiopia, Nigeria, and a dozen other African countries, in November 1972 Mobutu recognized the PRC. The following January, he visited Beijing, where he received a thirty-year interest-free loan.[35] When Roberto, following in his patron's footsteps, visited Beijing in December 1973, the Chinese, who were "attempting to curry favor" with Mobutu, promised him military aid. The fall of Caetano spurred them into action. On June 3, 1974, the Zairean daily *Salongo* reported that Beijing had pledged to send 112 military instructors to train the FNLA in Zaire and that the first contingent had already arrived. In early August a second group arrived, followed, in early September, by 450 tons of weapons. "The Chinese no doubt . . . saw in the FNLA a means to compete with Soviet interests in Angola as represented by the MPLA," an NSC document noted. "[The] FNLA's fortunes," it added, "were beginning to improve."[36]

The only Angolan rebel movement that received virtually no outside aid during the war of independence was UNITA. From the very beginning of its armed struggle, in late 1966, UNITA was based in eastern Angola, and, after losing Zambia's support in 1967, it was left to its own devices except for some "token support" from Beijing.[37]

Friend and foe alike acknowledged the intelligence and the charisma of the leader of UNITA, Jonas Savimbi. "Savimbi is an impressive figure," the U.S. ambassador in Zambia reported after meeting him in January 1975. "Savimbi is very intelligent," Lara agreed.[38] Unlike Neto, who spent very little time with his guerrillas inside Angola, and Roberto, who never set foot in Angola during the war of independence, Savimbi, as a South African journalist observed, "spent most of his time leading his troops in the field." Savimbi himself boasted, in a clear swipe at Neto and Roberto, "I alone remained in the bush for six years."[39] Less clear, however, is exactly what he was doing there. In July 1974 the Paris-based weekly, *Afrique-Asie*, published four letters allegedly exchanged between Savimbi and Portuguese officials in 1972 that seemed to prove that he had colluded with Lisbon.[40]

Savimbi immediately denounced the documents as forgeries, and his many supporters and sympathizers in the West have consistently dismissed them, casting aspersions on *Afrique-Asie*, a left-wing magazine with frank sympathy for the MPLA. The documents have been dismissed or ignored by scholars in the United States.[41]

This is baffling. Many well-placed and decidedly nonleftist Portuguese officials have attested to Savimbi's links with Lisbon. In his memoirs, published a few months after the April coup, Caetano praised General José Bethencourt Rodrigues, who had been the Portuguese commander of the Eastern Military Zone of Angola in 1971–73. Bethencourt's mission, Caetano wrote, "was to . . . pacify the region, [and] he succeeded, including coming to an understanding with UNITA." General Francisco da Costa Gomes, the commander in chief in Angola from May 1970 through August 1972, wrote that UNITA "had signed an agreement in the second half of 1971, which had led to a suspension of military operations." The documents published in *Afrique-Asie* were not forgeries, Pompílio da Cruz, a prominent right-wing Portuguese settler in Angola, explained: after the fall of Caetano, a Portuguese officer had "disloyally, with the perfidy of a venomous beast, leaked photocopies of letters exchanged between the Portuguese authorities and Dr. Jonas Savimbi." In 1979, the mainstream Lisbon weekly, *Expresso*, printed several more documents detailing Savimbi's cooperation with the Portuguese. Since then, several Portuguese officials who were involved have provided additional testimony. Many details are still missing, but, as *Expresso* pointed out in 1979, "The fact that Savimbi collaborated with the Portuguese colonial authorities has been so amply proved that no one can question it in good faith."[42]

The first contacts between Savimbi and the Portuguese occurred in 1969. In August the U.S. consul general reported that the Portuguese governor had said that "contacts are still maintained with Savimbi."[43] It is not known who approached whom, or whether these contacts continued over the next two years. All we know is that there were virtually no clashes between the Portuguese and UNITA during this period. The Portuguese were focusing on the MPLA, and UNITA was just trying to survive the assaults of the MPLA and FNLA. According to U.S. officials, it had about 300 combatants. "The organization is so small, as a military force," INR remarked in September 1971, "that it is difficult to know with any certainty just what it does consist of and where it operates."[44]

In late 1971 the Portuguese decided to enlist UNITA in their war against the MPLA in the east. "Jonas Savimbi was a very ambitious man, and he led a small group," explained General Costa Gomes, who presided over the mission, called Operation Timber.[45] The Portuguese followed two parallel tracks: the first, to secure UNITA's aid against the MPLA; the second, eventually to bring Savimbi and UNITA back into the colonial fold.

Within a few months the first track had reached a successful conclusion. In early February 1972 Savimbi proposed that "our forces [UNITA and Portuguese] cooperate against preestablished objectives. We would be willing to provide guides to enemy zones. . . . I am sure that with our cooperation the MPLA . . . would . . . be eliminated from the East."[46] The Portuguese responded favorably. They agreed not to harass UNITA within specified borders, "where it could even receive some humanitarian and logistical assistance." In return, UNITA promised to attack guerrillas of the other two movements and to inform the Portuguese command about the movements of MPLA and FNLA forces.[47] Savimbi proved to be a loyal ally. He "told us where the 'squadrons' of the MPLA, as he called them, were," Costa Gomes wrote. UNITA, another Portuguese officer remarked, "gave the Portuguese forces the decisive weapon in that kind of war: information about the guerrilla base camps."[48] On September 26, 1972, Savimbi wrote to General Joaquim da Luz Cunha, who had just replaced Costa Gomes as Portuguese commander in chief in Angola: "We want the decisive eradication of war from this eastern sector. We have done everything we could to weaken the forces of the common enemy. . . . We will never make the mistake of taking up arms against the authorities. Instead, we will use our arms as vigorously as possible to force the MPLA to abandon the east."[49] In November 1973, the U.S. consul general in Luanda reported that Savimbi had "avoided armed combat, at least since the beginning of last year, against Portuguese troops. There is news of ambushes mounted by his men against groups of MPLA and FNLA."[50]

The second track was less successful. One may wonder whether Savimbi was sincere when he proclaimed his desire to return, one day, to Portuguese sovereignty, or whether he was buying time until Portuguese rule collapsed. In the meantime, he enjoyed the best of two worlds: helping destroy his rivals, while safeguarding his own weak military forces.

In June 1973 a *Washington Post* journalist, Leon Dash, was shepherded by

UNITA guides from Zambia into their territory. "[I] spent the next ten weeks living with the guerrillas and traveling as an observer with their heavily armed, self-sufficient bands, which appear to move at will in a vast domain of virtually trackless forest and plain," he wrote. While he never claimed to have witnessed a clash between UNITA and the Portuguese, his series (which was not published until December) conveyed the image of an aggressive UNITA fully engaged in fighting the colonial troops. This, however, was very far from the truth.[51]

Had Dash undertaken his journey a few months later, he might have witnessed fighting. "In the last quarter of 1973," Costa Gomes writes, "we violated the agreement [with Savimbi]." Joaquim da Silva Cunha, overseas minister from 1965 to November 1973, when he became Caetano's last defense minister, explains what had happened: "UNITA, which remained in its area with our permission because it was assisting us in the war against the MPLA, was . . . involved in negotiations with us, which were developing slowly but surely, to return its leader, Jonas Savimbi, and his men to the Portuguese community." But in September 1973 a new Portuguese commander in the east, General Abel Barroso Hipólito, launched an offensive against UNITA, "even though he had been told in Lisbon about the importance of those negotiations and despite his instructions." And so Savimbi became a freedom fighter. "It was sheer lunacy," another Portuguese general remarked. "UNITA was on our side, but . . . Barroso Hipólito said that for him all the Angolan rebels were the same." Barroso Hipólito was recalled to Lisbon. "I sacked him," said Costa Gomes, who had become the chief of the general staff of the Portuguese armed forces.[52] Contacts between Savimbi and the Portuguese authorities were reestablished early in 1974. "Things were, therefore, on the way to returning to the previous situation and negotiations were under way," Silva Cunha writes, when Caetano was overthrown on April 25, 1974.[53]

UNITA was the weakest of the rebel movements at the time. "Unlike the other two main groups, UNITA had only a small armed force (600–800 men) on April 25 [1974]," U.S. consul general Killoran reported. "These men had much less combat experience than FNLA or MPLA troops."[54] A few days after Caetano's ouster, however, Savimbi took advantage of the festive mood of the Portuguese troops to carry out his most successful military operation: UNITA captured an entire company of Portuguese soldiers, disarmed and stripped them, so that they returned completely naked to their barracks.[55] With that brilliant stroke, Savimbi refurbished his credentials as a freedom fighter, just before signing a cease-fire with his erstwhile allies, the Portuguese, on June 14.

Although the FNLA and the MPLA did not sign cease-fires until October, the Portuguese suspended offensive operations shortly after the fall of Caetano. During the summer of 1974 UNITA began organizing politically, especially among the Ovimbundu in the central highlands, and the FNLA began moving troops from Zaire into the Bakongo regions of northern Angola, while the MPLA was virtually inactive, paralyzed by internal strife. It was not until September, at a conference of the top guerrilla commanders and urban cadres, that Neto was able to reassert control.[56]

Four months later, on January 15, the Alvor agreement between Portugal and the three Angolan liberation movements was signed. It was, U.S. intelligence remarked, "a complex and delicate mechanism." A Portuguese high commissioner would govern the country until independence on November 11, 1975. He would be assisted by a transitional government headed by a presidential council composed of a representative each from the FNLA, MPLA, and UNITA. The cabinet would include twelve ministers, three for each movement and three for the Portuguese. There would be a 48,000-man army: 24,000 Portuguese and 8,000 from each movement. (All Portuguese troops in excess of 24,000 would leave Angola by April 30, 1975, and the rest would be withdrawn gradually between October 1, 1975, and February 29, 1976.) Elections for a Constituent Assembly, which would select the country's first president, would be held by October 31, 1975.[57]

THE MPLA'S FRIENDS

By the time the transitional government took office on January 31, the MPLA had begun the slow process of transforming its motley forces into a regular army, the FAPLA (Popular Armed Forces for the Liberation of Angola). Because this required external aid, it had also begun to repair its relations with friendly governments, which had been disrupted by its leadership crisis.

In the 1960s, the MPLA had received some Soviet and Soviet-bloc aid. The paucity of this aid was consistent with Soviet policy toward sub-Saharan Africa. The disappointments of the early 1960s—crowned by the twin blows of the Simbas' debacle in Zaire and Nkrumah's overthrow in Ghana—had led to a significant diminution of Soviet interest in the region in the second half of the decade, precisely when the MPLA finally had guerrillas in the field. In March 1973 Assistant Secretary Newsom told British officials that "we [the United States] were surprised by the low level of Soviet . . . support for the liberation movements operating against Portuguese territories." Of course, this was not true everywhere; the Soviets were not niggardly in their support of the PAIGC in Guinea-Bissau, but they were impressed neither with the MPLA's military performance nor with its leaders, particularly Neto. "Moscow had never trusted Neto," a former Soviet official recalled in his memoirs. They also disliked Lara, who, they believed, was partial to European-style social democracy. Moreover, they suspected that Neto and his group were pro-Chinese. This was ironic: the Chinese had given some assistance to the MPLA in the early 1960s, but by 1963 they suspected that the MPLA was pro-Soviet and relations had become, in Lara's words, "tenuous."[58]

The MPLA itself fostered this impasse with the two Communist giants by its proud and stubborn refusal to criticize either one publicly. A former MPLA official, Ndunduma, who was the leader of a group of MPLA students in Yugoslavia, recalled that in 1967 he received a telegram telling him to go to the main railway station in Belgrade to meet Neto, who was arriving from Moscow. Ndunduma thought it was strange that Neto would arrive by train, but later learned that in Beijing the Chinese had pressured Neto to condemn Soviet revisionism, he had refused, and the Chinese had refused to provide any aid; in Moscow, Neto's next stop, the Russians had pressured him to condemn the Chinese, he had refused, and decided to forgo the plane ticket to Belgrade the Soviets had offered him and to travel instead by train, which he could afford with his own money.[59]

The incident illuminates both Neto's personality and the travails of a small, proud, and unsuccessful guerrilla movement. "Our relationship with the Russians was difficult," a senior MPLA commander, Ndalu, remarked. "Neto was very strong-willed; he didn't accept orders. The Soviets (and the Chinese) wanted to involve us in a war that was not ours [the Sino-Soviet clash]. Neto didn't bend for the Russians, and he didn't bend for the Chinese."[60]

In 1972, when the MPLA was reeling from the Portuguese assault and was torn by internal strife, Moscow stopped giving it any aid. (Norwegian scholar Odd Arne Westad, who has had access to Soviet documents, writes that the Soviet Union continued to send "a trickle of military and financial support," but the MPLA leaders claim that the aid was completely cut off.) In Lara's words, "The Soviets dropped us. We assumed it was over."[61]

Chronic Soviet suspicions that the MPLA was pro-Chinese had probably been fanned by an ephemeral thaw in the MPLA's relations with Beijing. Following a July 1971 trip to Beijing of a five-man delegation led by Neto, twelve MPLA military commanders spent nine months in China for political and military training and other MPLA guerrillas were trained by Chinese military instructors in Tanzania. "The Russians didn't like it," Ndalu recalled.[62]

This may have contributed to the suspension of aid, Lara speculated, but "it was primarily due to our internal difficulties." In the struggle between Neto and Chipenda (from 1972 to 1974), the MPLA was for all practical purposes split in two and the Soviets favored Chipenda, apparently giving him a small amount of financial aid.[63]

Through those difficult years, the MPLA's closest friend was Yugoslavia, which played an important role in African liberation wars. President Josip Broz Tito "clearly enjoys his role as a patriarch of guerrilla liberation struggle," the U.S. ambassador in Belgrade remarked.[64] Yugoslavia had been a strong supporter of the Algerian rebels fighting against French rule;[65] it gave valuable assistance to the PAIGC; and it stood by the MPLA "even, and especially, in our most difficult moments," Ndalu said. In 1972–74, "when the Soviet Union stopped its aid and the other Soviet bloc countries followed suit, Yugoslavia alone in the socialist camp continued to help us," another MPLA official recalled. "I must emphasize," Neto declared in 1977, "how constant, firm, and generous . . . Yugoslavia's help was during our war of liberation." This help, he added, "was extraordinary."[66]

The Soviets' interest in the MPLA resumed, according to Westad, shortly after the fall of Caetano, but they insisted that the rival MPLA factions unite before they would provide any aid. Meanwhile they did nothing. "We had the feeling they had abandoned us," Lara said, remembering the summer of 1974. "Right when we needed a lot of weapons, we couldn't get them." Finally, after Neto had regained control of the movement, the Soviets relented, accepting that unity was a chimera, and, as Westad writes, they "threw their weight squarely behind Neto's group." In December 1974, according to Westad, Moscow "drew up an elaborate plan for supplying the MPLA with heavy weapons and large amounts of ammunition."[67]

The MPLA had also been exploring the possibility of Cuban aid. Its relations with Cuba had become more distant after the departure of the Cuban military instructors from the Congo in 1967.[68] "The Cubans didn't cultivate the relationship," Lara observed. The MPLA did not maintain an office in Havana, as it did, for example, in Belgrade, and Havana's assistance was very modest. A few MPLA guerrillas received military training in Cuba, and Cuba consistently supported the MPLA (and Neto) at international conferences, at the United Nations, and in the nonaligned movement.[69]

When I first queried Cuban officials about the slackening of ties with the MPLA, they talked geography. After 1966 the focus of the MPLA's effort was the eastern front, and its rear guard was Zambia, and there was no Cuban presence in Zambia, even though the two countries had established diplomatic relations in 1972.[70] This explanation is not persuasive. There was a Cuban embassy in Dar-es-Salaam, which was an important center of MPLA activities; furthermore, there is no indication that the Cubans tried to establish an embassy in Lusaka. When they did, in 1975, they were immediately successful.

More to the point, writes Mabeko Tali, reflecting the views of the MPLA leaders, "The state of the relationship between Cuba and the MPLA had cooled."[71] Both sides had been stung by their experience in Brazzaville in 1965–67: the Cubans were disappointed, and the MPLA resentful. In March 1972, Neto told the Cuban chargé in Brazzaville "that while one cannot say that the relations between Cuba and the MPLA are bad or cold, it's obvious that they are not like what they were a few years ago." Neto remarked that when he had visited Cuba in January 1966, "he had gotten the impression that Fidel and the other Cuban leaders were disappointed in the African national liberation movements and wary of them because of their very bad experiences in Zaire and in their dealings with other movements in Africa. Neto added that he understood that there was indeed ample reason to be disillusioned by what had happened in Zaire, but that they [the MPLA] were a serious movement, that they were really fighting, and that they did not understand this impasse that had developed between Cuba and the MPLA."[72]

A few weeks later, perhaps in response to Neto's complaint, Havana expressed its desire to send several men to Angola to learn about the progress of the war. The MPLA agreed, in principle, but did nothing. Given the MPLA's disarray at the time, this was not surprising. The Cubans did not press the issue and relations remained distant. Their attention had shifted to the far more success-ful struggle in Guinea-Bissau, and the weakness of the MPLA in the early 1970s "did not encourage us to increase our aid," as Carlos Cadelo, who was the Central Committee staffer on Angola, remarked.[73]

The fall of Caetano brought no immediate change. An MPLA delegation visited Cuba for the celebrations of July 26, 1974, and brought a request from Neto for economic aid, military training, and weapons. "We said yes," Cadelo recalled. But nothing happened. In early October the Cuban ambassador in Dar-es-Salaam, Héctor Ramos Latour, informed Havana that Neto had requested "urgently" five Cuban military officers to help organize the FAPLA. Castro was consulted and responded favorably.[74] Then he had second thoughts. Ten years earlier, he had sent instructors to help the Zairean rebels on the basis of second-hand information and before any Cuban had ever set foot in Zaire. Now, he was more cautious. Instead of sending the five officers, he instructed Ramos Latour to inform Neto that he wanted to send a military officer who would speak with the MPLA leaders in Dar-es-Salaam and travel around Angola in order to see the situation on the ground, which no Cuban had yet done. Neto gave his approval and told Ramos Latour "that they could receive the compañero in the second half of November." Havana sent Major Alfonso Pérez Morales (Pina), who had served with the PAIGC guerrillas in Guinea-Bissau, and Cadelo. "We wanted to send a political analyst and a military officer," Risquet explained. Together they would assess the situation and suggest what Cuba could do to help the MPLA.[75]

CHAPTER TWELVE
THE GATHERING STORM:
ANGOLA, JANUARY-OCTOBER 1975

Cadelo and Pina arrived in Dar-es-Salaam in late December 1974. In meetings with Neto and other senior MPLA officials, they learned that an MPLA delegation was preparing to go to Moscow to ask for Soviet military aid and that Neto was going to meet Holden Roberto and Savimbi in Mombasa on January 3, 1975, to forge a common position for the upcoming negotiations with the Portuguese at Alvor. Neto welcomed Cadelo and Pina's desire to go to Angola. "He said we should verify for ourselves everything he had told us so that we could be sure we had a clear view of the situation in Angola."[1]

Traveling with Tanzanian documents that identified them as Angolan refugees (courtesy of the MPLA), Cadelo and Pina flew to Lusaka on January 3.[2] From there, they were driven to Kassamba, the major MPLA camp near the Angolan border, where they joined a convoy of trucks taking hundreds of refugees back to Angola. They were the first Cubans to enter Angola since Moracén and his friends had left Cabinda at the end of 1965.[3] They traveled incognito, but some Portuguese officers who sympathized with the MPLA knew who they were. "[António] Rosa Coutinho [the Portuguese high commissioner] himself knew we were there," Cadelo recalled. "I mean, he knew that two Cubans were there, looking into helping the MPLA. He didn't know whether we were fat or thin, white or black, but he knew we were there."[4] In Luanda they met with Xiyetu, the chief of staff of the fledging FAPLA (the MPLA's army), and other top MPLA officials who told them that by independence day, in November 1975, they would have an army of 20,000 men. Xiyetu "immediately told us what they needed from us: military training at every level . . . [and], as soon as possible, the training of ninety security personnel." He stressed "that the training had to take place in Angola, because it was impossible to take the cadres out of the country."[5]

On January 22, after two weeks in Angola, Cadelo and Pina were back in Dar-es-Salaam, where they met Neto again. Neto told them that until independence the MPLA was going to focus on organizing in three areas: political, trade union, and military. He wanted Cuba's assistance to prepare political and trade union cadres. Neto also explained that the military plan that Xiyetu had outlined in Luanda was their "ultimate objective," but that they would be unable to achieve it with the weapons they expected from Moscow and Belgrade. He added that they were going to sign a military protocol with the Soviet Union very soon and that then they would know exactly what weapons they were going to receive. "What we ask Cuba will be contingent on this."[6] Neto then handed Cadelo and Pina a letter to the Cuban government:

Dear Comrades,

Given the situation on the ground of our movement and our country, and taking into account the results of the exploratory trip of the official Cuban delegation [Cadelo and Pina], we are sending you a list of the urgent needs of our organization. We are confident that you will give it immediate consideration.

1. The establishment, organization, and maintenance of a military school for cadres. We urgently need to create a company of security personnel, and we need to train our military staff.

2. A ship to transport the war matériel that we have in Dar-es-Salaam to Angola. The delivery in Angola, if it were in a Cuban ship, could take place outside of territorial waters.

3. Weapons and transportation for the Rapid Deployment Unit [Brigada de Intervención] that we are planning to organize, as well as light weapons for some infantry battalions.

4. Transmitters and receivers to resolve communication problems of widely dispersed military units.

5. Uniforms and military equipment for 10,000 men.

6. Two pilots and one flight mechanic.

7. Assistance in training trade union leaders.

8. Assistance in organizing schools to teach Marxism. . . .

9. Publications dealing with political and military subjects, especially instruction manuals.

10. Financial assistance while we are establishing and organizing ourselves.

We also urge the Communist Party of Cuba to use its influence with its friends and allies, especially from the Socialist camp, to encourage them to grant useful and timely aid to our movement, which is the only guarantee of a democratic and progressive Angola in the future.

Comrades, accept our revolutionary greetings and convey the good wishes of the combatants of the MPLA and of the new Angola to Prime Minister Fidel Castro.[7]

In conversations with Neto and other senior MPLA officials in Luanda and Dar-es-Salaam, other matters were considered, particularly the possibility that Cuba send military instructors to Angola. Xiyetu, who had led the MPLA delegation that had just returned from Moscow and Belgrade, told Cadelo and Pina that the talks had been constructive. The Soviets would provide military aid, but could promise only that it would arrive "within five months." They were also willing to assist in the creation of an elite "rapid, efficient, and well-armed" force of 2,250 men with its own means of transportation, a project that Neto was particularly eager to implement. They wanted, however, to train and equip the men in the Soviet Union, and the Angolans wanted the training close to home. "Training this force in the USSR creates problems for the Angolans," Cadelo and Pina reported, "because it would mean that a large part of their force would be very far away and could not be counted on in a crisis."[8] The project, then, was up in the air.

On one point Neto was definite: while waiting for the Soviet weapons to arrive, he wanted Cuba to provide $100,000 to ship the weapons the MPLA had in Dar-es-Salaam, its major arsenal, to Angola. "This was one of Neto's two priorities," Pina recalled. "The other was that Cuba send spare parts for the vehicles that were in terrible disrepair."[9]

And so Cadelo and Pina concluded their mission with two items: Neto's letter and a vague idea about military instructors. As Cadelo noted, "Even though Neto gave us a letter with some concrete demands, it was not really clear what the best form of cooperation with Cuba would be, or how and when it should be implemented." Xiyetu agreed: "In the conversations with Cadelo and Pina we spoke in very general terms; we didn't have concrete plans." Lúcio Lara explained, "We didn't know yet exactly what we were going to do. That's why we were hesitant and vague."[10]

From Dar-es-Salaam, Cadelo and Pina flew to Mozambique "to learn," a Maputo daily explained, "about Frelimo, Mozambique, and its people." They returned to Cuba at the beginning of March and on the 21st presented a report to Osmany Cienfuegos, the Central Committee member who had been Castro's point man for Africa in the mid-1960s and had recently resumed that role, and to Raúl Díaz Argüelles, who was the head of the Décima Dirección, the special task force in charge of all Cuban military missions abroad.[11]

Their report was optimistic about the MPLA's long-term prospects and the likelihood of the October elections being held. "We didn't think there would be a civil war in the near future," Cadelo recalled. "We thought it wouldn't happen for two or three years." Apparently, this was also the Soviet view: the Soviet embassy in Brazzaville, Westad writes, "did not expect a full scale civil war to break out before Angola achieved its independence in November." More important, this was the view of the MPLA. "We expected elections and not the civil war," Lúcio Lara recalled. "We believed that peace would hold at least through the elections," Xiyetu agreed.[12]

Cadelo and Pina reported that while the FNLA was militarily stronger than the MPLA (Neto himself had told them as much), the MPLA had better long-term prospects. "This movement," they wrote, "is the best structured politically and militarily, and enjoys extraordinary popular support." By contrast, they explained, the FNLA lacked support beyond the two northern provinces peopled by Bakongo. UNITA, they concluded surprisingly, "could count only on minimal support from the black population." The Portuguese military in Angola, which was scheduled to remain in the country until February 1976, was in the sway of young, left-leaning officers who had contempt for Holden Roberto's kowtowing to Mobutu and Savimbi's erstwhile collaboration with the colonial authorities. They were sympathetic to the MPLA, particularly in the east and in Cabinda ("where we traveled in the Portuguese military commander's personal car"). Cadelo and Pina knew that Admiral Rosa Coutinho, whose sympathy for the MPLA had aroused a storm of complaints from the FNLA and UNITA, was being replaced by a more neutral high commissioner, General António da Silva Cardoso. But Silva Cardoso, Xiyetu had told them in Luanda, was reputed to be "progressive and honest" and the majority of his officers sympathized with the MPLA.[13]

The presence of Portuguese in key administrative positions and of over 20,000 Portuguese troops seemed to guarantee the continuation of peace through independence day and beyond. In the meantime the MPLA would strengthen itself politically and militarily. The MPLA, Neto had told Cadelo and Pina, intended to "do political work among the population so that it would hold the key positions that would assure its continuation in power by democratic means." At the same time, it would create an army to be prepared if war came.[14] Furthermore, it was likely that the FAPLA would be strengthened by the addition of the 2,000- to 3,000-strong group of Katangan gendarmes living in Angola. These Zairean exiles, who had been well trained by the Portuguese to fight against Roberto's FNLA, were now engaged in secret talks with the MPLA. Although the previous November Mobutu had urged them to return to Zaire, saying they would be granted total amnesty, they did not trust him, and with good reason: in 1968 almost 1,000 of them had been executed, usually after hideous torture, after Mobutu had promised them amnesty in 1967. Therefore, they wanted to remain in Angola and they sought the support of the MPLA. "The compañeros of the MPLA," Cadelo and Pina reported, "are eager to respond to their overtures, so that, if necessary, they could count on their assistance."[15]

HAVANA'S LANGUOR

After receiving Cadelo's and Pina's report, the head of the Décima Dirección, Díaz Argüelles, presented "a draft proposal for military aid . . . to the MPLA for the period from May 1975 through 1976, and the creation of a military mission."[16] But nothing happened. Cuban officials say that they were waiting for the Angolans to clarify their requests,[17] but Havana neither asked for clarification nor sent Neto the $100,000 he had specifically requested.

It is difficult to explain this. Perhaps Cadelo's and Pina's report dulled the sense of urgency, as did their behavior after they had concluded their conversations with the MPLA leaders in Dar-es-Salaam, going, for almost a month, to Mozambique, and cabling Havana only a short report about the MPLA in the interim. Furthermore, the Angolans waited until May before reiterating their request.[18]

In Luanda, time and again, I asked the same question: why didn't the MPLA press Cuba for aid after Cadelo's and Pina's visit? Soft-spoken, incisive, and patient, Lúcio Lara helped me to see the situation through MPLA eyes. After talking to him and to other leaders of the MPLA, I finally began to understand that their behavior was the result of pride, self-confidence, and miscalculation.

In the early months of 1975, the MPLA did not consider Cuba its most important potential source of aid. When Cadelo and Pina arrived, "We asked for help," Lara explained. When Cuba failed to answer, Lara's son added, "We didn't want to beg. This wasn't just Neto's reaction, but that of most of the leaders."[19] Furthermore, because the MPLA did not expect war in the near future, it felt little urgency. And it expected Belgrade and Moscow, not Havana, to be its major benefactors. "We needed weapons," Lúcio Lara told me. "We weren't very concerned about getting instructors." And Cuban instructors "could have irritated Portugal and African countries."[20] Besides, Moscow was willing to help with the training. In March approximately 100 MPLA members left for the Soviet Union. "It was a compromise solution," Xiyetu remarked. The previous January the Soviets had agreed to instruct the 2,250-man elite brigade Neto wanted, but they insisted that the training take place in the Soviet Union. The MPLA had wanted it to be closer to home, so it sent only the cadres for specialized training.[21]

Furthermore, Yugoslavia had given the MPLA the $100,000 Neto had requested from Castro, and a senior FAPLA commander, Dangereux, had successfully overseen the transfer of the weapons from Dar-es-Salaam to Angola in late April.[22]

There was, therefore, no need to knock at Cuba's door again. Pride, self-confidence, and the illusion that war could be postponed made the MPLA think that it did not have to beg.

THE CIVIL WAR BEGINS

In fact, the war could not be postponed. The first clashes were in Luanda, just weeks after the transitional government took power. With over 550,000 residents, Luanda was the prize: the economic, political, and demographic capital of the country. A large majority of blacks and mulattoes (who together composed about 75 percent of the city's population) supported the MPLA, but in those first months of 1975 the FNLA was, militarily, the dominant liberation movement in the city. "Its well-armed troops in their impeccable uniforms" had begun arriving in Luanda in October 1974 aboard planes of the Zairean air force. The FNLA was hoping to compensate for its lack of political appeal with military muscle, but the brutality and arrogance of its soldiers increased the population's hostility. Distracted by its internal strife, the MPLA had sent troops to Luanda later and in far smaller numbers, and UNITA, which had almost no troops, had only a symbolic military presence in the capital.[23] Chipenda, Neto's defeated rival for the MPLA's leadership, sent a group of armed men to Luanda to establish a military presence there, even though the Alvor agreement recognized the FNLA, UNITA, and the MPLA "as the sole legitimate representatives of the people of Angola." After losing the struggle for control of the MPLA, he had cast his lot with Mobutu and Roberto.[24]

It is difficult to reconstruct what took place in Angola during the first ten months of 1975, as the hope of Alvor collapsed into the grim reality of civil war. Press coverage was scant and unreliable. There were very few journalists on the scene, and most of them knew virtually nothing about Angola, stayed only a few days, and did not venture beyond the capital. Why should it have been otherwise? Angola seemed to be just one more bush war in Africa, of little international relevance and scant interest for American and European readers who were saturated with news about the fall of Saigon, the investigations of the CIA in the U.S. Congress, the leftward plunge of Portugal, and the travails of détente. The sheer size of the country and the inadequacy of its communication network (including the collapse of its telephone system) made reporting outside Luanda a daunting challenge. The press most useful to the scholar is off the beaten path—not the *New York Times* or the *Washington Post*, but the two Luanda dailies *Provincia de Angola* (despite a marked bias for the FNLA) and *O Comércio*, the Portuguese dailies *Jornal Novo* and *Jornal do Comércio*, and two South African papers with correspondents in Luanda, the *Rand Daily Mail* and the *Cape Times* (despite their frank anti-MPLA bias). *Le Monde* should be added to the list not for the regularity of its coverage, but for the quality of its infrequent articles.[25]

Furthermore, few scholarly works clarify the events of the first ten months of 1975 in Angola. The three major exceptions are a chapter by John Marcum, the foremost historian of the Angolan war of independence; a slender book by journalists Colin Legum and Tony Hodges; and a longer study by the German sociologist Franz-Wilhelm Heimer, one of the few foreign scholars who had done extensive research in Angola before 1975.[26] Newly declassified U.S. and Cuban documents and interviews with protagonists help to flesh out the story.[27]

Peace in Angola depended on the movements' willingness to abide by the Alvor agreement and on Portugal's willingness to use its troops, if need be, to uphold it. The Transitional Government took over on January 31 in an atmosphere of deep mistrust. The FNLA had the military edge; the MPLA, the political and administrative advantage. "CIA operatives found the MPLA to be the better organized group up and down the line," U.S. Defense Intelligence Agency (DIA) analyst William Thom asserted.[28]

This was bound to increase the FNLA's uneasiness with the political process. Meanwhile, growing numbers of young people, and even children, swelled the ranks of the Poder Popular, an unwieldy coalition of semiautonomous paramilitary groups that rallied around the MPLA in the shantytowns of the capital. On January 26, the FNLA attacked the government radio station, destroyed the equipment, and kidnapped the assistant director, an MPLA member. "He was tortured and then, after the intervention of the Portuguese authorities, he was freed," a senior Portuguese officer wrote.[29] On February 13, the MPLA attacked and seized Chipenda's headquarters in Luanda.[30] Major fighting broke out on March 23, when the FNLA attacked MPLA installations in the capital, and it raged for several days, particularly in the slums. "The estimated 35,000 Portuguese soldiers still on duty in Angola . . . hold the key to peace," the *Rand Daily Mail* observed. But the Portuguese troops, as Neto fumed, assumed "an attitude of criminal passivity toward the violence." With the decisive help of the Poder Popular, the FAPLA units in the capital repelled the FNLA.[31] "It seems pretty certain that the latest troubles were begun by the FNLA," the *Cape Times* conceded. This was also Washington's view: "The recent clashes in Luanda may have been intended by FNLA as a show of force to impress Portuguese officials and the MPLA and to improve FNLA's security and bargaining positions," three senior aides told Kissinger. "Alternatively, they may have been the first move in an attempt to destroy the MPLA's military capacity."[32]

The Portuguese succeeded in bringing about a shaky truce on April 1. "Luanda, these days, has an air of extreme unreality," the Lisbon daily *Jornal Novo* declared in late April. "In the white center of the city, there is almost no tension: the restaurants and nightclubs are always packed and the shops are full of luxuries. In the slums everything is different." There, the FNLA tried to establish control by bringing in more troops and intensifying its terror against an increasingly hostile population, "as if to punish it," Heimer wrote, "for siding overwhelmingly with the MPLA."[33] By the end of April the cease-fire had broken down as the FNLA launched a coordinated series of assaults on MPLA headquarters in nearly all the shantytowns of Luanda. Once again the Portuguese troops failed to intervene. The fighting spread to several other cities until another cease-fire took hold around May 12.[34]

Meanwhile Zairean troops had been infiltrating into northern Angola. Portugal had given up trying to police the border. Angola "was being subjected to a silent invasion by soldiers from Zaire," Neto warned. "One reliable source in Luanda puts the number of Zairean soldiers in Angola at 1,200," Colin Legum wrote in the *Observer* on May 18. A high-level Portuguese delegation flew to Kinshasa at the end of May but failed to convince Mobutu to remove his troops.[35]

In late May a third round of fighting broke out. This time, the initiative was the MPLA's, which had decided to launch, Politburo member Iko Carreira explained, a "counteroffensive to create a cordon sanitaire around Luanda and to beat the FNLA wherever the MPLA had military superiority." The MPLA claimed it was retaliating for months of FNLA aggression. Its attacks, however, reflected more than exasperation. It had finally understood that a full-fledged military confrontation with the FNLA was unavoidable, and, at the same time, the military balance was shifting in its favor. The arrival of weapons from the Soviet Union and, more important, from Yugoslavia had greatly reduced or even eliminated the FNLA's advantage in hardware, and the FAPLA's defensive victories in Luanda had shattered the popular perception that the FNLA was invulnerable. Furthermore, the FAPLA's massive recruitment, particularly in the slums, had swelled its ranks, and this green army could count on the support of the Katangans, who had rallied to the MPLA. Finally, pressure from the population, which deeply resented the brutality of the FNLA, pushed the MPLA to attack. "Senhor presidente," an Angolan journalist told Neto in February, "the population considers the passivity of the MPLA to be weakness. . . . It feels insecure because the FNLA can operate at will with no response from the MPLA." Neto's aide Paulo Jorge remembered this factor to be critical. "We realized that the people were surprised that we were not responding to the FNLA attacks. There was very strong pressure in Luanda for us to respond." Lara agreed: "They wanted us to fight." The pressure from the population strengthened the hand of those MPLA leaders who argued that they had to counterattack.[36]

This round of fighting lasted several days, in Luanda and several other cities, and it subsided with a cease-fire on June 7. "The National Front's [FNLA's] military position has been seriously weakened since the sharp clashes of late May and early June," DCI William Colby reported.[37] U.S. officials lamented Roberto's continued absence from Angola; he had last visited his country, according to U.S. intelligence, in 1956. "Roberto's refusal to appear in Angola, because he fears assassination and realizes that he probably cannot 'turn out the crowds' as his rivals have been able to do, has hurt his own political image, and he has found it difficult to coordinate his group's political and military operations from Zaire," an NSC task force on Angola noted in mid-June. "The strength of the FNLA continues to suffer from Holden's refusal to move from Zaire to Angola to take direct control of FNLA activities," Kissinger stressed a few days later.[38]

How different was Savimbi. Fearless, charismatic, he was crisscrossing Angola. He used his eloquence and his political skills to build a network of support for UNITA. "Since the coup in Lisbon, Savimbi has emerged as the most active and politically skillful of Angola's three nationalist leaders," the NSC task force noted.[39] With the weakest military of the three movements, UNITA avoided the fighting; Savimbi instead waxed lyrical about peace, hitting all the right notes—democracy, free elections, unity.[40] More discreetly, UNITA was consolidating its power by very effective means: "In quite a number of Ovimbundu villages, individuals who refused to adhere to UNITA, or simply stood in the way of local UNITA representatives, were executed on the pretext of their being sorcerers," Heimer writes.[a] Savimbi was also strengthening UNITA's ties with the FNLA. "Holden and Savimbi are now working well together behind the scenes," Kissinger noted at a National Security Council meeting in late June. Savimbi was also courting South Africa.[41]

The Portuguese, who despised Roberto as a puppet of Mobutu, would have

a. Heimer, *Decolonization*, p. 62. Savimbi's major biographer, and erstwhile admirer, asserts that in the 1980s Savimbi was still executing "sorcerers and witches"—those who questioned his absolute rule and their families—by having them publicly burned at the stake. (Bridgland, "Savimbi.")

liked to forge some sort of understanding between Savimbi and the MPLA. But they could not overcome the burden of the past. Because of Savimbi's "well-known collusion with the Portuguese colonial troops before April 25," a top Portuguese official noted, it was "extremely difficult to make the MPLA swallow the idea of an alliance with UNITA."[42]

Four weeks of uneasy peace followed the June 7 cease-fire between the FNLA and the MPLA. On July 9, mortar fire again shook Luanda. The initiative was, once again, the MPLA's. After a few days of bitter fighting, the MPLA expelled the FNLA from Luanda. The *Rand Daily Mail* reported, "Portuguese officials say that the MPLA's tactics have been better than the FNLA's, their leaders superior and their soldiers . . . better motivated." The FAPLA had also enjoyed the massive and active support of the population. "Just a few weeks ago," the Lisbon daily *Jornal Novo* wrote on July 15, "the political leaders of the FNLA were boasting about the power and discipline of the 'glorious ELNA' [the FNLA army] and its 'brave and heroic freedom fighters,' while calling the MPLA soldiers 'armed cowboys' and 'pimps.' . . . Now the 'armed cowboys' and 'anarchists' have smashed the 'glorious ELNA' in Luanda. . . . Enjoying strong popular support, the men of the MPLA have the skill and motivation that the ELNA troops lack. The latter have very good weapons and very nice uniforms, but little else." From Kinshasa, Holden Roberto declared "total war."[43]

ENTER CUBA

Only then, in the second half of July, did Cuba rally. The MPLA had repeated its request for Cuban help in May, when Neto happened to meet Cuban deputy prime minister Flavio Bravo in Brazzaville. But Havana decided to wait until late June, when Cadelo would meet Neto at the celebration of Mozambique's independence, before responding. In Maputo Neto again asked the Cubans for assistance.[44]

Havana's response was sluggish. "We decided to send the money to transport the weapons," Cadelo remarked, "but there were only $20 bills in the bank." On July 25 Cadelo and Comandante Augustín Quintana (of the Décima Dirección of the armed forces) left for Angola with $100,000 in $20 bills.[45]

They flew to Lisbon and were about to continue to Luanda when they received a message from Havana instructing them to wait for five senior military officers from Cuba. "They were going to pin down exactly what aid the MPLA wanted, what objectives they expected to achieve with it, and what their timetable was." The group was led by Díaz Argüelles, the head of the Décima Dirección. Cadelo and Quintana flew with them to Angola.[46] "We arrived in Luanda, Angola, on Sunday, August 3, and established contact with the MPLA," Díaz Argüelles reported to Raúl Castro.

> They immediately took us to a hotel. When President Neto heard about it, he sent for us and put some of us up in his house and the others in another

compañero's house. In our first conversation with Neto . . . we explained the purpose of our visit, which we based on the following points:

a) The request made by the MPLA . . . in January and the request made later in Mozambique by Cheito [Xiyetu], the chief of staff of the FAPLA.

b) These requests were somewhat contradictory: during the January visit the MPLA asked [Cadelo and Pina] for aid and for the training of cadres in Cuba and in Angola, and in Mozambique it asked only for the training of cadres in Cuba.

c) We wanted to clarify what aid we should offer, given the FNLA's and Mobutu's aggression against the MPLA and the possible course of events before independence in November. We knew that the forces of reaction and imperialism would try with all their might to prevent the MPLA from taking power because it would mean a progressive government in Angola. Therefore we were bringing Neto the militant solidarity of our Commander in Chief, our party, and our government, and we gave him the $100,000.

In the course of this conversation the Angolans complained about the paucity of aid from the socialist camp, and they pointed out that if the socialist camp does not help them, no one will, since they are the most progressive force [in the country], whereas the imperialists, Mobutu and . . . [one word sanitized] are helping the FNLA in every way possible. They also complained that the Soviet Union stopped helping them in 1972 and that the military aid it is now sending is paltry, given the enormity of the need.[47]

Neto wanted Cuban military instructors. He did not have a precise figure in mind, but he was thinking of less than 100 men dispersed among many small training centers. He also wanted weapons, clothing, and food for the recruits. On the basis of this request, Díaz Argüelles drafted a proposal for a military mission "that would include 65 officers and 29 noncommissioned officers and soldiers."[48]

On August 8, Díaz Argüelles and his group returned to Cuba. "We told Fidel," Cadelo recalled, "that if South Africa and Zaire invaded, the Cuban instructors would have two alternatives: to fight a guerrilla war or withdraw to Zambia. We urged Fidel to open an embassy in Zambia at once. (We had only a nonresident ambassador based in Dar-es-Salaam, while Zambia's ambassador to Cuba was based in Canada.) Fidel agreed. We proposed as ambassador a compañero from the Décima [Dirección] who spoke English well—perhaps he wasn't the most accomplished diplomat, but he was the man for the job."[49]

He was Major Eduardo Morejón, who had just returned to Cuba after two years with the Cuban military mission in South Yemen. He was helping plan the military mission in Angola when Díaz Argüelles called him. "It took me by surprise," he recalled. "I thought he was going to send me to Angola, but he said, 'You've got to open our embassy in Zambia.' My job was to organize a network of support in case our men had to withdraw from Angola." In late August he and three other Cubans left for Lusaka.[50]

Meanwhile Díaz Argüelles's proposal for a military mission had been dramatically expanded in Havana. The revised plan called for the dispatch of 480 men who would create and staff four training centers (Centros de Instrucción Revolucionaria, or CIRs), which would train some 5,300 Angolans in three to six months. Cuba would supply the weapons for the instructors and for the recruits in the CIRs, as well as enough food, clothing, camping gear, toiletries, medicine, cots, and bedclothes for six months. The CIRs would open in mid-October. Following the Cuban model, the instructors would teach and, if necessary, fight alongside their students.[51] In other words, Cuba decided to offer Neto almost five times as many instructors as he had requested. (Guevara's column in Zaire and Risquet's column in the Congo had also been larger than requested.) "If we were going to send our men," Risquet explained, "we had to send enough to fulfill the mission and to defend themselves, because too small a group would simply have been overwhelmed."[52]

Contrary to the widespread belief that Cuba rushed to the aid of the MPLA, Havana had responded slowly. "The explanation for this is in Havana; you must search for it there," Lúcio Lara said time and again when I asked him why the Cubans had taken over six months to respond to Neto's request for aid.[53]

Unfortunately the Cuban documents I have seen do not explain this delay, and I have not been able to interview the protagonists who could provide an answer, notably Fidel and Raúl Castro. Perhaps Cuba was reluctant to be drawn into what could become an open-ended conflict. Perhaps it was reluctant to jeopardize relations with the West at a moment when they were markedly improving: for the first time since 1959, the United States was interested in a modus vivendi with Cuba; the Organization of American States was preparing to lift its sanctions; and the West European governments were offering Havana low-interest loans. Perhaps Cuba feared that the dispatch of military instructors would offend friendly African countries like Tanzania. Perhaps the attention of the Cuban leaders was distracted by the preparations for the first Congress of the Cuban Communist Party, to be held in December. "The revolution was institutionalized in 1975," Risquet remarked. "It was a year of never-ending work. This may have played a role. And the situation in Angola was quite confused. In the first months of 1975 there was very little discussion in the sessions of the political bureau about Angola. Our focus was on domestic matters."[54]

None of these explanations is fully satisfying. By preparing to host a conference for the independence of Puerto Rico in September 1975, Havana had already signaled that there were limits to the price it would pay for a modus vivendi with Washington.[55] By sending troops to Syria in October 1973—troops that might well have become involved in a major clash with the Israelis—Cuba had demonstrated its continued willingness to take risks for a cause it believed just. Some will claim that Castro did not move sooner to help the MPLA because the Soviet Union did not want him to. But can one seriously argue that he needed Soviet permission to send $100,000 to Neto? In the absence of a definitive explanation, one can only note that the Cuban leaders were focusing on domestic matters and that relations with the MPLA since 1967 had not been close. As a senior MPLA official pointed out, "Cuba wasn't focusing on Angola; they [the Cubans] were embroiled in other things; and in Africa they'd focused on Guinea-Bissau."[56] In July, when Cadelo and Quintana left for Angola with the $100,000 stuffed in their pockets and Díaz Argüelles on their heels, Cuba had finally made its choice.

THE WAR SPREADS

While the Cubans rallied, Roberto's troops advanced on Luanda. "Nothing can stop us," the FNLA boasted. On July 24 it took the crossroads town of Caxito, forty-two miles north of Luanda and key to an attack on the capital, "since," as a DIA analyst noted, "the approach to Luanda from the east was blocked by the Dembos forest, a longtime MPLA stronghold."[57] On July 27 Roberto entered Angola for the first time in more than fourteen years to take command of his troops.[58] "The highway from Luanda to the north will henceforth be named Holden Roberto Highway," Johnny Eduardo, Roberto's top lieutenant, announced at a press conference. "And the city of Caxito will henceforth bear the name of that brave fighter, Holden Roberto," he added. A few days later, however, the MPLA stopped the advance. The MPLA, Heimer wrote, "had won this phase despite a persisting, though no longer dramatic, inferiority in equipment and foreign military personnel mainly because its troops were fighting on their own ground, were better motivated, better led, and, being urban, somewhat more adept at learning military techniques."[59]

Savimbi, who had been engaged in secret talks with Roberto, the South Africans, and Mobutu, joined forces with the FNLA in early August.[60] UNITA's few troops remained in central and southern Angola, where they fought against the MPLA.

The war was spreading throughout Angola. In a country twice the size of Texas, *Le Monde* noted, the two sides were waging "a poor man's war."[61] While on paper the three armies numbered tens of thousands, the real number of combatants was dramatically lower. In the largest battle fought before independence—at Quifangondo, on November 10—the combined size of the two forces was less than 5,000 (including more than 1,000 Zaireans). More often, the number on each side of a given battle was in the hundreds. They fought for the control of towns, bridges, and key communication points—crucial dots in Angola's vast expanse.

"The largely undisciplined ex-guerrilla forces, plus a mix of new recruits with no military experience, made the job of creating a regular army a major challenge for each nationalist movement," DIA analyst Thom writes. "This placed a high premium on military training assistance along with the receipt of arms and supplies. Training cannot be overemphasized as an important factor in building the military capabilities of all three groups."[62] Until late August, however, no foreign instructors had set foot in Angola; FNLA troops were being trained by the Chinese in Zaire, and about 100 MPLA military cadres were in the Soviet Union. This was, at the time, the extent of foreign training.

The dearth of foreign instructors and the lack of expertise in the use of modern weapons increased the importance of Zairean troops, for it was they, and a handful of Portuguese mercenaries, who knew how to operate the heavy weapons that the FNLA had been receiving. "Zaire is practically a party to the struggle," the *Washington Post* reported in late August.[63] But Mobutu's freedom of maneuver was constrained by a severe economic and political crisis at home. "Our Embassy [in Zaire] has reported Mobutu . . . 'weakened,' his friends in 'disarray,' his popular support 'eroded,' elements in the army and party leadership 'alienated,' army loyalty 'strained,' a 'climate of confusion and muffled resentment,' . . . etc.," Assistant Secretary for African Affairs Nathaniel Davis noted on July 12. Another report, a few days later, added: "Mobutu is clearly in a quandary. Because of economic difficulties, he has been forced to cut back drastically on his substantial aid to the FNLA at a time when the FNLA has met serious reverses."[64]

It was just at that moment, on July 18, that President Ford approved covert aid to Roberto and Savimbi.[65] On July 29 the first C-141 left the United States for Kinshasa with arms for the FNLA and UNITA. "Two more C-141 flights were being put together on a high-priority base," John Stockwell, the chief of the CIA Task Force on Angola, writes. "Approximately two weeks ago," the Lisbon weekly *Expresso* reported on August 30, "massive amounts of war material" began flowing from Zaire to the air force base of Negage, near Carmona, the major town of the north. "According to eyewitness accounts," the *Rand Daily Mail* noted, this material included "light tanks, armoured cars and jeeps, uniforms, munitions, trucks, anti-tank weapons and heavy mortars."[66]

The Portuguese had withdrawn their troops from Carmona and Negage on August 4, abandoning the entire north to the FNLA.[67] There were still 26,000 Portuguese soldiers in Angola, a senior aide told Kissinger on August 15. Twelve thousand were "in the immediate Luanda area. The rest of them are scattered around the country and have not done anything effective, except to protect the white citizens who are tending to gather in population centers preparatory to evacuation. That has been about their sole activity." Throughout 1975, Portugal was consumed by internal strife and incapable of enforcing the Alvor agreement. "The major Portuguese Government objective in Angola is to get out," the NSC noted, "with honor if possible, but in any case to get out." *Le Monde* reported from Luanda, "Rather relaxed, with long hair and bushy beards, the young Portuguese draftees do not look aggressive. This war which is spreading like a flood does not interest them. . . . Lisbon has neither the means nor the will to play cop." Therefore, the exodus of the whites accelerated on "mercy flights" organized by the Portuguese government. "Telephone lines are down throughout Angola," the *Rand Daily Mail* reported in early August. Rumors were rampant.[68]

Adding to the confusion, on August 9 South African troops moved some thirty miles inside Angola to occupy the Calueque and Ruacana dams, which were part of the South African–financed Cunene River hydroelectric project. The Portuguese, who were not informed until August 12, offered only a feeble protest. The South Africans claimed they were protecting their investment; the MPLA wondered whether it was the prelude to a new phase in the war.[69]

THE CUBAN MILITARY MISSION

On August 21 Díaz Argüelles was back in Luanda as the head of the fledgling Cuban Military Mission in Angola (MMCA). He reported to Abelardo (Furry) Colomé, the first deputy minister of the Cuban armed forces. His handwritten reports from late August through October describe the evolution of the military mission.[70]

Díaz Argüelles's first order of business was to obtain Neto's approval for the proposed 480-man mission and CIRs. "Comrade Neto accepted our offer with great emotion," he informed Colomé in late August. "He was moved. He asked me to tell Fidel that they accept everything." One of Neto's close aides recalled that "we were very pleasantly surprised when we saw that Fidel was proposing a much more serious plan than we had envisioned. Neto called it 'a much better plan.' "[71] By then, the MPLA had concluded that the United States was providing "massive" support to the FNLA. Mobutu "does not have the financial means to provide the FNLA with the kind of help it is now getting," a senior MPLA official told U.S. consul general Killoran on August 19. "He must be getting assistance, and he must be getting it from the U.S."[72]

In his next letter, dated September 2, Díaz Argüelles proposed that the four CIRs be located in Cabinda, a few miles south of the port of Benguela, and near the towns of Henrique de Carvalho in eastern Angola and of Salazar, 143 miles east of Luanda. He also offered his assessment of the military situation. "I believe," he wrote, that the MPLA "will defeat the FNLA in short order unless Mobutu intervenes in full force. . . . Once our people and matériel arrive, and once we have streamlined the military training, we will be able to crush the FNLA and UNITA." He was worried, however, about foreign intervention. "We do not know how Mobutu, South Africa, the Portuguese, and the imperialists will respond if the FNLA and UNITA are facing an imminent defeat," he wrote. "Zaire and South Africa might intervene on behalf of the FNLA and UNITA, with the support of the United States and possibly France and West Germany." In that case the MPLA, even with the support of the Cuban instructors, would be overwhelmed. Díaz Argüelles was concerned that Cuba's plan had not taken these dangers into account. "Yesterday [September 1] I met with the political bureau [of the MPLA]. They asked how long it would take us to train the recruits, and I told them three months." Because it was expected that the CIRs would begin functioning on October 15, the first batch of recruits would not be ready until January 1976. If there were large-scale foreign interventions in support of Roberto and Savimbi, however, "we could be fighting before November." Therefore, Díaz Argüelles urged Havana to consider sending troops. The following day, he repeated: "We expect that our men will be participating directly in the fighting, and we think that it will not be long before they [the MPLA] ask us to send troops." He also relayed Neto's plea: that "our Commander in Chief intervene [with the socialist bloc] on the MPLA's behalf in order to get more effective aid."[73]

By the time Díaz Argüelles wrote these reports, Fidel Castro had been considering a large-scale Cuban military intervention in Angola for over two weeks. According to Westad, who cites a Soviet document,

> On August 15 Castro sent a message to Leonid Brezhnev arguing the need for increased support for the MPLA, including the introduction of Cuban special troops. The Cubans had already developed a fairly detailed plan for transporting their troops to Luanda (or Congo), for supplies, and for how the Cuban soldiers would be used on the ground in Angola. Castro wanted Soviet transport assistance, as well as the use of Soviet staff officers, both in Havana and Luanda, to help in planning the military operations. The Cubans underlined to the Soviets the political strength of the MPLA, and the threat which foreign assistance to the FNLA/UNITA alliance posed to socialism and independence in Angola.[74]

The Soviet leaders worried that the dispatch of Cuban troops would hurt détente and offend most African countries, and they were not convinced that the situation in Angola warranted it.[75] Castro's timing was poor. The ailing Brezhnev was focused on the strategic arms limitation talks (SALT II) with the United States and the February 1976 congress of the Communist Party of the Soviet Union. As DCI Colby told the NSC in late July 1975, "He knows it is his last Congress—they occur every five years—and he doubtless sees it as the occasion for securing his place in Soviet history. . . . [He] wants to go before the Congress proclaiming the success of detente." As if to confirm Colby's words, on August 13, two days before Castro sent his message to Brezhnev, Soviet ambassador Anatoly Dobrynin delivered a message from Brezhnev to Ford "suggesting a visit [to Washington] late in November or during the first half of December." Dobrynin explains in his memoirs that "It was important for the Politburo and Brezhnev personally to have achieved significant progress by then [before the February party congress] in relations with the United States. A meeting with Ford, the Politburo hoped, would produce a SALT agreement."[76] Clearly, Castro and Brezhnev were on different wavelengths.

In the meantime, the MMCA was beginning to get organized. The most urgently needed specialists flew to Angola on commercial flights. By September

2, the MMCA had twenty-nine members, including Díaz Argüelles.[77] Because foreigners needed Portuguese visas to enter Angola, the Cuban government had asked senior Portuguese officials to make sure that there would be no obstacles. Admiral Rosa Coutinho, commander of the Portuguese navy, had arrived in Cuba on August 18. "He and Fidel spoke at length," Risquet recalled.[78] And the first members of the MMCA encountered no difficulties. But this soon changed. Portugal's "ardent summer" was ending with the defeat of those groups most sympathetic to the MPLA. Portuguese prime minister General Vasco Gonçalves, who was close to the Communists, was forced to resign on August 29. "There are changes in the visa requirements," a Cuban official cabled from Lisbon on September 4. "There may be delays." In Havana, the Portuguese ambassador promised "that unless he received new instructions he would continue to grant [the Cubans] the visas [to Lisbon]," but it became increasingly difficult to obtain visas in Lisbon for Luanda. Comandante Ramón Espinosa, who was to head the CIR of Cabinda, flew from Havana to Lisbon on September 5 with six of his men and had to wait eight days there. "We had expected to continue without delay for Luanda, but it turned out that getting the visas was no easy task," he recalled. Nevertheless, by late September there were about fifty Cubans in Angola.[79]

For Díaz Argüelles and those members of the MMCA who were in Angola, September had been a month of preparation and waiting. They had decided where the four CIRs would be located, what matériel would be needed from Cuba, and how to assure the logistics of the operation—from unloading the ships to transporting the men and the equipment to the CIRs—in a country that seemed to lack everything. They had to be discreet, trying to maintain their cover and avoid provoking the Portuguese. And they had to familiarize themselves with the terrain in which they would have to operate.[80]

Meanwhile in Cuba the remaining 430 members of the MMCA were being selected. Three ships—*Vietnam Heroico, La Plata,* and *Coral Island*—left Cuba between September 16 and 20 with almost 300 instructors and the matériel for the CIRs.[81] Castro was worried about the Portuguese response to the arrival of the ships. "We must avoid at all costs an armed clash with the Portuguese," he stressed, "because whatever the outcome, it would hurt us, because it would give the impression that we are invading [Angola]. . . . As soon as our people disembark, they must be taken to the camps of the MPLA [the CIRs] as quickly as possible. . . . Once they are there . . . if the Portuguese attack, it would be an attack on the MPLA and we would join in the fighting without any hesitation."[82]

While the ships steamed toward Africa, two Cuban planes with the remaining 142 instructors flew to Brazzaville.[83] Castro had decided that the CIR of Cabinda would have almost as many instructors as the three other CIRs combined. "The MPLA thought they were needed elsewhere," Risquet remarked, "but we were worried that if they lost Cabinda they would never retake it."[84] The 2, 900-square-mile enclave of Cabinda was separated from the rest of Angola by the Congo River and a Zairean corridor 40 miles wide. Its population of 80,000 was linked demographically to the Congo and Zaire, and a large Cabindan community had settled over the years in and around Pointe Noire. In 1966 Gulf Oil discovered substantial oil reserves offshore. By 1974 Gulf was pumping 150,000 barrels a day from these fields. Cabinda, the London *Times* noted in 1975, "has an income from oil taxes and royalties (all from the Gulf Oil Company's concession) of $450 million a year."[85] Not surprisingly, Cabinda's two neighbors were not unmindful of this. "Both the Congo and Zaire . . . look covetously at Cabinda's oil," the NSC had noted in June 1975.[86] Both sought to gain influence in the province by supporting rival separatist groups, both of which claimed to be the true Front for the Liberation of the Enclave of Cabinda (FLEC).

CABINDA

The two FLECs had once been united. The original FLEC had been created in August 1963 with the blessings of Congolese president Fulbert Youlou, who had hoped that an independent Cabinda would become part of the Congo, a wish his successors shared.[87]

The war had left Cabinda largely undisturbed. The FNLA had launched a few raids from Zaire in 1961–64, and the MPLA had fought in the province in 1965, before shifting its efforts to eastern Angola. Perhaps in response to the collapse of the eastern front, in 1973–74 it revived low-intensity guerrilla warfare in Cabinda, and when Caetano fell, it was the only guerrilla movement in the province.[88]

The FLEC had been dormant throughout the war, but as soon as Caetano was overthrown, it sprang to life. With the encouragement of the Congolese, it selected Auguste Tchioufou, a Cabindan native who had lived his whole adult life in the Congo, as its leader. Tchioufou was the deputy director general of Elf-Erap, the Brazzaville subsidiary of the French oil company Elf. He demanded "immediate and full independence for Cabinda," and the Congolese government echoed that "one cannot deny Cabinda the right to be independent." Lacking an army of its own, the FLEC borrowed one: a few hundred former Special Troops—black soldiers who had fought under the Portuguese against the MPLA in the enclave. By late 1974, they were patrolling the streets of Cabinda city on behalf of the FLEC.[89]

The MPLA complained bitterly. Then it acted. On November 1 MPLA guerrillas descended on Cabinda city, seizing the airport, the radio station, and the main administrative buildings as the Portuguese soldiers looked on. After a few shots, the FLEC fled to the Congo, leaving the MPLA and the Portuguese in control. "The situation is absolutely calm," *Provincia de Angola* reported on November 4.[90] Brazzaville was unfazed. In late December 1974 President Marien Ngouabi publicly referred to Cabinda as an autonomous country. "This," Neto told Cadelo and Pina, "is the most eloquent proof that the Congo has not renounced its claim to Cabinda."[91] The following January, the FLEC replaced Tchioufou with Alfred Raoul, who was even more acceptable to Brazzaville. A retired Congolese military officer, he had been the Congo's prime minister from August 1968 to December 1971. "President Ngouabi would like to see Cabinda established as an independent state under a leadership influenced by and beholden to the Congo," the NSC remarked. "Eventually, Ngouabi believes, this could lead to a political union between the Congo and Cabinda. To achieve this end, the Congolese . . . have a former Premier of the Congo, Alfred Raoul, ready to step in as the first President of Cabinda." Neto had other ideas. "We are ready to respond to any attack, from Zaire or from the Congo," he told *Expresso*. "We have the weapons and the soldiers, and we are not afraid of fighting. . . . We are shocked by the Congo's policy."[92] Undaunted, Brazzaville continued to give the FLEC generous financial aid and some military assistance.[93]

Cabinda was too rich a prize for Mobutu to forgo. In late 1974 a group of FLEC members who had broken with Tchioufou appeared in Kinshasa. Their leader, Luis Ranque Franque, lavished praise on Mobutu, "champion of African freedom, lover of Africa,"[94] and Mobutu responded with money and weapons.

The situation for Mobutu, patron of both Ranque Franque's FLEC and the FNLA, was awkward. Initially he prohibited the FNLA from entering the territory. During their visit to the enclave in mid-January 1975, Cadelo and Pina had been struck by "the failure of the FNLA to open a political office in Cabinda or to send troops there."[95] Finally, in late January, Mobutu had relented and a small FNLA force had entered Cabinda, where it coexisted uneasily with the MPLA. Fighting erupted, however, in early June, and three days later the MPLA ejected the FNLA. Gulf Oil continued pumping, undisturbed.[96]

Mobutu, meanwhile, was busy organizing an army for his FLEC. "In the forests of Zaire, some sixty miles from the Cabinda border, some 800 to 2,000 Cabindan guerrillas are training," the *New York Times* reported in July. U.S. officials put the number more soberly at "several hundred."[97]

Both the Congo and Zaire endorsed the Alvor agreement, which stated that Cabinda was "an integral and inalienable part" of Angola, but both also stressed Cabinda's right to secede and each supported its FLEC. The MPLA openly criticized both countries. "Cabinda is a problem," Lara told a Portuguese daily in May, "that has been created by two of our neighbors: the Zaire of Mobutu, and the Congo of Marien Ngouabi." As a Cuban official pointed out, the Congo's ambitions over Cabinda were particularly unfortunate because the Congo was the only country bordering on Angola that was not hostile to the MPLA. Because Portuguese troops were still stationed in Angola's deepwater ports and airports, virtually the only way for the MPLA to receive weapons from abroad was to have them sent to the Congo, from where they could be smuggled into Angola. Ngouabi, however, resented the MPLA's unbending opposition to his Cabindan dreams. He would no longer accept, he told the Soviet ambassador, that Neto "on the one hand demands assistance from the Congo, [and] on the other makes accusations against us."[98]

The importance of Cabinda, coupled with the serious threats to its security, explains why Cuba wanted to send half its instructors there. The only practical way for the instructors and the equipment to get there, however, was through the Congo. This required Ngouabi's permission.

In his September 2 report to Colomé, Díaz Argüelles expressed his hope, and that of the political bureau of the MPLA, that Castro could sway Ngouabi, who was going to Cuba in mid-September. "Everything depends on our—Cuba's—efforts with Ngouabi."[99]

Relations between Havana and Brazzaville had cooled markedly after the overthrow of Massamba-Débat in 1968. But Ngouabi's policies were remarkably similar to those of his predecessor, and his rhetoric even more radical. Relations between the two countries gradually improved, particularly after Havana's appointment of Arquimedes Columbié as ambassador in July 1974. "Columbié was a superb diplomat," the director of African affairs in the Cuban Foreign Ministry recalled. In February 1975 the two governments signed a military protocol whereby Cuba granted sixty scholarships in Cuban military schools to Congolese officers. By sending so many officers, the Congolese defense minister told Flavio Bravo, the Congo was demonstrating its confidence in Cuba.[100] What convinced Ngouabi, however, to accede to the Cubans' request about Cabinda was self-interest.

Mobutu and Ngouabi "have assured one another that neither will move to annex the territory by force," the NSC had reported in June. "Nevertheless, the possibility clearly exists for an eventual Congolese-Zairian clash over Cabinda."[101] It must have slowly dawned on Ngouabi that if he persisted in seeking Cabindan independence, he would face Mobutu alone. Not only was the Congo a dwarf compared to its neighbor, but Mobutu was supported by a coalition that included the United States, France, and South Africa.[102] It was in Havana in September that Ngouabi finally faced the fact that an independent Cabinda would be Mobutu's puppet, not his. On his return to the Congo, he stated with flat realism that there was "not an Angolan problem and a Cabinda problem. There is only one problem: that of the independence of Angola." The Congo forbade all FLEC activity in its territory, and Alfred Raoul was recast as the Congolese ambassador to Brussels.[103] Henceforth Brazzaville gave the MPLA unwavering support, serving as the rear guard for the Cuban-FAPLA defense of Cabinda and providing every kind of assistance for the planes and ships that brought aid for the MPLA. "My contacts with Ngouabi before he went to Cuba had been infrequent," Ambassador Columbié reported in January 1976. "Since he returned, our contacts have been intense, to the degree that now I can see him whenever necessary. . . . This is due, without doubt, to his trip to Cuba and the very close cooperation between our two countries in helping Angola."[104] Castro had made it a little easier for Ngouabi to abandon his Cabindan ambitions and to defy Mobutu by pledging a "very significant" increase in Cuba's economic aid and promising to send a military unit to the Congo as protection against a possible attack by a vengeful Zaire.[b,105]

THE INSTRUCTORS ARRIVE

Two weeks after Ngouabi's trip to Havana, on October 1 and 3, the two Cuban planes with the instructors for Cabinda landed at Brazzaville. On October 11, a Cuban ship, the *La Plata*, arrived at Pointe Noire. Columbié was waiting. "I coordinated the unloading of the *Plata* with Silvain Goma, chief of staff [of the Congolese army]," he informed Havana. "They helped us in every way possible to unload and transport the cargo." Two other ships, the *Vietnam Heroico* and the *Coral Island*, had docked at a deserted beach near Porto Amboim, south of Luanda, on October 5 and 8 respectively.[106]

The three ships had brought the weapons and equipment for the CIRs, including 12,000 Czech rifles for the Angolans. (According to a 1965 Cuban-Soviet protocol, Cuba could not send weapons it had received from the Soviet Union to a third party without Soviet permission.) Because Díaz Argüelles had realized that the MPLA did not have enough vehicles to transport the instructors and the cargo to the CIRs, Havana had sent trucks aboard the ships. "The distances here are very great," Díaz Argüelles told Colomé, "and there are neither mechanics nor spare parts. . . . Comandante, this is the largest operation we have ever undertaken and we are doing it in the worst possible conditions and circumstances. With little time to plan and virtually no knowledge of or experience in the country, . . . we have had to improvise as we go. . . . It is a task of enormous magnitude. . . . I have taken the steps necessary to start the training on October 15."[107]

By October 18–20, almost on schedule, the instructors, recruits, and equipment were in place, and the four CIRs were ready to start operations. The MMCA had almost 500 men, including 17 in a medical brigade and 284 officers. (The original figure of 480 had been increased by a few pilots sent at Díaz Argüelles's request to fly the small civilian planes that the MPLA had acquired, and by some specialists in air traffic control and handling cargo at ports.) There were 191 Cubans in the CIR in Cabinda, and 66 or 67 in each of the other three. The remaining Cubans were at headquarters in Luanda or dispersed throughout the country.[108]

About 100 more Cubans were expected to join the MMCA. On September 25, Xiyetu, the chief of staff of the FAPLA, had told Díaz Argüelles that Moscow had

b. Because military developments in Cabinda and northern Angola in the first half of November had weakened Mobutu, Ngouabi felt that "for the time being, Zaire does not directly threaten the Congo." Therefore, he asked that the Cuban military unit be stationed not in the Congo but in Cabinda, coming to the defense of the Congo "if need be." Castro complied. (Columbié to Carlos Rafael [Rodríguez], Nov. 18 [quoting Ngouabi] and 20, 1975; Cienfuegos to Columbié, Havana, Nov. 22, 1975.)

promised to send five BM-21s (multiple rocket launchers), ten T-34s, twenty-five 76-mm artillery pieces, ten armored cars, and two planes by independence day. "They [the MPLA] want us to supply all the necessary personnel for all these weapons," Díaz Argüelles reported.[109] "I recommend that we agree," he cabled Colomé. "If we don't, they won't be able to use the equipment . . . until the Soviets have finished training the Angolans." On October 5 Havana approved the request.[110]

THE WAR INTENSIFIES

The MPLA had succeeded in reestablishing a degree of order in Luanda in the midst of the war, even executing some of its own soldiers convicted of crimes. "Here [in the capital] the Popular Movement has won a reputation for efficiency and discipline," the New York Times reported on September 22. "There has been little looting, and factories and shops abandoned by Portuguese are still undamaged." In a similar vein, Jornal Novo remarked, "In the areas controlled by the MPLA . . . calm and order are gradually returning. Crime has plummeted in Luanda since the FAPLA began patrolling the city. This is not the case in Nova Lisboa [UNITA's capital], for example, where life has become practically impossible." The MPLA "has shown itself more capable of administering the areas" than the FNLA and UNITA, the conservative Daily Telegraph conceded.[111]

In late August the MPLA and UNITA had made a serious attempt to come to some sort of political accommodation: two senior MPLA leaders, Lopo do Nascimento and Carlos Rocha, had met two UNITA leaders, José N'Dele and Fernando Wilson, in Lisbon for several days' talks under the auspices of Portuguese president Costa Gomes. On his return to Luanda, on August 31, Lopo do Nascimento told waiting journalists that "in the sessions held among the three parties—the MPLA, Portugal, and UNITA—we reached a degree of understanding that will make it possible to move beyond the current military confrontation and political impasse between our two movements." UNITA's N'Dele echoed these sentiments in a press conference in Lisbon.[112] This alarmed Washington. "We wanted no 'soft' allies in our war against the MPLA," Stockwell explains. Accordingly, a CIA officer "promptly interrogated Savimbi." Savimbi claims that he ignored the CIA's threats and that the main reason for the breakdown in the conversations with the MPLA was the latter's intransigence. Costa Gomes, on the other hand, blamed UNITA. In fairness, however, as Neto told Díaz Argüelles, the MPLA was also divided about the talks.[113] Following the collapse of the talks, Lisbon announced that its troops would leave Angola by November 11, 1975, and not by February 29, 1976, as stated in the Alvor agreement.[114]

The major military challenge to the MPLA came not from Savimbi's hollow army, but from Roberto's well-equipped forces. The FNLA controlled Angola's two northern provinces bordering Zaire, where it had its supply line in men and matériel. It was stiffened by Zairean troops and by several score of former

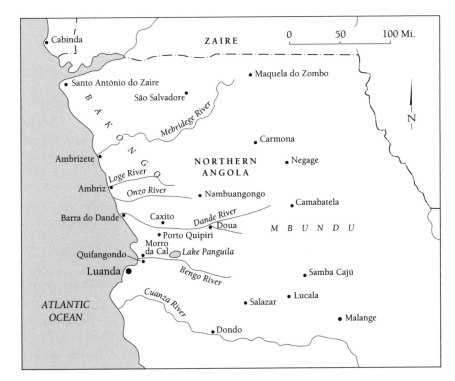

Northern Angola

Portuguese officers and mercenaries belonging to the Liberation Army of Portugal, a shadowy organization of the extreme right. "Well armed, the FNLA has but one obsession: Luanda," *Le Monde* reported in late August. "We have tanks," Roberto's top lieutenant boasted. "We will take Luanda, and it will be a bloodbath." A Portuguese spokesman explained that if the FNLA entered Luanda, Portuguese troops "would intervene only to protect the whites and would not get involved in the fighting between the two liberation movements. Our job," he added, "is to safeguard the evacuation of the white population."[115]

Over the next two months a seesaw battle flared north of Luanda. It was fought along the coastal road that led from the north to the capital, and the most contested terrain lay between Caxito and Quifangondo, "a scruffy little village"[116] thirteen miles north of Luanda, where the capital's water supply was located. Beyond Quifangondo lay Luanda, the prize.

There are no exact figures, and no authoritative sources, but the evidence suggests that, thanks to the U.S. weapons and Mobutu, Roberto enjoyed superiority in heavy weapons and in personnel trained to use them. A journalist from *Le Monde*, who spent a few days at the front in early September with the FNLA, wrote: "Operated by Zairean soldiers, the [FNLA's] artillery is not very accurate, but it nevertheless makes an impression on the enemy." The MPLA, he added, "clearly does not have . . . similar weapons." The *Rand Daily Mail* agreed: the

MPLA "lacks some of the heavy equipment of the FNLA," it noted on August 27. The playing field was leveled, however, because, as the CIA noted, the MPLA's troops were "better organized and better led" than those of the FNLA. "The competence of the FNLA's military organization," DIA analyst Thom remarked, "was apparently exceedingly low. Although arms and ammunition were provided in a timely manner, the FNLA lacked the logistics system to effectively distribute them. Further, the FNLA did not master the rudiments of organization for a successful military effort. Leadership, discipline, maintenance, and command, control and communications were all lacking. The FNLA also had the poorest quality soldiers generally."[117]

At the end of August, the FNLA launched an offensive against Luanda from Caxito. By September 4 it had arrived just north of Quifangondo. Then, just when Roberto saw Luanda in his grip, a new FAPLA unit joined the battle. The Ninth Brigade had "armored cars, artillery, and mortars," a Luanda daily explained.[118] It was led by a prestigious commander, Ndozi, and it included approximately 100 Angolans who had just returned with Ndozi from specialized training in the Soviet Union. (This was the only group to do so between the fall of the Portuguese dictatorship and Angola's independence.) It was an approximate version of that "rapid, efficient, and well-armed" elite force that Neto had been so eager to create back in January when Cadelo and Pina had visited him. "It was called the Ninth Brigade," one of its officers recalled, "in the hope of confusing the enemy, to make him think there were other brigades, when in fact there were none."[119]

In late August the weapons for the brigade—ten armored cars (BRDM-2), artillery (82-mm mortars and twelve 76-mm guns, antiaircraft weapons, and light infantry weapons—had arrived aboard a Soviet ship. An Angolan landing craft brought them from Pointe Noire to Cabo San Braz, eighty-two miles south of Luanda.[120]

The Ninth Brigade launched its attack on September 7. Surprised by the MPLA's sudden strength, the FNLA withdrew in haste. On September 8 the FAPLA entered Caxito. The FNLA was thrown back to its position of mid-August—more than forty miles north of Luanda.[121] In its hasty retreat, Stockwell notes, "it left behind crates of munitions which bore fresh U.S. Air Force shipping labels. The MPLA displayed these trophies to western journalists."[122]

Roberto had suffered "a very bad defeat," INR director Bill Hyland told Kissinger on September 11, "and, as of yesterday, Mobutu was considering that he might have to intervene with his forces thinly disguised to save the situation." Using weapons received under the U.S. military assistance program (MAP) to fight in Angola would violate the MAP agreement, Assistant Secretary for African Affairs Davis warned, but Hyland was philosophical. "After all, who will know that Mobutu's units [in Angola] have American equipment?" Or even that they were Zairean troops? "I mean, it won't be that clear. . . . They're not going to be flying Zairean flags." Kissinger was not impressed by Davis's legalism. "Is our missionary bureau," he asked Davis, referring with thinly disguised contempt to the Africa Bureau, "going to keep its mouth shut on the subject?"[123]

The seesaw battle rocked on. More weapons arrived for Roberto from the United States (and some also from a new ally, South Africa). Mobutu committed fresh troops. "There are about 1100 Zairean troops in support of the Nationalists [FNLA]," DCI Colby reported. The FNLA retook Caxito and pushed toward Luanda.[124] Only the Ninth Brigade stood between Roberto and the capital. Its core of Soviet-trained specialists was supplemented by what Ndalu, the brigade's chief of staff, called a "part-time infantry." He explained: "Sometimes I had 1,000, sometimes 100. They'd disappear whenever they felt like it; they'd go to Luanda for the weekend." Nevertheless, on September 26 the Ninth Brigade stopped the FNLA's advance at Morro da Cal, three miles north of Quifangondo, and they did it alone.[125] The brigade had only one foreign adviser: Yuri, a Soviet colonel who had arrived in Angola in September. Throughout the campaign he advised Ngongo, who was in charge of the brigade's artillery. The Angolan officers who knew Yuri praise him warmly. "Yuri was wonderful; he was extremely capable," Kianda said. "Yuri was an outstanding artilleryman," Rui de Matos remarked. "Yuri was a great guy, and he was brilliant," Ngongo added. He was the only Soviet military adviser in Angola before independence.[126]

Through the first half of October, Roberto's troops were unable to advance despite their superior numbers. Mobutu, beset by domestic woes, was able to commit only a limited number of his mediocre troops, not enough to smash the MPLA.

As the November 11 independence day approached, Roberto's impatience grew. "The FNLA . . . will be in the capital on Tuesday," he announced on Friday, October 17. Over the next few days, he kept repeating that his troops would enter Luanda "within 24 hours."[127] On October 23 Roberto's forces—about 3,500 men, including some 1,200 Zaireans[128]—attacked Morro da Cal. Its 1,100 defenders, who included about 40 Cubans from the CIR of Salazar, withdrew to Quifangondo, where they held the line. This was the first time that Cubans participated in the fighting. "The enemy showed very little ability to maneuver or shoot," Díaz Argüelles reported, "and little will to advance if faced with any resistance." Five days later, a second group of Cuban instructors fought, with the MPLA, east of Quifangondo to recover the village of Quiangombe.[129]

The MPLA had been gaining ground on the other fronts. "The area controlled by UNITA is shrinking like a burst balloon," Le Monde had noted in mid-September. "The military situation favors the MPLA," Díaz Argüelles wrote on October 1.[130] U.S. intelligence agreed. In a lengthy September 22 report, the Bureau of Intelligence and Research of the State Department warned: "Since the outbreak of fighting in Angola in March, the MPLA has achieved an almost unbroken series of military successes. . . . It is in complete control of Luanda and the surrounding areas. . . . In the past two months it has won virtually complete control of the coast from Luanda south to the Namibian border and thereby has gained unimpeded access to five major ports." It was also in control of Cabinda, from which it could not be dislodged "without strong outside backing—i.e., direct Zairian military intervention." It held key areas in eastern Angola (including virtually all the diamond-rich Lunda district). From its positions along the southern coast it was extending its control "well into the interior," threatening UNITA's core areas. Finally, the report pointed out, "Of major political significance is the fact that the MPLA controls 9 of Angola's 16 district capitals and is contesting a 10th at Luso in eastern Angola." Looking back to the Lisbon talks of late August, the report noted that "High-ranking Portuguese officials . . . have in recent weeks been actively promoting the creation of a coalition between the MPLA and UNITA. . . . Neto is on record as having endorsed such a coalition, but Savimbi's intransigent opposition and the MPLA's growing strength now make the likelihood of such an arrangement all the more remote."[131]

By mid-October, with the MPLA continuing to gain ground, a conservative British newspaper observed, "FNLA and UNITA know that they must improve their positions by Nov. 11 or risk being left out in the cold," while the *Rand Daily Mail* reported that the MPLA was "making a vigorous four-pronged drive on Nova Lisboa," UNITA's capital in the central highlands.[132] D-Day, the day on which Angola would become independent, was fast approaching. From Luanda, *Le Monde*'s René Lefort wrote: "In the upper right-hand corner of the two Angolan dailies controlled by the MPLA, there is a black box counting down the number of days until the fateful date of November 11. . . . The MPLA is now in control of twelve of the country's sixteen provinces, every important urban center, with the exception of Nova Lisboa, almost all the industrial and mining centers, beginning with the oil fields of Cabinda, and all the important ports on the Atlantic."[133] The FNLA and UNITA had only a tenuous hold on the remaining four provinces, the Brazilian mission in Luanda warned, and they "both sought foreign intervention because they knew that, without it, they would not be able to dislodge the MPLA from its controlling position."[134]

It has been written that the MPLA was winning because of the Cuban troops. Of the many accounts that have made this point, that of the prominent Norwegian scholar Odd Arne Westad deserves serious attention, because he is the only researcher who has had access to the relevant Soviet archives.[c]

Westad argues that "the first Cuban combat troops arrived in Luanda in late September and early October" aboard Cuban ships and "several Soviet aircraft." His source is an interview with Georgi Kornienko, the head of the American department of the Soviet Foreign Ministry in 1975. Kornienko's account is corroborated by a document: on November 4 the Soviet ambassador in Brazzaville, Yevgeny Afanasenko, informed Moscow that he had been told by his Cuban

---

c. Westad was allowed to take notes but not to photocopy documents. He told me that when he tried to reexamine them on a later visit to the archives, he was refused permission.

counterpart, Columbié, that "a Cuban artillery regiment is already fighting in Luanda."[135]

Kornienko, who was recalling events that had occurred almost twenty years earlier, could have confused his dates, mistakenly remembering that the Cuban troops had begun to arrive in September when they had in fact not appeared until November. Afanasenko's report, however, cannot be so easily explained away. It was written at the time, and it reports a conversation with an important and well-informed Cuban official. Yet it contradicts all of Díaz Argüelles's reports written from late August through late October.

I cannot solve the puzzle. I can only say that while Westad has only one document to support his thesis, I have all Díaz Argüelles's reports and that, whereas Westad was allowed only to take notes from the documents he saw, I have photocopies of all the documents I use. Among these documents are several reports in which Columbié describes the growth of the Cuban presence in Angola and refers to conversations with Afanasenko, but none that refers to the alleged exchange. (One possible explanation is that Columbié told Afanasenko that Cubans from the CIR of Salazar were fighting north of Luanda—as was indeed the case by late October—and that Afanasenko misunderstood or misspoke in his November 4 report.)

U.S. intelligence reports shed some light on the issue. In January 1976 Kissinger told Congress that "In August [1975], intelligence reports indicated the presence of Soviet and Cuban military advisers, trainers and troops, including the first Cuban combat troops." He was rewriting history: in the summer of 1975 U.S. intelligence told a different story.[d] An August 20 CIA report concluded, "What seems . . . likely is that the Soviets have asked Cuba to help out with advisers and technicians. . . . [sanitized] Officials of the Ministry of Information, which is controlled by the MPLA, have tried to pass them off as tourists." On September 22, an INR report claimed that "the Soviet and other allied countries, notably Cuba, have provided technicians and advisers to assist in military planning and logistics. While most are based in the Congo, there is increasing evidence that some foreign advisers are present with MPLA units inside Angola." On October 11 the CIA *National Intelligence Daily* specified that "a few Cuban technical advisers have been operating with the Popular Movement [MPLA] inside Angola for some time." There was no mention of Cuban troops, or even of large numbers of instructors, until early October, when a significant number of Cuban advisers did indeed arrive.[136]

The MPLA leaders I have interviewed confirm that the Cuban troops did not arrive until November, as does Robert Hultslander, the CIA station chief in

---

d. Kissinger, Jan. 29, 1976, U.S. Senate, Committee on Foreign Relations, Subcommittee on African Affairs, *Angola*, p. 10. In his memoirs, Kissinger cites one of my articles to support his claim that the Cuban intervention "began in May, accelerated in July, and turned massive in September and October," which is precisely the opposite of what my article said. (Kissinger, *Renewal*, p. 820.)

Luanda from early August to November 3, 1975. "I agree with the history as you present it," he wrote me after reading a draft of this chapter, "and with your conclusions regarding the assistance provided by Cuban forces, which I believe did not arrive in any numbers until we departed. . . . Although we desperately wanted to find Cubans under every bush, during my tenure their presence was invisible, and undoubtedly limited to a few advisors." Hultslander had cleared this letter with the CIA before he sent it to me.[137]

It has also been argued that the Portuguese helped the MPLA.[138] In fact, the support that Cadelo and Pina had observed during their January 1975 trip had long disappeared. "The Portuguese do not appear to be playing any favorites in the current faceoff between the MPLA and the FNLA," a senior aide told Kissinger in early May. "Despite covert backing of the MPLA in the past, insofar as Lisbon now has a policy it is one of impartiality between the factions," DCI Colby confirmed the following month.[139] In fact, as DIA analyst Thom observed, the only known case of significant Portuguese military action against any of the three movements in 1975 was an attack on MPLA headquarters in Luanda (Vila Alice) in late July.[140]

Finally, it has been said that the MPLA was winning because the Soviet Union and other foreign supporters had given it superiority in weapons. The evidence, however, suggests that the MPLA had no such advantage.[141] A better explanation for its success was given by Hultslander, who wrote that the MPLA leaders "were more effective, better educated, better trained and better motivated" than those of the FNLA and UNITA. "The rank and file also were better motivated (particularly the armed combatants, who fought harder and with more determination)." As Heimer observed, "In the military conflict, the MPLA proved to have the better chances as long as external support was approximately equal on both sides because its political and military leadership was better qualified and its troops on the whole better motivated."[142]

And so, despite Mobutu's efforts and the U.S. covert operation, the MPLA was winning as independence day approached. The FAPLA "appeared to be heading for a military walkover," Legum wrote.[143] But this was to change, dramatically. On October 14, South Africa invaded.

CHAPTER THIRTEEN
SOUTH AFRICA'S FRIENDS

For Pretoria, the collapse of the Portuguese dictatorship was a disaster. It turned friends into foes and opened gaping holes in the buffer zone that protected it from the hostile continent to its north. As Mozambique swung to the left and Angola descended into civil war, the instability in Rhodesia and Namibia assumed a more ominous and urgent hue. South Africa's defenses were crumbling.

Namibia, or South West Africa, had become a South African mandate after the First World War, and it had been ruled as the country's fifth province. In June 1971 the International Court of Justice decreed that South Africa was illegally occupying Namibia and ordered it to withdraw immediately. The UN Security Council endorsed the ruling in October. The mounting international clamor was accompanied by growing unrest among Namibia's African population, long quiescent under Pretoria's harsh rule, and by the rising influence, at home and abroad, of the South West Africa People's Organization (SWAPO), a liberation movement that drew most of its support from the Ovambo people, who straddled the border between Namibia and Angola and made up 46 percent of Namibia's population of 900,000. SWAPO began guerrilla activity in 1966 from bases in Zambia, which meant that fighters had to pass through either southeastern Angola or Namibia's Caprivi strip, a 250-mile panhandle squeezed between Angola, Zambia, and Botswana and dotted with South African military bases.[1]

The Portuguese had been neighborly to the South Africans. Not only did they share intelligence, but they allowed the South Africans to conduct search-and-destroy operations against SWAPO in southeastern Angola. Caetano's overthrow changed this. In September, the Portuguese informed Pretoria that its patrols would no longer be allowed in Angola. "On October 26 the last South African liaison officers left the territory," a South African scholar writes. "In November SWAPO camps of up to seventy men were already in place." Unrest increased in Namibia, particularly among Ovambos, and by the end of 1974 more than 3,000 youths had gone to Angola, many of them to join SWAPO.[2]

Nine years earlier, on November 11, 1965, Rhodesian prime minister Ian Smith had unilaterally and illegally declared the British colony independent in order to prolong white rule. Stoutly refusing to deploy military force against the white rebels, London promised to bring down the Smith regime through economic sanctions. But the mandatory sanctions imposed by the UN Security Council proved ineffectual, in part because Pretoria defied them and also extended Salisbury military aid. Beginning in September 1967, South African police were deployed in Rhodesia against the black insurgents. "The full extent has never been disclosed," a South African scholar has noted, "but it is accepted that every year from 1967 to 1975 there were about two thousand South African police in Rhodesia." Pretoria also loaned Salisbury helicopters and spotter planes, as well as pilots to fly them.[3]

Ian Smith's other stalwart supporter was the Portuguese colony of Mozambique. "Our relations with Mozambique were second only to those with South Africa," he wrote.[4] In part this was economic: 80 percent of Rhodesia's foreign trade went through Mozambique.[5] And in part it was military: Lisbon welcomed and assisted the Smith government's attacks against the Rhodesian rebels' bases in Mozambique. As in Angola, the coup in Portugal changed all this. Lisbon told Salisbury to halt all operations in Mozambique,[6] and a few weeks later it agreed to hand power to Frelimo on June 25, 1975.

This sent shock waves through the embattled Smith government. A leftist Mozambique could become a haven for Rhodesian guerrillas and a barrier to Rhodesia's trade. "We had survived because of assistance from South Africa and Portugal," Ian Smith explained. "With the collapse of Mozambique, only South Africa remained."[7]

SOUTH AFRICAN DÉTENTE

Pretoria responded to the elimination of its buffer zone by dangling economic aid and trade concessions in front of its black neighbors and launching a flurry of diplomatic activity to improve its relations with them.[8]

But its relationship with Ian Smith could have stymied all these efforts. "South Africa, in search of 'detente' with Black Africa, is prepared to ditch us," the head of Rhodesian intelligence wrote in his diary on December 1, 1974. Ian Smith had become a liability. Encouraging the transition to majority rule in Rhodesia would minimize South Africa's chances of ending up with a radical regime in Salisbury and demonstrate Pretoria's newfound goodwill toward black Africa. Peaceful coexistence with its neighbors would be based on absolute respect for the internal system of each state, particularly, that is, for South Africa's minimally revamped apartheid regime. "Domestic politics must not obstruct international cooperation," Prime Minister John Vorster told *Le Monde*.[9]

Zambian president Kaunda "seized on this opening in South Africa's policy," U.S. intelligence reported, "to enlist Pretoria's aid in pressing Rhodesia to negotiate." In September 1974 Zambia and South Africa opened secret talks and, on February 9, 1975, "in a major step towards southern African detente," Pretoria's foreign minister flew to Lusaka and openly met with President Kaunda, the foreign ministers of Zambia, Botswana, and Tanzania, and representatives of Rhodesia's guerrilla movements. It was, wrote the *Zambia Daily Mail*, "a historic visit."[10] Two days later the Rhodesian government announced that "some elements" of the South African police had begun to withdraw from "certain forward positions on the Zambezi River," which separated Rhodesia and Zambia, and on March 8 the commander of the Rhodesian army stated that the South African police were "no longer taking part in the maintenance of law and order in Rhodesia," but had been confined to camps in noncombat areas. "They have done us proud over the past several years," he added wistfully. Smith flew to Cape Town for talks with Vorster. "South Africa," an embittered Smith wrote, "controlled our lifeline and had already made it clear to us that, if need be, they were prepared to use this control to force us to co-operate."[11]

Détente extended to Mozambique. South African officials assured Kaunda that they "would not allow mercenaries to operate from their soil" against Mozambique and resisted the temptation "to take action, covert or overt, to interfere" in the country's decolonization.[12] "We would be less than honest if we did not acknowledge that Prime Minister Vorster, regardless of our diametrically opposed positions on apartheid, has honoured his word on the concrete issues we have dealt with under difficult circumstances," Zambian foreign minister Vernon Mwaanga told the OAU the following April.[13] Vorster could afford to be magnanimous. "Looking to the future, South Africa is fairly confident that its financial tentacles will be sufficient to grasp an independent Mozambique in a close if cool embrace," the *Zambia Daily Mail* remarked in an incisive article. In 1971, the last year for which figures are available, South Africa had contributed 42 percent of Mozambique's GDP (mainly through the income from more than 115,000 Mozambican contract workers in the South African mines, the harbor and railway taxes levied on South African trade traveling through Maputo, and tourism). "Mozambique cannot stand on its legs without cooperating with South Africa," South African officials said.[14]

ANGOLAN TEMPTATIONS

Angola's economy, on the other hand, was far less dependent on South Africa, and this meant Pretoria had less leverage there. It had, however, more at stake in Angola than in Mozambique because of the threat posed by SWAPO to its continuing control of Namibia. And the confused situation in Angola, where three groups were vying for power, offered Pretoria an opportunity to interfere when two of these groups—the FNLA and UNITA—came courting. UNITA took the lead.

The story of Savimbi's relations with Pretoria, long shrouded in mystery and obfuscation, has been recently unveiled. In 1978 the South African Defense Ministry commissioned a study by Professor F. J. du Toit Spies on South Africa's role in the 1975–76 Angolan civil war. As "official historian," Spies had access to government archives, including those of the armed forces. His report was approved by a supervisory committee that was led by an army general and included representatives from the Ministries of Defense and Foreign Affairs and from academia, and after a ten-year delay caused by the continuing war in Angola, it was published in 1989 as *Operasie Savannah* (the South African code name of its Angolan operation). A member of Spies's supervisory committee,

Commander Sophie du Preez, also published a book, *Avontuur*, in 1989 that is based on essentially the same documentation, but focuses more on the human side of the war. Together, these two books provide a fascinating, if partial, account of South Africa's role in Angola. While both are very discreet about Pretoria's dealings with the United States and other friendly governments during the operation, they are much more candid about other issues, including Savimbi's relations with Pretoria.[15]

Savimbi first approached the South Africans in the summer of 1974 through Portuguese settlers living in Angola.[16] Contacts between senior UNITA officials and South African representatives were followed by meetings between Savimbi and midlevel South African officials from Military Intelligence and the Bureau of State Security (BOSS) on February 12, 1975, in Cangumbe near Luso; on March 17–18 in Gaborone; and on April 12 in London. In these meetings, Savimbi delineated, with increasing zest, his vision of an Angola that would maintain friendly relations with South Africa based on the principle of non-interference and would join South Africa and other countries in the region in an anti-Communist bloc. The wary South Africans wanted to know about his relations with SWAPO. Savimbi was frank: in the past he had cooperated with SWAPO, but no longer. "He promised to do everything in his power to prevent armed units of SWAPO from entering South West Africa [Namibia]."[17] In return, he needed money and weapons. Pretoria obliged with a few arms and some money to keep its options open.

Meanwhile, Roberto approached the South Africans, stressing his desire to have friendly relations and his hostility toward SWAPO, and he was also given small amounts of weapons and money.

In late May 1975 Vorster asked for a full report on the situation in Angola from the South African Defense Force (SADF) and BOSS. The report, presented on June 26, concluded that civil war in Angola was inevitable and that the MPLA would win, with Soviet help. Only South African assistance to a united FNLA-UNITA front, the report asserted, might prevent an MPLA victory. Pretoria could, on the other hand, choose a hands-off policy, but this "would without doubt encourage a takeover by a pro-communist force friendly to SWAPO."[18]

At Vorster's request General Constand Viljoen, the army's director of operations, and General Hendrik van den Bergh (the head of BOSS and one of Vorster's closest advisers) prepared a list of weapons for Savimbi and Roberto, with a total price tag of 20 million rand ($14.1 million). On July 14 Vorster approved the list, with the proviso that the weapons be bought abroad in order to hide Pretoria's involvement. The decision had been reached without any dissent.[19]

THE U.S. RESPONSE

After receiving the June 26 report, Vorster decided to sound out the Ford administration about collaboration in Angola.[20] By then, the United States was itself considering intervention.

Nixon's Africa policy had been characterized by apathy and a tilt toward the white regimes—South Africa, Rhodesia, and Portugal. Anxiety that the continent was threatened by a Communist offensive had receded before Nixon came to power. In October 1967 the CIA had observed that the Soviet Union had been "burned by several misadventures" in Africa and that the Chinese had suffered "humiliating setbacks" there.[21] The rebels' defeat in Zaire in 1965, followed by the consolidation of Mobutu's regime, had been an important signpost, as had been the fall of the "radical" leaders, communism's Trojan horses (Ben Bella in 1965, Nkrumah in 1966, and Mali's Modibo Keita in 1968), and the failure of the guerrillas in Angola, Mozambique, and Rhodesia. What is most striking about the reams of documents on Angola and Mozambique in the Kennedy and Johnson presidential libraries is the change in the U.S. assessment of Portugal's ability to maintain control over its colonies. The pessimism of the early 1960s had faded. In 1967, a National Intelligence Estimate predicted, "No liberation movement is likely to expand its operations sufficiently to raise the costs of white resistance to an intolerable level."[22] Why care about Africa, if the Communist threat had been defanged? "Africa in the 1973 edition of the Key Intelligence Questions hardly rated a mention," DCI Colby wrote. "They [top U.S. officials] weren't interested in it [Africa]," recalled Larry Devlin, who was the Africa division chief of the CIA's Directorate of Operations in 1971–74.[23] This complacency was shared by the U.S. Congress and public.

In their tilt toward Africa's white regimes, U.S. officials tried to avoid unnecessarily offending black governments. This was not easy. For example, the secret sale of two Boeing 707s to Portugal in July 1970 was leaked to the *Washington Post* in January 1971.[24] The State Department claimed that the planes were purely commercial, "but the truth was different," Portuguese ambassador João Themido wrote. "Those planes would transport troops between Lisbon and Africa." Not surprisingly, as a 1971 State Department memorandum noted, the United States was "identified with the Portuguese in both their [Portuguese] and insurgent eyes."[25]

Even more offensive to Africans was the Byrd amendment, approved by Congress in November 1971, which exempted chrome from the mandatory UN sanctions against Ian Smith's illegal government in Rhodesia. As a former U.S. ambassador to Zambia pointed out, "The action placed the U.S. in the select company of South Africa and Portugal in open and voluntary breach of sanctions. Indeed, the U.S. became the only country in the world in explicit legislative defiance of its obligations under the [UN] Charter respecting sanctions."[26] A few months later, from his post in Lusaka, a U.S. official remarked with uncommon frankness: "developments in our foreign relations in recent years clearly have made U.S. support of self determination for the African countries remaining under minority rule less plausible. The U.S. should take some measures to restore credibility to our policy and to make it at least somewhat effective in encouraging change." This did not happen. "Our relations with Africa overall are going downhill," Assistant Secretary Newsom told Kissinger in October 1973. "The gap between the Africans' preoccupations and our policy responses is widening. . . . Our credibility on moral questions of racial equality is challenged."[27]

The Portuguese coup took Washington by surprise. "No expert had predicted it, and even the second-guessers could not find the usual intelligence report that turns out to have been totally ignored," INR director Hyland wrote. "Portugal was on the back, back burner, of no special concern, watched over by a sleepy American embassy. The Caetano regime was, after all, the successor to the reliable dictatorship of Salazar, and was thought to be reasonably sound and secure."[28] When Caetano fell, the United States was caught with bad cards in Africa—its association with the fallen dictatorship and virtual ignorance about the rebel movements in the Portuguese colonies.

The U.S. presence in Angola was limited to a consulate in Luanda. "It was a very small consulate," recalled Richard Post, who was the U.S. consul general there in 1969–72. "There were five US officials in all, including myself, the code clerk and a secretary," Post's successor, Everett Briggs (1972–74), said. The consulate reported directly to the State Department in Washington, but "in Washington nobody cared, nobody gave a damn about our reports," observed Edward Fugit, who doubled as vice-consul and political officer in Luanda in 1973–75.[29] The CIA had opened an office in Luanda in 1964, "chiefly to report on various African liberation movements," explained Hultslander, who became station chief there in 1975. The midlevel case officer who was assigned to the office "spent most of his time with American and European businessmen and missionaries. I understand that during his three years he provided information for only a dozen disseminated reports. This is probably more an indication of lack of interest in Washington than the competence of the officer." The station was closed in 1967 "to humor the Portuguese and the Agency was forced to rely on 'off-shore' coverage."[30] What coverage there was was provided by the CIA station in Lisbon, and it was perfunctory. "The CIA man from Lisbon came down occasionally," Consul General Post recalled. "They [CIA officials in Lisbon] weren't spending the time to stay on top of it," Vice-Consul Fugit remarked. "They were following the war by asking the Portuguese [intelligence and military] in Lisbon. Their reporting was very second-hand." The CIA station in Lisbon was very small and very dependent on the Portuguese for information. DCI Colby explained, "Portugal had been such a backwater that in 1973 I suggested closing our station there."[31]

Successive U.S. administrations had had to grapple with the question of what type of contact they should maintain with nationalist movements fighting against colonial rule. In a forceful November 1962 memo, Assistant Secretary Mennen Williams had argued,

> As our experience with Algeria shows, to cut ourselves off from contact with nationalist leaders during the pre-independence period at the behest of the metropolitan power is to impose serious handicaps on our relations with the

nationalist government after independence. Despite this object lesson, we have progressively succumbed to Portuguese pressure to a point at which even covert contact with Angolan and Mozambican nationalists is being challenged within the U.S. Government. Unless we are willing to abandon these nationalists to the Communists, we must re-establish and expand our contacts with them, overtly as well as covertly.[32]

A few months later, the able U.S. consul general in Maputo, Thomas Wright, had echoed Williams's words. "The importance of our maintaining close continuous contact with the nationalist groups cannot be overemphasized," Wright wrote. "Failure to maintain this liaison not only leaves us flying blind but exposes them to the blandishments of the more radical African leadership as well as extending an open invitation for their subversion by the Sino-Soviet bloc. . . . A do-nothing policy on our part will not insure a continuation of even the unsatisfactory status quo," he warned. "On the contrary, it is much more likely to result in such frustration and disillusionment as to US African policy as to leave us helpless spectators when the change does take place."[33]

The Kennedy administration had groped with this question without finding an answer, as a memo written by Robert Kennedy two days before his brother's assassination indicates. "I gather that we really don't have much of a policy," he observed.[34]

Nor did the Johnson administration resolve the question. In December 1968, a senior State Department official suggested that the United States "should discreetly develop and maintain unobtrusive but useful contacts with the leaders of the African nationalist movements of southern Africa, avoiding, however, any implication of advocacy or support of violence." But the sense of urgency had passed. The Nixon administration looked askance at embassy contacts with African rebel leaders, particularly those of the Portuguese colonies. "Out of deference to our ally, Portugal, we have held the insurgent leaders at arm's length," Assistant Secretary Newsom noted in 1972. "I don't know if it was ever written down," his successor, Donald Easum, remarked, "but the message was clear: Such contacts were frowned upon."[35]

Accordingly there were virtually no contacts with the Angolan rebel movements. In 1969, Stockwell, then a CIA officer in southern Zaire, wrote an intelligence report about a visit he made to an FNLA camp near the Angolan border. "The chief of station, Kinshasa, sent me a note in the classified pouch advising that the agency wasn't interested in Angolan revolutionary movements, and that my visit was unfortunate because it could have been misconstrued. We didn't support the black fighters and we didn't want our NATO ally, Portugal, picking up reports that we were visiting Angolan rebel base camps."[36]

Even Roberto was kept at arm's length. Since at least 1961, the CIA had maintained "an intelligence-collection relationship with Holden [Roberto]," paying him a yearly subsidy that began at $6,000 and increased over time to a far more substantial amount. "Roberto is a valuable asset who has proved himself trustworthy over a period of years," a U.S. official noted in 1962. But the relationship was also an embarrassment. "Portuguese intelligence was sufficiently good that they had knowledge of our contacts with Roberto," recalled Everett Briggs, who served in the U.S. embassy in Lisbon in the mid-1960s. "The Portuguese foreign minister would wave the dossier [about U.S. contacts with Roberto] in front of the hapless US ambassador and say 'you pay him more than I make!'" Therefore, in 1970 the payment was slashed to "about $1,000 monthly."[37]

Zambia was the rear guard of the MPLA, which had opened the eastern front in 1966, but the U.S. embassy in Lusaka made no attempt to establish contact with the movement's leaders. "We didn't have contacts with the MPLA," the embassy's DCM, Harvey Nelson, remarked. "We may have run into them once in a while at an embassy reception but that was it! The embassy wasn't able to follow the war in Angola. If we'd been more aggressive, if we'd gotten into the field, we could have done it. But we didn't. It was too dicey because of the attitude back in Washington—fear of repercussions on our relations with Portugal and South Africa."[38] Too much initiative might have hurt an officer's career.

FIRST STEPS

U.S. interest in Africa did not suddenly spike after the fall of Caetano.[39] U.S. officials, and public opinion, were preoccupied with far more momentous issues—from Watergate to war in the Middle East. Nor did the transition from Nixon to Ford, four months after the coup in Portugal, lead to a reevaluation of U.S. policy toward the continent. It was not until late 1974 that the Ford administration began to focus on the repercussions of the coup, and its attention riveted on Portugal itself, where the Communist Party was in the ascendant. For Kissinger, Portugal became an obsession. Its colonies, however, remained on the back burner. "While I was in Lisbon, there was no sense of concern from Washington about them," recalled Richard Post, who was DCM there through December 1974. "I was the old Africa hand—I would have been very aware of it if there had been any concern!" Luanda "was still a backwater post," added Tom Killoran, who was appointed consul general there in mid-1974 even though he had never worked on Africa. And, from Lusaka, DCM Nelson saw "not much change [in U.S. policy] after the fall of Caetano."[40]

Donald Easum, who had replaced Newsom as assistant secretary for African affairs in early 1974, was the most senior of a small group of State Department officials who understood that things were bound to change in southern Africa, fast, and that U.S. policy, too, must change. "The entire . . . situation is changing very rapidly, and it's going to change regardless of our policies," he told Kissinger. The United States, he argued, should harden its position toward South Africa, push for majority rule in Rhodesia, and develop a friendly policy toward Frelimo.[41] He focused much more on Mozambique, which was slated to become independent in June 1975, than on Angola, which seemed a more distant problem. "I don't recall writing recommendations about Angola," he said. What he did do was to shoot down the recommendations of Larry Devlin, the African division chief in the CIA's Directorate of Operations, and of Jim Potts, Devlin's successor.[42]

Devlin wanted to reopen the CIA station in Luanda. Easum was opposed, and Devlin did not press the issue.[43] In July 1974 Devlin retired, and his successor, Potts, began arguing that the United States should give financial aid to Roberto. "He said Roberto was a good guy," Easum recalled, "who would play an important role, and we should strengthen that role." If Easum had agreed, the next step would have been a joint proposal by the CIA and the Africa Bureau to the 40 Committee, the top-level review board chaired by Kissinger that approved "all major and/or politically sensitive covert action programs."[44] Easum, however, disagreed. "My long-held view was that Frelimo, the PAIGC and the MPLA had valid objectives and that their ideology was something we didn't need to worry about, and that we needed to be supportive. I discussed them [Potts's ideas] with my people [senior officials in the Africa Bureau] and they agreed with me. I believed that the MPLA was a better partner for the US than the FNLA."[45] Back in Washington after two years as consul general in Luanda, Briggs, who considered the FNLA utterly corrupt and racist, had a sinking feeling when he was debriefed by CIA officials in Langley in September 1974. "I realized that the CIA was so taken with their puppets [FNLA] that there was no way you could tear them loose." It was as if Roberto's consistent history of corruption and ineptitude had failed to make any impression.[46]

For a time, however, the CIA was stymied by Easum's resistance. To Easum's knowledge, Potts "didn't go higher," that is, directly to Kissinger. (Y, a senior CIA officer who was involved in the Angola operation and has asked not to be named, pointed out that the appropriate bureaucratic procedure would have been for Potts to go to DCI Colby and for Colby to have raised it with Kissinger or one of Kissinger's top deputies. Y believed that Potts did speak with Colby. It is unclear whether Colby wasn't yet interested or whether he did pursue the matter, without results. What is clear, Y argues, is that if Easum had been supportive it would have been much easier to bring the matter to the 40 Committee.)[a,47] Lacking 40 Committee approval, the CIA could only increase the feeding money it was doling out to Roberto. On July 7, 1974, it raised the payment to $10,000 per month. Meanwhile, Stockwell writes, given that the CIA station in Luanda remained closed (it was reopened in March 1975) and that the CIA's "intelligence reporting on Angola was predominantly from Zairian and

a. A 1975 intelligence report noted, "Before covert operations are presented to the Director [of Central Intelligence] for submission to the 40 Committee, an internal CIA instruction states that they *should* be coordinated with the Department of State." 40 Committee approval was required only for "major and/or politically sensitive covert action programs." (U.S. Senate, Staff Report, *Covert Action*, p. 41, emphasis in the original.)

FNLA sources," the agency's dependence on Roberto increased.[48] Hultslander, who was appointed Luanda station chief in late July 1975, confirms Stockwell's account: "Responding to the worsening crisis," he explains, "the Agency decided to send a few officers to Luanda on temporary duty in March 1975. I followed as quickly as possible, arriving in early August. To the best of my knowledge, the bulk of the CIA's reporting in 1974 and 1975 did in fact come from Kinshasa. Holden Roberto was well known to the US government which enjoyed good access to Roberto and his chief lieutenants, facilitated by . . . Mobutu." The reporting from Kinshasa did little to change the CIA's opinion of the MPLA. Devlin believed that it "was Soviet-controlled," and Potts agreed with him. "The briefings and orientation I received prior to arriving in Luanda," Hultslander recalled, "emphasized the communist orientation of the MPLA, and convinced me of the urgent need to stop the MPLA from taking power." This conviction was as firm as the evidence supporting it was weak. "The coverage of Angola was very poor throughout," Devlin observed.[49]

In December 1974, Kissinger got rid of Easum, appointing him ambassador to Nigeria. Easum's exile was not caused by differences over Angola—Kissinger had not yet focused on that country—but by his efforts to move U.S. policy toward South Africa, Rhodesia, and Mozambique in a more liberal direction.[50] To replace Easum, Kissinger chose Nathaniel Davis, who had been the U.S. ambassador to Guatemala in 1968–71 and to Chile in 1971–73 and was widely praised as "a star in the service." He was also rumored, unfairly, to have been involved in the CIA plots against Allende. In a vain effort to prevent the appointment, Charles Diggs (D.-Mich.), chair of the House Foreign Affairs Subcommittee on Africa, cabled Kissinger, "It would be sheer arrogance to impose his selection upon an African Bureau still on the defensive Re: Easum." But Kissinger wanted Davis. "He used to comment that the Africa Bureau was full of missionaries," Davis remembered. "His intention [in appointing me] was to get someone who didn't have those sorts of ties to Africanists and to the whole African point of view." The "Allende man," as the *Zambia Daily Mail* called him, was sworn in on April 2.[51] By then, the United States had become involved, albeit tentatively, in the Angolan crisis. Deputy Assistant Secretary Edward Mulcahy, who had become the acting assistant secretary after Easum's departure, had sided with Potts, and the CIA and the Africa Bureau had drafted a joint proposal for the 40 Committee. They wanted to give Roberto and Savimbi $300,000 and $100,000 respectively for nonmilitary aid. Colby presented their proposal to the 40 Committee on January 22, "just at the end of the meeting," according to Y, who was present. Colby explained that the CIA had received " 'some very disturbing intelligence' " that the Soviet Union had begun shipping weapons to the MPLA through the Congo. He argued that " 'it was clear that Neto wasn't our man,' " and that CIA support for Roberto and Savimbi would be " 'a token' which would give the United States 'some capital in the bank' " with two of Angola's future leaders. "It was presented as a pre-electoral move," added

Hyland, who was also present. "It all sounded pretty innocuous. After all he [Roberto] used to be on the payroll for Kennedy." Savimbi would get less because he was still an unknown quantity and tainted by his earlier contacts with the Chinese.[52]

The 40 Committee authorized the $300,000 for Roberto but vetoed the $100,000 for Savimbi. "They didn't explain why they cut out Savimbi," Mulcahy remarked. "I think it was because they ran out of time." The likely reason, Y agreed, "is that probably Kissinger had heard of Roberto before, but he had never heard of Savimbi."[53]

It was just a week after the Alvor agreement, and 24,000 Portuguese troops were going to remain in Angola to enforce the accord. "Most local sources are optimistic that civil war can be avoided in the short term," Consul General Killoran had reported from Luanda, "but there is a good deal of concern about long range prospects for continued peace."[54] Washington could have used its influence to try to maintain peace. Instead, in an almost careless spasm, it gave money to Roberto. "There was very little discussion," Hyland recalled. "The amount of money was so small by the standards of a covert operation."[55] Senior U.S. officials were distracted by other, far more pressing concerns: the danger of war in the Middle East, the leftward drift in Portugal, the threats to détente, and the Cyprus question. And as 1975 began, Vietnam came unstuck. A Communist offensive, which had begun with limited objectives in mid-December, gathered momentum and Saigon responded more feebly than anyone had expected. In mid-March, while Kissinger was traveling through the Middle East in his interminable shuttle diplomacy, South Vietnam's president, Nguyen Van Thieu, ordered his troops to withdraw from the central highlands. As retreat turned into rout, Thieu lost half of his country and half of his army in a matter of days. Angola must have seemed terribly unimportant to the weary traveler aboard his Boeing 707.

The United States had, as yet, no Angola policy. The 40 Committee's decision to fund Roberto was an ad hoc move, not the beginning of a covert operation. Yet Roberto was likely to interpret it as an indication of unconditional U.S. support, which would strengthen his desire to seek a military solution, unless Washington sent a strong signal to the contrary. No such signal was forthcoming. When the U.S. ambassador to Zaire, Deane Hinton, visited Luanda in February 1975, the Portuguese high commissioner pleaded with him to urge Mobutu not to interfere in Angola.[56] Washington refused. In March, Zairean troops entered Angola. "The Portuguese have . . . asked us to raise the subject [Zaire's aid to the FNLA] with Mobutu (which, thus far, we have declined)," an aide told Kissinger three months later.[57]

In late March, the FNLA attacked the MPLA in Luanda. Washington expressed no disapproval. From Lisbon, U.S. ambassador Frank Carlucci warned that Portugal was unlikely to use force to uphold the Alvor agreement. "Even in the improbable event that GOP [government of Portugal] decided to risk troops in major action for sake of civil order in Africa," he added, "it may reasonably be assumed that Portuguese troops would not obey the order."[58]

The Luanda fighting spurred Assistant Secretary Davis, INR director Hyland, and chief of the Policy Planning Staff Lord to try to get Kissinger's attention. On April 4 they wrote a memo to the secretary: "The shakiness of the truce [between the MPLA and the FNLA] . . . has pointed to the continued potential for widespread violence in Angola. If civil war breaks out, and barring outside intervention, the FNLA may have the military force to defeat MPLA. . . . In a prolonged conflict between the two movements, each would probably have to have foreign military assistance." The MPLA would be likely to seek Soviet aid. "The USSR, most probably, would provide assistance but will attempt to keep its involvement indirect to avoid any prejudice to its delicately balanced policy toward Portugal." The time had come, Davis, Hyland, and Lord concluded, for the United States to pay attention to Angola. "We must decide on a U.S. position. . . . Specifically, at what level, if any, should we covertly support FNLA's Holden Roberto or other Angolan leaders?"[59]

The other Angolan leader was, of course, Savimbi, who was already seeking U.S. aid. "Our perception of Savimbi is hazy; almost all our information is second-hand," an intelligence officer warned on April 29. "We know he is ambitious. . . . He clearly is extremely flexible in pursuit of his objectives. It is therefore difficult to accept without reservations any of the political convictions claimed by or attributed to him." Indeed, the six-page document reveals how little U.S. intelligence knew about Savimbi.[60] In a May 1 memo to Kissinger, written at the secretary's request ("You asked me to look further into the background of Jonas Savimbi and report to you"), Assistant Secretary Davis noted,

the CIA has produced an informal assessment [of Savimbi] . . . and so has INR. . . . These memos give a favorable picture of Savimbi's personality, public presence, political drawing power, and flexibility of maneuver. They also suggest opportunism, and solicitation of covert funding in all quarters. . . .

Savimbi's efforts to obtain funds and arms have taken him to Belgium, Paris, London, etc. Reportedly he has plans to visit Peking . . . [sanitized]. The South Africans have expressed interest in providing financial assistance [sanitized].

The wide knowledge of Savimbi's solicitations and subventions makes me skeptical that U.S. support could long be kept secret. Our consul in Luanda reports that the soliciting agent who recently approached him was not discreet. [sanitized]. . . . If we launch a program of covert support for Savimbi, I think we must reckon with probable disclosure. At most we would be in a position to commit limited resources, and buy marginal influence. [sanitized] We might find ourselves drawn in deeper very fast, as the fighting produces more intense pressures for arms and ammunition—as well as money. The political price we might pay—as reports of bloodshed and alleged atrocities multiply—would, I believe, exceed the possibility of accomplishment. . . .

The foregoing represents my own view, as opinions on our desired posture toward Savimbi are somewhat divided in AF [the Africa Bureau of the State Department].[61]

Kissinger read this memo with the echo of Zambian president Kaunda's urgent plea on Savimbi's behalf still ringing in his ears. Kaunda had arrived in Washington on April 18 for a two-day state visit. A deeply religious man who was sympathetic to the West, he had been offended by Nixon's policy toward southern Africa. "He [Kaunda] kept me waiting for twenty-one days before I was allowed to present my credentials," Jean Wilkowski, who had arrived in Lusaka as U.S. ambassador in 1972, complained. "The Chinese ambassador only waited two days. Kaunda wanted to send a message. We got off to a very rocky start." Kaunda wanted to persuade the United States to support majority rule in southern Africa, but the administration was not moved.[62]

In the spring of 1975, as Angola was sliding toward civil war, Kaunda suddenly mattered. When he arrived in the United States, "The Americans rolled out the red carpet . . . in a display of warmth not accorded any visiting African dignitary since Richard Nixon went to the White House in 1969," Colin Legum reported from Washington. Kissinger even went to the airport to greet him, and Ford hosted a formal White House dinner in his honor instead "of the more usual breakfast or lunch accorded to African leaders."[63] At the dinner, Kaunda rose to toast his hosts. Asking Ford's forgiveness for his "candor," he openly expressed "our dismay" over U.S. policy in Africa and called "upon America not to give any support to the oppressors."[64] This was his public message; in private he urged Ford to provide military aid to Savimbi. Perhaps he was motivated by antipathy toward Neto, or perhaps he feared that Neto was too close to the Soviet Union, or perhaps he, or some of his advisers, were influenced by Tiny Rowland, the British financier who had large economic stakes in Zambia and was a strong supporter of Savimbi. Certainly Kaunda was swayed by Savimbi's charm, charisma, and eloquent declarations in favor of peace in Angola. U.S. officials concluded, "Kaunda has developed a personal animosity toward Neto. . . . As his disenchantment with Neto and the MPLA grew, Kaunda became increasingly impressed with . . . Savimbi."[65]

Kaunda's unexpected plea brought Angola to the attention of top policy makers just as the wave of renewed fighting between the FNLA and MPLA raised further doubts about the likelihood of a peaceful solution. In a May 6 memorandum, written while fighting raged in Luanda and other Angolan towns, the Africa Bureau of the State Department noted that "an agreement [among the parties] on elections [was] increasingly unlikely. . . . Prospects appear to be mounting . . . for an escalation of violence." It was time for the United States to assess its options. Kissinger's sense of urgency was tempered, however, by the pressure of other crises (Saigon fell on April 30) and by the news that the civil war in Angola was moving in the right direction: on May 13, Mulcahy told him, "FNLA (and UNITA) seems to be in the ascendancy."[66]

On May 26, at Kissinger's request, an NSC interagency task force chaired by Davis was established and told to prepare a report on U.S. interests and policy options in Angola by June 30.[67] In his memoirs, Kissinger alleged that Davis "managed to delay my dealing with Angola by nearly ten weeks because he opposed the decision he feared I would make. He simply used the splendid machinery so methodically to 'clear' a memorandum I had requested [the task force report] that it took weeks to reach me."[68] In fact Davis submitted his report on June 13, two weeks after he had been given his charge and two weeks before the deadline Kissinger himself set. The formulation of U.S. policy toward Angola was delayed not by Davis but by Kissinger's failure to focus on it.

The Davis report identified three options for the United States. The first was neutrality: "Under this option we would choose not to involve ourselves in the Angolan situation. We would support neither the FNLA nor UNITA. We would indicate our desire to enter into diplomatic relations with whatever government is established in Angola."[69]

The second option was to "promote a peaceful solution through diplomatic/political measures. . . . Under this option we could: urge Portugal to play a stronger—but impartial—role; encourage Portugal to press the USSR to reduce its support of MPLA; encourage interested Africans to seek Soviet reduction of its support to MPLA; we could privately approach, or build public pressure on, the USSR to reduce its support of MPLA; or, ultimately, support or promote a UN mediation effort."[70]

The third option was to "Actively support one or more of the liberation groups. . . . We could channel military aid through Zaire and, conceivably, Zambia, to FNLA and UNITA. We could directly provide military equipment and supplies including heavy weapons to one or both groups."[71]

Within the task force, opinion was divided: in a memo to Kissinger, the NSC Africa staff person, Hal Horan, noted that both the Treasury and JCS representatives preferred the first option: "Treasury argued that our interests in Angola are minimal and do not warrant our becoming involved in a difficult situation. The JCS representative summed up his view as supporting a policy of 'studied indifference.' No other agency held this view, although 'neutrality' was recognized as a serious option." Most task force members, however, preferred the second option, diplomacy. There was "little support" for option three—a covert operation.[72]

On June 19 the NSC's Senior Review Group—high-level representatives from various agencies chaired by Kissinger—reviewed the report. At the meeting, Kissinger conceded that "it appears that most favor trying a diplomatic effort." He went on, however, to express his reservations: "But I am concerned that the NSSM [the report's] response is weak on just how we can proceed with such an effort. I wonder how much leverage we have, for example, with the Portuguese, or Mobutu, or the Soviets." To address these concerns, the task force was told to prepare a paper elaborating the options that would be presented to an NSC meeting scheduled for June 27.[73] This paper, which was essentially an expansion of options two and three—diplomacy and covert operations—was ready on June 25. It boldly advised against a covert operation. "The uncertainties of the situation in Angola make the risks of becoming directly involved greater than the probable gains to be derived therefrom," it said. "We would have to commit US resources and prestige in a situation where the outcome would still be in doubt and over which we can exercise only limited influence at best. In any case, we could not realistically consider any direct, overt military support, such as arms shipments or commitment of US personnel. Any assistance would have to be covert, and military assistance would have to be channeled through third parties." The paper also noted that "it was essential" that the United States ascertain "what role Zaire is likely to play and what recent changes may have taken place in Mobutu's attitude towards Angolan developments and towards an increased U.S. role in Angolan affairs."[74]

MOBUTU'S RESPONSE

Mobutu was at that very moment making his views abundantly clear to Kissinger's special envoy, Sheldon Vance, a former U.S. ambassador to Zaire (1969–73). The collapse of Portuguese rule in Angola had presented both an opportunity and a threat to Mobutu. If Roberto won, Mobutu would extend his influence over Angola and possibly even grab Cabinda. But if Neto won, Cabinda would be lost and Angola would turn into a springboard for Zaire's enemies. Mobutu feared Neto, whom he considered radical and likely to seek revenge for Zaire's persecution of the MPLA. As Mobutu became involved in the civil war on Roberto's behalf, his fear of retribution increased, as did his desire to see the MPLA crushed. "Mobutu regards an Angola dominated by the MPLA's Agostinho Neto as intolerable," Kissinger told the NSC on June 27.[75]

In 1973 Mobutu, the child of the CIA, had begun trying to project himself as a champion of the Third World who could deal with both West and East. He had been received like a hero in China and North Korea. He had once been, in the words of the U.S. secretary of state, "a staunch personal advocate of the Israeli cause," but in order to strengthen his radical credentials, he expelled the Israeli trainers "for his so-called elite division" and turned the training over to North Koreans. "It was an act of folly," the U.S. ambassador, Deane Hinton, remarked. "Among other problems, to put it mildly, there was an entirely new doctrinal approach and an even worse language problem!"[76] As Zaire's economic crisis deepened in 1974—the result of extreme economic mismanagement, rampant corruption, and the fall of copper prices—and the United States responded not with significant economic aid but with Hinton's lectures on the virtues of economic austerity, Mobutu's criticism of the United States grew increasingly brazen. In January 1975 he lashed out at U.S. policies in Africa in front of a large U.S. congressional delegation and the diplomatic corps. "Your country did not help

Africa to gain its freedom!" he thundered. "In some cases, the United States has even worked against the interests of Africa, as, for example, with Rhodesian chrome [the Byrd amendment]." He condemned U.S. passivity toward South African apartheid, the firing of Assistant Secretary Easum, and the appointment of Nathaniel Davis.[77]

What angered Mobutu was not Washington's failure to help in the struggle against apartheid, but its failure to help him smash the MPLA in Angola. By the spring of 1975, Zaire was doing its best to help Roberto, but Washington had done virtually nothing. As Mobutu's frustrations grew, so did the intensity of his rhetoric. He proclaimed his country's "active solidarity" with North Korea, extended the hand of friendship to the Palestine Liberation Organization, and greeted the Communist victory in Vietnam "with joy," declaring, "All the revolutionaries of the world have celebrated enthusiastically the victories so longed for of our brothers and sisters of Vietnam and Cambodia." It was strong stuff, but it "didn't get Washington's attention," remarked Lannon Walker, who was the DCM in Kinshasa. "Kissinger wasn't looking at Angola, and he certainly wasn't looking at Africa or Zaire, despite everything that was going on in southern Africa." What Mobutu got, rather than help in the struggle against the MPLA, was an economic austerity plan. Hinton and Walker delivered it in early June. "Hinton had put his economic plan [for Zaire] together," Walker explained. "He told me, 'Let's go to see Mobutu, explain the trouble he's in to him, and point him to the IMF.' And so off we went! Hinton told Mobutu in his heavily accented French, 'Monsieur le président, you're sick and you need a good doctor. And the best doctor is the IMF.' Mobutu said, 'Ah bon,' and left the room. It was the straw that broke the camel's back."[78]

A few days later, Mobutu upped the ante: he accused the CIA of encouraging a group of Zairean officers to organize a coup against him, and he expelled Hinton. "The courageous decision of our leader is justified because the ominous shadow of the notorious American diplomat was behind the bloody hand of the CIA, pulling the strings of the sinister plot," *Elima* explained.[79]

"I honestly doubt that Mobutu believed that the US had been plotting against him," Walter Cutler, the director of the Central Africa office in the State Department, observed. "What he had at the time was a feeling of neglect; he felt that we weren't giving him the attention he deserved. He wanted to get our attention; he was frustrated. And he was unhappy with Hinton. . . . He was unhappy with the relationship. Mobutu, who is a mastermind at political manipulation, took the risk of blowing up this failed coup into a crisis with the United States. . . . He wasn't getting much from us at the time. There may have also been some genuine fear—maybe 20% paranoia and 80% sheer political manipulation."[80]

It was a bold move. Mobutu threw down the gauntlet at a moment when his country was mired in economic and political crisis and his hold on power shaky. DCM Walker expected the State Department to respond with a strong rebuke.[81] Instead Kissinger caved. Mobutu's vulnerability and Kissinger's belated interest in Angola saved him.

Kissinger's response verged on panic. "His reaction was, 'My God, this is not the time to have a major crisis and an estrangement with Mobutu,'" Cutler recalled. "There was a risk of Soviet penetration in Central Africa, and Zaire, already weakened by an economic crisis, could be next." Hinton believed that "the odds on Mobutu's survival 'have shifted markedly' and 'he could be thrown out at any moment.'"[82]

This is why Sheldon Vance ended up as Kissinger's special envoy to Zaire listening to Mobutu's suggestions, while in Washington the Davis task force was completing its report for the upcoming NSC meeting on Angola. Vance, who had gotten along famously with Mobutu when he had been ambassador to Zaire, landed in Kinshasa on June 21, four hours after Hinton had departed.[83] DCM Walker, who accompanied Vance, recalls vividly how Mobutu began the conversation. "'Before you start,'" he told Vance, "'I want you to know I have already forgiven you Americans, but I will never forget.'" This ended all discussion of the incident. Then they got down to business. "Two-hour breakfast meeting with Mobutu this morning (June 23) was friendly throughout and he asked me to meet with him again tonight at 6:30," Vance cabled Kissinger.

> After he greeted me warmly, I told Mobutu that the Secretary had asked me to come to Kinshasa for the following purposes:
> (1) To find out from Mobutu what was troubling him, leading to his accusations about coup plotting.
> (2) To stress the importance we attach to Zaire and Mobutu.
> (3) To convey our desire to work with him, provided he wishes it.
> (4) To stress the importance of Angola in the Secretary's mind and his desire to have Mobutu's analysis and policy plans.

Mobutu's answer was relayed by Kissinger at the June 27 NSC meeting. "He [Mobutu] said the Soviets continue to pour arms and other assistance into Angola for Neto," Kissinger stated. "His own ability to continue to aid Holden is restricted by his own low stock of weapons and a scarcity of money. He explained it would be very grave for Zaire if the Soviets controlled Angola, and they would if Neto became master of the country." Mobutu wanted the United States to help Savimbi and Roberto, possibly through Zaire. ("It is known that the U.S. has helped Zaire militarily and that Zaire has helped Roberto, so the modalities of our possible assistance are clearly indicated," Mobutu had told Vance.)[84]

Angola would provide the joint endeavor that would reestablish U.S.-Zairean friendship. "An important side benefit [of the covert operation]," the NSC noted, "would be improved US-Zaire relations."[85] Kissinger urged Ford to approve a $50 million assistance package for Mobutu. Failure to provide the assistance, he told the president, "could have severely negative, immediate consequences on our political and economic interests in Zaire." When Secretary of the Treasury William Simon suggested that the aid be at least linked to Mobutu's acceptance of an IMF reform package, Kissinger said that Mobutu would probably refuse any conditions, and "that if he does, the stakes are so important that we must offer our assistance anyway." (Ford approved the aid "without conditions.")[86] Kissinger may also have been thinking of the point made by the Davis task force that aid to Mobutu would "enable him to provide military and other support to FNLA and UNITA." He told the June 27 NSC meeting on Angola, "One of the most interesting proposals in that paper might be to extend aid to President Mobutu as an offset to enable him to provide military and other support to Holden and Savimbi."[87]

KISSINGER'S DECISION

The NSC meeting took place under twin shadows: Mobutu's situation was deteriorating while Neto's was improving. "In recent fighting, the MPLA has bested its rival, the FNLA, in numerous clashes in Luanda, northern Angola and Cabinda," Kissinger announced.[88] The minutes of the meeting have been very heavily sanitized, but some key points emerge: Ford knew nothing about Angola; Kissinger dominated the meeting; Ford followed Kissinger's lead. Kissinger presented the recommendations of the Davis task force, dismissing the first (neutrality) out of hand and saying bluntly, "As for the second course [diplomacy], my department agrees, but I don't." The next long paragraph, presumably his description of the third option, is deleted. Ford responded by asking the CIA—which favored covert action—and not the Davis task force, which favored diplomacy, to draft a paper on Angola for the July 14 meeting of the 40 Committee. The paper should "look at the levels that would be required in assisting Holden Roberto and Jonas Savimbi; look at supplying assistance, both directly and through third parties (e.g. Mobutu of Zaire); . . . examine other assistance that may be needed other than arms, such as shoring up the Movement's capacity to enforce discipline, perhaps through third parties; . . . examine whether we should inform others (e.g., President Kaunda of Zambia) of our intentions." The focus was now entirely on a covert operation.[89]

The CIA paper for the 40 Committee has not been declassified; only brief excerpts have been quoted or paraphrased by critics such as Stockwell and particularly Davis, whose biting critique, which he sent on July 12 to the State Department's representative on the 40 Committee, Under Secretary Sisco, has been declassified. Yet only the bare outlines of the plan can be discerned, and it is difficult to assess its arguments. "The CIA paper," Davis wrote, "envisages covert CIA-organized military training, organization, orientation and leadership" of the FNLA and UNITA, as well as the participation of "former Portuguese and Zairian officers and non-coms" (an idea, he observed, that "has obvious hazards"). The plan assigned a key role to Mobutu ("Zaire is the key chosen instrument for everything," Davis wrote) and a supporting role to Zambia. It also stated that the "'Soviets enjoy greater freedom of action in the covert supply of arms, equipment and ammunition' and 'can escalate the level of their aid more readily than we.'" It is not clear why the CIA plan would have said that Moscow could escalate the level of its aid more readily than Washington. No one at the time even thought that Cuba might intervene, and geography favored the United States. Three of Angola's neighbors—Zaire, Zambia, and South Africa—were strong supporters of UNITA and the FNLA. Only the Congo, which bordered the Cabinda enclave, gave lukewarm support to the MPLA. (Furthermore, according to Stockwell, the paper also said that a U.S. program of $40 million would likely match any increase in Soviet aid to Neto.)[90]

In his critique, Davis drew attention to UNITA's military weakness. Savimbi, he noted, had only 500 to 800 guerrillas at the time of the Portuguese coup; "while he claims large numbers of unarmed troops now, they have not done any substantial fighting, have been defeated when caught up in violence, and have mostly not been tested or trained with real weapons." And he expressed healthy skepticism about Roberto. "He is accused of cowardice in refusing to return to Angola. His leadership is reported to be faltering, and that of his subordinates to be 'abysmal.'" Davis warned that "Unless we are prepared to go as far as necessary, in world balance of power terms, the worst possible outcome would be a test of will and strength which we lose. The CIA paper makes clear that in the best of circumstances we won't be able to win. If we are to have a test of strength with the Soviets, we should find a more advantageous place."[91] Not everyone was so pessimistic. When I queried Mulcahy on this point, for example, he laughed. "I'm an optimist! I thought the operation would succeed. No one expected it to fail—the idea was that we would win." Y agreed and pointed out that "nobody knew how much the Soviets would provide in aid to the MPLA" if they were confronted with serious opposition from the United States. Furthermore, he mused, "nobody [at CIA, the State Department] knew how much the United States was going to provide." The CIA plan was just a blueprint, with a lot of blank spaces that Kissinger could fill in as he saw fit. The 40 Committee could allocate more money and introduce modifications en route, according to the circumstances.[92]

Apparently, the CIA paper said nothing about South Africa, even though Pretoria was obviously a major player in the region and the CIA had been asked by the NSC on June 27 to assess "What response [to a covert operation] could we expect from the Soviets, from the MPLA, *third countries*, particularly African, the US Congress and the public."[93] This striking omission fits a pattern: in the declassified record South Africa is virtually invisible. Yet Pretoria decided in mid-July to provide military assistance to Savimbi and Roberto, and a well-informed scholar, James Roherty, asserts that Vorster sounded out Washington beforehand.[94] Even if we dismiss Roherty's account and assume that Vorster did not consult the Americans, it is difficult to believe that the CIA did not approach the South Africans. (Relations between BOSS and the CIA were notoriously close.) This oversight would be even more striking because Kissinger and the other supporters of the covert operation could harbor no illusions about Zaire. "Ambassador Hinton's view," Davis noted in his July 12 critique, "is that . . . 'Mobutu's arrest and torture of a number of highly respected officers and his subsequent dismissal of a dozen additional general officers cannot help but have shaken his officer corps.'" Zaire's weakness had been a consistent refrain of the embassy through the spring. "Our reports," DCM Walker recalls, "made it clear that Mobutu was in bad shape, his armed forces in shambles."[95]

Are we to assume, then, that no one in Washington even wondered about what Pretoria would do? "I doubt we overlooked them," Davis commented. "There was an inhibition about being explicit about cooperating with South Africa. I can think of no better way of getting the goat of the Africanists. I'm sure a lot was discussed without me because they knew what my position was." Walker, who favored a covert operation, agreed. "The idea of working with South Africa in Angola was really tabu among Africanists; it was really the show stopper. Would have cost too much with the Africans. If I had been told, I would have been very opposed." While few might have dared to disagree openly with Kissinger, strong opposition in the ranks would have increased the danger of leaks.[96]

The written record, spare as it is, is contradictory. On the one hand, the report of the Davis task force asserts, surprisingly, "Pretoria is concerned that a communist or otherwise unfriendly regime in Luanda might support guerrilla activity in Namibia and foster serious problems along that border. However, South Africa does not seem to be planning action to counter this threat and, in fact, gives little indication that it sees any need to formulate an Angolan policy at all." By July 16, however, Davis was writing to Kissinger, "South Africa is reported to be giving Roberto some support." And Chester Crocker, who became Ronald Reagan's assistant secretary for African affairs and had access to the classified record, writes that through the late spring of 1975, "an intense debate over Angolan developments had been underway within the South African government. Pretoria was in close contact with *all the Western and African players*, and was actively courted by FNLA and UNITA leaders as well as certain African governments to throw its weight into the balance. . . . By July . . . Pretoria began providing clandestine aid to the FNLA and UNITA. Zairean army units had started to deploy across the border into northern Angola in support of the FNLA. *Washington, of course, was well aware of these moves: our winks and nods formed part of the calculus of Angola's neighbors.*"[97]

Is it a giant leap, then, to suspect that Pretoria's moves also formed part of Washington's calculus when the 40 Committee met on July 14, and that the lack of evidence is a reflection of how little has been declassified and of the extreme discretion with which such sensitive matters were handled?

There are no available records of the July 14 meeting of the 40 Committee. "The meeting was inconclusive," writes Davis, who had asked to be included but was not invited. "A small ad-hoc working group was then formed to refine the covert action proposal and answer the questions not satisfactorily resolved. I attended two sessions of this working group."[98] Meanwhile, from Angola came news that the MPLA had won the battle of Luanda, and from Kinshasa an "alarmed" Mobutu continued to press "for a concrete demonstration of U.S.

support for his efforts to prevent a takeover of Angola by the MPLA."[99] On July 17 the 40 Committee met again and approved the revised CIA plan. The next day President Ford authorized the disbursement of $6 million (followed by another $8 million on July 27 and $10.7 million on August 20).[100] The CIA covert operation in Angola dubbed IAFEATURE had begun.

FRIENDS

The United States was in the lead, flanked by Zaire and South Africa. England and France took up the rear. This was the coalition that was forming in the summer of 1975 behind UNITA and the FNLA. "They are the same, those who yesterday . . . supported Salazar and Caetano, and today are against the MPLA," Neto remarked.[101]

By July, Crocker asserts, the British and the French governments had begun "their own clandestine assistance programs." British companies joined in to help UNITA. When Stockwell flew from Lusaka to Silva Porto in Angola's central highlands to meet Savimbi in August 1975, he flew in a small Lear jet with a British crew on loan from the British commercial conglomerate Lonrho. Lonrho "was betting on Savimbi to win the war," Stockwell remarked. "Special access to Angolan minerals would be prize aplenty."[102]

France coveted Cabinda's oil. "The Cabindan affair puzzles Paris," *Le Monde* explained in August 1975, "because Brazzaville and Kinshasa, both special friends of France, have contradictory views about the future of the enclave."[103] Paris, however, had already decided to back Kinshasa.[104] Not only was Zaire, with all its mineral riches, a far more attractive partner than the Congo, but its friends, too, were more attractive: South Africa, the United States, Roberto, and Savimbi.

Paris, therefore, helped the FNLA and UNITA. When the Portuguese empire collapsed, "though we were helpless to prevent Mozambique falling victim to Marxism and famine, the least we could do was to try to counter the Soviet and Cuban ascendancy in Angola," the director of French intelligence, Alexandre de Marenches, wrote. So France sent weapons to Savimbi and, through Mobutu, to Roberto. "I am sorry to say," Marenches added, "that there was no coordination between American services and our own." There was, in fact, a one-sided partnership. "The CIA briefed the French intelligence service in detail about its Angola program," Stockwell complained, "while the French listened carefully but told the CIA nothing about their own activities in Angola and Cabinda." In September 1975 Neto told *Le Monde*, "It appears that it is France's destiny to help the reactionary forces in Africa."[105]

The odd men in this company were the Chinese, who had about 200 military instructors training the FNLA in Zaire by the end of 1974. "The Chinese recently agreed to continue this assistance until the end of 1975," the Davis task force noted in June 1975. The following month, Beijing, which had already supplied arms to the FNLA (and, to a lesser degree, to UNITA), acceded to a new request from Roberto and went "out of its way to make sure the supplies were received quickly."[106] China's assistance was welcomed by U.S. officials, but there was no consultation or coordination between the two governments. Relations between Washington and Beijing, which had blossomed in 1971–72, had lost momentum by 1973–74, and "a certain immobilism and cooling of atmosphere" had set in because of domestic difficulties in both countries, Chinese dissatisfaction with continuing U.S. ties with Taiwan, and Beijing's fears that the United States was playing the China card in its pursuit of détente with the Soviet Union. In Africa "more than elsewhere," the State Department's briefing paper for Ford's December 1975 trip to Beijing noted, the "radically different approaches to Third World issues" of Washington and Beijing were apparent. The Chinese supported armed struggle against the white regimes, and "their strident political rhetoric emphasized the conflict of the LDC's [less developed countries] with the developed world." They supported the FNLA because Roberto's (and Mobutu's) victory would strengthen the anti-Soviet forces in central Africa, but they kept the Americans at arm's length. The briefing paper pointed out that "Secretary Kissinger's efforts to engage PRC Foreign Minister Ch'iao Kuan-hua in a discussion of Angola during their late-September meeting in New York did not succeed in overcoming Ch'iao's reserve, although he was clearly interested in hearing our views." Instead, Ch'iao warned Kissinger against enlisting "the help of South Africa. This is short sighted," he said.[107]

PRETORIA AND WASHINGTON MEET IN ANGOLA

U.S. aid began reaching Roberto and Savimbi in early August, a most opportune time. The MPLA had won the battle of Luanda, the FNLA was eager to recover the initiative by attacking the capital, and UNITA had joined the war against the MPLA. Stockwell details how the $14 million that had been approved in late July was allocated: $8 million for arms and the planes to transport them from Kinshasa to Angola; $2.75 million in cash to Mobutu to encourage him to send more arms to the FNLA and UNITA; $2 million doled out at $200,000 a month to both Roberto and Savimbi to cover operating costs. "The [CIA] chiefs of station [COS] in Kinshasa and Lusaka insisted on controlling these funds, and specified that Roberto and Savimbi should not be told how much they were to receive," Stockwell writes. "Each COS claimed one of the movements, Roberto belonged to Kinshasa and Savimbi to Lusaka. Each COS wanted to dole money to his leader, or to be able to make cash purchases on his leader's behalf."[108] Meanwhile, in Washington, the State Department was preparing to sound out key members of Congress for a $50 million emergency aid package for Mobutu.[109]

That same August, Pretoria's first arms shipments reached the FNLA and UNITA. Some SADF officers, however, were already saying that Vorster should also send military instructors. "If you give a man a weapon, you must also show him how to use it. Otherwise it is useless," they argued. On September 3, a senior officer involved in the operation, Commander Jan Breytenbach, submitted a proposal to the army's director of operations, General Viljoen. "'I think,' he wrote, 'that the success of the operation depends on good leadership, that is white South African command at every level, and also on logistical support.'"[110] The following day, Vorster authorized the SADF to provide military training, advice, and logistical support to UNITA and the FNLA. "In turn, they [the FNLA and UNITA] would help expel SWAPO from southern Angola."[111]

The first South African special forces, led by Breytenbach, were immediately dispatched to Angola to begin training FNLA forces. "In a small place called Mpupa on the Cuito River about 70 kilometers north of the South West Africa border, I came face to face with the first FNLA soldiers," Breytenbach writes. "I stared distastefully and with sick foreboding at the most miserable, underfed, ragged and villainous bunch of troops I had ever seen in my life." For the next few weeks the South Africans fed, armed, and trained their charges at Mpupa and organized them into small units. "They were totally dependent on South Africa for weapons, ammunition and general equipment," Spies writes. South African officers and noncommissioned officers and also former officers of the Portuguese secret police were put in command of the companies and platoons. South Africans also went to the southern town of Serpa Pinto to train other FNLA forces. "The FNLA soldiers were told that the instructors were mercenaries."[112]

Meanwhile, on August 22 the SADF launched operation Sausage II, a major raid on SWAPO camps in southern Angola. "These forces have entered Angolan territory," an MPLA communiqué said nine days later, "and the Portuguese authorities have not said anything." Finally, on September 5 a communiqué from the Portuguese Foreign Ministry stated: "During this current week we brought to the attention of the South African government some evidence that . . . mercenaries and unidentified forces were infiltrating into southern Angola from Namibia." Pretoria had replied, the communiqué said, that it "does not allow mercenaries or other forces to operate from its territory or territory under its control."[113] That would be the last word, as far as the Portuguese were concerned. Throughout September, the SADF launched raids across the border to eliminate SWAPO. UNITA and the FNLA, "both now allies of the Republic of South Africa," helped locate the SWAPO camps, Spies wrote. The Portuguese said nothing. "It was as if nothing had happened," Lara said.[114]

On September 17 Generals van den Bergh (the head of BOSS) and Viljoen flew to Kinshasa to meet Savimbi. It was the first time that top South African officials had met him, and, true to form, he won them over. For the South Africans, Breytenbach wrote, Savimbi "had become the new star in the sky." Viljoen and van den Bergh were dazzled by his personality, his grasp of military matters, his sympathetic understanding of Pretoria's need to smash SWAPO, and his emphasis on an anti-Communist bloc that would include South Africa, Angola, Zaire, and Zambia. A few days later, twenty-five South African military instructors (officers and noncommissioned officers) arrived at Capolo, eighty miles south of Silva Porto in the central highlands, to train UNITA troops. "They were given false names and were told to speak only English . . . and anything identifiable was removed from their equipment," Spies wrote. They "were ordered . . . to describe themselves, if asked, as English." They were in good company. "By this time," du Preez explained, the CIA was already training recruits at Capolo. "And in the following weeks South Africans and Americans worked side by side—each under his own cover."[115]

This is not what the Ford administration later told Congress. From Kissinger down, U.S. officials stoutly maintained that there had been no cooperation whatsoever between the United States and South Africa and that CIA activities within Angola had been limited to intelligence gathering. Neither statement was true.[116]

A glaring weakness of IAFEATURE was, as Stockwell writes, "a lack of information about our allies and about the interior of Angola. We were mounting a major covert operation program to support two Angolan liberation movements about which we had little reliable intelligence. Most of what we knew about the FNLA came from Roberto . . . and it was obvious that he was exaggerating and distorting facts in order to keep our support. We knew even less about Savimbi and UNITA." Once the CIA began sending weapons to the FNLA and UNITA, it discovered, as Davis had earlier warned, that they lacked the skill, leadership, and discipline to conduct an effective military campaign. This inexorably led to the introduction of the CIA's own paramilitary experts into the FNLA and UNITA commands. "We called the advisors we placed inside Angola 'intelligence gatherers,' although their intelligence effort was always subordinate to their advisory capacity," Stockwell explains. "To cite a few examples: . . . CIA communication officers trained FNLA and UNITA technicians at the Angolan advance bases, . . . CIA paramilitary officers were training UNITA forces in Silva Porto and the FNLA in Ambriz in the use of infantry weapons."[117]

Stockwell is a controversial source. He left the CIA in 1977, a bitter critic of the agency and of IAFEATURE, and proceeded to write a scathing book about the operation, the only insider's account we have. Some critics accuse him of distorting the truth; Y, for example, asserts that there were no CIA paramilitary officers inside Angola.[118]

DIA analyst Thom, however, disagrees: "By November, four companies of 108 [UNITA] men each were being trained every two weeks by US and South African instructors."[119] And Fred Bridgland, a British journalist who covered the Angolan war and became Savimbi's official biographer, describes an encounter with a CIA paramilitary officer in Silva Porto (which was at the time Savimbi's military headquarters):

A fawn Range Rover raced up and out stepped Skip, who passed himself off to reporters as an American journalist but who, fresh from the failure of Vietnam, was now the CIA's resident liaison man with Savimbi. . . . Some of Skip's military "advisers" were straight out of the American nightmare—for example, an unsmiling tough in his late twenties who wore a black Texan cowboy hat, high-heeled boots and studded jeans and walked with a mean swagger while his tight, sour, gum-chewing face sent the message: "Look at me, admire me, but don't speak to me." Other CIA specialists wore huge silver or wooden crosses flapping on their chests and told inquisitive reporters they were there to check on the fates of their Christian "flocks."[120]

Given this evidence, Hultslander's judgment seems fair. "Although I take great issue with Stockwell's 'defection,'" he wrote me, "I remember that his book, *Search*, which I read carefully shortly after it was published, was largely accurate. He took part in the Washington debate, and probably reported accurately on the meetings he attended. He was also charged with implementing the covert action program, and from my own limited knowledge, I believe his account to be accurate." When I asked Hultslander whether there were CIA paramilitary officers in *Angola*, he answered, "We had no paramilitary presence in *Luanda*."[121]

The parallelism between Pretoria and Washington is striking. Both launched their covert operations at roughly the same time—in mid-July—and both had a military presence in Angola by early September. How the cooperation between them unfolded remains murky. Stockwell writes that the South Africans "came into the conflict cautiously at first, watching the expanding U.S. program and timing their steps to the CIA's." According to Spies, "at the beginning, there were no direct contacts between the two governments at the usual Foreign Ministry and ambassadorial levels." An important role was played by Zambia. "Between July and December 1975," Bridgland writes, "Brand Fourie, then the top civil servant in the South African Foreign Ministry, made more than twenty clandestine trips to Zambia to liaise with Kaunda and Jean Wilkowski, the US ambassador to Lusaka. Wilkowski, big and bossy and with all the mannerisms of an English girl guide leader, was an almost constant presence in Kaunda's State House headquarters at the time."[122]

The SADF and the CIA did more than work side by side in Angola. When the first U.S. weapons started arriving at Kinshasa's airport, the CIA station in Kinshasa began "pleading for airplanes to fly military supplies to the FNLA and UNITA bases inside Angola," Stockwell explains. The Pentagon refused to lend its planes, and so as early as August a loose cooperative effort began: "The South African Air Force . . . the Zairian Air Force . . . and CIA planes on contract all made deliveries into Angola on behalf of the anti-MPLA coalition," DIA official Thom writes. "South Africa was isolated," General Viljoen explained many years later. "Although it was done secretly, it was good for South Africa to be cooperating with a big force like the U.S., even though it was clandestine."[123]

Weapons and instructors were not enough, however, to stem the tide. By early October 1975, with independence day looming, the MPLA was winning. The first clash between South Africans and FAPLA occurred on October 5, when UNITA forces led by a SADF major and nineteen South African advisers manning a handful of armored cars confronted an MPLA advance on Nova Lisboa, Savimbi's capital. The battle "made it clear that UNITA . . . was not able to resist the FAPLA without help," Spies writes. A few South Africans could not redress the balance. "The choice lay between active South African military participation on the one hand and—in effect—acceptance of an MPLA victory on the other."[124] Unable to countenance the latter, Pretoria escalated. A South African column (called Zulu) entered Angola from Namibia on October 14.

Pretoria's decision to send troops into Angola, unlike the decision to provide weapons, had been sharply debated among the few principals who were in on the secret. The driving force in favor of escalation was the military, led by Defense Minister P. W. Botha; Hendrik van den Bergh was opposed, as was Foreign Minister Hilgard Muller, who was, however, largely excluded from the decision. Vorster, a strong prime minister, sided with Botha.[125] Among the key considerations reassuring him was the fact that South Africa was not alone. Key African presidents (Mobutu, Kaunda, Senghor, and Ivory Coast's Félix Houphouët-Boigny) were urging Pretoria to intervene.[126] And, above all, there was the United States. "The United States, at the highest level, requested assistance, or rather requested South Africa to go in and assist UNITA," a senior South African official recalled. But the story is shrouded in obfuscation. Kissinger maintains his total innocence. "We had no foreknowledge of South Africa's intentions, and in no way cooperated with it militarily," he told Congress in 1976. Twenty years later, in his memoirs, he was even more specific: he learned of the invasion only at the end of October, two weeks after it had begun.[127]

Other U.S. officials have been more forthcoming. Chester Crocker wrote, "The United States and other Western governments had done nothing to discourage Pretoria's mid-October intervention." Stockwell, after writing that "I saw no evidence that the United States formally encouraged them [the South Africans] to join the conflict," added: "On two occasions the BOSS director visited Washington and held secret meetings with [CIA Africa division chief] Jim Potts. . . . The COS, Pretoria, was ordered to brief BOSS about IAFEATURE, and nearly all CIA intelligence reports on the subject were relayed to Pretoria so his briefings would be accurate and up to date. . . . Thus, without any memos being written at CIA headquarters saying 'Let's coordinate with the South Africans,' coordination was effected at all CIA levels and the South Africans escalated their involvement in step with ours." Stockwell, a task force chief, was not in a position to know what went on at more exalted levels. He did not even know what Potts, who ran the operation and played his cards very close to his chest, told van den Bergh.[128] Ed Mulcahy, who was acting assistant secretary for African affairs, was also out of the loop. A few days after the South African invasion had begun, he recalled, "I was told by a very senior administration official that Kissinger should have let me know about the talks he was having with the South Africans. (The official didn't say whether Kissinger was having these talks directly or through back channels.)" The senior administration official was, apparently, very discreet, as was Mulcahy, twenty years later, in telling me about the episode. And so was Joe Sisco, under secretary of state in 1975. At the end of a one-hour conversation which was largely off the record, he summed up U.S.–South African cooperation in 1975 on Angola for the record. "A reasonable premise," he told me with a smile, "is that while it cannot be demonstrated that the administration explicitly took steps to encourage South Africa's intervention, it certainly did not discourage it."[129]

There is no smoking gun. We do not know whether any written document exists, for instance on the conversations between Potts and van den Bergh, nor do we know whether Kissinger used a back channel. South Africa's ambassador to the United States, Pik Botha, was not in on the secret until November and the U.S. ambassador, William Bowdler, has consistently refused to grant interviews. Fortunately for Kissinger, Pretoria reluctantly concluded that it must be discreet when it came to its foreign partners in the Angolan venture: "It is not in the general interest to say very much about this," Defense Minister Botha stated in late January 1976, and Vorster made the same point a few days later: "The Angola matter," he told Parliament, "is an exceptionally delicate matter. Even on this occasion there are things that I simply dare not say. South Africa's involvement was not an isolated involvement; others were also involved. I am not going to mention their names." On one occasion, however, P. W. Botha broke his silence. "Against which neighboring states have we ever taken aggressive steps?" he asked the South African Parliament on April 17, 1978. "I know of only one occasion in recent years," he said, "when we crossed a border and that was in the case of Angola when we did so with the approval and knowledge of the Americans. But they left us in the lurch. We are going to retell that story: the story must be told of how we, with their knowledge, went in there and operated in Angola with their knowledge, how they encouraged us to act and, when we had nearly reached the climax, we were ruthlessly left in the lurch."[130]

CHAPTER FOURTEEN
PRETORIA MEETS HAVANA

When the South African column, Zulu, entered Angola on October 14, the MPLA controlled the few towns, the major villages, and the few roads in the south of the country. It also held the entire coast from Namibia to Quifangondo, north of Luanda. UNITA's territory had shrunk to parts of central Angola, threatened by the FAPLA. In the north, the FAPLA's elite force, the Ninth Brigade, held back Roberto and his Zairean allies. It was still, however, a poor man's war. South of Luanda there were only weak FAPLA units, badly armed and poorly trained. They were strong enough to defeat UNITA, but were no match for the South Africans.

Zulu advanced at full speed, forty or forty-five miles a day, smashing through scant and ineffective resistance. For a few days the column moved west just north of the border, seizing Pereira de Eça on October 19 and Roçadas a day later.[1]

With the South African invasion, the second phase of the Angolan war began. Foreign troops would take center stage, as a bush war escalated into an East-West crisis. Scores of journalists descended on Angola, but covering the war proved extremely difficult. "A complete breakdown of internal communications, together with the withdrawal of all Portuguese forces from the interior of the country, makes it impossible to find out what the real military situation is," the London *Times* observed on November 6. "One of the more bizarre aspects of the war in Angola is that hardly anyone has seen it," the *New York Times* echoed two months later. "Journalists have been kept away from all fronts by the three warring factions."[2] Press coverage was correspondingly shallow. The best was provided by the *Rand Daily Mail* and the *Cape Times*, which were kept relatively well informed by South African officials, who also set strict limits on what could be published. The two Luanda dailies, *Diário de Luanda* and *Jornal de Angola*, are interesting only as mouthpieces of the MPLA. American newspapers are far more useful for their coverage of the debate in the United States about Ford's policy in Angola than for their coverage of the war.

The books and essays that deal with this second phase of the war—from the entry of Zulu in October 1975 to the South African retreat in late March 1976—reflect the dearth of available primary sources. The major exceptions are four accounts by South African authors: the two semiofficial histories of Operation Savannah by Spies and du Preez, and two books of memoirs by Commander Jan Breytenbach, who led one of Zulu's units. While these authors are frankly sympathetic to the South African viewpoint, their bias is tempered by their professionalism. Also useful are, with the same qualifications, the accounts of three well-connected South African journalists who specialized in military matters: Ian Uys, Helmoed-Römer Heitman, and Willem Steenkamp.[3]

It is these South African authors who make it possible to follow the advance of Zulu in the initial stages of the invasion. There were no journalists in southern Angola at the time—or, at least, none filed any report; the telephone system did not work, and press coverage was extremely hazy. The reports of the Cuban military mission are not informative (which is not surprising given that there were no Cubans in southern Angola), and declassified U.S. diplomatic reports are equally opaque.

THE SOUTH AFRICAN JUGGERNAUT

Zulu was composed of more than 1,000 black Angolans and a smaller number of white South African soldiers. The Angolans, led by SADF officers and noncommissioned officers, were FNLA guerrillas who had been trained by Breytenbach during the previous weeks, and former Flechas, a special military unit of black Angolans who had fought for the Portuguese during the war of independence, many of whom had fled after the fall of Caetano to Namibia, where the SADF had welcomed them and provided training.[4]

It is unclear how many SADF soldiers were initially in Zulu. Spies, the official historian of Operation Savannah, gives no figures. Du Preez mentions 150, but provides no details. What is known is that Pretoria immediately began sending reinforcements. Roçadas, for example, fell on October 20 to a battle group that had entered Angola soon after Zulu. This battle group, which included a squadron of armored cars, infantry, and a mortar unit, was, Breytenbach explains, "a purely South African force." After Roçadas, it became part of Zulu.[5]

Furthermore, in mid-October SADF planes transported about 100 South African soldiers, twenty-two Eland-90 armored cars, and other war matériel for a second task force, Foxbat, to Silva Porto, Savimbi's military headquarters in central Angola. Foxbat absorbed the UNITA troops that the South Africans had been training at Silva Porto and began receiving SADF reinforcements within a few days. It is likely that by the end of October more than 1,000 SADF soldiers were in Angola (most with Zulu, the others with Foxbat) and their number was rapidly increasing.[6]

The size of the SADF presence was a function of Pretoria's evolving aims. The plan for Operation Savannah, which had been approved by Vorster in late September, included four phases, each more ambitious than the preceding one. The first three aimed to eliminate the FAPLA from, respectively, the border area, the southwestern region, and, finally, the central region. "Phase 4 provided for the capture of Luanda, the ultimate military objective," South African scholar Deon Geldenhuys writes. Vorster called the shots, deciding whether and when to move from one phase to the next.[7]

"The advance was far more rapid than expected," Breytenbach recalls. After the fall of Roçadas, on October 20, Zulu veered northwest deep into Angola. Sá

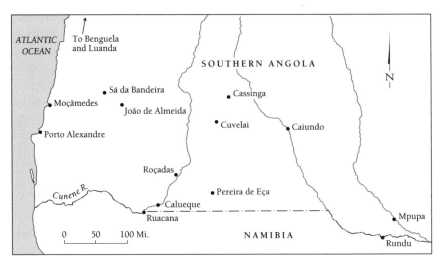

The South African Advance into Southern Angola

da Bandeira fell on October 24, Moçâmedes, the major port of southern Angola, on October 28. "Phases 1 and 2 of the operational plan had been successfully concluded," du Preez writes. It had taken less than two weeks.[8]

"Zulu's spectacular early success in southern Angola can be attributed to several factors," DIA analyst Thom explains. "First was the size of its units. . . . Second, Zulu troops were well organized, trained, and led by capable SADF officers and NCOs. Third, they had the advantage of aerial resupply. . . . Finally, as the campaign developed, increasingly better weapons were provided." The South Africans' Eland-90 armored cars, heavy guns, well-trained crews, and planes were technologically far superior to anything the FAPLA could muster. The weather cooperated: "We were deep into October and the rains had not yet come," Breytenbach recalled.[9]

The MPLA tried to put the best possible face on it. On November 1, its spokesperson downplayed FAPLA's retreat and emphasized that "the invasion exposes the dirty plot the imperialists have been hiding for a long time."[10]

The South Africans told a different story. Their soldiers had been ordered to say they were mercenaries from any English-speaking country but South Africa.[11] This deception was made easier by the absence of Portuguese troops along Zulu's path. By mid-October there were only 10,000 Portuguese soldiers still in Angola, and they were passive spectators eagerly awaiting November 11, independence day, when the last of them could leave the country. As their numbers shrank, so too did the area in which they were stationed. During the second week of October they withdrew from southern Angola, except for a 150-man paratroop unit and a corvette at Moçâmedes.[12] On the evening of October 27, Spies writes, the Portuguese captain in command of the paratroop unit and a naval officer "with a white flag" went to meet Zulu as it approached the town.

The captain "was clearly loath to get involved in a battle," and the naval officer even more so. Speaking English, Zulu's commander, Colonel Koos van Heerden, ordered the Portuguese captain "to keep his soldiers . . . in their barracks if they wanted to avoid being shot at and threatened the naval officer 'to blow his ship out of the sea' if it was still in the harbor at daybreak. When the sun rose, the ship was gone." After Zulu entered Moçâmedes early on October 28, the Portuguese paratroopers left on two cargo planes, leaving their supplies behind.[13] Upon his arrival in Luanda, the Portuguese captain stated that the "column is led by English speaking officers who, he believes, are South Africans."[14] Deaf to the MPLA's assertions that South Africa had invaded, the Western press explained that FNLA and UNITA troops, stiffened by South African and Portuguese mercenaries, were on the offensive.[15]

Even as Moçâmedes fell, the commander of the Cuban military mission (MMCA), Díaz Argüelles, underestimated the gravity of the threat. There were no Cubans in southern Angola, so he had no clear idea of the strength of the column and he did not realize that it included South African troops. In his analysis of the month of October he concluded that the MPLA's successes elsewhere in Angola were "more important than the advantage gained by the enemy by its capture of the south. Despite the fiasco in the south, the MPLA still has the advantage, ten days before independence. The enemy, ill prepared and dispirited, including the Zairean army units . . . is giving us breathing space to train the [MPLA] battalions."[16] By the time Díaz Argüelles wrote this report, Zulu was racing toward the coastal city of Benguela, an MPLA stronghold 218 miles north of Moçâmedes.

On November 2–3, at the crossroads town of Catengue, 43 miles southeast of Benguela, several hundred FAPLA tried to halt Zulu's advance. For the third time since the onset of the civil war (the first had been at Quifangondo on October 23), Cubans—thirty-five or forty instructors from CIR 2, which was located south of Benguela—participated in the fighting. "We were facing the best organized and heaviest FAPLA opposition to date," Breytenbach wrote. But the FAPLA and Cubans were outgunned and outnumbered, and they withdrew. Four Cubans died, seven were wounded, and thirteen were missing in action.[17]

In Kinshasa, *Elima* praised "the troops of the FNLA and UNITA, whose striking power and cunning have stunned the observers." Savimbi vowed, "Some time ago I promised you that there would be military surprises in Angola. We are now witnessing the disintegration of Neto's troops on Angolan territory. Today I promise you even greater surprises before November 11, because we know that there are only nine days left."[18]

The news of FAPLA's retreat from Catengue shocked Benguela, where the MPLA enjoyed "strong support," as the *Rand Daily Mail* reported. "We had thought that we couldn't lose—now the enemy was coming to us!" recalled Conceição Neto, a young member of the local MPLA militia. Before daybreak on November 5, the FAPLA abandoned Benguela, as well as Lobito, Angola's major commercial port, nineteen miles north. Conceição Neto left as well, with several friends from the militia.[19] But the South Africans, "sobered by the strength of the resistance at Catengue," did not enter Benguela immediately. They asked Pretoria for heavier guns and were assured that they would be sent at once. When Conceição Neto arrived in Lobito at dawn on November 6, "the city was paralyzed, waiting." She fled north to Novo Redondo. That same day, Zulu entered Benguela. On the seventh, Lobito fell. Only the fourth and final phase of the South African plan was left: Luanda.[20]

Pretoria decided to push forward. On the day Lobito fell, Breytenbach recalls, a C-160 brought "the high brass . . . we discussed further operations in a relaxed atmosphere, the Brigadier [General] as pleased as punch on the progress so far. . . . We were, evidently, on our way to Luanda. Fresh troops were being deployed from South Africa and the whole campaign was beginning to look more South African than Angolan." The American and French governments, Spies explains, pressed the South Africans to keep going. "Both asked South Africa to 'chalk up a success against Luanda.' "[21]

Roberto was also on his way to Luanda, or so he hoped. On November 6, the FNLA had attacked Quifangondo again, only to be repelled by the MPLA,[22] but Roberto remained confident: U.S. planes were bringing more weapons to Kinshasa, South African planes were helping ferry these weapons to Roberto (and to Savimbi) in Angola, and Mobutu was sending fresh troops. "Zaire Joins Angola War," was the headline in the *Cape Times* on November 7, as it announced that "at least two battalions of President Mobutu's infantry are backing up the FNLA force poised to launch an attack on the capital."[23] Roberto was also buoyed by the more discreet arrival of twenty-six South African military personnel, including General Ben de Wet Roos, several officers, and heavy weapons specialists, who flew in with some heavy guns for the final assault on Luanda. Also joining Roberto, at his headquarters in Ambriz, were several CIA paramilitary officers.[24]

Some 2,000 Portuguese troops remained in Luanda,[25] but a spokesman of the Portuguese high commissioner announced that they would not intervene if the FNLA attacked. The fundamental task of the Portuguese troops in Luanda, Vitor Crespo, Portugal's minister of foreign aid, explained, was to protect "the Portuguese citizens who were still being evacuated."[26] On November 3, all evacuations ended and U.S. consul general Killoran and the other eight members of the consulate's staff flew out of Luanda as ordered by the State Department. There were no U.S. officials left in the city.[27]

The MPLA had started preparing for the independence celebrations in Luanda. "Squads of street cleaners are attempting to remove the rubbish that has accumulated during weeks of neglect," the London *Times* reported. Beneath the surface, "The tension in Luanda is terrible," a Cuban journalist wrote. The enemy was threatening from the north and rolling in from the south. The MPLA said very little about the South Africans' advance, and rumors spread. "Every day in Luanda the most diverse and at times ridiculous rumors swirl around, and they are unfortunately believed by many," *Jornal de Angola*, one of the two dailies still being published in the capital, reported on November 7. "Let's not help the enemy any longer," it admonished. "Let's denounce the rumormongers." But it said nothing about the enemy advancing from the south.[28]

OPERATION CARLOTA

That same day, November 7, Cuban soldiers boarded two planes for Angola. Fidel Castro had decided to send troops to Angola on November 4: a 652-man battalion of the elite Special Forces of the Ministry of the Interior would fly to Luanda, and an artillery regiment would follow by sea.[29] Operation Carlota had begun.

In Havana I have been unable to see any document about the Cuban decision to send troops or to interview any of the men who made it. According to Michael Wolfers and Jane Bergerol, two journalists who had good contacts with the MPLA, as Zulu was closing in on Benguela the MPLA's political bureau "met in an emergency session" and listened as Neto announced that they had to ask Cuba for troops. "There was unanimous agreement," Wolfers and Bergerol write. A member of the MPLA's Central Committee, Onambwe, "was entrusted with the task of bearing the request for help to Cuba."[30]

I hoped, therefore, that interviews with MPLA leaders in Luanda would allow me to shed some light on the Cuban decision. I was particularly eager to hear Onambwe's account of his conversation with Castro.

Onambwe, however, categorically denied that he had flown to Havana to deliver a request for Cuban troops. He told me he had not gone to Cuba until mid-December, and then only as a member of the MPLA delegation led by Lúcio Lara to the First Congress of the Cuban Communist Party (PCC). Xiyetu, chief of staff of the FAPLA, and two members of the MPLA's political bureau in 1975— Lara and Ludy Kissassunda—adamantly confirmed Onambwe's account.[31]

The MPLA's political bureau, they explained, never formally requested Cuban troops. The leaders of the MPLA and of the FAPLA informally discussed the need for Cuban reinforcements with the Cuban military mission (MMCA). The Cuban instructors agreed. " 'To mount an effective resistance we need a lot more aid,' " they told Lara. From Havana, the high command of the armed forces told the MMCA to prepare to defend the main approaches to Luanda and to continue the work in the CIRs. "We are studying the possibility of sending reinforcements," it added. After Catengue, Díaz Argüelles urged Castro for troops.[32]

Castro would have preferred to wait until independence, but the battle of Catengue changed his mind. "It was then that we understood that the South Africans had invaded," Risquet recalled. Castro realized that unless he acted at once, the South Africans would take Luanda. He decided to send the Special Forces and the artillery regiment. "We told the MMCA to inform the Angolans and to urge them to take control of the airport. We had to choose: either withdraw the instructors and abandon Angola, or send in the Special Forces." The decision was made hurriedly and under pressure, with the feeling that time was running out.

The sudden arrival of Cuban troops in November 1975 halted the South African advance on Luanda, doomed Kissinger's covert operation in Angola, and stunned U.S. officials. Americans found it hard to believe that the small Caribbean island would dare send troops to faraway Angola on its own initiative; it made more sense, and was more satisfying, to conclude that Castro was just a Soviet proxy, acting on Brezhnev's orders. No one said so more loudly than Henry Kissinger. But Havana had acted without even informing Moscow, and twenty-five years later Kissinger wrote in his memoirs that Castro "was probably the most genuine revolutionary leader then [1975] in power." (Cartoon by Wright for the *Miami News;* reprinted in the *Washington Post,* December 7, 1975).

It was taken by Fidel Castro without consultation with the political bureau, probably after speaking with his closest advisers, particularly his brother Raúl.[33]

Castro was convinced that the United States was involved in the South African invasion. As he later told Senator Frank Church (D.-Idaho), he could "not believe that South Africa, . . . always . . . so cautious on such matters, would have sent forces without the complicity of Kissinger." Nevertheless, given the recent U.S. debacle in Vietnam, the recession in the United States, Moscow's achievement of strategic parity, and Ford's lack of a political mandate, he considered a U.S. military response (in Angola or in Cuba) to the dispatch of Cuban troops unlikely. He did expect Washington to apply political pressure on him, and he was worried that Pretoria, urged on by Washington and possibly Paris, would escalate its involvement and that his troops might face the full force of the South African army.[34]

The Cubans assert that they did not inform the Soviets until after the decision had been made. "That was a decision of ours," Castro has said. "The only thing that came from the Soviet Union was worries. They conveyed them to us in 1975, but it was an absolutely free and sovereign decision by our country."[35] This may seem surprising, given the risks of the operation and the closeness of Cuban-Soviet ties. Soviet sources, however, confirm the Cuban account. Arkady Shevchenko, who was an adviser of Soviet foreign minister Andrei Gromyko in 1970–73 and then undersecretary-general of the United Nations until 1978, when he defected to the United States, writes that in 1976 Vasily Kuznetsov, acting foreign minister, asked him to join a group reviewing Soviet policy in Africa. Shevchenko asked Kuznetsov, " 'How did we persuade the Cubans to provide their contingent?' . . . Kuznetsov laughed . . . [and] told me that the idea for the large-scale military operation had originated in Havana, not Moscow." Likewise, Anatoly Dobrynin, former Soviet ambassador to the United States, states in his memoirs: the Cubans sent their troops "on their own initiative and without consulting us." Even Kissinger, who liked to dismiss the Cubans as Soviet proxies, has reconsidered. "At the time, we thought he [Castro] was operating as a Soviet surrogate. We could not imagine that he would act so provocatively so far from home unless he was pressured by Moscow to repay the Soviet Union for its military and economic support. Evidence now available suggests that the opposite was the case."[36]

There are probably two reasons why "Castro acted without prior consultation with Moscow" (to quote yet another Soviet official). On the one hand, there was very little time—the South Africans were closing in on Luanda; on the other, Castro had made his decision. Consulting the Soviets would run the risk of a negative or dilatory answer; the previous August, when Castro had wanted to send troops to Angola, Brezhnev had said no. Better, then, to act first and tell the Soviets later. At the same time, the very closeness of the relationship may have led Castro to be confident that, confronted with the fait accompli, Moscow would support him. "They were told quickly," Risquet said, "because we wanted their help." In Moscow the news "was greeted without enthusiasm," a senior Soviet official recalled.[37]

At 6:45 P.M. on November 4, a few hours after Castro had decided to send troops to Angola, a Britannia turbo prop left Havana for Brazzaville with about 100 Cubans on board. These were the heavy weapons specialists that the MPLA had requested in late September. Also on board was Major Lucas Molina, the first officer de enlace sent to Angola.[38] (Officers de enlace were sent by the Cuban high command to a war zone to observe the situation, have access to all information, speak to the local commanders, and fly back and report to Havana.)

To reach Luanda or Brazzaville from Havana, the old, lumbering Britannia had to refuel twice. Cuba had an agreement with Barbados that its passenger planes could refuel at Bridgetown. After a brief stopover there and a much longer stop in Bissau, the plane landed at Brazzaville on November 6 at 7:30 P.M.

(local time). "Ambassador Columbié and the entire embassy staff were waiting for us," Molina wrote in his report. Columbié had instructions to send several of the Cubans to Pointe Noire, where they would be trained by Soviet instructors in the use of a new weapon, the Flechas C-2M, an improved version of the surface-to-air missiles that the Cubans had used in Guinea-Bissau in 1973 and 1974. (The training had to take place in Pointe Noire because the Soviets refused to send military personnel to Angola until November 11, with the sole exception of Yuri.) Molina and the remaining Cubans flew a few hours later to Luanda in a small plane piloted by Cubans. They arrived on November 7.[39] That same day, in Cuba, the first company of Special Forces, 158 men dressed in civilian clothes, boarded two Britannias for Angola.[40]

Before they left, Castro addressed them. "He spoke above all about the South African invasion," recalled one of the officers, René Hernández Gattorno. "He said that some of the Cuban instructors had died, that it was a difficult situation, that we must stop the South Africans before they reached Luanda, and that many of us would not return. He said that it was very hard for him to say this and not go with us." Castro, perhaps remembering Che's experience in Zaire, told the Special Forces that if Luanda fell they would fight a guerrilla war as long as the MPLA fought, but that if the MPLA stopped fighting, they would withdraw. The only possible safe haven was Zambia, where Cuba had just opened an embassy, but it would be very difficult to get there. As the battalion's deputy commander, José Luis Padrón, pointed out, "It was a risky operation. The Special Forces had no rear guard; there was no way to evacuate them. Once we got to Angola, the door closed behind us."[41]

The flight took almost forty-eight hours. After refueling in Barbados and Bissau, they waited for nightfall in Brazzaville, and then flew without lights along the coastline to Luanda.[42]

The MPLA had taken over the airport of Luanda in the early hours of November 6. ("The Portuguese withdrew after what was reported to be an exchange of epithets and some firing," the *New York Times* wrote.) The next day the FAPLA replaced the Portuguese in the port of Luanda after both sides faced each other with guns at the ready. "Dr. Neto's forces," *Le Monde* noted, "are now in position to receive the war matériel they need for the defense of their capital."[43]

The two Britannias landed at Luanda airport in the evening of November 9. The Special Forces immediately went to Grafanil, the military camp on the outskirts of Luanda that housed the MMCA. There they donned their uniforms and received their weapons. A few hours later—shortly after 8 A.M.—the company was in position behind the defenders of Quifangondo, "ready to intervene if the enemy succeeded in breaking through our defenses."[44]

THE BATTLE OF QUIFANGONDO

Holden Roberto had decreed that his forces would take Luanda on November 10, on the eve of independence. "In addition to his horde of partly trained and

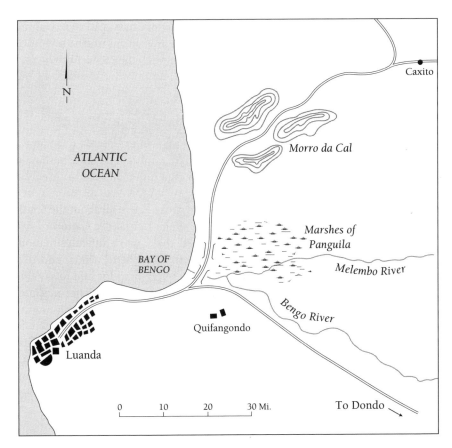

The Battle of Quifangondo, Angola

mostly completely unsophisticated Bakongo tribesmen," South African military analyst Steenkamp writes, "he had about 120 Portuguese mercenaries, his contingent of faint-hearted Zaireans and a few resident advisers, among them the South African group led by General Roos and a small CIA contingent." The South Africans and the Portuguese were in charge of the tanks and the artillery. On October 25 and again on November 4 the director of operations of the South African army, General Viljoen, flew to Ambriz to speak with Roberto. "Viljoen's patience with Roberto was astonishing," two South African analysts observe. But it was to no avail.[45] "Unlike Savimbi who . . . relied on his South African advisers' professional knowledge, Roberto insisted on going his own way," Steenkamp laments. Between Roberto and Luanda lay Quifangondo, a village in the middle of a broad marshy plain with one narrow road through it. "In vain Roberto's Portuguese officers suggested a flanking attack through the swamps, while Roos mooted a wide swing around in the east. . . . Roberto shrugged off all such subterfuges in favor of an advance straight down what later became known as 'Death Road.'"[46]

Angolan rebel leader Holden Roberto had decreed that he would seize Luanda, the stronghold of the rival Popular Movement for the Liberation of Angola (MPLA), by November 10, 1975, the eve of independence. He had confidence in his army of 2,000 Angolans, 1,200 Zairean soldiers supplied by his Zairean patron Mobutu, 120 Portuguese mercenaries, and a few South African and CIA advisers. But on November 10, at Quifangondo, thirteen miles north of Luanda, a smaller force of MPLA guerrillas stiffened by Cuban artillerymen turned Roberto's advance into a rout. In 1977 Fidel Castro visited Quifangondo, where Ndalu, who had been the chief of staff of the MPLA troop there, explains the course of the battle. Angola's president, Agostinho Neto, stands to the left of Castro. Ndalu is to Castro's right.

And death road it was. "God made Quifangondo for a victorious battle," Risquet observed.[47] When I visited Quifangondo, in 1997, I understood what he meant. The village is protected on all sides. The river Bengo flows two and a half miles to the northwest. A sole bridge spans it. All around, marshes. To the south, a small hill allows an unimpeded view of the plain beyond. A sign, half lost in the grass, reminds the visitor that this was the observation point for the FAPLA and Cubans during the battle of Quifangondo. On November 7 the *La Plata* brought six Soviet BM-21s (multiple rocket launchers) to Luanda, and they were immediately sent to Quifangondo, where they were manned by twenty Cuban specialists from the group that had flown in with Molina.[48]

At dawn on November 10, three South African bombers flew over the FAPLA positions at Quifangondo. It was the first time in the war that planes were used to attack the enemy, but the desire to maintain deniability hindered the operation. The planes flew very high overhead, dropped only a few bombs, and flew away. None hit its target.[49]

Undeterred, Roberto ordered his men to attack. The CIA advisers "watched the column's movement across the valley," Stockwell writes.[50] Quifangondo was defended by 850 FAPLA, 200 Katangans, 88 Cubans, and Yuri, the Soviet adviser. (Behind the first line of defense were 120 Cubans from the just arrived Special Forces.) The Cubans were in charge of the heavy weapons: the BM-21s and 120-mm mortars. The BM-21s "played havoc with the morale of Roberto's mainly unsophisticated troops," Steenkamp writes. "Artillery fire rained on the attackers as they approached the Bengo river, and one by one the armoured cars were knocked out. . . . Soon soldiers began trickling away, including all those detailed to help the South African artillerymen. . . . When the trickle turned into a flood, Roos ordered the artillerymen to fall back."[51]

INDEPENDENCE

That same day, at 6 P.M., "one of the most unusual acts of decolonization ever witnessed in Africa" (as the *Times* deemed it) took place in Luanda. In a brief ceremony at the governor's palace "at which no Angolans were present," the Portuguese high commissioner, Admiral Leonel Cardoso, announced that in the name of the Portuguese president he was transferring sovereignty to the "Angolan people." Cardoso's statement, noted the *Times*, "was in accordance with Portugal's policy not to hand over power to any one of the three liberation movements."[52]

The Portuguese flag was lowered, and Cardoso left the palace in a black limousine, surrounded by his troops. Several helicopters flew over the column as it made its way to the harbor, where three troop transports were waiting. "That was how Portugal today ended, with little glory and certainly no pomp and ceremony, nearly five centuries of colonial rule here," Agence France Press mused.[53]

A few hours later, at midnight, "a huge cheer was heard," the *World* reported from Luanda, "as Dr. Neto announced: 'In the name of the people of Angola, before Africa and the world, I proclaim the independence of Angola." The People's Republic of Angola (PRA) was born.[54] For their part, FNLA and UNITA announced the formation of a Democratic People's Republic of Angola with a temporary capital at Huambo (the former Nova Lisboa), but the representatives of the two movements were unable to conceal their distaste for each other. It was "a totally unnatural alliance," writes Savimbi's biographer, "urged upon reluctant partners by the CIA and other clandestine foreign services." The *Rand Daily Mail* observed, "even if the FNLA takes Luanda soon and the MPLA is routed, a fight to the finish between UNITA and the FNLA cannot be ruled out." As if fulfilling the prophecy, FNLA and UNITA "engaged in bitter fighting" in Huambo on November 10.[55]

THE BATTLE OF CABINDA

In the meantime, the Cubans and the FAPLA were fighting to maintain their control of Cabinda. "It is increasingly likely," U.S. intelligence had noted in late September, "that Mobutu will move to secure the Cabinda enclave, notwithstanding the certain international repercussions of such a move." In fact, Mobutu was acting with Washington's consent. "Seeing his chance in October to annex the MPLA-held Cabinda," Stockwell wrote, "Mobutu approached the CIA. We promptly flew in a one-thousand-man arms package for use in the invasion, and CIA officers of the Kinshasa station began to visit the FLEC training camp to coordinate." The invasion was originally set for October, the CIA reported, "but was postponed at least twice because of logistic [sic] problems." By late October, a heterogeneous force had congregated near Cabinda's borders: Zairean soldiers, FLEC guerrillas, and a dozen French mercenaries sent by the notorious Bob Denard, who had been a leader of the CIA's "White Giants" in Zaire, to give the FLEC some backbone.[56]

"These Frenchmen may in fact have been hired by the French intelligence service [SDECE]," Stockwell wrote. "French agents were appearing in Kinshasa and in Angola, but CIA intelligence on the subject was sketchy."[57] It was a good guess. Denard was not just a mercenary. Colonel Maurice Robert, who headed SDECE's Africa division from 1960 to 1973, told a French tribunal in March 1993 that he had recruited Denard in 1968 and "subcontracted" covert actions to him. Denard told the tribunal: "From 1968, I always had direct personal contact with the officer-in-charge, Colonel Maurice Robert. Every time I had an operation that was within the political framework, I had first to get the green light from the French services. Well, sometimes it was more like an amber light, but I never did—nor ever would—act against France." In the case of Angola, he added, he was "in close contact" with SDECE.[58]

Beginning on November 8, the mercenaries, Mobutu's troops, and FLEC launched an attack on Cabinda, which was defended by approximately 1,000 FAPLA and 232 Cubans. In the early hours of November 12, after Quifangondo had been defended and independence declared, the Cubans and FAPLA went on the offensive in the enclave. Within a few hours, Zaireans, FLEC, and mercenaries had withdrawn in disorder across the Zairean border. "The operation has failed miserably," wrote René Dulac, the leader of the mercenaries sent by Denard. This was "a blow to Mobutu," the CIA stated.[59] Nothing, however, stopped Gulf Oil, except President Ford. "Cabinda's oil production, entirely from offshore fields, has not been seriously affected by the military situation," the CIA reported on November 14, and was running "to about 140,000 barrels a day."[60] But a month later, at the request of the Ford administration, Gulf suspended operations in Cabinda and put the $125 million in taxes and royalties it owed the State of Angola in escrow, to be paid when Angola had a government "generally recognized by the world community."[61]

THE CENTRAL FRONT

The Special Forces had not been needed to defeat Mobutu and Roberto in Cabinda and at Quifangondo, but a far greater challenge threatened the MPLA

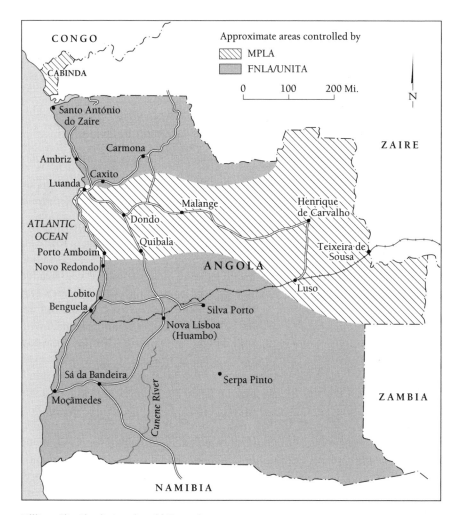

Military Situation in Angola, mid-November 1975

from the south. On November 10, Zulu began advancing from Lobito toward Novo Redondo, eighty-three miles to the north, on the coastal road to Luanda. The next day, the column was ambushed fifteen miles south of Novo Redondo by the Cuban instructors from the CIR of Benguela. The enemy was "well-dug and camouflaged," Breytenbach writes, and inflicted losses on Zulu with "accurate and effective" fire that delayed its advance for a few hours.[62] The Cubans then fell back to Novo Redondo, which a small group of FAPLA led by Commander Kassanje was preparing to defend. Kassanje had been the MPLA's political leader in Benguela; when Zulu had closed in on the city, he had fled to Novo Redondo, but he would not flee again. He organized the defense of Novo Redondo while the FAPLA commanders who had also fled from Benguela turned tail again, in disarray. "I saw Monty [Jorge de Morais, the commander of the central front] drive away, northward. Our confidence in the leaders of the FAPLA was zero, except for a few like Kassanje," recalled Conceição Neto, who spent independence day in Novo Redondo.[63] On November 12, she left the city in a pickup truck with seven or eight others; they drove north, toward Porto Amboim, thirty-seven miles from Novo Redondo, beyond the River Queve.

As we approached the bridge on the Queve, we suddenly saw the Cubans with two trucks and heavy weapons. They were alone, they had gotten out of the trucks, and they were there in the underbrush at the ready. It was a very sad moment, it filled us with shame: they were going to fight and we were fleeing, once again. We were convinced that all was lost, that there was no way to prevent the South Africans from reaching Luanda. We had also heard that north of Luanda the situation was very bad. So when we saw the Cubans coming to fight, we felt ashamed—ashamed and full of despair: we didn't think the Cubans could stop the South Africans.[64]

These Cubans were the Special Forces, who had left for Novo Redondo immediately after the battle of Quifangondo. A rough division of labor was being established: the Cubans went south, against the South Africans, and the FAPLA's elite Ninth Brigade remained in the north to counter Roberto.[65]

Through most of November 12, the FAPLA and the Cubans held Zulu at bay. Kassanje died fighting. Then they fell back. On November 13, Zulu occupied Novo Redondo.[66] "The fast moving armoured column spearheading the attack on Luanda has reached a crucial point in its advance on the capital," the *Cape Times* reported on November 14. The fall of Porto Amboim, just 160 miles south of Luanda, was imminent, it predicted. "The town is an important road junction," and after its fall the armored column would split in two parts, one going north to Luanda, the other northeast to Dondo, which controlled the electric supply of the capital. The *Rand Daily Mail* had already announced that Porto Amboim had fallen: "A fast-moving armored column, including former Portuguese officers and White mercenaries, is closing in on Luanda from Porto Amboim." Savimbi tasted victory: Luanda "will be completely isolated," he promised, "without food, electricity or water."[67]

Between Novo Redondo and Porto Amboim flows the Queve. It was there, on the northern shore of the river, that the Cubans made their stand after the fall of Novo Redondo. The second and third companies of the battalion of Special Forces, which arrived in Luanda from November 11 to 16, went straight to the Queve. They had to hold the line, they were told, "whatever the cost."[68]

Zulu advanced along the coastal road toward Porto Amboim; the Cubans blew up the bridge on the Queve. "Ahead we could see the bridge, well and truly destroyed," Breytenbach writes. "Our progress to Port Amboim and points further north had been effectively stopped along that particular route." Leaving some forces behind at Novo Redondo, Zulu turned east, searching for a road to Luanda. But Díaz Argüelles shifted his forces—the Special Forces and the instructors from the CIR of Benguela—eastward, toward the town of Quibala,

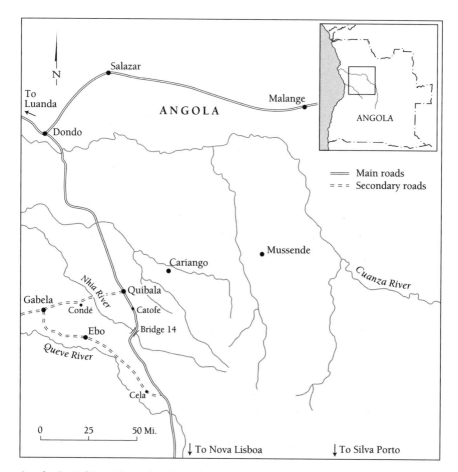

Angola, Central Front, November–December 1975

which sat astride the only other paved road to Luanda. "There were three or four bridges between Porto Amboim and Quibala," the deputy commander of the Special Forces, Padrón, recalled. "We blew them up and gained time." Díaz Argüelles left a few men in key locations while half his force shadowed the South Africans on their march eastward. "We were defending a 100-mile-long front with a few hundred Cubans and about 400 FAPLA," Padrón explained.[69] The South Africans overestimated the enemy's strength. Reflecting the SADF's perception, Steenkamp writes, "a strong enemy force occupied the northern bank [of the Queve]." The weather helped the defenders. "The rainy season had started in all earnest," Breytenbach writes. "Inland, in the valleys, the going would be muddy and soft."[70]

The South Africans were impressed by the Cubans. After a detailed briefing from Vorster, the *Cape Times* reported on November 21 that "FNLA and UNITA commanders greatly admired the courage of what they said were mercenaries from Cuba fighting with the MPLA." (Major South African newspapers were briefed by government officials about the SADF presence in Angola, were forbidden under the country's stringent security laws to mention it, and used FNLA and UNITA as code words for SADF.) The official South African historian of the war, Spies, writes, "The Cubans rarely surrendered and, quite simply, fought cheerfully until death."[71]

THE BATTLE OF EBO

Seeking to outflank Díaz Argüelles, the South Africans shifted their focus to Quibala. Foxbat, the battle group that had been pushing northward from Silva Porto, had already occupied the town of Cela, south of Quibala, on the road to Luanda. Cela, which had a very good airfield, became the headquarters of Foxbat. Reinforcements from the coast (from Zulu) and from Namibia streamed into it. "The war had achieved a more South African flavour over the past few weeks or so," writes Breytenbach, who arrived at Cela on November 23 from Novo Redondo. "In fact it struck me forcibly that most of the troops around Cela were white troops and not blacks." Cargo planes from Namibia "droned in and out of Cela in accordance with a steady schedule," Breytenbach noted, but when he arrived at Cela "there was a panic on."[72] The South Africans had just suffered a bloody defeat, near the village of Ebo.

Trying to surprise the enemy, Foxbat had sent a column on a winding road from Cela northwest toward Gabela; from there it was to have headed east to Quibala. Díaz Argüelles, however, outsmarted them. "We heard that the South Africans were advancing toward Gabela," recalled René Hernández Gattorno, who was with Díaz Argüelles at Catofe, the forward position of Quibala.[a] Díaz Argüelles decided to reconnoiter the likely route the South Africans would take. One and a half miles north of Ebo, on the road to Gabela, a small wooden bridge crossed the Mabassa, a narrow but deep river. "'Okay René,'" Díaz Argüelles told Hernández Gattorno, "This is where we've got to stop them."[73] The ambush was laid. Hidden along the shore, seventy Cubans, manning the BM-21s and antitank rockets, waited, while a group of FAPLA infantry was ready to fight if the South Africans crossed the river.[74]

In the early morning of November 23, the South Africans advanced toward the bridge. First came the armored cars, then the infantry and the artillery. "'I'm at the bridge. There's nothing on it. I'm going on,'" the South African commander in the lead car radioed. The next moment, his car was hit. The battle was on. "The enemy advanced with the infantry and the armored cars against our positions," Díaz Argüelles reported. White South Africans manned the

a. When Cuba decided to send troops to Angola, it also appointed a more senior officer, *primer comandante* Leopoldo Cintra Frías, to head the MMCA. Díaz Argüelles became the commander of the central front. He was killed on December 11, 1975.

armored cars and artillery; the infantry was black—UNITA and FNLA—with white officers and noncommissioned officers.[75]

By 4 P.M. the battle had ended. One Cuban had died and five had been wounded. The FAPLA, which had not had to fight, suffered no casualties. According to Hernández Gattorno, the South Africans and their allies suffered more than thirty dead and thirty wounded. Not so, writes Breytenbach, who spoke with the survivors shortly after the battle: the column's casualties were "between 80 and 90 killed or wounded." They also lost seven or eight armored cars.[76]

"The sun set that evening on a black Sunday for South Africans," du Preez intoned. Díaz Argüelles, on the other hand, was ebullient. "I don't think they'll attack again," he wrote the new head of the MMCA. "But don't worry: if they do, they won't get through."[77]

Two decades later, Iko Carreira, who was the MPLA's minister of defense in 1975, wrote: "The battle of Ebo was a turning point for Angola, and the victory was due, above all, to Díaz Argüelles, who became a legend in modern Angolan history."[78]

Breytenbach arrived at Cela just in time to witness the precipitous retreat of the column from Ebo. "Guns and armored cars careered past us heading for the rear, followed by infantry in civilian trucks. . . . Blood was dripping from one of the trucks which was filled with wounded." Shocked by this first defeat, overestimating the number of enemy troops, and fearing a counteroffensive, Foxbat dug in, preparing to repel an attack that never came, unaware that their humiliation had been inflicted by only seventy Cubans. "The battle of Ebo unsettled the South Africans. They stopped their offensive. This was a mistake," Padrón remarked.[79]

This pause in the offensive gave the Cubans time to build up their forces. There were approximately 1,300 Cubans in Angola,[80] including a few hundred in Cabinda and north of Luanda, and the MMCA was anxiously awaiting the arrival of the artillery regiment that Castro had ordered to Angola on November 4: 1,253 men with heavy weapons who had left Cuba on board the *Vietnam Heroico*, the *Imías*, and the *Océano Pacífico* from November 11 to 13. The three ships reached Luanda between November 27 and December 1.[81]

The MMCA was also waiting for more Soviet weapons. While the weapons were sent to the MPLA, it was understood that they were also for the Cubans; indeed, in many cases they were the only ones who knew how to operate them. "The Soviet embassy in Brazzaville is handling Soviet aid to Angola," Ambassador Columbié reported on November 28. "The Soviet military specialists in Luanda [who had begun arriving after independence day] report to the Soviet military attaché in Brazzaville [Colonel Vladimir Saenko], and it is the Soviet ambassador [Afanasenko] here [Brazzaville] who is in contact with Neto and who lets Moscow know what aid the MPLA needs from the USSR." On November 21, Afanasenko, who had just returned from Luanda, told Columbié that the head of the MMCA had informed him that the Cuban troops "required certain weapons urgently and that he was going to ask Moscow to send them." Afanasenko added, somewhat cryptically, "that to render effective aid to Angola it was necessary for Fidel Castro himself to make the necessary arrangements with Moscow."[82]

Colonel Saenko, who had accompanied Afanasenko to Luanda, told Columbié that the city "seemed tranquil, and the water and electricity services were functioning, but that the situation was difficult. He said that the enemy forces in the south are strong and well armed, and . . . are supplied by air and by ship . . . while our [Cuban] troops lack all sorts of weapons, vehicles, and men." Saenko also told Columbié "that the Cubans should get the weapons that are being sent because they are bearing the brunt of the fighting." On November 28, the new head of the MMCA, Abelardo (Furry) Colomé, met Afanasenko and Saenko and "suggested . . . the military equipment that was needed to start offensive operations," Columbié reported. "The ambassador seemed very receptive, jotted it down, and promised to inform Moscow that very night."[83]

On December 6, the FAPLA received an important shipment of Soviet weapons. "Our older brothers [the Russians] have said that ten planes with ten BM-21s, twenty 76-mm artillery pieces, twenty 82-mm mortars have arrived," Colomé cabled Havana. More weapons were promised: "Today I spoke with our older brothers; they told me that they had asked [Moscow] for twenty tanks and fifty vehicles to be sent immediately by plane, but they haven't received an answer yet. If they arrive, the situation will turn decisively in our favor."[84]

Colomé, the first deputy minister of the armed forces, had arrived in Luanda in late November to take charge of the MMCA. A few days later, Jorge Risquet, a member of the Secretariat of the PCC, arrived to head the Cuban civilian mission.[85] Risquet had long-standing ties with Neto and the MPLA: for eighteen months, beginning in mid-1965, he had headed the Cuban mission in the Congo, which had been the main rearguard base of the MPLA and Neto's home. Risquet had worked closely with the MPLA leadership, while Cuban instructors had trained the MPLA guerrillas in the Congo and fought alongside them in Cabinda. It was because of these long-standing ties that he had been selected to head the Cuban mission in Angola. "No one was allowed to volunteer to go to Angola because everyone wanted to go," he recalled. "So, when I brought a photo of Neto and me to a meeting of the political bureau, some people complained that I was volunteering, but I told them, 'I'm a special case, because I'm a friend of Neto.' "[b,86]

---

b. Until Risquet's arrival, Columbié was the key civilian official in Africa with responsibility for Angola. Cuba had had an ambassador in Zaire since 1974, Lazaro Mora, but he was an onlooker, because the MPLA's rear guard was the Congo, and Zaire was enemy territory. Except for a brief visit to Luanda in May 1975, in which he had no in-depth

Meanwhile more Cubans were arriving in Angola. Among them were reservists. "We included reservists because they have more training than regular soldiers," a Cuban officer explained. "The soldier is a recruit, an eighteen-year-old kid. The reservist is a more mature man who has had three years of military service and regular training after that."[87]

The diaries of two reservists tell how they ended up in Angola. Before dawn on November 5 they were told to report to a military camp in the suburbs of Havana, where they were told that they had been selected for a "delicate" and "very serious" internationalist mission. They were also told that "anyone who didn't want to go would be allowed to leave. . . . The mission was voluntary."[88] After a fortnight of intensive training, "they took us to the theater where we were told that we were going to listen to a recorded speech of the Commander in Chief. . . . The entire battalion fell silent as we began to hear the voice of Fidel. It was a stirring moment. It was the speech he had given to the compañeros who had left for Angola before us. An hour went by, and some more time—I couldn't say how much—and suddenly from the right side of the theater, where there is a big door, we could hear some cars arriving and doors opening and suddenly . . . the Commander in Chief appeared!" Fidel was followed by Raúl Castro, Colomé, Osmany Cienfuegos, and others. "We all stood and broke into uproarious applause."[89] Castro began to speak.

He explained the situation in Angola to us. He told us about the battles that had just taken place in the north and the south, and about how our troops were playing a decisive role. . . . Then he spoke to us about the importance of Cabinda and said that we were going there, that our task was to prevent the enemy from entering that province and also to protect our Congolese brothers from a possible attack by South African troops. He stressed that if Cabinda fell into the hands of Angola's enemies, Angola would lose almost all its riches. . . .

He told us to be careful, that he didn't want corpses or suicidal missions and that he trusted us because most of us were workers and students. He kept talking to us; he told us some stories about the Cuban revolution, he compared Cabinda with Girón [the Bay of Pigs], he compared Mobutu with Pinochet, and then he compared the ship *Sierra Maestra* with the yacht *Granma*. He told us that the *Sierra* would take us to the Congo, that it was a long, uncomfortable, and dangerous trip, and that just to arrive . . . at Pointe Noire would be a triumph for us and a victory for the Angolan people.[90]

---

conversations with MPLA officials, his role was limited to desultory and infrequent conversations with Zairean Foreign Ministry officials and FNLA representatives. (Interviews with Mora, Oramas, and Cadelo. For Mora's visit to Luanda, see *Provincia de Angola*, May 7, 1975, p. 3, and *O Comércio*, May 16, 1975, p. 3. None of the Angolans I interviewed remembered Mora's visit or recognized his name.)

At 7 A.M. on November 22 the *Sierra Maestra* steamed from Mariel with more than 700 members of a regiment of motorized infantry. The remainder left for Pointe Noire aboard three other ships by November 28. Because the MMCA feared that Mobutu would launch another attack against Cabinda with French mercenaries, the regiment's task was to defend the enclave and, "if necessary," the Congo. The four vessels reached Pointe Noire between December 9 and 30.[91]

THE SADF ON THE CENTRAL FRONT

Cabinda, however, was no longer in danger. Except for a few small hit-and-run attacks, the war there was over. Nor would Mobutu attack the Congo. He had his hands full with Luanda. "During the first three weeks of November," Spies writes, "the three Zairean battalions that attacked Luanda had shrunk from a total of 1209 men to 609. About fifty had been killed or wounded in the fighting. The rest had fled."[92] On December 4, the Ninth Brigade went on the attack. Two days later, FNLA and Zaireans abandoned Caxito. For the rest of the month, the Ninth Brigade pushed northward. The advance was slow—the enemy had laid mines and blown up bridges—but steady. "The situation on the northern front continues to reflect the enemy's low morale and poor skill," Havana noted on December 21.[93] The South Africans agreed. Having concluded that Roberto and his army were beyond salvation, the SADF had decided in late November that it was time for Brigadier Roos and his men to exit discreetly, before they were marooned in northern Angola or found themselves in Cuban hands. Having been told by the army command on November 24 to figure out his own escape route, Roos turned to the CIA operatives in Ambriz, who "had promised to help him to get out. To his anger and dismay he learned that . . . the Americans had quietly decamped without any prior warning." And so, at dawn on November 28, a South African frigate came to get Roos and his men near the northern town of Ambrizete. Two days later, they landed at Walvis Bay in Namibia.[94]

The South Africans turned all their attention to the central front. "Indications are that South Africa is becoming more deeply involved militarily," the U.S. State Department noted on December 1.[95] Numbering 2,900, the South African soldiers in Angola had the edge over the Cubans in both numbers and equipment. "Two things are giving us trouble," Colomé cabled Havana on December 11: "the maneuverability of the [South African] AML-90s [armored cars] and the fact that our artillery still isn't as effective as it needs to be."[96] The South Africans, however, were unable to break through the Cuban defenses. In part this was due to the weather: "It was mud and more mud everywhere," Breytenbach writes, "through which the infantry had to squelch on foot. It was impossible for any vehicles, including armored cars, to move off the road. As a consequence, all the fighting took place on narrow fronts up and down the main road arteries." The Cubans held fast. "The MPLA forces," the *Observer* reported from Luanda on December 7, "have halted the enemy column's advance for three weeks, roughly along the line of the Queve river." Reporting from Johannesburg on December 11, the London *Times* gave a similar assessment: "During the past two weeks, there has been a dramatic change in the military situation. . . . In the south the armoured column of FNLA, UNITA and white mercenary forces[!] . . . has been halted in its tracks south of Porto Amboim. Another force, which was heading for the Cambambe dam and hydro-electric scheme at Dondo . . . has hit solid MPLA opposition near Gabela [that is, at Ebo]."[97]

In a May 1976 debate in the South African Parliament, Defense Minister Botha let it be known that the SADF had not taken Luanda because "the Americans told him to stop." This is flatly contradicted by the South Africans' determined efforts to advance northward after their capture of Novo Redondo. In February 1977 the SADF tried a different tack: "The South Africans and their allies could have conquered all of Angola," but Savimbi had discouraged them because he still hoped to reach a peaceful settlement with the MPLA that would spare his country further bloodshed. This is flatly contradicted by Savimbi's triumphant cries in early November 1975 about the imminent fall of Luanda.[98]

On December 12 the South Africans launched a powerful attack against the Cuban-FAPLA positions on the Nhia River, south of the village of Catofe on the road from Cela to Quibala, and "succeeded in breaking through our [Cuban] defenses, inflicting heavy losses in men and matériel." The South Africans, however, were unable to exploit this victory. Not only did they not reach Quibala, ten miles north of Catofe, but they didn't even enter Catofe: "We were able to stop them at a few hundred yards from Catofe," a Cuban officer recalled. Du Preez agreed: Catofe could not be taken, she conceded at the end of her detailed account, because of the Cubans' spirited defense.[99] The South Africans remained "bogged down," the U.S. State Department noted on December 20, along a "front" that stretched eastward from the Queve River estuary to the Nhia River and farther east to the town of Cariango. This was not a continuous front, DIA analyst Thom observed, "as there were too few troops available to both sides, but there were dispersed fortified points centered mostly at key towns or bridges."[100] Hundreds of miles farther east a 370-man South African task force with heavy guns, code-named X-Ray, and UNITA troops seized Luso, a major town on the Benguela railway, on December 11, but were unable to exploit this success. Their mission was to control the railway line all the way from Luso to Zaire, but they had to stop halfway because of the enemy's growing resistance. On December 27, X-Ray was ordered back to Luso.[101]

THE PRESS DISCOVERS THE SOUTH AFRICANS

The big lie was unraveling. On November 14 Fred Bridgland, Reuters's special correspondent, filed a story from Lobito announcing that South African regular troops—not mercenaries—were leading the advance on Luanda. Reuters, however, rewrote his story. "Reuters was still nervous about stating categorically that South Africa had invaded Angola," Bridgland recalled. "So the story that the agency's international subscribers received began this way: 'Columns of ar-

The two South African soldiers in this photo were captured by the Cubans in central Angola on December 13, 1975, and shown to the press three days later. "They were irrefutable proof," a Luanda daily said, that South Africa had invaded Angola, something Pretoria had fiercely denied until that moment. "A single photograph in the South African newspapers this week," the Johannesburg *Rand Daily Mail* wrote, "brought home . . . the implications of this country's involvement in the Angolan conflict. Here were the first South African soldiers in a quarter of a century to be taken prisoner of war. . . . Somehow nothing before—not even any of the tragic deaths in unidentified 'operational areas'—has conveyed to the same degree the direct human consequences of becoming embroiled with antagonists in southern Africa." (*Rand Daily Mail* [Johannesburg], December 19, 1975.)

mored vehicles manned by white personnel are slicing across great tracts of Angola through the defences of the marxist-oriented MPLA, informed sources said. The major unanswered question is the origin of the white soldiers.'" This version appeared in the major European and U.S. newspapers. "For days afterwards the story was reworked," Bridgland writes. "On November 22 I finally persuaded the agency to name the South Africans and the next day the story appeared on the front page of the *Washington Post*."[102]

Actually it was on page 18. Still, a major Western newspaper had finally announced that "South African regular troops are fighting hundreds of miles inside Angola."[103] Not all major newspapers followed suit. The *New York Times*, for example, continued to downplay the South African role. Pretoria "evidently has permitted a small number of mercenaries to aid rival Angolan groups in the south," it noted in a December 9 editorial, while lashing out at Cuba and the Soviet Union: "this blatant military intervention by white powers from distant continents in the internal affairs of a black African country is the kind of aggression that the UN was created to oppose." It took three more days before it was ready to say that "about 1,000" South African soldiers were in Angola. The London *Times* was equally obtuse. It printed Bridgland's Reuters story on November 15; over the next three weeks, when referring to the "mysterious armoured column of white troops," it variously noted that its members were mercenaries; that South African troops might be involved; that "there is now little doubt that South Africa is involved in Angola, but to what extent is not certain"—only to return full circle on December 11 with a reference to the "armoured column of FNLA, UNITA and white mercenary forces."[104]

Until December 18 the South African press breathed not one word about the SADF advance in Angola. It printed, however, terse statements released by the SADF about the death of servicemen in unspecified "border" and "operational" areas.[105] As the death toll in these "border" areas mounted, so too did uneasiness in South Africa. Then, on the morning of December 16, four South African POWs were displayed to the press by the FAPLA in Luanda. They had been captured, the POWs explained, between Cela and Quibala, about 440 miles inside Angola. This was "irrefutable proof," *Diário de Luanda* wrote, of South Africa's aggression. Two of the prisoners were flown to Lagos, where they were shown to the Nigerian authorities and the international press.[106] "A single photograph in South African newspapers this week," the *Rand Daily Mail* wrote,

brought home, perhaps more than anything else so far, the implications of this country's involvement in the Angolan conflict. The photograph showed two young South African Defence Force men in handcuffs.

Here were the first South African soldiers in a quarter of a century to be taken prisoner of war—two bewildered youngsters enduring public humiliation; paraded before an international audience by their MPLA captors. . . .

Somehow nothing that has gone before—not even any of the tragic deaths in unidentified "operational areas"—has conveyed to the same degree the direct human consequences of becoming embroiled with antagonists in southern Africa.[107]

On December 17 Defense Minister Botha announced that "In the exigency of the circumstances, it is necessary to extend the services of a limited number of national servicemen [draftees on 12-month tours of active duty] for 1 month." Furthermore, he added, "During 1976 a number of citizen forces units [army reserves] will also serve in the operational area. As a result of long distances and traveling time involved, as well as other requirements, it will be necessary for those units to be called up for twelve weeks instead of three weeks." The SADF "had been caught in a manpower squeeze," Steenkamp remarked.[108]

White South Africans, the *Rand Daily Mail* lamented, "are facing the chilliest winds for decades. . . . We meet Christmas with families already in mourning for a mounting number of young lives that have recently been lost in vaguely defined 'operational areas.' "[109]

Chill winds were buffeting Savimbi as well. The capture and display of the South African prisoners was humiliating, because he had vehemently denied that South African forces were helping UNITA and had challenged the MPLA to produce a single South African prisoner. He had asserted that far from helping UNITA, South Africa was targeting it because of its commitment to SWAPO. (He had been more candid with U.S. ambassador Wilkowski in Lusaka, admitting that "There had been clashes between UNITA and SWAPO forces." Savimbi, Wilkowski remarked, was "too dependent upon South African goodwill" to worry about SWAPO.) Even after the display of the South African POWs in Luanda, he stubbornly persisted: "We are very much aware that South Africa has penetrated Angola," he told the Uganda radio in Kampala, "but since all its troops are equipped with very sophisticated weapons we cannot fight them." All rumors of South African aid to UNITA were Communist propaganda.[110]

As Savimbi squirmed, the FAPLA grew more confident. In the terrible days after Zulu had struck, the FAPLA had been impotent as the white column had rolled northward. Now they were no longer alone. The "superb Cuban fighters" (as the *Cape Times* described them)[111] gave the FAPLA heart. From the front, *Le Monde*'s correspondent reported:

> A Cuban soldier died in the fighting. On his grave, there is neither a cross nor an epitaph: just an Angolan flag. After the ceremony, the chief of the Cuban unit . . . simply asked permission to dig more graves for "those who will die." Whether true or not, this story has impressed the Angolan combatants, who have repeated it to us all along the central front, between Quibala and Porto Amboim. Its icy realism leaves them stunned. Thousands of stories like it stress the courage and organization of the Cubans and are repeated time and again. "Our relationship to the Cubans is like that of students to their teachers," a FAPLA commander told us. Without any bitterness or animosity, he merely stated that at this phase of the war it could not be otherwise.[112]

The Cubans, whose numbers had been steadily increasing, were preparing to seize the offensive. By late December, there were some 3,500 to 4,000 Cubans in Angola, including 1,000 in Cabinda. This must have given them approximate numerical parity on the central front with the 3,000 South Africans.[113] "I have just returned from a tour of Quibala, Catofe, Conde, Ebo, Gabela, Porto Amboim," Risquet wrote Fidel Castro on December 30. "The morale of the [Cuban military] commanders with whom I spoke . . . is very high: they are optimistic and full of ideas about how to attack the enemy. The morale of the soldiers and officers with whom I spoke was equally high. . . . This high morale, the large number of our troops, the large supply of matériel, the nature of the terrain, and the material and psychological condition of the enemy lead me to conclude that there are no big problems for our line at Amboim-Ebo-Quibala-Cariango; that we have recovered the initiative in the south; that in the next few days our 'active defense' will gain ground there."[114]

The following day, December 31, Cuban infantry seized the Morros de Medunda, two strategic hills between Quibala and Cela. The next morning, the South Africans counterattacked. After reconquering one of the Morros, they launched several hundred men on the other. As the South Africans and their Angolan allies closed in, the commander of the platoon of Cubans on the Morro ordered his men to take refuge in a cave and asked the Cuban artillery, which was located behind the hill, to fire on his own position. They hesitated, and he asked again. Then they opened fire and stopped the enemy. The Cubans remained in possession of the Morro.[115]

DISINFORMATION

That same day, Savimbi turned the tables on Pretoria: a UNITA communiqué in Lusaka branded the South Africans "invaders." South Africa, it explained, "had invaded southern Angola in July 1975. UNITA and the MPLA had tried to repel the invasion but had been defeated"; UNITA forces had remained in the south and were fighting against the South Africans in guerrilla operations. The claim was so absurd it made Savimbi look like a fool, but it probably originated not in his fertile imagination, but in the disinformation campaign of the CIA station in Lusaka. "The propaganda output from [the] Lusaka [CIA station] was voluminous and imaginative, if occasionally beyond credibility," Stockwell wrote.[116] It occasionally even confused other U.S. intelligence agencies. For example, in late November 1975, a UNITA communiqué announced that twenty Soviet military advisers, thirty-five Cubans, fifteen Mozambicans, three Congolese, and one Brazilian had been captured when Savimbi's forces had taken the town of Malange, 240 miles east of Luanda, and that a document had been found, written by Neto, "promising the Russians and other foreign mercenaries full control of Malange if they secured it from UNITA/FNLA attacks." The U.S. Defense Intelligence Agency noted that UNITA's claim "of capturing a group of foreign personnel in Malange may be exaggerated. Nevertheless it draws attention to the existence of communist presence and assistance to the Popular Movement [MPLA] in Angola." The UNITA communiqué, however, had been written by the CIA station in Lusaka. Malange had not fallen, and no foreign military advisers had been captured.[117] "Another Lusaka fabrication," Stockwell related, "accused Cuban soldiers of committing atrocities in Angola. It mentioned rape and pillage. Then its stories became more specific, 'reporting' a (totally fictitious) incident in which Cuban soldiers had raped some Ovimbundu girls. Subsequently it wrote that some of those same soldiers had been captured and tried before a tribunal of Ovimbundu women. Lusaka kept this story going endlessly throughout the program."[118]

Stockwell's "description of the incredible, anti-MPLA propaganda coming out of Lusaka was accurate," Hultslander noted. "This was not one of the agency's finest hours."[119]

ZULU AND THE PRESS

As 1975 came to a close, the tide had turned against Washington and Pretoria. It had turned on the battlefield, where the Cubans had stopped the South African advance, and it had turned on the propaganda front: the Western press had noticed that South Africa had invaded Angola.

The press's failure to report on the SADF invasion for more than five weeks deserves an explanation. Some journalists knew about the South Africans' presence and chose to remain silent. Ambassador Wilkowski reported from Lusaka that on November 15 Andrew Jaffe, Nairobi bureau chief for *Newsweek*, had told an embassy official that he had "definite information" that approximately 1,000 South African troops were deep inside Angola. "Jaffe uncertain how much he can report about South African presence in Angola without jeopardizing his future access to sources," Wilkowski cabled.[120] In the event Jaffe—or his editors—chose to equivocate. On December 1 *Newsweek* merely noted that "some reports indicated that South African troops may have entered the war," and it was not until December 29 that it flatly stated that South African troops were involved in the fighting.[121]

Other journalists may have worried, like Jaffe, about the repercussions of telling the truth, but the silence was too widespread to be explained simply by this. Certainly the government press of Tanzania, which was fiercely hostile to South Africa, would not have been afflicted by similar doubts. And yet as late as November 22, the Tanzanian government *Daily News* called Zulu the "white mercenary–led 'flying column' " and said nothing about the SADF.[122]

It was the same in oil-rich Nigeria, which was an outspoken foe of South Africa. For over a month, the Nigerian government and press said nothing about the South African invasion, but "deplored the support given by the Soviet Union to one of the liberation movements."[123] Apparently Lagos believed that South African military interference was limited to raids against SWAPO in southern Angola. It was only on November 23, Nigerian foreign minister Joe Garba writes, that "we . . . learned that South African troops had advanced from the Cunene river and were moving rapidly toward Luanda." Thereafter Nigeria threw its full weight behind the MPLA.[124]

This extraordinary silence seems due, therefore, above all to the fact that there were no journalists or other independent observers at the front and that distances and transportation problems made covering the war extremely difficult. (Bridgland's scoop had been due to ingenuity and good luck.) Even the MPLA failed to realize for several days that the whites in the invading column were not mercenaries: it did not denounce the South African invasion until October 23, nine days after it had begun.[125]

Furthermore, most foreign observers found it difficult to believe that South Africa had invaded Angola. Pretoria had been proceeding toward détente at full throttle. Vorster had not interfered in Mozambique, and he had continued to nudge the Rhodesian government toward black majority rule. On July 31 the minister of police had announced that the South African police units that were still in Rhodesia had been recalled home. In Lusaka, President Kaunda said, "I welcome this move because it lessens the areas of differences between South Africa and Zambia. . . . If any white man in South Africa can change matters for the better, that man is Mr. Vorster."[126] In September the Ivory Coast information minister visited South Africa for ten days, and in October the president, Houphouët-Boigny, urged black African states to open diplomatic relations with South Africa.[127] It was difficult to imagine that, in the midst of this détente offensive, Vorster would invade Angola. Of course, even fewer suspected that Vorster's key détente partners—Zaire, the Ivory Coast, and Zambia—were urging him on.[128]

While some newspapers were less gullible than others (the *Washington Post* less than the *New York Times*, and *Le Monde* less than the London *Times*), without the Cuban intervention, the South Africans would have seized Luanda before anyone reported that they had crossed the border. The CIA covert operation in Angola would have succeeded.

CHAPTER FIFTEEN
CUBAN VICTORY

The Americans who planned the covert operation in Angola had overlooked Castro. A June 10, 1975, intelligence memo listing the "MPLA's partisans" had included several African states, the Soviet Union, "Eastern European states, Communist parties and others on the left in Western Europe." But not Cuba. "Cuba didn't even enter into our calculations," Deputy Assistant Secretary Mulcahy, one of the advocates of the covert operation, recalled.[1]

In late August U.S. intelligence began reporting the presence of a "few Cuban technical advisers" in Angola.[2] In early October the CIA promptly reported the arrival of the *Vietnam Heroico* and the *Coral Island* near Porto Amboim with the instructors on board. On October 11 the *National Intelligence Daily* noted that a "sizable force of Cuban 'volunteers' recently arrived in Angola" aboard two Cuban ships. "One of the two ships is a cargo vessel and presumably was used to transport arms and equipment; the other carries cargo but also has facilities for 240 passengers and a history of involvement in clandestine operations."[3]

The news failed to raise alarm bells in Washington. On October 14 South Africa invaded Angola and Zulu began rolling northward. The next few weeks must have been a period of quiet satisfaction in Washington as the Angolan towns fell in rapid succession and Zulu closed in on Luanda. The "few hundred Cuban military personnel" in Angola (according to an October 25 CIA estimate) seemed impotent against this onslaught. "The news is changing for the better militarily," Mulcahy told Kissinger on November 5, reporting on the fall of Benguela. At that same meeting Assistant Secretary for Inter-American Affairs William Rogers inveighed against the Cuban presence in Angola. ("It is obscene . . . the rawest kind of intervention.") Kissinger remained calm; he was, after all, winning. U.S. officials did not imagine that Castro might raise the stakes. "No one thought the Cuban troops would intervene," Mulcahy recalled. Kissinger concurs: "The intervention of Cuban combat forces came as a total surprise," he writes in his memoirs.[4]

Why was the United States caught so off guard? First, there was no historical memory. U.S. officials knew that Cubans had fought in Guinea-Bissau and Zaire and had trained MPLA guerrillas in the Congo, but they had not focused on it, and it did not enter the calculations of the men who planned IAFEATURE. "In the 1960s there was no sense of a Cuban danger in Africa; their intervention in Angola was a real surprise," observed former State Department official Paul O'Neill. "During my tenure as Director of Southern Africa Office [of the State Department from July 1973 to June 1975] we were aware that there was some

Soviet/East European support for the MPLA, but I don't recall any discussion of a Cuban role before I left. Aside from the Soviet Union, we would discuss the possible role of East Germany. I don't recall any concern about a Cuban role. Before I left, when people in the Africa Bureau [of the State Department] talked of the Soviet Bloc role in Angola, they thought of the Soviets, the East Germans, not of Cuba. I don't recall that we knew of Cuba's ties with the MPLA, but even if we knew it didn't worry us."[5]

Furthermore, in 1975 the United States and Cuba were engaged in conversations about normalizing relations. INR director Hyland claims that when he raised the possibility that Cuba might help the MPLA, Assistant Secretary Rogers argued that Havana would not do anything that would jeopardize either these talks or the thaw in its relations with Western Europe and Latin America.[a,6] Finally, Washington's complacency was strengthened by the lack of any contrary evidence. The CIA did not report any Cuban military presence in Angola until very late in the game, for the very simple reason that there was none to report.

KISSINGER RESPONDS

It took a few days before the significance of the arrival of Cuban troops registered in Washington. On November 10, the day after the first Special Forces landed in Luanda, Roberto was routed at Quifangondo. "We had to figure out what happened to Roberto," Edward Fugit, a member of the Interagency Task Force that oversaw IAFEATURE, recalled. "It took a couple of days to find out how bad the defeat was." Furthermore, the news from the front was still good. On November 13, Zulu took Novo Redondo, overwhelming the FAPLA and Cuban defenders. "Militarily the situation goes well for the good guys," Mulcahy told Kissinger. If Zulu continued to advance, Roberto's debacle would be a minor glitch. On November 14, the CIA reported that the Cuban presence in Angola was growing, but it still did not mention combat troops: the Cubans, it said, "appear to be:—Preparing anti-aircraft defenses in Luanda.—Staffing a former Portuguese air base.—Serving as advisers with Popular Movement [MPLA] units in the field.—Providing medical assistance to Popular Movement forces.—Operating a tactical radio network." The report also noted that "the tide has turned, at least temporarily against" the MPLA. "Castro is gambling that the Popular Movement's fortunes have not already passed the point of no return."[7] This would depend on whether his troops could stop the South Africans.

Pretoria was optimistic. When the Cubans blew up the bridge between Novo Redondo and Porto Amboim, Zulu veered east, trying to outflank the Cubans. "In some ways the situation looked relatively favorable," Steenkamp remarks.

a. Rogers freely acknowledges that he did not imagine that Cuba would intervene in Angola. He is very skeptical, however, that the conversation as retold by Hyland ever took place. (Tel. interview with Rogers.)

"There was still a chance of conquering Luanda and the few remaining MPLA-held regions." Furthermore, the American and the French governments were "still urging the South Africans to stay on." On November 14, Spies writes, Vorster decided to continue the offensive against Luanda and on November 17, General Viljoen flew to Kinshasa to inform Mobutu, Savimbi, and the CIA station chief there, Stuart Methven. The decision, he reported, was met with general satisfaction.[8]

Two developments signal that in late November Washington realized that the situation on the ground had changed significantly. First, the United States approached the Soviets to urge mutual restraint in Angola. "We initiated the diplomacy toward Moscow on November 20," Kissinger writes. On that day "an unsigned note—officially more than a conversation, less than a letter—was handed to [Soviet ambassador] Dobrynin at the State Department warning that Soviet actions in Angola were passing all 'reasonable bounds.'"[9]

The administration also decided to increase military aid to the FNLA and UNITA. On November 27, Ford approved an additional $7 million for IAFEA-TURE, bringing the total to $31.7 million. This depleted the CIA Contingency Reserve Fund for fiscal year 1975, which meant that additional funds had to be approved by Congress.[10] The Defense Appropriation Bill for fiscal year 1976 was pending before the Senate, and the CIA budget was buried in it. Ford wanted Congress to approve $28 million for IAFEATURE. It was the first time that the administration asked Congress for money for the covert operation.

Immediately thereafter Ford left for his first trip to China, where he met Mao Zedong and other top Chinese leaders and was lectured on U.S. lack of resolve vis-à-vis the Soviet Union. On his return, Ford told the Republican congressional leadership, "There is a very strong anti-Soviet attitude. It is almost unbelievable. The Chinese . . . urged us to prevent Soviet expansion anywhere, but especially in the Middle East, the Pacific and in Africa."[11]

On October 27, however, two weeks after the South Africans had invaded Angola and a month before Ford's trip, the Chinese instructors who had been training the FNLA had left Zaire. At a press conference at Kinshasa airport, the group's leader had "expressed happiness over their pleasant stay in Zaire" and announced that their task had been accomplished. Their public departure at such a critical juncture was motivated by their determination not to be associated with the South African invasion that was bound to become public. Noting that the Chinese had "opted out of the crucial showdown" under way in Angola, the State Department briefing paper for Ford's visit to Beijing warned, "We doubt that you should raise African issues, unless developments in Angola enable you to point to it as an example of our effectiveness in blunting Soviet intervention."[12]

Ford, however, did raise the issue with Mao Zedong, hoping to enlist Chinese aid for the deteriorating Angolan situation. In his memoirs, Kissinger writes that Mao was receptive. While nothing definitive was arranged, "at that moment, in the Chairman's study, the mood was still upbeat." China wanted to cooperate with the United States in Angola. Two weeks later, however, the U.S. Senate defeated Ford's request for additional funds for IAFEATURE, "thwarting," Kissinger wrote, "an attempt to collaborate with China."[13]

This grossly overstates the case. Mao had been sympathetic but noncommittal.[14] The following day, Vice-Premier Deng Xiaoping explained clearly that China could not help in Angola. (Kissinger does not include this in his memoirs.) "The relatively complex problem is the involvement of South Africa," he said. "And I believe you are aware of the feelings of the black Africans toward South Africa." Kissinger promised that the United States would push South Africa out of Angola "as soon as an alternative military force can be created." Ford joined in: "We will take action to get South Africa out, provided a balance can be maintained for their not being in." It was a meaningless promise: no alternative military force could be created, and the Chinese knew it. If the Americans could get South Africa "out of Angola as soon as possible . . . this would be good," Deng said. Until then, the Chinese would do nothing. They would not even pressure their African friends—Mozambique and Tanzania—to reconsider their support for the MPLA. "Please understand this with regard to African countries—even the small ones," Deng told Ford and Kissinger: "they are extremely sensitive on matters involving national pride."[15]

While Ford was traveling, the Senate was considering his request for additional money for the covert operation in Angola. Congress had consistently shown a deep lack of interest in and ignorance of Africa. Most members could not distinguish, Senator Joseph Biden (D.-Del.) quipped, "between 'Angola' and 'Mongolia.'" Dick Clark (D.-Iowa), chair of the Senate Foreign Relations Subcommittee on Africa, recalled, "I knew nothing about Africa. I had not been there, had not studied it and wasn't particularly interested in . . . it."[16] Seeking to educate himself and his colleagues, in June and July 1975 he held hearings on U.S. policy toward southern Africa. During five of the ten sessions (two dealt with Angola), he was the lone senator present. Four subcommittee members put in brief appearances (one each), and Senator Biden attended three sessions.[17] These were the only congressional hearings that dealt with Angola until November 1975. Between July 25 and October 31, 1975, the CIA briefed nineteen senators and fifty-six representatives about IAFEATURE, but this failed to shake Congress from its lethargy. "Congress was very passive," Mulcahy recalled. "There wasn't much interest in Angola."[18]

Senator Clark and other members of Congress later claimed that the CIA briefings had saddled them with "the illusion of co-responsibility for the covert action without having any say in the decision." Because the members who were briefed were sworn to secrecy, Clark argued, "there is no way the Congress can properly use it [the information about covert operations] to oppose or influence policy."[19]

The Senate Foreign Relations Committee's chief of staff, Pat Holt, begged to differ. "That was a disingenuous statement," he observed. "If someone disapproved [of a covert operation], the remedy was to take it up with the White House or the State Department." The evidence indicates that only two members of Congress who were briefed on IAFEATURE before November, Biden and Clark, expressed any reservations. Furthermore, when the operation was made public on the front page of the New York Times on September 25, 1975, for all members of Congress to see, it provoked hardly a ripple of interest. "The truth," as Holt said, was that "Congress was not concerned about Angola until the shit hit the fan."[20]

By December, when the administration turned to Congress for money for IAFEATURE, Congress saw a prescription for disaster and paid attention. The evidence of the South African invasion of Angola was overwhelming, and the stench of U.S. collusion with Pretoria hung in the air. Worse, the growing numbers of Cuban troops had derailed the CIA's plans, and the administration seemed at a loss about what to do next.

Seeking to rally wavering senators, administration officials beat the drums, none as loudly as the ambassador to the United Nations, Daniel Patrick Moynihan. "If Soviet neocolonialism succeeds [in Angola] the world will not be the same in the aftermath," he warned television viewers on Sunday, December 14. "Europe's oil routes will be under Soviet control as will the strategic South Atlantic, with the next target on the Kremlin's list being Brazil." Asked whether President Ford agreed with Moynihan, White House deputy press secretary William Greener answered, "Yes."[21]

These dire predictions notwithstanding, on December 19, the Senate refused to approve the $28 million by a 54-22 vote.[22] (On January 27, in a "resounding rebuff" to Ford, the House endorsed the Senate action by 323 votes to 99.)[23]

Some members of Congress feared a new Vietnam. They believed, the Wall Street Journal wrote contemptuously, that "If we send some bullets, we will be stepping on a slippery slope and will end up with 500,000 American troops slogging through the jungles of Africa." Others, the New York Times noted, "had the November [1976] elections on their minds and the possibility of vulnerability at the polls if they voted for more money for Angola." But many others simply wondered how a few million dollars worth of arms could, as Congressman Stephen Solarz (D.-N.Y.) asked Assistant Secretary William Schaufele, "stem the tide which had been unleashed, as it were, by the presence of well-trained and well-equipped Cuban forces?" Senator Jesse Helms (R.-N.C.), who voted against the administration's request even though he was in sympathy with its Angola policy, wrote to Ford that approving the money would have been "an exercise in futility . . . just throwing good money after bad."[24]

Kissinger blamed Congress for the U.S. failure in Angola. He testified in January 1976 that the administration's policy had begun to pay off when the Senate suddenly pulled the plug. "The [Soviet] airlift was interrupted from December 9 until December 24," he asserted. "At that point, the impact of our domestic debate overwhelmed the possibilities of diplomacy. After the Senate vote to block further aid to Angola, the Cubans more than doubled their forces and Soviet military aid was resumed on an even larger scale."[25]

This may appear to be rather predictable bluster, but Risquet confirmed, "Yes, it's true, there was a Soviet pause, for which we received no explanation."[26]

According to a respected study by Bruce Porter, "Cuba's airlift of soldiers to Angola also ceased over the same period [December 9 to 24]," which "would seem to be evidence of the close coordination that took place between Havana and Moscow."[27] It would also suggest that, had the Senate approved the aid requested by the administration, Kissinger's policy might have saved Angola.

In fact, however, there was no interruption in the flow of Cuban troops, and Porter's much-quoted statement is a textbook illustration of how history should not be written. His one source was an article by Cubanologist Nelson Valdés, and he did not check Valdés' sources—a March 5, 1976, article in *Diario de las Américas* and a December 17, 1975, article in the *Miami Herald*. The *Diario de las Américas* article does not mention any interruption in the airlift. The *Miami Herald* article does. It quotes "reliable sources" who said that after a "lull in the troop flights for most of last week," two Cuban flights outbound for Guinea-Bissau "refueled in Barbados Saturday [December 13]." According to the *Herald*, therefore, the lull had lasted not two weeks, but less than one.[28] This is consistent with what the CIA reported two days before the *Herald* article: "Cuba appears to have resumed its troop airlift to Angola via Barbados after a three-day hiatus."[29]

This is also consistent with the facts about the pace of the airlift, and it constitutes no "lull." In November and December there were only two or three Cuban flights per week to Angola. In the period of December 9 to 24, when, according to Porter, the Cubans had suspended their flights to Angola, the State Department reported that two Cuban planes had transited through Guyana and three more Cuban planes had landed in the Azores on their way to Angola.[30] Cuban documents tell a similar story of four plane trips from Havana to Luanda on December 19, 20, 22, and 23, respectively: the first, with 94 military personnel; the second, with "105 compañeros"; the third, with 65 passengers; and the fourth, with 4 passengers and communication equipment. Furthermore, on December 10 a Cuban ship, the *Agate Island*, left Mariel for Pointe Noire with troops on board.[31] To put it simply, there was no lull in the dispatch of Cuban troops.

If the U.S. Congress had not lost its nerve, these troops would have been in for a nasty surprise in Angola, or so Kissinger claims, for the first time, in the last volume of his memoirs. On December 16, 1975, French president Giscard d'Estaing had told him that "he would assist by making available auxiliary (French African or Moroccan) troops and a number of Alouette helicopters [with French crews] armed with S-11 missiles." Six days later, however, the Senate voted down the $28 million, and Giscard drew back.[32]

I asked William Schaufele, who was then the assistant secretary for African affairs, if he could confirm Kissinger's account. "This [the possibility that

France might help] was talked about in kind of philosophical terms," Schaufele told me. "Some of us would sit around and kick around possible options. But on my end, I didn't see anything very concrete. We didn't take it very seriously." Of course, Kissinger may have kept Giscard's promise a secret, but it is difficult not to be skeptical. As Schaufele pointed out, "the French were too prudent [to do it]."[33]

The same applies to Giscard's "auxiliary troops." It is true that in April 1977 Morocco, under pressure from the United States and France, sent 1,500 men to Zaire to fight against the Katangan rebels who had entered from Angola. But they went to push weak rebel forces back into Angola, and they went, formally, at the request of the legal government of Zaire.[34] In 1975, however, they would have faced thousands of Cubans, and they would have gone as Pretoria's de facto allies. The events of 1977 might have inspired Kissinger's account of a promise made in 1975, but the circumstances were completely different.

Kissinger had another arrow in his quiver, which he glosses over in his memoirs: in response to the arrival of the Cubans, the administration tried to raise a mercenary army, just as Johnson had done in Zaire in 1964.[35] As in 1964, it was stipulated that no American could join, and the word "mercenary" was neatly airbrushed out of the discussion. CIA Africa division chief Potts "forbade its use in cables, memoranda and files, at headquarters and in the field. Thereafter the mercenaries who were hired and sent to Angola were to be called 'foreign military advisers.'"[36]

The CIA scrambled for mercenaries. The CIA deputy director, General Vernon Walters, who had been army attaché in Brazil in the mid-1960s, "felt sure he could influence the Brazilian military command to help us recruit," Stockwell writes, but the Brazilians politely refused to receive him and rebuffed his suggestions. The CIA also turned to French intelligence, which introduced CIA case officers to Denard and, according to Stockwell, "for $500,000 cash—paid in advance—he agreed to provide twenty French mercenaries who would 'advise' UNITA on short-term contracts." Denard confirms that the CIA gave him $400,000 to raise mercenaries for UNITA. He succeeded in rallying about two dozen who were on the ground in Angola in January 1976.[37]

The CIA also hammered out a program to recruit 300 Portuguese mercenaries, but by the time the first 13 had made it to Kinshasa the war in the north had virtually ended; they flew back without setting foot in Angola. The total bill for the abortive Portuguese mercenary program came to $569,805.[38]

The major recruiting center for mercenaries, however, was England, through a shadowy group called Security Advisory Service (SAS), which officially worked for the FNLA. In the latter half of January 1976, about 140 mercenaries left England for Zaire and then for the front. (Another 60 followed in early February.)[39] "I certainly deplore the recruitment of mercenaries," British foreign secretary James Callaghan told the House of Commons on January 28, "just as I deplore the entry of the Cubans upon the scene." A few days later, Prime Minister Harold Wilson confirmed that fourteen British mercenaries had been executed

The Christian Scienc

The United States responded to the sudden arrival of Cuban troops in Angola in late 1975 by trying to raise an army of mercenaries in France, Portugal, and Brazil. In the end, however, the most successful recruiting drive was in England. (This cartoon by Guernsey LePelley first appeared in *The Christian Science Monitor* on February 5, 1976, and is reproduced by permission. Copyright © 1976 The Christian Science Monitor. All rights reserved. Online at csmonitor.com.)

Many Americans criticized Kissinger's response to the arrival of Cuban troops ("Soviet mercenaries") in Angola as too weak. They argued that he was hobbled by his obsession with détente. This view was dominant among South African whites, and the *Rand Daily Mail*, a prominent liberal paper from Johannesburg, shared the opinion. ("Knuckle-rapping" by Bob Connolly, *Rand Daily Mail* [Johannesburg], November 27, 1975.)

by a firing squad of their own comrades in northern Angola. The prime minister, however, failed to explain his government's role in the mercenary story. "Scotland Yard," the *Daily Telegraph* wrote on February 13, "[is] 'extremely concerned' about how mercenaries left Britain without passing through passport or immigration controls. Of the 43 men who returned to London from Angola on Tuesday [February 10], it is understood that only 10 had passports. A number of those returning were found to be wanted by police." As *Jeune Afrique* pointed out, "When one knows how fussy British immigration authorities can be, one must marvel at the special treatment [accorded the mercenaries]."[40] Two of the mercenaries confirm that the immigration authorities had been extraordinarily obliging. They write that on Saturday, January 17, 1976, the day before the first batch of recruits left London for Kinshasa,

> it was discovered that a number of mercenaries . . . [including one of the authors] didn't have valid passports. . . . The Immigration Office at Heathrow Airport . . . said it would be acceptable for the men to travel without passports as long as they carried identification supplied by Security Advisory Service and their entry was unopposed by the country of disembarkation. Obviously

the men were not going to be refused entry into Zaire, but there was the complication that they would have to stay overnight in Brussels in order to catch their connecting flight to Kinshasa the following morning. The Belgian embassy was hastily consulted and, after some delay, permission was obtained for the mercenaries to enter Belgium using documents issued by SAS.[41]

At the Brussels airport the mercenaries were treated with "friendly courtesy." The Belgian Foreign Ministry noted that while the recruitment of mercenaries on Belgian soil was illegal, allowing properly documented mercenaries to travel through Belgium was not.[42] The problem, of course, was that many of the mercenaries were not properly documented.

Instructions must have come from above—that is, from the British and Belgian governments. The U.S. embassy in London seemed to suggest as much, when it told Washington the following March, "Britain's direct involvement in Angola was little and unhappy. And its last involvement—the haphazard introduction of largely British mercenaries to rescue the FNLA—ended in squalid tragedy."[43] Whether the British and the Belgian governments were acting on their own or working with the United States is unclear.[44] What is certain is that the entire episode generated a grand total of fewer than 250 mercenaries, including Denard's Frenchmen and the 13 Portuguese.[b]

And so Kissinger's response to Castro's intervention was to throw mercenaries and weapons at the problem. But, as House Speaker Carl Albert pointed out, "You either do enough or you're better off not doing anything."[45] Enough would have meant persuading Pretoria, in November, to expand dramatically its military presence in Angola so that it could overwhelm the Cuban troops before they received reinforcements. "We should assign a major role to South Africa in restoring freedom in Angola," Senator Helms urged Ford. There is little doubt that Ford would have been happy to oblige. "They [the South Africans] are fighting [in Angola] to keep the Soviet Union from expanding, and we think that's admirable," he told Mao Zedong.[46] But to sway Vorster, Washington would have had to have openly endorsed the South African invasion and to have assured Pretoria that it would provide military assistance if the Soviet bloc escalated—both of which were politically impossible.

It is unlikely that Kissinger thought his response to Castro's intervention would be adequate. He may have hoped that the additional money might bring about a miracle. (There is a parallel with his request for additional aid for South Vietnam in early 1975. "If we had the $722 million, we could have gotten a negotiation," he told Ford as South Vietnam crumbled.) Above all, however,

b. After reading this section, Robert Hultslander, who was the CIA station chief in Luanda, commented: "To the best of my knowledge, you accurately describe the agency's involvement in the last ditch attempt to raise a mercenary force." (Hultslander, fax to Piero Gleijeses, Dec. 22, 1998, p. 5.)

Kissinger sought to shift the blame to Congress. "We would have defeated the Soviets in Angola if Congress had not stopped our assistance," he told a Chinese official in an oft-repeated refrain.[47]

THE OFFENSIVE IN THE NORTH

By the time the British mercenaries arrived in northern Angola in late January 1976, the FNLA was crumbling. At the very end of December, 300 Cubans had been sent to the northern front. Neto and Castro wanted to capture Carmona, Holden Roberto's capital, before the OAU emergency summit on Angola began on January 10 in Addis Ababa.[48] On January 1, two columns launched the offensive. One, led by the Cuban Víctor Schueg, advanced from Samba Cajú toward Carmona with about 1,000 FAPLA infantry and 250 to 300 Cubans manning the artillery and tanks. The other, Ndozi's Ninth Brigade, went north from Caxito along the coast with 1,200 FAPLA and a handful of Cuban advisers. On January 4, Schueg took Carmona and pressed northward along the inland road to the Zairean border. The FNLA's morale was "plummeting," the CIA noted. "The once proud and powerful FNLA army . . . has been reduced to a disorganised, demoralised rabble fleeing into the northern jungle," the *World* reported.[49]

In a January 7, 1976, letter to Castro, Risquet drew the lessons of the successful offensive against Carmona. "The great positive lesson," he wrote,

> is that our respect for the lives and proper treatment of our prisoners caused the enemy to surrender in droves. It is worth noting that they would find out where the Cubans were so they could surrender to us. . . . On the negative side, FAPLA soldiers and civilians looted some abandoned houses and stores, and stole some cars, etc. In a few isolated cases, Cuban soldiers joined in. . . . We will have to work to make sure that that is not repeated. . . .
>
> I stressed to Neto that the way we treat the population is key to gaining their support. . . . I stressed how the thuggish behavior of the FNLA (robberies, assaults, murders, rapes, unbelievable savagery) engenders widespread hatred even among people who are not politicized. Later, there will be [time for] propaganda, political education, . . . but simply treating people well . . . can garner the massive support of the population.[50]

Over the next few weeks, Ndozi and Schueg continued to advance toward Zaire along the coastal and inland roads respectively. "Only natural obstacles, like destroyed bridges, are slowing the advance of the MPLA," the Brazilian embassy in Luanda wrote. The *Washington Post* reported that the FNLA "often did not even bother to fight and sometimes simply abandoned towns 24 hours or more before the Popular Movement actually arrived. . . . The Zairean army, which was supposed to have provided artillery and armored vehicle support, also fled and in many cases fled first." The FNLA guerrillas and the Zaireans paused only to loot and rape. They "pillaged the towns to which they withdrew and that they are still holding," the *New York Times* wrote. "Refugees report that these towns . . . have been completely sacked and that their populations have fled. . . . The Zaire army units were said to have been the most active element in the looting."[51] Meanwhile, relations between Mobutu and Roberto were souring. "In recent months Mobutu has become increasingly disillusioned with Holden's military performance," the U.S. embassy in Kinshasa reported on January 29. "Holden, for his part, has become increasingly critical of the FAZ's [Zairean army's] performance in the field."[52]

The British mercenaries could not stop the Cubans. While the FNLA representatives in London bragged about an attack in which eighty Cubans died without a single mercenary casualty and claimed that "[the] only [mercenary] injury so far has been a sprained wrist,"[53] the mercenaries were in fact being cut to pieces. "The exercise was characterized by murderous inefficiency at every stage—from the recruiting in London to the operational direction in northern Angola," the *Washington Post* explained in February. "The poor quality of the recruits—some of them literally lured from London pubs with the offer of easy money and high living—stimulated violent recriminations among the mercenary leaders that led to the execution of 14 of the mercenaries." On February 10 forty-five "limped home [to London] on crutches and wheelchairs."[54] In South Africa, "Mad Mike" Hoare of Zaire fame put his "Wild Geese" on alert and made noises about joining the fight for Mobutu in Angola. Hoare's men were "graying at the temple but like old crocodiles still dangerous," *Newsweek* wrote. But nothing happened. "The geese have not yet flown to Angola," the *Times* reported in mid-February. Wisely, they remained cooped up at home.[55]

Seeking to extricate himself from the debacle, Mobutu announced on February 3 that he would no longer allow mercenaries to transit through Kinshasa. "The original decision to permit British mercenaries to enter had been made in the absence of President Mobutu," Foreign Minister Nguza Karl-i-Bond declared. Twenty-two mercenaries, who arrived on February 16 from London, were promptly deported.[56] This was the ignominious end of the story. "The last remaining British mercenaries in northern Angola have withdrawn and are to return to Britain," the *Guardian* reported from Kinshasa on February 17.[57]

In late February both Schueg and Ndozi reached the Zairean border. "Northern Angola has been completely liberated," Angolan defense minister Iko Carreira declared on February 26.[58]

SOUTH AFRICA RETREATS

South of Luanda, on the central front, the Cubans and the FAPLA faced not the effete Zaireans, but the South Africans, supported by the FNLA and UNITA. The entente between Roberto and Savimbi, cobbled together in August 1975, was fragile and strained. On December 1 Roberto flew to Huambo to attend the inaugural ceremonies of the joint UNITA-FNLA cabinet that had finally been agreed upon after difficult negotiations. "He arrived after dark over Huambo in a Fokker Friendship F-27 flown by American pilots, together with an accompanying aircraft containing foreign correspondents brought from Kinshasa," the *Rand Daily Mail* reported from Huambo. "The UNITA-staffed control tower at the largely derelict Huambo airfield failed to turn on landing lights for Dr. Roberto, and the FNLA leader had to turn tail and fly back to Kinshasa . . . in a great rage."[59] As their fortunes deteriorated, the mutual antipathy between the two movements increased and erupted into "a true pitched battle" in Huambo on Christmas Eve. Fighting between the erstwhile allies soon spread to Sá da Bandeira and Moçâmedes, escalating into a "war within a war" from which UNITA emerged victorious within a few days.[60]

In early January, as FNLA and UNITA battled each other, the FAPLA and the Cubans launched small offensive probes to the south. On January 16 the South Africans withdrew from Cela. Nine days later, after several skirmishes with the retreating South Africans, the Cubans entered Novo Redondo.[61] "If life is harsh in Novo Redondo today, those who remain say it was even harsher before Luanda's army took over," *Newsweek*'s Loren Jenkins wrote a few weeks later. "The pro-Western troops looted the town, commandeered provisions from merchants and indulged in an orgy of violence before they left. . . . The local South African commander intervened only once—to save the life of a Portuguese banker who refused to open his vaults."[62]

What were the South Africans' plans as they withdrew from Cela and Novo Redondo? The international press was full of rumors. "South Africa seems poised to intervene on a larger scale in Angola," *Le Monde* predicted on January 16, while the *Rand Daily Mail* remarked: "An indication of the seriousness of the situation . . . is that one of the most extensive military call-ups in South Africa's history is now taking place." In the meantime South African troops were involved in heavy fighting in the east. "Today I saw several convoys of Mercedes lorries driven by white soldiers moving . . . toward the battle zone," the correspondent of *Agence France-Presse* reported from Luso on January 14.[63]

The Cubans did not know what to expect. "We were aware that the South Africans were withdrawing," a classified Cuban history of the war asserted, "but it was not clear whether this was a full retreat [all the way to Namibia] or just a falling back to a new line." Therefore, Havana kept sending men and matériel to Angola. "Fidel thought, 'If we have to fight a decisive battle [against the South Africans] we will have to be strong,'" Risquet explained. "Furthermore, we thought that the South Africans might give up if they saw us coming with a massive force."[64]

In fact, the worst was over. In late December, Vorster held three meetings with Foreign Minister Muller, Defense Minister P. W. Botha, BOSS head van den Bergh, and other senior officials from the SADF, the Foreign Ministry, and BOSS. The debate was heated. The Foreign Ministry and BOSS favored withdrawing from Angola, while P. W. Botha and the SADF were opposed. The hard-liners' hand was strengthened by the urgent pleas of Mobutu, Savimbi, and the United States, including, Spies writes, a direct appeal from National Security Adviser Brent Scowcroft to Roelof Botha, South Africa's ambassador in Washington, who flew home just in time to attend the third of these meetings, on December 30, at which Vorster decided to withdraw to a line thirty to fifty miles north of the Namibian border.[65]

The decision was driven by South Africa's isolation. The U.S. Senate vote on December 19 cutting further funds for IAFEATURE had "deeply disappointed and greatly angered" Vorster and his advisers, Geldenhuys wrote. "The South Africans, facing tough fighting with the Cubans . . . wanted firm assurances from Washington that they would be assisted if the fighting escalated," INR director Hyland recalled. The Ford administration, however, was eager to distance itself from South Africa. So was Mobutu. "If it is true that South Africa is intervening in Angola, no self-respecting African country could tolerate it," he declared with customary hypocrisy. "When the chips were down, there was not a single state prepared to stand with South Africa," the *Cape Times* remarked. A member of the South African Congress put it graphically: "Where was America? Where were Zaire, Zambia . . . and South Africa's other friends? They were nowhere to be seen, not a whisper of public support was heard. The halls of power echoed with silence. We stood naked in the world."[66]

The situation on the battlefield also affected the South Africans' calculus. Through November and December, the SADF had tried to break through the Cuban defenses and push toward Luanda, but the Cubans had held firm, even though they were inferior in number and weaponry. Now more and more Cuban troops kept arriving and more weapons poured in from the Soviet Union. "The Cubans," the chief of the SADF remarked, "are highly trained soldiers, using a wide range of sophisticated weapons." Consequently, as DIA analyst Thom put it, South Africa had "to decide if it was willing to bring in more men and equipment to stay in the game." Sobered by the Cubans' performance and by the West's cold shoulder, Pretoria chose to fold.[67]

Having made the decision to withdraw, Vorster postponed implementation until after the OAU emergency session in Addis Ababa. Vorster "hoped to strengthen the position of UNITA and the FNLA in a possible settlement," writes Geldenhuys. The conference, however, did not even call for a negotiated solution. While the MPLA failed to obtain the OAU's recognition of its People's Republic of Angola (PRA)—22 states voted in favor, 22 against, and 2 abstained—it was clear that it was only a matter of time, perhaps of days, before the PRA would get 2 more votes and be admitted as a member of the OAU. On January 14, the day after the conference ended in disarray, Vorster gave the order to withdraw.[68]

By early February the SADF had fallen back to the extreme south of Angola. On February 3, Defense Minister Botha told the *Washington Post* that between

In mid-January 1976 the South African troops withdrew from central Angola. Were they on their way back to Namibia or were they falling back to more favorable positions in southern Angola? As Cuban troops poured into Angola, the two most senior Cuban officials in the country, Jorge Risquet (to Castro's right, with glasses) and Furry Colomé (to Risquet's right), flew to Moscow on February 24 to brief Fidel Castro, who was attending the 26th Congress of the Communist Party of the Soviet Union.

4,000 and 5,000 South African troops were holding the southernmost strip of Angola up to fifty miles deep and stretching from the Atlantic to Zambia. They would remain there until Pretoria had received assurances from Luanda that the area would not "provide bases for terrorists [SWAPO guerrillas] striking across the border" into Namibia and that the Cunene dams, just above the Namibian border, would continue to provide electricity to northern Namibia.[69]

Bereft of the South African shield, UNITA and the FNLA promptly crumbled. The Cubans and FAPLA entered Huambo on February 8, Lobito and Benguela on the 10th, Sá da Bandeira on the 16th, and Moçâmedes on the 17th. "The speed of MPLA's advance has taken everyone by surprise," the *Sunday Times* noted on February 15. "It is now less than 150 miles from the South African troops, who are stationed up to 30 miles from the Namibian border. It could be only a matter of days before the Cubans bump up against the South Africans."[70] Would the SADF withdraw as the Cubans and FAPLA approached? If not, the Cubans would have to fight a major battle in territory close to the enemy's rear guard. "The imminent clash with troops of the racist South African regime requires a massing of forces and special preparations," the Angolan defense minister explained.[71] To this end, Cuban troops kept pouring into Angola through February and March. They were joined by symbolic contingents from Guinea-Bissau and Guinea.[72]

As the final battle loomed on the southern front, Western countries began to recognize the MPLA government. The French, typically, stole the march, on February 17, even though the Common Market had previously agreed to act in concert. (Britain, Denmark, Ireland, Italy, the Netherlands, Norway, and West Germany followed suit over the next two days, as did non-EEC members Sweden, Switzerland, and Canada.)[73]

The French had informed the CIA in mid-January that they were disengaging from Angola.[74] In mid-March, Denard's mercenaries, who had been helping UNITA in the south, did likewise. "It was time to repatriate the team," Denard explained, and "to cash the indemnities of our dead and wounded and everybody's wages." They had not contributed very much. It had not been one of the CIA's best investments. As Stockwell reckoned, "twenty-two had eventually been sent into Angola at a cost of over $500,000 [paid by the agency]; two had been killed in action."[75]

On March 9, Gulf Oil released the tax and royalty payments it owed Angola from escrow; it resumed operations in April, unaware that it owed a debt to the Cubans. The previous December, when Gulf had suspended operations in Cabinda, Neto had considered seizing its holdings and had sent feelers to Rumania to see whether it would be willing to operate the Cabinda oil fields. The Cubans, recognizing that "the socialist countries have little expertise in offshore oil exploitation," had urged Neto not to be rash. "I explained to him," Risquet wrote Castro, "that turning to the socialist countries should be the *last resort*, to be taken only after he had tried unsuccessfully with Gulf Oil, other capitalist companies, Nigeria and Algeria, OPEC, etc. . . . I will return to this subject in my next conversation [with him]. . . . I am confident that I can take care of it." Neto had been patient, and the Ford administration had finally acceded to Gulf's repeated requests to resume operations in Cabinda. "Gulf concluded its negotiations with the MPLA and did pretty well," Assistant Secretary Schaufele told Kissinger in April 1976.[76]

Meanwhile the advance of the FAPLA and Cubans in southern Angola slowed down as they approached the SADF. The South Africans, a Cuban general recalled, "[had] laid a lot of mines in our path." Furthermore, Cuban deputy prime minister Flavio Bravo explained, it was "extraordinarily difficult to supply the Cuban and FAPLA units because of the distances and the destroyed bridges." But the main reason for the delay was political. "We are not planning any military clash with the South African troops in the immediate future," Bravo said. Instead, it was "necessary to strengthen our international campaign to increase the pressure on South Africa to withdraw its troops from Angola."[77] While Pretoria and Luanda engaged in indirect negotiations via the British and the Soviet governments about an SADF withdrawal from Angola, Castro flew to

By early March 1976 the South African troops had withdrawn from central Angola, but they continued to occupy the southernmost strip of the country. From Conakry, on March 15, Castro issued a public warning to South Africa: withdraw or face a Cuban attack. Thousands of well-armed Cuban soldiers making their way toward the South African positions lent weight to his words. On the day of his speech, Castro visited President Agostinho Neto of Angola (to his left) and the presidents of the two countries that had sent troops to fight alongside the Cubans in Angola, Luís Cabral of Guinea-Bissau (to Neto's left) and Ahmed Sékou Touré of Guinea (to Castro's right).

Conakry to meet with Neto and the presidents of the two other countries that had sent troops to help the MPLA, Guinea, and Guinea-Bissau.[78] From Conakry, on March 15, he addressed a public warning to South Africa. "The imperialists are worried," he stated.

There are powerful revolutionary forces in southern Angola and they are gaining strength every day. President Neto has publicly declared that he will not destroy the Cunene dams . . . or cut off the electricity supplied by these dams to the Namibian people. . . . Therefore there can be no pretext what-soever for the fascist government of South Africa, which already oppresses twenty million Africans . . . and illegally occupies Namibia . . . to also occupy . . . any Angolan territory.

If the Cunene dam becomes a battlefield because of the South African racists' decision to continue to occupy one inch of Angola, the responsibility will be South Africa's. If the war extends to Namibia because of the South African racists' decision to continue to occupy one inch of Angola, the responsibility will be South Africa's. If black Africa forms an all-African army to settle accounts once and for all with apartheid because of South Africa's decision to continue to occupy one inch of Angola, the responsibility will be South Africa's.[79]

The notion of a multinational African army liberating South Africa was far-fetched, but thousands and thousands of well-armed Cuban troops were, in fact, marching toward the Namibian border.

On March 25 Defense Minister Botha told the South African Parliament: "Seen as a whole, the assurances by the government of the People's Republic of Angola amount to this—that it will not damage the hydroelectric project . . . and that it will respect the international boundary. . . . In these circumstances, the Government has decided that all our troops will be out of Angola by Saturday 27 March 1976."[80]

On March 27, "in a cloud of dust," the last sixty South African military vehicles crossed the border near the Ruacana dam, where P. W. Botha stood on a makeshift dais and saluted. "Angola may well be regarded as South Africa's Bay of Pigs," a retired South African general lamented.[81] As a final indignity, the withdrawal occurred just as a special session of the UN Security Council met to consider "the act of aggression committed by South Africa against the People's Republic of Angola." On March 31, in a 9-0 vote, the Security Council branded South Africa the aggressor and demanded that it compensate Angola for war damages. The Chinese delegate did not vote, but he made his feelings amply clear in the debate, lashing out at "Soviet social-imperialism and its [Cuban] mercenaries" for their "towering crimes" against Angola. His diatribe could not obscure a basic fact: in Angola, Beijing had been on the side of South Africa's clients, and the well-publicized departure of the Chinese instructors in late 1975 could not dispel the smell of collusion with the apartheid state. "Next to us they have been the most discredited in Angola," Kissinger told Ford.[82]

The United States, South Africa's partner in the invasion, abstained in the Security Council vote, as did France, Britain, Italy, and Japan. "South Africans are at present in particularly bruised mood," the U.S. embassy cabled from Cape Town. "Failure of the 'western countries' (read US) to block UNSC resolution branding South Africa as aggressor in Angola and calling for reparations highly resented."[83]

Pretoria lost more than international standing in Angola. As the Cuban and FAPLA units mopped up southern Angola, SWAPO's guerrillas followed them, making their way to the Namibian border. "Our independence will not be complete until South Africa is liberated," Neto had told a visiting East German official in February 1976. "[We] will help our brothers in Namibia with all the means at our disposal. . . . The struggle is not over with the liberation of Angola."[84] He kept his word. As a South African general writes, "Many military observers consider 27 March 1976 to be the date on which the [SWAPO] insurgency war really started in all seriousness. . . . For the first time they obtained what is more or less a prerequisite for successful insurgent campaigning, namely a border that provided safe refuge."[85]

Beyond Namibia, the tidal wave unleashed by the Cuban victory washed over South Africa. The legacy of Angola, the *Rand Daily Mail* warned, was "The blows to South African pride. The boost to African nationalism which has seen South Africa forced to retreat." U.S. officials remarked that Angola had "blurred the image of South African and mercenary invincibility." For South African blacks, the SADF seemed suddenly vulnerable. "Their [the SADF] racist arrogance shrank when our MPLA comrades thrashed them in Angola," the African National Congress stated in one of the several pamphlets it issued to celebrate the event.[86]

"In Angola Black troops—Cubans and Angolans—have defeated White troops in military exchanges," a South African analyst had observed in February 1976. "Whether the bulk of the offensive was by Cubans or Angolans is immaterial in the color-conscious context of this war's battlefield, for the reality is that they won, are winning, and are not White; and that psychological edge, that advantage the White man has enjoyed and exploited over 300 years of colonialism and empire, is slipping away. White elitism has suffered an irreversible blow in Angola and Whites who have been there know it."[87] The "White Giant" had retreated for the first time in recent history—and Africans celebrated. "Black Africa is riding the crest of a wave generated by the Cuban success in Angola," noted the *World*, South Africa's major black newspaper. "Black Africa is tasting the heady wine of the possibility of realizing the dream of 'total liberation.'" The effect of this heady wine was evident in the *World* itself: over the past few months its tone had become more firm, more outspoken. "We must expect a hardening of the attitudes of our own Non-Whites," a South African member of parliament warned.[88]

Within a few months, South African blacks had celebrated Mozambique's independence under Frelimo and the SADF's humiliation in Angola. "They began to show in their speeches and attitudes," the *Observer* noted, "that they felt they no longer had to submit passively to the traditional power exercised by whites. A new sense of black consciousness began to spread widely."[89] The principal of a black high school in Soweto told a *New York Times* journalist in late February 1976 that Angola "was very much on the minds of his 700 students . . . 'it gives them hope.'"[90]

Three months later, Soweto exploded. One of the sparks that ignited the fire was Angola. "It makes us all think," a young black man from Soweto had mused in February. "In Rhodesia they are talking and after 10 years they have nothing. In Angola and Mozambique they fought, and they have won."[91]

CHAPTER SIXTEEN
REPERCUSSIONS

The story of foreign intervention in Angola is complex and important, for in the details of who did what when lie some of the bitter debates of the Cold War. It is therefore necessary to examine the levels and timing of outside support to the two Angolan sides, focusing especially on the role of the Soviet Union. It is also important to analyze the U.S. decision to launch IAFEATURE, and the reluctance of the U.S. press to report it. Finally, the degree of cooperation between Cuba and the Soviet Union in Angola must be assessed.

OUTSIDE SUPPORT: WEAPONS

To examine the extent of foreign intervention in the Angolan war, one must distinguish between two phases. The second, which began in mid-October 1975, is the easier to characterize: there is no question that in this phase Soviet-bloc involvement in men and matériel far outweighed that of the West, and that foreign troops—Cubans and South Africans—were the true protagonists on the battlefield. The real questions about foreign involvement concern the first phase, from the summer of 1974 to early October 1975.

While there is a reasonable degree of certainty about the timing and the levels of aid provided by the United States to UNITA and the FNLA in this first phase, the extent of Soviet aid to the MPLA is far more controversial.

U.S. officials have claimed that Moscow began sending weapons to the MPLA in October or November 1974.[1] Westad, who had access to Soviet documents, places the Soviet decision to give weapons to the MPLA in December 1974, which is consistent with Cuban and Angolan sources.[2]

The thornier issue, however, is to determine the amount of aid the Soviet Union provided in this phase. In an important book he coauthored with fellow journalist Tony Hodges, Colin Legum states that "the first definite evidence of sizeable Russian and Yugoslav arms reaching Angola goes back to 25 March 1975, when 30 Russian cargo planes arrived in Brazzaville." (Legum's only source is a report by a Brigadier W. F. K. Thompson in the April 11, 1975, issue of the *Daily Telegraph*.) In April, Legum asserts, a Greek-registered ship left Dar-es-Salaam with military supplies for the MPLA, and two Yugoslav ships and a Soviet ship unloaded arms at Pointe Noire. In July a Cypriot ship offloaded its supplies in Luanda. "All this," he concluded, "is sufficient evidence that a steady flow of Russian arms . . . had begun to reach the MPLA during the first half of 1975. This flow became a flood from the middle of October."[3] Hodges states that in March "several Soviet planes" had delivered arms to the MPLA in Brazzaville and adds to Legum's list of the "steady flow" a chartered aircraft, four Soviet ships, two East German ships, and one Algerian ship. His sources are Legum and a September 25, 1975, article in the *New York Times* by Leslie Gelb.[4] John Marcum, too, sees the arrival of the Soviet planes at Brazzaville as a turning point: "In March, Soviet deliveries began to increase. They went by air to Brazzaville." Other shipments, including heavy weapons, arrived aboard Soviet ships in April. Gelb's September 25 article is his only source.[5] To recap, then, the March arrival of the Soviet planes in Brazzaville, which apparently signaled the beginning of large-scale Soviet involvement, is based on two sources: the April 11 *Daily Telegraph* article and Gelb's September 25 *New York Times* article.

I was puzzled by the fact that the arrival of the thirty Soviet planes had not been reported in any of the French, Portuguese, South African, U.S., or African newspapers I had read, so I turned to the *Daily Telegraph* to see for myself what Brigadier Thompson had to say. I found no article by a Brigadier Thompson and no report whatsoever about the arrival of the Soviet planes—not on April 11, or on any other day in 1975. Gelb's September 25 article in the *New York Times*, on the other hand, exists. His sources, he explained, were four U.S. officials who spoke off the record. These officials may have told the truth, or they may have distorted it for perfectly understandable reasons.

The point is neither to suggest that there was no Soviet military aid to the MPLA nor to cast aspersions on the integrity of these journalists. The point is that assertions that rest on dubious evidence have hardened into accepted facts in most accounts of the war.[6]

Other observers, as authoritative as Legum, Hodges, and Marcum (but less frequently cited by U.S. authors), have reached a different conclusion, specifically that through the spring of 1975 the main supplier of weapons to the MPLA was Yugoslavia, which was not a member of the Soviet bloc and was certainly not acting on behalf of the Soviet Union. The German sociologist Franz-Wilhelm Heimer writes that "the deliveries of weapons from Yugoslavia seem to have been decisive [in strengthening the FAPLA]." Mabeko Tali, the foremost authority on the MPLA, agrees: "Yugoslavia tried to alleviate the cruel lack of weapons that debilitated the MPLA by sending a ship loaded with arms." Colonel Ernesto Melo Antunes, who became Portugal's foreign minister in March 1975 and whom Kissinger considered a "moderate," goes further. Through the summer of 1975, he asserts, "the big cargo of weapons . . . for the MPLA came from Yugoslavia."[7]

U.S. documents written at the time are not very helpful. What little has been declassified indicates that U.S. officials did not know how much aid Moscow was extending to the MPLA. "The Soviet Union . . . has lately provided the movement [MPLA] with considerable new military equipment," the Davis task force stated on June 13, but it added, "We are unable to determine the quantity of military assistance being provided by the USSR and other communist sources." A June 27 document asserted that Soviet military aid was "of major significance," while one of July 15 termed it "modest."[8]

According to the MPLA leaders I have interviewed, the first shipment of weapons came from Algeria, in response to a request for aid made by Neto in December 1974. The ship arrived in early 1975 at Barra do Dande (near Caxito) with, according to Lúcio Lara's classified history of the MPLA, "our first . . . half a dozen small armored cars" aboard. They were "very old," Onambwe recalled. The ship also brought mortars, light weapons, and a few infantry transports. In late April, the Yugoslav ship *Postoyna* arrived in Luanda. The Portuguese turned it back; it proceeded to Pointe Noire, where it unloaded armored cars, a few recoilless cannons, and machine guns; from there, in two trips, a landing craft smuggled the weapons to Cabo San Braz, halfway between Luanda and Porto Amboim. This was the "big cargo" mentioned by Colonel Antunes. (A scale model of the *Postoyna* is displayed in the War Museum in Luanda.) Some Soviet shipments also arrived, but they were of lesser importance. "Until August 1975 [when the Cuban military mission was established] the country that helped the MPLA the most was Yugoslavia," Paulo Jorge remarked. In early August, the MPLA leaders complained to Díaz Argüelles that the military aid the Soviet Union was sending was "paltry, given the enormity of the need." The first important Soviet shipment arrived at Pointe Noire at the end of August with weapons for the Ninth Brigade.[9] The first weapons from Cuba arrived in October, when Cuban ships brought arms for the recruits in the CIRs.

One other country, the German Democratic Republic (GDR), sent weapons to the MPLA before independence. Several documents in the East German archives make it possible to retrace this aid step by step and also, therefore, to assess the accuracy of U.S. reports on Soviet-bloc arms deliveries to the MPLA. According to an August 20, 1975, CIA report, for example, an East German ship had unloaded military equipment "in Luanda harbor itself."[10]

The GDR documents indicate that the first shipment of aid arrived in January 1975: photographic material, two tons of blankets for children, half a ton of tangled fleece, and 6.5 tons of ready-to-cook dishes with meat added. A second ship followed in April: five tons of medicine, bandages, medical-technical equipment, and five and a half tons of textiles. Two more ships arrived, in May and June respectively. They brought typewriters, communication equipment, shoes, clothing, camping and sports gear, fifteen ambulances, and food. There were no weapons. Other nonmilitary aid was sent on five flights between July and December 1975.[11] Military aid did not begin until September, contrary to CIA reporting.

Quite frankly, this is surprising. One would expect the East Germans to smuggle in weapons, not blankets. The documents do not explain why the military aid began so late, but they leave no room for doubt about when it began or the amounts involved. Following an urgent plea by Neto that had been conveyed by MPLA defense minister Iko Carreira during a visit to Berlin in late August, the political bureau approved the delivery of 6 million marks ($2,290,000) of military aid on September 9, 1975. That same month the *Vogtland* left for Pointe Noire with its cargo of "noncivilian goods" worth 6.6 million marks ($2,523,000). This was the only military aid the GDR sent before Angola's independence.[12]

Unlike the FNLA and UNITA, the MPLA could receive weapons only by sea or air. This created problems, Iko Carreira told East German officials, "because the airspace and the coasts . . . are controlled by Portugal." This meant that weapons for the MPLA had to be sent to the Congo, and from there smuggled on small boats into minor ports.[13]

Obviously, this was feasible. The weapons of the *Postoyna* were unloaded at Pointe Noire and spirited into Angola. The weapons of the Ninth Brigade also found their way from Pointe Noire to Angola. Still, the logistical abilities of the MPLA should not be exaggerated; it would have been a daunting task, for example, to smuggle the weapons from the thirty Russian cargo planes that had, allegedly, arrived at Brazzaville in March 1975. Furthermore, until late September, the MPLA's relations with the Congo were strained, and Soviet influence with the Congolese government was limited. Soviet officials complained that "there are pro-Chinese elements within the government and the [ruling] party [of the Congo]."[14] As Westad writes, "The MPLA ran up against increasing problems in securing their Soviet lifeline through the Congo. . . . By early August [1975] the Congolese had informed Afanasenko that they would not accept Soviet plans for large-scale support of the MPLA through Congolese territory."[15] The Congolese changed their attitude only after Ngouabi's visit to Cuba in mid-September.

What can one conclude from this fragmentary evidence based on uncertain sources? First, one should note that not one of the available U.S. documents from the March–October 1975 period claimed that the MPLA enjoyed superiority in weapons over its rivals, nor did those few journalists who spent some time at the front. The reports of Díaz Argüelles in September–October 1975— written for his superiors in Havana, not for public dissemination—stressed the FNLA's superiority in hardware.[16]

Second, despite U.S. denials, a close look at U.S. government sources indicates that until October the FNLA and UNITA received at least as much military aid as the MPLA. According to a February 1976 State Department memorandum, "by independence day on November 11, 1975, MPLA had received from the Soviet bloc military hardware valued at $81 million." Assistant Secretary Schaufele told a House committee in January 1976, "By comparison, U.S. assistance amounted to only $32 million."[17] The CIA, however, systematically undervalued the cost of the weapons it sent to the FNLA and UNITA. For example, the *New York Times* noted, "the retail cost of a new .30-caliber carbine is $76, and the inventory value of each of the 20,000 such weapons now stored by the CIA is $15." Therefore,

Marcum concluded, "After adjusting for what appeared to be a consistent under-valuation of materiel sent, real American assistance appeared to be about twice the figure of $32 million eventually acknowledged."[18] We know, furthermore, that in July 1975 Pretoria decided to give Savimbi and Roberto $14.1 million in weapons.[19] Even if we assume that this was all the aid Pretoria gave until it invaded, we would still arrive at $78 million from the United States and South Africa alone. If we include China, France, England, West Germany, and Rumania,[a] it is likely that total aid to Savimbi and Roberto was well over $81 million. It is also possible, of course, that the figure of $81 million that U.S. officials gave for the amount of aid the MPLA received from the Soviet bloc was an overstatement and that the FNLA and UNITA had a clear edge in armament. This would be consistent with the reports from the battlefield.

OUTSIDE AID: INSTRUCTORS AND TROOPS

The evidence is far less murky in the case of foreign military instructors and troops. Chinese instructors were the first to arrive, in the summer of 1974; they stayed in Zaire, never entering Angola. They were also the first to leave, on October 27, 1975.[b]

South African instructors, CIA paramilitary personnel, and the first members of the Cuban military mission (MMCA) began arriving in Angola at roughly the same time, in late August 1975. With the exception of Yuri, no Soviet military advisers arrived until after independence. As Raymond Garthoff, the author of a superb study on U.S.-Soviet relations in the 1970s, writes, "The Soviets were scrupulous about not introducing their own military advisers until Angola was juridically independent." According to Westad, Soviet advisers began arriving in Luanda on the evening of November 12. Judging from the fragmentary evidence that is available, there were soon scores of Soviet instructors teaching the FAPLA how to use the Soviet weapons and Soviet technicians repairing equipment.[20]

Zaire was the first to send troops. They entered Angola in March 1975 and

a. Through most of 1975 Rumania gave military aid to UNITA and the FNLA, and medical aid to the MPLA. In December it shifted gears, concluded "that the right thing to do is to help the MPLA," and ended all aid to FNLA and UNITA. (Sardañas to Columbié, Brazzaville, Dec. 17, 1975, p. 3 quoted, MINREX; Velazco San José to Columbié, Havana, July 1, 1975, MINREX; Marcum, *Angolan Revolution*, 2:264–66.)

b. North Korean instructors also trained the FNLA in Zaire. Unlike the Chinese, who came with the express purpose of training the FNLA, the North Koreans were already in Zaire to train Mobutu's elite division, the Kamanyola. In December 1975 the North Korean ambassador in Kinshasa told his Cuban colleague "that they [North Koreans] had begun to withdraw their military instructors from Zaire and would all be out by the end of the month. He said that they support the MPLA and the Congo and that they wouldn't give Zaire anything that could be used against either of them." (Mora to Roa, Kinshasa, Dec. 4, 1975. See also Klinghoffer, *Angolan War*, pp. 107–8.)

were fighting by the summer. Next came the South Africans, in mid-October, and the Cubans in early November. The record is clear: it was the South African invasion that triggered the dispatch of Cuban troops.[21]

Outside interference, however, did not cause the civil war. The MPLA—aware of the FNLA's military superiority and of its own long-term strength—wanted to avoid an armed clash, and the FNLA, for the same reasons, wanted to precipitate one. Roberto would have resorted to force without any outside involvement. Moreover, even if, by some miracle, there had been no civil war before independence, it strains credulity to imagine that the losers at the polls would have peacefully accepted their defeat. Given the crushing legacy of political underdevelopment bequeathed to Angola by the Portuguese and the hatred among the three rebel groups, Angola was a most unlikely place for this kind of miracle to occur.

ELECTORAL SPECULATIONS

It is almost conventional wisdom that UNITA would have won at least a plurality in any elections because it drew its support from the Ovimbundu, Angola's largest ethnic group with some 35 percent of the total population, whereas the MPLA's base was among the Mbundu (about 20 percent) and the FNLA's among the Bakongo (from 13 to 15 percent).[22] Reality, however, was more complicated. The MPLA was strong in the country's urban centers irrespective of ethnicity. In May 1975 U.S. consul general Killoran warned from Luanda to beware of simplistic arithmetic: "I have reports that MPLA is making inroads among the Ovimbundu in urban areas and among the young," he cabled. Looking back, two decades later, Killoran laughed. "Everyone was always quoting these very precise statistics," he recalled. "I fell into that trap a few times. But it was nonsense. Everything was very fluid."[23]

Christine Messiant, the author of one of the best studies on Angolan society, and Conceição Neto, a former MPLA militiawoman who has become one of Angola's foremost historians, agree with Killoran. Except for the Bakongo, there was no strong ethnic tradition in Angola in 1974. "Ethnicity . . . was not a paramount identification," Messiant writes.[24] Killoran, Messiant, and Conceição Neto do not claim to know who would have won, had elections been held. They merely stress that it was impossible to know.[c]

c. In 1992, the MPLA defeated UNITA in the only elections that have taken place in Angola, receiving 53.7 percent of the vote in the congressional races (UNITA garnered 34.1 percent) and 49.6 percent in the presidential elections. Savimbi got only 40.1 percent of the presidential vote and refused to accept the results, plunging the country again into civil war. (For an excellent analysis of the elections and their historical context, see Messiant, "Angola: les voies." See also Anstee, *Orphan*. Anstee was the special representative of the secretary-general of the United Nations for Angola and head of the UN Angola Verification Mission, which observed the elections and certified them as "overall free.")

By the time Ford approved the covert operation in Angola in July 1975, the elections had become moot. The country was in the throes of civil war, and the MPLA was winning.

Consul General Killoran, who was one of the few U.S. officials with firsthand knowledge of the Angolan movements, believed that the MPLA was "the best qualified of the three movements to run the country" and that the United States would be best served by working with it. His views were not well received in Washington. "The State Department was very uncomfortable with the Luanda consulate's contacts [with the MPLA] and its reporting on the MPLA in early 1975," Robert Hultslander, the CIA station chief in Luanda, writes. "The Agency considered much of Consul General Killoran's reporting on the MPLA to carry a leftist bias; in fact [CIA] Task Force officers warned me to be very careful sharing information with Killoran, as he was 'sympathetic' to the MPLA. . . . In the interest of candor, I must admit that Killoran and I were frequently at loggerheads over what I initially perceived as his MPLA bias." But eventually, Hultslander adds, "I came to share Killoran's assessment that the MPLA was the best-qualified movement to govern Angola." The chair of the Senate Foreign Relations Subcommittee on Africa, Dick Clark, who visited Luanda at the end of August 1975, noted, "The CIA station chief thought we were creating a disaster by supporting Savimbi and Roberto. . . . [Killoran and Hultslander] were convinced our government was making a big mistake." Hultslander explains, "I did my best to . . . defend the covert action program during my all-night session with Clark at Killoran's Luanda residence. My heart was not in it, however, and I finally admitted that I personally thought our support of Roberto and Savimbi would prove disastrous. This position, as you can imagine, caused me problems with my superiors, and infuriated Kissinger."[25]

Killoran and Hultslander were atypical. Most U.S. officials disliked the MPLA because of its "strong Marxist strain" and ties with the Soviet Union, but they did not consider it a threat to U.S. interests. "An MPLA government would be no worse than many governments in West and East Africa that have sought Soviet or Chinese aid," Under Secretary Sisco noted on July 15.[26]

Furthermore, both supporters and opponents of the covert operation agreed that U.S. interests in Angola were minor. The representatives from the Treasury and the JCS in the Davis task force deemed U.S. interests "minimal" and recommended a policy of "studied indifference." Davis, Hyland, and Lord wrote in their April 4 memo to Kissinger, "Our strategic interests are marginal."[27]

This, however, was not the point. Prestige was. As the State Department explained to the Senate Foreign Relations Committee in December 1975, "the credibility of our policies throughout the world" was at stake. "In Africa and elsewhere, this means showing that the United States, despite recent reverses in Southeast Asia and our preoccupations at home, is still able to react when a power—the Soviet Union in this instance—moves to upset the international political environment."[28]

Considerations of prestige became all the more compelling after the Communist victory in Indochina. At an NSC meeting less than three weeks before the fall of Saigon, DCI Colby warned against the dangers of overreaction. "Mr. President," he said,

> there is the question of how these recent events [in Vietnam] may affect the attitudes of other nations toward us. In general, the current debacle is seen not as a turning point, but as the final step on a particular path that most governments had long seen coming. . . . Adjustments were already being made. . . . Soviet, Chinese, and other Communist leaders, for their part, will not automatically conclude that other U.S. commitments are placed in question, unless U.S. public reaction points to a repudiation of other foreign involvement, or internal U.S. recriminations are so divisive as to raise doubts of the U.S. ability to develop any consensus on foreign policy in the near future.

It was a sober assessment. Kissinger immediately took him to task. "I want to take issue with the estimate of the Director of Central Intelligence regarding the impact on our worldwide position of a collapse of Vietnam," he said. "It was his judgement that the world reaction would be negligible, based on the fact that everybody had been anticipating what would happen. Let me say that . . . no country expected so rapid a collapse. . . . Especially in Asia, this rapid collapse and our impotent reaction will not go unnoticed. I believe that we will see the consequences although they may not come quickly or in any predictable manner. . . . I believe that, even in Western Europe, this will have a fall out."[29]

For Kissinger, the final debacle in Vietnam was both a national and a personal humiliation. It undermined his standing at home and his influence in an assertive Congress. It gave heart to the critics of détente who called for a stronger policy toward the Soviets.

The ghost of Vietnam would be exorcised by a display of American power. "In the wake of our humiliating retreat from Cambodia and Vietnam, our allies around the world began to question our resolve," Ford wrote in his memoirs. "The British were concerned. So, too, were the French. Our friends in Asia were equally upset. In the Middle East, the Israelis began to wonder whether the U.S. would stand by them in the event of war." And then there were the Chinese, who berated America's lack of resolve. "Mao's theme is our weakness," Kissinger told the president in October 1975. "We are the 'swallow before the storm.' We are ineffectual. What we say is not reliable."[30]

Against this backdrop, Angola began to acquire a particular significance. It offered both opportunity and risk: America's resolve would be tested. Even the Davis task force, which was opposed to the covert operation, had noted that it "could be a signal to the USSR, Portugal, our NATO allies and others that recent events in Southeast Asia have not sapped the U.S. will to act to protect or promote U.S. interests anywhere in the world, including countries of marginal interest to the U.S." Kissinger made the point forcefully at the June 27 NSC meeting, the meeting that tilted the debate in favor of IAFEATURE. "Playing an active role [in Angola] would demonstrate that events in Southeast Asia have not lessened our determination to protect our interests," he asserted. "In sum we face an opportunity—albeit with substantial risks—to preempt the probable loss to Communism of a key developing country at a time of great uncertainty over our will and determination to remain the preeminent leader and defender of freedom in the West."[31]

When the administration decided to launch IAFEATURE, in July 1975, it knew that Moscow was already giving military aid to the MPLA and that the United States was not (except for the $300,000 approved for Roberto in January). Kissinger brushed aside the fact that by July the Chinese, Zaireans, French, British, and South Africans were also intervening. For him the essential fact was that the Soviets were playing and the Americans were not.

Kissinger also saw pro-American stability in Africa threatened by an MPLA victory in Angola. Zambia and Zaire were applying pressure. "Our failure to heed President Mobutu's repeated requests for help in Angola created strains in our traditionally close relations with this important power in Africa," noted the State Department's December 1975 briefing paper. "Similarly, President Kaunda . . . in April asked us to assist moderate elements in Angola. It was clear that the establishment of a radical and potentially hostile regime in Angola could have grave consequences for the security and stability of both Zaire and Zambia." Furthermore, Kissinger feared that an MPLA victory would have destabilizing effects throughout southern Africa. It "would increase the prospects for violent rather than peaceful change [in southern Africa] and perhaps fatally undermine the incipient trend toward detente between South Africa and Black African states."[32] Neto had made no secret of his hostility to South Africa. "I asked [him] about detente in Southern Africa," Killoran reported in mid-May 1975. "Neto does not see how it can work: nothing fundamental has changed in South Africa; apartheid is still the official policy. [South African] detente is a chimera and after one or two years of no progress black Africa will once again be supporting armed struggle."[33]

Another factor that motivated Kissinger was the dearth of good alternatives. By the time the decision to launch IAFEATURE was made the civil war had begun in earnest. If the Davis task force could say on June 13 that "hopes for a peaceful transition have dimmed,"[34] by early July these hopes were certainly dashed. And by then the MPLA had the upper hand and the alternative the Davis task force had favored—diplomacy—did not look very promising. Too many countries were already involved. A diplomatic solution would require them all to stop providing military assistance more or less simultaneously. It also would require the Portuguese to use force, if necessary, to stop the civil war, and Washington knew that the Portuguese had "neither the will nor the wherewithal" to intervene.[35]

If the United States had wanted to try a diplomatic solution, the best time would have been January, in the afterglow of Alvor, before the civil war began. Instead, the administration had given $300,000 to Roberto in January, with no strings attached. In their April 4 memo, written after the first major FNLA attack against the MPLA, Davis, Hyland, and Lord still felt that there was a chance, "however slim, that the struggle for power in Angola will be political rather than military." With this memo they were trying to catch Kissinger's attention, but he was, as Davis later recalled, "distracted by a lot of other things." There was "a lack of focus on the part of Kissinger," Mulcahy agreed. "He was gone most of the time, a quick trip here, a quick trip there. He didn't designate anyone [to take charge of Angola]." Kissinger's lack of focus was also due to overconfidence. His aides had served him poorly, he complained on July 14, as he learned of the MPLA's victory in Luanda. "I was told for six months that Roberto was in great shape. . . . The conventional wisdom until two months ago is [sic] that Holden Roberto was doing great." Why bother about the civil war in Angola, if the outcome was going to be positive?[36]

The difficulty, and the significance, of getting the top-ranking officials to focus on an issue is not unique to the Ford administration. In his memoirs, Robert Pastor, the NSC aide for Latin America in the Carter administration, tells a similar story. Through late 1978 and early 1979, he and other high-ranking officials (like Assistant Secretary for Latin American Affairs Viron Vaky and deputy NSC adviser David Aaron) were alarmed by the growing crisis in Nicaragua. But they could not get the attention of the "principals" (President Carter, NSC adviser Zbigniew Brzezinski, Secretary of State Cyrus Vance), who were focused on other, momentous issues: the Camp David negotiations, relations with China, SALT II. Hence U.S. policy toward Nicaragua was paralyzed.[37] Something similar happened in 1975 in the case of Angola, but while there were several principals in 1978, in 1975 there was only one: Henry Kissinger. "Kissinger tended to address questions when he was ready to," Davis remarked. "It was very difficult to force Henry Kissinger into a decision if he wasn't ready to make one." And, Y noted, "if you didn't have the attention of Kissinger in this [kind of] situation, there was no point in thrashing it out with a lot of other people. He was the only one who counted." Kissinger, however, was not ready to focus on Angola until June, when the crisis was, in Under Secretary Sisco's words, "ripe." The civil war had broken out, the Soviets were helping the MPLA, Kaunda's plea in April had been reinforced by Mobutu's tantrum in June (when he expelled the U.S. ambassador). Above all, Sisco explained, "our guys were losing."[38]

The discussion about Angola began very late and ended very quickly. When the Davis task force presented its report on June 13, the CIA alone was in favor of a covert operation. Two weeks later, Davis alone was against it. In the meantime Kissinger had taken a stand. "And when Henry makes his desires known, then that sure turns it around," Davis remarked. "Henry Kissinger was a very strong personality in a very strong position." In 1975 only two State Department officials were prepared to challenge Kissinger. From Luanda, Killoran boldly repeated that the MPLA was the best of the three movements. Washington did not reply. "Everything I sent, I never heard anything about. It was like sending all that stuff into a black hole," he recalled. "No one wanted to believe the consulate's reporting, and Killoran's courageous and accurate reporting was ignored," Hultslander explained. "He sacrificed his career in the State Department when he refused to bend his reporting to Kissinger's policy."[39]

The other State Department official who stood up to Kissinger was Davis. Davis did not share Killoran's respect for the MPLA, but he opposed the covert operation. He was articulate and persistent. After his July 12 critique of the CIA paper, he sent two more memos to Sisco, with copies to Kissinger, over the next four days, criticizing the idea of a covert operation. When he learned that Ford had approved IAFEATURE, he submitted his resignation. A handwritten note by Deputy Under Secretary Lawrence Eagleburger to Kissinger attests to Davis's persistence: "Nat Davis has asked if you would read over his memo to Sisco, giving his views on the Angola issue. I've had further talks with Nat, but have not convinced him to withdraw his position [resignation] or to agree to a month delay."[40]

Davis's courageous stance destroyed his career and earned him Kissinger's lasting enmity. In his memoirs, the former secretary portrays him as a gutless bureaucrat, who "had no stomach for covert operations" and resorted to every trick in the book to delay his boss's efforts to do the right thing.[41]

For Kissinger, critics like Davis were at best naive. There was a Cold War on, and the Soviet Union was intervening in Angola while the United States was not. Therefore, a vital interest was indeed at stake: prestige.

This point cannot be dismissed lightly. If the United States had failed to intervene, it would have lost face with those who supported UNITA and the FNLA: South Africa, China, France, England, possibly Belgium, certainly Zaire, Zambia, and a handful of other African countries. Perhaps, too, the Soviet Union would have seen it as a sign of weakness.

U.S. prestige would be even more hurt, however, if the United States intervened and failed. This was Davis's point. "If we are to have a test of strength with the Soviets, we should find a more advantageous place," he wrote in his July 12 critique.[42] What was the likelihood of the covert operation succeeding? If we believe Kissinger's claim that IAFEATURE did not include collaboration with South Africa, then the former secretary is guilty of exactly the charge he leveled against Davis: naiveté. Without the South African dimension, Kissinger was committing the prestige of the United States to a covert operation that was built on sand: UNITA was weak, the FNLA incompetent, and Mobutu unreliable.

Kissinger was not, however, naive: Pretoria was part and parcel of IAFEATURE. The United States and South Africa proceeded in lockstep during the summer, sending weapons and then military instructors to their Angolan clients. Nevertheless, by early October the MPLA was winning because UNITA, the FNLA, and Mobutu were as inept as Davis had said. But Pretoria's invasion, launched on October 14 with Washington's blessing, set things right. By early November Zulu was closing in on Luanda. A few more days, and IAFEATURE would have succeeded.

But would it have been a Pyrrhic victory? Certainly Washington was aware of the extreme sensitivity of the partnership, a fact that is revealed by the extraordinary secrecy that enshrouds it to this day. Would collaboration with the pariah—even if successful—have carried a prohibitive political cost for the United States?

Not necessarily. By November 13 Zulu had been in Angola for five weeks and the world press was writing only of a "mystery column" led by white mercenaries. It was not until November 23 that the South African invasion was exposed by the *Washington Post*. By then, Pretoria and its clients, the FNLA and UNITA, could have consolidated their victory, muting any belated outrage at South Africa's bold grab, particularly if the SADF had withdrawn quickly from Luanda. And, of course, U.S. officials would vehemently have denied any involvement with the South Africans. Arguably, few African governments would have been duped, but so what? They needed economic aid. Confronted with the fait accompli, they might have been tempted to do in 1975 what they had done in 1965 despite their disgust at Johnson's use of mercenaries in Zaire: accept the American victory and move on. (Furthermore, with the possible exception of oil-rich Nigeria, African governments would have been hard put to retaliate against the United States.) The prestige of the United States would have suffered, but not the kind of prestige that interested Henry Kissinger. What concerned him was respect for U.S. power, not admiration of American virtue.[43] Who else would have been outraged? American public opinion? But Americans cared little about Africa. The American press and the U.S. Congress did not turn against the covert operation until it had become clear that it was failing. Had it succeeded, few would have been eager to explore the South African connection.

It seems fair, therefore, to conclude that IAFEATURE could have succeeded and the cost for the United States—at least in the short and medium term—would have been low. But just as victory was within sight, Cuban troops stopped Zulu along the Queve River and derailed IAFEATURE. This was the plan's great flaw: it did not take Castro into account. Kissinger's aides had let him down: no one at the State Department, at the NSC, or in the intelligence community had warned him about Cuba. This was an egregious lapse, given Cuba's past activities in Africa and long-standing ties with the MPLA, but just as Kissinger would have reveled in the glow of victory, so too must he bear responsibility for failure.

Before closing the ledger, we must consider one more fact: Kissinger's Angola policy was amoral. He committed the United States to a policy that was inimical to the interests of the people of Angola. As Killoran and Hultslander argued, the MPLA was by far the best of the three Angolan movements. As the U.S. State Department noted, it commanded "the allegiance of most of the best educated and skilled people in Angola."[44] And while some MPLA leaders were self-serving and corrupt, as a group they towered over the FNLA and UNITA in their honesty and commitment to the welfare of Angola. Roberto and his aides were thugs—brutal, corrupt, and inept. Savimbi remains a warlord whose consuming passion is absolute power.[45] The United States bore no responsibility for the outbreak of the civil war, but Kissinger did his best to smash the one movement that represented any hope for the future of Angola.

While it may be tempting to retort that the MPLA has not, in fact, delivered on this promise, as a whirlwind of violence, corruption, and incompetence has engulfed Angola for the past two decades, it is important to bear in mind that Angola and the MPLA have been deformed by the descent of the Cold War upon them. The MPLA bears a grave responsibility for its country's plight, but the relentless hostility of the United States forced it into an unhealthy dependence on the Soviet bloc and encouraged South Africa to launch devastating military raids in the 1980s.

Beyond the desire to give U.S. prestige a shot in the arm, Kissinger justified his policy by arguing that an MPLA victory would encourage armed struggle and subvert Vorster's détente in southern Africa. He was right, but South Africa's détente was, as Neto said, a "chimera," and violence was inevitable as long as apartheid ruled South Africa, a racist regime dominated Rhodesia, and Namibia was occupied. Just as the MPLA's victory in Angola brought hope to South African blacks, strengthened SWAPO, and spurred the United States to seek majority rule in Rhodesia, so IAFEATURE's success would have strengthened the forces of racism and apartheid in southern Africa. And what for? To teach Brezhnev the rules of détente?

Nat Davis was right when he argued that a covert operation was not America's best option in Angola. "You may ask me the question: 'What is the alternative?' Do we simply lose?" he later asked the officers at the Naval War College. The alternative, he said, was "to pass," not to engage the power and the prestige of the United States when no vital U.S. interests were at stake and where the United States held bad cards.[46]

It is always dangerous to engage in counterfactual history, but it seems safe to venture that if Kissinger had followed Davis's advice, the other foreign powers—East and West—would have limited their intervention in Angola. Left to their own devices, without the comfort of Washington's embrace, Mobutu would have been more cautious. The South Africans would have sent arms, they might have sent a few instructors, but they would not have dared send troops. Without the South African invasion, the MPLA would have won by independence day, without Cuban troops. The Angolan conflict would have continued to be, largely, a "bush war" among rival Angolan groups, not an East-West conflict decided by foreign troops and Soviet hardware. Savimbi's and Roberto's frustrated patrons would certainly have been displeased by Washington's failure to join them, but it is difficult to argue that the damage to U.S. prestige would have been serious or lasting. And U.S. prestige would have increased among most African countries had Washington stood squarely behind the OAU's calls for foreign powers not to interfere in Angola.

Furthermore, through 1975, the Soviets warned the Cubans that Neto was unreliable and prone to be swayed by Washington and other Western powers. On one point they were right: Neto, though a Marxist, was not an admirer of the Soviet Union; he was interested in Angola's well-being, and he knew that his country needed the West. He was, in fact, a pragmatic nationalist who understood that it was in Angola's interest to establish a working relationship with the United States. "Once, when I talked with Neto, I asked him why he was anti-USA," Killoran recalled. "He told me, 'We aren't so anti-US that we can't see where our interests lie.' He knew that they needed the West."[47]

All this was lost on Kissinger. He dealt with momentous matters and important leaders—détente, SALT, Israel, Brezhnev, Mao Zedong, Giscard. He was not interested in Angola, its ragtag liberation movements ("cut-throats," he called them),[48] or the welfare of the people of the region. Angola was but a pawn in the game. Morality took second place to power, just as, in Kissinger's world, order preceded justice. To "pass" in Angola would have been a sign of maturity, not weakness, but it was not Kissinger's style.

To be sure, the paper that the CIA prepared outlining the covert operation was couched in very vague terms. According to Davis, it suggested that "arming Roberto and Savimbi could 'discourage further resort to arms and civil war' " and "that restoration of some sort of triangular 'balance' . . . will produce a peaceful, negotiated, collective solution."[49] This became the official rationale for the administration's Angola policy. "The program [covert operation] is not intended to crush the MPLA," the State Department told the Senate Foreign Relations Committee in December 1975. "Rather, our limited commitments have been geared to our limited objectives: 1) preventing the MPLA and its Soviet and Cuban backers from achieving a quick military takeover of Angola; and 2) sufficiently redressing the balance among Angola's political movements to facilitate a political solution in which the MPLA does not dominate UNITA and FNLA." Kissinger repeated this defense of his policy to the Senate Foreign Relations Subcommittee on Africa a month later: "In Angola we have consistently advocated a government representing all three factions. We have never opposed participation by the . . . MPLA," he said. "Our immediate objective was to provide leverage for diplomatic efforts to bring about what we consider a just and peaceful solution. . . . We wanted the greatest possible opportunity for an African solution."[50]

This insults the intelligence of Henry Kissinger. By July Angola was in the throes of a full-fledged civil war and the administration knew that there was virtually no chance of a peaceful transition. "All hope for a peaceful solution was gone once they began fighting in Luanda back in March," mused Y, who helped draft the CIA plan. Furthermore, as Davis pointed out, providing weapons was a strange way to seek peace. ("So far, the arming of the various factions has fed the civil war, not discouraged it," he wrote.) Mobutu, who would be the main conduit of U.S. aid to Roberto and Savimbi, had made it absolutely clear that he was not interested in peace: he wanted to destroy the MPLA. Nor did Kissinger, judging from Davis's July 12 memo, hold out any hope for peace. "I believe the Secretary is right in his conviction—if I understand his views—that if we go in, we must go in quickly, massively and decisively enough to avoid the tempting, gradual, mutual escalation that characterized Vietnam during the 1965–67 period."[51]

Furthermore, IAFEATURE included not one nod toward a peaceful solution. U.S. officials intervened to scuttle any possibility of agreement between the MPLA and UNITA in September and delivered arms, not admonitions, when the South Africans raced toward Luanda and Roberto's forces attacked Quifangondo a few weeks later. The United States approached the Soviet Union to search for mutual restraint only on November 20, after the Cuban troops had landed.

I shared my doubts with Under Secretary Sisco, in a one-hour interview that was mostly off the record. Finally he answered, on the record, that while the United States had hoped for a peaceful and democratic solution, by the time it embarked on the covert operation it knew that it was not in the cards. "If you ask, did we hope for a peace between Savimbi and Roberto," he said, "the answer is yes. Including Neto? The answer is no."[52]

The CIA's talk of a peaceful solution was a smokescreen. "As is typical of such clandestine operations," Hyland writes, "the policy discussion was cryptic."[53] Just as it was better not to mention any possible collusion with South Africa, so it was better to shroud IAFEATURE in a mist of peace. This was particularly true in light of the Hughes-Ryan amendment, passed by Congress in December 1974, which stipulated that the CIA had to report "in a timely fashion, a description and scope" of covert operations to eight congressional committees. And Congress, in the wake of Vietnam and Watergate, was an unreliable partner. "It can be assumed," the Davis task force warned, "that there would be strong Congressional opposition to any US involvement in support of one of the contending factions [in Angola]."[54] Through the summer and the fall of 1975, the administration briefed the relevant congressional committees about IAFEATURE, but the briefings were less than candid. Representative Diggs, who chaired the Congressional Black Caucus and was a bitter foe of South Africa, would have strenuously objected had he known the true scope of the operation. "[We were told that] South Africa was not going to be any part of this. . . . So we were not going to 'be embarrassed' by South Africa," Senator Biden noted in January 1976. Hyland recalls that in late July 1975 he briefed the Senate Foreign Relations Subcommittee on Africa about IAFEATURE. "No one objected, and if there were any reservations, they were not voiced. . . . The senators who later became strong critics may have had a point. If they had been informed by the White House or the State Department that we were determined to wring a military victory out of the mess in Angola, they might have registered reservations and objections much earlier."[55] Congress's interest in Africa was virtually nonexistent; all that was needed was reassurance that no major complications would arise from IAFEATURE. The smokescreen was a pacifier.

THE U.S. PRESS AND IAFEATURE

The Angola debacle unfolded as Ford prepared to seek the Republican nomination for the 1976 presidential elections. Predictably, he tried to shift the burden of failure to Congress. As he signed the bill forbidding covert aid to the Angolan factions on February 10, 1976, Ford lashed out: "The Soviet Union and their Cuban mercenaries" had won because members of Congress had "lost their guts." This was "a tasteless and tactless charge," the *Washington Post* wrote, "made, one is forced to suspect, to protect his right flank against Ronald Reagan [in the Republican presidential primaries]. . . . In fact, if 'guts' is the issue, one can imagine several more valid tests. It would take 'guts' for the President to admit he made a mistake in Angola." Columnist Anthony Lewis was biting: "The phrasing had the delicacy of Joe McCarthy's."[56]

Beyond Ford's immediate concern—the polls—loomed a larger issue, the credibility of the United States. "Do we really want the world to conclude that if the Soviet Union chooses to intervene in a massive way, and if Cuban or other troops are used as an expeditionary force, the United States will not be able to muster the unity or resolve to provide even financial assistance?" Kissinger asked in a whirlwind of appearances in Congress and on television. Arthur Schlesinger retorted, dryly, "We may well raise graver doubts about our 'credibility,' by giving inadequate aid to a side that goes on to lose than by giving no aid at all."[57]

Many U.S. newspapers criticized the administration harshly. Others lambasted Congress. Still others damned both the weak-kneed Congress and Kissinger's effete interpretation of détente. In short, the debate in the U.S. press was robust and wide ranging. It was, however, a debate that had been long in coming.

In his July 12 critique of the CIA plan for IAFEATURE, Assistant Secretary Davis had written that the risk of disclosure was great. There was the danger of leaks from members of the administration and Congress. Furthermore, he noted, "We would have to reveal our plans and arrangements to senior officials of at least four governments or Movements, of uncertain orientation, reliability and reputation for discretion. Even the purely external signs on the ground of changed military capabilities would almost certainly be immediately apparent."[58]

Davis was both right and wrong. Abroad, the covert operation became common knowledge in less than a month. The large amounts of war matériel that began to flow from Kinshasa to northern Angola in early August aroused suspicions. Even the friendly *Zambia Daily Times*, which opposed the MPLA, noted on August 23 that "the United States is already providing arms for the . . .

FNLA."[59] At home, however, the press was less alert or, perhaps, more discreet—just as it had been a decade earlier in the case of the covert operation in Zaire.

Among American newspapers, the New York Times offered by far the best and most extensive coverage of the war in Angola, and it was the New York Times that first revealed the existence of a U.S. covert operation there. In a front-page article on September 25, Leslie Gelb wrote that "millions of dollars are being poured covertly into Portugal and Angola by East and West," including the Soviet Union and the United States. (The Soviets, he hastened to say, were "far more" involved in both Portugal and Angola than the Americans.)[60] The article provoked nothing but total silence. "It was, and still is, a mystery to me why the Gelb report had so little public impact in the United States when it was published," Nathaniel Davis writes.[61] The explanation is suggested by a stern editorial in the Washington Post that appeared two days after Gelb's article. The editorial endorsed the covert operation in Portugal, but not that in Angola. "The operation there seems much closer to the questionable crudely anti-communist adventures that have so marred the CIA's past," it observed. But this was not the point. The point was that the secret had been betrayed: "The disclosures illuminate the strange new semi-public setting in which 'secret' operations must now be devised. . . . Some would consider this anticipation of exposure as a healthy deterrent or even as just retribution for past excesses. We find it deplorable. The United States still has, we believe, reason to conduct certain covert operations abroad—Portugal is an excellent example. It should not be necessary to point out that covert operations must be covert. 'National security' unquestionably has been overworked as a rationale for secrecy but it has not lost all validity."[62]

The Christian Science Monitor, the Wall Street Journal, the Chicago Tribune, the Los Angeles Times, the Nation, the Village Voice, the New Republic, Newsweek, and Time apparently agreed with the Post. All of them ignored Gelb's article.[63] And so did the New York Times, except for two passing references on October 16 and October 26, until a November 3 editorial that included the first hint of criticism of U.S. policy: "Zaire and China support FNLA and there have been reports of American aid to both FNLA and UNITA. . . . With bitter experience of intervention in a complicated civil war in Asia, the United States should take great care to avoid involvement in this equally complex civil war in Africa."[64]

The Times offered no further criticism of the administration's Angola policy for more than a month. On November 7 it reported, without comment, that Under Secretary Sisco and DCI Colby had told a closed session of the Senate Foreign Relations Committee that the administration was covertly supplying arms to UNITA and the FNLA. On November 9 it seemed to forget this, stating that the FNLA was supported by Zaire and "probably indirectly by the United States."[65] Over the next month, the New York Times increased its coverage of the war in Angola in response to the arrival of Cuban troops and the growing involvement of the Soviet Union, and it reported the administration's harsh criticism of Havana's and Moscow's adventurism extensively. Only rarely did it mention that the United States was providing aid to the FNLA and UNITA and these references were usually cushioned by the adverb "indirectly" and by the explanation that the amount was quite modest—"paltry," when compared with Soviet aid to the MPLA. Moscow was the villain. Not one question was raised about the aim of U.S. policy. The administration's claim that it was sending arms in order "to create a stalemate . . . so as to get all the parties together in a coalition" was repeated unquestioningly. A good illustration of the *Times*'s approach is its November 26 editorial: "Soviet imperialism has re-entered the African continent in crude force, this time in . . . Angola. . . . The interventionists, the provocateurs of civil war in Angola are not American; it is not Washington that is trying to capitalize, for its own great power interests, on the misery of an ill-prepared African society struggling for national identity and sovereignty." The editorial did not add that the United States was intervening in the conflict; neither Zaire nor South Africa was mentioned.[66]

The same complacency characterized the *Washington Post*, the *Christian Science Monitor*, the *Wall Street Journal*, the *Chicago Tribune*, the *Los Angeles Times*, *Newsweek*, and *Time*. On the few occasions they mentioned U.S. support to the FNLA and UNITA, they stressed that "the Soviets have outspent the U.S. many times over." And with the exception of the *Washington Post*, there was no hint of criticism of the U.S. role, and the administration's explanation of its policy was stolidly echoed. "The United States," the *Christian Science Monitor* stated on November 12 in a typical editorial, "reportedly has indirectly channeled military aid to the FNLA and UNITA as a means of strengthening them sufficiently to work out a coalition government with the MPLA. . . . Secretary of State Kissinger has expressed concern about the substantial military aid given to the . . . [MPLA] by the Soviet Union and Cuba. He says the U.S. has no interest in Angola except that its independence be respected."[67]

But like the U.S. Congress, the press finally awoke. Things got rough. On December 14, the *New York Times* published a major article on the covert operation—the first since Gelb's September 25 piece. While it did not criticize the administration's Angola policy directly, it revealed that it had caused rifts within the State Department and had led Davis to resign. Two days later, an editorial bluntly criticized the lack of public debate on U.S. policy "toward the catastrophic civil war in Angola," and raised questions "about what US interests are at stake in Angola" and the appropriate means to defend them—questions that the editors could have raised two months earlier.[68] The difference, of course, was that, like Congress, the press had no interest in discussing the operation or its rationale as long as the policy appeared to be successful.

The African American press had also shown very little interest in the Angolan conflict. It was the South African invasion and revulsion at the fact that "the U.S. and South Africa have climbed into the same bed," as the *Pittsburgh Courier* put it, that transformed the issue from a remote African civil war into racial conflict. As a result, in December, the African American press turned decisively against the administration's policy.[69] Likewise, the seventeen members of the Congressional Black Caucus became very vocal after months of silence.[70]

As the debate ground on through the winter and the early spring of 1976, the administration had nothing to show for its pains: not only had it failed to bloody the Soviets' nose, but it had inflicted an unnecessary humiliation on the United States. It was not the first time that Washington had pursued a policy in Africa that offended many Africans (Zaire, in 1964–65, was equally distasteful), but it was the first time that the United States had been roundly defeated. Kissinger's and Ford's attempts to control the spin proved counterproductive. Their claims of concern about the welfare of the people of Angola provoked scorn in Africa. The Nigerian president bitterly dismissed America's "crocodile tears" and Nyerere noted that, "During the armed liberation struggle, the . . . Americans . . . were not prepared even to donate a single quinine tablet for the fighters."[71]

While African leaders denounced the United States, the Ford administration denounced Cuba and the Soviet Union. It vented its spleen at Castro in small ways (calling off an exhibition baseball series between the two countries) and big, announcing that there would be no improvement in relations for the foreseeable future.[72]

According to U.S. officials Castro's role was despicable, but the real villain was the Soviet Union. Cuba, Kissinger explained, "was acting merely as the 'client state.'" Using its "Cuban mercenaries," Moscow had flouted the principles of détente, echoed Ford.[73] But it was not clear what was the appropriate punishment. As Garthoff points out, Ford had "in effect two possible sticks—a cutoff of grain sales or holding back on SALT, both of which represented palpable Soviet interests. Both, however, were also *American* interests," and, in an election year, the grain sales were also a palpable Ford interest. "There isn't the slightest doubt . . . [that] the Soviets could get along without American grain," Ford told the American Farm Bureau Federation, while Kissinger argued forcefully, within the administration and in public statements, that there was "no alternative" to dialogue with the Soviet Union on SALT.[74]

Kissinger and Ford, therefore, stressed the gravity of the Soviet offense in Angola, but did not respond with effective sanctions. The result was unsettling. A columnist aptly noted that while Ford and Kissinger continued "to shake their fists at both Congress and the Russians," the sense of impotence and frustration among the American public grew, discrediting the administration and hurting détente. It was all grist to the mill for the administration's conservative critics, who had always opposed détente.[75]

CUBAN-SOVIET RELATIONS AND ANGOLA

"Kissinger and I wondered," INR director Hyland recalled, "why the Russians thought Angola worth the trouble it created between us and them on détente."[76]

Hyland's question is all the more pertinent when one realizes that the Soviets did not trust the MPLA. They had not trusted its leaders during the war of independence against Portugal, and they still didn't trust them in 1975. "A Soviet source has informed me," Ambassador Columbié cabled Havana in December 1975, that Moscow "is presently very worried because Sweden has recognized the MPLA [government]. While on the one hand they consider it a positive step, on the other hand they consider it dangerous, because of . . . the influence they [the Swedes] could acquire over President Neto and other MPLA leaders." The Soviets were also wary of Brazil, which had recognized Neto's People's Republic of Angola with suspicious speed. "Even though it seems that the initiative came from them [the Brazilians]," Ambassador Afanasenko told Columbié, one could not exclude the possibility that they had done it at the behest of the United States, "which knows that it would be fairly easy for the Brazilians to manipulate the MPLA leadership." Neto's close adviser, Lúcio Lara, remained, as always, Moscow's bête noire. Afanasenko told Columbié "that the fact that Lara played an important role in the party [MPLA] worried him." The Soviets distrusted not only Lara, but also his wife, who was of Jewish descent and, Afanasenko explained, the daughter of a former "German social democrat leader." And they continued to distrust Neto. Before 1974 they had suspected him of being pro-Chinese; now they worried that he might be swayed by the Americans. "It is very important to be aware," they told Columbié, "of Neto's relations with the Yankees."[77]

Why then would the Soviets endanger détente on behalf of a movement they didn't even trust?

Until the relevant Soviet documents are declassified, any discussion of Soviet motivations must remain tentative.[78] But even educated guesses require, first, some determination of what the Soviet Union actually did. The available evidence suggests that, contrary to what U.S. officials have claimed, until October 1975 Soviet bloc aid to the MPLA was at most equal to the aid the United States and its friends gave the FNLA and UNITA. In other words, Soviet policy was cautious, and if the Soviets violated the spirit of détente, so too did the United States.

The Ford administration blamed Moscow for the dispatch of the Cuban troops, but we now know that that the Cubans acted on their own, without consulting Moscow. Moreover, by early November the Soviets must have known that South Africa had invaded Angola, that Zulu was closing in on Luanda, and that the MPLA was threatened with imminent ruin.[79] And yet they still did not approach Havana to resurrect Castro's August proposal for the dispatch of Cuban troops. They merely sent weapons that the inexperienced FAPLA could not use. This restraint may have been motivated, above all, by Brezhnev's desire to conclude the SALT II negotiations before the February 1976 Congress of the Soviet Communist Party. "On November 8," Kissinger writes, "Dobrynin delivered an 'oral message' from Brezhnev to Ford saying that he was prepared to break the SALT deadlock on the basis of concessions by both sides and suggesting that I meet with him in December in Moscow for that purpose."[80]

Arguably, Soviet policy became less cautious after Castro had begun sending his troops. But even on this point there is room for disagreement. According to Westad,

> During the week before independence, large groups of Cuban soldiers had started arriving in Luanda onboard Soviet aircraft. The Soviets had organized and equipped these transports, although the operation was technically directed by the Cubans themselves. . . . After the creation of the MPLA regime the Politburo authorized the Soviet General Staff to take direct control of the trans-Atlantic deployment of additional Cuban troops, as well as the supplying of these troops with advanced military hardware. The massive operation . . . transported more than 12,000 soldiers by sea and air from Cuba to Africa between late October and mid-January 1976.[81]

U.S. and Cuban documents, however, tell a different story: "In January 1976," noted a National Intelligence Estimate, "the Soviets . . . began providing an airlift for Cuban forces between Cuba and Angola." Until then, all Cuban troops went to Angola on Cuban ships and Cuban planes, without any assistance from the Soviet Union. For example, on January 3, 1976, the State Department estimated that there were "as many as 7,500 Cubans in Angola . . . 4,200 Cubans may have gone to Angola on 14 sailings by *Cuban* ships and another 3,300 aboard 43 aircraft flights."[82] These flights, another report noted, were aboard three Britannias and two IL-18s belonging to Cubana de Aviación.[83] Because of their limited range, the Britannias and the IL-18s needed to refuel twice en route to Luanda. The second stop presented no difficulties: both Guinea-Bissau and Guinea were steadfast in their support for the MPLA. But finding an airport for the first stop posed a problem. Initially the Cubans used Barbados's Bridgetown airport. To hide the military nature of the flights, the troops dressed in civilian clothes and remained on the planes, staying well clear of the door, while in transit.[84] At first, U.S. intelligence was not sure of their destination. "The planes most likely went to Africa," the CIA reported on November 14, "but we do not have positive confirmation that they did so." Eventually, however, the nature of the flights became obvious. "Bridgetown is the refueling stop for Cubana flights to Africa," a December 1, 1975, State Department cable noted. Two weeks later, on December 16, another State Department cable said, "to date there have been 33 Cubana airlines flights to Africa, probably to Angola. These flights transited Barbados." Under U.S. pressure Barbados withdrew its landing permission from Cuba on December 17. "Cuba may have serious problems in continuing its airlift," the CIA observed the following day.[85] The Western press, which was closely following the fortunes of the Cuban airlift, agreed. "Barbados' refusal to allow Cuban troop carriers to use its refuelling facilities may force Russia into the more uncomfortably active role of lending the Cubans their AN-22 long-distance transport aircraft," noted the *Economist*, while the *Daily Telegraph* wrote on December 19: "Russia will almost certainly take over the Cuban airlift of troops and supplies to Angola following Barbados's angry refusal on Wednesday to allow any more Cuban troop planes to refuel at Seawell near Bridgetown."[86]

The loss of Barbados led Cuba to approach several other countries for landing rights. Trinidad refused. Cape Verde offered the Isla de Sal, but reneged a few days later after Washington applied pressure. Finally, Guyana stepped into the lurch. "When Barbados closed its airport to us," recalls General Juan Escalona, "Fidel sent me to Guyana, to ask President Forbes Burnham to allow our planes to land there." Burnham agreed. The first flight refueled in Guyana on December 18 or 19. But when Washington learned of Burnham's transgression, it applied pressure on him and asked Venezuela, Guyana's big neighbor, to help in turning the screws. Venezuelan president Carlos Andrés Pérez warned Burnham "that the favorable treatment on petroleum sales that the GOG [government of Guyana] is seeking . . . would be in jeopardy if 'one drop of Venezuelan oil' went to fuel Cuban aircraft." Burnham gave in. In the end, "only two Cuban flights transited Guyana," Kissinger observed. On December 20, Portugal allowed Cuban planes to refuel at the Azores, but the U.S. embassy in Lisbon protested and the Portuguese caved. "Last Cuban flight to stop in Azores was on Jan. 14," Kissinger said.[87]

Havana had also turned to Moscow. In late December the army chief of staff, General Senén Casas, spoke in Moscow with General Viktor Khulikov, the chief of the general staff, "in order to explore the possibilities of Soviet assistance to the airlift." The Soviet response was dilatory. Finally, on the morning of January 6, the Soviet ambassador in Havana, Vitali Vorotnikov, told a senior Cuban military officer that he had a message for Raúl Castro: Aeroflot would provide ten charter flights to transport the Cubans to Angola. The planes, two IL-62s, which could carry 162 passengers each, would fly directly to Conakry (Bissau's airport was too small) and from there to Luanda. "I told him [the ambassador] that this was very good news," the officer reported, "especially at a time when the U.S. was pressuring several governments not to let us use their airports."[d,88]

The first IL-62 left Havana on January 9 with Cuban troops and Soviet pilots.[89] (The Cubans had not yet been trained to fly the IL-62s.) The United States knew immediately. A January 13 State Department cable noted, "Cuba may have *begun* to use 200 passenger capacity IL-62 aircraft (Soviet) in its airlift support operations. The IL-62 has double the capacity of Bristol Britannias and IL-18s which Cuba has previously employed and has a longer range as well. IL-62 left Havana for Luanda Jan. 10 and Jan. 11."[90]

In late January, the *Christian Science Monitor* summed up the story well:

d. Sékou Touré was a firm MPLA supporter and Soviet planes used in the Angola airlift were already refueling at Conakry airport. When Washington expressed its "disappointment and irritation" at this transgression and warned that it would affect relations between the two countries, Touré was defiant, informing the Soviet ambassador: "You have permanent and unconditional permission [to use Conakry airport] for all flights relating to Angola." (Darío to Roa, Conakry, Dec. 29, 1975, quoting the Soviet ambassador; for the text of the U.S. note, see Darío to Osmany, Conakry, Dec. 30, 1975.)

"Using old British Britannia turboprop aircraft, which have long served as the backbone of Cubana de Aviación . . . Cuba began an air ferry of troops. The Britannias are lumbering old planes that cannot make the transatlantic crossing without refueling stops. For a time Barbados was used, but the government there ordered a stop to the practice. Trinidad and Tobago also refused permission. Then the government of Guyana allowed refueling rights . . . but this is tapering off. Now Soviet IL-62 jet craft, with transatlantic range, are being used."[91] On one point the article was mistaken. The IL-62 flights had already ended, since Moscow had offered only ten flights and these had all taken place by January 16. "The Soviets have now recalled IL-62s," Kissinger noted on January 31.[92] Cuba was again on its own.

Unable to find an airport for the second stop, the Cubans outfitted the Britannias with additional fuel tanks in order to increase their range. They flew from Holguín, in eastern Cuba, directly to Bissau—a very risky operation.[93] Meanwhile, the Cuban government scrambled to get more IL-62 flights from the Soviet Union. On January 31 Raúl Castro wrote to Severo Aguirre, Cuba's ambassador in Moscow, "Ask for a meeting with Katushev [Soviet Central Committee member in charge of foreign relations] . . . to raise the question of our leasing three IL-62s as long as the present emergency in Angola lasts." The Soviets did not respond until February 10. The next day, Fidel Castro cabled Colomé, the head of the Cuban military mission in Luanda: "Up to ten IL-62 flights will be arriving soon. After that, we will rely on one IL-62 we have leased [from the Soviets]."[94]

Three weeks earlier, on January 16, Havana and Moscow had signed a military protocol. Article 1 stated that the Soviet Union would give weapons worth 35 million rubles ($25 million) to Cuba by the end of the month. Soviet planes and ships would deliver the weapons directly to the Cubans in Angola.[95] In late January, two Soviet ships left the Soviet Union for Angola with a cargo of forty-three tanks, twelve BM-21s, seventeen BTRs, and other weapons.[96] This was the first Soviet shipment of weapons to the Cuban troops in Angola. "Commander in Chief," Risquet wrote to Fidel Castro on January 29, in a letter that sheds some light on the triangular relationship between Cubans, Angolans, and Russians,

1. Furry [Colomé] and I spoke with Neto alone . . . and we informed him of your decision to send more troops, fully armed, in order to amass the forces necessary to both free the country from the South African and Zairean invasions and to be in a position to counter any possible increases in their forces.

We told him [Neto] that some of the new Cuban troops would arrive by boat with their weapons and the rest would fly to Luanda, where they would collect the weapons that the Soviet Union is going to send for them.

We explained that this would save us the time, expense, and risk of having the Soviets send the weapons to Cuba and then transporting them to Angola with the troops.

Neto understood and approved our plan without qualm or hesitation.

2. Three days later, the Soviet general [head of the Soviet military mission in Angola] told us he too would like to inform [Neto], on behalf of the USSR, about the delivery of the Soviet weapons to the Cubans in Angola. We agreed that the most appropriate way would be that he, Furry, and I meet again with Neto alone. And so we did. The general explained in some detail what weapons were being sent.

Neto raised no objection whatsoever, wrote down the most important weapons, said that he would inform the Political Bureau of this increase [of men and arms], and appeared very satisfied with it, as an additional guarantee to counter whatever the South Africans, the Zaireans, and the Imperialists might do. . . .

3. Nevertheless, taking into account the concern you expressed in your cable of yesterday, when Oramas and I met today with the president to discuss other matters (SWAPO, Katangans, etc.), I returned to it as if in passing, and I gave him a list of the weapons that would be arriving on future Soviet ships and that are for the Cuban troops. . . .

We told him that the Cuban troops, with all these weapons, would remain in Angola for as long as it took and for as long as he considered necessary, and that we would train the Angolan personnel to operate the tanks, the planes, Katiuskas, mortars, guns, etc. And that if the weapons delivered to the PRA [People's Republic of Angola] were to prove insufficient for the future Angolan army, the USSR would always be ready to provide what was required, etc. etc.

That is, our conversation was absolutely brotherly and without the smallest misunderstanding or reproach. However, we wanted to be absolutely clear—and we left the list as written evidence—so that there could be no misunderstandings, now or in the future.[97]

Therefore, one must distinguish between two kinds of Soviet deliveries of weapons to Angola: those to the FAPLA, which began sometime in 1975 and gained momentum in the fall, and those to the Cuban troops, which began in late January 1976. Of course, this distinction is blurred by the fact that many of the weapons sent to the Angolans were used by the Cubans because they were too sophisticated for the FAPLA.

More significant, however, is the fact that the Soviet airlift of Cuban troops did not begin until January. For two months, amid growing difficulties, the Cubans sent their troops to Angola on Cuban planes—perhaps they didn't turn for help to the Soviet Union, or they did and were turned down, or they received hints not to ask. With infuriating consistency, Cuban officials have refused to enlighten me about the reasons for the Soviets' failure to provide more timely assistance, even though the documents that I have obtained from the Cuban archives make it plain that this assistance was sorely needed. Fidel Castro touched briefly on this matter in 1992: "The Soviets were not at all sympathetic to the transportation of our troops to Angola. . . . What there was was a great deal of criticism by the Soviets in connection with the activities we were carry-ing out." And he mentioned it again in 1999, during an interview for the CNN series on the Cold War: "We acted . . . but without their cooperation. . . . Quite the opposite! There were criticisms."[98]

This paints a complex picture: Moscow increased its military aid to the MPLA in November and December, but provided no assistance to the airlift of the Cuban troops that would defend Luanda from the South Africans. And for two critical weeks—from December 9 to 24—Moscow even stopped sending weap-ons to Angola, at a time when the SADF was still trying to break through the Cuban defenses. The least that can be said, until the Soviet archives are open, is that Moscow was not an enthusiastic participant. Arguably, Soviet restraint was caused by concern about the impact on détente, or by irritation with Castro's unilateral decision, or by doubts about the Cubans' ability to stop the South Africans, or by reservations about the MPLA.

Whatever tension may have existed in 1975 between Moscow and Havana about Angola, it had dissipated by February 1976, both because the operation had been successful and because it had become clear that SALT II was not going to be concluded quickly. Despite Kissinger's earnest desire to move forward, Ford had caved to the conservatives and had virtually suspended work on the treaty until after the November presidential elections. In Moscow this strength-ened the hard-liners who, in Dobrynin's words, argued that "the United States was . . . busy consolidating its positions in Egypt and elsewhere, and had actively overthrown a socialist government in Chile that came to power legally. So how could the Americans see our support for the newly formed government in Angola as a violation of detente? Must we yield to American arrogance and their double standard?" Brezhnev, who had hoped to crown the party Congress with a SALT treaty, would instead deliver a success in Angola, burnishing Mos-cow's credentials as the champion of Third World liberation.[99] The gap between Castro and Brezhnev had narrowed. Relations were also helped by the fact that the Cubans—unlike their behavior in the 1960s—went to great lengths to as-suage Soviet sensitivities. "The Soviet cadres in Angola," writes Westad,

were, by 1976, very satisfied with the way both Angolans and Cubans had respected Moscow's political primacy during the war. . . . The Soviet repre-sentatives often expressed a certain degree of surprise to Moscow at how harmonious were relations with the small Caribbean ally. The Soviet-Cuban "close coordination in Angola during the war has had very positive results," [the chargé d'affaires in Luanda, G. A.] Zerev told his superiors in March 1976. Soviet diplomats and officers lauded the Cubans for their bravery and for their ability to function as a link between Moscow and Luanda while at the same time "respecting" the paramount role of the CPSU leadership. The overall Cuban-Soviet relationship improved significantly in the wake of the Angolan operation, up to a point which had not been reached since the 1962 missile crisis.[100]

Westad points out, correctly, that Cuba followed a two-track approach toward Moscow in Angolan matters. On the one hand, it stressed Moscow's primacy, both in the socialist family and as Angola's paramount ally. On the other hand, it defended the MPLA's efforts to define its own path, which was not in lockstep with Moscow. "For leaders like Agostinho Neto and Lúcio Lara," Mabeko Tali remarked, "the inspiration in their relations with the Soviets was the spirit of independence of Tito's Yugoslavia."[101]

This underlying tension was laid bare during an attempted coup in Luanda on May 27, 1977. Much about the coup remains obscure, but two key points are clear. First, the plotters sought closer ties with the Soviet Union and enjoyed the sympathy, if not the active support, of the Soviet embassy. Second, the Cubans played a decisive role in defeating the revolt.[102] As Ambassador Andrew Young told a Senate subcommittee in 1978, "The Cubans and the Russians haven't been always united in Angola. . . . When there was a recent coup attempt against Neto, it was pretty clear from African sources that the Russians were behind that coup. Yet, the Cubans sided with Neto."[103]

In the 1960s, Cuba would probably have embroidered its role in the coup with snide remarks about the less than honorable role played by the Soviets. The Cuba of the 1970s was more restrained. A few days after the failed uprising, Raúl Castro replied to his Soviet counterpart, who had asked for the Cuban assessment of the revolt, in impeccable fashion: his letter contained no reference whatsoever to Moscow's role, but detailed what the Cuban troops had done "at the request of President Neto in order to reestablish order."[104]

CHAPTER SEVENTEEN
LOOKING BACK

 uba's intervention in Angola did not occur in a vacuum. While it caught Washington flat-footed, it fit, in fact, into the continuum of Cuba's relations with Africa, the Soviet Union, and the United States.

THE CUBAN-SOVIET RELATIONSHIP IN THE 1960S

As a senior U.S. intelligence officer noted in 1967, Cuba's "heavy dependence on the Soviet Union for survival . . . [was] incontrovertible reality."[1] Soviet aid kept the Cuban economy afloat, and Soviet weapons kept the Cuban soldiers armed. Was Cuba, therefore, a Soviet puppet? No, according to U.S. intelligence, which pointed to Castro's resistance to Soviet advice and his open criticism of the Soviet Union. "He has no intention of subordinating himself to Soviet discipline and direction, and he has increasingly disagreed with Soviet concepts, strategies and theories," a 1968 study concluded, reflecting the consensus of the intelligence community. Castro had no compunction about purging those who were most loyal to Moscow or about pursuing economic policies that ran counter to Soviet advice. Soviet officials "muttered about pouring funds down the Cuban rathole" and footed the bill, the State Department noted. Castro also criticized the Soviet Union as dogmatic and opportunistic, niggardly in its aid to Third World governments and liberation movements, and overeager to seek accommodation with the United States. He made no secret of his displeasure with the inadequacy of Moscow's support of North Vietnam, and in Latin America he actively pursued policies that went against Moscow's wishes.[2]

If we take the major West European countries as our frame of reference, in the 1960s Cuba was not as submissive to the Soviet Union as Italy was to the United States. Rome's leaders boasted that they had "always supported the United States" and that Washington was "the North Star to our foreign policy."[3] Nor was it as deferential as the British or West German governments, which carefully avoided open criticism of the United States and generally followed Washington's lead. It was more like de Gaulle's France, which felt free to criticize the United States and to pursue policies that irritated Washington. But perhaps the most fitting comparison is Israel. Israelis and Cubans were both dependent on the economic and military largesse of a foreign patron and yet both retained their independence.

To explain why the Soviets put up with "their recalcitrant Caribbean ally,"[4] the director of the State Department's Bureau of Intelligence and Research (INR) wrote in 1965 that they were "inhibited by Castro's intractability" and by geography—Cuba was an isolated outpost "in the American front yard." After noting that "the frictions in the Soviet-Cuban relationship" were "substantial and deeply rooted," he continued, "For all the problems it has brought with it, the Cuban revolution has had a buoying effect on Soviet morale, marking, for the Soviets, the onward march of socialism to the very doorstep of the bastion of capitalism. The adverse consequences to the Soviet Union in the rest of the world of a break with Cuba would be considerable, particularly coming on top of the Sino-Soviet split and the erosion of the Soviet position as close to home as Albania and Rumania." Almost three years later, addressing the same question when there were even greater strains in the Cuban-Soviet relationship, the CIA concluded that while the Soviets still saw some advantages in their relations with Cuba—as a symbol of Soviet ability "to support even remote allies," and for its "nuisance value" vis-à-vis the United States—it was the political cost of withdrawal that kept them tied to their expensive adventure: "How could the Soviets pull out of Cuba and look at the world or themselves in the morning? It would be a confession of monumental failure—the first and only socialist enterprise in the New World abandoned—and it would seriously damage Soviet prestige and be widely interpreted as a victory of sorts for the United States."[5]

Dealing with Cuba, however, meant dealing with Castro, the fiercely independent "personification of the [Cuban] Revolution."[6] Castro's hold over Cuba remained "unassailable," the CIA concluded in 1966: "Ardent 'Fidelistas'" were in control "in all areas of national life," the military and security forces were "fervently loyal," and Castro continued to enjoy "a large degree of popular support, especially among the youth, the peasants, and the poor working class." The Soviets were stuck: "they have little practical choice except to keep backing Fidel."[7]

This subtle analysis of the Cuban-Soviet relationship did not trickle up to the top levels of the U.S. government. U.S. policy makers did not focus on whether Castro was a Soviet puppet or an independent-minded Soviet ally. The difference would have been relevant only if they had intended to negotiate with him—and they did not.

CUBA IN AFRICA: BEFORE ANGOLA

It is not easy to determine what motivated Castro to pursue his independent policy in Africa because all aspects of this policy were closely held covert operations in the 1960s. Only Fidel and Raúl Castro and, until 1965, Che Guevara, were involved in the formulation of the policy. No written record of their discussions is available, and none may exist.

My repeated requests to interview Fidel and Raúl Castro were ignored or rebuffed. This forced me to rely more than I might otherwise have done on U.S. documents, particularly those of the CIA and the INR. The gap between these reasoned, insightful evaluations and those of U.S. policy makers is striking.

Occasionally, CIA and INR analysts stressed Castro's ego—"his thirst for self-aggrandizement"—as a motivating factor for his foreign policy activism, but the explanation they posited again and again was "his sense of revolutionary mission."[8] As the chair of the Board of National Estimates told the director of Central Intelligence in September 1963, "He [Castro] is first of all a revolutionary."[9] Report after report stressed the same point: Castro was "a compulsive revolutionary,"[10] a man with a "fanatical devotion to his cause,"[11] who was "inspired by a messianic sense of mission."[12] He believed that he was "engaged in a great crusade."[13] The men who surrounded Castro shared his sense of mission: "revolution is their *raison d'etre*."[14]

According to U.S. officials, this "messianic compulsion to lead 'revolution'" was one of Castro's "two basic goals or drives." The other was "the survival of the [Cuban] Revolution": he was "intent upon making it economically viable" and he was "determined to win prestige and preserve for Cuba what he conceives of as an independent status."[15] Quoting Castro himself, U.S. analysts noted that he saw Cuba as "'a small country, attacked, blockaded, against which a policy of undeclared war is being followed,'"[16] and that he believed that the survival of the revolution depended on "'other Cubas' succeeding on the continent. . . . [Castro thought] that the US would ultimately be forced to come to terms with Cuba when it has to deal simultaneously with 'several' other revolutionary regimes."[17]

These two drives—self-preservation and revolutionary zeal—shaped Castro's foreign policy. In a lengthy 1964 analysis, the CIA wrote:

Castro has made it clear on a number of occasions, publicly and especially privately, that he is not, and resents being considered a Soviet puppet. . . . Castro's goal appears to be to build in Cuba a unique Communist system. He also obviously aspires to a leading role in what he genuinely seems to believe is an approaching and inevitable "anti-imperialist revolution" in all of Latin America and, in fact, throughout all the underdeveloped world. . . .

Castro's efforts to identify his regime with other underdeveloped nations of the world seem to be related to his strong desire not to appear to be a Soviet puppet and his concept of world history in which he places himself in the vanguard of irrepressible worldwide revolutionary movement. He envisages a new kind of communism—adapted to the peculiarities of individual nations and to present day conditions—toward which all the emerging nations are moving.[18]

When Che Guevara went to Africa in December 1964, U.S. intelligence experts followed his trip closely. With more wisdom than Che's later biographers, they never claimed that Guevara was looking for a way out and acting independently of Fidel Castro. On the contrary, INR director Hughes noted that "Che Guevara's three-month African trip was part of an important new Cuban strategy." This strategy, he argued, was based on Cuba's belief that Africa was ready for revolution and that it was in Cuba's interest to spread revolution there: it would win Havana new friends and it would weaken U.S. influence on the continent. Hughes made only one oblique reference to the Soviet Union: "Cuba's African strategy is designed to provide new political leverage against the United States and the socialist bloc. . . . The Cubans doubtless hope that their African ties will increase Cuba's stature in the nonaligned world and help to force the major socialist powers to tolerate a considerable measure of Cuban independence and criticism."[19] This search for "political and psychological leverage against both the US and the USSR"[20] was a recurring theme when U.S. intelligence officers examined Cuba's motivations in Africa or Latin America. Not once did they suggest that Cuba was acting at the behest of the Soviet Union.

Their analysis was astute: idealism and pragmatism were the engines behind Cuba's activism in the Third World. (They were fueled by a profound overestimation of the revolutionary potential of Latin America and, in 1965, of Africa.) This activism had roots in Cuba's prerevolutionary past. Approximately 1,000 Cubans had crossed the ocean to defend the Spanish republic against Francisco Franco in 1936–39,[21] and many other Cubans had joined in the antidictatorial wars of their Caribbean neighbors in the 1940s. Cuba's greatest hero, José Martí, had projected his own role on a continental scale—to defend "our America" against the "turbulent and brutal" North American empire.[22]

Castro was heir to this tradition. In 1947 he was one of hundreds of Cubans who volunteered to fight against Trujillo for the liberation of the Dominican Republic. The wave of hope that his victory over Batista aroused throughout Latin America, making him "a destroyer of the old order and . . . a champion of social revolution,"[23] increased his confidence and heightened his sense of mission. Of course, there was ego—but above all there was, as U.S. intelligence acknowledged, mission. As Hughes wrote, Castro and his cohorts were "dedicated revolutionaries, utterly convinced that they can and must bring radical change to Latin America some day."[24]

U.S. hostility spurred Castro to expand his vistas beyond the Western Hemisphere: it would have been suicidal to respond directly to the American assault—by attacking the U.S. base at Guantanamo, striking the U-2s that flew over the island, or providing material assistance to radical groups in the United States. Cuba could strike only in the periphery—in Latin America, in Africa, even in Asia. (It offered to send volunteers to fight in Vietnam.)[a] As one of the volunteers said, by challenging "the Yankees along all the paths of the world," Cuba would divide their forces, "so that they wouldn't be able to descend on us (or on any other country) with all their might."[25] This would help Cuba, and it

a. Hanoi, however, accepted only civilians; Cuban doctors and other experts went to North Vietnam. A small number of Cuban military personnel went to North and South Vietnam "to learn from the Vietnamese experience." At least four were killed on July 19, 1966, by U.S. bombs near Hanoi. (Interview with a Cuban officer [quoted]; MINFAR, list of dead with biographical notes, n.d., ACC. See also Denney [INR] to SecState, "Cuban Foreign Policy," Sept. 15, 1967, Pol 1 Cuba, SNF, NA, and Denney [INR] to Acting Secretary, "What Vietnam Means to Cuba," Apr. 3, 1968, ibid.)

would also help those struggling for social justice and national sovereignty in foreign lands.

At times realpolitik clashed with revolutionary duty and the former prevailed. The Mexican government did not join the U.S. crusade against Cuba, and in return Cuba did not criticize Mexico's corrupt and repressive regime or support armed struggle there. But at other times revolutionary duty prevailed. In 1961 Cuba risked de Gaulle's wrath to help the Algerian rebels, and in 1963 it went to the defense of the Algerian Republic, even though this jeopardized an important sugar contract with Morocco.

The Cuban leaders were convinced that their country had a special empathy for the Third World and a special role to play on its behalf. The Soviets and their East European allies were white and, by Third World standards, they were rich; the Chinese suffered from great-power hubris and were unable to adapt to African and Latin American culture. By contrast Cuba was nonwhite, poor, threatened by a powerful enemy, and culturally Latin American and African. It was, therefore, a special hybrid: a socialist country with a Third World sensitivity in a world that, according to Castro, was dominated by the "conflict between privileged and underprivileged, humanity against 'imperialism,'"[26] and where the major fault line was not between socialist and capitalist states but between developed and underdeveloped countries.

History, geography, culture, and language made Latin America the Cubans' natural habitat, the place closest to Castro's and his followers' hearts, the first place they tried to spread revolution. But Latin America was also the place where their freedom of movement was most circumscribed: Castro was, as the CIA observed, "canny enough to keep his risks low" in the U.S. backyard. This is why fewer than forty Cubans fought in Latin America in the 1960s; why Cuba was extremely cautious about sending weapons to Latin American rebels; and why Castro did nothing when revolution in neighboring Santo Domingo in April 1965 seemed to offer "a classic opportunity to provide assistance to a leftist insurrection."[27]

In Africa, Cuba incurred fewer risks. Whereas in Latin America Havana was operating against legal governments, flouting international law, and facing the condemnation of the governments of the hemisphere, in Africa it was confronting a colonial power or defending established states. Only in Zaire did Cuba help insurgents fighting against an independent government, but it was a government that was considered illegitimate by many African states, and Cuba's intervention was coordinated with Tanzania and Egypt. Above all, in Africa there was much less risk of a head-on collision with the United States. In fact, except for fleeting moments (Algeria in October–November 1963 and Zaire in September 1965), U.S. officials barely noticed the Cubans in Africa.

This is not to say that these operations were risk-free. There was always the possibility that the Americans would respond—particularly in Zaire, where the United States was deeply committed. And there was the danger that the 1,400 Cubans who went to Algeria in 1963, to Zaire and the Congo in 1965, and to

Guinea-Bissau in 1966–74 would suffer heavy casualties. Their mission was, in Castro's words, to "Train and Fight; Fight and Train."[28] It turned out differently: the Cubans did not have to fight in Algeria and in the Congo, and the Simbas' collapse in Zaire cut short an operation Havana had thought would last several years. As a result, the human toll was low: six Cubans dead in Zaire and nine in Guinea-Bissau.

Lack of opportunity limited Cuba's military interventions. As a result, the economic burden had been relatively light, making it possible to carry out the African policy without Soviet assistance. To be sure, Cuban and Soviet policies ran along parallel tracks in Africa; both supported the Ben Bella regime in Algeria and both helped the Simbas in Zaire and the PAIGC in Guinea-Bissau. Cuba, however, was pursuing its own goals, often informing Moscow only after decisions had been made. When the Soviets asked Castro not to withdraw the Cuban column from the Congo in December 1966, for example, he disregarded their request.[29]

What did these missions achieve? In Algeria the Cubans may have helped restrain Morocco, and in the Congo they provided valuable aid to the MPLA. The most successful effort was in Guinea-Bissau, where the Cuban contribution was critical. Zaire was a fiasco, but even there the volunteers behaved with discipline and commitment, despite their bitter disappointment with the Simbas. Throughout, the Cubans showed empathy and sensitivity that set them apart from their socialist allies and their Western foes. As a PAIGC leader said, "The Cubans understood better than anyone that they had a duty to fight and help their brothers become free."[30]

It is impossible to know what would have happened to Cuba's foreign policy activism had the costs suddenly escalated—that is, had the United States been willing to consider a modus vivendi if Castro had abandoned his support for revolution abroad. INR director Hughes wrestled with this question in the spring of 1964:

> On the one hand, they [Cuba's leaders] are still dedicated revolutionaries. . . . Many would rather be remembered as revolutionary martyrs than economic planners. Yet on the other hand these same men are aware that the current pressing problems demand amelioration that can only be brought by muting the call to revolution, by attempting to reach live and let live arrangements with the US, and by widening trade and diplomatic contacts with the free world.
>
> Tensions between the two paths, between peaceful coexistence and the call for violent revolution will continue to exist within the Cuban hierarchy, both within and between individuals, for the foreseeable future.[31]

In the months that followed this report, Castro tried again to open conversations with the United States. Hughes noted in an August 1965 analysis, "one of the most fascinating and little explored events of the last year was Castro's offer in July . . . of 'extensive discussions of the issues' dividing Cuba and the US.

Castro implied an offer to withhold material support from Latin American revolutionaries if the US and its allies would cease their support of anti-Castro activities." Washington responded by demanding "as preconditions for US-Cuban talks," not only that Cuba "cease subversion in Latin America," but also that it "break with the Russians"—an impossible demand, as Hughes pointed out, since it meant asking Castro to renounce Soviet support before negotiations with Washington had even begun. Castro finally gave up in the early fall, "because of the lack of US interest in his proposals. Castro's experience in the peace offensive," Hughes concluded, "may well have persuaded him that it was futile to court . . . the US."[b,32]

ANGOLA

By the early 1970s, reeling from the failure of his revolutionary offensive in Latin America and of his economic policies at home, Castro had softened his attitude toward the Soviet Union. Cuban criticism of Soviet policies ceased, and Havana acknowledged Moscow's primacy within the socialist bloc. Castro was no longer reminiscent of the obstreperous de Gaulle but of the better-behaved British and West Germans.

In August 1975, when Castro first considered sending troops to Angola, he asked Brezhnev to endorse the operation. In the 1960s, he had never sought Moscow's approval before embarking on a military mission in Africa, but in the 1960s Cuba had never undertaken such a major and risky operation. To ask for Soviet support in these circumstances was not subservience but common sense. When Brezhnev said no, Castro stepped back. At the time, the MPLA was winning.

Three months later, the South African invasion presented Castro with a stark choice: intervene or seal the fate of the MPLA. It was a defining moment. Castro defied the Soviet Union. He sent his troops on Cuban planes and Cuban ships, without consulting Brezhnev, hoping that Moscow would come around, but without any assurance that it would. He was no client. "He was probably the most genuine revolutionary leader then [1975] in power," Henry Kissinger opined in his memoirs.[33]

b. Two years later another senior intelligence officer noted, "The US has consistently laid down two firm conditions for any relaxation of tensions: that Cuba halt its assistance to subversives, and sever its 'ties of dependence' with the Soviet Union. The first might conceivably be met. Whatever his ulterior reasons, Castro has in fact during certain periods de-emphasized his export of revolution and hinted that Cuban assistance to Latin subversive groups might be negotiable. . . . Cuba's ties to the Soviet Union are, however, of necessity less subject to negotiation. . . . For Castro unilaterally to break (or even offer to break) these ties would not only represent an unlikely ideological turnabout, but it would signify throwing himself on the economic mercy of Washington with no advance guarantee that the US would reopen the old Cuban sugar quota or in other ways assist the economy." (Denney [INR] to SecState, "Cuban Foreign Policy," Sept. 15, 1967, p. 23, Pol 1 Cuba, SNF, NA.)

It is difficult to assess the costs of Operation Carlota for Cuba. The Ford administration responded by freezing the normalization process, but a modus vivendi with the United States was far less important than it would have been in the 1960s, when Cuba had been the target of U.S. paramilitary operations, the Cubans had lived in constant fear of U.S. military strikes, and their foreign trade had been crippled by U.S. pressure on third countries. Furthermore, the normalization process resumed when Jimmy Carter became president in 1977.

Similarly, while there is no doubt that Operation Carlota had a negative effect on Cuba's relations with Western countries, the only concrete cost was Bonn's decision to cancel its projected development aid program, and the amount involved was small. To Washington's regret, "Cuba's adventurism" did not affect the island's trade or financial relations with Western countries. America's allies, the NSC noted, continued "to base their financial decisions on economic factors, believing Cuba is a good credit risk because of its impeccable repayment record with the West, and that the USSR would stand behind Cuba's debt obligations."[34]

According to U.S. officials, the 30,000 Cubans who went to Angola between November 1975 and March 1976 suffered "few casualties"—at most 200 dead, including 16 prisoners who had been captured by the South Africans, handed over to UNITA, and executed.[35] Two soldiers deserted.[36] Pretoria kept three Cuban POWs. They were exchanged on September 2, 1978, with the eight South African soldiers who had been captured by the Cubans during the war.[37]

There is no hard data about the reaction of the Cuban population to Operation Carlota. "The general feeling is one of pride," the *Washington Post* reported in February 1976. Two years later, a major NSC study concluded, "The average Cuban may not care much about Marxism-Leninism, but the role Cuba is playing in Africa appeals to his sense of nationalist pride." This pride, the NSC expert on Latin America remarked, had even infected the Cuban community in the United States, which was notorious for its hostility to Castro: "On the issue of Cuban involvement in Africa, their views range from ambivalent to undisguised pride. I suspect this may be reflective of the views of many Cubans in Cuba."[38]

Victory in Angola boosted Cuba's prestige in the Third World. In the words of a prominent South African member of Parliament, "The Cubans are now the people who are regarded as heroes in the Black world." In 1976 the fifth summit of the nonaligned movement praised Cuba for its intervention "against South Africa's racist regime and its allies." Cuba was chosen to host the next summit in 1979 (and therefore to chair the movement in the 1979–82 period). Tanzanian president Nyerere, who in 1975 had swung in support of the MPLA only after realizing that South Africa had invaded Angola, urged Havana to keep its troops in Angola to protect it from South Africa and to help SWAPO, the Namibian liberation movement. "'Tell Fidel that we want the Cubans to train SWAPO,'" he told the Cuban ambassador.[39]

The Soviet leaders' initial displeasure with Castro's decision to send troops to Angola had turned into warm approval by early 1976, as they concluded that Operation Carlota had achieved an important victory for Soviet foreign policy. Soviet approval was reflected in generous economic agreements with Cuba in April 1976, followed by the delivery of new, more sophisticated weapons for the Cuban armed forces.[40] Increased Soviet economic aid helped compensate Cuba for the cost of uprooting thousands of skilled workers first to fight in Angola and, later, to help fill the gaps left by the flight of the Portuguese population.

Ninety percent of the Portuguese living in Angola in April 1974 had left by November 1975, taking with them "almost everything that made the system of government and the economy work."[41] The country was left bereft of skilled workers, including health care personnel.

Cuban doctors began arriving in Angola in late November 1975, while the South Africans were still trying to break through the Cuban defenses. The following July *Jeune Afrique*, not a friend of Havana's presence in Africa, wrote: Huambo [Angola's second city] lives in fear that the Cuban doctors may leave. 'If they go,' a priest said recently, 'we'll all die.' . . . [When] a Cuban medical team arrived on March 7, only one Angolan doctor and a Red Cross mission were left [in Huambo]. The latter . . . left at the end of June. The Cuban medical teams play a key role throughout the country." A year later, President Carter's special assistant on health reported that an Angolan doctor had told him that the "most important contribution [to Angola's medical services] has been from Cuba with no strings attached. We only had 14 doctors, but now we have more than 200, thanks to Cuba."[42]

Raúl Castro, who visited Angola from April 19 to June 7, 1976, endorsed the plea of the Angolan leaders for greater Cuban assistance. By year's end, 1,400 Cuban experts were working in Angola. This aid was free.[43]

CONSIDERATIONS ON U.S. POLICY

Americans—government officials, journalists, the public—had paid scant attention to sub-Saharan Africa before the Cubans landed in Angola.[44]

African Americans, who could have been the natural constituency for Africa in the United States, were focused on their struggle for equal rights at home. They had little time for African issues, even for those where race was paramount, in South Africa, the Portuguese colonies, and Rhodesia. This was true of the NAACP and the other mainstream civil rights organizations, of most individual leaders, and certainly of the rank and file. "Through all those years I felt frustrated, very much so, because of the lack of interest [among African Americans]," Congressman Diggs, one of the few black leaders with a sustained concern for Africa, recalled. "I felt very lonely. There's no question about it."[45]

Even radical African Americans had only tenuous ties with Africa, with the major exception of Malcolm X in the last months of his life. Stokely Carmichael's fling with the PAIGC was an overture followed by silence. Eldridge Cleaver and other Black Panthers went to Algeria seeking refuge and help for their struggle in the United States, and were disappointed.[46]

The lack of interest in Africa in the U.S. Congress was legendary. When it came time to appoint the chairs of the Senate Foreign Relations subcommittees, Africa was the booby prize. The first chair, John Kennedy, accepted the job in May 1959 on the condition that he would not have to hold any hearings. (During his chairmanship, the subcommittee met only once, briefly.)[c] Dick Clark, who chaired the subcommittee at the time of the covert operation in Angola, was a first-term senator when he was appointed in early 1975. "The senior members of the committee pick the subcommittees they want," he wrote, "and by the time they got down to me, the only subcommittee no [one] else wanted was Africa."[47]

Congress's lack of sensitivity about African concerns found its most notorious expression in the 1971 Byrd amendment, which exempted Rhodesian chrome from the mandatory sanctions imposed by the UN Security Council and afforded Salisbury "much needed foreign exchange," as well as "moral and psychological support," as a State Department official noted. Several attempts to repeal the amendment were defeated in 1972–74.[48]

In November 1974, in the wake of Watergate, the American people elected what was arguably the most liberal Congress since the end of World War II. Ten months later, on September 25, 1975, the House voted on yet another bill to repeal the Byrd amendment. "Today the House has the opportunity . . . to deliver a timely prod to Rhodesia's illegal white regime to negotiate realistically with the African leaders," the *New York Times* wrote. The bill failed. As the *Rand Daily Mail* observed, the House had granted Ian Smith "a political victory . . . of immense psychological value."[49]

Against this backdrop, why should the White House have cared about Africa, unless it perceived a Communist threat there? American economic interests were minor—in 1973, for example, sub-Saharan Africa claimed no more than 3 percent of total U.S. private investment overseas and only 4 percent of total U.S. trade—and public concern nonexistent.[50]

c. Richard Mahoney writes that when the subcommittee was created in May 1959, Kennedy, who had spoken out forcefully in favor of Algerian independence, "was the natural choice to head it" (Mahoney, *JFK*, p. 28). But the account of a senior committee staffer rings more true: "Nobody wanted to be chairman. So Fulbright told Carl Marcy [the committee's chief of staff], 'Tell Jack Kennedy that he's got to do it. He's junior on the committee [he was just beginning his second term as senator] and he never comes to the meetings anyway, so he's got to do it.' Marcy relayed the request more diplomatically. Kennedy asked, 'How often does it have to meet?' and Marcy said, 'As often as you want.' So Kennedy asked, 'Suppose I never want it to meet?' And Marcy replied, 'Then it never meets.' Kennedy said, 'OK, I'll do it.'" (Interview with Pat Holt; see also Pat Holt, OH, pp. 52–53.) On the subcommittee meeting only once under Kennedy, see Mahoney, *JFK*, p. 28.

Presidents Kennedy and Johnson had believed that Africa should be the responsibility of the Europeans. "We were a junior partner in Africa throughout the period of the Kennedy and Johnson administrations," Secretary Rusk remarked. "I felt that . . . we should work out some sort of division of labor. After all, the Europeans do very little in aid to Latin America . . . [and] to Asian countries, and we were very heavily involved with the Asian countries. And so it seemed to me that we should expect and allow Europe to play the major role in Africa."[51]

The numbers bear this out. From 1960 to 1968 aid worth more than $11 billion was given to sub-Saharan Africa; the U.S. share was only $2.1 billion.[52] "We must live and deal with the cold truth that the overwhelming theme of current U.S. relations with most of Africa is that we have promised much and delivered little," the NSC Africa specialist remarked in late 1967. The following year Congress cut the aid package. "Our most nagging problem in Africa is to make words do in place of money," another NSC aide wrote. The assistant secretary for African affairs tried to do just that when he visited sixteen African countries in mid-1968. "In response to deep concern about the level and direction of our foreign aid policy," he reported, "I explained with frankness the problems we are now experiencing, such as the heavy financial burden of the Vietnam war, our balance of payments deficit, and the threat of inflation. I emphasized, however, the transitory nature of these problems. . . . We will face a real crisis of responsiveness if we are not able within a year or two to at least restore past levels of aid." He also warned, "Any reversal of direction or loss of momentum by a future Administration with respect to civil rights and equal opportunity could deal a heavy blow to our relationships in Africa."[53]

During the Nixon presidency aid was not restored to its pre-1968 level, and there was a loss of momentum on civil rights. The morale of the Africa Bureau of the State Department (AF) suffered accordingly. "AF has been a very well run Bureau," a Policy Planning Staff study noted in 1974. "Its main difficulty is not internal or organizational, but external due to the fact that US relations with Africa have generally been considered less important than US relations with other regions. AF knows this and, as a result, tends to be somewhat defensive on issues arising between itself and other Bureaus . . . [and to] accept inter-bureau compromises detrimental to itself out of fear that a Seventh Floor decision would be even more detrimental."[54]

President Ford followed Nixon's lead. "The Africans are disappointed with the amount and kind of development assistance they are receiving from the US and with our lack of support for (or opposition to) their stepped-up efforts to bring about majority rule throughout Africa," Assistant Secretary Davis and Policy Planning director Lord told Kissinger in April 1975.[55]

That the Africans were disappointed did not matter, however, as long as the continent was safe from the Communist threat. After an initial flurry of anxiety during the headlong rush toward independence, U.S. policy makers were confident that Africa was not in peril. The one running sore in the 1960s and early 1970s was the rebellion in the Portuguese colonies. Kennedy defined the U.S. position: the weapons Washington gave to Portugal could not be used in Africa; if Lisbon violated this stipulation, the United States would complain, but not too vigorously, because Portugal was in NATO and the fortunate owner of the Azores. Johnson continued this policy, and Nixon tilted it even more toward Lisbon. But the keynote of U.S. policy toward Portuguese Africa from the mid-1960s to April 1974 was consistent: complacency. Washington was confident that the rebels would not win, at least in the foreseeable future.

The major armed conflict in Africa in these years was the Nigerian civil war, which raged from mid-1967 to January 1970—a human tragedy but not a Cold War crisis. Both the United States and the Soviet Union supported the Federal Military Government. Therefore, it attracted little attention from top U.S. policy makers.[56]

From 1959 to 1975, the United States faced only two important Cold War crises in Africa: the first in Zaire, and the second in Angola.

The analysis of the U.S. intervention in Zaire in 1964–65 uncovers several abiding themes in U.S. foreign policy. First, there is a striking gap between intelligence and policy. Second, this gap can be sustained as long as the costs can be kept low; that is, the overwhelming power of the United States in the Third World often means that U.S. policy makers pay no price for sloppy and wrongheaded thinking. Finally, the fact that the costs were very low muted debate at home and made it possible to transform a power play based on fuzzy thinking into a noble deed.

The intelligence gap was evident in July and August 1964, when the Simba revolt suddenly engulfed Zaire. Like their European counterparts, CIA and INR analysts reported that the revolt was "largely tribal" and the Communist role "marginal."[57] But as intelligence changed into policy, nuance was lost: Washington hastily concluded that Zaire was threatened by a Communist takeover. The explanation for this break in communication can only be tentative. There was no question that the rebels were unfriendly to the United States; they claimed to be followers of the late Lumumba, Zaire's first prime minister, whom Washington had branded an African Castro and whom U.S. officials had tried to murder. Given the necessary tentativeness of intelligence reports about fast-developing events and the mind-set in Washington, this easily slid into thinking that the rebels were Communists. Given their lack of knowledge, the policy makers fell victim to their propensity to equate anti-Americanism in the Third World with communism. They had little time for reflection; the Zairean crisis had erupted suddenly in the midst of a crowded agenda, and it required a rapid response lest the rebels win while Washington cogitated. It was safer to assume the worst.

Occasionally reality surfaced. At the August 11, 1964, NSC meeting on Zaire, for example, Secretary Rusk said that "the present trouble is tribal unrest and rebel bands moving freely in the absence of effective police." He went on to say, however, "we must assume that if disintegration continues the Communists will take over."[58] Rusk did not explain why, and no one asked.

The policy makers' knee-jerk reaction was reinforced by domestic consider-ations. At best, the rebels' victory would have meant an unpleasant neutralist regime in a country where both Eisenhower and Kennedy had struggled to impose a pro-American government, and this—a White House aide wrote in a revealing memo—"would be hard to explain politically in US."[59] The moment was particularly delicate: the November presidential elections approached and Lyndon Johnson did not want to give Republican challenger Barry Goldwater any ammunition to fuel the charge that he was soft on communism.

Imperial hubris made a sober decision even less likely—the greatest democ-racy on earth and the leader of the Free World should not have to accept the unsavory compromises that lesser powers had to endure. In the glare of this hubris, the subtle distinctions of the intelligence reports disappeared.

It came down, in the end, to a question of costs. The Europeans would not send troops to crush the revolt, and Washington was loath to send American soldiers; even the dispatch of four transport planes and fifty-six paratroopers to guard them had raised hackles in the U.S. Congress and the American press. Had U.S. troops been the only way to prevent a Simba victory, Johnson and his advisers might have paused to consider the findings of U.S. intelligence about the rebels, instead of fixating on the "Communist" label, and they might have allowed events in Zaire to run their course. The administration, however, hit on an imaginative solution—mercenaries. If the cost of victory could be kept low, then there was no reason to compromise.

Once the decision had been made, in August 1964, there was no need to reconsider. A mercenary army was quickly assembled, and it soon became obvious that it would win the war for the United States. Furthermore, by early 1965 there was clear evidence that Soviets and Chinese were sending weapons to the rebels, and this seemed to confirm the wisdom of policy makers' initial decision. No one paused to consider that this aid might have been triggered by Washington's actions.

What struck me as I read the thousands of pages of U.S. documents on the Zairean revolt is the degree of consensus: not one U.S. official questioned any aspect of the policy, and if the administration's "liberals"—Assistant Secretary Williams, his deputy Wayne Fredericks, and USIA director Rowan—had any qualms about using the mercenaries, they kept their counsel.[d] The only concern through the months that followed the initial decision was to keep the costs low—and this meant leaving the fighting to the mercenaries, pushing the Bel-

d. In a letter to the author, however, Fredericks suggested that there were "differ-ences of opinion within the USG [U.S. government] on Congo [Zaire] policy" (May 28, 1992). If so, they were so subtle or subterranean that U.S. policy makers were not aware of them. Thus Under Secretary Ball told Fredericks (who was, apparently, a dissenter) that "he and Fredericks saw eye to eye and he had complete confidence in Fredericks, and his judgment." (TelConv, Fredericks and Ball, Nov. 11, 1964, 3:45 P.M., Ball Papers, box 2/3, LBJL.) Interviews with Ball, Komer, Godley, and Blake confirmed the lack of dissent.

gians to the fore, and hiding the role of the United States as the mercenaries' patron.

The administration's caution paid off. The mercenaries won the war and only five Americans lost their lives: three missionaries and another civilian hostage who were killed by the Simbas in the wake of the U.S.-Belgian raid on Stanleyville in November 1964, and one CIA contract officer whose plane was hit by the rebels.[60]

The covert operation provoked an uproar in Africa, but the storm did not last. Those African countries that felt humiliated and threatened by U.S. policy in Zaire accepted the inevitable because, as an NSC official said, "They had their own problems to worry about and because we were successful."[61] The Simbas' disarray and lack of charismatic leaders, along with Tshombe's removal, made it easier for the Africans to turn a blind eye to what happened in Zaire. The West Europeans welcomed a rebel defeat as long as they did not have to send troops. Success, Washington concluded, paid off.

Moreover, success justified the policy: U.S. policy makers convinced themselves that in defending the interests of the United States, they had also served the interests of the Zairean people. They had helped the legal government of Zaire defeat an assault instigated by international communism and had saved the country from savagery and mayhem. In their self-congratulations, they overlooked several facts that were well documented in CIA and State Department reports: the legal government of Zaire was the product of U.S. interference in 1960–61; the 1964 revolt had been provoked by the government's thievery and savagery, not by international communism; and the rebels' atrocities were more than matched by those of the Zairean army and the mercenaries.

But who would challenge the official story? Once it became clear that no U.S. troops would be sent to Zaire and that the mercenaries would defeat the rebels, Congress readily endorsed the administration's policy. As did the American press. With the exception of a few African American newspapers, it overlooked the atrocities of the mercenaries and failed to report that a major U.S. covert operation was under way in Zaire. This skewed coverage did not encourage debate in the United States and certainly did not help create an educated public.

It was in Zaire that Cuba and the United States first clashed in Africa, but it was an oddly muted confrontation. Guevara's column arrived in the spring of 1965, almost a year after the U.S. intervention had begun. U.S. officials were not even aware of the Cubans' presence until the following July, and, except for a brief moment in September, they were not worried about it. When they thought of a Communist threat, they thought of Moscow and Beijing, not Havana.

IAFEATURE AND DÉTENTE

In 1975, after a ten-year "lapse," Africa became again, an NSC study noted, "a locus of competition between the USSR and the United States" as the Angolan civil war exploded.[62]

This time there was no gap between U.S. intelligence and policy makers. Both analysts and policy makers failed to include the Cubans in their calculations and both concluded that an MPLA regime in Angola did not threaten significant U.S. interests. But for Henry Kissinger this was irrelevant: U.S. policy toward Angola would be determined not by what happened there, but by his conception of the U.S. position in the world at the time.

In order to understand the U.S. decision to intervene in Angola, it is therefore important to look at the state of the Cold War, of détente, in those crucial months of 1975 in which the Angolan decisions were made. The paradoxical result is that the more deeply one looks at the evidence, the harder it is to understand the decision to launch the covert operation.

Détente had lost much of its luster in the United States by January 1975, despite the fact that the Soviet Union had been steadily losing ground. In the Middle East the United States had become, in Kissinger's words, "the dominant world power."[63] The bloody military coup that overthrew President Allende in September 1973 had reestablished pro-American stability in Chile and dashed Soviet hopes of peaceful transition to socialism in the Third World. A year later, the U.S. Congress had stymied Soviet hopes for U.S. trade and investment by imposing humiliating conditions that Moscow was bound to reject. And when Brezhnev and Ford had agreed on a framework for a SALT II treaty at Vladivostok in December 1974, "it was the Soviets who had made almost all concessions," Kissinger noted. Even Defense Secretary James Schlesinger—not a fan of détente—had applauded the agreement. "Mr. President," he told Ford, "You've got the high ground. . . . You can say categorically that you have not put the U.S. in a position of inferiority."[64]

But Kissinger's successes in the Middle East had come at a price: American supporters of Israel, fearful that détente was weakening U.S. backing for the Jewish state, joined hands with conservatives who considered Kissinger soft on the Soviet Union and with liberals who assailed his silence on human rights violations in the Soviet Union as amoral and inconsistent with American values.

Watergate dealt a further blow to détente: Nixon went down in disgrace in August 1974 and in November Americans elected a Democratic Congress eager to assert influence over foreign policy and deeply suspicious of the secretive modus operandi Nixon and Kissinger favored. This resurgent Congress faced a weakened executive: a president who had never been elected to national office and who was burdened by his pardon of Nixon; a secretary of state scarred by the battles of the previous fifteen months; and a secretary of defense who had little sympathy for Kissinger or for détente. A severe economic slump contributed to the sense of malaise and undermined public confidence in the new administration. The collapse of South Vietnam in April 1975 swelled the ranks of the critics of détente and further tarnished Kissinger's aura. "Let us talk not of détente or of past achievements," Schlesinger told Ford in a clear jab at Kissinger. "We need to challenge the Soviet Union. . . . We want to preserve détente, but it cannot be a one way street."[65]

Vietnam provided the gloomy backdrop to a series of crises that faced the United States in 1975 in Latin America, Europe, and the Middle East. It was in this context that the decision was made to launch a covert operation in Angola.

In Latin America the Panama Canal negotiations dominated all other issues. While considered essential to quell rising frustration in the hemisphere, these talks were political dynamite, especially with the presidential elections approaching.

In Europe, the administration was deeply worried about what Ford called the "underside or belly of NATO":[66] relations between Greece and Turkey were strained to the breaking point over Cyprus; Franco's health was fast declining; the Portuguese Communist Party was gaining strength; and in Italy the Communists seemed on the verge of joining the government.

Finally, there was the Middle East. On March 24, 1975, Kissinger returned to Washington after three weeks of "extremely disappointing" shuttle diplomacy. His step-by-step negotiations between Egypt and Israel had ground to a halt. "Our role and the whole strategy we had followed for eighteen months . . . has been disrupted," Kissinger told the NSC.[67]

By Kissinger's own reckoning, not one of these foreign policy crises had been provoked by the Soviet Union. In the tense debate within the NSC over the Panama Canal negotiations, the Soviet Union was not mentioned once. As Kissinger writes, Moscow had nothing to do with the outbreak of the Cyprus crisis and "was kept at arm's length" throughout.[68] The success of the Italian Communist Party was due to its moderate and pragmatic policies and its growing independence from the Soviet Union—which caused deep concern in Moscow—not to Brezhnev's intrigues. And while Kissinger was deeply concerned by the Portuguese Communists' inroads, he believed nonetheless that Moscow was behaving with restraint. The Soviets had "exploited" the situation in Portugal, but they had not created it, he told the NSC. The available evidence confirms that the Soviet role was modest.[69]

It was not the Soviets, moreover, who had thrown a monkey wrench into Kissinger's shuttle diplomacy in the Middle East. The problem, Kissinger told the cabinet on March 26, was Israel. The Israelis had been "'not only . . . unreasonable, . . . [but] disastrous."[70]

The Soviets were bystanders in the Middle East, but not at the Helsinki summit or the SALT negotiations.

American critics of détente railed against both, calling the July 1975 Helsinki summit's acceptance of the inviolability of the European borders a second Yalta, another craven capitulation to Soviet power. In their indignation, they failed to note that the act included provisions for the protection of human rights in the member countries. Kissinger was more perceptive than his critics. "They are bitching now about the borders we did nothing to change when we had a nuclear monopoly," he told the cabinet on his return from Helsinki. "The borders were legally established long ago. All the new things in the document are in our favor—peaceful change, human contacts. . . . At the Conference . . . it was the West which was on the offensive."[71]

Meanwhile the administration was growing increasingly fractured over the SALT negotiations. Defense Secretary Schlesinger wanted the United States to adopt a tougher position, while Kissinger announced on *Meet the Press* in October 1975, "most of the significant concessions over the last 18 months in the [SALT] negotiations have been made by the Soviet Union."[72]

As South Vietnam crumbled in the spring of 1975, Kissinger had been bleak: henceforth the Soviet Union would see "the US as weak and unwilling to stand up for its commitments anywhere in the world."[73] Nevertheless, in Western and Eastern Europe, in Latin America and the Middle East, the United States had fared well in 1975, and the Soviet Union had made no inroads. "If they [the Soviets] were to draw a balance sheet, they would not have too much to count," Kissinger told Ford in September 1975.[74] The Portuguese Communist Party had been defeated by late 1975, the Italian Communists had been kept out of the government, Helsinki would loosen Soviet control over Eastern Europe, Panama was quiet, and the crisis in Cyprus was abating. In the Middle East, the negotiations that had been paralyzed by Israel's intransigence resumed in June 1975, and in early September an agreement between Israel and Egypt was signed in Geneva. Once again, the Soviet Union had been left out in the cold.

As the civil war in Angola gained momentum in the spring of 1975, Kissinger suddenly paid attention, and his reaction is puzzling. While his assessment of Soviet policy in Europe, Latin America, and the Middle East was astute and sober, he appears to have had a knee-jerk overreaction in Angola.

It is unclear whether Kissinger truly believed that a Soviet power grab was occurring in this remote African country. What is clear is that he chose Angola as the place to show America's resolve in the wake of Vietnam. In Angola, he would take the offensive; he would send a signal.

The available evidence indicates that the Soviets intervened in Angola slowly and reluctantly. Their aid to the MPLA began in early 1975, well after Beijing had sent instructors and weapons to Roberto's FNLA. In August, despite evidence of growing external support for the FNLA and UNITA, Brezhnev rejected Castro's proposal for the dispatch of Cuban troops. Until mid-October 1975 the war remained largely a struggle among Angolans, and the MPLA was winning.

It was at this point that the real power grab occurred: with Washington's encouragement, South Africa invaded Angola. Cuba responded by sending troops, the South Africans were forced to retreat, and the United States suffered a humiliating defeat.

As U.S. officials had predicted, the MPLA victory did not threaten major U.S. interests in Angola. Luanda's economic ties continued to be with the West, the Soviet Union gained no naval bases, and the Angolan government soon sent signals of its willingness to improve relations with the United States. The real costs were self-inflicted: the United States had intervened and failed, it had acted clumsily, and—worse—it had been in cahoots with South Africa. The fiasco greatly strengthened the critics of détente and contributed to Ford's decision to suspend the SALT negotiations and put détente in the deep freeze. The best epitaph to Kissinger's Angola policy was offered by Kissinger himself. "It wouldn't be the first time in history," he rued in January 1976, "that events that no one can explain afterwards give rise to consequences out of proportion to their intrinsic significance."[75]

THE REPERCUSSIONS OF DEFEAT AND VICTORY

The major consequence of Angola—beside its effect on détente—was to bring Africa to the forefront of U.S. concerns. In November 1975, as Cuban soldiers halted the South African advance on Luanda and doomed Washington's power play, U.S. officials were shocked. Cuba became, for the first time, an important factor in U.S. policy making in Africa. This was evident most dramatically in Rhodesia.

"The Soviet/Cuban intervention in Angola has drastically affected the determinants of our policies toward Rhodesia," Assistant Secretary Schaufele warned Kissinger in April 1976. "Our essentially passive stance no longer is the most appropriate approach." Policy Planning director Lord agreed: "The ultimate nightmare to be avoided is Soviet/Cuban combat intervention in Southern Africa with widespread African support."[76]

Prodded by the Cuban victory in Angola, Kissinger went on his first official visit to Africa in late April 1976. Rhodesia was the top item on his agenda. "If the Cubans are involved there, Namibia is next and after that South Africa itself," he told the NSC before his departure. "On my African trip, I will identify with African aspirations." This included a pledge to finally repeal the Byrd amendment. As *Newsweek* put it, "dropping Washington's traditional, if unstated, support for the white regimes seemed a reasonable price to pay for thwarting the Communists." It was painful, but necessary, Kissinger told the NSC on his return. "I have a basic sympathy with the white Rhodesians but black Africa is absolutely united on this issue, and if we don't grab the initiative we will be faced with the Soviets, and Cuban troops."[77]

Many Americans were outraged. Ronald Reagan denounced any move to repeal the Byrd amendment. Looking nervously at Reagan's challenge in the primaries, Ford backpedaled, and Congress did not even consider a bill to repeal the amendment. It was only in March 1977, with a new president and a new Congress, that the Byrd amendment was finally repealed. Among the many factors that shaped Jimmy Carter's policy toward Rhodesia was fear that a prolonged war would provide an opening for the Cubans, who were hovering in the background, training Rhodesian, Namibian, and South African guerrillas at a military school in Boma, in eastern Angola. This was "possibly the largest school of this kind in the world," Risquet told the Soviet ambassador in Luanda.[78]

Secretary of State Kissinger was notorious for his lack of interest in Africa. The Cuban victory in Angola changed this. In late April 1976 he went on his first official visit to Africa and pledged tough, tangible U.S. actions to help bring about majority rule in Rhodesia. "I have a basic sympathy with the white Rhodesians," he told the National Security Council on his return from Africa, "but . . . if we don't grab the initiative we will be faced with the Soviets, and Cuban troops." Many Americans considered this rank appeasement. Kissinger's African trip had been "ill-timed because it had a 'devastating effect' on Southern states," the House minority whip, Robert Michel (R.-Ill.), declared. In May 1976 Kissinger defended his new African policy before the Senate Foreign Relations Committee. (Library of Congress, Washington, D.C.)

Angola widened Castro's horizons. In March 1976, as Cuban troops approached the Namibian border, a prominent American journalist had written, "Vistas that might seem dazzling to Fidel Castro's eyes will open up with the victory in Angola. . . . For Fidel Castro there is no 'darkest Africa.' It is all ablaze with lights—the campfires of fellow revolutionaries. . . . So long as Castroite Cuba exists there will be armed Cubans in Africa, and they will be much more than shock troops for the Russians. Fidel Castro sees them as standard bearers for the nonaligned countries of the third world."[79]

One year later Castro told Honecker, "In Africa . . . we can inflict a heavy defeat to the entire policy of the imperialists. . . . We can free Africa from the influence of the U.S. and the Chinese." But, he added, "all this must be discussed with the Soviet Union. We follow her policy and her example."[80]

He was bowing to reality. Cuba could offer large-scale aid to its African friends only with Soviet economic and military help. Castro was not offering to do the Soviet bidding; he was seeking to enlist Soviet support for the policy he wanted to carry out.

After Angola, Cuba's largest military intervention was in Ethiopia, where in 1978 16,000 Cuban troops helped repulse the invading Somali army. The operation was strictly coordinated with and supported by the Soviet Union. Tens of thousands of Cubans armed with Soviet weapons remained in Angola through the 1980s. Smaller military missions were active in the Congo, Guinea, Guinea-Bissau, Mozambique, and Benin. Cuban military instructors trained Namibian, Rhodesian, and South African guerrillas.

Cuba's military presence in Africa was accompanied by a massive program of technical assistance: tens of thousands of Cuban experts—mainly in the fields of health, education, and construction—worked in Angola, Mozambique, Cape Verde, Guinea-Bissau, Guinea, Ethiopia, São Tomé and Príncipe, Tanzania, the Congo, and Benin. At Tindouf, in southwest Algeria, Cuban doctors cared for the tens of thousands of refugees who had fled the Western Sahara, occupied by Moroccan troops. Thousands of African students (their number peaked at 18,075 in 1988) studied in Cuba on full scholarships paid for by the Cuban government.

This much is known, but the full story of Cuba's policy in Africa after 1976 remains to be written.[81] Given its extremely controversial nature, to do so will require studying thousands of pages of documents and writing hundreds of pages—that is, another book. Arguably the most controversial question to be addressed will be one that has been a recurring theme in this book: was Cuba acting as a Soviet proxy? A preliminary inquiry indicates that in answering this question, there was once again a gap between U.S. policy makers and the assessment of intelligence analysts. For example, President Carter and his top aides responded to the Cuban intervention in Ethiopia much as President Ford and his top aides had responded to the Cuban intervention in Angola: Castro was Brezhnev's puppet; "the Cuban proxy," as National Security Adviser Brzezinski put it, had acted at Moscow's behest. But an NSC interagency study warned, in words strikingly similar to those used by the CIA in the aftermath of Angola, that "Cuba is not involved in Africa soley or even primarily because of its relationship with the Soviet Union. Rather, Havana's African policy reflects its activist revolutionary ethos and its determination to expand its own political influence in the Third World at the expense of the West (read U.S.)."[e] The same point was made in a perceptive September 1979 memo by the NSC expert on Latin America: "Let me suggest that we try to use a different term to refer to the Cubans than that of 'Soviet puppet,'" he told Brzezinski. "The word 'puppet' suggests that the Cubans are engaging in revolutionary activities because the Soviets have instructed them to do it. That, of course, is not the case."[82]

e. An October 1976 National Intelligence Estimate had told Ford, "Soviet-Cuban cooperation in supporting a national liberation movement there [in Africa] may be repeated if suitable opportunities arise, but only when both countries judge such activity to be in their interest. . . . This collaboration . . . will not be automatic. Moscow and Havana will each want to be sure that such an undertaking furthers its own interests." (NIE, "Soviet Military Policy in the Third World," Oct. 21, 1976, pp. 3, 32, MF 00500, NSA.)

This sober advice was disregarded by the Carter, Reagan, and Bush administrations. The idea that Castro was Moscow's puppet was a comforting myth, and, as former under secretary George Ball has written, "Myths are made to solace those who find reality distasteful and, if some find such fantasy comforting, so be it."[83]

With the collapse of the Soviet Union, the "dazzling vistas" that had seduced Castro disappeared. Cuba withdrew its soldiers and its technical experts from Africa. Only fragments of the once massive aid program remained. The largest was in Guinea-Bissau, where Cuban military instructors and doctors had helped the PAIGC defeat the Portuguese and then trained the army, provided almost half of the country's doctors, and founded its medical school.[84] Only the medical mission remained when I visited Bissau in 1996.[85] The Cuban military instructors had been replaced by Portuguese, and the Cuban embassy, once influential, lacked funds, personnel, and contacts. Twenty-eight Cuban doctors remained, living extremely frugal lives, funded in part by Havana and in part by a Dutch aid agency and the World Health Organization. They were the representatives of a nation that many Guineans, desperate for Western aid, wanted to forget, and the fact that they did not charge their patients did not sit well with their Guinean colleagues who had discovered the virtues of private practice. They continued to staff the medical school that had been named after Raúl Díaz Argüelles, who had been in charge of the Cuban military mission in Guinea-Bissau and had died on an Angolan battlefield in December 1975, but the plate bearing his name has long since disappeared. Why remind potential donors that Cuba, the pariah, had played such a large role in the birth of the country?

THE SILENCE

It is the end of the Cold War that made it possible to conduct the research for this book. Until the early 1990s, secrecy enveloped Cuba's policies in Africa. Only Operation Carlota had been discussed in public, and only in a cursory fashion. The famous Colombian novelist Gabriel García Márquez had written a short account of the operation based on what Cuban officials had told him.[86] Out of deference to the MPLA's sensitivities, the few Cuban publications about Operation Carlota had consistently understated the role played by the Cuban troops and given the credit instead to the MPLA.[87]

While this stereotyped version of Operation Carlota became part of the official discourse of the Cuban revolution, the earlier operations remained virtually ignored. When Rodríguez Peralta, the Cuban captain who had been captured in Guinea-Bissau in 1969 and spent the next five years in captivity, flew to Bissau in January 1977 as a guest of the Guinean government, *Granma* printed two short articles about his trip saying that he had been received by President Luís Cabral, that he had been awarded the Amílcar Cabral medal (the country's highest distinction), and that Luís Cabral had referred to "the disinterested aid that Cuba has given to Guinea-Bissau from the time of our war of independence to the present." *Granma* did not explain, however, what this aid had been, it did not reveal that Rodríguez Peralta (or any other Cuban) had fought in Guinea-Bissau, and it did not say why he had received the prestigious medal.[88] The Bissau newspaper, *Nõ Pintcha*, on the other hand, published several long articles on Rodríguez Peralta's visit and printed the full text of Cabral's speech. "We know," he said,

that we were able to fight and triumph because other countries and people helped us . . . with weapons, with medicine, with supplies. . . . But there is one nation that in addition to material, political, and diplomatic support, even sent its children to fight by our side, to shed their blood in our land alongside that of the best children of our country.

This great people, this heroic people, we all know that is the heroic people of Cuba; the Cuba of Fidel Castro; the Cuba of the Sierra Maestra, the Cuba of Moncada. . . . Cuba sent its best sons here to help us in the technical aspects of our war, to help us wage this great struggle . . . against Portuguese colonialism.

One of the sons of Cuba who fought and shed his blood in our land is here with us: our brother and comrade Pedro Rodríguez Peralta, who was wounded and captured . . . on November 18, 1969, and spent five years in Portugal in the prison of Caxias.

On this day on which we honor our heroes and our martyrs . . . the government of the Republic of Guinea-Bissau has decided to give our comrade Comandante Pedro Rodríguez Peralta the Amílcar Cabral medal of bravery.[89]

Despite these public accolades, the Cuban silence continued through the 1980s—about Cuba's aid to the Guinean rebels, about Che's column in Zaire, about Risquet's column in the Congo, and even about the aid given to Algeria during the 1963 Desert War.

"We thought it would be much more dignified if the people we had helped talked about it [our aid]," Risquet explained.[90] More dignified, and safer—being silent meant avoiding saying something that might offend friendly African governments or that might provide the United States with useful intelligence. Furthermore, there was no urgency: Cuban soldiers and doctors were still carrying Cuba's banner in Africa. And because their leaders were silent, the Cuban volunteers who had carried out the missions said nothing. The culture of silence enveloped the island. It was the reticence of a government, and of a people, who have long lived under the siege of an implacable foe.

What has changed? Not the hostility of the United States. But the Soviet empire has collapsed, the Soviet economic subsidy has evaporated, Cuba is bankrupt, the greatest domestic achievements of the Cuban revolution—in health, in education—are crumbling.

Cuba has withdrawn from Africa. Its troops are gone, its experts are gone. Cuba is on the ropes, condemned by the United Nations for its human rights record, and searching for acceptance in a world dominated by the United States.

The Africans are not rushing to tell Cuba's story. In the official history of the Angolan Armed Forces, for example, the Cuban role in 1975–76 is virtually overlooked. And in a Portuguese television documentary on the war of independence in Guinea-Bissau, not one of the former PAIGC guerrillas interviewed mentioned Cuba's contribution. I watched the program with Víctor Dreke, the discreet and stoic man who had created the Cuban military mission in Guinea, and I wondered what he must have felt.

As their world collapsed, the Cuban authorities began to reconsider their silence. A few articles and memoirs by participants in the African missions began appearing. And in 1993 the Cuban authorities decided to open their archives. They did so in a hesitant, contradictory way—something that I vehemently complained about during my six years of research. As I finish this book, however, it is only fair that I express my respect for the man who bore the brunt of my complaints. Jorge Risquet had received from "his compañeros" (he never explained who they were) a broad mandate to give me access to the archives. Over six years of haggling, he demonstrated flexibility and intelligence, and the ability to bridge the divide that separates us.

Had the Cuban government maintained the wall of silence, the foot soldiers never would have spoken. But as the government softened its position, many stepped forward. They were proud of their past, and they wanted it to be recorded.

NOTES

PROLOGUE

1. Macmillan, Aug. 22, 1959, letter, quoted by Horne, *Harold Macmillan*, p. 182.

2. Stengers, "Precipitous Decolonization," p. 330 quoted.

3. Herter quoted in NSC meeting, Mar. 24, 1960, p. 9, WF, NSC Series, box 12, DDEL; Nixon quoted in NSC meeting, Apr. 14, 1960, p. 15, ibid.; NIE, "The Probable Interrelationships of the Independent African States," Aug. 31, 1961, pp. 2, 6, NSF, NIE, box 8, LBJL.

4. Africa Bureau, DOS, "Outlines of U.S. Policy and Operations Concerning Africa," Sept. 22, 1961, enclosed in McGhee to Rostow, Sept. 22, 1961, NSF, box 2, JFKL.

5. Quoted by Skinner, "African, Afro-American, White American," pp. 388-89. See also CIA, ONE, "The Addis Ababa Conference and Its Aftermath," July 11, 1963, NSF, box 3, JFKL.

6. Eisenhower quoted in NSC meeting, Mar. 24, 1960, p. 10, WF, NSC Series, box 12, DDEL; "National Security Implications of Future Developments Regarding Africa," p. 7, enclosed in Boggs, memo for the NSC, Aug. 10, 1960, WHO, Office of the Special Assistant for National Security Affairs, NSC Series, Policy Papers Subseries, box 28, DDEL.

7. NIE, "Probable Developments in Colonial Africa," Apr. 11, 1961, p. 2 quoted, NSF, NIE, box 8, LBJL; Sakwa, "U.S. Policy towards Portugal," Jan. 17, 1962, NSF, box 154, JFKL; "The White Redoubt," June 28, 1962, enclosed in Owen to McGhee et al., July 6, 1962, NSF, box 2, JFKL; Hughes (INR) to SecState, "Prospects for Angolan Nationalist Movement," Nov. 5, 1963, NSF, box 5, JFKL.

8. Ben Bella, *Revolución* (Havana), Oct. 17, 1962, p. 7.

9. Quotations from CIA, DI, "Some Aspects of Subversion in Africa," Oct. 19, 1967, p. 5, NSFCF, box 78, and Comandante Reinerio Jiménez (quoting Osmany Cienfuegos), in "Versión taquigráfica de la reunión en el EMG con el comp. Risquet. (Enero 18/1967)," p. 18, enclosed in Ulises to Tomassevich, Jan. 18, 1967, ACC.

10. *NôPintcha* (Bissau), Apr. 2, 1986, p. 7.

11. Interview with McIlvaine, who was U.S. ambassador in Conakry in 1966-69.

12. "The Department of State during the Administration of President Lyndon B. Johnson, November 1963-January 1969," vol. 1, ch. 5, "The Place of Africa in US Foreign Policy," unpaginated, Administrative History of the Department of State, LBJL.

13. Colby, *Honorable Men*, p. 368.

14. Quotations from interview with Mulcahy; CIA, *National Intelligence Daily*, Oct. 11, 1975, p. 4, NSA; Kissinger, *Renewal*, p. 815.

15. Quotations from Roger Sargent, *Rand Daily Mail* (Johannesburg), Feb. 13, 1976, p. 13, and *World* (Johannesburg), Feb. 24, 1976, p. 4.

16. Interview with Agramonte.

17. Until the early 1990s, no author writing about Cuban foreign policy had access to Cuban documents. With this proviso, the most important works on Cuban policy in Africa were William Durch's careful "The Cuban Military in Africa and the Middle East: From Algeria to Angola," William LeoGrande's brilliant *Cuba's Policy in Africa*, and Carlos Moore's *Castro, the Blacks, and Africa*. In the early 1990s, three researchers gained access to Che Guevara's unpublished manuscript about his activities in Zaire in 1965, copies of which exist in several private collections in Havana. In 1994 Paco Ignacio Taibo published a garbled account of Che's time in Zaire, based on the manuscript (*El año que estuvimos en ninguna parte*). In 1997 Taibo, Jorge Castañeda, and Jon Lee Anderson used the manuscript in their biographies of Che.

The only scholarly work published in Cuba on Cuban policy in Africa is Gisela García's slim but pathbreaking *La misión internacionalista de Cuba en Argelia (1963-1964)*, published in 1990. (García also wrote an article on Che in Zaire, "El Che en el corazón de Africa," but this is less valuable because she was not able to use primary sources.) When it became clear that Che's manuscript was going to become public, the Cubans published a semiofficial account of Che's Zairean episode (William Gálvez, *El sueño africano del Che*), and then a version of Che's own manuscript (*Pasajes de la guerra revolucionaria: Congo*). Four books and about twenty newspaper articles by participants have also been published. They are cited in the relevant endnotes.

18. About 90 of the more than 3,000 pages of documents that I have received were lightly sanitized after I had read them. Frequently the edited lines contained the remarks of a foreign leader criticizing his own political allies. In the case of three intelligence documents, the sanitized paragraphs would have revealed sources. In other cases the lines (or words) sanitized included comments about African or Asian countries that, the censors believed, would unnecessarily complicate Cuba's contemporary foreign relations.

19. See chapter 4, n. 80, and chapter 12, footnote c.

CHAPTER ONE

1. Rabe, *Eisenhower*, p. 175. On Wilson and Haiti, see Schmidt, *United States*; on Wilson and the Dominican Republic, see Calder, *Impact*, and Gleijeses, *Dominican Crisis*, pp. 15-20; for the best discussion of Wilson and Mexico, see Mitchell, *Danger of Dreams*, pp. 160-215. The only president who had deviated, briefly, from the norm was Truman in 1945-47. The best historical overview of U.S.-Latin American relations is Schoultz, *Beneath the United States*.

2. Quotations from "Unofficial Visit of Prime Minister Castro of Cuba to Washington—A Tentative Evaluation," enclosed in Herter to Eisenhower, Apr. 23, 1959, *FRUS 1958-60*, 6:483, and Special NIE, "The

Situation in the Caribbean through 1959," June 30, 1959, p. 3, NSA.
Any study of Fidel Castro is bound to suffer from the lack of Cuban documents. With this proviso, Szulc's *Fidel* is the best biography. (See also Clerc, *Les quatre saisons*; Quirk, *Fidel Castro*; Balfour, *Castro.*) The most important studies of Cuba for the period considered in this book are Domínguez, *Cuba*; Karol, *Guerrillas*; Halperin, *Rise*; Gonzalez, *Cuba*; Mesa-Lago, *Revolutionary Change*; Mesa-Lago, *The Economy*; Lévesque, *L'URSS et la révolution cubaine*; Moniz Bandeira, *De Martí a Fidel.*

3. Jefferson to Madison, Apr. 27, 1809, in Washington, *Writings*, 5:444 (emphasis in original). On relations between the United States and Cuba from Jefferson through Eisenhower, see Benjamin, *United States*; Thomas, *Cuba*, pp. 93-1371; Foner, *History*; Pérez, *Cuba*; Pérez, *1898*; Gellman, *Roosevelt*; Paterson, *Contesting Castro*; Welch, *Response*; Rabe, *Eisenhower*, pp. 117-73; Wayne Smith, *Closest of Enemies*, pp. 13-67; Morley, *Imperial State*, pp. 40-130.

4. Adams to Nelson, Apr. 28, 1823, in Worthington Ford, *Writings*, 7:373.

5. Martí to Manuel Mercado, May 18, 1895, in Martí, *Epistolario*, 5:250.

6. Szulc, *Fidel*, p. 13.

7. Castro to Celia Sánchez, June 5, 1958, in Franqui, *Diary*, p. 338. The United States cut off arms supplies to Batista in March 1958, but the U.S. Military Assistance Advisory Group remained. (See Paterson, *Contesting Castro*, p. 242.)

8. Eisenhower press conference, Oct. 28, 1959, in U.S. General Services, *Public Papers: Dwight D. Eisenhower, 1959*, p. 271; Mitchell, "Remember the Myth," *News and Observer* (Raleigh), Nov. 1, 1998, G5.

9. NSC meeting, Jan. 14, 1960, *FRUS 1958-60*, 6:742-43.

10. Braddock to SecState, Havana, Feb. 1, 1960, *FRUS 1958-60*, 6:778.

11. Gray (Eisenhower's special assistant for national security affairs) to Wilson (assistant director, DDEL), Dec. 3, 1974, p. 1, Gray Papers, box 2, DDEL.

12. Recent literature on the Bay of Pigs includes Kornbluh, *Bay of Pigs*; Blight and Kornbluh, *Politics*; Vandenbroucke, *Perilous Options*, pp. 9-50; Gleijeses, "Ships"; Bissell, *Reflections*, pp. 152-204; Lynch, *Decision*; Rodríguez, *La batalla.*

13. Goodwin, memo for president, "Conversation with Commandante Ernesto Guevara of Cuba," Aug. 22, 1961, *FRUS 1961-63*, 10:642-45.

14. INR/ONE working group, "Facts, Estimates and Projections," May 2, 1961, app. A, p. 2, enclosed in Boggs to NSC, May 4, 1961, FOIA 1995/3520.

15. NIE, "The Situation and Prospects in Cuba," Mar. 21, 1962, p. 23, NSF, NIE, box 8/9, LBJL; interview with Bundy.

16. The best discussion of Kennedy's policy toward Latin America is Rabe, *Most Dangerous.* See also Scheman, *The Alliance.*

17. Assistant to the head of the CIA unit working on Cuban operations quoted in U.S. Senate, Select

Committee, *Alleged Assassination Plots*, p. 141 (hereafter U.S. Senate, *Alleged Assassination Plots*). See also Bissell, *Reflections*, p. 201.

18. Quotations from Schlesinger, *Robert Kennedy*, p. 516; Bissell, *Reflections*, p. 201; interview with Helms. On Mongoose, see Chang and Kornbluh, *Cuban Missile Crisis*, pp. 9-75; Corn, *Blond Ghost*, pp. 67-96; Blight and Kornbluh, *Politics*, pp. 107-32; Hersh, *Dark Side*, pp. 267-93; Rodriguez and Weisman, *Shadow Warrior*, pp. 99-114; U.S. Senate, *Alleged Assassination Plots*, pp. 139-70.

19. Quotations from Lansdale, "Memorandum for Members, Caribbean Survey Group," Jan. 20, 1962, *FRUS 1961-63*, 10:721, and Special NIE, "The Situation and Prospects in Cuba," Nov. 28, 1961, p. 1, FOIA 1984/1516.

20. Quotations from CIA officer Sam Halpern, in Blight and Kornbluh, *Politics*, p. 117; NIE, "The Situation and Prospects in Cuba," Mar. 21, 1962, p. 21, NSF, NIE, box 85, JFKL; "Minutes of the Meeting of the Special Group (Augmented) on Operation Mongoose, 4 October 1962," Oct. 4, 1962, NSC 145-10001-10023, JFKAC, RG 263, NA; Helms, memo for the record, "Mongoose Meeting with the Attorney General," Oct. 16, 1962, *FRUS 1961-63*, 11:46.

21. Che Guevara to Daniel [René Ramos Latour], Dec. 14, 1957, in Franqui, *Diary*, p. 269. On Raúl's membership in the PSP's youth group, "Information über eine Aussprache mit dem Generalsekretär der Sozialistischen Volkspartei Kubas, Blas Roca, am 13.6.61 in Havanna," GDR AA, A 16339.

22. Guevara to Daniel, Dec. 14, 1957, in Franqui, *Diary*, p. 269.

23. The only discussion of Soviet relations with Cuba in this period that uses Soviet archival sources is Fursenko and Naftali, *"One Hell of a Gamble."* Unfortunately, this pathbreaking study is marred by serious factual mistakes about the Cuban revolutionary process. (See Tad Szulc's excellent review, "The Most Dangerous Game," *WP Book World*, June 29, 1997, p. 4.) No authoritative Cuban sources are available.

24. Fursenko and Naftali, *"One Hell of a Gamble,"* p. 39.

25. Hernández de Zayas, "Sobre la vida de un revolucionario: el comandante Angelito," p. 11. This is the only biography of Colonel Angelito Martínez (Francisco Ciutat), who led the first group of Spanish officers.

Fursenko and Naftali write that Raúl Castro had requested in April 1959 that Moscow send a group of military officers of Spanish extraction and that within a few weeks such a group had arrived *("One Hell of a Gamble,"* pp. 11, 12). Yet Hernández de Zayas's essay indicates that Colonel Angelito Martínez led the first group of Spanish officers and that they arrived on March 4, 1960—that is, almost one year later.

26. Hughes (INR) to Acting Secretary, "Daniel's Conversation with Castro," Dec. 13, 1963, pp. 2, 4, NSFCF, box 17; DOS, MemoConv, Kennedy, Adzhubei, et al., Jan. 30, 1962, ibid. For Adzhubei's

report to Khrushchev, see Fursenko and Naftali, *"One Hell of a Gamble,"* pp. 152-53.

27. McNamara's foreword, in Chang and Kornbluh, *Cuban Missile Crisis*, pp. xi-xii. On the Missile Crisis, see Fursenko and Naftali, *"One Hell of a Gamble,"* esp. pp. 166-315; Garthoff, *Reflections*; Blight, Allyn, and Welch, *Cuba on the Brink*; May and Zelikow, *The Kennedy Tapes*; Gribkov and Smith, *Operation ANADYR*; Brenner, "Thirteen"; [Cuban government], *Peligros*; Gaddis, *We Now Know*, pp. 260-80.

28. Parrott, minutes of the meeting of the SGA (the special group that oversaw Mongoose), Feb. 26, 1962, NSC 145-10001-10272/175, JFKAC, RG 263, NA. See also Hershberg's probing "Before."

29. Castro's remarks at the Havana Conference on the Cuban Missile Crisis, Jan. 11, 1992, in Chang and Kornbluh, *Cuban Missile Crisis*, p. 339, and Castro to Khrushchev, Oct. 31, 1962, in Blight, Allyn, and Welch, *Cuba on the Brink*, p. 491. For the ditty, see Castañeda, *Compañero*, p. 229; confirmed in conversations in Cuba.

30. Kennedy to Khrushchev, Oct. 27, 1962, in "Back from the Brink," p. 51.

31. Gaddis, *We Now Know*, p. 279.

32. For Kennedy's press conference, see U.S. General Services, *Public Papers: John F. Kennedy, 1962*, pp. 830-38. Khrushchev's requests and Kennedy's rebuffs can be easily verified in the letters printed in "Back from the Brink." See also Beschloss, *Crisis*, pp. 561-68, and Blight, Allyn, and Welch, *Cuba on the Brink*, p. 420 n. 63. Both Secretary Rusk, at a closed Senate hearing in January 1963, and Secretary McNamara, at an international conference thirty years later, stated that "there was no non-invasion guarantee by the Kennedy administration," because the U.S. conditions had not been met (Rusk, Jan. 11, 1963, in U.S. Senate, Committee on Foreign Relations, *Executive Sessions*, pp. 3-33; McNamara, in Blight, Allyn, and Welch, *Cuba on the Brink*, p. 384 quoted).

33. Fitzgerald (chief, Special Affairs Staff) and Cooper (assistant deputy director intelligence) to DCI, Dec. 9, 1963, p. 2, FOIA.

34. Castro, Jan. 15, 1963, speech, *Revolución* (Havana), Jan. 16, 1963, p. 8.

35. Quotations from [CIA] Annex 3, enclosed in Bundy, "The Cuban Problem," Apr. 21, 1963, NSF, box 38, JFKL, and Miller, *Soviet Relations*, pp. 93-94.

36. Kennedy, June 10, 1963, in U.S. General Services, *Public Papers: John F. Kennedy, 1963*, p. 461; Khrushchev, in Beschloss, *Crisis*, p. 601.

37. Beschloss, *Crisis*, p. 624.

38. Quotations from Kent to DCI, Sept. 4, 1963, p. 3, NSC 145-10001-10126/205, JFKAC, RG 263, NA, and "Review of the Cuban Situation and Policy," p. 1, enclosed in Bundy, memo to the NSC, Mar. 11, 1963, NSF, Meetings and Memoranda, box 314, JFKL.

39. Quotations from [CIA], "Review of Current Program of Covert Action against Cuba," [Jan. 27, 1964], p. 7, NSFCF, box 24/25, and Parrott, "Sabotage Program, Cuba," June 19, 1963, NSC 145-10001-10194/208, JFKAC, RG 263, NA. In 1998 the CIA declassified several thousand pages of documents on covert operations against Cuba under Kennedy (many heavily sanitized), but they are only the tip of the iceberg. Three books that convey the flavor of the secret war against Castro in 1963 are Corn, *Blond Ghost*, pp. 96-119; Evan Thomas, *The Very Best*, pp. 291-310; Ayers, *The War*.

40. Interview with Bundy; McCone, memo of meeting with president, Aug. 23, 1962, *FRUS 1961-63*, 10:955.

41. Denney (INR) to SecState, Sept. 15, 1967, pp. 3-4, Pol 1 Cuba, SNF, NA; Castro quoted in Fursenko and Naftali, *"One Hell of a Gamble,"* p. 141.

42. Hughes (INR) to SecState, Apr. 17, 1964, p. 10, FOIA 1996/668.

43. Quotations from Castro, July 26, 1966, speech, *Granma* (Havana), July 27, 1966, p. 3; interview with Fernández Mell; Guevara, "Proyecciones sociales del Ejército Rebelde," Jan. 27, 1959, p. 20, in Guevara, *Escritos*, vol. 4.

44. Alfredo Maneiro in Blanco Muñoz, *La lucha armada: hablan 6 comandantes*, p. 349. The absence of documentation has made all studies of the guerrilla wars in Latin America in the 1960s and particularly of the Cuban role in them provisional. The most important are Gott, *Rural Guerrillas*; La critique; Goldenberg, *Kommunismus*, pt. 3; Lamberg, *Die Guerilla*; Allemann, *Macht*; Wickham-Crowley, *Guerrillas*. The only Cuban contribution to the subject, Alberto Prieto's *Guerrillas*, is shallow and riddled with factual mistakes.

45. Quotations from Castro, Feb. 22, 1963, speech, *Revolución*, Feb. 23, 1963, p. 4; NIE, "Latin American Reactions to Developments in and with Respect to Cuba," July 18, 1961, p. 3, NSF, NIE, box 8/9, LBJL; CIA, DI, "Cuban Subversive Activities in Latin America: 1959-1968," Feb. 16, 1968, pp. 1-2, NSFCF, box 19.

46. CIA, DI, "Cuban Subversive Activities in Latin America: 1959-1968," Feb. 16, 1968, p. 3 quoted, NSFCF, box 19; CIA, "Cuban Training of Latin American Subversives," Mar. 27, 1963, V.P. Security File, box 9, LBJL; CIA, OCI, "Survey of Latin America," Apr. 1, 1964, p. 84, NSFCF, box 1; Hughes (INR) to SecState, "An Outline Guide to Communist Activities in Latin America," Oct. 20, 1964, NSFCF, box 2; CIA, no title, [mid-1967], NSF, Intelligence File, box 2/3, LBJL; CIA, DI, "The Communist Insurgency Movement in Guatemala," Sept. 20, 1968, NSFCF, box 54.

47. One of them, Alberto Castellanos, was captured, sentenced to five years, and freed in December 1967. Throughout his ordeal, he maintained his cover as a Peruvian student. The other Cuban, Hermes Peña, was killed in a skirmish. He carried a brief diary that did not betray his nationality. (Interview with Castellanos; Peña's diary is printed in Mercier, *Las guerrillas*, pp. 153-64.)

In an outburst of revolutionary enthusiasm, in the eight months after the fall of Batista scores of Cubans joined the expeditions that set off from Cuba to overthrow the governments of Panama, the Dominican Republic, and Haiti and the group that was preparing to invade Nicaragua from Honduras. (Only the expeditions against Trujillo and Somoza had

Castro's support.) (See Piñeiro, "Inmortalidad," p. 42; Brache, *Constanza*; Gómez Ochoa, *Constanza*; Anderson, *Che*, pp. 394-97, 418-19, 439-40; Cordero Michel, "Las expediciones"; Diederich and Burt, *Papa Doc*, pp. 135-47; Borge, *La paciente impaciencia*, pp. 147-50.) The swift failure of these expeditions was followed by a lull that lasted more than one year, until Cuban support for armed struggle in Latin America began in earnest in 1961, in a much more hostile international environment.

48. CIA, OCI, "Survey of Latin America," Apr. 1, 1964, p. 84, NSFCF, box 1.

49. CIA, "Arms Traffic in the Caribbean Area, 1963," May 18, 1964, p. ii, NSFCF, box 31/32. See also Hughes (INR) to SecState, "Clandestine Arms Traffic in Latin America and the Insurgency Problem," Nov. 29, 1963, NSFCF, box 24/25; Read to Bundy, Feb. 13, 1964, ibid.; CIA, "The President's Intelligence Checklist," Nov. 29, 1963, JFK-M-02 (F2), CIA Miscellaneous Files, JFKAC, RG 263, NA; CIA, Daily Summary, Dec. 9, 1963, ibid.

50. See the accounts of three Venezuelan guerrilla commanders: Anselmo Natale and Luis Correa in Blanco Muñoz, *La lucha armada: hablan 6 comandantes*, pp. 199-200, 211-15, 225-26, 285-89, and Guillermo García Ponce in Blanco Muñoz, *La lucha armada: hablan 5 jefes*, pp. 368-70. See also Portillo, *Venezuela-Cuba*, pp. 75-76.

51. For the Dominican Republic, see Gleijeses, *Dominican Crisis*, pp. 100-103, 108-14, and Special NIE, "Instability and Insurgency Threat in the Dominican Republic," Jan. 17, 1964, NSF, NIE, box 8/9, LBJL. For Argentina, see chapter 2.

52. Attwood, "Memorandum on Cuba," Sept. 18, 1963, *FRUS 1961-63*, 11:868-70.

53. Attwood to Chase, Nov. 8, 1963, *FRUS 1961-63*, 11:880.

54. Attwood to Chase, Nov. 22, 1963, *FRUS 1961-63*, 11:893.

55. Quotations from Attwood to Chase, Nov. 22, 1963, *FRUS 1961-63*, 11:893, and Attwood to Stevenson, Dec. 9, 1963, ibid., p. 903. See also Chase to Bundy, Oct. 21, 1963, ibid., p. 877; Bundy, memo for the record, Nov. 12, 1963, ibid., pp. 888-89; Chase to Bundy, Nov. 19, 1963, NSFCF, box 21; Attwood, *Reds*, pp. 142-48; U.S. Senate, *Alleged Assassination Plots*, pp. 173-74; Howard, "Castro's Overture"; Kornbluh, "JFK and Castro."

56. Hughes (INR) to Acting Secretary, "Daniel's Conversation with Castro," Dec. 13, 1963, p. 1, NSFCF, box 17. See also Jean Daniel, "Unofficial Envoy"; Jean Daniel, "Two Interviews: Castro's Reply to Kennedy Comments on Cuba," *NYT*, Dec. 11, 1963, p. 1.

57. Bundy, quoted in Chase, "Meeting with the President, December 19, 1963," *FRUS 1961-63*, 11:907.

58. Eckel, "Memorandum for the Record: Cuban Operations," Nov. 12, 1963, *FRUS 1961-63*, 11:887.

59. J. S. Earman (inspector general, CIA), "Report on Plots to Assassinate Fidel Castro," May 23, 1967, p. 94, MF 0995, NSA.

60. Chase to Bundy, Nov. 25, 1963, *FRUS 1961-63*, 11:890.

61. Attwood to Stevenson, Dec. 9, 1963, *FRUS 1961-63*, 11:904.

62. [Chase], "Negotiations with Castro—Possible Scenario for First Steps," Apr. 21, 1964, quoted, NSFCF, box 21; Chase to Bundy, Dec. 2, 1963, *FRUS 1961-63*, 11:897; Chase to Bundy, Dec. 11, 1963, NSFCF, box 21; Chase, memo for the record, Jan. 24, 1964, ibid.

63. Quotations from Johnson to Fulbright, Dec. 2, 1963, in Beschloss, *Taking Charge*, p. 83, and White House, memo for the record, "Cuba meeting," Feb. 19, 1964, p. 3, NSFCF, box 24. For the consensus of the intelligence community, see CIA, "Cuba—A Status Report," Dec. 12, 1963, NSFCF, box 29; "Meeting with President Johnson," Dec. 19, 1963, *FRUS 1961-63*, 11:904-9; "Minutes of the Special Group Meeting, 13 February 1964," Feb. 14, 1964, NSC 145-10001-10221/135, JFKAC, RG 263, NA; CIA, OCI, "Survey of Latin America," Apr. 1, 1964, p. 79, NSFCF, box 1; Hughes (INR) to SecState, Apr. 17, 1964, FOIA 1996/668.

64. DOS, MemoConv (Johnson, Rusk, Alec Douglas-Home, et al.), Feb. 12, 1964, FOIA 1996/1453. A plethora of documents in the Johnson Library illustrates the administration's pressure on third-country governments and firms to eschew business with Cuba. (See esp. NSFCF, boxes 16-20, 26-28.) On continuing paramilitary operations, see esp. NSFCF, boxes 22 and 24/25; CIA Miscellaneous Files, JFKAC, RG 263, NA.

65. See Woodward (U.S. ambassador, Madrid) to SecState, May 25, 1964, NSFCF, box 21; Hughes (INR) to Acting SecState, June 2, 1964, ibid.; Stevenson to President, June 16 and 26, 1964, ibid.; Hughes to Acting SecState, "Castro Proposes US-Cuban Rapprochement," July 6, 1964, NSFCF, box 24/25; [GDR], "Informationsbericht des ADN-Korrespondenten in Havanna v. 29.7.1964," GDR AA, A3177(1); Rusk to Amembassy Conakry, Oct. 28, 1964, FOIA 1995/1351; Denney (INR) to SecState, "Cuban Foreign Policy," Sept. 15, 1967, Pol 1 Cuba, SNF, NA. See also *NYT* May 22, July 6, 7, 22, 1964 (all p. 1).

66. DOS, Policy Planning Council, "Caribbean: Cuba" (draft outline), Feb. 13, 1964, pp. 13, 6-7, 8-9, 10, NSFCF, box 26.

67. Castro to Johnson ("Verbal message given to Miss Lisa Howard of ABC News on February 12, 1964, in Havana, Cuba"), NSFCF, box 21 (emphasis in original).

68. Quotations from CIA, memo for DCI, "Current Thinking of Cuban Government Leaders," Mar. 5, 1964, pp. 1-2, JFK-M-07 (F1), CIA Miscellaneous Files, JFKAC, RG 263, NA, and McCone (DCI) to Secretaries of State and Defense and to the Special Assistant to the President for National Security Affairs, Mar. 4, 1964, p. 2, NSC 145-10001-10111/91, JFKAC, RG 263, NA.

69. Watson (British ambassador, Havana) to Foreign Minister Butler, Aug. 5, 1964, pp. 3 and 6 quoted, FOIA 1998/3232; Watson, "Cuban Foreign Policy," July 20, 1964, enclosed in Whitehead to Follestad,

Aug. 10, 1964, FOIA 1998/3233; Watson, "Cuban Foreign Policy," Aug. 19, 1964, enclosed in Whitehead to Follestad, Aug. 24, 1964, FOIA 1998/3234.
70. Szulc, *Fidel*, pp. 593-94.
71. Hughes (INR) to SecState, Apr. 17, 1964, pp. 10-11, FOIA 1996/668.
72. Lechuga, *En el ojo*, pp. 282-306.
73. Rabe, *Most Dangerous*, pp. 193, 197.
74. Fursenko and Naftali, *"One Hell of a Gamble,"* p. 141.
75. CIA, OCI, "Latin American Communist Developments," Mar. 15, 1966, p. 2 quoted, NSFCF, box 2; CIA, DI, "Castro and Communism: The Cuban Revolution in Perspective," May 9, 1966, NSFCF, box 19; Piñera, *Utopia*, pp. 62-67. (Piñera, a top aide of the Argentine Communist leader Vittorio Codovilla, was involved in the preparation of the conference.)
76. CIA, DI, "Cuban Subversive Activities in Latin America: 1959-1968," Feb. 16, 1968, p. 3, NSFCF, box 19. See also Hughes (INR) to SecState, "Latin American Communists Hold Strategic Conference," Jan. 22, 1965, NSFCF, box 31/32; CIA, OCI, "Cuban Subversion in Latin America," Apr. 23, 1965, ibid.
77. Johne (GDR ambassador, Havana) and Kulitzka (the embassy's first secretary), "Über die Entwicklung der Republik Kuba im Jahre 1964 und einige Entwicklungstendenzen für das Jahr 1965," Jan. 21, 1965, pp. 9-10, 13-14, SED, DY30 IVA 2/20/270. For Castro's Jan. 2, 1965, speech, see *Revolución*, Jan. 4, 1965, pp. 3-5.

CHAPTER TWO

1. Interview with Bangaly, one of the fifteen students from Guinea; Republic of Guinea, Ministère des Affaires Etrangères et de la Coopération, "Memorandum sur la Coopération entre la République de Guinée et la République de Cuba," Conakry, July 1994, Private Collection, Conakry.
2. Interviews with DGI officers Estrada and Cárdenas.
3. Interviews with DGI officers Estrada, Cárdenas, Urra, Carretero, and Duany. On the absence of DGI stations in Africa except in Algeria until 1965, see also CIA, DI, "Cuban Meddling in Africa," Mar. 24, 1967, p. 3, NSFCF, box 19. On the lack of an Africa department in the DGI until 1965, see also CIA, OCI, "Cuban Subversion in Latin America," Apr. 23, 1965, NSFCF, box 31/32. For claims that there were Cuban military instructors in Ghana, see Lang, "Les Cubains," p. 23, and Robbins, *Cuban Threat*, p. 61. For a list of Cuban embassies, see Hughes (INR) to SecState, "An Outline Guide to Communist Activities in Africa," May 15, 1964, p. 13, NSFCF, box 76, and Williams to SecState, July 7, 1965, MWP, box 13.
4. Ball to Accra, Nov. 22, 1963, Pol 7 Cuba, SNF, NA; Rusk, Circular Telegram (to eleven U.S. embassies in West Africa), Nov. 29, 1963, ibid.; Palmer (U.S. ambassador, Lagos) to SecState, Nov. 29, 1963 (quoted), ibid.; Kaiser (U.S. ambassador, Dakar) to SecState, Dec. 27, 1963, ibid.
5. CIA, OCI, "Weekly Cuban Summary," May 5, 1965, FOIA; [British embassy, Havana], "Communist Subversion Threat to Africa," Apr. 1965, enclosed in Vertretung der BRD bei der NATO to AA, Paris, May 26, 1965, FRG, AA Afrika Allg. 1965. See also "Country Internal Defense Plan," enclosed in Amembassy Pretoria to DOS, Dec. 18, 1962, FOIA; CIA, OCI, "Cuban Training and Support for African Nationalists," Jan. 31, 1964, NSCF, box 24; Hughes (INR) to SecState, "Cuba and Africa," Jan. 5, 1965, ibid.; CIA, DI, "Some Aspects of Subversion in Africa," Oct. 19, 1967, NSCF, box 78. On the British embassy's role, see Hershberg, "Their Men."
6. Hughes (INR) to SecState, Apr. 17, 1964, pp. 7 and 12 quoted, FOIA 1996/668. The only two studies of Cuba's relations with Algeria worth citing are Durch, "The Cuban Military," pp. 43-45, and, above all, García Blanco, *La misión*. Cuba's first ambassador to Algeria, Jorge Serguera (1963-65), has written his memoirs, *Caminos*. Unfortunately, the few useful tidbits are buried in an avalanche of philosophical verbiage and self-aggrandizement. Factual errors compound the problem.
7. Jorge Ricardo Masetti, *Los que luchan*, *Granma* (Havana), Sept. 7, 1968, p. 7; Jorge Masetti, *La loi*, pp. 130-32. Before the creation of the DGI, there had been a smaller intelligence unit, Departamento M, also under Piñeiro. In June 1961, M became part of the newly created Ministry of the Interior and was revamped as the DGI.
8. Hiram Prats, OH, n.d., pt. 1, p. 1 quoted, and pt. 2, pp. 6-7, AIHC. See also Pedro Labrador Pino, OH, Aug. 29, 1985, p. 1, AIHC, and Jorge Serguera, OH, Mar. 6, 1985, pp. 1 and 33, AIHC.
In 1985, the Centro de Estudio de Historia Militar, a branch of the Ministry of Armed Forces, conducted a series of interviews with Cubans who had been involved in Algeria. These interviews are in the AIHC.
9. *Revolución* (Havana), Feb. 14, 1962, p. 10, and Feb. 20, suppl., pp. 2-3 quoted. See also Prats, OH, pt. 2, p. 2.
10. Roberto González Gómez, letter to Piero Gleijeses, Havana, July 7, 1994. In the first seven months of 1957 there were four major articles about Algeria in *Bohemia* (Havana): Feb. 3, pp. 67, 81-82; Apr. 14, pp. 68, 91-93; June 23, pp. 110-12; July 7, pp. 8-9, 128-31. In addition, there was on average one shorter article every two weeks in the international section of the magazine. This pattern holds true through the fall of Batista.
11. Silvino Sorhegui to the Cuban embassies abroad, circular cable, Havana, June 28, 1961, MINREX, and Pervillé, "L'insertion," pp. 381, 385. For an indication of press coverage, see the weekly *Verde Olivo* (Havana) in the last year of the war: Mar. 19, 1961, p. 80; Apr. 16, pp. 24-26; Oct. 8, pp. 61-66; Oct. 15, pp. 50-55; Nov. 5, pp. 36-37; Jan. 21, 1962, pp. 54-55; Feb. 25, pp. 47-49; Apr. 1, pp. 32-34. (This list includes only the major articles.)
12. Interview with Risquet.
13. Ben Bella, quoted in Merle, *Ahmed Ben Bella*, pp. 153-56. See also Mohammed el Hadi Hadj-Smaïne, who accompanied Ben Bella to Cuba, quoted in "La seule erreur," p. 49; Ben Bella, "Ben Bella parle," pp. 51-52; Ben Bella, "Ainsi"; Porter (U.S. ambassador, Algiers) to SecState, Oct. 22, 1962, FOIA.

14. *Revolución*, Oct. 17, 1962, p. 6.
15. Ibid., p. 7. For the text of the communiqué, see *Revolución*, Oct. 18, 1962, p. 4.
16. Mrs. I. J. Overman to the President, Oct. 18, 1962, WHCF, box 41, JFKL. For more, see ibid.
17. Schlesinger, *A Thousand Days*, p. 565.
18. *CSM*, Oct. 18, 1962, p. 1.
19. "Discussion of Strategy and Action Plan for Algeria," Feb. 2, 1963, p. 3, NSF, Meetings and Memoranda, box 34, JFKL. See also Komer to Bundy, Dec. 12, 1962, and Komer to the President, Dec. 12, 1962, both enclosed in National Security Action Memorandum no. 211, Dec. 14, 1962, NSF, Meetings and Memoranda, box 33, JFKL; Root to SecState, Algiers, Feb. 6, 1963, MWP, box 24; Rusk, memo for president ("Plan of Action for Algeria"), [Feb. 1963], FOIA 1985/1592.
20. *Revolución*, Oct. 17, 1962, pp. 6-7.
21. Ibid., Oct. 18, 1962, p. 8. Of 2,500 doctors in Algeria in January 1962, only 600 remained six months later, when the country became independent. Of these, 285 were Algerian; many of the others were "volunteers who had come for a short period." (*Le Peuple* [Algiers], Aug. 20, 1963, p. 3 quoted, and Aug. 21, p. 3. See also Bennoune, *The Making*, p. 245.)
22. Interview with Perelló.
23. Interviews with Cedeño, Morejón, and Perelló; *Revolución*, May 20, 1963, p. 1, and May 24, p. 3. On Castro's planned visit to Algiers, which did not take place because of time constraints, or, two scholars write, on the urgent advice of Khrushchev, who believed that a plot was afoot to assassinate Castro during the trip, see *La Dépêche d'Algérie* (Algiers), Apr. 22, 1963, p. 1, and May 24, p. 8; *Le Monde*, May 24, 1963, p. 2; Fursenko and Naftali, *"One Hell of a Gamble,"* p. 331.
24. See *Revolución:* May 18, 1963, p. 1; May 20, p. 1; May 22, p. 2; May 24, p. 4.
25. Gabriel Molina, "La asistencia médica de Cuba a Argelia," *Revolución*, June 23, 1964, p. 5.
26. José Ramón Machado Ventura, note to Piero Gleijeses, Havana, July 12, 1995, p. 1. In 1959 there were approximately 6,000 doctors in Cuba. By late 1962, about 1,500 had left, "and an equal number had asked to leave. The most we could do was to delay their departure for a while" (ibid.; see also "En Síntesis," *Colaboración Internacional* [Havana], April 1980, p. 37).
27. Interview with Dr. Pablo Resik Habib by Hedelberto López Blanch. I would like to thank Mr. López Blanch, one of Cuba's foremost investigative journalists, for sharing his notes with me.
28. Interview with Cedeño. "A comrade from the Foreign Ministry gave us a lecture about Algeria. This is all the preparation that we received" (interview with Perelló). "It was a terrible lecture. Nothing they said had anything to do with what we found" (interview with Morejón).
29. Interviews with Cedeño and Perelló. On the arrival of the mission and its first days in Algiers, see also *Alger Républicain:* May 25, 1963, p. 1; May 27, p. 5; May 28, p. 3; May 31, p. 1; *Le Peuple*, May 25,

1963, p. 1, and May 28, p. 3; *La Dépêche d'Algérie*, May 25, 1963, p. 8.
30. Interviews with Perelló, Morejón, and Cedeño. "Our policy has always been to give the same stipend to all civilian internationalists, irrespective of their qualifications." (Interview with Benítez y de Mendoza, deputy minister of the Ministerio para la Inversión Extranjera y la Colaboración Económica. See also "Informe al Comité Central sobre la colaboración civil con Angola," 1978, pp. 55-56, ACC.)
31. Interviews with Cedeño, Perelló, and Morejón.
32. Interview with Cedeño.
33. Ibid. On Che's visit to Algeria, see *Revolución:* July 2, 4-6, 8, 10-16, 24, 1963; see also Amembassy Algiers to SecState, July 27, 1963, Pol 7 Cuba, SNF, NA.
34. Quotations from *Le Peuple*, May 28, 1965, p. 3, and from the interview with Resik by López Blanch. Havana paid for everything until 1978: travel expenses, salary in Cuba, stipend in Algeria. The Algerians took over payment in 1978, and the terms were finally codified in 1980. ("Protocolo que rige las condiciones de empleo, trabajo y remuneración de los expertos cubanos en los servicios argelinos de salud," Havana, Mar. 30, 1980, MIECE, and interview with Benítez y de Mendoza.)
35. Quotations from interview with Perelló and Jaime Sarusky, "Los médicos cubanos en Argelia," *Revolución*, suppl., Dec. 16, 1963, p. 11. The press rarely covered the Cuban medical missions in Algeria. The articles by Molina (see n. 25) and Sarusky are the most informative, but see also Moreno Luna, "Les Médecins Cubains en Algérie," *Le Peuple*, Dec. 25, 1964, p. 5, and Caridad Martínez, "Una experiencia para toda la vida," *Colaboración Internacional*, July-Sept. 1983, pp. 11-12.
36. Interview with Perelló.
37. Interviews with Perelló (quoted), Cedeño, Morejón, and with two doctors and a nurse who were in Algeria with later medical missions: Ulloa (1965-66), José Lara (1971-73), Amaro (1969-70).
38. *Revolución*, June 12, 1964, p. 1.
39. Interview with Resik by López Blanch. The medical missions in Algeria ended in 1992. This was due, in part, to economic considerations: there had been a dramatic devaluation of the dinar—from 4.77 dinars per $1 in 1985 to 24.42 dinars per $1 in 1992 (*International Financial Statistics*, June 1992, pp. 70-71). "Since the payment was calculated in dinars, this meant that we were receiving almost nothing." Furthermore, the turmoil in Algeria created very serious concerns for the security of the Cuban personnel (interview with Benítez y de Mendoza).
40. Jean Lacouture, *Le Monde*, May 26, 1963, p. 1.
41. "The Addis Ababa Conference," n.d., p. 4 quoted, enclosed in Brubeck to Bundy, May 27, 1963, FOIA 1976/169E. On Ben Bella's commitment to African liberation, see the excellent overview in Grimaud, *La politique*, pp. 263-79; Ottaway and Ottaway, *Algeria*, pp. 144-48, 162-229; Mortimer, "Foreign Policy," pp. 229-78; and, for background, Chick, "L'Algérie."

42. Hughes (INR) to Acting Secretary, "Algeria's Ben Bella: An Interpretation and Estimate," May 28, 1964, p. 1, NSFCF, box 79.

43. On the Ben Bella administration, see Quandt, *Revolution*, pp. 204-35; Chaliand and Minces, *L'Algérie*, pp. 23-85; Ottaway and Ottaway, *Algeria*, pp. 1-195.

44. Hughes (INR) to SecState, "Polarization in North Africa: Implications for the US," Jan. 6, 1965, p. 4, FOIA 1978/205c.

45. See Reyner, "Morocco's International Boundaries," and Trout, *Morocco's Saharan Frontiers*.

46. Quotations from *Le Petit Marocain* (Casablanca), Oct. 2, 1963, p. 3, and Oct. 7, pp. 1 and 3. For the Moroccan occupation of Hassi-Beida and Tindjoub, see Centre National de la Recherche Scientifique, *Annuaire*, p. 312.

47. *NYT*, Oct. 20, 1963, p. 17.

48. There is no comprehensive study of the 1963 border war. The best press coverage is in *Le Monde* and the *New York Times*. The most detailed chronology is Centre National de la Recherche Scientifique, *Annuaire*.

49. Quotations from CIA, OCI, "Consequences of Algerian Coup," June 19, 1965, p. 2, NSFCF, box 79, and *NYT*, Aug. 2, 1964, p. 5.

50. Reinerio Placencia, in "Entrevista realizada a un grupo de compañeros de la misión internacionalista en Argelia," Nov. 29, 1985, p. 12, AIHC.

51. *Times* (London), Oct. 28, 1963, p. 10. On the Algerian and Moroccan armed forces, see also DOS, Policy Planning Council, "North Africa in the Mediterranean Littoral," Sept. 23, 1963, pp. 12-13, 24-25, NSF, box 3, JFKL; Hughes (INR) to SecState, "Soviet Military Aid to Algeria," Aug. 6, 1964, NSFCF, box 79; *NYT*, June 30, 1963, 4:10, and Apr. 16, 1964, p. 28.

52. *Le Petit Marocain*, Oct. 11, 1963, p. 4.

53. *Verde Olivo*, Oct. 13, 1963, p. 51.

54. Flavio Bravo to Raúl Castro, Algiers, Oct. 21, 1963, p. 1; *Revolución*, Nov. 2, 1963, p. 2 (quoting Serguera).

55. Serguera, OH, Mar. 6, 1985, p. 8.

56. Gabriel Molina, OH, n.d., p. 3, AIHC.

57. Mesa and Perozo were killed in a clash with Batista's troops, which were supported by two tanks, on November 5, 1958 ([Cuban government], Comisión de Historia de la Columna 19 "José Tey," *Columna 19*, pp. 299-304).

58. Serguera, OH, Mar. 6, 1985, pp. 8-9. Molina confirms Serguera (Molina, OH, pp. 3-4).

59. See Blake to Fredericks, Dec. 12, 1963, FOIA 1993/146, and Ferguson (U.S. ambassador, Rabat) to SecState, Jan. 29, 1964, NSFCF, box 16.

60. Special NIE, "The Effects of Hurricane Flora on Cuba," Nov. 15, 1963, p. 3, FOIA, 1987/1210.

61. Labrador Pino, OH, pp. 2-8 quoted. The following interviews conducted by members of the Centro de Estudios de Historia Militar were also particularly useful for Cuba's aid during the 1963 war: "Entrevista colectiva sobre la misión internacionalista en Argelia," Oct. 30, 1985 (hereafter "Entrevista colectiva"); "Entrevista realizada a un grupo de compañeros de la misión internacionalista en Argelia," Nov. 29, 1985 (hereafter "Entrevista"); Lieutenant Colonel Melquiades González, OH, Dec. 16, 1985; all located in the AIHC. Also very useful is the "Diario del Instructor Revolucionario Pedro Rodríguez Delgado," PCH (hereafter "Diario"), which covers Oct. 13, 1963-Apr. 1, 1964.

62. Labrador Pino, OH, pp. 9-10; interview with Santamaría. The four who spoke with Ben Bella were Santamaría, Bravo, and Martínez (the three senior members of the group) and Serguera (interviews with Santamaría and Labrador Pino). Angelito Martínez, who had arrived in Cuba in March 1960, had become a comandante in the Cuban armed forces. He remained in Cuba until 1977, when he went back to his native Spain. In the mid-1980s, he returned to Cuba, where he died in November 1986 (Hernández de Zayas, "Sobre la vida").

63. Labrador Pino, OH, p. 11.

64. Luis Francisco Díaz, in "Entrevista," p. 109.

65. Reinerio Placencia, in "Entrevista," pp. 121-23. See also Jesús Díaz, ibid., pp. 75-76, and Melquiades González, OH, pp. 3-4.

66. Pedro Rodríguez Fonseca, in "Entrevista colectiva," pp. 3-4.

67. Quotations from Rodríguez Delgado, "Diario," entries of Oct. 14 and 16, 1963. See also ibid., entry of Oct. 17; [no first name] Velázquez, in "Entrevista colectiva," pp. 34-35; Eloy Cruz in ibid., pp. 42-44; José Luis Rodríguez Rivero in ibid., pp. 46-48.

68. See "Relación del personal del Grupo Especial de Instrucción," AIHC, and Flavio Bravo to Raúl Castro, Algiers, Oct. 21, 1963, p. 1.

69. See *Le Peuple*, Nov. 1, 1963, p. 1, and Nov. 5, p. 1; Root to SecState, Algiers, Oct. 8, 1963, Pol 7 Cuba, SNF, NA.

70. Interview with Ameijeiras.

71. Raúl Castro to Flavio Bravo and Jorge Serguera, Havana, Oct. 20, 1963, pp. 3-5.

72. Quotations from Pedro Rodríguez Delgado, "Entrevista colectiva," p. 19; Labrador Pino, OH, p. 13; interview with Ameijeiras. The experience of the *González Lines* was similar. (See Rodríguez Delgado, "Diario," entries of Oct. 29 and 30, 1963, and Velázquez, "Entrevista colectiva," p. 39.)

73. Interview with Ameijeiras. For press reports, see *Daily Telegraph* (London), Oct. 26, 1963, p. 16; *NYT*, Oct. 27, 1963, p. 1, and Oct. 30, p. 3; *Le Petit Marocain*, Oct. 28, 1963, p. 3; *Le Monde*, Oct. 30, 1963, p. 2; Oct. 31, p. 6; Nov. 1, p. 2; *Times*, Oct. 28, 1963, p. 10, and Oct. 30, p. 7.

74. Quotations from Amconsul Oran to DOS, Nov. 8, 1963, Pol 32-1 Alg-Mor, SNF, NA, and Ball to Amembassy Algiers, Oct. 30, 1963, Def 19-6 Cuba-Alg, SNF, NA. See also Ferguson to SecState, Rabat, Oct. 24, 1963, ibid.; DOS to Amembassy Moscow and Amembassy Cairo, Oct. 25, 1963, Pol 32-1 Alg-Mor, SNF, NA; Porter to SecState, Algiers, Oct. 29 and 31, 1963, Def 19-6 Cuba-Alg, SNF, NA; Ball to Amembassy Algiers, Oct. 29, 1963, ibid.; British embassy Algiers to FO, Nov. 4, 1963, FO 371/173131, PRO.

75. Ben Bella, "Ainsi."

76. Flavio Bravo to Raúl Castro, Algiers, Oct. 21, 1963, pp. 1, 3 (emphasis in original).

77. Rodríguez Delgado, "Diario," entry of Nov. 11, 1963; Velázquez, "Entrevista colectiva," p. 39.

78. Quotations from Flavio Bravo to Raúl Castro, Algiers, Oct. 31, 1963, p. 1; Melquiades González, OH, pp. 20-21; interview with Ameijeiras. On Operación Dignidad, see Flavio Bravo to Raúl Castro, Algiers, Oct. 21, 1963, p. 3; García Blanco, La misión, pp. 27-28, 34; Serguera, OH, Sept. 13, 1985, pp. 1-3.

79. See Wild, "Organization," and Touval, Boundary, pp. 255-62.

80. See, for example, Williams to Ferguson, Oct. 25 and 29, 1963, MWP, box 11.

81. Interview with Ameijeiras.

82. Quotations from the Times, Oct. 22, 1963, p. 8, and Hughes (INR) to SecState, "Polarization in North Africa: Implications for the US," Jan. 6, 1965, p. 4, FOIA, 1978/205c. Cuba and Egypt were the only countries that sent troops. The first Egyptian soldiers did not reach Algeria until the end of October. "Even though we came from much farther away, we were the first to arrive," remarks Ameijeiras. (Interview with Ameijeiras. See also Amembassy Cairo to SecState, Oct. 28, 1963, Pol 32-1 Alg-Mor, SNF, NA; British embassy Algiers to FO, Nov. 4, 1963, FO 371/173131, PRO; Amconsul Oran to DOS, Nov. 8, 1963, Pol 32-1 Alg-Mor, SNF, NA; CIA, ONE, "Nasser's Policy and Prospects in Black Africa," Jan. 9, 1964, FOIA 1977/20E; Le Petit Marocain: Oct. 28, 1963, p. 3; Nov. 6, p. 3; Nov. 12, p. 1; Times, Oct. 30, 1963, p. 7, and Nov. 2, p. 7; Le Monde, Oct. 30, 1963, p. 2, and Nov. 3, p. 11.)

83. Foreign Minister Abdelaziz Bouteflika, Le Peuple, Nov. 23, 1963, p. 3. The French archives for the period are still closed, but there are numerous U.S. reports on the French position in Pol 32-1 Alg-Mor, SNF, NA. French neutrality was motivated, a French official explained, by de Gaulle's belief that "we must avoid at all costs being cut off from Algeria" (Porter to SecState, Algiers, Oct. 31, 1963, ibid.). See also Blankenhorn (FRG ambassador, Paris) to AA, Oct. 16, 1963, FRG, AA MF 00004-2; Hoffmann (FRG embassy, Algiers), Oct. 22, 1963, FRG, AA MF 00004-3; Wauthier, Quatre présidents, pp. 156-57.

84. Williams to Ferguson, Oct. 25, 1963, pp. 1-2 quoted, MWP, box 11; Berramdane, Le Maroc, pp. 264-68. See also the cables and memos in FRUS, 1961-1963, 21:13-17, 23-30, 30-34, and in Pol 32-1 Alg-Mor, SNF, NA.

85. Interview with Ameijeiras.

86. Times, Oct. 28, 1963, p. 10 (quoted), and Oct. 30, p. 7. See also Evans (British embassy, Algiers) to FO, "State of Algerian and Moroccan Armed Forces," Nov. 20, 1963, FO 371/173131, PRO; Hughes (INR) to SecState, "Soviet Military Aid to Algeria," Aug. 6, 1964, NSFCF, box 79; Le Petit Marocain, Oct. 28, 1963, p. 3, and Oct. 31, p. 3; CSM, Oct. 29, 1963, p. 2; Le Monde, Nov. 1, 1963, p. 2; NYT, Oct. 30, 1963, p. 3.

87. Boumedienne to Raúl Castro, Algiers, Nov. 20, 1963.

88. Interview with Ameijeiras; Ulises Rosales del Toro to Raúl Castro, "Informe resumen," Bedeau, Mar. 30, 1964, pp. 10-11.

89. Quotations from Rodríguez Fonseca, in "Entrevista colectiva," p. 11, and Rodríguez Delgado, "Diario," entry of Mar. 5, 1964; interview with Perelló.

90. Rodríguez Delgado, "Diario," entries of Nov. 22 (quoted), 27, 29, 30, 1963; of Dec. 5, 1963; of Feb. 19, 21, 28, 1964.

91. Ibid., entry of Dec. 8, 1963.

92. Interviews with DGI officers Estrada, Cárdenas, and Montero; Ulises Rosales del Toro to Raúl Castro, "Informe resumen," Bedeau, Mar. 30, 1964, p. 10 quoted.

93. Quotations from Hughes (INR) to SecState, "Soviet Military Aid to Algeria," Aug. 6, 1964, p. 2, NSFCF, box 79, and interview with Ameijeiras.

94. Quotations from Rodríguez Delgado, "Diario," entries of Mar. 12, 29, 30, and Apr. 1, 1964.

95. Le Petit Marocain, Nov. 1, 1963, p. 4 quoted. See also Hess (FRG embassy, Rabat) to AA, Dec. 5, 1963, FRG, AA MF 00004-3; CIA, "Daily Summary," Dec. 6, 1963, JFK-M-02 (F2), CIA Miscellaneous Files, JFKAC, RG 263, NA; Rusk to Amembassy Rabat, Dec. 11, 1963, Pol 17 Cuba-Mor, SNF, NA; Blake to Fredericks, Dec. 12, 1963, NSFCF, box 18; Ferguson to SecState, Rabat, Jan. 11 and 13, 1964, Pol 17 Cuba-Mor, SNF, NA; Porter to SecState, Algiers, Jan. 14, 1964, ibid.; Sanne (FRG embassy, Rabat) to AA, Feb. 2, 1964, FRG, AA MF 00001-5; Le Petit Marocain, Jan. 14, 1964, p. 1; Le Monde, Dec. 23, 1963, p. 6; Revolución, Feb. 27, 1964, p. 1, and Mar. 11, p. 2.

96. Hughes (INR) to Acting Secretary, "Algeria's Ben Bella: An Interpretation and Estimate," May 28, 1964, p. 3, NSFCF, box 79.

97. Ben Bella, Le Peuple, Feb. 23, 1965, p. 3.

98. Ibid., Oct. 14, 1964, p. 3.

99. Quotations from CIA, OCI, "Ben Bella's Relations with the Soviet Bloc," June 3, 1964, p. 4, NSFCF, box 79, and Hughes (INR) to SecState, Apr. 19, 1965, p. 6, NSFCF, box 20.

100. Quotation from interview with Urra. The ambassador in Cairo, Luis García Guitart, was a prominent university professor who lacked ties with the Cuban leadership. Armando Entralgo, who represented Cuba in Accra, was a young Foreign Ministry official.

101. Interviews with DGI officers Urra (quoted), Estrada, and Cárdenas.

102. Interview with Estrada.

103. Ben Bella, "Ainsi," quoted; Ben Bella, "Ben Bella parle," p. 53.

104. Le Peuple, Aug. 4, 1963, p. 1.

105. Quotations from interview with Urra; CIA, OCI, "Weekly Cuban Summary," Dec. 30, 1964, p. 2, NSFCF, box 33/37; Serguera, OH, Mar. 6, 1985, p. 24. Drawn to conspiratorial activities, Serguera neglected less exciting work like attending to the needs of the Cuban medical mission. In early 1964 Oscar Oramas, a young Foreign Ministry officer who had no ties to the DGI, was appointed deputy chief of mission and took over the routine business of the embassy.

106. Interviews with Urra (quoted), Estrada, and Carretero; Serguera, *Caminos*, pp. 53-67; Colomé in Báez, *Secretos*, pp. 24-25; Ulises Estrada, "La política internacionalista de Cuba en los años 60/70," pp. 5-8, PCH. See also chapter 5, n. 5.

107. Interview with Urra; Serguera, *Caminos*, pp. 145-47.

108. Quotations from Hughes (INR) to SecState, "Cuba and Africa," Jan. 5, 1965, p. 3, NSFCF, box 24, and from interviews with Estrada, Urra, and Oramas. See also Serguera, *Caminos*, pp. 243-44, and the accounts of the Venezuelan guerrilla commander Luis Correa in Blanco Muñoz, *La lucha armada: hablan 6 comandantes*, p. 306, and the Venezuelan Oswaldo Barreto, who participated in the operation in Algeria, in Kalfon, *Che*, p. 391.

109. Hughes (INR) to SecState, "Che Guevara's African Venture," Apr. 19, 1965, NSFCF, box 20.

110. This paragraph is based on the two folders labeled "Operación Triángulo," ACC; Risquet, *El segundo frente*, pp. 26-29; interview with Estrada, who was in charge of the operation; Serguera, OH, Mar. 6, 1985, p. 23.

111. Quotations from Ottaway and Ottaway, *Algeria*, p. 231, and Bundy, memo for president, Jan. 5, 1965, NSFCF, box 79. For key documents, see RWK [Komer], memo for record, Jan. 15, 1964, ibid.; Porter to SecState, Algiers, May 11, 1964, FOIA 1978/258A; CIA, OCI, "Ben Bella's Relations with the Soviet Bloc," June 3, 1964, NSFCF, box 79; Root to DOS, June 29, 1964, ibid.; Hughes (INR) to SecState, "Ben Bella Heading into Stormy Seas," Sept. 10, 1964, FOIA 1978/259A; Komer, memo for record, Nov. 19, 1964, NSF, Name File, box 6, LBJL; DOS, MemoConv (Rusk, Guellal, et al.), Apr. 16, 1965, NSFCF, box 79; Porter to SecState, Algiers, May 12, 1965, ibid.; INR, "Political Dynamics Study on Algeria," n.d., enclosed in Hughes to SecState, June 19, 1965, ibid. The most comprehensive overview of U.S. relations with Ben Bella's Algeria is Rahmani, "Algerian-American Relations," 1:188-261.

112. *Le Monde*, Nov. 8, 1963, p. 1.

113. *NYT*, June 21, 1965, p. 3.

114. *Revolución*, June 28, 1965, pp. 4-5.

115. Interview with Oramas, the chargé.

116. *Revolución*, July 1, 1965, p. 1, and July 5, p. 1.

117. Watson (British ambassador, Havana) to Dawbarn, Apr. 12, 1966, FO 371/190372, PRO.

118. Flavio Bravo to Raúl Castro, Algiers, Oct. 21, 1963, pp. 2-3. Fursenko and Naftali write that during his first trip to the Soviet Union, in May 1963, Castro had urged Khrushchev to provide military assistance to Algeria *("One Hell of a Gamble,"* p. 331).

119. See Hughes (INR) to SecState, "Soviet Military Aid to Algeria," Aug. 6, 1964, NSFCF, box 79.

120. "Texto del discurso pronunciado por el comandante Ali Hamlat, en el acto central organizado por el MINFAR, con motivo del primero de Noviembre / 1984," p. 9, AIHC.

121. Interviews with Estrada and Cárdenas.

122. Porter to SecState, Algiers, Oct. 6, 1962, 033.51511/10-662, Central Decimal File, NA.

CHAPTER THREE

1. Hughes (INR), "The Communist Specter Looms in Zanzibar," Jan. 13, 1964, NSFCF, box 103. On the Zanzibar revolution, see Lofchie, "Zanzibari Revolution"; Wilson, *United States Foreign Policy*; Clayton, *The Zanzibar Revolution*, and the memoirs pf tje US vice-consul (Petterson, *Revolution*). For the best press coverage, see the *Tanganyika Standard* (Dar-es-Salaam), Jan.-Apr. 1964.

2. CIA, OCI, "Cuban Training and Support for African Nationalists," Jan. 31, 1964, NSFCF, box 24/25. Actually the office opened on January 12, 1962. (See *Revolución*, Jan. 13, 1962, p. 9.)

3. Interview with Devlin.

4. Leonhart (U.S. ambassador, Dar-es-Salaam) to SecState, Jan. 28, 1964, NSFCF, box 103.

5. Quotations from Leonhart to SecState, Jan. 26, 1964, sec. 2, p. 1, NSFCF, box 103; *Tanganyika Standard*, Jan. 28, 1964, p. 1; "Visit of Prime Minister Douglas-Home, February 12-13, 1964: Background paper. East Africa and Zanzibar," Feb. 7, 1964, p. 1, FOIA 1995/ 3199. See also CIA, "Communist Involvement in Recent East African Events," Feb. 5, 1964, NSFCF, box 77.

6. Quotations from Rusk to Bruce, Feb. 1, 1964, NSFCF, box 103; Williams to Harriman, Feb. 1, 1964, MWP, box 12; Bundy, memo for president, Feb. 4, 1964, NSF, McGeorge Bundy, box 18/19, LBJL; Rusk to Bruce, Mar. 29, 1964, p. 1, NSFCF, box 103; DOS, MemoConv, Apr. 29, 1964, FOIA 1964/00174. See also Williams to SecState, Jan. 23, 1964, MWP, box 29; TelConv, Ball and Harriman, Jan. 26, 1964, Ball Papers, box 4, LBJL; Ormsby Gore (British ambassador, Washington, D.C.) to FO, Jan. 28, 1964, FO 371/176514, PRO; FO to Washington, D.C., Jan. 29, 1964, ibid.; Ball to Bruce, Jan. 29, 1964, NSFCF, box 103; Rusk to Bruce, Feb. 1 and 4, 1964, ibid.; Johnson to British Prime Minister, enclosed in Rusk to Amembassy London, Feb. 5, 1964, ibid.; Williams to Harriman, Feb. 12, 1964, MWP, box 12; Rusk to Amembassy Dar-es-Salaam, Mar. 6, 1964, NSFCF, box 103; Carlucci (U.S. chargé, Zanzibar) to Williams, Mar. 9, 1964, MWP, box 28; Rusk to Amembassy London, Mar. 27, 1964, NSF, Memos to the President, box 1, LBJL; Bruce to SecState, Mar. 31, 1964, ibid.; Millard (FO, London) to Killick, Apr. 2, 1964, FO 371/176601, PRO.

7. *NYT*, Jan. 15, 1964, p. 1 (p. 3 quoted), and Jan. 19, p. 1. See also *WP*, Jan. 15, 1964, p. 9; Jan. 18, p. 8; Jan. 31, p. 13; *CSM*, Jan. 17, 1964, p. 4, and Jan. 21, p. 1; *WSJ*, Jan. 15, 1964, p. 1; *Newsweek*, Jan. 27, 1964, pp. 34-35; *U.S. News & World Report*, Jan. 27, 1964, p. 6.

8. *NYT*, Jan. 23, 1964, p. 1.

9. Interviews with DGI officers Estrada and Cárdenas. (Both note that Field Marshal Okello had never set foot in Cuba.) See also Köhler (GDR office, Cairo), "ZNP Sansibar," Oct. 22, 1962, GDR AA, A14187; "Informationsbericht über Sansibar," n.d., SED, DY30 IVA 2/20/966; Fritsch (GDR ambassador, Zanzibar), "Innen- und aussenpolitische Entwicklung der Volksrepublik Sansibar," n.d., ibid.

10. Quotations from Lofchie, "Zanzibari Revolution," pp. 925-26, and DOS to All African Diplomatic Posts, Jan. 30, 1964, p. 3, NSFCF, box 103. For Nyerere's comments, see Leonhart to SecState, Jan. 20, 1964, NSFCF, box 100. According to the CIA, there were four Cuban diplomats at the Dar-es-Salaam embassy, including the chargé (CIA, "Communist Involvement in Recent East African Events," Feb. 5, 1964, Annex A, NSFCF, box 77). On the absence of DGI officers in sub-Saharan Africa, see chapter 2, n. 3. On Tanzania's distant relations with Cuba, see Leonhart to SecState, Mar. 5, 1964, Pol 17 Cuba-Tangan, SNF, NA.

Many years after serving as the Cuban chargé in Dar-es-Salaam in 1963-64, Juan Benemelis moved to Miami, where he wrote a fantastic exposé of Cuba's activities in Africa. (Benemelis, *Castro*, see pp. 85-96 for his account of how Cuba masterminded the Zanzibar revolution.)

11. Interview with Serguera.

12. See *Revolución*, Jan. 16, 1964, p. 5, and *Tanganyika Standard*, Jan. 20, 1964, p. 1. U.S. documents confirm the lack of a Cuban embassy. See, for example, Rusk to Amembassy Bangkok et al., Apr. 3, 1964, NSFCF, box 103. See also Bailey, *The Union*, p. 72, table 19.

13. Carlucci to SecState, Mar. 26, 1964, NSFCF, box 103; Hughes (INR) to Acting Secretary, "Growing Communist Influence in Zanzibar," Apr. 15, 1964, p. 4, ibid. See also Ball to Amembassy Paris, Apr. 13, 1964, ibid., and NSC meeting, Apr. 5, 1964, NSF, NSC Meetings File, box 1, LBJL.

14. Ball to Amembassy Dar-es-Salaam, Apr. 18, 1964, NSFCF, box 103. See also "Talk between Sir Saville Garner and Mr. McGeorge Bundy at the White House, on April 17 [1964]," FO 371/174226, PRO.

15. For the transcripts, see Beschloss, *Taking Charge*.

16. Johnson, May 27, 1964, conversation with Russell, quoted by Beschloss, *Taking Charge*, p. 365, and Johnson, May 27, 1964, conversation with Bundy, ibid., p. 370.

17. Harriman, quoted by Abramson, *Spanning the Century*, p. 632.

18. On U.S. policy toward Zaire in 1960-63, see Mahoney, *JFK*, pp. 34-156 (p. 43 quoted); Kalb, *Congo Cables*; Gibbs, *Political Economy*, pp. 77-144; Weissman, *American Foreign Policy*; Mollin, *Die USA*, pp. 389-468; Michael Williams, "America." The most authoritative source on Soviet policy toward Zaire in 1960-63 is Namikas, "The Cold War and the Congo Crisis," chs. 2-6. (Namikas is the only scholar who has used the very limited evidence available in the Russian archives.) For the domestic situation in Zaire in the same period, see CRISP: *Congo 1960*, *Congo 1961*; *Congo 1962*; *Congo 1963*. See also Willame, *Patrice Lumumba*. On the controversial role of the United Nations in Zaire, see also Urquhart, *Ralph Bunche*, pp. 298-347; Rikhye, *Military Adviser*; O'Brien, *To Katanga*; de Witte, "De Lumumba à Mobutu."

19. *NYT*, Jan. 19, 1961, p. 7 quoted; Heinz and Donnay, *Lumumba*; Brassinne and Kestergat, *Qui?*, pp. 84-209; de Witte, *L'assassinat*.

20. CIA, Information Report, Oct. 18, 1962, FOIA 1982/1507.

21. Odom, *Dragon Operations*, p. 4; DOS, MemoConv (Kennedy, Mobutu, et al.), May 31, 1963, pp. 3-4, NSF, box 29, JFKL.

22. Quotations from CIA, DI, "The Political Situation and Prospects in the Congo," Feb. 20, 1964, p. 1, NSFCF, box 81, and Ball to Amembassy Brussels, Jan. 29, 1964, NSFCF, box 16. For Zairean politics in 1964-65, see CRISP, *Congo 1964* and *Congo 1965*; Verhaegen's *Rébellions* and "Conditions"; Coquery-Vidrovitch, Forest, and Weiss, *Rébellions-Révolution*; Fox et al., "La deuxième"; Young, "Rebellion."

U.S. policy toward Zaire in 1964-65 has received remarkably short shrift, but see Weissman, *American Foreign Policy*, pp. 211-56; Gibbs, *Political Economy*, pp. 146-64, is particularly strong on Belgian business interests in Zaire. There are two excellent studies of the U.S.-Belgian raid on Stanleyville in November 1964: Wagoner, *Dragon Rouge*, and Odom, *Dragon Operations*.

Memoirs by protagonists in the crisis are not very helpful. The best are those by mercenaries who served in Zaire (see n. 64). Accounts by U.S. and foreign officials are shallow (the one exception is Vandewalle, *L'Ommegang*), as are those of journalists who covered the story. (The best are Reed, *111 Days*; Kestergat, *Congo Congo*, and Le Bailly, *Une poignée*.)

23. Quotations from Rose (British ambassador, Leopoldville) to FO, Feb. 12, 1964, p. 4, FO 371/176648, PRO; NSC meeting, Apr. 3, 1964, pp. 7, 8, NSF, NSC Meetings File, box 1, LBJL; *Le Soir* (Brussels), May 6, 1964, p. 3 (quoting Mobutu). See also Gullion (U.S. ambassador, Leopoldville) to SecState, Feb. 4, 1964, FOIA 1976/268B; Williams to Harriman, Mar. 17, 1964, MWP, box 12; Godley (U.S. ambassador, Leopoldville) to SecState, Apr. 3, 1964, Harriman Papers, box 543, LOC; MacArthur (U.S. ambassador, Brussels) to SecState, Apr. 3, 1964, ibid.; Spaak to Belgian embassy Washington, D.C., Apr. 4, 1964, MAE 18.293 II (c); CIA, OCI, "The Security Situation in the Congo," June 12, 1964, NSFCF, box 81.

24. Quotations from Rose, "Congo (Leopoldville): Annual Review for 1964," Leopoldville, Jan. 12, 1965, sec. 1, p. 2, FO 371/181656, PRO (hereafter Rose, "Congo–1964"), and *WP*, Nov. 25, 1964, p. 1 (quoting the consul, Michael Hoyt, who had been held prisoner by the rebels for almost four months). See also Hoyt, *Captive*, pp. 176, 232-36.

25. Rose, "Congo–1964," p. 2.

26. Quotations from Godley to Williams, June 16, 1964, MWP, box 29; *Le Monde*, July 30, 1964, p. 1; FRG embassy Leopoldville to AA, June 23, 1964, p. 2, FRG, AA 90.08.

27. Verhaegen, "La Première République," p. 126; *Daily Nation* (Nairobi), July 30, 1964, p. 11; Rose to Millard, Leopoldville, Aug. 28, 1964, FO 371/176697, PRO.

28. Dean to Amembassy Leopoldville, July 2, 1964, DOS MF 8503217.

29. Quotations from Special NIE, "Short-Term Prospects for the Tshombe Government," Aug. 5, 1964, NSF, NIE, box 8, LBJL; Amembassy Leopoldville to DOS, Joint Weeka no. 10, Sept. 20, 1964, DOS MF 8503217; CIA, DI, "The Security Situation in the Congo," June 17, 1964, p. 3, FOIA 1978/135B; Godley to SecState, Aug. 5, 1964, NSFCF, box 81; Rose, "Congo—1964," p. 2. On the attitude of the population, see also CIA, OCI, "Situation in the Congo," Aug. 26, 1965, NSFCF, box 85; Kerchove (Belgian ambassador, Leopoldville) to Spaak, Sept. 4, 1964, MAE 18.288 (X); Godley to SecState, Dec. 4, 1964, NSFCF, box 85; CIA, DI, "The Congo: Assessment and Prospects," Dec. 31, 1964, NSFCF, box 87; CIA, OCI, weekly report, "The Situation in the Congo," Mar. 10, 1965, ibid. (hereafter CIA, "Situation," followed by date); Blake to DOS, "The Congolese Rebellion: Current Status and Outlook," Leopoldville, Mar. 3, 1966, DOS MF 8705067/1.

30. Quotations from Hoffacker, "What Should Be U.S. Policy vis-à-vis Tshombe in Future Contingencies?," n.d., enclosed in McElhiney to Palmer, Dec. 3, 1964, DOS MF 8503217, and Godley to SecState, July 1, 1964, p. 2, ibid.

31. Quotations from Special NIE, "Short-Term Prospects for the Tshombe Government," Aug. 5, 1964, NSF, NIE, box 8, LBJL; interview with DCM Blake; Williams to Harriman, July 24, 1964, MWP, box 12. On Tshombe's appointment, see also NSFCF, box 81; DOS MF 8503217; MWP, box 12; MAE 18.288 (IX and X) and 18.289.

32. Ahmed Ben Bella, quoted in *CSM*, Mar. 17, 1965, p. 1.

33. Broadcast of July 14, 1964, quoted in CRISP, *Congo 1964*, p. 456.

34. Special NIE, "Short-Term Prospects for the Tshombe Government," Aug. 5, 1964, NSF, NIE, box 8, LBJL. For the best newspaper accounts on the fall of Stanleyville, see *Courrier d'Afrique* (Leopoldville): Aug. 5, 6, 7, 1964, all p. 1. For two eyewitness testimonies, see Hoyt, *Captive*, pp. 37-69, and Nothomb, *Dans Stanleyville*, pp. 40-78.

35. Quotations from Brubeck, memo for president, June 15, 1964, p. 1, NSFCF, box 81, and Denney (INR) to Harriman, "Chinese Communist Involvement in Congolese Insurrections," Aug. 11, 1964, p. 2, ibid. See also Hughes (INR) to SecState, "Appraisal of Congolese Insurgency," Aug. 7, 1964, ibid.; CIA, "Situation," Aug. 27 and Sept. 3, 1964. See also n. 79.

36. Denney (INR) to Harriman, "Congo Contingency: Possible Alternatives Ahead," Aug. 15, 1964, p. 1, NSFCF, box 82.

37. *WP*, Sept. 25, 1964, p. 24 (ed.).

38. Godley to SecState, Aug. 2, 1964, NSFCF, box 81.

39. Harriman to MacArthur, Aug. 4, 1964, NSFCF, box 81; Rusk to Amembassy Brussels, Aug. 6, 1964, ibid.

40. Brubeck, memo for president, Aug. 6, 1964, NSFCF, box 81; Rusk to Amembassy Brussels, July 31, 1964, ibid.

41. "Exposé de Monsieur P. H. Spaak," Sept. 4, 1964, p. 11, MAE 149.1.

42. Quotations from Rusk to Amembassy Brussels, Aug. 6, 1964, NSFCF, box 81; MacArthur to SecState, Brussels, Aug. 6, 1964, ibid.; interview with Ball. See also Amembassy Paris to SecState, Aug. 7, 1964, NSFCF, box 81; MacArthur to SecState, Aug. 7, 1964, ibid.; Harriman to Bundy, Aug. 11, 1964, ibid.; Tasca to Harriman, Aug. 11, 1964, Harriman Papers, box 448, LOC; McGhee (U.S. ambassador, Bonn) to SecState, Aug. 14, 1964, NSFCF, box 81; Under Secretary Cartens to Westrick, Aug. 14, 1964, in Institut für Zeitgeschichte, *Akten 1964*, 2:232-34; Amembassy Paris to SecState, Aug. 26, 1964, NSFCF, box 82.

43. Quotations from interview with DCM Blake and from Williams to Rusk, Aug. 7, 1964, MWP, box 12.

44. MacArthur to SecState, Brussels, Aug. 5 (sec. 1, p. 2, quoted) and 8, 1964, NSFCF, box 81.

45. Quotations from Rose to FO, Leopoldville, Sept. 7, 1964, FO 371/17665, PRO; MacArthur to SecState, Brussels, Aug. 6, 1964, NSFCF, box 81; "Exposé de Monsieur P. H. Spaak," Sept. 4, 1964, p. 10, MAE 149.1. See also MacArthur to SecState, Aug. 8, 1964, NSFCF, box 81; Dean to SecState, July 16, 1964, DOS MF 8503217; Spaak to Belgian embassy Washington, D.C., July 29, 1964, MAE 18.293 II (c); Belgian embassy Leopoldville to MAE, July 1, 1964, MAE 18.288; *Le Monde*, Aug. 8 and 9, 1964, both p. 1; *Le Soir*, Aug. 8, 1964, p. 1.

46. Quotations from interview with DCM Blake; FRG embassy Paris, Aug. 8, 1964, FRG, AA 90.08; DOS, MemoConv (Rusk, Alphand, et al.), Jan. 11, 1965, FOIA 1995/860; "Points on Meeting to Be Held on January 7 between the Prime Minister and Governor Harriman," Jan. 6, 1965, FO 371/181609, PRO.

47. Scheyven (Belgian ambassador, Washington, D.C.) to MAE, Aug. 21, 1964, MAE 18.293 I (a).

48. Brubeck, memo for president, Aug. 6, 1964, NSFCF, box 81.

49. Johnson to Reuther, Aug. 9, 1964, in Beschloss, *Taking Charge*, p. 510.

50. NSC meeting, Aug. 11, 1964, NSF, NSC Meetings File, box 1, LBJL. An earlier NSC meeting had dealt only peripherally with Zaire (see NSC meeting, July 28, 1964, ibid.).

51. NSC meeting, Aug. 11, 1964, NSF, NSC Meetings File, box 1, LBJL.

52. Author's name deleted, memo for Bundy, Aug. 14, 1964, NSFCF, box 81. See also Harriman to Bundy, Aug. 4 and 11, 1964, ibid.; Brubeck, memo for president, Aug. 6, 1964, ibid.; Rusk to Amembassy Leopoldville, Aug. 13, 1964, ibid.; Amembassy Leopoldville to SecState, Aug. 15, 1964, ibid.; Godley to SecState, Aug. 24, 1964, NSFCF, box 82. See also Kerchove to Spaak, Leopoldville: telegram nos. 2857, 2859, 2882, 2890, Aug. 15-18, 1964, all MAE, 18.288 (X).

53. NSC meeting, Aug. 11, 1964, p. 1, NSF, NSC Meetings File, box 1, LBJL; Godley to SecState, Aug. 15, 1964, NSFCF, box 81.

54. Godley to SecState, Aug. 5, 1964, NSFCF, box 81.

55. Rusk to Amembassy Leopoldville, Aug. 6, 1964, NSFCF, box 81.

56. Quotations from Williams to SecState, Aug. 7, 1964, MWP, box 12; Rusk to Harriman, Aug. 7, 1964, NSFCF, box 81; Vandewalle, *L'Ommegang*, p. 201; Wilson, FO minutes, "White Mercenaries in the Congo," Aug. 28, 1964, FO 371/176683, PRO. On U.S. overt military aid, see Godley to DOS, "Belgian Presence and Belgian Policies in the Congo," Dec. 2, 1965, DOS MF 8503217; CRISP, *Congo 1964*, pp. 357-59, 363-64; CRISP, *Congo 1965*, pp. 300-301; Gérard-Libois, "L'aide extérieure (II)," pp. 1-4.

57. Quotations from *Cape Times* (Cape Town), Aug. 25, 1964, p. 3; *Jeune Afrique*, Sept. 7, 1964, p. 7; *Cape Times*, Aug. 27 and Sept. 2, 1964, both p. 1; Godley to SecState, Aug 26, 1964, NSFCF, box 82; *Le Courrier d'Afrique*, Aug. 28, 1964, p. 1. See also *Cape Times*, Aug. 28, 1964, p. 13; Aug. 29, p. 1; Sept. 1, p. 3; Sept. 2, p. 15; Sept. 4 and 8, both p. 1; Sept. 9, p. 3; *Rhodesia Herald:* Aug. 24, 28, and Sept. 2, 1964, all p. 1; *Le Courrier d'Afrique*, Aug. 26, 1964, p. 1; *Le Soir*, Sept. 2, 1965, p. 3; *Le Progrès* (Leopoldville), Sept. 8, 1964, p. 1. See also CIA, Intelligence Information Cable, Aug. 24, 1964, NSCF, box 82; Pearson (U.S. consulate, Salisbury) to SecState, Aug. 24, 1964, ibid.; Godley to SecState, Aug. 24, 1964, ibid.; CIA, "The Congo Situation," Aug. 29 and 31, 1964, NSFCF, box 87.

58. Quotations from *Le Courrier d'Afrique*, Aug. 10, 1964, p. 1; *Le Soir*, Aug. 28, 1964, p. 3; "Congo C-130 Crisis," July 1967, Tab. 1, "Background," p. 1, NSF, NSC History, "Congo C-130 Crisis," box 15, LBJL. For Mobutu's October statement, see *Le Progrès*, Oct. 16, 1964, p. 6.

59. Rusk to Amembassy Kinshasa, Aug. 26, 1967, NSFCF, box 86.

60. USARMA Leopoldville to RUEPDA/DA, December 1964, NSFCF, box 85. (The feelings were mutual: see Hoare, *Congo Mercenary*, pp. 36, 126.)

61. Germani, *Weisse Söldner*, p. 103.

62. The letter and the reply are printed in Mockler, *The Mercenaries*, p. 244. It was not U.S. policy to exclude blacks: their inclusion was repugnant to the white mercenaries, particularly the dominant South African and Rhodesian element.

63. "Escale à Léo," *Jeune Afrique*, Aug. 8, 1965, p. 19.

64. Germani, *Weisse Söldner*, pp. 8, 60, 8. *Weisse Söldner*, Hoare's *Congo Mercenary*, and Puren's *Mercenary Commander*, pp. 174-224, are interesting, if not reliable. Two other memoirs by mercenaries (Schramme, *Le Bataillon Léopard*, pp. 129-232, and Müller, *Les nouveaux mercenaires*) are self-serving tales of very little value.

65. Quotations from Godley to SecState, Dec. 13, 1964, NSFCF, box 85, and from CIA, Intelligence Information Cable, "Situation Report of Stanleyville, 11-14 January 1965," ibid.

66. Godley to SecState, Aug. 26, 1964, NSFCF, box 82; Carlo Gregoretti, "Una guerra privata in cinemascope," *L'Espresso* (Rome), Dec. 20, 1964, p. 7.

67. *Observer* (London), Aug. 29, 1965, p. 2. The *Observer* explained that the photographs, which had been taken as souvenirs "for the men to send home to their families," had been provided by a mercenary who had become "so disgusted at the atrocities that he now wants to do all he can to expose them." (Ibid. See also *Observer*, Sept. 5, 1965, p. 31.)

68. Peter Lloyd-Lister, "Stop Our Young Men from Going to the Congo," *Cape Times*, Aug. 14 and 21, 1965, both p. 2; FO Minutes, "West Africa and the Congo. Impressions of Nigeria and the Congo by Colin Legum on his recent visit," Apr. 30, 1965, p. 1, FO 371/181632, PRO.

69. Godley to SecState, Oct. 30, 1965, NSFCF, box 85; tel. interview with Lloyd Garrison, who was the *New York Times* correspondent in Zaire in 1964-65. The best sources on the campaign are the reports on "The Situation in the Congo" by the CIA, OCI (NSFCF, box 87). By far the most useful memoir by a participant is Vandewalle, *L'Ommegang*. Good secondary accounts are CRISP, *Congo 1964*, pp. 349-411, 535-36; CRISP, *Congo 1965*, pp. 43-58, 89-160; Wagoner, *Dragon Rouge*; Odom, *Dragon Operations*.

70. Quotations from Rusk to Amembassy Leopoldville, Aug. 15, 1964, NSFCF, box 81, and *NYT*, Apr. 26, 1966, p. 1. See also Spaak to Belgian embassy Leopoldville, Oct. 1, 1964, MAE 18.289 (III); CIA, "Situation," Oct. 27, 1964; Ball to USUN, Dec. 11, 1964, NSFCF, box 22; Vandewalle, *L'Ommegang*, pp. 63-64; Puren, *Mercenary Commander*, pp. 174-95; Wagoner, *Dragon Rouge*, pp. 33-34, 76, 90; García, "Operación"; Gup, *Book*, pp. 143-56; Marchetti and Marks, *CIA*, pp. 117-18.

71. Quotations from Wagoner, *Dragon Rouge*, p. 66, and CIA, "Situation," Nov. 17, 1964, p. 3.

72. Odom, *Dragon Operations*, p. 33.

73. See Spaak, *Combats*, 2:275; Schoenbaum, *Waging*, p. 380.

74. Vandewalle, *L'Ommegang*, p. 417. See also Wagoner, *Dragon Rouge*, p. 198, and Verhaegen, *Rébellions*, 1:323-27, 2:651-54.

75. Rose, "Congo–1964," p. 3 quoted. See also n. 79.

76. Ben Bella, *Jeune Afrique*, Jan. 10, 1965, p. 7, and Nyerere, *Standard*, Nov. 27, 1964, p. 1. (In November 1964, the *Tanganyika Standard* became the *Standard*.)

77. Quotations from GDR embassy Moscow, "Aktenvermerk über eine Konsultation mit dem Leiter der 2. afrikanischen Abteilung des MID, Genossen Sitenko, am 16. September 1964," Sept. 17, 1964, p. 3, GDR AA, A1154, and Quilitzsch (counselor, GDR embassy, Moscow), "Aktenvermerk über ein Gespräch mit Genossen Kurdjukow, stellvertretender Leiter der 2. Afrikanischen Abteilung in MID, am 27 November 1964," Dec. 2, 1964, pp. 1-3, ibid.

78. Winzer (first deputy foreign minister) to Ulbricht, Dec. 14, 1964, GDR AA, A14593; "Vorlage für das Politbüro des ZK der SED," Berlin, Dec. 30, 1964, ibid.; "Gesprächskonzeption für die erste Unterredung mit dem Vertreter der Revolutionären Regierung der Volksrepublik Kongo, Bagira, am 14.1.1965," Berlin, Jan. 13, 1965, ibid.; "Vermerk über

die erste Verhandlungen mit dem Vertreter der Revolutionären Regierung der Volksrepublik Kongo, Herrn Casimir M'Bagira, am 14.1.1965," Berlin, Jan. 14, 1965, ibid.; "Vermerk über das anlässlich der Unterzeichnung des Protokolls mit dem Vertreter der Volksrepublik Kongo, Herrn M'Bagira, geführte Gespräch am 19. Januar 1965," Berlin, Jan. 19, 1965, ibid.

79. See CIA, OCI, "Chinese Communist Activities in Africa," June 19, 1964, NSFCF, box 76; Rusk to Amembassy Brussels, Aug. 15, 1964, NSFCF, box 81; CIA, OCI, "Brazzaville's Move to the Left," Oct. 30, 1964, NSFCF, box 83; CIA, OCI, "Situation in the Congo," Dec. 30, 1964, NSFCF, box 87; CIA, DI, "The Congo: Assessment and Prospects," Dec. 31, 1964, ibid.; CIA, OCI, "Situation in the Congo," Jan. 19, 1965, ibid.; CIA, OCI, "East African Involvement in the Congo," Feb. 18, 1965, FOIA 1977/9F; CIA, OCI, "Tanzanian Support for the Congo Rebels," Apr. 7, 1965, NSFCF, box 87; CIA, ONE, "Prospects in Brazzaville," May 17, 1965, NSFCF, box 85; CIA, OCI, "Tanzania Taking the Left Turn," May 21, 1965, NSFCF, box 100; CIA, DI, "The Southern Sudan Problem and Its Relationship to the Congo," May 28, 1965, NSFCF, box 87; CIA, ONE, "A Reassessment of Julius Nyerere," June 10, 1965, NSFCF, box 100; CIA, OCI, "Consequences of Algerian Coup," June 19, 1965, NSFCF, box 79; CIA, OCI, "Situation in the Congo," July 1, 1965, NSFCF, box 85; CIA, OCI, "The Congo since the Mobutu Coup," Feb. 11, 1966, ibid. The CIA weekly reports on Zaire (see n. 69), which always include a 2-to-3-page section on "The Rebels and Their Sympathizers," provide a convenient guidepost.

80. *NYT*, Dec. 13, 1964, 4:4; CIA, DI, "The Congo: Assessment and Prospects," Dec. 31, 1964, p. 7, NSFCF, box 87; tel. interview with Godley.

81. For reports, see *Le Soir*, June 16, 1964, p. 3; *Le Progrès*, Aug. 5 and 6, 1964, both p. 1; *Le Courrier d'Afrique*, Aug. 12, 1964, p. 1.

CHAPTER FOUR

1. Guevara, Oct. 29, 1961, speech, in Guevara, *Escritos*, 5:315-16. See also Porra, "L'Afrique du Che."

2. *Verde Olivo* (Havana), June 28, 1964, pp. 51-52.

3. *Revolución* (Havana), Dec. 9, 1964, p. 1.

4. United Nations General Assembly, Official Records, 19th sess., plenary meetings, Dec. 11, 1964, 10:30 a.m., pp. 7-14, and Dec. 11, 1964, 3:30 p.m., pp. 5-9. On a few occasions, I have modified the UN translation in order to adhere more closely to the Spanish version published in *Revolución*, Dec. 12, 1964, pp. 1, 2, 10.

5. Rusk to U.S. embassies in Africa, Dec. 24, 1964, NSFCF, box 20. Guevara's trip can be followed in *Revolución*, Dec. 19, 1964-Mar. 15, 1965, as well as from the reports of the U.S. embassies in the countries he visited.

26. Quotations from Knox to SecState, Cotonou: Jan. 22, 1965, 1:50 p.m.; Jan. 26 and Jan. 23, 1965. See also Knox to SecState: Jan. 22, 5 p.m., Jan. 29 and

Apr. 6, 1965; Harriman to Knox, Jan. 27, 1965 (all Pol Cuba-Dahomey, SNF, NA).

7. *Le Peuple* (Algiers), Jan. 26, 1965, p. 3, and Jan. 30, p. 3; *Revolución*, Feb. 3, 1965, p. 1.

8. Quotations from CIA, DI, "Chinese Communist Activities in Latin America," Apr. 30, 1965, p. 3, NSFCF, box 2; conference communiqué printed in *Revolución*, Jan. 19, 1965, p. 1; Johne (GDR ambassador, Havana) and Kulitzka (the embassy's first secretary), "Über die Entwicklung der Republik Kuba im Jahre 1964 und einige Entwicklungstendenzen für das Jahr 1965," Jan. 21, 1965, p. 15, SED, DY30 IVA 2/20/270.

9. CIA, DI, "Chinese Communist Activities in Latin America," Apr. 30, 1965, p. 4, NSFCF, box 2. See also CIA, OCI, "Weekly Cuban Summary," Feb. 3 and Mar. 31, 1965, NSFCF, box 33/37; Johne to Stibi, Havana, Feb. 22, 1965, SED, DY30 IVA 2/20/270; "Informationsbericht des ADN-Korrespondenten in Havanna," Mar. 3, 1965, ibid.; Johnson, *Communist China*, pp. 160-63.

10. *Revolución*, Mar. 2, 1965, p. 1.

11. Kulitzka, "Einschätzung zum Brief Ernesto Guevara an die Wochenzeitung `Marcha' (Uruguay)," Havana, Oct. 26, 1965, p. 2, GDR AA, A3363 (2).

12. *Revolución*, Feb. 25, 1965, p. 5.

13. Porter to SecState, Algiers, Feb. 25, 1965, NSFCF, box 20; Hughes (INR) to SecState, "Che Guevara's Blueprint for Afro-Asian Liberation," Feb. 26, 1965, p. 2, NSFCF, box 24/25.

14. Hughes (INR) to SecState, "Che Guevara's African Venture," Apr. 19, 1965, NSFCF, box 20. See also Hughes to SecState, "Cuba and Africa," Jan. 5, 1965, NSFCF, box 24/25; CIA, Intelligence Information Cable, Jan. 15, 1965, NSFCF, box 20; Amembassy Conakry to DOS, Jan. 26, 1965, ibid.; DOS to All African Posts, Jan. 29, 1965, NSFCF, box 18; Howe to DOS, "African Travels of Che Guevara," The Hague, Feb. 16, 1965, NSFCF, box 20; Porter to SecState, Algiers, Feb. 25, 1965, ibid.; Hughes to SecState, "Che Guevara's Blueprint for Afro-Asian Liberation," Feb. 26, 1965, NSFCF, box 24/25; Finletter to SecState, Paris, Apr. 7, 1965, Pol 7 Cuba, SNF, NA.

15. Risquet interview in Deutschmann, *Changing*, p. 2.

16. The literature on the Congo for the years covered in this book (1960-76) is poor. The best sources are Gauze, *Politics*, pp. 88-238; Decalo, *Coups*, pp. 39-88; Kissita, *Congo*, pp. 38-122; Amin and Coquery-Vidrovitch, *Histoire*, pp. 55-152; Bazenguissa-Ganga, *Les voies*, pp. 65-236; Nkouka-Menga, *Chronique*, pp. 57-159.

17. Quotations from Decalo, *Coups*, p. 54, and Amembassy Brazzaville to SecState, June 28, 1963, p. 6, FOIA 1981/526B.

18. DOS to Bundy, "Government Crisis in Congo (Brazzaville)," Aug. 19, 1963, p. 1 quoted, NSF, box 29, JFKL; Foccart, *Tous*, p. 789; Foccart, *Foccart*, 1:274-75, 481; Boutet, *Les Trois*.

19. [CIA], "Alphonse Massamba-Debat," [Aug. 1963], NSF, box 29, JFKL.

20. CIA, ONE, "Prospects in Brazzaville," May 17, 1965, pp. 5-6, NSFCF, box 85.

21. CIA, OCI, "Brazzaville's Move to the Left," Oct. 30, 1964, p. 5, NSFCF, box 83 (for the army's size, see ibid., p. 1); Lissouba, *Congo*, p. 89.

22. *La Semaine Africaine* (Brazzaville), May 17, 1964, p. 3; Koren (U.S. ambassador, Brazzaville) to SecState, May 11, 1964, Pol 17 Congo-Cuba, SNF, NA.

23. Amembassy Brazzaville to SecState, Jan. 7, 1965, p. 1 quoted, NSFCF, box 20. On the Congo's request, interviews with Serguera and Risquet; Serguera, *Caminos*, pp. 226, 228-29, 231; Jorge Risquet, note to Piero Gleijeses, Havana, Aug. 1, 1995, pp. 1-2.

24. *Révolution Africaine* (Algiers), Mar. 28, 1964, p. 17 quoted. See also CIA, OCI, "Anti-Portuguese Campaign in Africa Shifts to Mozambique," Dec. 18, 1964, FOIA 1977/174B; Stewart (British consul, Luanda), "Political Changes in Angola during the Last Year," Jan. 9, 1965, FO 371/181969, PRO; Empson (British ambassador, Brazzaville) to Wilson, Jan. 29, 1965, FO 371/181970, PRO; Amconsul Luanda to DOS, Feb. 3, 1965, Pol 2 Ang, SNF, NA.

25. Interview with Lúcio Lara (quoted); Rivalta to Roa, Dar-es-Salaam, June 22, 1964, pp. 10-15, MINREX; interviews with Ndalu (the soccer star), Onambwe (one of the six), and Jorge, who represented the MPLA in Cuba in 1968-69; "Relación de becarios de Africa que cursan estudios en nuestro país," Dec. 4, 1969, unpaginated, PCH; Rius, *Angola*, pp. 125-29; *A Provincia de Angola* (Luanda), Jan. 31, 1975, pp. 2, 10. One of the six, Mario Alberto de Assis, left Cuba before completing his medical studies. After graduating, the others received military training before leaving Cuba. Four of the six (Ndalu, Onambwe, Juan de Matos, and Saydi Mingas) became prominent MPLA leaders in the early 1970s. On Ndalu's soccer exploits, see also *Revolución*, Dec. 13, 1963, p. 11, and *Granma* (Havana), Jan. 10, 1966, p. 10.

26. Quotations from Lúcio Lara, "A história do MPLA," n.d., p. 100, and interview with Lúcio Lara. I would like to thank Dr. Christine Messiant of the Centre d'Etudes Africaines of Paris for sharing Lara's important, unpublished document with me.

27. Interview with Lúcio Lara, with Ruth Lara's interjections. See also Carreira, *O Pensamento*, pp. 35-36.

28. I first heard this story from two Cuban officials who asked not to be named. With a stern face, Lúcio Lara told me that the story was not true. Three other Angolans who were in positions to know laughed and said that it was indeed true, but also preferred to remain anonymous. On the *New York Times* story, see Paterson, *Contesting Castro*, p. 76, and Franqui, *Cuba*, pp. 87-88.

29. Interviews with Serguera and Risquet (who in July 1965 was briefed by Fidel Castro).

30. CIA, OCI, "Weekly Cuban Summary," Jan. 6, 1965, p. 9, NSFCF, box 33/37; Leonhart (U.S. ambassador, Dar-es-Salaam) to SecState, Jan. 4, 1965, Pol Cuba-Tanzan, SNF, NA.

31. *Nationalist* (Dar-es-Salaam), Jan. 13, 1965, p. 4 (ed.).

32. CIA, special memorandum, "Implications of Growing Communist Influence in URTZ," Sept. 29, 1964, pp. 11, 3, 4, NSFCF, box 100.

33. Quotations from CIA, OCI, "Tanzania Taking the Left Turn," May 21, 1965, pp. 1-2, NSFCF, box 100. The best study on Nyerere's foreign policy in the 1960s is Niblock, "Aid."

34. For a full list, see "Jahresbericht 1965 des Generalkonsulats der Deutschen Demokratischen Republik in der Vereinigten Republik Tansania," Dar-es-Salaam, Jan. 3, 1966, p. 50, SED, DY30 IVA 2/20/963.

35. CIA, OCI, "Weekly Cuban Summary," Mar. 10, 1965, p. 6, NSFCF, box 33/37.

36. Interview with Rivalta.

37. Ibid.; Oliva interview in Gálvez, *El sueño*, p. 51 quoted; Rivalta to Roa, Dar-es-Salaam, May 4, 1964, MINREX. For the date of Rivalta's arrival, see Leonhart to SecState, Dar-es-Salaam, Mar. 5, 1964, Pol 17 Cuba-Tangan, SNF, NA.

38. Quoted in *Revolución*, Jan. 18, 1965, p. 1. See also *Revolución*, Dec. 28, 1964, p. 6; Jan. 19, 1965, p. 1; Feb. 1, p. 12; Feb. 19, p. 1; Mar. 25, p. 1; "Che Guevara en Afrique," *Révolution Africaine*, Dec. 26, 1964, pp. 12-13; *L'Essor* (Bamako), Jan. 5, 1965, p. 1.

39. Che Guevara, "Pasajes de la guerra revolucionaria (Congo)," [Dar-es-Salaam, Dec. 1965 or early 1966], pp. 13-14, PCH (hereafter Guevara, "Pasajes").

40. Ibid., pp. 13-14.

41. Ibid., p. 12.

42. "Niederschrift über das Gespräch zwischen Genossen Erich Honecker und Genossen Fidel Castro am Sonntag, dem 3. April 1977, von 11.00 bis 13.30 Uhr und von 15.45 bis 18.00 Uhr, im Hause des ZK," Berlin, Apr. 3, 1977, p. 32, SED, DY30 JIV 2/201/1292.

43. For example, Frelimo made the unlikely claim that in the period November 17-22, 1964, its guerrillas killed 59 Portuguese soldiers and wounded several, at the cost of only 2 wounded. Another communiqué stated that between December 19 and 24 Frelimo killed 124 Portuguese soldiers and wounded many others at the cost of 1 guerrilla killed (*Nationalist*, Dec. 5, 1964, p. 1, and Jan. 8, 1965, p. 8).

44. Interview with Ferrer. Beginning in April 1965, Ferrer was Cuba's liaison with Frelimo.

45. Interview with Marcelino dos Santos.

46. Shore, "Resistance," p. xxx quoted; Gunn, "Cuba," pp. 79-80.

47. Interview with Ferrer.

48. Interviews with Estrada, Ferrer, and Marcelino dos Santos; see also n. 107.

49. Frelimo, "Documents of the 2nd Congress," Niassa, Mozambique, July 1968, p. 17, SED, DY30 IVA 2/20/948.

50. Interview with Tschamlesso. For Kabila's biography, see Verhaegen, *Rébellions*, 1:520.

51. Guevara, "Pasajes," pp. 12-13. On Soumialot, see Verhaegen, *Rébellions*, 1:524-25.

52. Interview with Tschamlesso.

53. Guevara, "Pasajes," p. 14.

54. "Informe al Acto Central por la Conmemoración del XX aniversario de la formación, salida y cumplimiento de misión internacionalista de la Columna Especial Número Uno en el Congo Leopoldville," [Havana, 1985], pp. 1-2, PCH (hereafter "Informe al Acto").

There were three Petis ("Peti" is an acronym for Punto de Entrenamiento de Tropas Especiales e Irregulares) in Pinar del Río. Each specialized in a particular kind of training.

55. Che Guevara, "Evaluación del personal a mis ordenes," [Dar-es-Salaam, Dec. 1965 or early 1966], PCH.

56. Víctor Dreke, letter to Piero Gleijeses, Havana, Oct. 20, 1994.

57. Interviews with Dreke, Agramonte, and Lieutenant Erasmo Vidiaux, who belonged to the group chosen by Terry.

58. Interview with Zerquera. See also Rafael Zerquera: "Kumy habla de Tatu," *Vanguardia* (Santa Clara, Cuba), Oct. 7, 1990, p. 4, and "Una casi desconocida epopeya," *Tribuna de la Habana*, Oct. 8, 1990, pp. 4-5.

59. The pages that follow are based on "Informe al Acto" and on interviews with the following members of the column: Dreke, Agramonte, Vidiaux, Torres, Chivás, Hernández Betancourt, Chaveco, Moracén, Olachea, Veitía, Monteagudo, Marín, Medina Savigne, Morejón Gibert, Vaillant. In order to avoid long, repetitive notes, I identify the interviewee only when there is a direct quote.

60. Interview with Moracén. The figure of 113 is from "Informe al Acto," p. 2.

61. Quotations from "Informe al Acto," p. 2, and interview with Dreke.

62. Interview with Vidiaux.

63. Interviews with Olachea and Dreke.

64. "Informe al Acto," p. 3.

65. Nine men were left behind: six who had failed the physical demands of the training and three who had asked to withdraw from the mission. For security reasons, it was decided that they would remain in the Petis until the column had returned from Zaire ("Informe al Acto," p. 2; interviews with Dreke and Vidiaux). Luckily for them, the column was back in less than one year.

66. On "Pasajes," see chapter 4, footnote a.

67. Interview with Risquet.

68. Serguera, *Caminos*, p. 199.

69. Interview with Ferrer, who was assigned to the operation in April 1965.

70. Che to Fidel Castro, [Nov. 4, 1965], in Guevara, "Pasajes," p. 120; interview with Rivalta.

71. Interview with Rivalta, who accompanied Che to Cairo.

72. Heikal, *The Cairo Documents*, pp. 343-57.

73. Ben Bella, "Ainsi." This is the article in which Ben Bella made the implausible claim that he had had no forewarning of the Cuban military aid that arrived in October 1963. (See chapter 2.)

74. Interview with Rivalta.

75. Interviews with Rivalta, Ferrer, and Fernández Padilla. (Ferrer and Fernández Padilla joined the embassy staff in April and September 1965 respectively.)

76. Castañeda, *Compañero*, p. 287.

77. Nyerere had pledged to the Zanzibari leaders that in exchange for the closing of the GDR embassy there, he would allow a general consulate in Dar-es-Salaam. When Bonn tried to blackmail him by threatening to reduce economic aid, Nyerere replied, on March 1, 1965, that Tanzania would no longer accept West German economic aid. The two governments later agreed that aid in the pipeline would be disbursed, but no new agreements would be signed. (See GDR AA, VVS Archiv [Tanganyika/Sansibar]; SED, DY30 IVA 2/20/963; Institut für Zeitgeschichte, *Akten 1965*, pp. 72-76, 213-18, 293-95, 408-11, 422-25, 841-45, 1046-49, 1279-80, 1367; Niblock, "Aid," pp. 207-63.)

78. See Castañeda, *Compañero*, pp. 301-2, and Anderson, *Che*, p. 639. Both Castañeda and Anderson interviewed Alekseev in Moscow.

79. See chapter 5.

80. Lise Namikas, who was in Moscow from September 1998 to April 1999 researching Soviet policy toward Zaire in 1960-65, found no documents that shed light on the 1964-65 period (see Namikas, "The Cold War and the Congo Crisis," ch. 7). The Cuban semiofficial account of the operation, Gálvez's *El sueño*, is silent on the Soviet role.

81. CIA, OCI, "Survey of Latin America," Apr. 1, 1964, p. 4, NSFCF, box 1; NSC, "Discussion of Proposed Cuban Resolution," Mar. 5, 1964, p. 2, NSFCF, box 24.

82. *NYT*, Apr. 3, 1964, p. 11. On U.S. support for the coup, see Leacock, *Requiem*, ch. 10; Parker, *Brazil*, pp. 57-87; Hershberg, "'The Best,'" pp. 68-74.

83. Connell-Smith, *The United States*, p. 240.

84. On U.S. pressure on these governments, see the following boxes of documents: Pol Cuba, SNF, NA; Pol 2 Cuba, SNF, NA; Pol Cuba 17, SNF, NA; Pol 17 Bol-Cuba, SNF, NA. On Mexico's cooperation with the United States against Cuba, despite its OAS vote, see Pellicer, *México*.

85. Jova (DCM, U.S. embassy, Chile) to SecState, Oct. 28, 1964, p. 2, FOIA 1995.

86. There were senior U.S. officials who advocated military strikes against Cuba. For example, after the discovery of the Venezuela arms cache, the head of the State Department's Policy Planning Council, Walt Rostow, proposed that U.S. planes attack a Cuban military installation while others fly over Havana to drop leaflets denouncing Castro. Should the Cubans dare to oppose the U.S. aircraft entering their air space, Rostow wrote, "we shall be prepared to respond with overwhelming force." (Rostow to Mann, Feb. 21, 1964, p. 3 quoted, FOIA 1996/1676; Rostow to Bundy, Feb. 21, 1964, NSFCF, box 24/25; U. Alexis Johnson to SecState, Feb. 25, 1964, Pol Cuba-US, SNF, NA.)

87. Interview with Risquet.

88. [Name deleted], quoted in Crimmins to Adams et al., Jan. 28, 1965, NSFCF, box 33/37.

89. Quotations from CIA, OCI, "Weekly Cuban Summary," Jan. 6, 1965, p. 1, NSFCF, box 33/37, and

"Informationsbericht des ADN-Korrespondenten in Havanna," Jan. 4, 1965, SED, DY30 IVA 2/20/270. For Castro's January 2 speech, see *Revolución*, Jan. 4, 1965, pp. 3-5.

90. CIA, OCI, "Weekly Cuban Summary," Dec. 9, 1964, p. 4, NSFCF, box 33/37; interview with Risquet; "Aus der Aussprache mit Genossen Fidel Castro am 14. November 1968 während des Mittagessens im Gürtel von Havanna," pp. 4-5, SED, DY30 IVA 2/ 20/ 265.

91. Quotations from CIA, OCI, "Weekly Cuban Summary," Mar. 3, 1965, p. 7; Mar. 10, p. 1; Mar. 17, p. 1; Mar. 31, p. 2; Apr. 7, pp. 1-3; all NSFCF, box 33/ 37.

92. On the Soviet response, see Gaiduk, *The Soviet Union and the Vietnam War*, pp. 22-72.

93. See Gleijeses, *Dominican Crisis*, chs. 4-11.

94. CIA, OCI, "Weekly Cuban Summary," May 5, 1965, p. 2, NSFCF, box 33/37; Watson (British ambassador, Havana), quoted in Sutherland to Smith, May 14, 1965, NSFCF, box 18.

95. *Egyptian Gazette* (Cairo), Feb. 2, 1965, p. 1.

96. See chapter 1.

97. *Revolución*, Dec. 15, 1964, p. 2.

98. Kent to DCI, Sept. 4, 1963, p. 4, JFKAC, RG 263, NA.

99. Interview with Dreke. For a full expression of this view, see "Mensaje a los pueblos del mundo del comandante Ernesto Guevara a través de la Tricontinental," *Granma*, Apr. 17, 1967, pp. 3-5.

100. CIA, ONE, "Castro, Model 1966," Mar. 24, 1966, p. 5, FOIA 1993/2415.

101. Since 1964, when the Cubans took control of the Soviet SAMs on the island, they could have shot down the U-2s. Castro, however, submitted "to the humiliation of US U-2 flights," because he understood the price of defiance. As Dean Rusk said, "If they were to shoot down one of the U-2s, we would be obliged to strike back." (Quotations from Hughes [INR], "The Significance of the July 1964 OAS Foreign Ministers Meeting," Sept. 14, 1964, p. 4, NSFCF, box 24/25, and DOS, MemoConv [Rusk, Harlech, et al.], Oct. 27, 1964, Pol 31-1 Cuba-US, SNF, NA.)

102. See [CIA], "Preliminary report—Cuba/Red China involvement in promoting violence in the United States," July 26, 1967, NSF, Subject File, box 5, LBJL; [CIA], "Final report—Cuba/Red China involvement in promoting violence in the United States," July 26, 1967, ibid.; Cleaver, "Back to Africa," esp. pp. 216-19, 231; Gates, "After the Revolution," pp. 5-9; Reitan, *Rise*. See also chapter 9.

103. Hughes (INR) to SecState, "Che Guevara's African Venture," Apr. 19, 1965, pp. 1-2, NSFCF, box 20.

104. *Verde Olivo*, Dec. 6, 1964, p. 51.

105. Interview with Dreke.

106. Quotations from Rivalta to Roa, Dar-es-Salaam, June 22, 1964, pp. 2-3, MINREX, and interview with Estrada. On Serguera's previous trip to sub-Saharan Africa, see Serguera, *Caminos*, pp. 192-93, and Koren to SecState, Brazzaville, Sept. 25, 1964, Pol 17 Cuba-Alg, SNF, NA. (Serguera had also spent a couple of days in Zanzibar in January 1964.) On the language proficiency of the embassy's staff, interviews with Rivalta, Ferrer, and Fernández Padilla.

107. This account is based on documents in two folders labeled "Operación Triángulo," ACC; on Risquet, *El segundo frente*, pp. 26-29; on interviews with Estrada and with Agramonte, Moracén, and Veitía, three of the instructors on the *Uvero*. For the rebels of Guinea-Bissau, see chapter 9.

108. Interview with Estrada.

109. Quotations from interview with Estrada and "Entreprise Nationale de Transport Routier, de transit et de consignation maritime," no. 009814, May 14, 1965, "Operación Triángulo," ACC. See also "Ayuda brindada por la República de Cuba al Partido Africano por la Independencia de Guinea y las Islas de Cabo Verde (PAIGC)," p. 10, and Risquet, *El segundo frente*, p. 27. In his memoirs, Serguera acknowledges that he arrived late, but blames Piñeiro, who, he claims, did not adequately forewarn him that the *Uvero* was arriving (Serguera, *Caminos*, pp. 275-77).

110. See chapter 2.

111. See "M/N `Uvero.' Cruce del Ecuador," ACC.

CHAPTER FIVE

1. Interview with Dreke.

2. Ibid. The date is from Dreke, in Carrasco, "Tatu," p. 33.

3. Castro in Minà, *Encounter*, p. 223.

4. Guevara, "El Patojo," *Verde Olivo* (Havana), Aug. 19, 1962, p. 38.

5. Interview with Estrada. On Operation Segundo Sombra, see Anderson, *Che*, pp. 537-60, 573-79, 587-94; Castañeda, *Compañero*, pp. 237-40, 246-51; Piñera, *Utopía*, pp. 49-56. For Cuban accounts, see Piñeiro, "Mi modesto homenaje," pp. 17-18; Piñeiro, *Barbarroja*, pp. 50, 87-88; Molina, *Jorge Ricardo Masetti*, *Granma* (Havana), Sept. 7, 1968, p. 7; and the sources listed in chapter 2, n. 106. For relevant U.S. documents, see NSFCF, box 1. For press reports, see *La Nación* (Buenos Aires): Mar. 2, 6-8, 11, 15, 19, 24, Apr. 17, 19-22, 25, May 4, 18, 1964.

6. Quotations from Pompeyo Márquez in Blanco Muñoz, *La lucha armada: hablan 5 jefes*, p. 119, and Piñeiro, "Inmortalidad," p. 42. See also the Venezuelan guerrilla commander Luben Petkoff, in Blanco Muñoz, *La lucha armada: hablan 6 comandantes*, pp. 149-50.

7. For the failure of Operation Matraca in Peru in mid-1963, see Gott, *Rural Guerrillas*, pp. 390-97; Mercado, *Las guerrillas*, pp. 55-60; Vázquez-Viaña and Aliaga Saravia, "Bolivia," pp. 4-5. On Cuba's role, see Gálvez, *El sueño*, pp. 48-49; Ulises Estrada, "La política internacionalista de Cuba en los años 60/ 70," pp. 6-7, PCH; Jesús Lara, *Guerrillero*, pp. 50-51.

8. Quotations from Castro in Minà, *Encounter*, p. 223, and Anderson, *Che*, p. 596. Castañeda's biography is *Compañero*. Other useful biographies are Taibo, *Ernesto Guevara*, Kalfon, *Che*, Tutino, *Guevara*, Cormier, *Che Guevara* (for the early years).

9. Anderson, *Che*, pp. 594-616, 623-29 (pp. 596, 597 quoted); Castañeda, *Compañero*, pp. 235-306.

10. Castañeda, *Compañero*, p. 249; see also Franqui, *Vida*, p. 329.

11. Interview with Fernández Mell.

12. Castañeda, *Compañero*, pp. 295-98.

13. CIA, OCI, "Weekly Cuban Summary," Mar. 3, 1965, p. 15; Mar. 17, p. 12; Mar. 24, p. 14; Mar. 31, p. 4; Apr. 7, p. 5; all NSFCF, box 33/37. *Revolución* (Havana): Feb. 27, 1965; Mar. 9, 11, 19, 20, 22-24, 26, 27, 29-31; Apr. 1-3, 7; all p. 1.

14. I have a photocopy of the passport Che Guevara used with the April 1, 1965, exit stamp from Cuban immigration. It is a diplomatic passport with a photograph of Che in disguise and the false name, Juan Soto (courtesy of María del Carmen Ariet of the *Archivo Personal del Che Guevara* in Havana). The April 1 date is also accepted by both Castañeda (*Compañero*, p. 301) and Anderson (*Che*, p. 629).

15. *Revolución*, Feb. 25, 1965, p. 1; Feb. 26, p. 8 (quoted); Mar. 2, p. 1; Mar. 8, p. 12.

16. Hughes (INR) to SecState, "Castro Decries Disunity of Communist World," Mar. 15, 1965, FOIA 1996/3134; DOS, "Political Currents in the Cuban Leadership," Mar. 1965, NSFCF, box 33/37; Hughes to SecState, "Che Guevara's African Venture," Apr. 19, 1965, NSFCF, box 20. For Castro's Mar. 13, 1965, speech, see *Revolución*, Mar. 15, 1965, p. 3.

17. Quotations from Johne (GDR ambassador, Havana) to Stibi, May 19, 1965, p. 5, SED, DY30 IVA 2/20/283, and from "Informationsbericht des ADN-Korrespondenten in Havanna," June 15, 1965, p. 1, SED, DY30 IVA 2/20/285. See also Korth (GDR chargé, Havana) to Stibi, June 16, 1965, p. 6, SED, DY30 IVA 2/20/270; "Hausmitteilung für Honecker," Berlin, Dec. 9, 1965, SED, DY30 IVA 2/20/63.

18. Kulitzka (first secretary, GDR embassy, Havana), "Aktenvermerk über eine Unterhaltung mit dem Stellvertreter des hiesigen sowjetischen Botschafters, Genossen Ministro Consejero N. A. Belous, am 29. Juli 1965," Aug. 2, 1965, pp. 9-10, GDR AA, A3242(2).

19. Interview with Risquet. On Raúl Castro, see Kulitzka, "Einschätzung zum Brief Ernesto Guevara an die Wochenzeitung `Marcha' (Uruguay)," Havana, Oct. 26, 1965, p. 4, GDR AA, A3363 (2), and Kulitzka, "Aktenvermerk über ein Gespräch mit dem Stellvertreter des sowjetischen Botschafters, Genossen Lebedev, am 27. Oktober 1965," Havana, Nov. 1, 1965, p. 3, GDR AA, A3242(1).

20. Castañeda, *Compañero*, pp. 287-88. I have tried repeatedly, but unsuccessfully, to interview Aragonés to clarify this matter.

21. See *Le Peuple* (Algiers), Jan. 26, 1965, p. 3, and Jan. 30, p. 3. For Che's movements in January, see *Revolución*: Jan. 2, 5, 8, 16, 18, 19, 20, 22, 25, 1965, all p. 1; Jan. 27, p. 5; Jan. 28, p. 1. Che's movements were also reported by the press of the countries he visited: *L'Essor* (Bamako), Jan. 4, 1965, p. 9, and Jan. 5, p. 1; *Dipanda* (Brazzaville), Jan. 2, 1965, p. 1; *La Semaine* (Brazzaville), Jan. 10, 1965, p. 3; *Horoya* (Conakry), Jan. 9, 1965, p. 1, and Jan. 16, p. 1; *Ghanaian Times* (Accra): Jan. 16, 1965, p. 1; Jan. 18, p. 12; Jan. 19, p. 3; Jan. 20, p. 3; Jan. 21, p. 12; Jan. 23, p. 2; Jan. 25, p. 2; *Evening News* (Accra): Jan. 15, 1965, p. 2; Jan. 18, p. 2; Jan. 19, p. 1; Jan. 20, p. 1; Jan.

25, p. 1. In other words, there was nothing secretive in Che's movements.

22. Anderson, *Che*, p. 628. See also Piñeiro, "Inmortalidad," p. 43; Castro in Minà, *Encounter*, p. 223.

23. Anderson, *Che*, pp. 627-28.

24. Hamadi Ben Milad, "Che Guevara: l'avenir de l'Afrique c'est le socialisme, puis le communisme," *Jeune Afrique*, Mar. 21, 1965, pp. 22-23.

25. Interview with Dreke (quoted); Castro, *Granma* (Havana), Oct. 4, 1965, p. 3.

26. On Che's brief "period of doubt" in Fidel's leadership, in late 1957, see Anderson, *Che*, p. 294.

27. *Granma*, Oct. 4, 1965, p. 1.

28. Roberto González Gómez, letter to Piero Gleijeses, Havana, July 7, 1994.

29. Che Guevara, "Pasajes de la guerra revolucionaria (Congo)," [Dar-es-Salaam, Dec. 1965 or early 1966], p. 15, PCH (hereafter Guevara, "Pasajes").

30. Interview with Dreke, who adds that for the same reason Che included three other personal aides who were not part of the initial column (Angel Hernández Angulo, Carlos Coello, and Harry Villegas). On Papi, see López et al., *Mártires*, 2:148-54; *Granma*, July 30, 1969, pp. 1-3; Mariano Rodríguez Herrera, "Ricardo: un extraordinario combatiente," *Bohemia* (Havana), July 30, 1982, pp. 78-79; Rodríguez Herrera, *Ellos*, pp. 67-81.

31. Interviews with Dreke (quoted), Rivalta, Rivalta's aide Ferrer, and with the following members of the column: Chivás, Torres, Vidiaux, Hernández Betancourt, Chaveco, Zerquera, Marín, Medina Savigne, Monteagudo, Morejón Gibert, Olachea, Vaillant; see also "Informe al Acto Central por la Conmemoración del XX aniversario de la formación, salida y cumplimiento de misión internacionalista de la Columna Especial Número Uno en el Congo Leopoldville," [Havana, 1985], p. 3, PCH (hereafter "Informe al Acto").

32. For the full list, see chapter 7, n. 51.

33. Interviews with Dreke (quoted) and Rivalta; Guevara, "Pasajes," p. 15. On the incident with the knapsack, interview with Dreke and Anderson, *Che*, pp. 337-38.

34. Guevara, "Pasajes," p. 15.

35. Interview with Tschamlesso.

36. CIA, OCI, weekly report, "The Situation in the Congo," Apr. 14, 1965, p. 2 quoted, and Apr. 28, 1965, NSFCF, box 87 (hereafter CIA, "Situation," followed by date); Scholz, "Vermerk über ein Gespräch des Beauftragten der Regierung der DDR in der VAR, Dr. Ernst Scholz, mit General Olenga und Major Lambert Wemba am 26.4.1965," Cairo, May 2, 1965, GDR AA, VVS Archiv (VR Kongo); Scholz, "Vermerk über den Besuch des Vertreter der Revolutionären Regierung des Kongo, Herrn M'Bagira beim Beauftragten der Regierung der DDR in der VAR, Botschafter Dr. Ernst Scholz, am Mittwoch, den 5 Mai 1965," Cairo, May 12, 1965, ibid.; *Nationalist* (Dar-es-Salaam), Apr. 2, 1965, p. 6, and Apr. 27, p. 1.

37. Guevara, "Pasajes," p. 16 quoted; interviews with Dreke (quoted), Tschamlesso, and Rivalta.

38. Interview with Dreke (quoted); "Informe al Acto," p. 3.

39. Interviews with Torres (quoted), Zerquera (quoted), and with Morejón Gibert and Chivás, two other members of the group.

40. Guevara, "Pasajes," p. 15 quoted; Guevara, "Evaluación del personal a mis ordenes," [Dar-es-Salaam, Dec. 1965 or early 1966], PCH; Guevara, "Relación nominal," [Dar-es-Salaam, Dec. 1965 or early 1966], PCH. Che's translations into Swahili were not accurate.

41. Quotations from interviews with Dreke and Torres; see also Guevara, "Pasajes," p. 16. "We could not buy the knapsacks, boots, and the other equipment for the column all at once, but only in small quantities and using different compañeros in order not to provoke suspicions" (Oliva interview in Gálvez, *El sueño*, p. 52).

42. Interviews with Dreke and Ferrer (who joined the support group in April). The DGI officers flew on Aeroflot from Havana to Moscow and Cairo and on the Czech airline from Cairo to Dar-es-Salaam.

43. Guevara, "Pasajes," p. 16; interviews with Dreke and Tschamlesso.

44. Guevara, "Pasajes," pp. 16, 22, 25, 37; Kahama, diary, pp. 1, 3, 7, PCH; Paulu, "Diario de campaña," pp. 1, 6, PCH. "Diario de campaña" is the official diary of the column, which a Cuban, Emilio Mena (Paulu), kept at Dreke's request. (Next to Che's "Pasajes," this is the most important source on the Cuban campaign in Zaire.)

For security reasons the volunteers were not allowed to keep their own personal diaries. However, some could not resist the temptation and disobeyed the order. One of them was Kahama (Alberto Man Zuliman), and I have a copy of his diary.

45. On the Kwilu revolt, see Weiss, "Pierre Mulele," and Martens, *Pierre Mulele*, esp. pp. 132-287. See also chapter 3, n. 22.

46. CIA, OCI, "Tanzanian Support for the Congo Rebels," Apr. 7, 1965, p. 6, NSFCF, box 87. See also CIA, DI, "The Southern Sudan Problem and Its Relationship to the Congo," May 28, 1965, ibid.; Amembassy Brussels to SecState, Mar. 25, 1965, Harriman Papers, box 544, LOC; CIA, "Situation," Mar. 24 and 31, Apr. 7 and 21, 1965. See also *Le Courrier d'Afrique* (Leopoldville): Mar. 18 and 19, 1965, both p. 1; *Le Soir* (Brussels): Mar. 2, 1965, p. 3; Mar. 18, p. 3; Mar. 30, p. 3; Apr. 10, p. 2; Hoare, *Congo Mercenary*, pp. 176-224.

The Belgian historian Benoît Verhaegen, who is the foremost authority on the 1964-65 war in Zaire, is completing a study on this topic with a colleague (Verhaegen and Gérard-Libois, "Che Guevara"). With singular generosity, he has allowed me to read his working draft.

47. Hoare, *Congo Mercenary*, p. 239 quoted; Guevara, "Pasajes," pp. 148-49.

48. Oliva quoted in Gálvez, *El sueño*, p. 52; interview with Rivalta.

49. Quotations from interview with Dreke, and Guevara, "Pasajes," p. 29. According to an authorita-

tive Belgian study, the rebels had about 2,000 armed men (CRISP, *Congo 1965*, p. 141).

50. CIA, "Situation," Mar. 10, 1965; CIA, OCI, "Situation in the Congo," July 1, 1965, NSFCF, box 85; FRG embassy Leopoldville to AA, Sept. 16, 1965, p. 2 quoted, FRG, AA 90.08; Amembassy Leopoldville to DOS, Mar. 3, 1966, FOIA; Hoare, *Congo Mercenary*, p. 240.

51. Quotations from "Albertville et le Nord-Katanga," enclosed in Humblet (Belgian consul general, Elisabethville) to Spaak, May 5, 1965, p. 6, MAE 18.518/9, and Guevara, "Pasajes," p. 22. See also CIA, "Situation," Apr. 21, 28, and May 5, 1965; CIA, OCI, "Situation in the Congo," July 1, 1965, p. 2, NSFCF, box 85; Hoare, *Congo Mercenary*, pp. 239, 248.

52. Quotations from Paulu, "Diario de campaña," p. 2, and interview with Zerquera.

53. Interview with Dreke; Guevara, "Pasajes," pp. 17-18.

54. Interview with Dreke.

55. Interview with Tschamlesso; Guevara, "Pasajes," p. 18.

56. Interview with Tschamlesso.

57. *Nationalist*, May 6, 1965, p. 8 quoted; May 19, p. 3; May 21, p. 1. See also Scholz, "Vermerk über ein Gespräch des Beauftragten der Regierung der DDR in der VAR, Dr. Ernst Scholz, mit Herrn M'Bagira am 31.5.1965," Cairo, June 1, 1965, GDR AA, VVS Archiv (VR Kongo); Wildau, "Information über bestehende Differenzen in der Kongolesischen Befreiungsbewegung," Khartoum, July 7, 1965, SED, DY30 IVA 2/20/983; "Information über die letzte Entwicklung in der Führung der kongolesischen Befreiungsbewegung," Berlin, Sept. 18, 1965, ibid.; *Morning News* (Khartoum), May 23, 1965, p. 2; *Le Soir*, May 19, 1965, p. 4, and May 20, p. 2; *Le Monde*, May 20, 1965, p. 4.

58. Guevara, "Pasajes," p. 19.

59. Quotations from Guevara, "Pasajes," pp. 19-21, and interview with Zerquera.

60. Kahama, diary, entry of May 9, 1965, p. 1; Guevara, "Pasajes," pp. 21-23. On Mitoudidi, see Verhaegen, *Rébellions*, 1:176-77.

61. Quotations from Guevara, "Pasajes," p. 22; Kahama, diary, pp. 3-4; interview with Dreke. A sixteen-year-old aide of Mitoudidi, Ernest (Freddy) Ilanga, became Che's professor of Swahili and his interpreter. After falling sick, he was evacuated to Cuba, where he arrived in mid-November 1965. He is now a neurosurgeon in Havana. (Guevara, "Pasajes," p. 29; Freddy Ilanga: "Si repites este nombre te fusilo," *Vanguardia* [Santa Clara, Cuba], June 13, 1991, p. 2; "La incógnita del Tres," *Juventud Rebelde* [Havana], Apr. 27, 1997, p. 9; "Cuando el Che era Tatu," *Escambray* [Sancti Spiritus, Cuba], Mar. 28, 1997, p. 2.)

62. Guevara, "Pasajes," p. 25.

63. Ibid., pp. 26 and 28 quoted; Kahama, diary, p. 3; Paulu, "Diario de campaña," p. 4.

64. Guevara, "Pasajes," p. 26 (quoting from his diary).

65. Quotations from interview with Hernández Betancourt; Kahama, diary, p. 6; Guevara, "Pasajes," pp. 28, 29.

66. Paulu, "Diario de campaña," p. 2 quoted; Guevara, "Pasajes," pp. 30-31. On Mitoudidi's death, see also *La Révolution* (a rebel broadsheet that appeared erratically and was probably printed in Kigoma), n.d., pp. 6-7, PCH; Kahama, diary, p. 5.

67. Guevara, "Pasajes," pp. 31-34.

68. Ibid., p. 35.

69. Paulu, "Diario de campaña," pp. 5-6.

70. Quoted in Guevara, "Pasajes," p. 36; interview with Dreke.

71. Quotations from Paulu, "Diario de campaña," p. 6, and Guevara, "Pasajes," p. 36. See also Kahama, diary, pp. 6-7.

72. Quotations from interview with Vidiaux, and Guevara, "Pasajes," p. 45. See also Kahama, diary, p. 7, and interviews with Candebat and Monteagudo (two of the thirty-nine).

73. Kahama, diary, entry of July 4, 1965 (quoted), and interviews with Cubans who fought at Bendera: Marín (quoted), Dreke, Vaillant, Chivás, Morejón Gibert, Olachea. For two written accounts by participants, see Paulu, "Diario de campaña," pp. 7-14, and the statement by Sylvestre Mugabo, an aide of Mundandi who was captured by the mercenaries in mid-September, in British Defense Adviser in Leopoldville, "Maniema Rebels," Oct. 18, 1965, FO 371/181705, PRO. See also Guevara, "Pasajes," pp. 37-42; CRISP, *Congo 1965*, p. 139; *Le Courrier d'Afrique*, July 3, 1965, p. 1; Carrasco, "El combate."

74. Quotations from Rusk to All ARA Diplomatic Posts, July 7, 1965 (summarizing July 2 CIA report), Pol 23-7 Cuba, SNF, NA; British Defense Adviser in Leopoldville, "Maniema Rebels," Oct. 18, 1965, FO 371/181705, PRO; CIA, OCI, "Cuban Participation in the Congo Rebellion," Sept. 25, 1965, NSFCF, box 18. See also FRG embassy Leopoldville to AA, July 30, 1965 (which encloses excerpts from the diary), FRG, AA 90.08; Rusk to Amembassy Leopoldville, July 22, 1965, Pol 23-9 The Congo, SNF, NA; Kerchove (Belgian ambassador, Leopoldville) to MAE, Oct. 22, 1965, MAE 18.288 (XII); Campbell to Aspden, Nov. 10, 1965 (quoting from CIA liaison report of July 6, 1965), FO 371/181705, PRO; Guevara, "Pasajes," pp. 41, 53; *Standard* (Dar-es-Salaam), July 19, 1965, p. 1; *Nationalist*, July 20, 1965, p. 8; *Le Soir*, Aug. 20, 1965, p. 7; *NYT*, July 18, 1965, p. 58, and July 28, p. 39.

75. Almari to Kahama, July 4, 1965. (Kahama copied the note in his diary, p. 10.)

76. Kahama, diary, pp. 10-11.

77. Guevara, "Pasajes," pp. 42-43 (quoting from his diary).

78. Ibid., pp. 44-46.

79. Ibid., p. 46.

80. Ibid., p. 47.

81. For the incident, see Guevara, *El diario*, pp. 48-49, and the documents in Soria Galvarro, *El Che*, 3:49-52, 96-119.

82. Interviews with Dreke and Fernández Mell; Guevara, "Pasajes."

83. Interviews with Fernández Mell and Dreke, who adds that the Simbas in the Fizi-Baraka knew that the foreigners were Cubans, but at first they didn't know Che's identity. They knew him as Dr. Tatu, and they understood that he was the chief of the Cubans. Slowly the secret of Che's identity was revealed. Mitoudidi and Tschamlesso, and then local commanders, learned that Tatu was Che, and eventually it spread to the rank and file. For most Simbas, however, Che's name meant nothing.

84. Interview with Dreke.

85. Quotations from interview with Dreke; Guevara, "Pasajes," p. 57; British Defense Adviser in Leopoldville, "Maniema Rebels," Oct. 18, 1965, FO 371/181705, PRO. On the August 16 attack, see also Paulu, "Diario de campaña," pp. 27-29; *Le Soir*, Aug. 24, 1965, p. 3; *Le Courrier d'Afrique*, Sept. 30, 1965, p. 2; CRISP, *Congo 1965*, p. 141; Hoare, *Congo Mercenary*, pp. 247-48; Verhaegen and Gérard-Libois, "Che Guevara."

86. Guevara, "Pasajes," pp. 58, 60, 71.

87. Quotations from *Le Soir*, Sept. 9, 1965, p. 7, and Sept. 17, p. 2; Godley (U.S. ambassador, Leopoldville) to SecState, Sept. 21, 1965, no. 527, NSFCF, box 85. See also CIA, OCI, "Cuban Participation in the Congo Rebellion," Sept. 25, 1965, NSFCF, box 18; "Cuban Subversive Activities in Africa," enclosed in Smith [DDCI] to Ropa, Aug. 10, 1966, NSF Files of Edward Hamilton, box 1/3, LBJL; *Le Monde*, Sept. 9, 1965, p. 5; FRG embassy Leopoldville to AA, Sept. 16, 1965, FRG, AA 90.08; Verhaegen and Gérard-Libois, "Che Guevara."

88. Guevara, "Pasajes," pp. 64-65, 67; interviews with Frelimo leader Marcelino dos Santos and Víctor Schueg, one of the instructors; Schueg in Báez, *Secretos*, pp. 174-75. The figure of seven is from Gálvez, *El sueño*, p. 171. For Frelimo and Cuban military training, see chapter 10.

The column that had assembled at Peti-1 on February 2, 1965, included 113 men, but 9 of these had been left behind (see chapter 4, n. 65); at least 2 others had been detached from the column to go to the Congo.

89. Quotations from Fernández Mell, "Apuntes," n.d., p. 1, PCH, and Guevara, "Pasajes," p. 75. Also interview with Fernández Mell, and "Informe al Acto," p. 6.

90. Guevara, "Pasajes," p. 75 quoted; interviews with Fernández Mell and Dreke.

91. Particularly useful were interviews with Drs. Zerquera and Candebat, and with Dreke, Fernández Mell, and Fernández Padilla. For the full list of the doctors, see Guevara, "Evaluación del personal a mis ordenes," [Dar-es-Salaam, Dec. 1965 or early 1966], PCH, and "Columna `Patricio Lumumba': Planilla de Control," [Havana, 1985], PCH; Rafael Zerquera, "Una casi desconocida epopeya," *Tribuna de la Habana*, Oct. 8, 1990, pp. 4-5. The Haitian doctor, Adrien Sansaricq, eventually returned to his country and was killed by the Haitian army in 1969 (*NYT*, June 3, 1969, p. 17; Diederich and Burt, *Papa Doc*, pp. 385-88).

92. See chapter 8.

93. Interview with Risquet.

94. Wolf, *Spionagechef*, p. 387.

95. Quotations from interview with Ferrer, and Guevara, "Pasajes," p. 66. Also interviews with Rivalta and Dreke.

96. Interviews with Rumbau (the lead engineer), Escandón (another member of the group), and Fernández Padilla. See also Rómulo Rumbau, "Che y la misión en el Congo. Quince minutos para el tiro," *Vanguardia*, Oct. 24, 1990, p. 4.

97. Interviews with Fernández Padilla (quoted) and Escandón.

98. Interview with Fernández Padilla.

99. Interviews with Fernández Padilla, Rumbau, and Escandón.

100. Quotations from interview with Rumbau, and Guevara, "Pasajes," p. 125. See also Paulu, "Diario de campaña," p. 48.

101. Interviews with Fernández Padilla, Fernández Mell, and Dreke.

102. Guevara, "Pasajes," p. 90.

103. Ibid., p. 93.

104. Interview with Ferrer.

105. Ball to Amembassy Leopoldville, Sept. 29, 1965, Pol 23-9 The Congo, SNF, NA. See also *Revolución:* Sept. 1, 4, 11, 1965, all p. 1. While rivals, Soumialot and Kabila were formally part of the same government. Soumialot resided in Cairo but spent much of his time shuttling between friendly capitals. When he arrived in Havana on August 31, he was coming from Beijing, where he had spent ten days with five members of his government. From Cuba, he flew to the Soviet Union, where he spent two more weeks. (*Nationalist:* Aug. 20, 1965, p. 4; Aug. 26, p. 1; Sept. 15, p. 5; Sept. 27, p. 7.)

106. Guevara, "Pasajes," p. 93.

107. José Ramón Machado Ventura, note to Piero Gleijeses, Havana, July 12, 1995, p. 2 quoted; Guevara, "Pasajes," p. 93 (it was through Machado and through Fidel's letter that Che learned what had happened during Soumialot's visit); interview with Estrada. For Che's letter, see *Granma*, Oct. 4, 1965, pp. 3-4.

108. Castro in *Revolución*, Sept. 29, 1965, p. 4 quoted. For a careful description of speculations in the press and the U.S. government about Che's whereabouts, see Ryan, *The Fall*, pp. 30-39.

109. The Central Committee of the PCC included three members of Che's column: Dreke, Aragonés, and Fernández Mell.

110. Quotations from Martín Chivás, "El regreso de un amigo," *Trabajadores* (Havana), July 14, 1997, p. 9, and interview with Dreke.

111. Guevara, "Pasajes," pp. 95, 97.

112. Che to Fidel, Oct. 5, 1965, in ibid., pp. 93-95.

113. Fernández Mell to Guillermo García, Oct. 6, 1965, PCH.

CHAPTER SIX

1. Quotations from Spaak to Belgian UN delegation, Dec. 22, 1964, MAE 18.293 II (c); Rose (British ambassador, Leopoldville), "Congo (Leopoldville): Annual Review for 1964," Jan. 12, 1965, sec. 1, p. 4, FO 371/181656, PRO; CIA, OCI, "Situation in the Congo," July 1, 1965, p. 3, NSFCF, box 85; Godley to

SecState, Dec. 4, 1964, and Oct. 8, 1965 (quoting Mobutu), ibid.

2. Harriman to John Kennedy, Sept. 20, 1960, p. 4, Harriman Papers, box 405, LOC; *New York Herald Tribune*, May 28, 1963, p. 1 (quoting Rusk); Mennen Williams, OH, p. 77. Documents in the Kennedy Library (esp. NSF, boxes 2 and 3) and the Mennen Williams Papers (esp. box 16, NA) show the concern of both the Kennedy and Johnson administrations about the impact on Africans of the civil rights situation in the United States. See also Borstelmann, *Cold War* pp. 135-221 and Dudziak, *Cold War*, pp. 152-248.

3. *Tanganyika Standard* (Dar-es-Salaam), July 23, 1964, p. 1 quoted.

4. Rowan, memo for president, Aug. 14, 1964, Confidential File, Country 29, box 7, LBJL. In his autobiography, *Breaking Barriers*, Rowan overlooks the entire episode.

5. Godley to SecState, Dec. 13, 1964, NSFCF, box 85.

6. Amembassy Leopoldville to SecState, July 11, 1964, Pol 15-1 The Congo, SNF, NA; Nogueira, *Salazar: A Resistência*, pp. 570-71. On Tshombe's ties with Portugal, see ibid., pp. 357-58, 541, 560, 570-77, 601; Nogueira, *Salazar: O Último Combate*, pp. 50-52; Nogueira, *Um Político*, pp. 93, 95-96, 133.

7. Godley to SecState, Mar. 24, 1965, NSFCF, box 85; Leonhart (U.S. ambassador, Dar-es-Salaam) to SecState, Mar. 27, 1965, p. 2, NSFCF, box 100. Leopoldville's important newspaper, *Le Progrès* (which was pro-Mobutu and unsympathetic to Tshombe), had just published several front-page articles about Roberto's misadventures at Tshombe's hands: Feb. 3, 16, 18, 21, 23, 1965, all p. 1.

8. *Jeune Afrique*, Aug. 8, 1965, p. 19; Komer, memo for record, Jan. 21, 1965, NSFCF, box 85.

9. Quotations from DOS, MemoConv, "Tshombe Request for South African Assistance," Aug. 11, 1964, NSFCF, box 81; Godley to SecState, Aug. 24 and 23, 1964, NSFCF, box 82. For press reports, see *Cape Times* (Cape Town), Aug. 27, 1964, p. 1; *Egyptian Gazette* (Cairo), Aug. 24, 1964, p. 1, and Aug. 28, p. 2; *Daily Nation* (Nairobi), Aug. 24, 1964, p. 16, and Aug. 25, p. 11; *West Africa* (London), Aug. 29, 1964, p. 979.

10. Quotations from CIA, "Situation," Feb. 3, 1965, p. 3, and from interview with Devlin. On South Africa's involvement, see also CIA, OCI, weekly report, "The Situation in the Congo," Aug. 27, Nov. 10, and Dec. 30, 1964, NSFCF, box 87 (hereafter CIA, "Situation," followed by date); Godley to SecState, Feb. 9, 1965, NSFCF, box 85, and Mar. 3, 1965, NSFCF, box 87; Puren, *Mercenary Commander*, pp. 195-200, 207-8.

11. Quotations from Ball to Amembassy London, Jan. 28, 1965, NSFCF, box 85, and Harriman to Amembassy Brussels, Dec. 14, 1964, p. 2, ibid.

12. Ramsden (British embassy, Brussels) to Le Quesne, Apr. 9, 1965, FO 371/181705, PRO.

13. See Williams to Harriman, July 24, 1964, p. 1 quoted, MWP, box 12; McSweeney to SecState, July 13 and 28, 1964, DOS MF 8503217; Spaak to Belgian

embassy Washington, D.C., July 29, 1964, MAE 18.293 II (c); Brubeck, memo for president, Aug. 6, 1964, NSFCF, box 81; Godley to SecState, Aug. 15, 1964, ibid.

14. Spaak to Kerchove, Sept. 17, 1964, MAE 18.289 (III); Kerchove (Belgian ambassador, Leopoldville) to Spaak, Aug. 28, 1964, MAE 18.288 (X); Vandewalle, *L'Ommegang*, p. 209. See also Spaak to Belgian embassy Leopoldville, Aug. 28, 1964, MAE 18.289 (III), and Aug. 31, 1964, MAE 18.518/9; Kerchove to Davignon, Sept. 10, 1964, MAE 18.288 (X); *Le Courrier d'Afrique* (Leopoldville), Sept. 2, 1964, p. 1; *Le Monde*, Dec. 29, 1964, p. 4. For the 1936 law, see Amembassy Brussels to SecState, Jan. 30, 1976, DOS MF 8904623/1.

15. Godley to SecState, Dec. 13, 1964, NSFCF, box 85, and Godley to DOS, "Belgian Presence and Belgian Policies in the Congo," Dec. 2, 1965, DOS MF 8503217. For the breakdown by nationality, see Godley to SecState, Oct. 28, 1964, NSFCF, box 83, and Nov. 18, 1965, NSFCF, box 85; CIA, "Situation," Jan. 19, 1965; Blake to DOS, "The Congolese Rebellion: Current Status and Outlook," Leopoldville, Mar. 3, 1966, DOS MF 8705067/1.

16. MacArthur (U.S. ambassador, Brussels) to SecState, Dec. 3, 1964, NSFCF, box 85, and Godley to SecState, Aug. 15, 1964, NSFCF, box 81.

17. Rusk to Amembassy Leopoldville, Jan. 6, 1965, NSFCF, box 85; Rowan to Amembassy Leopoldville, Dec. 29, 1964, ibid.; Ball to Amembassy London, Jan. 28, 1965, ibid.

18. Mason (British embassy, Leopoldville) to Le Quesne, June 26, 1965, FO 371/181705, PRO; *Sunday Tribune* (Durban), June 13, 1965, p. 2; *Le Figaro Littéraire* (Paris), Dec. 17, 1964, p. 9; Mason to Le Quesne, Leopoldville, June 26, 1965, FO 371/181705, PRO.

19. Quotations from Godley to SecState, Nov. 18, 1965, NSFCF, box 85; interview with Komer, the NSC official in charge of Africa; interview with DCM Blake.

20. CIA, "Situation," Jan. 27, 1965, p. 1 quoted; Ramsden (British embassy, Brussels) to Le Quesne, Mar. 30, 1965, FO 371/181707, PRO; "Assistance Technique Militaire au Congo," [June 1965], MAE 18.518/12; Godley to DOS, "Belgian Presence and Belgian Policies in the Congo," Dec. 2, 1965, DOS MF 8503217; Gérard-Libois, "L'aide (I)," pp. 19-25; Verhaegen, "L'Armée."

21. Godley to SecState, Aug. 26, 1964, NSFCF, box 82.

22. Mockler (*Mercenaries*, p. 247) prints the letter from which the quotation is taken. See also ibid., p. 245; Mallin and Brown, *Merc*, p. 110; Vandewalle, *L'Ommegang*, p. 201.

One American, however, slipped through: Samuel Shoesmith, who, Hoare recalled, "had emigrated hurriedly from the United States to the Northern Rhodesian copper belt" (Hoare, "Congo," p. 127).

23. McNamara, *In Retrospect*, p. 127.

24. *NYT*, Aug. 13, 1964, p. 28 (ed.); Stennis, Aug. 14, 1964, *CR*, 88th Cong., 2d sess., vol. 110, pt. 15:19531. See also Senator Michael Mansfield (D.-Mont.), Aug. 21, 1964, ibid., pt. 16:20884-87; *WP*, Aug.

15, 1964, p. 8, and Aug. 16, E6 (ed.); *NYT*, Aug. 15, 1964, p. 1, and Aug. 22, p. 1; *CSM*, Aug. 20, 1964, p. 16 (ed.); *WSJ*, Aug. 25, 1964, p. 12 (ed.); "President's Meeting with Congressional Leaders," Sept. 9, 1964, NSF, Files of Bromley Smith, box 1, LBJL.

25. TelConv, Lippmann and Ball, Aug. 25, 1964, 10:45 a.m., Ball Papers, box 2/3, LBJL; TelConv, Ochs and Ball, Aug. 21, 1964, 3:20 p.m., ibid. While the document identifies Ochs by his old family name, in the *New York Times* he appeared as Oakes.

26. *NYT*, Aug. 21, 1964, p. 28 (ed.).

27. *WP*, Mar. 14, 1965, p. 32, and Apr. 22, p. 25.

28. Quotations from "Red Arsenals Arm the Simbas," *Life*, Feb. 12, 1965, p. 31; Lloyd Garrison, "White Mercenary Finds a Weird War in Congo," *NYT*, Oct. 2, 1964, p. 6; Lloyd Garrison, "Congo Mercenary Kills Rebel Prisoner to Spare Him Torture," *NYT*, Oct. 25, 1964, p. 16. I examined the *New York Times*, the *Washington Post*, the *Christian Science Monitor*, the *Wall Street Journal*, *Time*, *Newsweek*, *U.S. News & World Report*, *Life*, the *Nation*, the *New Republic*, *Ramparts*, and the *Village Voice*. The *New York Times* covered the story almost daily through mid-1965 and less frequently for the remainder of the year. The *Washington Post* was second to the *New York Times* in the thoroughness of its coverage, with about one-third as much space devoted to the crisis. At the other end of the spectrum, the *Wall Street Journal* published only occasional articles. Among the magazines, *Time* and *Newsweek* covered the story regularly; *U.S. News & World Report*, the *New Republic*, and *Life* less so; the *Nation* carried only one article, *Ramparts* and the *Village Voice* none. I also examined five African American newspapers, and their coverage will be discussed later.

It is impossible to measure the depth of the concern felt by the American public about Zaire at the time since no public opinion polls were taken on the issue. However, judging by the extensive coverage in the U.S. press, the story did attract considerable interest.

29. Garrison, "White Mercenary," p. 6.

30. Garrison, "Congo Mercenary," p. 16. *Newsweek*'s senior editor, Arnaud de Borchgrave, must have traveled on the same plane: he also penned a sympathetic portrait of Wilson ("The Congo: Lousy Civilian," *Newsweek*, Oct. 12, 1964, p. 56). This was the only portrait of a mercenary that appeared in *Newsweek*. For a less romantic description of Wilson and of the battle for Lisala by a French journalist who covered the campaign, see Le Bailly, *Une poignée*, pp. 235-63.

31. "Conversations with Mercenaries," *Africa Today*, Dec. 1964, p. 8.

32. *NYT*, Dec. 2, 1964, p. 46; Dec. 21, p. 28; Dec. 6, 4:3; Jan. 7, 1965, p. 14; Jan. 19, p. 11.

33. *New Republic*, Dec. 12, 1964, pp. 3-4; *CSM*, Dec. 21, 1964, p. 1; *Newsweek*, Dec. 7, 1964, p. 48, and Dec. 14, p. 36.

34. *WP*, Apr. 25, 1965, p. 12.

35. In addition to "mercenaries, ammunition and supplies," the U.S. C-130s carried American journalists on their visits to the front (*NYT*, Jan. 23, 1965, p.

9; see also Godley to SecState, Nov. 17, 1964, NSFCF, box 83).

36. *Le Monde*, Nov. 28, 1964, p. 1 (ed.).

37. Quotations from *Muhammad Speaks* (Chicago), Dec. 18, 1964, p. 2, and Jan. 1, 1965, p. 6. See also Malcolm X, *Autobiography*, pp. 347-63; Clarke, *Malcolm X*, pp. 288-301, 335-42; Perry, *Malcolm*, pp. 314-18; *Egyptian Gazette*. Aug. 7, 1964, p. 2; Aug. 17, p. 5; Aug. 23, p. 2; Aug. 24, p. 4.

38. *WP*, Nov. 29, 1964, p. 36 quoted; *NYT*: Nov. 29, 1964, p. 5; Dec. 10, p. 58; Dec. 14, p. 3; Jan. 30, 1965, p. 4; *Afro-American* (Baltimore), Dec. 12, 1964, p. 14; *U.S. News & World Report*, Jan. 11, 1965, pp. 60-61; *Amsterdam News* (New York), Feb. 13, 1965, p. 1; American Negro Leadership Conference on Africa, "Resolutions," Sept. 24-27, 1964, pp. 1-2, 7-10, MWP, box 16.

39. Interview with Diggs. Diggs, an African American, was one of the few congressmen interested in Africa.

40. *WP*, Dec. 1, 1964, p. 14 (ed.).

41. Quotations from Bundy to SecState, Jan. 7, 1965, NSFCF, box 76, and from Komer to Bundy, Jan. 6, 1965, ibid.

42. Haynes to Bundy, Mar. 4, 1965, NSFCF, box 76. See also Williams to SecState, Mar. 2, 1965, MWP, box 13, and Komer and Haynes to Bundy, Mar. 30, 1965, NSFCF, box 76.

43. *Amsterdam News*. Aug. 8, 1964, p. 13; Sept. 19, p. 27; Oct. 3, p. 18. The coverage in the *Chicago Defender* and the *Pittsburgh Courier* was also superficial. *Freedomways*, a quarterly to the left of the *Crisis*, published an article on the April 1965 U.S. invasion of the Dominican Republic, which involved thousands of black soldiers and sailors (Jose Malcioln, "Notes on the Dominican Crisis," Fall 1965, pp. 517-24), but nothing on Zaire.

44. Quotations from *Afro-American*, Sept. 11, 1965, p. 20, and Dec. 5, 1964, p. 12, and *Muhammad Speaks*, Jan. 15, 1965, p. 7. See also *Afro-American*: Oct. 3, 1964, p. 20; Nov. 14, p. 12; Jan. 2, 1965, p. 20, and Jan. 23, p. 20; *Muhammad Speaks*, Dec. 18, 1964, p. 2; Mar. 19, 1965, p. 11.

45. "Hostages, Mercenaries and the CIA," *Nation*, Dec. 14, 1964, p. 454; "Red Arsenals Arm the Simbas," *Life*, Feb. 12, 1965, p. 31; *WP*, Nov. 15, 1964, E5; interview with Devlin.

46. Alsop, *"I've Seen the Best of It,"* p. 443 quoted. On the press's silence on the Guatemalan operation, see Gleijeses, *Shattered Hope*, pp. 258-62, 367-70; on the Indonesian operation, Kahin and Kahin, *Subversion*, esp. p. 158; on the Bay of Pigs, Bernstein and Gordon, "The Press"; Aronson, *The Press*, pp. 153-69; Salisbury, *Without Fear*, pp. 137-64.

47. Lord Harlech (British ambassador, Washington, D.C.), "Annual Review for 1964," Jan. 1, 1965, p. 4, FO 371/179557, PRO.

48. "Brief for the Secretary of State's visit to Brussels February 11/12 [1965]," n.d., quoted, FO 371/181692, PRO. On Africa's relations with the Tshombe government, see CRISP, *Congo 1964*, pp. 444-510, and CRISP, *Congo 1965*, pp. 264-91.

49. Komer, memo for president, May 31, 1965, NSF, Memos to the President, box 3, LBJL. See also Williams to Harriman, Dec. 11, 1964, MWP, box 12; CIA, OCI, "US Aid to Countries Aiding Congo Rebels," Dec. 15, 1964, enclosed in McCone to President, Dec. 16, 1964, NSFCF, box 87; Ball to Amembassy Cairo, Dec. 18, 1964, FOIA 1977/225G; Williams to Westerfield and Kling, Jan. 12, 1965, MWP, box 5; Williams to SecState, Jan. 18 and Mar. 25, 1965, MWP, box 13; Williams to Harriman, Feb. 3, 1965, ibid.; Komer, memo for president, Apr. 24, 1965, NSF, Memos to the President, box 3, LBJL. For the specific case of Egypt, see also Beat Bumbacher's well-researched *Die USA und Nasser*, pp. 175-223.

50. FO, Record of Conversation (Harriman and Thomson), Washington, D.C., Jan. 25, 1965, FO 371/181609, PRO; CIA, "Situation," Feb. 17, 1965; Spaak to MAE, Feb. 19, 1965, MAE 18.292 (V a); Godley to SecState, Mar. 31, 1965, NSFCF, box 85; FO, Record of Conversation (Williams and Thomson), London, Apr. 16, 1965, FO 371/181611, PRO; Foccart, *Foccart*, pp. 263-65, 308-12.

51. Attwood, *Twilight*, p. 276. The shift was timely: the failure of the rains throughout the country caused a serious food shortage and a pressing demand for U.S. food aid (see *Daily Nation*: June 9, 10, 15, 16, 18, 19, 1965).

52. Quotations from CIA, "Situation," May 5, 1965, p. 1, and Germani, *Weisse Söldner*, p. 159. See also CIA, "Situation," Dec. 30, 1964, Jan. 19 and 27, 1965; CIA, DI, "The Southern Sudan Problem and Its Relationship to the Congo," May 28, 1965, NSFCF, box 87; Williams to SecState, Sept. 3, 1965, MWP, box 14; Lessing, "Vermerk über ein Gespräch beim Stellvertreter des Vorsitzenden des Ministerrates Paul Scholz mit Herrn Casimir M'Bagira, Kongo, am 19.1.1965," Berlin, Jan. 19, 1965, GDR AA, A14593; Scholz, "Vermerk über ein Gespräch des Beauftragten der Regierung der DDR in der VAR, Dr. Ernst Scholz, mit General Olenga und Major Lambert Wemba am 26.4.1965," Cairo, May 2, 1965, GDR AA, VVS Archiv (VR Kongo); Wildau, "Information über bestehende Differenzen in der Kongolesischen Befreiungsbewegung," Khartoum, July 7, 1965, SED, DY30 IVA 2/20/983; British embassy Khartoum to FO, Feb. 6, 1965, FO 371/181718, PRO; FRG Interest Section Khartoum to AA, Sept. 18, 1965, FRG, AA 90.08.

53. Quotations from CIA, "Situation," Jan. 27, 1965, p. 5, and CIA, OCI, "Situation in the Congo," July 1, 1965, p. 5, NSFCF, box 85. See also CIA, "Situation," Feb. 3, 1965; CIA, ONE, "Prospects in Brazzaville," May 17, 1965, NSFCF, box 85; Dehennin (Belgian chargé, Brazzaville) to Spaak, Sept. 29, 1965, MAE 14.732.

54. DOS, MemoConv (Rusk, Guellal, et al.), Apr. 16, 1965, NSFCF, box 79.

55. CIA, OCI, "Consequences of Algerian Coup," June 19, 1965, p. 2 quoted, NSFCF, box 79; Amembassy Leopoldville to SecState, Oct. 29, 1965, DOS MF 8503217.

56. Interview with Devlin; Komer, memo for president, June 16, 1965, NSFCF, box 76.

57. Nyerere, quoted in *Tanganyika Standard*, Apr. 21, 1965, p. 1.

58. DOS, MemoConv, "Discussion of General African Situation," June 18, 1965, FOIA 1983/1196; Ronmeisl, "Auszug aus dem Aktenvermerk über ein Gespräch mit dem Leiter der 3. Afrikanischen Abteilung, Genossen Falin, am 9.8.65," Moscow, Aug. 11, 1965, GDR AA, A1168. On Tanzania's role, see also CIA, OCI, "Tanzanian Support for the Congo Rebels," Apr. 7, 1965, NSFCF, box 87; CIA, "Situation," Apr. 14, 1965; CIA, OCI, "Tanzania Taking the Left Turn," May 21, 1965, NSFCF, box 100; CIA, ONE, "A Reassessment of Julius Nyerere," June 10, 1965, ibid.; CIA, OCI, "Situation in the Congo," July 1, 1965, NSFCF, box 85; Komer to Bundy, Oct. 11, 1965, ibid.; Micheel, "Aktenvermerk über eine Unterredung zwischen dem Leiter der Delegation der Volksrepublik Kongo John Ali (wirklicher Name Jerome Kantarebe), und dem Stellvertreter des Ministers für Auswärtige Angelegenheiten Genossen Dr. Kiesewetter am 13. Mai 1965," Berlin, May 18, 1965, GDR AA, VVS Archiv (VR Kongo); Lessing to Kiesewetter, Dar-es-Salaam, Nov. 8, 1965, ibid.

59. Paulu, "Diario de campaña," entry of June 22, 1965, p. 5, PCH; Che Guevara, "Pasajes de la guerra revolucionaria (Congo)," [Dar-es-Salaam, Dec. 1965 or early 1966], p. 32, PCH (hereafter Guevara, "Pasajes").

60. Interviews with Blake (quoted), Devlin (quoted), Quintero (quoted), Hawes, and Halpern, a CIA officer involved in the Central American operation. See also CIA, "Situation," Mar. 10 and Apr. 14, 1965; CIA, OCI, "Tanzanian Support for the Congo Rebels," Apr. 7, 1965, NSFCF, box 87; CIA, OCI, "The Congo since the Mobutu Coup," Feb. 11, 1966, NSFCF, box 85; Humblet (Belgian consul general, Elisabethville) to Spaak, May 5, 1965, MAE 18.518/9; *Le Soir*, May 23, 1965, p. 2.

61. Guevara, "Pasajes," p. 147.

62. Ibid., pp. 94-95.

63. Interview with X.

64. Interview with Ferrer; Guevara, "Pasajes," p. 16.

65. Interview with Ferrer.

66. Interviews with Tschamlesso and Dreke; Guevara, "Pasajes," p. 21. "Mugabo [the Mundandi aide taken prisoner by the mercenaries] stated that the Cubans were known only by Swahili numbers" (British Defense Adviser in Leopoldville, "Maniema Rebels," Oct. 18, 1965, FO 371/181705, PRO).

67. Interview with Ferrer.

68. CIA, OCI, "Situation in the Congo," July 1, 1965, p. 2, NSFCF, box 85.

69. Ibid., Aug. 26, 1965, p. 4, NSFCF, box 85; British Defense Adviser in Leopoldville, "Maniema Rebels," Oct. 18, 1965, FO 371/181705, PRO.

70. Godley to SecState, Sept. 21, 1965, nos. 523 and 527 (quoted), NSFCF, box 85. See also Mason (British chargé, Leopoldville) to FO, Sept. 21, 1965, FO 371/181693, PRO, and Sept. 25, 1965, FO 371/181718, PRO; CIA, OCI, "Cuban Participation in the Congo Rebellion," Sept. 25, 1965, NSFCF, box 18;

Mason to Le Quesne, Oct. 8, 1965, FO 371/181693, PRO; Verhaegen and Gérard-Libois, "Che Guevara."

71. Interview with Devlin. See also CIA, "Weekly Summary," Oct. 8, 1965, p. 28, NSA; CIA, DI, "The Fall of Che Guevara and the Changing Face of the Cuban Revolution," Oct. 18, 1965, NSFCF, box 18; Hughes to SecState, "Guevara's Death—the Meaning for Latin America," Oct. 12, 1967, NSFCF, box 8.

CHAPTER SEVEN

1. Komer, memo for president, Sept. 27, 1965, p. 1, NSF, Files of McGeorge Bundy, box 19, LBJL.

2. Komer, memo for president, Oct. 4, 1965, p. 1, NSF, Memos to the President, box 5, LBJL; Mason (British chargé, Leopoldville) to Le Quesne, Oct. 8, 1965, FO 371/181693, PRO; Godley (U.S. ambassador, Leopoldville) to McIlvaine, Oct. 12, 1965, Harriman Papers, box 448, LOC; Komer, memo for president, Oct. 4, 1965, p. 1, NSF, Memos to the President, box 5, LBJL.

3. See Che Guevara, "Pasajes de la guerra revolucionaria (Congo)," [Dar-es-Salaam, Dec. 1965 or early 1966], pp. 88-147, PCH (hereafter Guevara, "Pasajes"); Paulu, "Diario de campaña," pp. 39-59, PCH; CRISP, *Congo 1965*, pp. 56-57, 143-44. Hoare, *Congo Mercenary*, pp. 248-72, is overblown but useful. The most informative newspaper articles are *Le Soir* (Brussels), Sept. 30, 1965, p. 2, and Oct. 13, p. 3; *Rhodesia Herald*, Sept. 30, 1965, p. 1; Oct. 1, p. 8; Oct. 12, p. 11; *Le Courrier d'Afrique* (Leopoldville): Sept. 28, 1965, p. 1; Sept. 30, p. 1; Oct. 11, p. 1; *Nationalist* (Dar-es-Salaam), Sept. 30, 1965, p. 8. When it is published, Verhaegen's account of the offensive will fill an important void (see chapter 5, n. 46).

4. Guevara, "Pasajes," p. 128.

5. Godley to SecState, Oct. 30, 1965, p. 2, NSFCF, box 85; Guevara, "Pasajes," pp. 114, 120.

6. Paulu, "Diario de campaña," p. 51. Dreke's Swahili nom de guerre was Moja, but the volunteers changed it to Moya.

7. Quotations from Fernández Mell to Guillermo García, Oct. 6, 1965, PCH, and interview with Dreke. Guevara, "Evaluación del personal a mis ordenes," [Dar-es-Salaam, Dec. 1965 or early 1966], identifies several of the Cubans on Che's list. See also Paulu, "Diario de campaña," pp. 51-52; "Informe al Acto Central por la Conmemoración del XX aniversario de la formación, salida y cumplimiento de misión internacionalista de la Columna Especial Número Uno en el Congo Leopoldville," [Havana, 1985], p. 7, PCH (hereafter "Informe al Acto").

8. On rebel infighting in these months, see Schedlich (first secretary, GDR office, Cairo), "Information über die letzte Entwicklung in der Führung der kongolesischen Befreiungsbewegung," Berlin, Sept. 18, 1965, SED, DY30 IVA 2/20/983; Schedlich, "Aktenvermerk über ein Gespräch mit Tshimbila, Präsident der PABECO, am 13.10.65," Cairo, Oct. 18, 1965, ibid.; Schedlich, "Aktenvermerk über ein Gespräch mit dem Vertreter der Revolutionären Regierung des Kongo in Kairo, Major Wambo, am 16.10.1965," Cairo, Oct. 23, 1965, ibid.; Schedlich, "Vermerk über ein Gespräch mit Herrn Ngoie, Herrn

Tshimbila und dem Nachfolger Pakassas, Herrn Mayinza Albert, am 23.11.65," Cairo, Nov. 24, 1965, ibid.; Scholz, "Vermerk über ein Gespräch des Beauftragten der Regierung der DDR in der VAR, Dr. Ernst Scholz, mit dem Berater für afrikanische Fragen des Präsidenten der VAR, Herrn Fayek, am Donnerstag, dem 17.2.1966," GDR AA, VVS Archiv (VR Kongo); FRG Interest Section Khartoum, Sept. 18, 1965, FRG, AA 90.08; CRISP, *Congo 1965*, pp. 162-200.

9. Quotations from Bundy, memo for president, Aug. 25, 1965, NSFCF, box 85, and Saunders to Bundy, Oct. 16, 1965, ibid.

10. Quotations from *NYT*, Oct. 25, 1965, p. 22, and *Standard* (Dar-es-Salaam), Oct. 30, 1965, p. 5 (quoting Nyerere). See also *Nationalist*, Oct. 15, 1965, p. 4; Leonhart (U.S. ambassador, Dar-es-Salaam) to SecState, Oct. 18, 1965, NSFCF, box 100; Godley to SecState, Oct. 29, 1965, DOS MF 8503217; Komer, memo for president, Nov. 1, 1965, NSF, Memos to the President, box 5, LBJL; Dehennin (Belgian chargé, Brazzaville) to Spaak, Nov. 2, 1965, MAE 14.732; Monnier, "L'Organisation."

11. Leonhart to SecState, Dar-es-Salaam, Oct. 31, 1965, p. 2 quoted, NSFCF, box 100; Fernández Padilla to Tatu, [late Oct.], quoted in Guevara, "Pasajes," p. 126; interviews with Rivalta and Fernández Padilla.

12. Guevara, "Pasajes," p. 126.

13. Guevara to Fidel Castro, [Nov. 4, 1965], in Guevara, "Pasajes," p. 128.

14. Rafael [Fernández Padilla] to Tatu, Nov. 4, 1965, in Guevara, "Pasajes," pp. 126-27.

15. Quotations from Rafael to Tatu, Nov. 9, [1965], ACC, and "Information über die Lage in Kongo-Leopoldville (Einschätzung der Befreiungsbewegung)," [early Nov. 1965], SED, DY30 IVA 2/20/983. See also Rafael to Tatu, [late Oct.], in Guevara, "Pasajes," p. 126; Rafael to Pablo [Rivalta], Nov. 9, 1965, ACC; Paulu, "Diario de campaña," entry of Nov. 4, 1965, p. 53; interview with Tschamlesso.

16. Guevara, "Pasajes," pp. 126, 134, 141. On Masengo, see Verhaegen, *Rébellions*, 1:521-22.

17. Rafael to Tatu, n.d., ACC. See also Guevara, "Pasajes," p. 136.

18. Tatu to Rafael, [Nov. 14, 1965], ACC.

19. Quoted in Guevara, "Pasajes," p. 138.

20. Guevara, "Pasajes," pp. 140-42 (p. 140 quoted); Paulu, "Diario de campaña," p. 57.

21. Quotations from Guevara, "Pasajes," p. 159; Rafael to Tatu, Nov. 19, 1965, in ibid., p. 143; Tatu to Rafael, Nov. 19, 1965, ibid.

22. Guevara, "Pasajes," p. 144.

23. Interviews with Fernández Mell (quoted) and Dreke.

24. Guevara, "Pasajes," p. 146. Four Cubans did not evacuate with the rest of the group. Three got lost during the retreat and had to be left behind. Che ordered thirteen of his men to stay in Kigoma and search for them. They were eventually found and returned to Cuba. The fourth, Aurino, is presumed dead. (See Paulu, "Diario de campaña," pp. 58, 60; "Informe al Acto," p. 7; Martín Chivás, "Feliz desenlace de incierto rescate," *Vanguardia* [Santa Clara, Cuba],

Dec. 1, 1989, p. 4; Roberto Pérez and Luis Aranda, "Shepua y Nyenyea vuelven a la vida," *Vanguardia*, Feb. 4, 1990, p. 3; interviews with Fernández Mell, who headed the group of rescuers, and with Chivás, who was his second-in-command. On Aurino, also interviews with Dreke, Marín, and Morejón Gibert.)

25. Benigno [Dariel Alarcón Ramírez], *Vie et mort*, p. 106. "Lawton" had been Changa's nom de guerre in the war against Batista. His real name was Roberto Sánchez Barthelemi.

26. See Debray, *Loués*, pp. 245-46, and Castañeda, *Compañero*, p. 285. Benigno's account first appeared in 1996 as *Vie et mort de la révolution cubaine* (pp. 101-12 on Zaire) and then, in 1997, in an enlarged Spanish edition, *Memorias de un soldado cubano* (pp. 97-108, 117). I quote from the French edition, except on the one occasion when the quotation appears only in the Spanish edition.

27. Benigno, *Vie et mort*, p. 103; Benigno, *Memorias*, p. 99.

28. Benigno, *Vie et mort*, pp. 107, 111.

29. Four died on June 29 at Bendera: Wagner Moro Pérez (Kawawa), Norberto Pío Pichardo Fortún (Ine), Víctor Valle Bellester (Thetahine), Crisójenes Vinajeras Hernández (Ansurine). Francisco Torriente Acea (Aurino) disappeared near Lulimba on October 14 or 15 as his group retreated after a clash with the mercenaries (see n. 24), and Orlando Puentes Mayeta (Bahasa) died on October 26 of wounds inflicted by mercenaries.

30. Thirteen of these interviews took place before Benigno defected (see the list of interviews in the bibliography).

31. Benigno, "El Che me cambió la vida," *Habanera* (Havana), Jan. 1995, pp. 12-19.

32. See Víctor Dreke, "Tatu: aquel hombre desconocido," *Vanguardia*, Nov. 29, 1989, p. 4, and "'Yo no me voy, primero me muero aquí,'" *Vanguardia*, Nov. 30, 1989, p. 4; Martín Chivás, "Feliz desenlace de incierto rescate," *Vanguardia*, Dec. 1, 1989, p. 4; Roberto Pérez and Luis Aranda, "Shepua y Nyenyea vuelven a la vida," *Vanguardia*, Feb. 4, 1990, p. 3; Luis Monteagudo, "Disparo al rostro de la selva," *Vanguardia*, June 14, 1990, p. 4; Rafael Zerquera, "Kumy habla de Tatu," *Vanguardia*, Oct. 7, 1990, p. 4, and "Una casi desconocida epopeya," *Tribuna* (Havana), Oct. 8, 1990, pp. 4-5; Rómulo Rumbau, "Quince minutos para el tiro," *Vanguardia*, Oct. 24, 1990, p. 4; Arcadio Hernández, "Tatu devuelve el jaque mate," *Vanguardia*, Oct. 25, 1990, p. 4; Catalino Olachea, "Las vivencias de Mafu," *Vanguardia*, Oct. 26, 1990, p. 4; Ramón Muñoz, "'Péganme un tiro y vayanse,'" *Vanguardia*, Dec. 23, 1990, p. 3; Harry Villegas, "El Doctor Tatu," *Vanguardia*, Oct. 8, 1991, p. 2, and "El Che en la memoria," *Trabajadores* (Havana), June 12, 1995, p. 9. See also Barreto, "Camarada Tato"; Carrasco, "Tatu"; Carrasco, "Che"; Carrasco, "El combate"; Freddy Ilanga, "Si repites este nombre te fusilo," *Vanguardia*, June 13, 1991, p. 2.

33. Guevara, "Evaluación del personal a mis ordenes," [Dar-es-Salaam, Dec. 1965 or early 1966], PCH. Che appended a handwritten note explaining

that he had listed the names in the order in which he had jotted them down in his pocket diary. Che considered only those Cubans who had been in Zaire to be members of the column. Therefore his list does not include the personnel of the support group, the two communications experts who were based at the embassy in Dar-es-Salaam and at Kigoma, and the Ministry of the Interior specialists who arrived in October to man the boats. The document was taped by Che, transcribed by Colman Ferrer, and corrected by hand by Che (interviews with Ferrer, Rivalta, and Fernández Padilla).

34. Che Guevara, "Relación nominal," [Dar-es-Salaam, Dec. 1965 or early 1966], PCH. Ferrer transcribed the document (see n. 33).

35. "Columna `Patricio Lumumba': Planilla de control," [1985], PCH. In a bureaucratic mix-up, the document was mistitled. The "Patricio Lumumba" column went to the Congo, not Zaire. The questionnaires, however, have been answered only by the personnel who went to Zaire or assisted Che's column from Tanzania.

36. Benigno is also the source for the imaginary quarrel between Che and Raúl Castro in the spring of 1965 (see chapter 5).

37. Castañeda, Compañero, p. 322; Paulu, "Diario de campaña," entry of Nov. 21, 1965, p. 59.

38. Interviews with Devlin and Hawes; see also Castañeda, Compañero, pp. 322-25. It should also be noted that the chain of command ran from Washington to Devlin in Leopoldville and from there directly to Hawes in the field.

39. Interviews with Fernández Padilla, Dreke, and Fernández Mell; Paulu, "Diario de campaña," entry of Nov. 21, 1965, pp. 58-59; "Informe al Acto," p. 7; Manuel Álvarez, the commander of the group of specialists from the Ministry of the Interior, in Gálvez, El sueño, pp. 290-91.

40. CIA, OCI, "The Situation in the Congo," Feb. 24, 1966, p. 1 quoted, NSFCF, box 85; CIA, OCI, "The Congo since the Mobutu Coup," Feb. 11, 1966, ibid. The United States encouraged the coup. (See Young and Turner, Rise, p. 53. On Mobutu's early contacts with the CIA, see Mahoney, JFK, p. 46.)

41. Paulu, "Diario de campaña," pp. 59-61; interviews with Fernández Padilla, Dreke, Ferrer, Zerquera, Hernández Betancourt, Chaveco, Morejón Gibert, Olachea, Torres, Fernández Mell, Marín, Medina Savigne, Monteagudo, Vaillant.

42. Paulu, "Diario de campaña," entry of Nov. 21, 1965, p. 59.

43. Interview with Ferrer (quoted); Pombo in Báez, Secretos, p. 477. Papi, Pombo (Harry Villegas), and Tuma (Carlos Coello) were three of the four personal aides who were with Che in Zaire. (See chapter 5, n. 30.) The story of the fourth, Sitaini, is discussed later in this chapter.

44. This and the next two paragraphs are based on an interview with Tony Pérez.

45. Interviews with Ferrer, Rivalta, and Fernández Padilla.

46. Castro Hidalgo, Spy, p. 54.

47. Interview with Dreke.

48. Interview with Fernández Mell; Guevara, "Pasajes," p. 160.

49. Interview with Rivalta.

50. Ibid.

51. In addition to the four aides who arrived with Rivalta, the support group included Ferrer, Estrada, Fernández Padilla, the embassy's encoder (Delfín), and four other DGI officers—Sandrino, Marcelo, Braulio Rodríguez, and César Vernier. (Interviews with Fernández Padilla, Rivalta, Estrada, and Ferrer.)

52. Interview with Torres.

53. Guevara, "Pasajes," p. 65.

54. "Informe al Acto," p. 5.

55. Guevara, "Pasajes," p. 103 quoted; interviews with Dreke, Fernández Mell, and Fernández Padilla; Kahama, diary, pp. 10-11.

56. "Mensaje a los Combatientes," Aug. 12, 1965, in Guevara, "Pasajes," pp. 59-60.

57. Guevara, "Pasajes," p. 94.

58. The worst infraction reported in any of the documents in my possession is the theft of a can of meat from the column's reserve supply by two Cubans. As punishment, they were sentenced to three days without food (Paulu, "Diario de campaña," entry of Aug. 6, 1965).

59. Interview with Fernández Mell. Given Cuban sensitivity about the issue, I prefer not to identify the person who first told me about the rajados.

60. Guevara, "Pasajes," pp. 45-46. See also Paulu, "Diario de campaña," p. 16, and the diary of Kahama, p. 11. In August two members of the column left Zaire: Ottu, "who had been sick for some time, and Sitaini, whose hiatus hernia allowed me to end the unpleasant situation created by his being here against his will" (Guevara, "Pasajes," p. 53).

61. Guevara, "Pasajes," pp. 49, 57 (quoted); Paulu, "Diario de campaña," pp. 16, 23, 24; diary of Kahama, p. 12.

62. "Mensaje a los Combatientes," Aug. 12, 1965, in Guevara, "Pasajes," pp. 59-60.

63. Guevara, "Pasajes," p. 75. The figure 128 is from Che's "Evaluación del personal a mis ordenes."

64. Interview with Chumi. I prefer not to give his real name.

65. Guevara, "Evaluación del personal a mis ordenes." The third doctor "rajado" was Fara. "He seemed ashamed of his decision, but he did not change it," Che wrote in "Evaluación." Like the others, Fara continued to work as a doctor.

66. Interview with Chumi. I have copies of three letters written by Chumi to his wife from Guinea-Bissau (dated Dec. 22-28, 1967; Mar. 20, 1968; and June 14, 1968).

67. Guevara, "Pasajes," pp. 158-59.

68. Thus, his evaluation of Fernández Mell noted that "he was overcome by skepticism" ("Evaluación del personal a mis ordenes").

69. Guevara, "Pasajes," p. 159.

70. Ibid., p. 105. The eighty-nine questionnaires in "Columna `Patricio Lumumba': Planilla Central" indicate that 57 percent of the members of the column were members of the PCC.

71. Guevara, "Pasajes," p. 110. See also Paulu, "Diario de campaña," p. 50.

72. Guevara, "Pasajes," pp. 160-61. Kabila seized power in 1997 and swiftly proved Che's prescience.

73. Interviews with Fernández Padilla and Rivalta. Relations between Cuba and China had continued to deteriorate in 1965 and reached an open break in January 1966.

74. See Guevara, "Pasajes," p. 143.

75. "Information über die Lage in Kongo-Leopoldville (Einschätzung der Befreiungsbewegung)," [Nov. 1965], SED, DY30 IVA 2/20/983.

76. Thus a Soviet ship reached Dar-es-Salaam in February 1965, five Soviet planes landed in March, and the Soviet arms freighter *Fizik Lebedev* arrived on April 15. (CIA, OCI, weekly report, "The Situation in the Congo," Mar. 10, Apr. 14 and 21, 1965, NSFCF, box 87; CIA, OCI, "Tanzanian Support for the Congo Rebels," Apr. 7, 1965, ibid.)

77. Interview with Fernández Padilla.

78. Guevara, "Pasajes," p. 126.

79. Interview with Rivalta.

80. Guevara to Castro, Oct. 5, 1965, in Guevara, "Pasajes," pp. 94-95; interview with Fernández Padilla.

81. Guevara, "Pasajes," p. 43.

82. Interview with Ferrer.

83. Haynes to Rostow, June 8, 1966, NSF, Name File, box 3, LBJL.

84. Hamilton to Rostow, Dec. 30, 1966, p. 3, FOIA 1966/1064. A penetrating discussion of the Godley incident is Pachter, "Our Man," pp. 114-18.

85. Quotations from Denney (INR) to SecState, "Trouble Ahead in Our Relations with Mobutu?," Oct. 12, 1966, p. 1, NSFCF, box 85; CIA, DI, "Mobutu and the Congo," June 23, 1967, p. 6, NSFCF, box 86; *NYT*, May 7, 1967, p. 7.

86. Quotations from Rusk to Kinshasa, July 6, 1967, p. 1, NSF, NSC History C-67, box 15, LBJL; McBride (U.S. ambassador, Kinshasa) to SecState, July 8, 1967, p. 1, NSFCF, box 86; Katzenbach, NSC meeting, July 13, 1967, p. 1, NSF, NSC Meeting File, box 2, LBJL.

87. Rostow, memo for president, July 6, 1967, NSF, NSC History, C-67, box 15, LBJL; Palmer to UnderSec, July 11, 1967, FOIA; Amembassy Brussels to SecState, July 29, 1967, FOIA; Rusk to Amembassy Athens, July 29, 1967, FOIA; Palmer to Kohler, Aug. 29, 1967, NSF, Intelligence File, box 2/3, LBJL; "Congo (K) Sitrep, 16 Hours EST, November 2, 1967," NSFCF, box 86.

88. Quotations from DIA, "Performance of the Congolese National Army (ANC) during the Bukavu Engagement," pp. 2, 3, enclosed in Hamilton to Rostow, Dec. 13, 1967, NSFCF, box 86; *NYT*, May 2, 1968, p. 46 (ed.); Rusk to Amembassy Kinshasa, Dec. 22, 1967, FOIA 1999/1963. On the revolt, see CRISP, *Congo 1967*, pp. 349-415; Clarke, *The Congo Mercenary*, pp. 73-78; Mockler, *The Mercenaries*, pp. 178-219. For accounts by mercenary leaders, see Puren, *Mercenary Commander*, pp. 225-319; Schramme, *Le Bataillon Léopard*, pp. 251-351; Lunel, *Denard*, pp. 325-90. On the amnesty, and its bloody aftermath, see also Braeckman, "La saga," p. 142.

89. Quotations from Rostow to Johnson, Apr. 25, 1968, NSFCF, box 86; Humphrey to Johnson, Jan. 12, 1968, pp. 25-26, NSFCF, box 77; "The Department of State during the Administration of President Lyndon B. Johnson, November 1963-January 1969," vol. 1, ch. 5, sec. C 1, n.d., unpaginated, Administrative History of the Department of State, LBJL.

90. CIA, DI, "Some Aspects of Subversion in Africa," Oct. 19, 1967, pp. 5, 6, and 8 quoted, NSFCF, box 78; CIA, DI, "Cuban Meddling in Africa," Mar. 24, 1967, NSFCF, box 19.

CHAPTER EIGHT

1. Interviews with Agramonte (quoted), Urra (quoted), Moracén, and Veitía (both were with Agramonte). The May 20 date is from MINFAR, "Las misiones internacionalistas desarrolladas por las FAR en defensa de la independencia y la soberanía de los pueblos," n.d., p. 15, AIHC (hereafter "Misiones"). For Urra's arrival, see also Amembassy Brazzaville to SecState, May 14, 1965, Pol 17 Cuba-Congo, SNF, NA.

2. Interview with Risquet. My comments on Risquet's personality are based on interviews with him and with a large number of Cubans who know him, including several who do not particularly like him. On Risquet's captivity, see "Causa seguida contra Pedro Oscar Fernández Padilla y Nilo Risket [sic] Valdés por delito de distribuir propaganda subversiva en Matanzas," Fondo Tribunal de Urgencia, Legajo 163, Archivo Histórico Provincial, Matanzas. (For Risquet's torture, see esp. the medical certificate of Jan. 11, 1957, in ibid., p. 9.)

3. Jorge Risquet, note to Piero Gleijeses, Havana, July 22, 1996 (quoted); Lagache in Kalfon, *Che*, p. 441.

4. Quotations from Jorge Risquet, note to Piero Gleijeses, Havana, Aug. 1, 1995, pp. 1-2, and "Discurso pronunciado por Raúl Castro Ruz en acto por el XX aniversario de la construcción de las columnas de combatientes internacionalistas cubanos que cumplieron misiones en el Congo Brazzaville y el Congo Leopoldville," Havana, Nov. 7, 1985, p. 7, ACC.

5. Quotations from interviews with Kindelán and Risquet. My information on the column's arrival in the Congo and its composition is from "Correo de Porfirio recibido 8/3/66," ACC, which lists all the Cuban personnel in the Congo with both their real names and their pseudonyms; Jorge Risquet, "Brizna de paja en la oreja," July 12, 1966, p. 66, ACC (hereafter "Brizna"); Risquet, *El segundo frente*, pp. 29-35; interviews with the following members of the column: Risquet, Kindelán, Urra, Agramonte, Moracén, Hernández Gattorno, Duany, Lemus, Veitía, Galindo, Arsides, Puente Ferro, Álvarez Cambras, Jacas, and Julián Álvarez.

6. Quotations from Foccart, *Tous*, p. 201; FRG embassy Brazzaville to AA, Sept. 16, 1965, p. 2, FRG, AA 90.47/65 - 623; Empson to Brown, Brazzaville, Sept. 24, 1965, FO 371/181988, PRO. See also Belgian embassy Brazzaville to Spaak, Sept. 10, 1965, MAE 14.732.

7. "Brizna," p. 66.

8. Desjeux, "Le Congo," p. 27. For my analysis of the Congo in the years covered in this chapter (1965-68), I rely on the secondary sources listed in chapter 4, n. 16, on Cuban documents, on U.S. reports (until diplomatic relations were suspended in August 1965), on reports from the British embassy in Brazzaville (until relations were broken in December 1965), and on reports from the Belgian and West German embassies. I was particularly impressed with the quality of the West German reports.

9. Quotations from Empson to Brown, Brazzaville, Sept. 20, 1965, FO 371/181676, PRO; Lessing, "Aktenvermerk über ein Gespräch mit dem Premier-Minister der Republik Congo/Brazzaville Herrn Pascal Lissouba am 10 Febr. 1965," Feb. 15, 1965, p. 2, GDR AA, VVS Archiv (VR Kongo); CIA, ONE, "Prospects in Brazzaville," May 17, 1965, p. 6, NSFCF, box 85.

10. Hasslacher (FRG ambassador, Brazzaville) to AA, "Politischer Jahresbericht 1965 über die Republik Congo-Brazzaville," Jan. 7, 1966, p. 9, FRG, AA 90.47 - 692 (hereafter "Bericht [1965]"); interview with Roy Haverkamp, a political officer at the U.S. embassy.

11. Komer to Bundy (quoting Ambassador Henry Koren), Aug. 6, 1965, NSFCF, box 85. See also Koren to SecState, Brazzaville: July 28 (nos. 44 and 45), July 31, Aug. 3, 1965, ibid.; TelConv, Secretary and Ball, Aug. 3, 1965, 6:10 p.m., Ball Papers, box 2, LBJL; TelConv, MacBundy and Ball, Aug. 4, 1965, 12:20 p.m., ibid.; TelConv, Ball and Myerson, Aug. 10, 1965, 6:10 p.m., ibid.; Rusk to Amembassy Brazzaville, Aug. 11, 1965, NSFCF, box 85; Amembassy Brazzaville to SecState, Aug. 13, 1965, ibid.; Le Monde, Aug. 15, 1965, p. 1; La Semaine (Brazzaville), Aug. 22, 1965, p. 3; NYT: Aug. 14, 1965, p. 1; June 7, 1977, p. 6; Nov. 4, p. 5.

12. Quotations from CIA, ONE, "Prospects in Brazzaville," May 17, 1965, p. 7, NSFCF, box 85; La Semaine, Jan. 3, 1965, p. 8 (quoting Massamba-Débat); Lessing, "Aktenvermerk über ein Gespräch mit dem Generalsekretär und amtierenden Aussenminister Herrn Gomez in Brazzaville am 8.2.65," Feb. 15, 1965, p. 2, GDR AA, VVS Archiv (VR Kongo). For interesting comments on the Congolese leaders' "hate and love" relationship with France, see FRG embassy Brazzaville to AA, "Zusammenfassender Bericht über die Republik Congo-Brazzaville seit der Augustrevolution von 1963," Jan. 21, 1965, p. 10 quoted, FRG, AA 90.47/65 - 623 (hereafter "Zusammenfassender Bericht"); "Bericht [1965]," pp. 10-11; FRG embassy Brazzaville to AA, "Politischer Jahresbericht 1966 über die Republik Congo-Brazzaville," Jan. 24, 1967, pp. 13-14, FRG, AA 90.47 - 726 (hereafter "Bericht [1966]").

13. Quotations from CIA, OCI, "Brazzaville's Move to the Left," Oct. 30, 1964, p. 3, NSFCF, box 83; Belgian embassy Brazzaville, "Rapport politique et économique sur le Congo en 1966," Jan. 28, 1967, p. 29, MAE 15.337; Haschke, "Vermerk über ein Gespräch des Genossen Dr. Quilitzsch mit dem Rat der Botschaft Kongos (B), Herrn Bikouta, am 15.3.66," Moscow, Mar. 17, 1966, p. 2, GDR AA, A1167; "Bericht [1965]," pp. 13-14.

14. Quotations from La Semaine, June 27, 1965, p. 3, and Aug. 21, 1966, p. 3. The list of Communist embassies is based on "Zusammenfassender Bericht," p. 8; Bayot (Belgian ambassador, Brazzaville) to Spaak, Apr. 22 and May 25, 1965, MAE 14.732.

15. Hasslacher to AA, July 7, 1966, p. 3 quoted, FRG, AA 90.47 - 549; CIA, DI, "Chinese Communist Activities in Africa," Apr. 30, 1965, FOIA 1977/7A; CIA, ONE, "Prospects in Brazzaville," May 17, 1965, NSFCF, box 85; Amembassy Brazzaville to DOS, June 23, 1965, Pol 17 Congo-USSR, SNF, NA; Koren to SecState, Brazzaville, Aug. 3, 1965, Pol 23-9 Congo, SNF, NA; FRG embassy Brazzaville to AA, Aug. 20, 1965, FRG, AA 90.47/65 - 623, and Oct. 6, 1966, FRG, AA Afrika Allg. 1966 - 692; USDAO [Defense Attaché Office] Cameroon, "Evacuation of Foreign Military Missions," Aug. 6, 1966, NSA; Risquet to Piñeiro, Aug. 15, 1966, ACC; Moracén, "Diario de campaña de Humberto Vazquez Mancevo" (hereafter Moracén, "Diario"), entries of July 27 and 28, 1966; "Brizna," pp. 8, 28; interviews with Urra, Risquet, and Moracén; Foccart, Tous, pp. 233-35.

16. Hasslacher to AA, Oct. 6, 1966, p. 4, FRG, AA Afrika Allg. 1966 - 692.

17. Amembassy Libreville (quoting French officials) to DOS, June 11, 1966, Pol 23 Congo, SNF, NA; Dehennin (Belgian chargé, Brazzaville) to Harmel, June 7, 1966, MAE 15.028.

18. NYT, Mar. 13, 1966, p. 21.

19. Interviews with the members of the column listed in n. 5.

20. Quotations from FRG embassy Brazzaville to AA, Apr. 28, 1967, FRG, AA 90.47 - 726, and Amembassy Kinshasa to DOS, May 9, 1968, p. 3 (quoting the Belgian ambassador in Brazzaville), Pol 2 Congo, NA. See also "Bericht [1965]"; FRG embassy Brazzaville to AA: Oct. 12, 1965, FRG, AA 90.47 - 623; Sept. 8, 1966, FRG, AA 90.47 - 687; Oct. 6, 1966, FRG, AA Afrika Allg. 1966 - 692; Belgian embassy Brazzaville to MAE, July 22, 1966, MAE 15.028; Amembassy Kinshasa to SecState, Jan. 20, 1967, Pol Congo, SNF, NA; CIA, DI, "Cuban Meddling in Africa," Mar. 24, 1967, p. 5, NSFCF, box 19; DOS, "Cuban presence in Congo (Brazzaville)," May 25, 1967, Pol 2 Congo, SNF, NA.

21. Dipanda (Brazzaville), Feb. 5, 1966, p. 6. See also FRG embassy Brazzaville to AA, Apr. 22, 1966, FRG, AA 90.47 - 686; Dehennin to Spaak, Mar. 5 and 7, 1966, MAE 15.028 (all Dehennin reports are from Brazzaville); "Bericht [1966]," p. 11; Amembassy Leopoldville to SecState, Apr. 15, 1966, Pol 15 Congo, SNF, NA. The army figure is from CIA, ONE, "Prospects in Brazzaville," May 17, 1965, NSFCF, box 85.

22. Interviews with Kindelán, Urra, and Risquet.

23. "Correo de Porfirio recibido 8/3/66," ACC; "Brizna," pp. 4, 12; interviews with Drs. Julián Álvarez, Puente Ferro, Jacas, and Álvarez Cambras; USRO/Paris to SecState, Feb. 10, 1964, Pol Congo-Cuba, SNF, NA; Granma (Havana), July 5, 1966, p. 12.

24. The account in this and the next paragraph is based on my interview with Julián Álvarez. Confirmed in all the essential points by interviews with Álvarez Cambras and Jacas.

25. Interviews with Puente Ferro, Álvarez Cambras (who married the daughter of one of the French doctors), Agramonte, and Urra; FRG embassy Brazzaville to AA, July 7, 1966, FRG, AA 90.47 - 549; "Brizna," pp. 16, 26; *La Semaine*, Feb. 28, 1965, p. 2; *NYT*, Mar. 6, 1965, p. 2; Bayot to Spaak, Brazzaville, June 1, 1965, MAE 14.732; Dehennin to Spaak, Dec. 31, 1965, ibid. (according to this report there were three, not two North Vietnamese doctors). The 850,000 figure is from "Bericht [1965]," p. 15.

26. Interviews with doctors Puente Ferro (quoted), Álvarez Cambras, and Julián Álvarez, and with Estrada and Duany, two DGI officers who participated in the operation. See also Dehennin to Spaak, Sept. 16 and Oct. 9, 1965, MAE 14.732; Empresa Cubana de Navegación, "Manifiesto de pasajeros congoleses," Havana, n.d., ACC; USRO/Paris to SecState, Jan. 28 and Feb. 10, 1966, Pol Congo-Cuba, SNF, NA; J' Transporte U/M 1546 to J' Servicios U/M 1546, Havana, Feb. 15, 1966; Estado Mayor General de las Fuerzas Armadas Revolucionarias, "Relación del personal especial que se encuentra en El Cano," Feb. 24, 1966; "Cuban Subversive Activities in Africa," enclosed in Smith (DDCI) to Ropa, Aug. 10, 1966, NSF, Files of Edward Hamilton, box 1/3, LBJL; CIA, DI, "Cuban Meddling in Africa," Mar. 24, 1967, FOIA 605/1996; Luis Hernández and Félix López, "Africa mía," *Juventud Rebelde* (Havana), Dec. 3, 1995, pp. 8-9.

27. Interviews with Estrada and Dreke; FRG embassy Brazzaville to AA, June 16, 1967, p. 1 quoted, and July 6, 1967, FRG, AA 90.47 - 726; "Bericht [1966]," p. 11; DOS to U.S. embassies Accra et al., Feb. 2, 1967, Pol Congo-US, SNF, NA.

28. Interview with Congolese scholarship student Oguemby. For the number of students in 1969, see "Relación de becarios de Africa que cursan estudios en nuestro país," Dec. 4, 1969, PCH. For the number of doctors, see "Listado de becarios extranjeros (por país)," archives of the Ministerio de Salud Pública, Havana. According to Congolese sources, there were sixty-one Congolese scholarship students in Cuba in 1970-71. Next to the USSR, Cuba gave the most scholarships to Congolese students (Eliou, *La formation*, pp. 174-84; Eliou, "La fuite," pp. 570, 574).

29. Quotations from *La Semaine*, Dec. 5, 1965, p. 8, and interview with Álvarez Cambras.

30. Helenio Ferrer and Rodolfo Puente Ferro to Machado Ventura, May 19, 1966, p. 2, PCH.

31. Helenio Ferrer, "Informe sobre campaña de vacunación (Continuación)," May 27, 1966, PCH; [Puente Ferro and Ferrer], "Projet de programme de vaccination contre la polyomelite dans la république du Congo-Brazzaville," n.d., ibid.; [Puente Ferro and Ferrer], "Quelques aspects du déroulement du programme de vaccination," n.d., ibid.

32. Quotations from Helenio Ferrer, "Informe sobre campaña de vacunación (Continuación)," June 3, 1966, p. 2, PCH, and *Bulletin quotidien de l'Agence Congolaise d'Information*, June 11, 1966, PCH. See also Ferrer to Machado Ventura, June 27, 1966, PCH, and Dehennin to Harmel, June 7, 1966, MAE 15.028. Also useful were interviews with Drs. Puente Ferro, Julián Álvarez, Jacas, and Álvarez Cambras, and with

Arsides, a Cuban soldier who helped administer the vaccine.

33. *Dipanda*, Aug. 6, 1966, p. 6.

34. The best secondary sources are Decalo, *Coups*, pp. 62-63; Kissita, *Congo*, pp. 80-81; "Congo Brazzaville: le mystère s'épanouit," *Le Mois en Afrique*, Sept. 1966, pp. 30-34. The best press coverage is by *Le Monde* and *Le Courrier d'Afrique* (Kinshasa). U.S. government reports provide only secondhand information because there was no U.S. embassy in the country.

35. Quotations from "Brizna," pp. 2 and 6, and from interview with Álvarez Cambras. Interview with Risquet.

36. "Brizna," p. 10 quoted; Amembassy Leopoldville to SecState, June 28, 1966, FOIA; Dehennin to Harmel, July 1, 1965, MAE 15.028; FRG embassy Brazzaville to AA, July 8, 1966, FRG, AA 90.47 - 686.

37. Interviews with Álvarez Cambras (quoted) and Lemus, who was the second-in-command at the radio; Dehennin to MAE, June 29, 1965, MAE 15.028; Dehennin to Harmel, July 1, 1965, ibid.; FRG embassy Brazzaville to AA, July 8, 1966, FRG, AA 90.47 - 686.

38. "Brizna," pp. 25 (quoted) and 61; FRG embassy Brazzaville to AA, July 4 and 8, 1966, FRG, AA 90.47 - 686; Dehennin to Harmel, July 1 and 8, 1966, MAE 15.028; *Dipanda*, July 9, 1966, p. 5; *Le Courrier d'Afrique*, July 4, 1966, p. 2, and Aug. 12, p. 5.

39. Quoted in "Brizna," pp. 43 and 53.

40. Quotations from Dehennin to MAE, July 4, 1966, MAE 15.028; FRG embassy Brazzaville to AA, June 30, 1966, FRG, AA 90.47 - 686; *Le Monde*, June 30, 1966, p. 5; Moracén, "Diario," entry of July 1, 1966.

41. "Brizna," pp. 28, 30.

42. Ibid., pp. 46-47.

43. Belgian embassy Brazzaville, "Situation à Brazzaville," June 30, 1966, MAE 15.028. See also FRG embassy Brazzaville to AA, July 7, 1966, FRG, AA 90.47 - 549. (According to this report, the total strength of the Congolese army was 1,600 men, all in the capital except for one unit in Pointe Noire.)

44. Quotations from FRG embassy Brazzaville to AA, July 8, 1966, p. 5, FRG, AA 90.47 - 686; *Le Monde*, July 5, 1966, p. 6; *Le Courrier d'Afrique*, July 4, 1966, p. 1.

45. "Brizna," pp. 53, 57-59; *Dipanda*, July 9, 1966, p. 6; Ngouabi, *Vers la construction*, pp. 16-17.

46. Quotations from Hunger, "Aktenvermerk über ein Gespräch des Genossen Seidel mit dem stellvertretenden Leiter der II. afrikanischen Abteilung des MID, Genossen Gnedych, am 20. September 1966," Moscow, Sept. 21, 1966, p. 3, GDR AA, A1167; Hasslacher to AA, July 8, 1966, p. 7, FRG, AA 90.47 - 686; Dehennin to Harmel, July 8, 1966, MAE 15.028; French ambassador in Brazzaville quoted in Godley to DOS, Sept. 1, 1966, p. 1, Pol 23 Congo, SNF, NA; Godley to DOS, July 14, 1966, Pol 23-9 Congo, SNF, NA.

47. Quotations from "Brizna," p. 63, and *Le Monde*, July 6, 1966, p. 5.

48. Quotations from Risquet to Piñeiro, Aug. 15, 1966, p. 1, ACC; USDAO [Defense Attaché Office] Cameroon, "Evacuation of Foreign Military Missions," Aug. 6, 1966, p. 1, NSA; Risquet to Piñeiro, Aug. 15, 1966, p. 3, ACC. See also Amembassy Paris to SecState, July 26, 1966, Pol 23-9 Congo, SNF, NA.

49. *Dipanda*, July 9, 1966, p. 2.

50. Quotations from Decalo, *Coups*, p. 58; "Brizna," pp. 59-60; interview with Urra.

51. *Le Courrier d'Afrique*, Aug. 19, 1966, p. 3.

52. Interview with Duany. On the UPC, see Eyinga, *L'U.P.C.*; Chaffard, *Les carnets*, 2:343-429; Gaillard, *Le Cameroun*; Joseph, *Radical Nationalism*.

53. Risquet to Gallego [Piñeiro], Aug. 15, 1966, ACC; Porfirio [Risquet] to Piñeiro, enclosed in Piñeiro to Cienfuegos, Sept. 13, 1966, ACC; Risquet, *El segundo frente*, pp. 161-82.

54. "Versión taquigráfica de la reunión en el EMG con el comp. Risquet. (Enero 18/1967)," enclosed in Ulises to Tomassevich, Jan. 18, 1967, ACC (hereafter "Versión"); Moya [Dreke] to Cienfuegos, Jan. 19, 1967, ACC; Risquet, *El segundo frente*, pp. 192-96.

55. Olivares to Castro, Moscow, n.d., enclosed in Piñeiro to Castro, Nov. 11, 1966, ACC.

56. About sixty Cubans remained behind; they were later reinforced by fifty more. See Borodin (captain, *Nadezhda Krupskaya*) and Risquet, "Acte," Pointe Noire, Dec. 15, 1966, ACC; "Brizna," pp. 66-68; "Relación del personal que se queda," n.d., ACC; Porfirio [Risquet] to Piñeiro et al., Dec. 20, 1966, ACC; "Versión," p. 1.

57. Lúcio Lara, "A história do MPLA," n.d., p. 86 (hereafter Lara, "História").

58. Ibid., pp. 49-50; Marcum, *Angolan Revolution*, 1:211-14, 2:44-45; Davezies, *Les Angolais*, pp. 30-33; Hughes (INR) to SecState, "OAU May Withdraw Recognition from Angolan Government in Exile," Mar. 12, 1968, Pol 30-2 Ang, SNF, NA; *Le Monde*, July 22, 1964, p. 4; Rossi, *Pour*, p. 70.

59. "Roberto Holden m'a dit," *Révolution Africaine* (Algiers), Aug. 29, 1964, p. 13.

60. Lara, "História," p. 85.

61. Kiluanji, *Trajectória*, p. 26. See also Carreira, *O Pensamento*, pp. 63-64; Empson to Wilson, Brazzaville, Jan. 29, 1965, FO 371/181970, PRO; Amconsul Luanda to DOS, Feb. 3, 1965, Pol 2 Ang, SNF, NA; "Chronology of Insurgent Activity in Cabinda," enclosed in Amcongen Luanda to DOS, Oct. 20, 1967, Pol 23-9 Ang, SNF, NA.

62. Quotations from interview with Moracén. See also Moracén, "Diario," entries of June 10, 12, 16, 17, 18, 19, 1965; also useful were interviews with Veitía (another of the six), Lúcio Lara, and MPLA guerrillas Tiro, Gato, and Kiluanji. I have copies of the identity cards of Veitía (Reinaldo Goncalves Lombelo) and Moracén (Humberto Macedo Vasques).

63. Quotations from Moracén, "Diario," entry of Sept. 1965, and interview with Moracén.

64. Interview with Lúcio Lara. In addition to Lara, my sources on the operation include the report by the Cuban officer in charge: Fernando Galindo, "A los compañeros: Cmdte. Rolando Kindelán [y] Cap. Jorge Risquet Valdes," Jan. 1, 1966, ACC (hereafter,

Galindo, "A los compañeros"); interviews with Angolan participants (Tiro, Gato, and Kiluanji—the last participated only in the planning); with Cuban participants (Galindo, Moracén, Veitía, Arsides, Duany, Julián Álvarez, Jacas, and Risquet—the last participated only in the planning).

65. Quotations from interviews with Lúcio Lara and Galindo.

66. Quotations from interviews with Lúcio Lara and Gato, and from Colonel Jeffries, U.S. Army attaché in Lisbon, "Cubans Reportedly with MPLA in Congo (B)," May 4, 1966, p. 2, NSA. My figure for the total strength of the MPLA is based on conversations with Moracén, Risquet, Lúcio Lara, Gato, Tiro, Kiluanji, and on Moracén, "Diario," esp. entry of June 16, 1965.

67. Quotations from Galindo, "A los compañeros," pp. 3, 4, 8.

68. Quotations from Mabeko Tali (the foremost historian of the MPLA), "Dissidences," p. 82, and Rufo [Kindelán] to Piñeiro, [early June], enclosed in Piñeiro to Cienfuegos, June 16, 1966, p. 3, ACC. On the MPLA's guerrilla war in Cabinda in 1965, see also [Portugal], Estado-Maior do Exército, "O caso de Angola," p. 21; Jika (an MPLA commander who fought in Cabinda), *Reflexões*, p. 65; Marcum, *Angolan Revolution*, 2:174-76; Summ (U.S. consul general, Luanda) to DOS, Oct. 30, 1965, Pol 2 Ang, SNF, NA. *Mayombe*, a novel by a former guerrilla, Pepetela, subtly addresses the ethnic tensions and other difficulties that the MPLA faced in Cabinda.

69. Quotations from interview with Risquet and from Rufo [Kindelán] to Piñeiro, [early June], p. 3, enclosed in Piñeiro to Cienfuegos, June 16, 1966, ACC. On the opening of the Third Region, see Heimer, *Entkolonisierungskonflikt*, pp. 104-8; Davidson, *Eye*, pp. 234-47; Barnett, *The Making*, pp. 86-105.

70. Interviews with Moracén and Risquet; Moracén, "Diario," entries of May 8, 12, 13, 1966.

71. Lara, "História," pp. 88-89. For the resumption of the ferry crossings, see *Le Courrier d'Afrique*, Nov. 5, 1965, p. 1, and Nov. 8, p. 1.

72. Rufo [Kindelán] to Piñeiro, [early June], enclosed in Piñeiro to Cienfuegos, June 16, 1966, p. 1 quoted, ACC; interviews with Lúcio Lara and Kiluanji (the column's second-in-command).

73. Quotations from Lara, "História," p. 89, and from interviews with Tiro (one of the column's officers) and Kiluanji. See also Moracén, "Diario," entries of June 2 through July 15, 1966, and Kiluanji, *Trajectória*, pp. 33-39. Also interviews with Moracén, Kindelán, and Lúcio Lara. For the August 16 date, see Comandante Camilo "Monstruo" to Comité Director of the MPLA, Oct. 8, 1966 (Spanish translation), enclosed in Piñeiro to Cienfuegos, Nov. 24, 1966, ACC (hereafter "Monstruo").

74. "Monstruo," pp. 1-2. See also [Portugal], Estado-Maior do Exército, "O caso de Angola," p. 19; Risquet to Piñeiro, Nov. 18, 1966, enclosed in Piñeiro to Cienfuegos, Nov. 24, 1966, ACC; FRG consulate Luanda to AA, Feb. 27, 1967, FRG, AA 90.23; Amcongen Luanda to DOS, Aug. 23, 1967, Pol 23-9 Ang, SNF, NA; Amconsul Luanda to DOS, Mar. 7, 1968, ibid.; Kiluanji, *Trajectória*, pp. 22, 40-48;

Davezies, *La guerre*, pp. 66-69, 85-88, 107-9; Marcum, *Angolan Revolution*, 2:176; José Antunes, *A guerra*, 2:994-95.

75. Lara, "História," p. 88.

76. "Monstruo," p. 5.

77. Quotations from diary of Irene Cohen, Nov. 20, [1966], PCH, and from Jiménez Rodríguez, *Heroínas*, p. 78; also interview with Ludy Kissassunda (one of the officers of the Kamy); Risquet to Piñeiro, Nov. 18, 1966, enclosed in Piñeiro to Cienfuegos, Nov. 24, 1966, ACC; "Misiones," p. 18.

78. Interview with Ludy Kissassunda. See also Neto, "Informe," in *Primer Congreso*, p. 8; Lara, "História," p. 96; Jiménez Rodríguez, *Heroínas*, pp. 78-82; Kiluanji, *Trajectória*, pp. 57-62.

79. Quotations from interview with Ludy Kissassunda and *Diário da Manha* (Lisbon), Mar. 28, 1967, p. 8. The Kinshasa press reported the arrest of the group and printed the names of the five women (*Courrier d'Afrique*, Mar. 4 and 6, 1967, both p. 1). See also Lara, "História," pp. 96-97; Amembassy Kinshasa to DOS, Mar. 6, 1967, Pol 30 Ang, SNF, NA; FRG embassy Brazzaville to AA, Mar. 9, 1967, FRG, AA 90.23; Jiménez Rodríguez, *Heroínas*, pp. 61-69, 89-90; Marcum, *Angolan Revolution*, 2:198.

80. Orlog (an officer of the Bomboko), "Memórias: Luta de Libertação Nacional," [1978 or 1979], pp. 2-3, private collection, Luanda (hereafter Orlog, "Memórias"); interviews with Moracén and Bomboko members Rui de Matos, Xiyetu, and Gato; transcript of the interrogation of Bomboko member Fernando Diogo, Apr. 11, 1969, enclosed in Amconsul Luanda to DOS, May 27, 1969, Pol 23 Ang, SNF, NA (hereafter "Diogo").

81. Interview with Xiyetu.

82. Quotations from Rui de Matos, quoted in Barnett, *The Making*, p. 78, and from interviews with Rui de Matos and Gato. Also interview with Xiyetu; "Diogo"; Lara, "História," pp. 100-101; Zengo, *Tragédia*, pp. 35-38, 59-60 (Zengo was a member of the MPLA underground in Kinshasa); FRG embassy Kinshasa to AA, Dec. 6, 1966, FRG, AA Portug. Gebiete; *Courrier d'Afrique*. Feb. 1, 1967, p. 1; Feb. 3, p. 1; Mar. 2, p. 1; *Diário da Manha*, Feb. 4, 1967, p. 3; FRG embassy Brazzaville to AA, Mar. 13, 1967, FRG, AA 90.23; Hansenne (Belgian chargé, Brazzaville) to Harmel, Mar. 14, 1967, MAE 15.337.

83. Quotations from Orlog, "Memórias," p. 4; Lara, "História," p. 102; interview with Lúcio Lara. Also interviews with Gato, Rui de Matos, and Xiyetu; "Diogo"; transcript of the interrogation of Bomboko member Felix Lembe, Feb. 28, 1969, enclosed in Amconsul Luanda to DOS, May 27, 1969, Pol 23 Ang, SNF, NA (hereafter "Lembe," followed by date of interrogation); Barnett, *The Making*, pp. 78-82; *La Semaine*, Jan. 14, 1968, p. 6, and Aug. 4, p. 5; *Granma*, Nov. 9, 1968, p. 7; Zengo, *Tragédia*, pp. 61-70.

84. Interviews with Lara, Xiyetu, Rui de Matos, and Gato; Orlog, "Memórias," p. 6; "Diogo"; "Lembe," Apr. 14, 1969; Zengo, *Tragédia*, pp. 71-82; Lara, "História," p. 103.

85. "Relación del personal que se queda," n.d.; interviews with Moracén, Lemus, and Agramonte; "Rap-

port-1967," p. 6; Amembassy Paris to SecState, Feb. 23, 1968, Pol 30-2 Ang, SNF, NA; Metten (Belgian chargé, Brazzaville) to Harmel, Aug. 9, 1968, MAE 15.337.

86. Emond (Belgian ambassador, Brazzaville) to Harmel, Nov. 13, 1968, MAE 15.337; Hughes (INR) to SecState, "Congo-Brazzaville's Provisional Regime Digs In," Dec. 3, 1968, p. 2 quoted, Pol 15 Congo, SNF, NA.

87. Quotations from Porfirio [Risquet] to Piñeiro, p. 3, enclosed in Piñeiro to Cienfuegos, Sept. 13, 1966, ACC, and from interviews with Kindelán and Galindo.

88. Dehennin to MAE, Oct. 18, 1965, p. 2 quoted, MAE 14.732. On the lack of relations between the two columns, interviews with Dreke, Fernández Mell, Fernández Padilla, and Risquet.

89. On the Mukwidi operation: "Versión," pp. 20-25; Risquet, *El segundo frente*, p. 256; interviews with Moracén, Montero, Risquet, and Julián Álvarez, who doubled as the doctor and political adviser of Mukwidi's group. On Mukwidi, see Martens, *Pierre Mulele*, pp. 160-61, 272-74, 305-8, 318-24.

90. Interviews with Montero (quoted), Risquet, Moracén, Urra, Agramonte, Lemus, and DGI officers Estrada and Cárdenas; Enrique Montero, "Sobre el tapiz rojo," PCH; "Versión," p. 24.

91. For Castro's frustration, see Neto, quoted in García Lara (Cuban chargé, Brazzaville) to Roa, Mar. 15, 1972, PCH, and Mabeko Tali, "Dissidences," p. 348. See also chapter 11.

92. Interviews with Kiluanji and Tiro. See also Lara, "História," p. 125; Massop (Cuban chargé, Dar-es-Salaam) to Cienfuegos, June 14, 1974; Mabeko Tali, "Dissidences," pp. 303-4. On life in the First Region from late 1966 through the end of the war, see Kiluanji, *Trajectória*, pp. 62-122.

CHAPTER NINE

1. Comandante Reinerio Jiménez (quoting Osmany Cienfuegos), in "Versión taquigráfica de la reunión en el EMG con el comp. Risquet. (Enero 18/1967)," p. 18, enclosed in Ulises to Tomassevich, Jan. 18, 1967, ACC (hereafter "Versión").

2. INR, "Africa: Prospects for Liberation from White Minority Regimes," Sept. 22, 1971, p. 8, Pol 13 Afr, SNF, NA. See also Bennett (U.S. ambassador, Lisbon) to DOS, Apr. 3, 1968, FOIA 1982/0392; Brown (U.S. ambassador, Dakar) to DOS, Jan. 23, 1969, Pol Port Guin, SNF, NA; Bennett to SecState, July 16, 1969, FOIA 1983/0449; Hughes (INR), "Portuguese Guinea: Talks about Talks," Mar. 3, 1970, FOIA 1982/ 1049; "Portuguese Guinea: Guidelines for Policy," enclosed in Irwin to Amembassy Lisbon, Oct. 2, 1970, FOIA 1982/1879; "Policy Planning Memorandum No. 1," enclosed in DOS to All African Diplomatic Posts, Lisbon, London, Paris, Rome, Dec. 2, 1971, Pol 1 Afr-US, SNF, NA; INR, "Portuguese Guinea: New Weapon Heightens Level of Combat," June 5, 1973, Pol 13-9 Port Guin, SNF, NA.

3. Piñeiro, in "Versión," p. 18. The best studies on the war of independence in Guinea-Bissau are Rudebeck, *Guinea-Bissau*; Chabal, *Amílcar Cabral*; Dhada, *Warriors*; José Antunes, *A guerra*. Of the many

accounts by journalists, the most important are Davidson, *No Fist*, Ledda, *Una rivoluzione*, Chaliand, *Lutte*, Venter, *Portugal's Guerrilla War*. The first three are sympathetic to the rebels, the last to the Portuguese. The literature on the war in Guinea-Bissau virtually overlooks the Cuban contribution, except for a cursory discussion by Oscar Oramas, who was Cuba's ambassador in Conakry in 1966-73 (Oramas, *Amílcar Cabral*, pp. 81-95).

4. Chabal, "People's War," p. 112; Entralgo to Roa, Dec. 13, 1963, in "Ayuda brindada por la República de Cuba al Partido Africano por la Independencia de Guinea y las Islas de Cabo Verde (PAIGC)," p. 5 (hereafter "Ayuda"); Brown to DOS, Dakar, Jan. 23, 1969, p. 6, Pol Port Guin, SNF, NA.

5. Chabal, *Amílcar Cabral*, p. 169. See also Chilcote, *Amílcar Cabral's Revolutionary Theory*, pp. 23-88; Mkandla, "The Thought"; McCulloch, *In the Twilight*.

6. Quotations from interview with Estrada and from Chabal, *Amílcar Cabral*, p. 98.

7. "Ayuda," pp. 2-6. Quotations are from Aug. 22, 1963, cable by Chargé Carballo and Dec. 13, 1963, cable by Ambassador Entralgo.

8. *Nô Pintcha* (Bissau), Oct. 9, 1975, p. 5.

9. CINCLANT to AIO Eight Four, May 1965, NSA.

10. Luís Cabral, *Crónica*, pp. 251-52 quoted; interviews with Dreke, who in 1966 headed the special unit that was in charge of training, and with Monteiro Santos, one of the Cape Verdeans. Two of the Cape Verdeans wrote about their experiences: Agnelo Dantas, "O primeiro juramento dos combatentes cabo-verdianos," *Voz di Povo* (Praia, Cape Verde), Jan. 16, 1988, p. 5, and Júlio de Carvalho, "Nunca é desejável que a intervenção policial sea repressiva," *Voz di Povo*, Jan. 30, 1988, p. 6. See also "15 de Janeiro: um marco importante da nossa história," *Voz di Povo*, Jan. 16, 1988, p. 11; Cardoso, *O partido*, pp. 18-19.

11. Quotations from INR, "Portuguese Guinea: What Chance for Negotiated Settlement?," Dec. 9, 1970, p. 4, Pol 10 Port, SNF, NA, and interview with Risquet. For Cabral's address, see Amílcar Cabral, *Guinée "Portugaise,"* pp. 41-62.

12. Interviews with Oramas and Vasco Cabral, who was a member of the five-man PAIGC delegation.

13. Luís Cabral, *Crónica*, p. 251.

14. Interview with Oramas.

15. X to M, [late 1965], quoted in "Ayuda," p. 7; interview with Oramas.

16. "Ayuda," pp. 12-14.

17. Interview with Oramas.

18. See *Revolución* (Havana), Oct. 14 (p. 16 quoted), 15, 17, 1960.

19. DOS, MemoConv (Bangoura, Rusk, et al.), Nov. 2, 1964, p. 1 quoted, Pol Cuba-Guin, SNF, NA. On Sékou Touré's foreign policy, see Leimgruber, *Kalter Krieg*, pp. 213-57; Camara, *La Guinée*, pp. 115-18, 130-252; Rivière, "La politique"; Harshe, "Non-Alignement"; Attwood, *Reds*, pp. 11-132.

20. Interview with Oramas; *Horoya* (Conakry), May 3, 1966, p. 1.

21. Interview with Galarza (quoted); "Ayuda," pp. 14-15.

22. Luís Cabral, *Crónica*, p. 252 quoted; "Ayuda," p. 15; interviews with Salavarría, who was on the plane, and with Galarza, Pina (Alfonso Pérez Morales), Mesa, and Drs. Camacho and Peraza, who were on the *Lidia Doce*, Orestes Carballo, "Dos fechas en una vida," *Vanguardia* (Santa Clara, Cuba), Nov. 30, 1990, p. 4.

23. "Ayuda," pp. 14-17.

24. Quotations from Luís Cabral, *Crónica*, p. 252, and Erasmo Vidiaux, "Diario de Vera," entry of Mar. 18, 1967, PCH. "Vera" was Vidiaux's nom de guerre.

25. Interviews with Galarza (quoted), Oramas, Dreke (head of mission, 1967-68), and Montero (head of mission, 1969-70). For the PAIGC's release of Portuguese prisoners, see *Dakar-Matin*, Mar. 16, 1968, p. 3; Dec. 13, p. 1; Dec. 28, p. 1; *El Moudjahid* (Algiers), Aug. 19, 1969, p. 1; *Le Monde*, Aug. 20, 1969, p. 5.

26. Quotations from CIA, DI, "Cuban Meddling in Africa," Mar. 24, 1967, p. 4, FOIA 1996/605, and interview with McIlvaine. See also Amembassy Conakry to SecState, July 27 and Aug. 11, 1966, Pol 30 Ghana, SNF, NA; "Cuban Subversive Activities in Africa," enclosed in Smith (DDCI) to Ropa, Aug. 10, 1966, NSF, Files of Edward Hamilton, box 1/3, LBJL; CIA, DI, "Some Aspects of Subversion in Africa," Oct. 19, 1967, NSFCF, box 78; CIA, NIE, "The Liberation Movements of Southern Africa," Nov. 24, 1967, NSF, NIE, box 8, LBJL; Amembassy Dakar to DOS, Sept. 13, 1968, and Jan. 23, 1969, Pol 13-9 Port Guin, SNF, NA; Amembassy Lisbon to U.S. Mission NATO, June 12, 1969, FOIA 1983/0447; Sonnenfeldt, memo for the record (Kissinger, Rui Patricio), Nov. 19, 1970, NSCF: Portugal, box 701, NP; INR, "Africa: Prospects for Liberation from White Minority Regimes," Sept. 22, 1971, Pol 13 Afr, SNF, NA; Knight (U.S. ambassador, Lisbon) to DOS, Oct. 19, 1971, FOIA 1982/1889, and Jan. 7, 1972, FOIA 1982/2672; INR, "Portuguese Africa: Growing Western Support for Liberation Movements," Aug. 21, 1972, Pol 13 Ang, SNF, NA.

27. Interviews with Pina, Mané, and Oramas. Artemio was probably chosen because the DGI wanted an intelligence officer to head the group (interview with Dreke).

28. Aurelio Ricard [Artemio] to Moya [Dreke], Havana, May 8, 1967, p. 3, PCH, and Moya to Artemio, Conakry, May 30, 1967, PCH.

29. Interviews with Mané (quoted), and with the Cubans Salavarría, Mesa, and Estrada (all of whom participated in the attack); MINFAR, "Las misiones internacionalistas desarrolladas por las FAR en defensa de la independencia y la soberanía de los pueblos," n.d., p. 20, AIHC (hereafter "Misiones").

30. Interview with Oramas.

31. Interview with Dreke (quoted); "Misiones," p. 21.

32. Interviews with Vidiaux (quoted) and Dreke.

33. Interview with Vidiaux.

34. Interviews with Dreke, Vidiaux, and Batista. See also "Ayuda," p. 20.

35. Interviews with Batista, Mané, Nino (João Bernardo Vieira), and Dreke.

36. "Ayuda," pp. 18, 20; interview with Dreke. In April 1967, 108 Cubans were attached to the MMCG, 38 of whom had come to train the militia of Guinea at Touré's request. "We thought there might soon be a military coup against Sékou Touré and if he were overthrown, the PAIGC would lose its rear guard." The project, however, was short-lived: the mercurial Touré soon lost interest, and in 1968 the Cuban instructors returned to Havana. (Interviews with Dreke [quoted], Oramas, Vidiaux, Estrada, and with the instructors Veranes and Vaillant. See [MMCG], "Plan de trabajo," Oct. 27, 1966, PCH; Moya to Jiménez, [late spring 1967], PCH; MINFAR, "Grupos y lugares donde se desarrolla la instrucción de milicia en la república de Guinea," Feb. 28, 1968, PCH.)

37. Moya to Ulises [Estrada], Conakry, Oct. 16, 1967, PCH.

38. Brown to DOS, Dakar, Jan. 3, 1969, pp. 2-3, Pol 19 Port Guin, SNF, NA. The United States had no representatives in Guinea-Bissau. Information on the war was gathered primarily by the U.S. embassies in Lisbon and Dakar.

39. Venter, *Portugal's Guerrilla War*, p. 15.

40. Brown to DOS, Dakar, Jan. 3, 1969, p. 4, Pol 19 Port Guin, SNF, NA.

41. *Diário de Notícias* (Lisbon), Nov. 30, 1969, p. 15.

42. Quotations from Hughes (INR) to SecState, "Portuguese Guinea: Peace Talks in the Offing?," Mar. 25, 1969, p. 1, FOIA 1982/1027, and from Chabal, *Amílcar Cabral*, p. 94.

43. Quotations from Pires, "Os antigos," pp. 8-9; Brown to DOS, Dakar, July 10, 1969, Pol 12-9 Port Guin, SNF, NA; Amílcar Cabral, quoted in "Stenographische Niederschrift der Beratung der Parteidelegation des ZK der SED unter der Leitung des Genossen Gerhard Grüneberg mit der Delegation der Afrikanischen Unabhängigkeitspartei Guineas und der Kapverdischen Inseln (PAIGC) unter der Leitung des Generalsekretärs der PAIGC, Amílcar Cabral, im Hause des ZK der SED am Donnerstag, dem 26.10.1972," Berlin, p. 6, SED, DY30 JIV 2/201/929; INR, "Portuguese Guinea: What Chance for Negotiated Settlement?," Dec. 9, 1970, p. 2, Pol 10 Port, SNF, NA.

44. Quotations from Fabião, "A descolonização," p. 308, and Spínola to Caetano, Nov. 11, 1970, in José Antunes, *Cartas*, 1:149. Alpoim Calvão, the Portuguese officer in charge of the operation, confirmed that had Cabral been in Conakry, "he would definitely have been killed." (*Público* [Lisbon], May 21, 1991, p. 19. See also Calvão, *De Conakry*, pp. 51-86.)

45. Yost to SecState, Nov. 8, 1970, p. 2, FOIA 1982/2654.

46. For Yost's statement, see United Nations, Security Council Official Records, 1563rd meeting, Dec. 8, 1970, pp. 5-7.

47. Quotations from Venter, *Portugal's Guerrilla War*, pp. 49, 80; Knight to DOS, Lisbon, Oct. 19, 1971, p. 3, FOIA 1982/1889; "Policy Planning Memorandum No. 1," p. 9, enclosed in DOS to All African Diplomatic Posts, Lisbon, London, Paris, Rome, Dec. 2, 1971, Pol 1 Afr-US, SNF, NA.

48. Sitkoff, *The Struggle*, p. 185.

49. For this and the next paragraph, interviews with Estrada (quoted), Dreke, Oramas, and DGI officer Cárdenas. (Amílcar Cabral told Oramas and Dreke of Carmichael's plans.) On Carmichael's trip to Cuba, Vietnam, and Africa, see *Granma*, June 25, 1967, p. 8; Aug. 18, p. 7; Aug. 30, p. 1; Sept. 9, p. 8; Sept. 12, p. 11; Sept. 27, p. 8; Nov. 21, p. 8. See also Hughes (INR) to Secretary, "Castro Adds the US to His Revolutionary List," July 27, 1967, NSF, Subject File, box 5, LBJL; Hughes to Secretary, "Stokely Carmichael," Aug. 2, 1967, ibid.; Foreign Broadcast Information Service, "Stokely Carmichael in Cuba," Aug. 11, 1967, ibid.; McIlvaine to SecState, Conakry, Oct. 3, 1967, ibid.

50. Quotations from Amembassy Conakry to DOS, Sept. 25, 1969, p. 2, and Mar. 3, 1966, Pol 13-9 Port Guin, SNF, NA; DOS, MemoConv (Cabral, Smith, et al.), Feb. 26, 1970, p. 2, FOIA 1982/1048; James Loeb (U.S. ambassador to Guinea, 1963-65), letter to the editor, *NYT*, Feb. 14, 1973, p. 40; interview with Todman.

51. Bennett to DOS, Lisbon, Apr. 3, 1968, p. 6, FOIA 1982/0392.

52. Quotations from Stevenson to SecState, no. 257, July 26, 1963, pp. 1-2 of sec. 1 and pp. 1-2 of sec. 2, Stevenson Papers, box WH-1, JFKL. See also Amembassy Lisbon to SecState, July 11, 1963, NSF, box 154, JFKL; Stevenson to SecState, no. 256, July 26, 1963, and Aug. 1, 1963, Stevenson Papers, box WH-1, JFKL; Hughes (INR) to SecState, "Focus on Portuguese Guinea," Aug. 16, 1963, ibid.; Elbrick to DOS, Lisbon, Aug. 17, 1963, NSF, box 154a, JFKL; Rusk to Amembassy Lisbon, Dec. 3, 1963, and May 4, 1964, NSFCF, box 203; Nogueira, *Diálogos*, 1:269 and 2:58-60.

53. Williams to Tyler, Apr. 8, 1964, p. 1, MWP, box 12, and Loeb to Williams, Conakry, June 19, 1964, p. 2, MWP, box 28; see also Williams to Loeb, June 30, 1964, MWP, box 12.

54. Stevenson to Kennedy, June 26, 1963, p. 2, NSF, box 154, JFKL; Leimgruber, *Kalter Krieg*, p. 105. For Kennedy's Portuguese policy, see ibid., pp. 92-127; Mahoney, *JFK*, pp. 187-222, 304-14; Marcum, *Angolan Revolution*, 1:181-87, 268-77; José Antunes, *Kennedy*. Noer, *Cold War*, pp. 61-125, and Schneidman, "American Foreign Policy," 1:56-267, cover both the Kennedy and Johnson years.

55. Quotations from Amembassy Dar-es-Salaam to SecState, Apr. 21, 1969, FOIA 1983/1209, and General Francisco da Costa Gomes, quoted in José Antunes, *Nixon*, p. 110.

56. *NYT*, Dec. 11, 1971, p. 16, and Dec. 18, p. 18 (ed.). The best studies on Nixon and Portugal are Schneidman, "American Foreign Policy," 2:278-375, and José Antunes, *Os Americanos*.

57. Cabral quoted in *NYT*, Feb. 2, 1972, p. 11. Portugal ended up not using the credits because it found better interest rates in Europe (José Antunes, *Os Americanos*, p. 216; Magalhães, "Portugal," pp. 35-37).

58. Davidson, *No Fist*, p. 62.

59. Quotations from *Nõ Pintcha*, Sept. 12, 1977, p. 1 (quoting Cabral), and interview with António Borges.

60. All the PAIGC officials whom I interviewed confirmed this. The Bissau newspaper *Nõ Pintcha*, which began publication in August 1975, ran well over 100 retrospective articles on the war over the next decade. Many refer to the Cuban military presence in Guinea-Bissau; not one mentions any other foreign presence.

61. Interview with Risquet. Cabral had gone to Brazzaville for a meeting of the Conférencia das Organizações Nacionalistas das Colónias Portuguesas (*La Semaine*[Brazzaville], Sept. 4, 1966, p. 5). French intelligence told the Americans that "Cubans [had] offered [to] provide [a] new contingent of instructors" to the PAIGC (Amembassy Libreville to SecState, Sept. 2, 1966, Pol 30-2 Ang, SNF, NA).

62. Interview with Dreke.

63. This figure is approximate and is calculated on the basis of the data in "Ayuda" and "Protocolo de asistencia técnica entre el partido comunista de Cuba y el Partido Africano por la Independencia de Guinea Bissao y Cabo Verde," Conakry, May 27, 1972, app. 1, MIECE, and interviews with the participants.

64. Quotations from interviews with Nino, Duky (Leopoldo Alfama), and Mané. This and the following four paragraphs are based on interviews with these senior PAIGC officials: Duky, Borges, Fidelis Cabral, Mané, Nino, Turpin, Vasco Cabral.

65. Interview with Nino.

66. For the military ranks of the volunteers: Dreke to Vice-Ministro para el Trab. Pol., Dec. 8, 1969, PCH; Moya to Vice-Ministro J' Dir. Política, "Informe," Aug. 14, 1970, PCH; "Ayuda"; interviews with volunteers.

67. Quotations from interview with Dreke and from Dantas, "O primeiro" (see n. 10). Interview with the Cape Verdean Monteiro Santos; Luís Cabral, *Crónica*, pp. 254-55, 281-83; "15 de Janeiro" (see n. 10); Cardoso, *O partido*, pp. 18-19.

68. Interview with Dreke.

69. Interview with Duky.

70. Interview with Montero.

71. Interview with Pereira. See also Dhada, "Guinea-Bissau's Diplomacy," and Valimamad, "Nationalist Politics," pp. 137-51.

72. Quotations from interview with Dreke and "Diario de Vera" [entry of mid-1968].

73. Interview with Dreke.

74. Ibid. The bridge was twelve miles from Bissau on the road from Bafatá to Bissau. It no longer exists.

75. "Resumen del discurso de Amílcar Cabral," Brazzaville, [Aug. 1966], pp. 1, 2, ACC; interviews with PAIGC leaders Vasco Cabral and Turpin.

76. Luís Cabral, *Crónica*, pp. 253 and 247; interview with Nino.

77. Interview with Peraza.

78. Interviews with Drs. Peraza (quoted), Camacho (who also went in the first group), and Pérez de León (who was with the second group of doctors).

79. Interviews with the Cuban doctors Peraza, Hechavarría, Candebat, Camacho, Romero, Pérez Capdet, and Pérez de León. For a vivid description

of one such hospital, see Sesana, *Liberate*, pp. 126-29.

80. Luís Cabral, *Crónica*, p. 253.

81. Interview with Romero.

82. Quotations from interview with Fidelis Cabral and from Spadafora, *Experiencias*, pp. 47, 50.

83. Interviews with PAIGC officials Fidelis Cabral, Nino, Ramos, Vasco Cabral, Pereira, and Arlette Cabral and with the Guinean doctors and physician's assistants listed in n. 90.

84. Interviews with the following Cuban and Guinean health personnel who worked at the Boké hospital: Pérez Capdet, Camacho, Furtado, Paulo Medina, Sousa Carvahlo, Alves; see also Luís Cabral, *Crónica*, and INR, "Africa: Prospects for Liberation from White Minority Regimes," Sept. 22, 1971, Pol 13 Afr, SNF, NA.

85. Luís Cabral, *Crónica*, p. 371 quoted, and interviews with Lopes Moreira (quoted) and Alves.

86. Luís Cabral, *Crónica*, pp. 297-98, 336-37, 341 (quoted); interviews with Hechavarría (Mariano Sixto); Pereira, Duky, Borges; Sesana, *Liberate*, pp. 37, 71-72.

Bowing to Portuguese pressure, in 1969 Dakar temporarily closed the hospital and arrested several PAIGC officials. The PAIGC had to evacuate more than 100 sick and wounded patients over 400 miles of very poor roads to Koundara (Lipinska, "Deux"; *NYT*, July 8, 1970, p. 10; INR, "Senegalese Support for the PAIGC," June 16, 1971, Pol 17 Port Guin, SNF, NA).

In the early 1960s, Senegal's president Léopold Sédar Senghor was very hostile to the PAIGC and Amílcar Cabral (whom he suspected of being a Communist), but during the war his opinion changed to one of high respect for Cabral and limited support for the PAIGC. See Chabal, *Amílcar Cabral*, pp. 84-85; José Antunes, *Nixon*, pp. 91-96.

87. I have reconstructed a list of forty-seven doctors, based mainly on interviews with Drs. Peraza, Hechavarría, Candebat, Camacho, Romero, Pérez Capdet, and Pérez de León and with MMCG heads Dreke, Vidiaux, and Montero. "Ayuda" gives only two exact figures: ten doctors went in 1966, and there were eight doctors and seven nurses in the spring of 1972. The May 1972 military protocol between Cuba and the PAIGC stated that Cuba would maintain a medical mission of seventeen members, including eight doctors ("Protocolo de asistencia técnica entre el partido comunista de Cuba y el Partido Africano por la Independencia de Guinea Bissao y Cabo Verde," Conakry, May 27, 1972, app. 1).

88. At Boké, two or three (Spadafora, Mihajlovic, and possibly a third); at Koundara, one or two; at Ziguinchor, possibly half a dozen.

89. Chabal, *Amílcar Cabral*, pp. 120-21; Rudebeck, *Guinea-Bissau*, pp. 186-201 (the best discussion of PAIGC medical care). See also Dhada, *Warriors*, pp. 61-72, 95, 115, 185, 187-96.

90. The next four paragraphs are based on interviews with two of the doctors (Paulo Medina and Venancio Furtado), the dentist (Gaudêncio de Sousa Carvahlo), and two of the physician's assistants

(Ernesto Lopes Moreira and Paulo Alves), as well as the curriculum vitae of Dr. Furtado.

91. Interview with Duky.

92. According to Rudebeck, there were 25 fully trained nurses and 215 nurses' aides in 1972 (Rudebeck, *Guinea-Bissau*, p. 199). Two years after the war, *Nõ Pintcha* reported that there were 38 nurses and 254 nurses' aides in the country (*Nõ Pintcha*, Oct. 19, 1976, p. 8).

93. For their abbreviated CVs, see Gleijeses, "The First Ambassadors," n. 114.

94. Interview with Pereira.

95. In my interviews, I asked all the Cubans who participated in any missions in Africa about the issues discussed in this section. In order to avoid long, repetitive notes, I identify the interviewee only when there is a direct quote or when I am dealing with an arcane issue.

96. Special NIE, "Cuba: Castro's Problems and Prospects over the Next Year or Two," June 27, 1968, pp. 4-5, NSF, NIE, box 8/9, LBJL.

97. Quotations from interviews with Montero and Cárdenas; Lieutenant Radamés Sánchez Bejerano to Raúl Castro, Havana, Oct. 23, 1965, PCH; Félix Barriento to Fidel Castro, Havana, Feb. 7, 1967, PCH.

98. Quotations from interviews with Estrada and Cárdenas.

99. Interview with Dreke.

100. Interviews with Dreke and Estrada.

101. Interview with Hechavarría.

102. "Diario de Vera," [entry of late 1967]. No mail was sent to or from the secret mission in Zaire.

103. Quotations from interviews with Estrada and Batista.

104. Conchita to Moya, Havana, Aug. 8, 1967, PCH.

105. Horacio to Vera, Mar. 31, 1967, PCH. Between June 1966 and June 1972 nine Cuban ships arrived at Conakry, at approximately eight-month intervals (see "Ayuda," esp. p. 15).

106. Interview with Hernández Gattorno.

107. Interview with Dreke.

108. This is based on my interviews with the volunteers and on two documents: enclosure in Dreke to Vice-Ministro para el Trab. Pol., Havana, Dec. 8, 1969, PCH, and Dreke to First Lieutenant Ulisis, Havana, Dec. 12, 1969, PCH.

109. Interview with Montero.

110. Interview with Urra.

111. Interview with Montero.

112. Quotation from interview with Pina.

113. Interview with Martínez Vaillant; confirmed by interviews with Mesa, Véliz, and Batista, all of whom had served on the committees.

114. Interviews with Pina and Hechavarría.

115. Quotations from interviews with Montero and Pérez de León.

116. INR, "Africa: Prospects for Liberation from White Minority Regimes," Sept. 22, 1971, p. 11, Pol 13 Afr, SNF, NA. See also n. 26.

117. *Diário de Notícias*: Nov. 21, 1969, p. 1; Nov. 24, p. 5; Nov. 28, p. 5; Amembassy Lisbon to USUN New York, Nov. 21, 1969, Def 9 Cuba, SNF, NA;

"Misiones," p. 22; [Portugal], Corpo das Tropas Pára-Quedistas, *História*, 4:167-69.

118. Falcón [Montero] to Vera [Vidiaux], Jan. 3, 1970, PCH.

119. Amílcar Cabral in U.S. House, Committee on Foreign Affairs, Subcommittee on Africa, *Report*, p. 13; *NYT*, Apr. 27, 1971, p. 13. See also "Pedro Peralta."

120. Interview with Cárdenas. My research confirms the silence of the Cuban press.

121. Post (DCM, Lisbon) to SecState, Jan. 2, 1974 (quoted); Scott (U.S. ambassador, Lisbon) to SecState, Jan. 22, 1974; SecState to Amembassy Lisbon: Nov. 22, 1973; Apr. 30, May 1 and 3, 1974; all NSCF: Portugal, box 701, NP. See also Congressmen Carl Albert, John Rhodes, et al. to Kissinger, Feb. 27, 1974, John Marsh Files, box 11, GRFL.

122. *Diário de Noticias*, Apr. 23, 1971, p. 4; *Granma*, Sept. 17, 1974, p. 1.

123. INR, "Africa: Prospects for Liberation from White Minority Regimes," Sept. 22, 1971, p. 4, Pol 13 Afr, SNF, NA.

124. Quotations from interview with Risquet; Hughes (INR) to SecState, "Focus on Portuguese Guinea," Aug. 16, 1963, pp. 7-8, Stevenson Papers, box WH-1, JFKL; Castro, in "Stenographische Niederschrift der Verhandlungen mit der Partei- und Regierungs-delegation der Republik Kuba in der DDR," June 20, 1972, p. 22, SED, DY30 JIV 2/201/919 (hereafter "Castro-Honecker, 1972"). Also interviews with Estrada and Cárdenas.

125. Quotations from "Castro-Honecker, 1972," p. 31, and Ibrahima, "Relaciones Guinea-Cuba," p. 33. Also interviews with Oramas and Bangaly, the director of the Western Hemisphere division of the Foreign Ministry of Guinea.

126. Declassified documents from the secret police archives in Lisbon reveal that the Portuguese and French secret services were planning an operation to overthrow Touré. Operation Safira was scheduled for June 1974, but the Portuguese dictatorship was overthrown the previous April. (See "PIDE e SEDEC.")

127. Interviews with Bangaly, Oramas, and Manuel Medina, deputy commander of the MMCG in 1973-74; "Castro-Honecker 1972," p. 30. The Cuban filmmaker Jorge Fuentes made a documentary, *Badenya* (Hermandad), about the construction of the airport of KanKan.

The Cubans also began providing some training to the militia, which Sékou Touré had revived after the November 1970 attack ("Castro-Honecker 1972," pp. 22-23; *Granma*, May 8, 1972, p. 1; interviews with Galarza, Martínez Vaillant, and Manuel Medina).

128. United Nations General Assembly, "Report of the Special Mission Established by the Special Committee at its 840th Meeting on 14 March 1972," UN document A/AC.109/ L.804, July 3, 1972, p. 19.

129. United Nations General Assembly, Official Records, 27th sess., Plenary Meeting, Nov. 14, 1972, 10:30 a.m.

130. The murder plot remains murky. For speculative theories, see Castanheira, *Quem?* For straightforward accounts based on the existing evidence, see Chabal, *Amílcar Cabral*, pp. 132-43, and José Antunes,

Nixon, pp. 249-50. Also useful was the secret report of the PAIGC's internal investigation: Fidelis Cabral, "Relatorio—Comissão de Inquerito," Conakry, June 9, 1973, private collection, Bissau.

131. INR, "Africa: Prospects for Liberation from White Minority Regimes," Sept. 22, 1971, p. 8, Pol 13 Afr, SNF, NA.

132 Quotations from Luís Cabral, *Crónica*, p. 433; Caetano, *Depoimento*, p. 179; Fabião, "A descolonização," p. 310. These were Strela missiles, the Soviet version of the SAM-7. The five planes were shot down between March 26 and April 6, 1973 (INR, "Portuguese Guinea: New Weapon Heightens Level of Combat," June 5, 1973, Pol 13-9 Port Guin, SNF, NA).

133. Spínola, *País*, pp. 53-54; Carvalho, *Alvorada*, pp. 107-8. (Carvalho served in Guinea-Bissau in 1971-73.) See also [Portugal], Estado-Maior do Exército, Comissão para o Estudo das Campanhas de África (1961-74), *Resenha*, 1:119, and the accounts of Air Force generals Manuel Diogo Neto and José Lemos Ferreira, in José Antunes, *A guerra*, 1:321 and 2:591-92.

134. Quotations from Vicente, *Gadamael*, p. 95; Spínola to Overseas Minister Silva Cunha, May 22, 1973, in Spínola, *País*, p. 57; MINFAR, "Realización de la Operación ` Amílcar Cabral,'" [1974], p. 90 (hereafter "Realización"); INR, "Portuguese Guinea: New Weapon Heightens Level of Combat," June 5, 1973, p. 1, Pol 13-9 Port Guin, SNF, NA. See also Silva Cunha, *O Ultramar*, pp. 52-56; Richard Lobban, "The Fall of Guiledje," *Africa*, Aug. 1973, pp. 36-37; [Portugal], Corpo das Tropas Pára-Quedistas, *História*, 4:212-27; Luís Cabral, "A Guiné," p. 52; Castanheira, *Quem?*, pp. 159-60. The number of Cubans who participated in the operation is from "Realización," p. 35. For a vivid account by a Portuguese officer of the diversionary offensive in the north, see Maia, *Capitão*, pp. 63-69.

135. *Nõ Pintcha*, Sept. 1976 (special issue), p. 15.

136. United Nations General Assembly, Official Records, 28th sess., Plenary Meeting, Nov. 2, 1973, 10:30 a.m., pp. 5-15. On the U.S. vote, see Transcripts of Secretary of State Henry Kissinger's Staff Meetings, 1973-1977, Oct. 2, 1973 (pp. 16-22), Oct. 29, 1973 (pp. 12-13), Dec. 3, 1973, (pp. 21-23); all box 1, NA.

137. Quotations from Bennett to SecState, Nov. 29, 1973, p. 3, Pol 17 Port, SNF, NA; Briggs (U.S. consul, Luanda) to DOS, July 17, 1973, Pol Afr-Ger W, SNF, NA; Newsom to SecState, Oct. 5, 1973, p. 6, Pol Afr-US, SNF, NA.

138. "Realización," p. 92.

139. *Granma*, Sept. 10, 1974, p. 1; Sept. 11, p. 1; Sept. 16, p. 6; Sept. 17, p. 1.

140. "Antwort des Generalsekretärs der PAIGC, Amilcar Cabral, auf die Ausführungen des Gen. Gerhard Grüneberg, Mitglied des Politbüros und Sekretär des ZK der SED, in der 2. Beratung zwischen den Delegationen der SED und der PAIGC am 27.10.1972 im Hause des ZK," Berlin, Oct. 30, 1972, p. 4, SED, DY30 IVB 2/2.023/87. See also "Die gegenwärtige Politik der PAIGC in Guinea-Bissau," n.d., ibid.; Amembassy Oslo to SecState, Mar. 29, 1972,

Pol 19 Port Guin, SNF, NA; INR, "Portuguese Africa: Growing Western Support for Liberation Movements," Aug. 21, 1972, Pol 13 Ang, SNF, NA; Luís Cabral, *Crónica*, pp. 333-36; Sellström, *Liberation*; Sellström, *Sweden*; Eriksen, *Norway*.

141. In 1969 there were thirty-six Guineans studying in Cuba; most had arrived in 1967 ("Relación de becarios de Africa que cursan estudios en nuestro país," Dec. 4, 1969, unpaginated, PCH). Scattered interviews indicate that many others went to Cuba before the end of the war. Twelve went in 1968 (interview with Arlette Cabral, a PAIGC official who was with them on the ship); seventeen went in September 1973 (interview with Mandjam Sambú, a member of the group).

142. *Nõ Pintcha*, Oct. 9, 1976, p. 1.

143. Like the Cubans, in the early 1970s the Soviet Union provided military aid to Guinea, the PAIGC's rear guard, against possible Portuguese attacks. (See Hall, "Naval Diplomacy," pp. 539-69; INR, "USSR-Guinea/Sierra Leone: New Twist to Gunboat Diplomacy," Jan. 18, 1972, Def 7 USSR, SNF, NA; INR, "USSR-Guinea: From Gunboat Diplomacy to Active Intervention," Feb. 9, 1973, ibid.)

144. MINFAR, List of dead with biographical notes, n.d., ACC. One doctor, the surgeon Miguel Angel Zerquera, died of malaria in Guinea-Bissau in April 1971.

145. Interviews with Torres and Hechavarría.

146. *Nõ Pintcha*, Nov. 29, 1975, p. 5.

147. Quotations from interview with Borges; Luís Cabral, *Crónica*, pp. 305-6; Pina in *Nõ Pintcha*, June 21, 1980, p. 3.

CHAPTER TEN

1. Cuba has not declassified documents pertaining to its relations with the United States or Latin America. Therefore this chapter relies largely on U.S. documents, and in particular on CIA reports, which are very often of high quality.

2. No documents are available on Che's thoughts and movements between his departure from Zaire and his arrival in Bolivia one year later. The account that follows is based on interviews. The semiofficial annotated chronology of Che's life by two Cuban journalists is marred by gross factual mistakes (Cupull and González, *Un hombre*, pp. 305-11).

3. CIA, DI, "Cuban Subversive Activities in Latin America: 1959-1968," Feb. 16, 1968, p. 3, NSFCF, box 19 (hereafter CIA, "Cuban Subversive Activities"). A few weeks after the Havana conference, Che was in Algeria, planning with Ben Bella for the arrival of a Cuban ship with weapons for the Venezuelan guerrillas (see chapter 2).

4. "Information zur Rede des 1. Sekretärs der Einheitspartei der Sozialistischen Revolution (PURS) und Ministerpräsidenten der Revolutionären Regierung der Republik Kuba, Genossen Dr. Fidel Castro," Berlin, Aug. 5, 1965, p. 5, GDR AA, A18130.

5. Juan Carretero, note to Piero Gleijeses, Havana, July 2, 1995 (hereafter Carretero to Gleijeses); interview with Carretero.

6. CIA, DI, "Cuban Subversive Policy and the Bolivian Guerrilla Episode," May 1968, pp. 13-14, 17, NSFCF, box 19.

7. Interviews with Carretero and Estrada.

8. Quotations from Castro in Minà, *Encounter*, p. 224, and from Carretero to Gleijeses.

9. Interviews with Estrada (quoted) and García Gutiérrez (Fisín).

10. Interview with Estrada (quoted); Carretero to Gleijeses; José Luis Ojalvo (DGI officer at the Cuban embassy in Prague in 1965-66), "Clandestino en Praga," *Juventud Rebelde* (Havana), June 14, 1998, special suppl., pp. 2-3. For the date of Che's departure from Tanzania, also interviews with Fernández Padilla and Ferrer, and Gálvez, *El sueño*, p. 356.

11. Interview with Carretero (quoted); Piñeiro, "Inmortalidad," p. 45; Tomassevich in Báez, *Secretos*, pp. 105-6.

12. Castro in Minà, *Encounter*, p. 225 quoted; Piñeiro, "Mi modesto homenaje," p. 17. While the literature on Che's guerrilla war in Bolivia is vast, there is no authoritative account of Havana's role, for the simple reason that the Cubans have declassified no documents. There is, however, an excellent account of the U.S. response to the Bolivian guerrilla war: Ryan, *The Fall*.

13. Debray, *Loués*, pp. 176-77. For speculations about the relationship between Castro and Guevara in 1966-67, see Tutino, *Guevara*, pp. 103-26; Benigno, *La vie*, esp. pp. 167-73; Castañeda, *Compañero*, 326-90; Geyer, *Guerrilla Prince*, pp. 307-18. In a special report on the diary Che kept in Bolivia, the CIA noted, "In the diary, Che mentioned frequent communications with Castro. . . . There were no indications of differences between the two men" (CIA, DI, "The Che Guevara Diary," Dec. 15, 1967, p. 6, NSFCF, box 19).

14. CIA, "Cuban Subversive Activities," p. 4; Bowdler to Rostow, Aug. 28, 1967, NSFCF, box 3.

15. For U.S. accounts, see CIA, ONE, "Latin American Insurgencies Revisited," Feb. 17, 1967, NSFCF, box 3; CIA, "Cuban Subversive Activities." For Cuban accounts, interview with DGI officer Montero; Raúl Menéndez Tomassevich and Ulises Rosales del Toro (two of the Cubans who went to Venezuela), in Báez, *Secretos*, pp. 107-9 and 498-99; Valdéz, "Briones Montoto"; López et al., *Mártires*, 2:115-31. For a Venezuelan account, see guerrilla commander Luben Petkoff in Blanco Muñoz, *La lucha armada: hablan 6 comandantes*, pp. 136-42, 148-54.

16. CIA, "Cuban Subversive Activities," p. 1.

17. Quotations from Hughes (INR) to SecState, May 9, 1967, p. 1, NSFCF, box 75, and CIA, DI, "Guatemala: A Current Appraisal," Oct. 8, 1966, p. 9, NSFCF, box 54. See also CIA, DI, "Instability in the Western Hemisphere," Dec. 9, 1966, NSFCF, box 2; CIA, "Status of Insurgency in Venezuela," Apr. 5, 1967, NSF, Intelligence File, box 2/3, LBJL; CIA, "Status of Insurgency in Colombia," Apr. 7, 1967, ibid.; CIA, "Cuban Subversive Activities"; CIA, DI, "The Communist Insurgency Movement in Guatemala," Sept. 20, 1968, NSFCF, box 54.

18. Castro, Aug. 10, 1967, speech, *Granma* (Havana), Aug. 11, 1967, p. 6.

19. CIA, "Cuban Subversive Activities," p. 1.

20. Castro, Aug. 10, 1967, speech, *Granma*, Aug. 11, 1967, p. 4. Two other classic examples of public castigation of the Soviet Union for its attempts to develop ties with the governments of Chile, Colombia, and Venezuela are Castro's speeches of July 26, 1966, and Mar. 13, 1967 (*Granma*, July 27, 1966, pp. 2-7, and Mar. 14, 1967, pp. 2-12). See also Hughes (INR) to SecState, "Cubans Hinder Soviet Efforts at Rapprochement with Latin American Countries," June 27, 1967, NSFCF, box 19; CIA, DI, "Latin American Solidarity Conference Resolution," Aug. 9, 1967, NSFCF, box 3; CIA, DI, "Latin America Looks to Eastern Europe," Mar. 29, 1968, ibid.

21. Quotations from "Informationsbericht des ADN-Korrespondenten in Havanna v. 11. Mai 66," GDR AA, A3363 (1) (quoting the Soviet ambassador), and Castro, Mar. 13, 1968, speech, *Granma*, Mar. 15, 1968, p. 7.

22. CIA, Board of National Estimates, "Bolsheviks and Heroes: The USSR and Cuba," Nov. 21, 1967, pp. 1-8 quoted, FOIA 1993/1807. See also CIA, Intelligence Information Cable, Oct. 6, 1967, NSFCF, box 19; Hughes (INR) to SecState, "Soviet-Cuban Relations after the Birthday Party," Nov. 21, 1967, ibid.; Hughes to SecState, "What Is Going On in Cuban-Soviet Relations?," Jan. 11, 1968, ibid.

23. Quotations from Castro, Jan. 2, 1968, speech, *Granma*, Jan. 3, 1968, p. 3; "Informationsbericht des ADN-Korrespondenten in Havanna v. 24.2.68," SED, DY30 IVA 2/20/285; Axen to Ulbricht, July 26, 1968, SED, DY30 IVA 2/20/265. According to U.S. intelligence, the Soviets were willing to increase oil deliveries to Cuba but not to the extent requested by Cuba (Hughes [INR] to SecState, "Cuba 1968—The Year of the Heroic Guerrilla," Jan. 1, 1968, NSFCF, box 19; Hughes to SecState, "Cuba: What Is Going On in Cuban-Soviet Relations?," Jan. 11, 1968, ibid.).

24. Quotations from Halperin, *Taming*, p. 302; Axen and Markowski, "Vorlage für das Politbüro," Berlin, Sept. 19, 1968, p. 3, SED, DY30 IVA 2/20/265; Denney (INR) to SecState, "Cuban Foreign Policy," Sept. 15, 1967, p. 1, Pol 1 Cuba, SNF, NA; Naumann to Markowski et al., Havana, Oct. 29, 1968 (quoting the Soviet chargé), SED, DY30 IVA 2/20/265. See also Sölle to Honecker, Berlin, Apr. 25, 1968, ibid.; "Information über das Gespräch des Genossen Prof. Albert Norden, Mitglied des Politbüros und Sekretär des Zentralkomitees der SED, mit Genossen Dr. Carlos Rafael Rodríguez, Sekretär des Zentralkomitees der Kommunistischen Partei Kubas, am 26. April 1968 im Hause des Zentralkomitees der SED," ibid.; "Information an die Mitglieder und Kandidaten des Politbüros," Berlin, Apr. 29, 1968, ibid.; "Konzeption für die Arbeit der Delegation des ZK der SED in Kuba," [Sept. 1968], ibid. For Nixon's statements on Cuba, see *NYT*: July 8, 1968, p. 32; Aug. 7, p. 28; Oct. 13, p. 76.

25. Karol, *Guerrillas*, p. 506.

26. Castro, Aug. 23, 1968, speech, *Granma*, Aug. 24, 1968, p. 2.

27. See, for example, Halperin, *Taming*, pp. 307-17; Clerc, *Fidel*, pp. 343-45; Bourne, *Fidel*, pp. 270-71; Theberge, *Soviet Presence*, pp. 63-64.

28. Castro quoted in "Aussprache mit einer Delegation der Kommunistischen Partei Kuba," Dec. 8, 1968, p. 7, SED, DY30 IVA 2/20/265.

29. Verner, "Bericht über die Reise der Delegation des Zentralkomitees der SED nach Kuba vom 11. bis 22. November 1968," Berlin, Nov. 29, 1968, p. 3 quoted, SED, DY30 IVA 2/20/265; "Aus der Aussprache mit Genossen Fidel Castro am 14. November 1968 während des Mitagessens im Gürtel von Havanna," ibid.; "Vermerk über die Abschlussaussprache mit der Delegation der KP Kuba am 11.11.68," ibid.

30. DOS, "Cuban Presence in Africa," Dec. 28, 1977, p. 4, FOIA, 1997/1334. See also DOS to All ARA Diplomatic Posts, Feb. 17, 1970, Pol Cuba-US, SNF, NA, and INR, "Cuba: Aid to Subversive Movements in Latin America at a Low Level," July 25, 1973, Pol Cuba-LA, SNF, NA.

31. See Ovalles, *Caamaño* (p. 13 quoted); Hermann, *Francis Caamaño*, pp. 347-465 (p. 426 quoted), and *Caracoles* (Hermann is one of the two survivors of Caamaño's guerrilla group); Mañon, *Operación*. For Cuban accounts, see Rius and Sáenz Padrón, *Caamaño*, pp. 173-329; Montero, "El legendario comandante."

32. Castro, July 26, 1973, speech, *Granma*, July 28, 1973, p. 4.

33. Havana radio, Aug. 4, 1970, quoted by Gonzalez, *Cuba*, p. 142 n. 59. For the Feb. 20, 1970, agreement with Chile, see *El Mercurio* (Santiago, Chile): Feb. 20, 1970, p. 3 (ed.); Feb. 21, p. 1; Feb. 22, p. 25.

34. Castro, in "Stenographische Niederschrift der Verhandlungen der Partei- und Regierungsdelegationen der Deutschen Demokratischen Republik und der Republik Kuba am 21. und 26. Februar 1974 in Havanna. Erster Tag: Donnerstag, den 21.2.1974," pp. 81-87, SED, DY30 JIV 2/201/1157.

35. Denney (INR) to SecState, "Cuban Foreign Policy," Sept. 15, 1967, p. 21, Pol 1 Cuba, SNF, NA.

36. "National Policy Paper—Cuba: United States Policy," draft, July 15, 1968, pp. 9-10, FOIA 1996/3108.

37. Castro, Mar. 13, 1968, speech, *Granma*, Mar. 15, 1968, p. 5.

38. Quotations from Castro, May 20, 1970, speech, *Granma*, May 21, 1970, p. 5, and Castro, July 26, 1970, speech, *Granma*, July 27, 1970, p. 5.

39. U.S. Senate, Committee on Foreign Relations, *Cuba: A Staff Report*, p. 1. On Soviet economic aid to Cuba, see CIA, DI, "Cuban Sugar Production in 1967 and Prospects for 1968 and 1970," Nov. 1967, NSFCF, box 19; Eliot to Kissinger, July 1, 1973, Pol 7 Cuba, SNF, NA; Miller, *Soviet Relations*, p. 96.

The quarterly economic reviews ("QER: Cuba, Dominican Republic, Haiti, Puerto Rico") of the *Economist Intelligence Unit* provide a convenient signpost for the evolution of the Cuban economy. See also Carnoy and Wertheim, "Cuba," pp. 21-52; Mesa-Lago,

Cuba, pp. 30-61; and several of the works cited in chapter 1, n. 2.

40. [Coordinator of Cuban Affairs], "Summary Statement of U.S. Policy toward Cuba," n.d., quoted, enclosed in Hilliker to Bundy, June 18, 1965, NSFCF, box 26/29; Bundy to President, June 26, 1965, and enclosed memo by DCI Raborn, NSFCF, box 24/25; Bundy to President, June 28, 1965, NSF, Memos to President, box 3, LBJL; Jessup to Moyers and Rostow, June 1, 1966, NSF, Intelligence File, box 2/3, LBJL; Brown, "Phantom Navy," pp. 61-62; Bundy, *Tangled Web*, p. 197; Hersh, *Price*, p. 251; Lynch, *Decision*, pp. 169-71.

41. The Church report states that "We have found concrete evidence of at least eight plots involving the CIA to assassinate Fidel Castro from 1960 to 1965" (U.S. Senate, Select Committee, *Alleged Assassination Plots*, p. 71). The report does not say, however, whether the plots continued after 1965.

42. Butterworth to DOS, Jan. 22, 1965, NSFCF, box 18. On relations between Canada and Cuba, see Kirk and McKenna, *Canada*.

43. "National Policy Paper—Cuba: United States Policy," draft, July 15, 1968, pp. 41-42, 52, FOIA 1996/3108.

44. *NYT*, July 13, 1974, p. 2.

45. DOS, "Cuba Policy," p. 1, enclosed in Gammon to Scowcroft, Aug. 15, 1974, NSATPF, box A6, GRFL.

46. Quotations from Kissinger to Nixon, Dec. 30, 1973, p. 1, NSATPF, box A4, GRFL; Kissinger to Ford, Aug. 12, 1975, p. 1, ibid.; Ingersoll to Ford, Feb. 25, 1975, p. 2, ibid. See also [DOS], "Cuba Policy," enclosed in Gammon to Scowcroft, Aug. 15, 1974; Springsteen to Scowcroft (and enclosures): Oct. 15 and Dec. 16, 1974; Feb. 7, 1975; DOS, MemoConv ("Licences for Participation by Chrysler de Mexico in Cuban Trade Fair"), Feb. 20, 1975; Rogers to SecState, Feb. 21 and Mar. 3, 1975; all NSATPF, box A6, GRFL.

47. *Le Monde*: Jan. 14 and 16, 1975, p. 1; Jan. 17, p. 36; Jan. 18, p. 3; Jan. 21, p. 5; *Observer* (London), May 25, 1975, p. 7 quoted; *Granma*: May 18, 1975, p. 1; May 20, p. 8; May 22, p. 1; May 26, p. 1. See also Lambie, "Western Europe."

48. On the visit, see *Granma*, June 30, 1975, p. 1, and July 2, p. 1.

49. Transcripts of Secretary of State Henry Kissinger's Staff Meetings, 1973-1977, Oct. 29, 1973, pp. 18-20, box 1, NA; DOS, "Cuban Presence in Africa," Dec. 28, 1977, FOIA, 1997/1334.

50. This paragraph and the next are entirely based on the trailblazing article by Kornbluh and Blight, "Dialogue with Castro." (Unless otherwise stated, all quotes are from the article.) See also Kissinger, *Renewal*, pp. 769-83.

51. DOS, "Cuba Policy," p. 5, enclosed in Gammon to Scowcroft, Aug. 15, 1974, NSATPF, box A6, GRFL. For the 1961 Che-Goodwin meeting, see chapter 1.

52. DOS, "Cuban Presence in Africa," Dec. 28, 1977, p. 5 quoted, FOIA, 1997/1334; see also Kissinger to Ford, Aug. 19, 1975, John Marsh Files, box 11, GRFL;

NSDM 305, Sept. 15, 1975, NSA: NSSM and NSDM, box 1, GRFL; Macdonald to Marsh (and enclosures), Mar. 25, 1976, Ron Nessen Papers, box 6, GRFL.

53. *Granma* reported on the visit briefly and factually (May 23, 1972, p. 6, and May 24, p. 5).

54. Castro, Jan. 3, 1973, speech, *Granma*, Jan. 4, 1973, pp. 2-3. According to a study by the staff of the Senate Foreign Relations Committee, in 1973 North Vietnam received $425 million in economic aid from the Soviet Union, that is, almost $200 million less than Cuba (*NYT*, Sept. 5, 1974, p. 8).

55. Interviews with Abdulkader Bajammal (who was a middle-ranking PDRY official) and with Eduardo Morejón, an officer in the Cuban military mission; "Convenio de asistencia y cooperación cultural, científica y técnica del gobierno revolucionario de la república de Cuba con el gobierno de la república Popular Democrática de Yemen," Havana, Nov. 7, 1972, MIECE; Fernández, *Cuba's Foreign Policy*, pp. 65-70; Berner, "Kubaner-Interventionen," pp. 330-31. In the archives of the SED there is rich documentation on the PDRY's relations with the Socialist bloc in the early 1970s: see esp. files DY30 IVB 2/20/285, DY30 IVB 2/20/445, DY30 IVB 2/20/89, DY30 IV 2/2.035/143.

56. This paragraph and the next are based on interviews with Moracén and Pérez de León (two officers who went with the force); MINFAR, "Las misiones internacionalistas desarrolladas por las FAR en defensa de la independencia y la soberanía de los pueblos," n.d., pp. 26-34, AIHC; Báez, *Secretos*, p. 383.

57. Durch, "The Cuban Military," p. 54.

58. CIA, "The Current Political Situation and Prospects in Tropical Africa," May 20, 1966, p. 6, NSFCF, box 76; Hunger, "Aktenvermerk über ein Gespräch des Genossen Dr. Quilitzsch mit dem Stellvertreter der II. Afrikanischen Abteilung des MID, Genossen Gnedyeh, am 5 August 1966," Moscow, Aug. 8, 1966, p. 4, GDR AA, A1167.

59. Interviews with DGI officers Estrada and Cárdenas; David Martin and Johnson, *Struggle*, pp. 27 and 146; CIA, DI, "Cuban Meddling in Africa," Mar. 24, 1967, NSFCF, box 19; CIA, DI, "Some Aspects of Subversion in Africa," Oct. 19, 1967, NSFCF, box 78; INR, "Africa: Prospects for Liberation from White Minority Regimes," Sept. 22, 1971, Pol 13 Afr, SNF, NA; "Vermerk," Mar. 13, 1978, SED, DY30 IV 2/2.035/127; "Vermerk über das Gespräch des Genossen Erich Honecker, Generalsekretär des ZK der SED und Vorsitzender des Staatsrates der DDR, mit Genossen Jorge Risquet, Mitglied des Politbüros und Sekretär des ZK der KP Kubas, am 17.4.1989," Berlin, Apr. 17, 1989, SED, DY30 JIV 958.

60. CIA, ONE, "A New Look at the Prospects for the African Nationalist Movements in Angola and Mozambique," Nov. 17, 1965, p. 11 quoted, FOIA 1984/0008; "Niederschrift über das Gespräch zwischen Genossen Erich Honecker und Genossen Fidel Castro am Sonntag, dem 3. April 1977, von 11.00 bis 13.30 Uhr und von 15.45 bis 18.00 Uhr, im Hause des ZK," Berlin, Apr. 3, 1977, p. 32, SED, DY30 JIV 2/201/1292; interviews with Marcelino dos Santos and Ferrer. On

Mondlane's relations with the United States, see Schneidman, "American Foreign Policy," 1:109-13, 241-43; Schlesinger, *Robert Kennedy*, p. 606; Evan Thomas, *Robert Kennedy*, pp. 144-45.

61. Quotations from interview with Marcelino dos Santos; Henriksen, *Revolution*, p. 187; interview with Risquet.

62. *People* (Freetown): July 22, 1972, p. 4, and Dec. 16, p. 1; Jan. 10, 1973, p. 3 quoted; *Daily Mail* (Freetown), Nov. 17, 1972, p. 2, and Jan. 6, 1973, p. 1. See also "Plan de trabajo para la ayuda militar a la república de Sierra Leone y al PAIGC de la llamada Guinea Portuguesa," [Apr. 1972]; "Protocolo de asistencia técnica entre la república de Sierra Leone y la república de Cuba," May 30, 1972; "Stenographische Niederschrift der Verhandlungen mit der Partei- und Regierungs-delegation der Republik Kuba in der DDR," Berlin, June 20, 1972, pp. 22-23, SED, DY30 JIV 2/201/919; Amembassy Freetown to DOS: Dec. 5, 1972, Jan. 2 and Feb. 27, 1973 (all Pol 23-3 SLeone, SNF, NA). Interviews with Martínez Vaillant, Galarza, and Urra, who served in the military mission.

63. Durch, "The Cuban Military," pp. 54-55; interview with Risquet.

64. The poverty of the sources is striking. I rely on Liniger-Goumaz, *Small*, pp. 57, 60, 82, 117-18; Liniger-Goumaz, *La Guinée Équatoriale*, pp. 144-46; interview with Urra; "Notas del CECE (Guinea Ecuatorial)," MIECE (for the technical assistance). Herbert Spiro, who was the U.S. nonresident ambassador in Equatorial Guinea in 1975-76, after a five-year stint as an Africa specialist with the State Department's Policy Planning Staff, told me, "I visited Equatorial Guinea twice. I never had any inkling of any Cuban presence there. Never heard of it, not even when I was at policy planning" (tel. interview with Spiro).

65. Interviews with Amaro (head of the Cuban nurses in Algeria, 1969-70) and with Drs. Ulloa (1965-66), Cedeño (1969-70), and José Lara (1971-73). For the size of the medical mission year by year, see "Notas del CECE (Argelia)," MIECE.

66. Levy Farah, Oct. 23, 1977, quoted in "Informe al Comité Central sobre colaboración civil con Angola," 1978, pp. 55-56, ACC. Instead, the stipend of the military personnel who belonged to the MMCG and to the column in the Congo varied according to rank (officers received roughly the equivalent of $30 per month, and soldiers $15). The Cuban troops who went to Algeria received a little money in local currency at the end of the mission, so that they could buy presents for their families. Those who went to Zaire received a Russian record player after the mission had ended.

67. I have relied on the country notes of the Comité Estatal de Colaboración Económica (CECE), MIECE, which are incomplete for the 1960s. For aid to Tanzania, see also CIA, DI, "The Current Disarray in Zanzibar," Dec. 2, 1968, NSFCF, box 100; Ramos Latour (Cuban ambassador, Dar-es-Salaam), "Tanzania: Resumen del año 1974," Jan. 22, 1975, MINREX; Oramas to Ramos Latour, Havana, Aug. 5, 1975,

MINREX; Ramos Latour to Roa, June 16, 1976, MINREX. For Mali, also interview with Rodríguez García, one of the two Cuban doctors assigned to Mali in 1965-66. For the Congo, see "Informe evaluativo de la situación económica de la R.P. del Congo en el año 1975," enclosed in Columbié (Cuban ambassador, Brazzaville) to Carlos Rafael Rodríguez, Jan. 9, 1976, MINREX; Columbié to Tabares, Jan. 17, 1976, MINREX; see also chapter 8. For Guinea, see also chapter 9. For Somalia, see also "Convenio de Colaboración en el campo de la industria azucarera entre el Ministerio de la Industria Azucarera de la República de Cuba y el de la República Democrática de Somalia," Mogadishu, Jan. 8, 1974, MIECE.

68. "Relación de becarios de Africa que cursan estudios en nuestro país," Dec. 4, 1969, PCH.

CHAPTER ELEVEN

1. Kissinger, *Renewal*, p. 709. On U.S. pressure, ibid., p. 520; José Antunes, *Nixon*, pp. 266-80; Magalhães, "Portugal," pp. 39-41.

2. Post (DCM, Lisbon) to SecState, Nov. 29 and Dec. 17, 1973, NSC Trip Files, box 43, NP; Kissinger, Report to President, Dec. 22, 1973, pp. 2-3, ibid.; Lord to SecState, "Status of Azores Base Negotiations," Mar. 8, 1974, PPS, box 345. U.S. officials estimated the cost of the equipment requested by Portugal at $190 million (Lord to SecState, Feb. 1, 1974, ibid.).

3. Interview with DePree; Lord, Transcripts of Secretary of State Henry Kissinger's Staff Meetings, 1973-1977, Jan. 28, 1974, pp. 4-5, box 2, NA (hereafter Transcripts, followed by date and box number).

4. Kissinger, Transcripts: Oct. 18, 1973, p. 21, box 1; Jan. 28, 1974, p. 4, box 2.

5. Kissinger, Transcripts: Oct. 15, 1973, p. 4, box 1; Nov. 26, 1973, pp. 3-4, box 1; Jan. 8, 1974, p. 14, box 2; Jan. 28, 1974, p. 14, box 2; Nov. 26, 1973, p. 4, box 1. On U.S.-European differences in the weeks that followed the cease-fire, Garthoff, *Détente*, pp. 450-54, and Kissinger, *Upheaval*, pp. 711-22.

6. Easum, DePree, Kissinger, Transcripts, Jan. 28, 1974, pp. 19, 23, 31, box 2.

7. Easum, Brown, Sonnenfeldt, Kissinger, Transcripts, Jan. 28, 1974, pp. 32-33, 44, 24, box 2.

8. Sisco and Kissinger, Transcripts, Jan. 28, 1974, pp. 16, 26, 27, 18, 29, box 2.

9. Kissinger, Transcripts, Jan. 28, 1974, pp. 9, 14, 31, 34, box 2. On the Defense Department's position, see also "NSSM 189: Azores Base Agreement Negotiations," Jan. 1974, pp. 50-51, enclosed in Hartman to Acting Secretary, Jan. 18, 1975, FOIA, and Lord to SecState, "Status of Azores Base Negotiations," Mar. 8, 1974, PPS, box 345.

10. Quotations from Rabenold, Mar. 14, 1974, in U.S. House, Committee on Foreign Affairs, Subcommittee on Africa, *The Complex of United States-Portuguese Relations*, p. 22; interview with Post; Todman to Easum, Mar. 27, 1974, PPS, box 345.

11. Interviews with DePree (quoted), Easum, and DePorte. (DePree and DePorte were the two PPS officials who had been assigned as support staff for the negotiations.)

12. Kissinger, memo for president, Apr. 29, 1974, p. 2, NSCF: Europe, box 701, NP.

13. On Portuguese decolonization, see MacQueen, *Decolonization*, Avillez, *Soares*, pp. 287-318; Ernesto Antunes, "A Descolonização," pp. 179-221; Associação 25 de abril, *Seminário*; Sánchez Cervelló, *A revolução*, pp. 261-327; Bragança, "Independence"; Silva, *A independência*.

14. Correia, "Portugal," p. 146.

15. Quotations from Amconsul Luanda to DOS, May 18, 1970, p. 5, Pol 30-2 Ang, SNF, NA, and Messiant, "Angola: The Challenge," pp. 140-41. For an overview of Angola's economy, see Barros, "Alguns"; Roque et al., *Economia*, pp. 23-76; DOS, "Country Summary–Angola," app. F, Mar. 20, 1980, DOS MF 8700220; Schümer, *Die Wirtschaft*; Henrique Guerra, *Angola*.

16. For population statistics, see Bender and Yoder, "Whites"; Heimer, *Entkolonisierungskonflikt*, pp. 42, 59; Wheeler, *Historical*, p. 39. For an excellent discussion of Angolan society in the years preceding the war of independence, see Bender, *Angola*, and Messiant, "1961." See also Pélissier, "Résistance," vols. 2 and 3.

17. Marcum, *Angolan Revolution*, 1:19.

18. Messiant, "Angola, les voies," pt. 1, p. 160; Heimer, "Décolonisation," p. 53.

19. The MPLA maintained a tenuous foothold among the Mbundu of Dembos-Nambuangongo (see chapter 8), but was unable to supply its guerrillas there, and these were, as the American consul in Luanda reported, exhausted, "dedicated to survival but incapable of offensive action" (Amconsul Luanda to DOS, Mar. 26, 1971, p. 2, Pol 30-2 Ang, SNF, NA).

20. Marcum uses public documents and the press very effectively, and is particularly knowledgeable about the FNLA. Messiant, "1961," and Heimer, *Entkolonisierungskonflikt*, focus respectively on the pre-1961 and post-April 1974 periods, but include valuable insights on the rebel movements during the war of independence.

21. Mabeko Tali, "Dissidences." (Mabeko Tali's dissertation has now appeared as a book, *Dissidências*.)There are many private collections of documents in Luanda. The best known is that of Lúcio Lara, which is rumored to fill sixty large boxes. In 1998, Lara began publishing these documents, beginning with a volume on the origins of the MPLA (Lúcio Lara and Ruth Lara, *Um amplo movimento*). See also Messiant's historiographical essay, "'Chez nous.'"

22. Bridgland, *Jonas Savimbi*. Three equally biased but far more superficial biographies of Savimbi are Loiseau and Roux, *Portrait*; Kalflèche, *Jonas Savimbi*; Vinicius and Saldanha, *Jonas Savimbi*. Savimbi's *Angola* includes several autobiographical chapters. Roberto has, as yet, inspired no biographers.

23. Quotations from Stewart (British consul, Luanda), "Political Changes in Angola during the Last Year," Jan. 9, 1965, FO 371/181969, PRO, and Neto, "A fase actual da nossa luta," in MPLA, "1a Assembleia Regional (1a e 2a Regiões)," Brazzaville, Feb. 22-25, 1968, in Mabeko Tali, "Dissidences," pp. 81-82.

24. CIA, OCI, "The Angolan Rebellion and White Unrest," Apr. 5, 1963, p. 2, NSF, box 5, JFKL; Hughes (INR) to SecState, "Prospects for Angolan Nationalist Movement," Nov. 5, 1963, p. 19, ibid.; Hilsman (INR) to SecState, Aug. 7, 1962, ibid. For Neto's poems, see Agostinho Neto, *Sagrada esperança*, and Trigo, *A voz*.

25. Lessing, "Bericht über den Besuch des Präsidenten der MPLA, Dr. Agostinho Neto, in der DDR vom 20. bis 23. Mai 1963," p. 5, SED, DY30 IVA 2/20/948; Davidson, *Eye*, p. 224.

26. Quotations from Carreira, *O Pensamento*, p. 31, and Ernesto Melo Antunes, in Avillez, *Do Fundo*, p. 29.

27. On Zambia's caution, see Amembassy Lisbon to SecState, Oct. 18, 1967, Pol 23 Ang, SNF, NA; DOS, MemoConv (Garin, Johnson), Feb. 28, 1969, NSCF: Europe, box 701, NP; INR, "Angola: An Assessment of the Insurgency," Sept. 16, 1970, Pol 23-9 Ang, SNF, NA; INR, "Zambia: Domestic Realities Overshadow the Campaign against the White-Ruled South," Aug. 14, 1972, Pol 1-3 Zambia, SNF, NA; Ramos Latour (Cuban ambassador, Dar-es-Salaam), "Informe sobre reuniones con movimientos de liberación acreditados en Tanzania–MPLA," [Sept. 1972], MINREX; interviews with MPLA commanders Rui de Matos and Ngongo.

28. Quotations from FRG consulate Luanda to AA, Sept. 26, 1966, p. 5, FRG, AA Portug. Gebiete; Amconsul Luanda to DOS, Nov. 13, 1968, p. 2, Pol 27 Ang, SNF, NA; Amconsul Luanda to DOS, Jan. 21, 1969, p. 3, Pol 23-9 Ang, SNF, NA; INR, "Angola: An Assessment of the Insurgency," Sept. 16, 1970, ibid.; Lúcio Lara, "A história do MPLA," n.d., p. 124 (hereafter Lara, "História"). See also FRG consulate Luanda to AA, Dec. 20, 1966, FRG, AA Portug. Gebiete; Van der Waals (a career military officer who was South Africa's vice-consul in Luanda in 1970-73), *Portugal's War*, pp. 149-54; Amembassy Lisbon to SecState, Oct. 18, 1967, Pol 23 Ang, SNF, NA. See also Amconsul Luanda to SecState: Nov. 28, 1967, Aug. 8, 1968, and Mar. 3, 1970, Pol 23-9 Ang, SNF, NA; Mar. 19, 1969, Pol 25 Ang, SNF, NA; Aug. 13, 1969, Pol 2 Ang, SNF, NA; Mar. 26, 1971, Pol 30-2 Ang, SNF, NA.

29. Quotations from Amconsul Luanda to DOS, Nov. 30, 1973, Pol 30-2 Ang, SNF, NA, and Neto to CPRFN, Mar. 26, 1974, in Mabeko Tali, "Dissidences," p. 117. On the MPLA's internal strife, see Mabeko Tali, "Dissidences," pp. 87-134, and Marcum, *Angolan Revolution*, 2:199-204, 248-50 (p. 201 quoted). On Zambia and the MPLA in this period, see also Massop (Cuban chargé, Mogadishu) to Cienfuegos, June 14, 1974 (relating a conversation with two senior MPLA officials); Mabeko Tali, "Dissidences," p. 111; Sánchez Cervelló, *A revolução*, p. 82; interview with Lúcio Lara.

30. Quotations from Costa Gomes, *Sobre Portugal*, p. 31; tel. interview with Briggs; annex IV, enclosed in DOS, "United States Policy toward Angola," Dec. 16, 1975, DOS MF 8704129/2; tel. interview with Killoran.

31. Tel. interview with Killoran; Robert Hultslander, fax to Piero Gleijeses, Dec. 22, 1998, p. 4.

32. See José Antunes, *A guerra*, 2:638-40; José Antunes, *Nixon*, p. 141; Silva Cunha, *O Ultramar*, pp.

39 and 59; João Guerra, *Memória*, p. 84; Nogueira, *História*, p. 358; Sánchez Cervelló, *A revolução*, pp. 79-80; Cann, *Counterinsurgency*, pp. 98-99. For sources on the Katangan gendarmes, see Gleijeses, "Truth," p. 71 n. 1.

33. Quotations from INR, "Angola: Two Liberation Groups to Merge," Jan. 5, 1973, p. 3, Pol 13 Ang, SNF, NA, and *Expresso* (Lisbon), Sept. 17, 1974, p. 18.

34. National Security Council Interdepartmental Group for Africa, "Response to NSSM 224: United States Policy toward Angola," June 13, 1975, enclosed in Nathaniel Davis to the Assistant to the President for National Security Affairs, June 16, 1975, NSA (hereafter NSC, "Response").

35. Quotations from DOS, MemoConv (Newsom, Le Quesne, et al.), Mar. 6-7, 1972, p. 1, Pol Afr-Chicom, SNF, NA, and INR, "Zaire: Mobutu Seeks a Wider International Role," Dec. 15, 1972, p. 5, Pol Zaire-A, SNF, NA. See also INR, "Africa: The PRC Presence," Jan. 3, 1972, p. 1, Pol Afr-Chicom, SNF, NA; DOS, MemoConv (Newsom, Ruyter, et al.), Mar. 21, 1973, ibid.; Vance (U.S. ambassador, Kinshasa) to SecState, Nov. 15, 1973, Pol 2-3 Zaire, SNF, NA; Dept. of the Army, Office of the Assistant Chief for Intelligence, "An Assessment of the Military Assistance Programs of the People's Republic of China," Nov. 15, 1974, MF 00319, NSA.

36. Quotations from USIB, *National Intelligence Bulletin*, Aug. 25, 1975, p. 7, MF 00360, NSA, and NSC, "Response," p. 7. See also *Salongo* (Kinshasa): June 3, 1974, p. 4; June 4, p. 2; Aug. 8, p. 2; *Elima* (Kinshasa), Sept. 12, 1974, p. 2; *Le Monde*, June 6, 1974, p. 4, and June 11, p. 15; Easum, Transcripts, July 11, 1974, p. 14, box 4.

37. On Chinese support: NSC, "Response," p. 52 quoted; Post (U.S. consul, Luanda) to DOS, Feb. 9, 1970, Pol 13 Afr, SNF, NA; INR, "Africa: Prospects for Liberation from White Minority Regimes," Sept. 22, 1971, ibid.; INR, "Africa: The PRC Presence," Jan. 3, 1972, Pol Afr-Chicom, SNF, NA. Kaunda broke relations with Savimbi after UNITA attacked the Benguela railroad. See Amembassy Lusaka to DOS, Feb. 13, 1967, Pol 2 Ang, SNF, NA; Amconsul Luanda to SecState, Oct. 19, 1967, Pol 30 Ang, SNF, NA; Amembassy Lusaka to DOS, Oct. 7, 1968, and Feb. 28, 1973, Pol 13 Ang, SNF, NA.

38. Wilkowski to SecState, Lusaka, Jan. 24, 1975, sec. 2, p. 2, DOS MF 8802086/2; Lara, "História," p. 94.

39. Moorcraft, *Nemesis*, p. 67; Savimbi, *Provincia de Angola* (Luanda), Mar. 14, 1975, p. 5.

40. "Angola: La longue trahison de l'U.N.I.T.A.," *Afrique-Asie* (Paris), July 8, 1974, pp. 8-17.

41. A welcome exception is Minter, *Operation Timber*, which includes the documents that have been published since 1974 and an excellent introduction.

42. Quotations from Caetano, *Depoimento*, pp. 180-81; Costa Gomes, *Sobre Portugal*, p. 32; Cruz, *Angola*, pp. 159-60; "'Operação Madeira' tenta portugalizar a UNITA," *Expresso*, Nov. 30, 1979, p. 8. *Expresso* published numerous documents in three consecutive issues: Nov. 17, 1979, pp. 18-19; Nov. 24,

pp. 25-26; Nov. 30, pp. 8-11 (hereafter "Operação Madeira," followed by date).

For testimonies by Portuguese officials, see Silva Cunha, *O Ultramar*, pp. 25-26, 61, 333-34; Costa Gomes, "Costa Gomes"; Correia, *Descolonização*, pp. 37-40; José Antunes, *A guerra*, 1:118-20, 408-9, 2:738; Correia, "Portugal," p. 150. See also João Guerra, *Memória*, pp. 168-73; Melo, *Os Anos*, 1:123-27. I have received a cache of documents on the subject from the journalist Augusta Conchiglia of *Afrique-Asie*, who has covered Angola for thirty years. Most of her documents have also been published by *Expresso*, and the general tenor of the story revealed in them is amply supported by the sources cited here.

43. Amconsul Luanda to DOS, Aug. 13, 1969, p. 4, Pol 2 Ang, SNF, NA. See also Savimbi, "Aos representantes do Governor-Geral," Angola, Mar. 3, 1969, courtesy of Augusta Conchiglia; Amembassy Lusaka to DOS, Oct. 7, 1968, Pol 13 Ang, SNF, NA; "Operação Madeira," Nov. 30, 1979, pp. 8-9.

44. INR, "Africa: Prospects for Liberation from White Minority Regimes," Sept. 22, 1971, p. 19 quoted, Pol 13 Afr, SNF, NA; DOS, Bureau of African Affairs, "U.S. Relations with the African Liberation Movements," n.d., enclosed in Rogers to All African Diplomatic Posts, Lisbon, London, Paris, Rome, Dec. 2, 1971, FOIA; INR, "Africa: The PRC Presence," Jan. 3, 1972, Pol Afr-Chicom, SNF, NA.

In the spring of 1970 the FNLA had begun operating in the east from bases in southern Zaire, but this was never more than a feeble effort (Sánchez Cervelló, *A revolução*, p. 79; Marcum, *Angolan Revolution*, 2:21-20).

45. Costa Gomes, "Costa Gomes," p. 6.

46. Savimbi to Portuguese authorities, [early Feb. 1972], in "Operação Madeira," Nov. 24, 1979, p. 26.

47. Correia, *Descolonização*, p. 38.

48. Costa Gomes, "Costa Gomes," p. 7; Correia, "Portugal," p. 150.

49. Savimbi, "Memorandum dirigido a sua excelencia o general Luz Cunha, comandante chefe das forças armadas em Angola, e a intenção de sua excelencia o general Bethencourt Rodrigues comandante da Zona Militar Leste," Sept. 26, 1972, courtesy of Augusta Conchiglia. This is one of the four letters published by *Afrique-Asie*.

50. Amconsul Luanda to DOS, Nov. 30, 1973, Pol 30-2 Ang, SNF, NA.

51. Leon Dash, "The War in Angola," *WP*, Dec. 23, 1973, p. 1 (quoted); Dec. 24, p. 1; Dec. 25, p. 1; Dec. 26, p. 1.

52. Quotations from Costa Gomes, *Sobre Portugal*, p. 32; Silva Cunha, *O Ultramar*, pp. 333-34; General Heitor Hamilton Almendra, in José Antunes, *A Guerra*, 2:738; Costa Gomes in ibid., 1:118-20.

53. Silva Cunha, *O Ultramar*, p. 334 quoted; Savimbi to Father António de Araujo Oliveira, Feb. 22, 1974, courtesy of Augusta Conchiglia.

54. Killoran to SecState, Luanda, Jan. 16, 1975, p. 3, DOS MF 8802086/2.

55. João Guerra, *Memória*, p. 416.

56. On developments in Angola from the fall of Caetano through the end of 1974, see Correia, *Descolonização*, pp. 73-131; Marcum, *Angolan Revolution*, 2:241-54; Sánchez Cervelló, *A revolução*, pp. 264-75; Mabeko Tali, "Dissidences," pp. 161-97; Soremekun, *Angola*, pp. 39-110.

57. Moose (INR), "The Angola Agreement," Jan. 23, 1975, p. 2 quoted, NSA. For the English text of the agreement, see U.S. Senate, Committee on Foreign Relations, Subcommittee on African Affairs, *U.S. Policy toward Southern Africa*, pp. 81-86. For the April 30 deadline, see Amembassy Lisbon to SecState, Mar. 28, 1975, DOS MF 8403582/2.

58. Quotations from DOS, MemoConv (Newsom, Le Quesne, et al.), Mar. 16, 1973, p. 3, Pol Afr, SNF, NA; Shevchenko, *Breaking*, p. 272; interview with Lúcio Lara. See also Lara, "História," p. 121; Westad, "Moscow," p. 22; Mabeko Tali, "Dissidences," pp. 158 and 342; Legum and Hodges, *After Angola*, p. 11; Albright, "Moscow's African Policy," pp. 40-42.

59. Interview with Ndunduma. I have been unable to confirm Ndunduma's story because both Neto and his close aide Anibal de Melo, who accompanied him on the trip (and was Ndunduma's source), are dead. I have found Ndunduma, however, to be a reliable source.

60. Interview with Ndalu.

61. Quotations from Westad, "Moscow," p. 23, and interview with Lúcio Lara. See also Amembassy Lusaka to DOS, Dec. 7, 1973, Pol 2-3 Zambia, SNF, NA; Díaz Argüelles to Raúl Castro, Havana, Aug. 11, 1975; Dobrynin, *In Confidence*, p. 360; Legum and Hodges, *After Angola*, p. 11; NSC, "Response," p. 49.

62. Interviews with Ndalu (quoted), Lúcio Lara (who was part of the Neto delegation), Ludy Kissassunda and Xiyetu (both members of the group that went to China for training), with MPLA commanders Rui de Matos and Onambwe, and with Ndunduma, who was a senior MPLA official in Lusaka. See also Jika, *Reflexões*, pp. 17, 100, and Júnior (who was the MPLA representative in Tanzania), *Lembranças*, pp. 118-19.

63. Interview with Lúcio Lara (quoted); Westad, "Moscow," p. 23.

64. Toon (U.S. ambassador, Belgrade) to DOS, Mar. 5, 1973, p. 2, Pol 7 Ang, SNF, NA.

65. See "Aktenvermerk über ein Gespräch des Kollegen Scharfenberg mit Herrn Si Oulhadi, Mitglied der Kommission für Auswärtige Angelegenheiten beim Politbüro der FLN am 7.3.1964," Algiers, Mar. 10, 1964, SED, DY30 IVA 2/20/803; Scharfenberg, "Bericht zur inneren Lage vor dem FLN-Kongress," Algiers, Mar. 13, 1964, SED, DY30 IVA 2/20/ 804; "Information über den Aufenthalt einer algerischen Partei- und Staats-delegation mit dem Präsidenten der Demokratischen Volksrepublik Algerien, Ben Bella, und der Spitze in der SFRJ," Belgrade, Mar. 18, 1964, ibid.

66. Quotations from interviews with Ndalu and Jorge and from Neto, "Informe," in *Primer Congreso*, p. 48. See also Mabeko Tali, "Dissidences," p. 346.

67. Quotations from interview with Lúcio Lara and from Westad, "Moscow," pp. 23-24. See also "Information des Mitglieds des Politbüros der Volksbefreiungsbewegung von Angola (MPLA), Iko

Carreira, zur gegenwärtigen Lage in Angola," p. 3, enclosed in "Vorlage für das Politbüro," Berlin, Sept. 3, 1975, SED, DY30 JIV 2/2A 1911.

68. On Cuba's relationship with the MPLA in 1965-67, see chapter 8.

69. Interviews with Lúcio Lara (quoted), with MPLA officials Jorge, Onambwe, and Ndunduma, and with Cadelo, who was the Cuban CC staffer in charge of Angola. See also [MINFAR], "Síntesis histórica de la ayuda internacionalista de Cuba a la R.P.A.," [1976], p. 3 (hereafter "Síntesis").

70. Interviews with Cadelo and Risquet. On the establishment of diplomatic relations, see *Granma*, July 19, 1972, p. 1.

71. Mabeko Tali, "Dissidences," p. 348.

72. García Lara (Cuban chargé, Brazzaville) to Roa, Mar. 15, 1972, PCH.

73. Interview with Cadelo (quoted); Ramos Latour, "Informe sobre reuniones con movimientos de liberación acreditados en Tanzania–MPLA," Dar-es-Salaam, [Sept. 1972], MINREX; Piñeiro to Raúl Castro, Havana, Nov. 22, 1972; Zorrilla (Cuban ambassador, Dar-es-Salaam) to Roa, Mar. 23, 1973; Massop to Cienfuegos, June 14, 1974 (see n. 29); "Síntesis," p. 3.

74. Quotations from interview with Cadelo and from Cienfuegos to Senén Casas, Havana, Nov. 22, 1974 (quoting from Ramos Latour's cable). See also "Síntesis," p. 3.

75. Quotations from Cienfuegos to Senén Casas, Havana, Nov. 22, 1974, and interview with Risquet.

CHAPETER TWELVE

1. "Conversación con Agostinho Neto, día 31 de diciembre de 1974," enclosed in [Cadelo and Pina], "Informe sobre la visita realizada a Angola," Mar. 21, 1975, pp. 27-31, p. 31 quoted (hereafter "Visita").

2. Tanzania, Aliens Travel Document of José Pina, with the entry and exit stamps of Zambia and Tanzania.

3. One Cuban, the wife of an MPLA member who had studied and trained in Cuba, had preceded them. She had arrived in Kassamba in the spring of 1972. In Kassamba, and other MPLA camps near the border, she worked as a nurse and later as a teacher. In December 1974 she arrived in Luso, a major town in eastern Angola, and it was there she met Cadelo and Pina at the beginning of their Angolan journey. (Interviews with Perera, her husband Onambwe, Pina, and Cadelo; Zorrilla [Cuban ambassador, Dar-es-Salaam] to Piñeiro, Nov. 25, 1972.)

4. Interviews with Cadelo (quoted) and Pina.

5. "Reunión con Chieto [Xiyetu], Jefe del E.M.G.; Yica, Comisario Político del E.M.G.; N'Saji, Jefe Seguridad del E.M.G. y Lopo de Nascimiento, miembro del B.P.," enclosed in "Visita," p. 39. Xiyetu's name is João Luís Neto, but, like many other Angolans, he uses his nom de guerre. The Cubans called him Chieto.

6. "Conversación con Agostinho Neto al finalizar la visita a Angola," enclosed in "Visita," pp. 32-33.

7. Agostinho Neto, "Necesidades urgentes. Lista dirigida al: Comité Central del Partido Comunista de Cuba," Jan. 26, 1975, enclosed in "Visita," pp. 22-23.

8. "Reuniones con Chieto, Jefe E.M.G.; César Salomao (Yica), Comisario Político; Dangereux, Jefe E. M. del Frente Este y N'Zaji, Responsable de Seguridad del E.M.G.," [end Jan.], enclosed in "Visita," pp. 35-36 quoted; "Proyecto para la creación de las Fuerzas Armadas Regulares de 20,000 hombres antes de finalizar el periodo de transición," enclosed in "Visita," pp. 24-25; "Reunión con Chieto, Jefe del E.M.G.; Yica, Comisario Político del E.M.G.; N'Saji, Jefe Seguridad del E.M.G. y Lopo de Nascimiento, miembro del B.P.," enclosed in "Visita," pp. 39-40.

9. "Conversación con Agostinho Neto, día 31 de diciembre de 1974," enclosed in "Visita," p. 31; "Conversación con Agostinho Neto al finalizar la visita a Angola," enclosed in "Visita," p. 33; interviews with Pina (quoted) and Cadelo.

10. Quotations from Carlos Cadelo, note to Piero Gleijeses, Havana, [July 15, 1995], p. 7 (hereafter Cadelo to Gleijeses), and from interviews with Xiyetu and Lúcio Lara.

11. Interviews with Cadelo (quoted) and Pina. *Noticias* (Maputo): Jan. 28, 1975, p. 1 quoted; Jan. 29, p. 1; Feb. 1, p. 3; Feb. 2, p. 1; Feb. 3, p. 1. Their report is "Informe sobre la visita realizada a Angola," Mar. 21, 1975.

12. Quotations from interview with Cadelo; Westad, "Moscow," p. 24; interviews with Lúcio Lara and Xiyetu.

13. Quotations from "Visita," pp. 1, 9, 12, and from "Reunión con Chieto, Jefe del E.M.G.; Yica, Comisario Político del E.M.G.; N'Saji, Jefe Seguridad del E.M.G. y Lopo de Nascimiento, miembro del B.P.," enclosed in "Visita," p. 35. Rosa Coutinho left Angola on January 27, 1975. There are no reliable figures on the military strength of the three movements at the time of Alvor. For estimates, see Marcum, *Angolan Revolution*, 2:257, 435 nn. 129 and 130; "Visita," esp. pp. 2-5; Adelman, "Report," pp. 570-71; Legum and Hodges, *After Angola*, p. 50.

14. "Conversación con Agostinho Neto, día 31 de diciembre de 1974," enclosed in "Visita," p. 29 quoted.

15. "Visita," p. 13. On Mobutu's 1974 amnesty, see *Provincia de Angola* (Luanda), Dec. 23, 1974, p. 2; *Elima* (Kinshasa), Dec. 10, 1974, p. 8, and Dec. 18, p. 3. On the 1967 amnesty, see chapter 7. For the number of Katangans, I rely on Vance (U.S. ambassador, Kinshasa) to DOS, Mar. 5, 1970, Pol 1 The Congo-US, SNF, NA; Briggs (U.S. consul general, Luanda) to SecState, Mar. 15, 1973, Pol 30-2 Ang, SNF, NA; *Provincia de Angola*, Dec. 23, 1974, p. 2; Melo, *Os anos*, 1:122.

16. [MINFAR], "Síntesis histórica de la ayuda internacionalista de Cuba a la R.P.A.," [1976], p. 5 (hereafter "Síntesis").

17. Interviews with Risquet and Cadelo.

18. Interviews with Cadelo, Lúcio Lara, and Risquet.

19. Interviews with Lúcio Lara and Paulo Lara, who was a young guerrilla fighter at the time but, as Lúcio Lara's son, in a position to know the thinking of many MPLA leaders.

20. Interview with Lúcio Lara.

21. Interviews with Xiyetu (quoted) and four officers from the group that went to the Soviet Union: Ndalu (the chief of staff and second-ranking officer of the brigade); Rui de Matos (chief of operations and third-ranking officer); Ngongo (chief of the artillery and fourth-ranking officer); Kianda (Ngongo's deputy).

22. Dangereux chartered a DC-10 and loaded it with the weapons, uniforms, and medicine and, on April 21, flew to an abandoned area of Luso airport. FAPLA soldiers unloaded the weapons immediately. By the time the Portuguese impounded the plane, only the uniforms and medicine were aboard. (Interview with Xiyetu. See also *O Comércio* [Luanda], Apr. 23, 1975, p. 1; *Jornal do Comércio* [Oporto], Apr. 24, 1975, p. 16; *Guardian* [Manchester], Apr. 24, 1975, p. 3; *Daily Telegraph* [London], Apr. 26, 1975, p. 17.)

23. *Jornal Novo* (Lisbon), July 15, 1975, p. 1 quoted. On Luanda, see Messiant, "Luanda," and Cahen, "Syndicalisme."

24. See *Expresso* (Lisbon), Sept. 7, 1974, p. 18, and Nov. 30, p. 17; *Elima* Oct. 22, 1974, p. 3; Oct. 31, p. 7; Nov. 29, p. 1; Jan. 23, 1975, p. 7.

25. The leading Angolan daily, *A Provincia de Angola*, was bought by the FNLA in March with $50,000 provided by the CIA (see Mulcahy to SecState, May 13, 1975, PPS, box 368). In July it was taken over by the MPLA and renamed *Jornal de Angola*. The country's second-largest paper, Luanda's *O Comércio*, stopped publication on August 26. The MPLA controlled the only other Luanda daily, *Diário de Luanda*. Both Portuguese papers cited in the text had social-democratic leanings, and *Jornal Novo* was, in the words of an American journalist who followed the Portuguese scene closely, "the most outspoken organ of the democratic left [against the communists], along with the well-financed weekly *Expresso*." (Szulc, "Lisbon and Washington," p. 40. For the Portuguese press at the time, see Maxwell, *The Press*, esp. chs. 4 and 5.)

26. Marcum, *Angolan Revolution*, 2: ch. 6; Legum and Hodges, *After Angola*; Heimer, *Entkolonisierungskonflikt*. (The shorter English version, *Decolonization*, includes some additional material, but summarizes many points that are developed more fully in the German text. Hence it is best to use both.)

27. The reports of the Brazilian special mission in Luanda are of very modest utility. I would like to thank Professor James Hershberg, who generously shared these documents with me before depositing them at the National Security Archive in Washington, D.C.

28. Thom, "Angola's 1975-76 Civil War," p. 7.

29. Correia, "Portugal," p. 155 quoted; Killoran to SecState, Luanda, Jan. 29, 1975, DOS MF 8802086/2; *O Comércio*, Jan. 27, 1975, p. 5, and Jan. 28, p. 3.

30. See *Provincia de Angola*, Feb. 13, 1975, p. 2, and Feb. 14, p. 1; *O Comércio*: Feb. 13-15, 22, 24, 1975, all p. 1; *Jornal do Comércio*, Feb. 14, 1975, p. 12, and Feb. 15, p. 1; *RDM* (Johannesburg), Feb. 14 and 15, 1975, both p. 1. For other incidents, see *Provincia de Angola* Feb. 23, 1975, p. 1; Feb. 24, p. 5; Mar. 5, 11, 25, all p. 2; *O Comércio*, Feb. 24, 1975,

p. 2; Feb. 25, p. 8; Feb. 26, p. 8; Mar. 3, p. 3; *Jornal do Comércio*, Feb. 4, 1975, p. 8, and Feb. 5, p. 2.

On March 18, Chipenda formally joined the FNLA, which thereby gained a military presence in southeastern Angola. (See *Elima*: Feb. 22, 1975, p. 1; Mar. 23, p. 8; Apr. 18, p. 8; *Provincia de Angola*: Feb. 23, 1975, p. 1; Feb. 24, p. 1; Apr. 18, p. 1.)

31. Quotations from *RDM*, Mar. 28, 1975, p. 2, and *Times* (London), Apr. 1, 1975, p. 4 (quoting Neto). See also Killoran to SecState, Luanda, Mar. 25 and 27, 1975, DOS MF 8802141; Representação Especial do Brazil em Luanda, "Situação político-militar em Angola," Mar. 30, 1975, NSA; *Times*, Mar. 29, 1975, p. 4; *NYT*, Mar. 28, 1975, p. 2; *Expresso*, Mar. 28, 1975, p. 1; *Provincia de Angola*: Mar. 23, 1975, p. 2; Mar. 24, 25, 26, all p. 1; Apr. 4, p. 2; *O Comércio*: Mar. 24, 25, 27-29, 31, Apr. 2 and 7, 1975, all p. 1; *Jornal Novo*, May 22, 1975, p. 17; *Jornal do Comércio*: Mar. 27, 1975, p. 12; Mar. 28, p. 1; Mar. 29, p. 1; *RDM*: Mar. 25, 1975, p. 5; Mar. 31, p. 5; Apr. 1, p. 1; Apr. 2, p. 2.

32. *Cape Times*, Apr. 8, 1975, p. 10; Davis, Hyland, and Lord to SecState, Apr. 4, 1975, p. 3, DOS MF 8802915/2.

33. Quotations from *Jornal Novo*, Apr. 23, 1975, p. 14, and Heimer, *Entkolonisierungskonflikt*, p. 188.

34. *Jornal Novo*: Apr. 30, 1975, p. 17; May 2, p. 17; May 5, p. 3; May 6, p. 17; May 10, p. 18; May 13, p. 1; May 14, p. 17; May 16, p. 17; *Expresso*, May 17, 1975, p. 18; *Le Monde*, May 3, 1975, p. 6, and May 15, p. 1; *Times*, May 5 and 6, 1975, both p. 6; *Zambia Daily Mail*, May 1, 1975, p. 2; *Provincia de Angola*: May 6, 1975, p. 17; May 9, 10, 13, all p. 3; *O Comércio*: Apr. 30, 1975, p. 2; May 1, 3, 4, all p. 1; May 8, p. 3; May 10, p. 2; *O Planalto* (Nova Lisboa), May 17, 1975, p. 2; *Jornal do Comércio*, May 1 and 3, 1975, both p. 1; *RDM*: May 2, 1975, p. 3; May 3, p. 2; May 5-7, all p. 1; May 8, p. 2; *Guardian*, May 3, 1975, p. 1, and May 5, p. 4.

35. Quotations from *Zambia Daily Mail*, Apr. 21, 1975, p. 1 (quoting Neto) and *Observer* (London), May 18, 1975, p. 5. On the delegation's visit to Kinshasa, see *Jornal Novo*, May 30, 1975, p. 1; *O Comércio*: May 29, 1975, p. 10; May 30, p. 1; June 2, p. 1; June 3, p. 1; *Elima*, June 3, 1975, p. 1; Correia, *Descolonização*, pp. 153-55.

36. Quotations from "Information des Mitglieds des Politbüros der Volksbefreiungsbewegung von Angola (MPLA), Iko Carreira, zur gegenwärtigen Lage in Angola," pp. 4-5, enclosed in "Vorlage für das Politbüro," Berlin, Sept. 3, 1975, SED, DY30 JIV 2/2A 1911; *O Comércio*, Feb. 13, 1975, p. 10; interviews with Jorge and Lúcio Lara. See also Heimer, *Entkolonisierungskonflikt*, pp. 193-94; *Jornal Novo*, May 9, 1975, p. 18, and May 31, p. 1; Mabeko Tali, "Dissidences," p. 330.

On the negotiations with the Katangans, see Heimer, *Entkolonisierungskonflikt*, pp. 193-94, and Mabeko Tali, "Dissidences," p. 353. On the foreign influx of weapons, see chapter 16.

37. "DCI briefing for 14 July SRG meeting," n.d., p. 2, NSA. On the clashes, see *Provincia de Angola*: May 31, 1975, p. 1; June 4, p. 1; June 6, p. 2; June 7, p.

1; June 8, p. 3; June 10, p. 2; June 12, p. 1; June 18, p. 2; *O Comércio*. May 29, 1975, p. 2; May 31, June 2, 4, 6, 7, 9, 11, all p. 1; *O Planalto*, June 12, 1975, p. 9; *Jornal Novo*. May 31, 1975, p. 17; June 2, p. 1; June 4, p. 16; June 7, p. 17; June 11, p. 21; *Jornal do Comércio*. May 30, 1975, p. 16; May 31, p. 1; June 5, p. 16; June 6, p. 8; June 7, p. 3; June 9, p. 1; *Expresso*, June 7, 1975, p. 16; *RDM*. May 30, 1975, p. 3; June 2, p. 3; June 3, p. 9; June 5, p. 1; *Guardian*, June 6, 1975, p. 4; Legum and Hodges, *After Angola*, pp. 50-51.

38. Quotations from National Security Council Interdepartmental Group for Africa, "Response to NSSM 224: United States Policy toward Angola," June 13, 1975, p. 8, enclosed in Nathaniel Davis to the Assistant to the President for National Security Affairs, June 16, 1975, NSA (hereafter NSC, "Response"); Kissinger [to Ford], "Meeting of the National Security Council, Friday, June 27, 1975, 2:30 p.m.," p. 2, NSA. For the 1956 date in the text, see Hughes (INR) to SecState, "Prospects for Angolan Nationalist Movement," Nov. 5, 1963, p. 18, NSF, box 5, JFKL.

39. NSC, "Response," p. 14.

40. Through the first half of 1975 *Provincia de Angola* and *O Comércio* reprinted the major speeches of Neto, Roberto, and Savimbi.

41. Kissinger [to Ford], "Meeting of the National Security Council, Friday, June 27, 1975, 2:30 p.m.," p. 3, NSA. On Savimbi and South Africa, see chapter 13.

42. Ernesto Melo Antunes, in Avillez, *Do Fundo*, p. 30 quoted; Sánchez Cervelló, *A revolução*, p. 267.

43. Quotations from *RDM*, July 19, 1975, p. 9, and from *Jornal Novo*, July 15, 1975, p. 1, and July 26, p. 19. See also *Jornal Novo*. July 11, 1975, p. 13; July 12, p. 1; July 14, p. 18; July 16, p. 1; *Jornal do Comércio*. July 12, 1975, p. 16; July 14, p. 20; July 15, p. 1; July 16, p. 19; *Le Monde*. July 13, 1975, p. 3; July 15, p. 1; July 16, p. 5; July 17, p. 4; July 18, p. 1; July 19, p. 4; *Guardian*, July 12 and 14, 1975, both p. 2; *Times*, July 14, 1975, p. 1, and July 15, p. 6; *Cape Times*. July 11, 1975, p. 5; July 12, 17, 21, all p. 1; *RDM*. July 12, 1975, p. 2; July 14, p. 1; July 15, p. 1; July 17, p. 2.

44. Cadelo to Gleijeses, p. 10; García Márquez, *Operación Carlota*, p. 8; interviews with Cadelo and Oramas, the director of Africa in the Cuban Foreign Ministry, who attended the meeting with Neto.

45. Interview with Cadelo.

46. [MINFAR], "Informe sobre las actividades ejecutadas por el Partido Comunista de Cuba y gobierno revolucionario para dar cumplimiento a la ayuda solicitada por el Movimiento Popular para la Liberación de Angola," n.d., p. 1 quoted (hereafter "Informe"); "Síntesis," p. 5; interviews with Cadelo and Schueg, another member of the group.

47. Díaz Argüelles to Raúl Castro, Havana, Aug. 11, 1975, pp. 1-2.

48. "Síntesis," p. 6 quoted; interviews with Cadelo, Schueg, Onambwe, Xiyetu.

49. Interview with Cadelo. While not close, relations between the two countries were friendly. (See Díaz Argüelles to Osmany Cienfuegos, "Informe sobre la Delegación del Gobierno de la República de Zambia," Havana, May 19, 1975; Ramos Latour to Roa,

Dar-es-Salaam, Aug. 13, 1975; *Zambia Daily Mail*, June 25, 1975, p. 1; *Times of Zambia*, Sept. 8, 1975, p. 1; Anglin and Shaw, *Zambia's Foreign Policy*, p. 326.)

50. Interview with Morejón.

51. See "Síntesis," pp. 6-7, and "Informe," pp. 1-2.

52. Interview with Risquet.

53. Interview with Lúcio Lara.

54. Interview with Risquet. In his capacity as a member of the secretariat of the PCC, Risquet attended the sessions of the Political Bureau.

55. The preparatory meeting for the conference was held in Havana in late March 1975. The conference was held on September 5-8. (See *Granma*. Apr. 1, 5, 15, 1975, all p. 1; Sept. 5, p. 1; Sept. 6, p. 8; Sept. 9, p. 2.) On the depth of the Cubans' commitment to Puerto Rican independence, see Bowdler to SecState, Sept. 14, 1978, National Security Affairs, Brzezinski Material, Country File, Cuba, box 13, Jimmy Carter Library.

56. Quotation from interview with Onambwe.

57. *Elima*, July 23, 1975, p. 1 (quoting FNLA communiqué); Thom, "Angola's 1975-76 Civil War," p. 22.

58. *Jornal do Comércio*, July 28, 1975, p. 20.

59. Quotations from *Elima*, July 26, 1975, p. 8 (quoting Johnny Eduardo), and Heimer, *Decolonization*, p. 73. For the fighting described in this paragraph, see *Jornal Novo*. July 31, Aug. 1 and 2, 1975, all p. 17; *Jornal do Comércio*. July 25, 26, 29, 1975, all p. 1; *Times*, July 26, 1975, p. 5; *Le Monde*, July 27, 1975, p. 6; *Cape Times*, July 26, 1975, p. 1; *RDM*. July 24, 1975, p. 7; July 26, p. 3; July 28, p. 2; July 30, p. 2.

60. On Savimbi's secret talks, see chapter 13.

61. *Le Monde*, Aug. 8, 1975, p. 1.

62. Thom, "Angola's 1975-76 Civil War," p. 6.

63. *WP*, Aug. 24, 1975, B1.

64. Davis to Sisco, July 12, 1975, p. 2, NSA; "[sanitized]—Angola," [late July 1975], pp. 3-4, NSA.

65. See chapter 13.

66. Quotations from Stockwell, *Search*, p. 58; *Expresso*, Aug. 30, 1975, p. 12; *RDM*, Aug. 23, 1975, p. 5.

67. See *Jornal Novo*, Aug. 6 and 7, 1975, both p. 17, and *Jornal do Comércio*, Aug. 6, 1975, p. 16.

68. Quotations from Mulcahy, Transcripts of Secretary of State Henry Kissinger's Staff Meetings, 1973-1977, Aug. 15, 1975, p. 10, box 8, NA; *Le Monde*, Aug. 8, 1975, p. 3; NSC, "Response," p. 20; *RDM*, Aug. 12, 1975, p. 5. The exodus of the whites can best be followed in *Jornal Novo*, May-Nov. 1975. An excellent account of Portugal's internal strife in 1975 is Maxwell, *The Making*.

69. *Jornal do Comércio*, Aug. 25, 1975, p. 2, and Sept. 5, p. 4; *RDM*, Apr. 1, 1976, p. 1; Spies, *Operasie*, pp. 44-48; du Preez, *Avontuur*, pp. 23-24; de Villiers and de Villiers, *PW*, pp. 242-44; P. W. Botha, Jan. 26, 1976, Republic of South Africa, *House of Assembly Debates*, col. 47; Wolfers and Bergerol, *Angola*, pp. 12-13.

70. See Díaz Argüelles to Colomé, [late Aug. 1975], 4 pp.; Díaz Argüelles to Colomé, Sept. 2, 1975, 14 pp.; Díaz Argüelles to Colomé, Sept. 3, 1975, 9 pp.

(signed by Díaz Argüelles but the handwriting is Cadelo's); Díaz Argüelles to Colomé, [late Sept. 1975], 5 pp.; Díaz Argüelles to Colomé, Oct. 1, 1975, 15 pp.; Díaz Argüelles to Colomé, [Oct. 15, 1975], 26 pp.; Díaz Argüelles to Colomé, [Oct. 16, 1975], 2 pp.; "Situación militar en Angola. Octubre/75," [Nov. 1?, 1975], 13 pp. Díaz Argüelles also cabled specific requests. See [MINFAR], "Solicitud de Argüelles," [Aug. 25, 1975, through Sept. 26, 1975]. In early November, a more senior officer replaced Díaz Argüelles as head of the MMCA.

Unless otherwise noted, all of Díaz Argüelles's reports cited in this chapter are from Luanda.

71. Díaz Argüelles to Colomé, [late Aug. 1975], pp. 1, 4; interview with Onambwe.

72. Killoran to SecState, Luanda, Aug. 20, 1975, p. 1 (quoting Luís de Almeida, the MPLA's chief of information services), and Aug. 21, 1975, NSA.

73. Díaz Argüelles to Colomé, Sept. 2, 1975, pp. 3, 5, 6, 9-10, 13, 12; Díaz Argüelles to Colomé, Sept. 3, 1975, p. 6.

74. Westad, "Moscow," p. 25. Westad explains that this document is a record of the conversation between the Soviet chargé and Osmany Cienfuegos, who had brought Castro's letter to the embassy. No copy of the letter is available in the Russian archives, and I have been unable to obtain either Cienfuegos's version of this conversation or a copy of Castro's letter.

CIA officials noted that in early September seven Cuban generals had disappeared from circulation. The agency later speculated that they must have gone to Angola ([CIA], "Cuba: Senior Officers reportedly in Angola," Nov. 25, 1975, NSA; USIB, *National Intelligence Bulletin*, Nov. 26, 1975, NSA). Actually, they had gone to the Soviet Union to take a two-year general staff course at the Voroshilov military academy. One of the seven generals, Raúl Menéndez Tomassevich, noted in an unpublished memoir that he had been appointed to head the MMCA in 1975—not by Castro, but by "the yankee press." In December 1975 *Newsweek* claimed that Menéndez Tomassevich and six other Cuban generals who had dropped out of sight the previous September were "running Castro's operation" in Angola. Menéndez Tomassevich remarked, "The CIA, if it was the source of the information, was completely off base, because we were all studying in Moscow at the Voroshilov military academy." (Quotations from *Newsweek*, Dec. 29, 1975, p. 33, and Menéndez Tomassevich and Garciga Blanco, "Patria Africana," pp. 11-12. See also Raúl Castro, "Del ministro de las Fuerzas Armadas Revolucionarias sobre la designación de jefes y oficiales de las FAR a cursar estudio en las academias del estado mayor general y de la defensa antiaerea de las fuerzas armadas soviéticas," Jan. 2, 1975.)

75. Westad, "Moscow," p. 25.

76. Quotations from Colby, NSC meeting, July 25, 1975, p. 2, NSAd, NSC Meeting Minutes, box 2, GRFL, and Dobrynin, *In Confidence*, p. 348.

77. "Síntesis," pp. 7-8.

78. Interview with Risquet (quoted); García Márquez, *Operación Carlota*, p. 10.

79. Quotations from Ernesto Antunes, "A Descolonização," p. 215; Cable no. 388, Lisbon, Sept. 4, 1975; Major Ernesto Llanes to Chief Department Foreign Relations (quoting Portuguese ambassador José Custódio de Freitas), Havana, Sept. 10, 1975; Espinosa, *La batalla*, p. 28. (Espinosa's memoir about Cabinda focuses on September-November 1975.) See also Bowen to Gondin, Lisbon, Aug. 27 and 30, 1975; Silvio to Bowen, Havana, Sept. 5 and 7, 1975; Bowen to Silvio, Lisbon: Sept. 5, 10, 18, 1975. Interviews with Cadelo, Burgos, Schueg, and Saucedo (MMCA members who arrived in Angola in August and September); Cadelo to Gleijeses, p. 12.

80. [Díaz] Argüelles, "Plan de medidas para asegurar la déscarga, traslado, ubicación y acondicionamiento de los medios materiales y personal cubano," [Sept. 1975].

81. [MINFAR], "Buques empleados para el traslado de fuerzas y medios `Operación Carlota,'" n.d.; "Informe," p. 3.

82. "En conversación con el Jefe Superior el 13.9.75 planteó," p. 1.

83. Colomé to Columbié, Havana, Sept. 28, 1975; Espinosa, *La batalla*, p. 209.

84. Interviews with Risquet (quoted) and Onambwe; "Síntesis," pp. 8 and 14.

85. *Times*, Aug. 4, 1975, p. 13.

86. NSC, "Response," p. 33.

87. See "Presidential Task Force on Portuguese Territories in Africa: Report," July 17, 1961, NSF, box 5, JFKL; Gullion (U.S. ambassador, Leopoldville) to SecState, Aug. 8, 1963, Pol 19 Ang, SNF, NA; Hughes (INR) to SecState, "Prospects for Angolan Nationalist Movement," Nov. 5, 1963, NSF, box 5, JFKL; Phyllis Martin, "Connection." For an overview of the Congo and Cabinda from 1960 through 1976, see Mabeko Tali, "Le Congo," pp. 112-39, and Maganga-Boumba, "Le Congo," pp. 105-40.

88. [Portugal], Estado-Maior do Exército, "O caso de Angola," pp. 20-21 quoted; interviews with Paulo Lara and Kianda (both fought in Cabinda in 1973-74); Mabeko Tali, "Dissidences," pp. 172-97; *Provincia de Angola*, Dec. 20, 1974, p. 5; Sousa, *Angola*, p. 36 (Sousa was the correspondent of *Provincia de Angola* in Cabinda from 1964 through September 1975).

89. Quotations from *La Semaine* (Brazzaville), Oct. 6, 1974, p. 6, and Nov. 17, p. 1. See also ibid.: July 7, 1974, p. 7; Aug. 25, p. 3; Oct. 27, p. 1; *Provincia de Angola*: Oct. 2 and 19, 1974, both p. 11; Oct. 29, p. 10; Nov. 29, p. 3; Sousa, *Angola*, pp. 20-25; Crimi, "Cabinda."

90. *Provincia de Angola*, Nov. 4, 1974, p. 5 quoted. See also ibid.: Nov. 1, 3, 4, 5, 6, 12, all p. 1; Nov. 17, p. 5; Nov. 28, p. 1; Dec. 7, p. 9; Dec. 14, p. 11; O *Planalto*, Nov. 19, 1974, p. 1; *La Semaine*, Nov. 24, 1974, p. 3, and Dec. 8, p. 1; *Le Monde*, Nov. 5, 1974, p. 7, and Nov. 19, p. 4; *Elima*: Nov. 5 and 8, 1974, both p. 1; Dec. 21, p. 5; Sousa, *Angola*, pp. 25-29; Correia, *Descolonização*, pp. 112-15. (Correia was a Portuguese officer who was sent from Luanda to Cabinda in early November to report on the incidents.)

91. "Conversación con Agostinho Neto, día 31 de diciembre de 1974," enclosed in "Visita," p. 27 quoted;

Ngouabi, *Vers la construction*, p. 204; "Rechenschaft Bericht II. Parteitag PCT, Dezember 1974," pp. 10-11, enclosed in "Arbeitsmaterial (Stand 20.12. 1974)," SED, DY30 IVB 2/20/292.

92. NSC, "Response," pp. 45-46; Neto, *Expresso*, Jan. 25, 1975, p. 17.

93. *Le Monde*, May 17, 1975, p. 6; NSC, "Response," p. 32.

94. *Elima*, Jan. 12, 1975, p. 8.

95. "Visita," p. 7 quoted; Marcum, *Angolan Revolution*, 2:254.

96. See *Provincia de Angola*. Mar. 8, 1975, p. 11; Mar. 18, p. 1; Mar. 24, p. 2; June 4, p. 3; June 5, p. 3; June 6, p. 2; June 11, p. 2; *O Comércio*. June 6, 7, 11, 1975, all p. 1; June 18, p. 3; Sousa, *Angola*, pp. 82-98; NSC, "Response," p. 33; *WP*, July 17, 1975, p. 20. UNITA's token military force in Cabinda withdrew from the enclave in early August. (See *Jornal Novo*, Aug. 9, 1975, p. 13.)

97. Quotations from *NYT*, July 13, 1975, p. 11, and NSC, "Response," p. 32. See also *Le Monde*, May 17, 1975, p. 6.

98. Quotations from art. 3 of the Alvor agreement; Lúcio Lara, in *Jornal Novo*, May 28, 1975, p. 17; Westad, "Moscow," p. 25 (quoting a June 14 report by Ambassador Yevgeny Afanasenko). See also Oramas to Columbié, Havana, May 28, 1975, MINREX.

99. Díaz Argüelles to Colomé, Sept. 2, 1975, p. 10.

100. Quotation from interview with Oramas. See also García Lara to Roa, Brazzaville, Feb. 12, 1971; "Reunión sostenida en el Comité Central del P.C.C. entre la delegación militar de la R.P.C. (Congo) y los Cos. Jorge R. Risquet y cdte. Escalona," [Havana, Oct. 1974]; "Reunión con el coronel Yoaquin Yombi Opango, ministro de defensa nacional de la República Popular del Congo (enero 2, 1975)"; "Entrevista con el Presidente Marien Ngouabi y la delegación cubana que asistió al segundo congreso del Partido Congolés del Trabajo," Jan. 2, 1975, enclosed in Columbié to Roa, Brazzaville, Jan. 12, 1975; "Protocolo de Asistencia Militar entre la República de Cuba y la República Popular del Congo," Feb. 19, 1975; Meléndez Bachs to Osmany Cienfuegos, Havana, Mar. 5, 1975.

101. NSC, "Response," p. 34.

102. On Mobutu's friends, see chapter 13. In 1975 the Congolese armed forces had about 5,500 men, whereas Zaire had 50,000 (Pabanel, *Les coups*, p. 23, table 1).

103. *La Semaine*, Sept. 28, 1975, p. 8 (quoting Ngouabi), and Oct. 19, p. 9; Soudan, "Guerre," p. 67.

104. "Resumen anual de las relaciones bilaterales entre Cuba y el Congo," p. 4, enclosed in Columbié to Carlos Rafael Rodríguez, Jan. 9, 1976. The reports of Columbié from late September 1975 include many examples of the Congo's aid to the MPLA. (All of Columbié's reports are from Brazzaville.)

105. See "Informe evaluativo de la situación económica de la R.P. del Congo en el año 1975," p. 15 quoted, enclosed in Columbié to Carlos Rafael Rodríguez, Jan. 9, 1976, MINREX; "Acuerdo de Colaboración económica y científico técnica entre el gobierno revolucionario de la república de Cuba y el gobierno de la república popular del Congo," Havana, Sept. 17, 1975, MIECE; Columbié to Carlos Rafael Rodríguez, Oct. 31, 1975; Osmany to Columbié, Havana, Nov. 7, 1975.

106. Columbié to Carlos Rafael [Rodríguez], Oct. 10, 1975 (quoted); Díaz Argüelles to Colomé, [Oct. 15, 1975]; [MINFAR], "Buques empleados para el traslado de fuerzas y medios `Operación Carlota,'" n.d.; Espinosa, *La batalla*, p. 209.

107. Díaz Argüelles to Colomé, [Oct. 15, 1975], pp. 5, 9-11, 12. See also Díaz Argüelles, cable of Sept. 14, 1975, in MINFAR, "Solicitud de Argüelles," [Aug. 25, 1975, through Sept. 26, 1975]; [MINFAR], "Composición de fuerzas y medios de la unidad incluyendo el incremento del Punto 4," [late Oct. 1975]. On the 1965 agreement, interview with Estrada, who was a senior intelligence officer at the time.

108. [MINFAR], "Composición de fuerzas y medios de la unidad incluyendo el incremento del Punto 4," [late Oct. 1975]; MINFAR, "Solicitud de Argüelles," [Aug. 25, 1975, through Sept. 26, 1975]; "Informe," p. 3; "Síntesis," pp. 11-12.

109. Cables of Sept. 25 (quoted) and 26, 1975, in MINFAR, "Solicitud de Argüelles," [Aug. 25, 1975, through Sept. 26, 1975].

110. Díaz Argüelles to Colomé, [late Sept. 1975], pp. 1-2 quoted, and "Informe," p. 3.

111. Quotations from *NYT*, Sept. 22, 1975, p. 2; *Jornal Novo*, Sept. 10, 1975, p. 14; *Daily Telegraph*, Oct. 10, 1975, p. 16. See also *Jornal Novo*, Sept. 13, 1975, p. 18, and Sept. 19, p. 17; *Le Monde*, Sept. 25, 1975, p. 3; Representação Especial [of Brazil] em Luanda, "Situação em Luanda," Sept. 23, 1975, NSA. In late August, the MPLA had executed six of its soldiers, who had been found guilty of murdering twelve civilians (*O Comércio*, Aug. 28, 1975, p. 1; *Diário de Luanda*, Aug. 28, 1975, p. 5; *Jornal de Angola*, Aug. 31, 1975, p. 3; *NYT*, Sept. 22, 1975, p. 2).

112. *Diário de Luanda*, Sept. 1, 1975, p. 2 quoted. See also *Jornal Novo*. Aug. 21, 1975, p. 14; Aug. 30, p. 14; Sept. 9, p. 14; Sept. 18, p. 1; *Jornal de Angola* Aug. 31, 1975, p. 3, and Sept. 4, p. 3; *Jornal do Comércio*, Sept. 2, 1975, p. 12; *O Comércio*, Aug. 28, 1975, p. 1.

113. Stockwell, *Search*, p. 193 quoted; Bridgland, *Savimbi*, p. 168; Costa Gomes, *Sobre Portugal*, p. 46. For Neto's comments, see Díaz Argüelles to Colomé, Sept. 3, 1975, pp. 5-6.

114. *Jornal Novo*, Sept. 19, 1975, p. 7.

115. Quotations from *Le Monde*, Aug. 20, 1975, p. 4, and Aug. 19, p. 3 (quoting Johnny Eduardo), and *Jornal do Comércio*, Sept. 9, 1975, p. 8.

116. *Daily News* (Dar-es-Salaam), Nov. 4, 1975, p. 4 (quoted).

117. Olivier Postel-Vinay, *Le Monde*, Sept. 10, 1975, p. 3; *RDM*, Aug. 27, 1975, p. 14; CIA, "Staff Notes: Soviet Union, Eastern Europe," Aug. 20, 1975, p. 2, NSA; Thom, "Angola's 1975-76 Civil War," p. 12.

118. *Jornal de Angola*, Sept. 12, 1975, p. 3 quoted; *Jornal Novo*, Sept. 12, 1975, p. 17.

119. Interviews with Kianda (quoted), Ndalu, Rui de Matos, and Ngongo.

120. Interviews with Ngongo, Kianda, Ndalu, and Rui de Matos; Avelino González to Colomé, Brazzaville, Sept. 3, 1975.

121. *Jornal Novo*, Sept. 10, 1975, p. 14; Sept. 12, p. 17; Sept. 22, p. 14; *Jornal do Comércio*, Sept. 11, 1975, p. 8; *Jornal de Angola*, Sept. 10, 1975, p. 1, and Sept. 11, p. 3; *Diário de Luanda*, Sept. 10 and 11, 1975, both p. 1; *Le Monde*, Sept. 13, 1975, p. 3.

122. Stockwell, *Search*, p. 201.

123. Hyland, Davis, and Kissinger, Transcripts of Secretary of State Henry Kissinger's Staff Meetings, 1973-1977, Sept. 11, 1975, pp. 27-29 quoted, box 8, NA; Davis and Kissinger, Sept. 4, 1975, pp. 33-34, ibid.

124. Washington Special Actions Group Meeting, Oct. 10, 1975, pt. 3, p. 2 (quoting Colby). On Pretoria's role, see chapter 13. On the fighting north of Luanda in the second half of September, see *Jornal Novo*, Sept. 22, 1975, p. 14; *Guardian*, Sept. 24, 1975, p. 4; CIA, *Intelligence Checklist*, Sept. 23, 1975, NSA; *Elima*, Sept. 23, 1975, p. 1; *Le Monde*, Sept. 23, 1975, p. 6; *Cape Times*, Sept. 25, 1975, p. 15; *Times of Zambia*, Sept. 26, 1975, p. 1; *RDM*, Sept. 25, 1975, p. 4, and Sept. 26, p. 3; "Síntesis," p. 9.

125. Interviews with Ndalu (quoted), Rui de Matos, Ngongo, Kianda, and Xiyetu; Díaz Argüelles to Colomé, Oct. 1, 1975, p. 2.

126. Interviews with Kianda (quoted), Rui de Matos (quoted), Ngongo (quoted), Xiyetu, and Ndalu.

127. Quotations from *Elima*, Oct. 21 and 23, 1975, both p. 1.

128. See Spies, *Operasie*, p. 132, and du Preez, *Avontuur*, p. 113.

129. Díaz Argüelles, "Situación militar en Angola. Octubre/75," [Nov. 1?, 1975], p. 3 quoted; "Síntesis," pp. 14-17; *Jornal de Angola*, Nov. 2, 1975, p. 2; *Diário de Luanda*, Nov. 1, 1975, pp. 6-7; and, for the recollections of a doctor who participated in the fighting, "Especialidad? Médico-morterista," *Granma*, Oct. 30, 1996, p. 4.

130. *Le Monde*, Sept. 13, 1975, p. 3; Díaz Argüelles to Colomé, Oct. 1, 1975, p. 11.

131. INR, "Angola: The MPLA Prepares for Independence," Sept. 22, 1975, pp. 4-5, NSA.

132. Quotations from *Daily Telegraph*, Oct. 10, 1975, p. 16, and *RDM*, Oct. 23, 1975, p. 21. See also Spies, *Operasie*, pp. 75-76, 83-85, and Representação Especial do Brasil em Luanda to Foreign Ministry, Oct. 3, 1975, NSA.

133. *Le Monde*, Oct. 23, 1975, p. 6. The two dailies (Luanda's only dailies) were *Jornal de Angola* and *Diário de Luanda*.

134. Representação Especial do Brasil em Luanda to Foreign Ministry, Oct. 24, 1975, p. 2, NSA.

135. Westad, "Moscow," p. 26.

136. Quotations from CIA, "Staff notes: Soviet Union–Eastern Europe," Aug. 20, 1975, p. 2, NSA; INR, "Angola: The MPLA Prepares for Independence," Sept. 22, 1975, p. 2; CIA, *National Intelligence Daily*, Oct. 11, 1975, NSA. See also Killoran to SecState, Luanda, Oct. 10, 1975, NSA; USIB, *National Intelligence Bulletin*, Oct. 25, 1975, NSA; "Cuban Military Personnel in Angola," [late Nov. 1975], PPS, box 372. The intelligence was reworked before it was provided to Congress in order to support the administration's account. (See CIA, "A Brief Chronicle of Events in Angola," enclosed in Mulcahy to Sisco, Dec. 17, 1975, MF 00549, NSA.)

The South African intelligence officer stationed in Luanda knew nothing about the Cubans' presence when he left on August 13, 1975 (du Preez, *Avontuur*, pp. 12, 30).

On January 11, 1976, *New York Times*'s David Binder reported from Havana that "In an informal talk last night," Carlos Rafael Rodríguez, deputy prime minister and Political Bureau member, said that Cuba's involvement in Angola "became substantial late last spring," when Neto asked Cuba for advisers "` and we sent 180—no it was 230—military men to Angola. They set up four training centers for Angolan fighters'" (*NYT*, Jan. 12, 1976, p. 7 quoted and Feb. 5, p. 12). This story was widely repeated. See *CSM*, Jan. 22, 1976, p. 9; Szulc, *Fidel*, p. 708; Valenta, "Soviet," pp. 100-101; Kissinger, *Renewal*, p. 806; Bennett, *Condemned*, p. 153.

Binder's account is flatly contradicted by the evidence. The Cubans began arriving in Angola in late August—as U.S. intelligence reported at the time. Furthermore, it strains credulity to imagine that Rodríguez, who was one of the most sophisticated Cuban leaders, would confide state secrets to an American journalist and, in the process, challenge his government's account of events.

137. Robert Hultslander, fax to Piero Gleijeses, Dec. 22, 1998, pp. 4, 6.

138. Kissinger, *Renewal*, p. 809; Greig, *Challenge*, p. 253; Charles, *Soviet Union*, p. 133; Meyer, *Facing Reality*, pp. 248-49.

139. Quotations from Deputy Assistant Secretary for African Affairs Mulcahy to Kissinger, May 7, 1975, p. 6, DOS MF 8403582/3, and Colby to Senior Review Group, June 24, 1975, NSA. See also "Portuguese Policy and Objectives in Angola," June 24, 1975, pp. 1-2, enclosed in Colby to Senior Review Group, June 24, 1975, NSA; Kissinger [to Ford], "Meeting of the National Security Council, Friday, June 27, 1975, 2:30 p.m.," p. 4, NSA; NSC, "Response," pp. 18-19; Díaz Argüelles to Colomé, Sept. 3, 1975, p. 4.

140. Thom, "Angola's 1975-76 Civil War," p. 22. The attack, in the morning of July 27, was in retaliation for an attack allegedly perpetrated by seven MPLA soldiers against a Portuguese patrol the previous night. (*Jornal do Comércio*, July 28 and 29, 1975, both p. 1; *Diário de Luanda*, July 28 and 29, 1975, both p. 2; *RDM*, July 28, 1975, p. 1; *Daily Telegraph*, July 28, 1975, p. 1.)

In his memoirs Pompílio da Cruz, a leader of a white separatist group that sought to impose a "Rhodesian solution," explains that the attack was actually carried out by members of his group, disguised in FAPLA uniforms (*Angola*, pp. 220-21).

141. See chapter 16.

142. Hultslander, fax to Gleijeses, Dec. 22, 1998, p. 3; Heimer, *Decolonization*, p. 82.

143. Legum in Legum and Hodges, *After Angola*, p. 15 quoted.

CHAPTER THIRTEEN

1. Du Pisani, *SWA/Namibia*, Soggot, *Namibia*; Ansprenger, *Die SWAPO.* Breytenbach, *Buffalo Soldiers*, p. 183 quoted.

2. Du Preez, *Avontuur*, pp. 2-3, 19-23 (p. 21 quoted); Burger, "Teeninsurgensie," pp. 187-99, 206-14, 277-97; Spies, *Operasie*, pp. 21-26, 40-41; Van der Waals (South Africa's vice-consul, Luanda, 1970-73), "Angola," pp. 465-69; José Antunes, *A guerra*, 1:400, 412; Soggot, *Namibia*, pp. 108-11; INR, "Angola: An Assessment of the Insurgency," Sept. 16, 1970, Pol 23-9 Ang, SNF, NA.

3. Burger, "Teeninsurgensie," p. 282 quoted; Dippenaar, *History*, esp. pp. 371-404 (this is the official history of the South African police); Ellert, *Rhodesian*, pp. 110-23 (Ellert was a senior Rhodesian intelligence official); DOS, "South Africa: Policy Review," June 1974, p. 14, enclosed in Easum and Lord to SecState, June 24, 1974, PPS, box 344; Cowderoy and Nesbit, *War*, pp. 50, 59; Seegers, "Revolution," pp. 250-51, 294; *Rhodesia Herald*, Aug. 2, 1975, p. 1; *Cape Times*, Aug. 2, 1975, p. 1.

4. Ian Smith, *Betrayal*, p. 226.

5. *NYT*, Mar. 4, 1976, p. 1.

6. Cilliers, *Counter-insurgency*, pp. 5-22; Ellert, *Rhodesian*, pp. 82-93.

7. Ian Smith, *Betrayal*, p. 186.

8. On the détente policy discussed in this and the next three paragraphs, see Anglin and Shaw, *Zambia's Foreign Policy*, pp. 272-309; Tamarkin, *Making*, pp. 20-77; David Martin and Johnson, *Struggle*, pp. 115-90; Ian Smith, *Betrayal*, pp. 159-75.

9. Quotations from Flower, *Serving*, p. 159, and *Le Monde*, Aug. 17, 1975, p. 3.

10. Quotations from INR, "Rhodesia: A Breakthrough toward Settlement?," Dec. 16, 1974, p. 4, NSA; *RDM* (Johannesburg), Feb. 11, 1975, p. 1; *Zambia Daily Mail*, Feb. 11, 1975, p. 1.

11. Quotations from *Rhodesia Herald*, Feb. 12, 1975, p. 1, and Mar. 11, p. 1; Ian Smith, *Betrayal*, p. 175.

12. Quotations from *Zambia Daily Mail*, May 3, 1975, p. 1, and INR, "Rhodesia: A Breakthrough toward Settlement?," Dec. 16, 1974, p. 4, NSA.

13. *Zambia Daily Mail*, Apr. 9, 1975, p. 1.

14. Ibid., Jan. 22, 1975, p. 4. See also Lord, Hyland, and Mulcahy to SecState, "Short-Term Assistance for Mozambique," Feb. 7, 1975, PPS, box 352; *Jornal Novo* (Lisbon), June 25, 1975, p. 11; *RDM*, Mar. 11, 1975, p. 15; Metrowich, *Frontiers*, pp. 80-87; Maxwell, "Legacy," pp. 17-18.

15. Spies, *Operasie*, p. xvi quoted; du Preez, *Avontuur*.

16. This and the next three paragraphs rely on Spies, *Operasie*, pp. 60-65, and du Preez, *Avontuur*, pp. 13-23.

17. Spies, *Operasie*, p. 62.

18. Ibid., pp. 63-64.

19. Ibid., pp. 64-65; Roherty, *State Security*, p. 73; Deon Geldenhuys, *Diplomacy*, p. 80.

20. Roherty, *State Security*, p. 73.

21. CIA, DI, "Some Aspects of Subversion in Africa," Oct. 19, 1967, p. 3, NSFCF, box 78.

22. NIE, "The Liberation Movements of Southern Africa," Nov. 24, 1967, p. 15, NSF, NIE, box 8, LBJL. See also CIA, "The Current Political Situation and Prospects in Tropical Africa," May 20, 1966, NSFCF, box 76; CIA, DI, "Some Aspects of Subversion in Africa," Oct. 19, 1967, NSFCF, box 78.

23. Colby, *Honorable Men*, p. 368; interview with Devlin.

24. *WP*, Jan. 5, 1971, p. 7.

25. Quotations from Themido, *Dez anos*, pp. 54-55, and DOS, Bureau of African Affairs, "U.S. Relations with the African Liberation Movements," n.d., p. 4, enclosed in Rogers to All African Diplomatic Posts, Lisbon, London, Paris, Rome, Dec. 2, 1971, FOIA.

26. Good, *U.D.I.*, p. 324. (Good was ambassador to Zambia, 1965-68.)

27. Reis, "The United States Stand on Self Determination in Africa," p. 4, enclosed in Amembassy Lusaka to DOS, Feb. 28, 1972, Pol 1 Afr-US, SNF, NA; Newsom to SecState, Oct. 5, 1973, Pol Afr-US, SNF, NA.

28. Hyland, *Rivals*, p. 131. See also José Antunes, *Os Americanos*, pp. 296-99, 305-12; U.S. House, Select Committee on Intelligence, *U.S. Intelligence Agencies*, pp. 777-811.

29. Quotations from interview with Post and tel. interviews with Briggs and Fugit.

30. Robert Hultslander, fax to Piero Gleijeses, Dec. 22, 1998, pp. 1, 2.

31. Quotations from interview with Post; tel. interview with Fugit; Colby, *Honorable Men*, p. 368. See also *CIA: The Pike Report*, p. 152; Stockwell, *Search*, p. 52; tel. interview with Briggs.

32. Williams to Rostow, Nov. 15, 1962, p. 3, MWP, box 10.

33. Wright to Williams, May 23, 1963, pp. 2-3, enclosed in Williams to Wright, June 3, 1963, MWP, box 28.

34. RFK to McGeorge Bundy, Nov. 20, 1963, NSA.

35. Quotations from DOS, Policy Planning Council, "National Policy Paper on Southern Africa," draft, Dec. 1968, p. 82, DOS MF 8403582/1; DOS, MemoConv (de Mello, Newsom, et al.), May 25, 1972, p. 2, Pol 7 Port, SNF, NA; interview with Easum.

36. Stockwell, *Search*, pp. 48-49.

37. Quotations from "Talking Points for Secretary Kissinger: National Security Council Meeting on Angola (Friday—June 27, 1975)," p. 1, enclosed in Horan to Kissinger, June 26, 1975, NSA; Deming to Williams, Mar. 16, 1962, p. 2, box 1, Lot 65 D 257, NA; tel. interview with Briggs; Mulcahy to SecState, May 13, 1975, p. 2, PPS, box 368.

Portuguese foreign minister Nogueira confirms Briggs's recollection: *Salazar: O Último Combate*, pp. 22-29, and *Diálogos Interditos*, 1:83-85, 102-19, 170-73. See also Anderson (U.S. ambassador, Lisbon) to SecState, June 12, 1964, NSFCF, box 81, and DOS, memo for Kissinger, Nov. 16, 1970, Pol 7 Port, SNF, NA.

38. Interview with DCM Nelson.

39. The literature on U.S. policy toward Angola in 1974-76 is abundant but suffers from lack of primary sources. It is only very recently that a significant body of relevant documents has been declassified. With this proviso, the best analysis is Garthoff's *Détente*, pp. 556-93. Two other valuable studies are Klinghoffer, *The Angolan War*, and Bender, "Kissinger in Angola." There are very few accounts by participants. INR director Hyland chose to be brief and above all very discreet (*Rivals*, pp. 130-47). NSC aide Rodman offered a loyal defense of Kissinger's Angolan policy that breaks no new ground (*More Precious*, pp. 163-82). Assistant Secretary for African Affairs Davis's brief account ("The Angolan Decision") is vindicated by the documents that have been declassified. Stockwell's *Search* has stood the test of time. The least reliable account is Kissinger's *Renewal*, pp. 791-833.

40. Interviews with Post (U.S. consul general in Luanda in 1969-72) and Nelson; tel. interview with Killoran. The best study on U.S. policy toward Portugal through the critical eighteen to twenty months that followed the Portuguese coup is Schneidman, "American Foreign Policy," 2:347-477.

41. Easum, in Transcripts of Secretary of State Henry Kissinger's Staff Meetings, 1973-1977, Dec. 5, 1974, p. 38 quoted, box 5, NA; interviews with Easum, and with Roy Haverkamp and Alfonso Arenales, respectively director and deputy director for Southern African Affairs at the Bureau of African Affairs; Schneidman, "American Foreign Policy," 2:438-41; Oudes, "The Sacking."

42. Interview with Easum.

43. Interview with Devlin.

44. Quotations from interview with Easum and from NSDM 40, Feb. 17, 1970, FOIA 1993/2310. The members of the committee were the national security adviser as chair, the attorney general, the under secretary of state for political affairs, the deputy secretary of defense, and the DCI (ibid.).

45. Interviews with Easum (quoted) and Arenales, one of the officials with whom Easum had spoken. See also Easum in U.S. House, Committee on Foreign Affairs, Subcommittee on Africa, *The Complex of United States-Portuguese Relations*, Oct. 8, 1974, p. 95.

46. Interview with Briggs.

47. Interviews with Easum (quoted) and Y.

48. Stockwell, *Search*, pp. 67 (quoted) and 258. For the $10,000 figure, see Mulcahy to SecState, May 13, 1975, PPS, box 368.

49. Hultslander, fax to Gleijeses, Dec. 22, 1998, pp. 2-3; interview with Devlin.

50. Interviews with Easum, Haverkamp, and Arenales; "Southern African Issues," enclosed in Easum and Lewis to Springsteen, Sept. 3, 1974, PPS, box 349; Schneidman, "American Foreign Policy," 2:438-41; Oudes, "The Sacking."

51. Quotations from *RDM*, Jan. 10, 1975, p. 1; Diggs to Kissinger, Jan. 21, 1975, in U.S. Senate, Committee on Foreign Relations, *Nomination*, p. 85; interview with Davis; *Zambia Daily Mail*, May 19, 1975, p. 4.

52. Quotations from interview with Y; Schneidman, "American Foreign Policy," 2:443 (quoting Colby); tel. interview with Hyland. Also interview with Mulcahy (who attended the meeting); Mulcahy to SecState, May 13, 1975, PPS, box 368; Hyland, *Rivals*, p. 137.

53. Interviews with Mulcahy and Y.

54. Killoran to SecState, Jan. 16, 1975, sec. 2, p. 2, DOS MF 8802086/2.

55. Tel. interview with Hyland (quoted); interviews with Mulcahy and Y.

56. Killoran to SecState, Feb. 25, 1976, sec. 1, p. 2, DOS MF 88013808/2.

57. Horan to Kissinger, June 18, 1975, p. 4, NSA.

58. Amembassy Lisbon to Kissinger et al., Mar. 28, 1975, pp. 1-2, DOS MF 8403582/2.

59. Davis, Hyland, and Lord to Kissinger, Apr. 4, 1975, pp. 1-5, DOS MF 8802915/2. For a similar plea ("we would be well advised to develop contingency plans in the event the transition to independence is not orderly"), see DOS, "Policy Guidelines for Sub-Saharan Africa" (draft), p. 33, enclosed in Davis and Lord to SecState, Apr. 3, 1975, PPS, box 351.

Due to the dearth of documents, there is no definitive account of Soviet policy toward Portugal in 1975. Garthoff writes that "although the Soviet Union had covertly provided routine financial support to the Portuguese Communist party, in all other respects it was careful not to interfere in Portugal." The statement about the "delicately balanced policy" indicates that this was also the view of the State Department. (Garthoff, *Détente*, p. 540 quoted; Szulc, "Lisbon and Washington"; Wettig, "Entspannungs- und Klassenpolitik"; Mansfield to Ford, Aug. 22, 1975, President's Handwriting File, box 7, GRFL.)

60. Kirk (INR) to Davis, Apr. 25, 1975, p. 1, DOS MF 8802915/2.

61. Davis to Kissinger, May 1, 1975, DOS MF 8802915/2. See also [CIA], Memorandum for: The 40 Committee, May 29, 1975, NSA.

62. Interviews with Wilkowski (quoted) and Nelson. Wilkowski arrived in Zambia on September 3, 1972, and presented her credentials on September 26 ("Jean M. Wilkowski," Apr. 11, 1975, Edward J. Savage Files, box 7, GRFL).

63. Legum, *Cape Times*, Apr. 25, 1975, p. 16.

64. *NYT*, Apr. 25, 1975, p. 35, prints a White House transcript of the speech; see also *Zambia Daily Mail*, Apr. 21 and 22, 1975, both p. 1.

65. National Security Council Interdepartmental Group for Africa, "Response to NSSM 224: United States Policy toward Angola," June 13, 1975, p. 45, enclosed in Nathaniel Davis to the Assistant to the President for National Security Affairs, June 16, 1975, NSA (hereafter NSC, "Response"). See also DOS (prepared for the Senate Foreign Relations Committee), "United States Policy toward Angola," Dec. 16, 1975, p. 2, NSA; *WP*, Jan. 6, 1976, p. 4; Kissinger, *Renewal*, pp. 795-98. On Tiny Rowland and Zambia, see Cronjé, Ling, and Cronjé, *Lonrho*, pp. 32-36. On Kaunda's support of Neto's enemies in 1973-74, see chapter 11.

66. Quotations from "Angola: Assessment," May 6, 1975, pp. 1, 3, enclosed in Mulcahy to SecState, May 7, 1975, DOS MF 8403582/3, and from Mulcahy to SecState, May 13, 1975, p. 3, PPS, box 368.

67. NSSM 224, May 26, 1975, NSA: NSSM and NSDM, box 2, GRFL.

68. Kissinger, *Upheaval*, p. 440.

69. NSC, "Response," pp. 55, 77.

70. Ibid., p. 79.

71. Ibid., pp. 81-82.

72. Horan to Kissinger, June 18, 1975, pp. 3, 4, NSA.

73. Scowcroft, "Talking Points for SRG Meeting on NSSM 224 Study–US Policy toward Angola. Thursday, June 19, 1975–11:00 a.m.," n.d., NSA. See also Horan to McFarlane ("Chronology of Consideration of NSSM 224"), Dec. 18, 1975, NSA.

74. "Special Sensitive Memorandum Regarding the Response to NSSM 224: ˙United States Policy toward Angola,'" n.d., enclosed in Springsteen to Scowcroft, June 25, 1975, pp. 11, 5, NSA.

75. Kissinger [to Ford], "Meeting of the National Security Council, Friday, June 27, 1975, 2:30 p.m.," p. 3, NSA.

76. Quotations from SecState, memo for president, July 28, 1970, p. 5, Pol 7 The Congo, SNF, NA, and Deane Hinton, letter to Piero Gleijeses, July 24, 1999. Mobutu first visited China in January 1973. In December 1974 he visited both China and North Korea (see *Salongo* [Kinshasa], Dec. 7-30, 1974).

77. *Elima* (Kinshasa), Jan. 22, 1975, p. 11.

78. Quotations from *Elima*, Jan. 31, 1975, p. 1, and May 22, p. 3, and interview with Walker. See also *Elima*: Mar. 11, 1975, p. 1; Apr. 3, p. 1; Apr. 13, p. 8; May 2, p. 2; May 18, p. 1; June 1, p. 13; June 3, p. 7; June 14, p. 10; June 29, p. 1.

79. *Elima*, June 22, 1975, p. 8. See also ibid.: June 16, 18-22; July 4-6; Sept. 2-3.

80. Interview with Cutler. See also Pachter, "Our Man," pp. 200-250.

81. Interview with Walker.

82. Quotations from interview with Cutler and from Davis to Sisco, July 12, 1975, p. 2 (quoting Hinton), NSA.

83. *NYT*, June 22, 1975, p. 15; *Elima*, June 22, 1975, p. 1.

84. Quotations from interview with Walker; Vance to SecState, Kinshasa, June 24, 1975, no. 5605, p. 1, NSA; Kissinger [to Ford], "Meeting of the National Security Council, Friday, June 27, 1975, 2:30 p.m.," pp. 3-4, NSA; Vance to SecState, Kinshasa, June 24, 1975, no. 5605, p. 2, NSA. See also Vance to SecState, Kinshasa, June 24, 1975, no. 5644, NSA.

85. "Talking Points for Secretary Kissinger: National Security Council Meeting on Angola (Friday, June 27, 1975)," p. 4, enclosed in Horan to Kissinger, June 26, 1975, NSA.

86. Quotations from Kissinger to Ford, July 17, 1975, James E. Connor Files, box 37, GRFL; Lynn to Ford, July 17, 1975, ibid.; Connor to Kissinger and Lynn, July 19, 1975 (quoting Ford), ibid.

87. Quotations from revised page 13 of "Special Sensitive Memorandum Regarding the Response to NSSM 224: ˙United States Policy toward Angola,'" n.d., enclosed in Springsteen to Scowcroft, June 26, 1975, NSA, and "Talking points for Secretary Kissinger: National Security Council Meeting on Angola (Friday, June 27, 1975)," p. 3, enclosed in unsigned White House memo, n.d., NSA.

88. Kissinger [to Ford], "Meeting of the National Security Council, Friday, June 27, 1975, 2:30 p.m.," p. 2, NSA.

89. Quotations from NSC meeting, June 27, 1975, NSAd, NSC Meeting Minutes, box 2, GRFL, and Horan, memo for file, June 30, 1975, NSA.

90. Davis to Sisco, July 12, 1975, quoted, NSA; see also Davis, "The Angola Decision," pp. 113-16, and Stockwell, *Search*, pp. 52-55, 180.

91. Davis to Sisco, July 12, 1975, p. 2, NSA.

92. Interviews with Mulcahy and Y.

93. Horan, memo for file, June 30, 1975, NSA (emphasis added).

94. Roherty, *State Security*, p. 73.

95. Quotations from Davis to Sisco, July 12, 1975, p. 2, NSA, and interview with Walker.

96. Interviews with Davis and Walker.

97. NSC, "Response," p. 49; Davis, July 16 memo to Sisco and Kissinger, quoted in Davis, "The Angola Decision," p. 116; Crocker, *High Noon*, p. 49 (emphasis added).

98. Davis, "The Angola Decision," p. 116.

99. "[sanitized]–Angola," [July 16, 1975], p. 6, NSA.

100. See Kissinger to the President, July 18, 1975, NSA, with Ford's signature alongside "Approve." (Unfortunately key portions of this document have been sanitized.) See also Stockwell, *Search*, pp. 47, 55, 162.

101. *Nõ Pintcha* (Bissau), Mar. 20, 1976, p. 4.

102. Quotations from Crocker, *High Noon*, p. 48, and Stockwell, *Search*, p. 139. See also Moss, "Castro's Secret War Exposed," *Sunday Telegraph* (London), Feb. 6, 1977, p. 8; Sitte, *Flug*, pp. 97-98; du Preez, *Avontuur*, p. 34; *WP*, Jan. 6, 1976, p. 4.

British economic interests in Angola were some £60 million (*Sunday Times* [London], Jan. 25, 1976, p. 10; Messiant, "1961," p. 16).

103. *Le Monde*, Aug. 10, 1975, p. 3.

104. The French had initially supported the Brazzaville FLEC, supplying weapons and helping arrange the dispatch of a small group of mercenaries to Brazzaville. (*Le Monde*, May 16, 1975, p. 7; *Le Soir* [Brussels], May 15, 1977, p. 3; Soudan, "Guerre"; Péan, *Affaires*, pp. 167-70; *Expresso* [Lisbon], May 31, 1975, p. 16, and Aug. 15, p. 7; Fournier and Legrand, *Dossier*, pp. 273-74.)

105. Quotations from Marenches, *Evil*, pp. 78-79, 81; Stockwell, *Search*, p. 192; *Le Monde*, Sept. 20, 1975, p. 6. On French aid to the FNLA and UNITA, see Frappat, "Le choc," pp. 219-21; Bach, "La France," p. 288; Gerald Ford, *A Time*, p. 345; Spies, *Operasie*, p. 55.

106. Quotations from NSC, "Response," p. 52, and USIB, *National Intelligence Bulletin*, Aug. 25, 1975, p. 7, MF 00360, NSA. See also *Le Monde*, Dec. 31, 1974, p. 3; *Elima*, June 3, 1975, p. 7; CIA, title and date deleted [summer 1975], MF 00315, NSA; Ebinger, "External Intervention," p. 689.

107. Quotations from "Brief History of Policy," p. 4, enclosed in "China: Current State of the Issue," Dec. 13, 1976, PPS, box 377; DOS Briefing Paper [for Ford's December 1975 trip to Beijing], n.d., pp. 1, 4, 5, PPS, box 373; White House MemoConv (Kissinger, Ch'iao Kuan-hua, et al.), New York, Sept. 28, 1975, p. 21, MF 00355, NSA. On relations between the Ford administration and Beijing, see Tyler, *A Great Wall*, pp. 183-225; Mann, *About Face* pp. 55-77; Burr, *Kissinger Transcripts*, chs. 6 and 8.

108. Stockwell, *Search*, p. 206.

109. The administration's informal soundings met with little success, and in October, in an "extraordinary move strongly endorsed" by Kissinger, the State Department urged key members of Congress to approve a $60 million emergency aid package "now, bypassing the normal, time-consuming Congressional review process." After praising Mobutu as a wise statesman and loyal friend of the United States, Deputy Assistant Secretary Mulcahy told the chair of the Senate Foreign Relations Subcommittee on African Affairs, "We do have, as you well know, Mr. Chairman, a warm spot in our hearts for President Mobutu." (Quotations from *NYT*, Oct. 16, 1975, p. 2, and Mulcahy testimony in U.S. Senate, Committee on Foreign Relations, Subcommittee on African Affairs and Subcommittee on Foreign Assistance, *Security Supporting Assistance*, Oct. 24, 1975, p. 32.)

110. Spies, *Operasie*, pp. 65, 67. Unless otherwise noted, the following account of South Africa's military steps is based on Spies, *Operasie*, pp. 43-44, 65-85; du Preez, *Avontuur*, pp. 23-31, 44-56, 63-67; Breytenbach, *Buffalo Soldiers*, pp. 15-37; Breytenbach, *Forged*, pp. 3-21, 63; Breytenbach, *Sword*, pp. 11-18; de Villiers and de Villiers, *PW*, pp. 248-51. Also useful were Uys, *Bushman*, pp. 23-29; Heitman, *War*, pp. 169-71; Steenkamp, *Border*, pp. 39-46; Stiff, *Silent War*, pp. 104-113

111. Du Preez, *Avontuur*, p. 28.

112. Quotations from Breytenbach, *Sword*, p. 13, and Spies, *Operasie*, pp. 68, 67.

113. Quotations from *Jornal de Angola*, Aug. 31, 1975, p. 3, and *Jornal do Comércio* (Oporto), Sept. 5, 1975, p. 4. See also du Preez, *Avontuur*, pp. 28-29; Spies, *Operasie*, pp. 43-44; *Jornal de Angola*, Aug. 29, 1975, p. 1, and Sept. 3, p. 3; *Diário de Luanda*, Aug. 28, 1975, p. 5; *O Comércio* (Luanda), Aug. 28, 1975, p. 2; *Times of Zambia*, Aug. 31, 1975, p. 1; *Jornal do Comércio*, Sept. 4, 1975, p. 5.

114. Quotations from Spies, *Operasie*, p. 43, and Lúcio Lara, "A história do MPLA," n.d., p. 162.

115. Quotations from Breytenbach, *Forged*, p. 21; Spies, *Operasie*, p. 70; Moss, "Castro's Secret War Exposed," *Sunday Telegraph*, Jan. 30, 1977, p. 8; du Preez, *Avontuur*, p. 45. "The radiotransmitters of UNITA, the SADF, and the CIA were located in three adjoining rooms. Major Van Heerden, the SADF's liaison officer, relates: `The Americans of the CIA were in the small room next door and across the hall was UNITA's radiotransmitter'" (du Preez, *Avontuur*, p. 48).

116. Kissinger, Jan. 29, 1976, in U.S. Senate, Committee on Foreign Relations, Subcommittee on Afri-

can Affairs, *Angola*, p. 13; Schaufele, Feb. 6, 1976, ibid., p. 176; Mulcahy, Jan. 26, 1976, in U.S. House, Committee on International Relations, *United States Policy on Angola*, p. 22. Kissinger and DCI Colby repeated this tale in their memoirs (Kissinger, *Renewal*, pp. 813, 820; Colby, *Honorable Men*, p. 374).

117. Stockwell, *Search*, pp. 90, 176-77.

118. Interview with Y.

119. Thom, "Angola's 1975-76 Civil War," p. 13.

120. Bridgland, *The War*, p. 6. See also *Los Angeles Times*, Dec. 21, 1975, p. 1, and Jan. 13, 1976, p. 10.

121. Hultslander, fax to Gleijeses, Dec. 22, 1998. pp. 4, 6 (emphasis added).

122. Quotations from Stockwell, *Search*, p. 185; Spies, *Operasie*, p. 260; Bridgland, "The Future," p. 33. Stockwell, *Search*, p. 89, and interview with Mulcahy confirm Wilkowski's involvement.

123. Quotations from Stockwell, *Search*, p. 59; Thom, "Angola's 19750-76 Civil War," p. 37; Viljoen interview in CNN, *Cold War*, p. 9.

124. Quotations from Spies, *Operasie*, p. 82, and Heitman, *War*, p. 170.

125. Deon Geldenhuys, *Diplomacy*, pp. 79-83; Deon Geldenhuys and Kotzé, "P. W. Botha," p. 39; du Preez, *Avontuur*, p. 12; Rees and Day, *Muldergate*, p. 67; de Villiers and de Villiers, *PW*, pp. 251, 275; Flower, *Serving*, p. 161.

126. The assertion of Anglin and Shaw that "there is no evidence of any direct Zambia-South Africa collusion over Angola" is contradicted by Savimbi's biographer, the head of the CIA Task Force, and well-informed South African authors, all of whom write that Kaunda urged Pretoria to intervene. (Anglin and Shaw, *Zambia's Foreign Policy*, p. 338 quoted; Bridgland, "The Future," p. 33; Stockwell, *Search*, p. 186; Fourie, "The Evolving Experience," p. 104; Deon Geldenhuys, *Diplomacy*, p. 76; *Times*, Feb. 17, 1976, p. 6.)

127. Pik Botha interview in CNN, *Cold War*, p. 9; Kissinger, Jan. 29, 1976, in U.S. Senate, Committee on Foreign Relations, Subcommittee on African Affairs, *Angola*, p. 13; Kissinger, *Renewal*, p. 820.

128. Crocker, *High Noon*, p. 49; Stockwell, *Search*, pp. 186-88. Potts chaired the interagency task group that oversaw the work of the CIA task force on Angola.

129. Interviews with Mulcahy and Sisco.

130. Botha, Jan. 27, 1976, Republic of South Africa, *House of Assembly Debates*, col. 114; Vorster, Jan. 30, 1976, ibid., cols. 364-65; Botha, Apr. 17, 1978, ibid., col. 4852.

CHAPTER FOURTEEN

1. See Spies, *Operasie*, pp. 86-93; du Preez, *Avontuur*, pp. 65-71; Breytenbach, *Forged*, pp. 22-42; Uys, *Bushman*, pp. 28-31.

2. *Times* (London), Nov. 6, 1975, p. 1; *NYT*, Dec. 31, 1975, p. 1.

3. Spies, *Operasie*; du Preez, *Avontuur*; Breytenbach, *Forged* and *Sword*, pp. 18-66; Uys, *Bushman*, pp. 26-43; Heitman, *War*, pp. 169-74; Steenkamp, *Border*, pp. 46-61.

4. Breytenbach, *Forged*, pp. 22-27. On the Flechas, see Uys, *Bushman*, pp. 1-25.

5. Quotations from du Preez, *Avontuur*, p. 33, and Breytenbach, *Sword*, p. 29.

6. See Spies, *Operasie*, pp. 82-83, 103; du Preez, *Avontuur*, pp. 52-56; Steenkamp, *Border*, pp. 45-46.

7. Deon Geldenhuys, *Diplomacy*, p. 80 quoted; Spies, *Operasie*, p. 86; du Preez, *Avontuur*, pp. 32, 63, 86; de Villiers and de Villiers, *PW*, pp. 254-55.

8. Breytenbach, *Forged*, pp. 43-65 (p. 62 quoted); du Preez, *Avontuur*, pp. 32 (quoted), 71-80; Spies, *Operasie*, pp. 93-101; Uys, *Bushman*, pp. 31-33.

9. Quotations from Thom, "Angola's 1975-76 Civil War," p. 26, and Breytenbach, *Forged*, p. 43.

10. *Jornal de Angola* (Luanda), Nov. 2, 1975, p. 2.

11. Spies, *Operasie*, p. 99; du Preez, *Avontuur*, p. 68.

12. *Jornal do Comércio* (Oporto), Oct. 18, 1975, p. 4; du Preez, *Avontuur*, p. 71.

13. Spies, *Operasie*, pp. 99-100. See also Breytenbach, *Forged*, p. 60; du Preez, *Avontuur*, p. 79; *Cape Times*, Nov. 3, 1975, p. 1; *Rhodesia Herald*, Oct. 29, 1975, p. 1.

14. *Observer* (London), Nov. 2, 1975, p. 6.

15. For a representative sample, see *Guardian* (Manchester), Nov. 4, 1975, p. 3; *Le Monde*, Nov. 7, 1975, p. 3; *Jornal Novo* (Lisbon), Nov. 6, 1975, p. 17; *Observer*, Nov. 9, 1975, p. 11; *NYT*, Nov. 9, 1975, p. 18; *Times*, Nov. 6, 1975, p. 5; *WP*, Nov. 7, 1975, p. 7.

16. Díaz Argüelles, "Situación militar en Angola. Octubre/75," [Nov. 1?, 1975], p. 10.

17. Breytenbach, *Forged*, p. 72 quoted; Spies, *Operasie*, pp. 114-18; du Preez, *Avontuur*, pp. 81-85; [MINFAR], "Síntesis histórica de la ayuda internacionalista de Cuba a la R.P.A.," [1976], pp. 17-18 (hereafter "Síntesis"); Wolfers and Bergerol, *Angola*, pp. 23-24 (pp. 20-25 provide an interesting account of the first two weeks of the invasion from the perspective of the MPLA).

18. *Elima* (Kinshasa), Nov. 2 and 3, 1975, both p. 1.

19. *RDM* (Johannesburg), Aug. 16, 1975, p. 2; interview with Conceição Neto.

20. Quotations from du Preez, *Avontuur*, pp. 85-86, and interview with Conceição Neto. See also Spies, *Operasie*, pp. 118-23; de Villiers and de Villiers, *PW*, p. 254.

21. Breytenbach, *Forged*, pp. 108-9; Spies, *Operasie*, p. 55.

22. Spies, *Operasie*, p. 133; MINFAR, "Resumen de los cables recibidos. Noviembre 75," entry of Nov. 6, 1975; [MINFAR], "Informe sobre las actividades ejecutadas por el Partido Comunista de Cuba y gobierno revolucionario para dar cumplimiento a la ayuda solicitada por el Movimiento Popular para la Liberación de Angola," n.d., p. 5 (hereafter "Informe").

23. *Cape Times*, Nov. 7, 1975, p. 1 quoted; Spies, *Operasie*, p. 130; du Preez, *Avontuur*, pp. 108, 112, 113; Stockwell, *Search*, p. 187.

24. Spies, *Operasie*, pp. 133-35; Stockwell, *Search*, pp. 176-77.

25. *Jornal Novo*, Nov. 10, 1975, p. 15.

26. *Elima*, Oct. 29, 1975, p. 1, and *Jornal do Comércio*, Nov. 3, 1975, p. 3 quoted.

27. See Killoran to SecState, Oct. 27, 1975; SecState to Killoran, Nov. 2, 1975, 00:20; Killoran to SecState, Nov. 2, 1975, 18:15; all NSA. See also Robert Hultslander, fax to Piero Gleijeses, Dec. 22, 1998, p. 1; *NYT*, Nov. 4, 1975, p. 10; *Jornal de Angola*, Nov. 2, 1975, p. 1. According to official Portuguese sources, 309,058 Portuguese citizens left Angola between the fall of Caetano and independence day; 235,315 of them were airlifted out (João Guerra, *Descolonização*, pp. 113, 118). The United States was one of the countries that, at Lisbon's request, participated in the airlift, and U.S. planes transported more than 30,000 returnees (Costa Gomes to Ford, [Dec. 3, 1975], enclosed in Springsteen to Scowcroft, Dec. 15, 1975, WHCF, Subject File, box 66, GRFL).

28. Quotations from *Times*, Nov. 6, 1975, p. 5; Taibo, *El hombre*, p. 30; *Jornal de Angola*, Nov. 7, 1975, p. 3. On the MPLA's silence, see *Jornal de Angola* and *Diário de Luanda*, the two newspapers that still appeared in the capital. For a vivid description of the mood in the capital, see Kapu<ac>sci<ac>nski, *Another Day.*

29. "Informe," p. 5; MINFAR, "Batallón de Tropas Especiales," n.d.

30. Wolfers and Bergerol, *Angola*, p. 30.

31. Interviews with Lúcio Lara, Onambwe, Ludy Kissassunda, and Xiyetu.

32. Quotations from interview with Lúcio Lara and from "Síntesis," p. 16. Also interviews with Onambwe, Ludy Kissassunda, and Xiyetu.

33. Interview with Risquet (quoted); "Informe," p. 5. As a member of the PCC's Secretariat, Risquet attended the meetings of the Political Bureau.

34. Church to Carter, Aug. 12, 1977, p. 2 quoted, enclosed in Dodson to Hutcheson, Aug. 17, 1977, FOIA 1997/1633; interview with Risquet; García Márquez, *Operación Carlota*, p. 15.

35. Castro's remarks at the Havana Conference on the Cuban Missile Crisis, Jan. 11, 1992, in Chang and Kornbluh, *Cuban Missile Crisis*, p. 334.

36. Shevchenko, *Breaking*, pp. 271-72; Dobrynin, *In Confidence*, p. 362; Kissinger, *Renewal*, p. 816. See also Westad, "Moscow," p. 21, and the testimonies of Karen Brutents, who was the deputy head of the CPSU Central Committee's International Department, and Georgi Kornienko, who was the head of the American Department of the Soviet Foreign Ministry, in Westad, "US-Soviet Relations," pp. 30-53.

37. Quotations from Pavlov, *Soviet-Cuban Alliance*, p. 102 (Pavlov became head of the Soviet Foreign Ministry's Latin American Department in 1987); interview with Risquet; Brutents interview in CNN, *Cold War*, p. 11.

38. Lucas Molina to Colomé, "Informe del cumplimiento de la misión en Luanda entre los días 4-18.11.75," Havana, n.d., pp. 1-4 (hereafter Molina to Colomé). For the MPLA's request, see chapter 12. On October 27, Columbié cabled Díaz Argüelles and Havana that a Soviet ship had left the Soviet Union with the weapons and would arrive at Pointe Noire the following week. (Columbié to Argüelles, Colomé,

and Osmany, Oct. 27, 1975, nos. 475 and 476. All of Columbié's reports are from Brazzaville.)

39. Molina to Colomé, pp. 1-4.

40. MINFAR, "Batallón de Tropas Especiales," n.d.

41. Interviews with Hernández Gattorno (quoted), Padrón (quoted), and three other witnesses: Special Forces officers Véliz and Suárez, and Hechavarría, one of the two physicians who accompanied the Special Forces.

42. Interviews with Padrón and Véliz.

43. Quotations from *NYT*, Nov. 7, 1975, p. 2, and *Le Monde*, Nov. 9, 1975, p. 3; see also *RDM*, Nov. 7, 1975, p. 1, and Nov. 8, p. 1; *Times*, Nov. 8, 1975, p. 4; *Jornal de Angola*, Nov. 7, 1975, p. 3.

44. Molina to Colomé, p. 7 quoted; MINFAR, "Resumen de los cables recibidos. Noviembre 75," entry of Nov. 9, 1975; interviews with Padrón and Schueg (third-in-command of the MMCA).

45. Quotations from Steenkamp, *Border*, pp. 48, 50, and de Villiers and de Villiers, *PW*, p. 256. See also Spies, *Operasie*, pp. 132-36; du Preez, *Avontuur*, pp. 114-16; *World* (Johannesburg), Nov. 18, 1975, p. 8, and Nov. 25, p. 4; *RDM*, Nov. 10, 1975, p. 3.

46. Steenkamp, *Border*, pp. 48, 50.

47. Interview with Risquet.

48. Molina to Colomé, p. 5; "Síntesis," p. 20.

49. See Spies, *Operasie*, pp. 136-37; du Preez, *Avontuur*, pp. 116-17; de Villiers and de Villiers, *PW*, pp. 257-58.

50. Stockwell, *Search*, p. 213.

51. Steenkamp, *Border*, pp. 48 and 50 quoted; Spies, *Operasie*, pp. 136-38; du Preez, *Avontuur*, pp. 116-19; MINFAR, "Resumen de los cables recibidos. Noviembre 75," entry of Nov. 11, 1975; [MMCA], "Fuerzas patrioticas participantes," n.d.; [MMCA], "Medios que se agregan (10-11-75)," n.d.; Buznego and Cardenas, "La batalla," pp. 25-26.

52. *Times*, Nov. 11, 1975, p. 1. On August 1, High Commissioner Silva Cardoso had been recalled to Lisbon. Leonel Cardoso had been appointed to replace him on August 28.

53. *Foreign Broadcast Information Service* (hereafter *FBIS*), 8, Nov. 11, 1975, E4.

54. *World*, Nov. 12, 1975, p. 4. For the most extensive coverage, see *Jornal de Angola*, Nov. 11, 1975, and *Diário de Luanda*, Nov. 12, 1975.

55. Quotations from Bridgland, *Savimbi*, p. 151; *RDM*, Nov. 10, 1975, p. 3; *Jornal Novo*, Nov. 12, 1975, p. 15. See also Savimbi, Angola, pp. 60-64.

56. Quotations from INR, "Angola: The MPLA Prepares for Independence," Sept. 22, 1975, NSA; Stockwell, *Search*, p. 164; CIA, *National Intelligence Daily*, Nov. 14, 1975, p. 4, NSA. See also Lunel, *Denard*, p. 448.

57. Stockwell, *Search*, p. 164.

58. Weinberg, *Last*, pp. 246, 248-49. On Denard's relations with SDECE, see also Marion, *La Mission*, pp. 102, 104, 123 (Marion was SDECE's director in 1981-82); Pean, *Affaires*, pp. 9-17; Pean, *L'homme*, pp. 300-302, 446, 454-58, 531-37.

59. Quotations from Lunel, *Denard*, p. 448, and CIA, *National Intelligence Daily*, Nov. 14, 1975, p. 4, NSA. See also Molina to Colomé, pp. 8-10; "Síntesis,"

pp. 20-21; Espinosa, *La batalla*, pp. 57-88; Díaz Argüelles to Colomé, Oct. 15, 1976, pp. 21-22.

60. CIA, *National Intelligence Daily*, Nov. 14, 1975, p. 4, NSA.

61. *WSJ*, Dec. 23, 1975, p. 2 quoted; *WP*, Dec. 20, 1975, p. 1; Stockwell, *Search*, p. 204. In September 1975 Gulf had paid quarterly royalties of $116 million to the Ministry of Finance of the Transitional Government in Luanda; the ministry, however, was controlled by the MPLA, the Transitional Government was defunct, and the money had gone into the MPLA's coffers (Legum and Hodges, *After Angola*, p. 12).

62. Breytenbach, *Forged*, p. 112 (he gives Zulu's losses as two armored cars and eighteen casualties). See also MINFAR, "Resumen de los cables recibidos. Noviembre 75," entry of Nov. 11, 1975; "Síntesis," p. 21; Spies, *Operasie*, pp. 124-26.

63. Interview with Conceição Neto. FAPLA officers confirmed this account and asked not to be named.

64. Interview with Conceição Neto.

65. Interviews with Kianda, Rui de Matos, Xiyetu, and Padrón.

66. See "Síntesis," p. 22; MINFAR, "Resumen de los cables recibidos. Noviembre 75," entries of Nov. 12 and 13, 1975; Spies, *Operasie*, pp. 124-28; Breytenbach, *Forged*, pp. 112-17.

67. *Cape Times*, Nov. 14, 1975, p. 1; *RDM*, Nov. 13, 1975, p. 4, and Nov. 14, p. 1 (quoting Savimbi).

68. MINFAR, "Resumen de los cables recibidos. Noviembre 75," entry of Nov. 13, 1975 (quoted); [MINFAR], "Batallón de Tropas Especiales," n.d.; interviews with Hernández Gattorno and Suárez, who arrived with the second company.

69. Quotations from Breytenbach, *Forged*, pp. 122-23, and interview with Padrón. See also MINFAR, "Resumen de los cables recibidos. Noviembre 75," entries of Nov. 13, 15, 17, 1975; Spies, *Operasie*, pp. 126-27; Uys, *Bushman*, p. 38; Wolfers and Bergerol, *Angola*, p. 39. Interviews with Véliz, Suárez, Cadelo, and Guerrero, another officer who fought under Díaz Argüelles.

70. Steenkamp, *Border*, p. 48; Breytenbach, *Forged*, p. 120. South African accounts of the campaign consistently overestimated the number of Cubans opposing the SADF in November and December.

71. Quotations from *Cape Times*, Nov. 21, 1975, p. 1, and Spies, *Operasie*, p. 108. For Vorster's November 19 briefing, see Heard (the editor of the *Cape Times*), *Cape*, p. 153; see also Sparks, *Mind*, pp. 305-6 (Sparks was the editor of the Johannesburg *Sunday Express*).

72. Quotations from Breytenbach, *Forged*, p. 131, and Breytenbach, *Sword*, p. 57. See also du Preez, *Avontuur*, pp. 124-33, 186, and Spies, *Operasie*, p. 128.

73. Interview with Hernández Gattorno (quoted); [MMCA], "Acciones combativas el día 18-11-75," n.d.; MINFAR, "Resumen de los cables recibidos. Noviembre 75," entry of Nov. 22, 1975; "Informe," p. 6.

74. My account of the battle of Ebo is based on a report from Hernández Gattorno to Díaz Argüelles, Nov. 23, 1975; two reports from [Díaz] Argüelles to Cintra Frías, both Nov. 23, 1975 (hereafter Argüelles to Cintra Frías [1] and Argüelles to Cintra Frías [2]); Cintra Frías to MINFAR, "Acciones combativas en Ebo. 23-11-75," n.d. All the reports are handwritten (the quality of the paper improves with the rank) and are in AIHC. Also interviews with Hernández Gattorno and with Guerrero (a Cuban captain who fought at Ebo). For South African accounts, see Spies, *Operasie*, pp. 180-91; du Preez, *Avontuur*, pp. 133-45; Breytenbach, *Forged*, pp. 130-32; Breytenbach, *Sword*, pp. 57-59.

75. Quotations from Spies, *Operasie*, p. 185, and Argüelles to Cintra Frías [1].

76. Hernández Gattorno to Díaz Argüelles, Nov. 23, 1975; interview with Hernández Gattorno; Breytenbach, *Forged*, p. 132 quoted; du Preez, *Avontuur*, p. 142. South African losses were four dead and eleven wounded; the other casualties were FNLA and UNITA soldiers (Spies, *Operasie*, p. 190).

77. Quotations from du Preez, *Avontuur*, p. 142; Argüelles to Cintra Frías [2]; Argüelles to Cintra Frías [1].

78. Carreira, *O Pensamento*, p. 141.

79. Quotations from Breytenbach, *Sword*, p. 58, and interview with Padrón. A light reconnaissance aircraft was shot down by the Cubans near Ebo on November 25. Two others crashed, one on October 29, 1975, and the other on January 4, 1976. These were the only aircraft the SADF lost during the campaign. (De Villiers and de Villiers, *PW*, pp. 254, 255; du Preez, *Avontuur*, pp. 57-58, 134, 144, 209; Spies, *Operasie*, pp. 194, 243.)

80. The MMCA had almost 500 men on November 4. To these must be added the Special Forces, the 100 specialists who arrived with Molina on November 7, and a few others.

81. [MINFAR], "Buques empleados para el traslado de fuerzas y medios `Operación Carlota,'" n.d.; MINFAR, "Transportación maritima," n.d.

82. Quotations from Columbié to Osmany [Cienfuegos] and Suárez, Nov. 28, 1975, and from Columbié to Carlos Rafael [Rodríguez] et al., Nov. 21, 1975, no. 575 (quoting Afanasenko). See also Columbié to Colomé and Osmany, Oct. 29 (nos. 486 and 487) and Nov. 26, 1975; Díaz Argüelles to Colomé, Nov. 17, 1975; Columbié to Carlos Rafael et al., Nov. 17, 18 (nos. 553, 554, 555, 556), and 21 (no. 576), 1975; Columbié to Osmany and Suárez, Nov. 28 and Dec. 2, 1975.

83. Quotations from Columbié to Osmany and Colomé, Nov. 25, 1975, nos. 593 and 594 (quoting the Soviet military attaché); Columbié to Osmany and Suárez, Nov. 28, 1975.

84. [MMCA], "Diario de las acciones combativas, Angola," entries of Dec. 6 and 7, 1975.

85. "Síntesis," pp. 23-24. Colomé replaced Cintra Frías, who in turn replaced Díaz Argüelles as commander of the central front. Díaz Argüelles became the commander of one of the three columns on this front.

86. Interview with Risquet.

87. Interview with Véliz.

88. "Los hombres nacen dos veces: cuando nacen de la madre y cuando son capaces de tomar una decisión como esta," diary of a Cuban combatant in Angola, pp. 1-2, PCH (hereafter "Los hombres"). See also Diary [untitled] of a Cuban combatant in Angola, p. 1, PCH (hereafter "Diary").

Unlike active duty troops, the reservists could refuse to go, but, as the *Washington Post* reported, "few do so when summoned for service" (*WP*, Feb. 22, 1976, p. 18).

89. "Diary," pp. 3-4.

90. "Los hombres," pp. 5-7. See also "Diary," p. 4.

91. "Síntesis," pp. 23, 25-26 (quoted); "Diary," p. 4; "Los hombres," pp. 6-12; MINFAR, "Resumen operativo del puesto de mando especial," Dec. 13, 1975, p. 3; MINFAR, "Parte operativo del puesto de mando especial," Dec. 19, 1975, p. 2; [MINFAR], "Buques empleados para el traslado de fuerzas y medios `Operación Carlota,'" n.d.

92. Spies, *Operasie*, p. 140.

93. MINFAR, "Parte operativo del puesto de mando especial," Dec. 21, 1975.

94. Steenkamp, *Border*, pp. 51-52 quoted; Spies, *Operasie*, pp. 140-42; du Preez, *Avontuur*, pp. 121-22; de Villiers and de Villiers, *PW*, p. 259.

95. SecState to All Diplomatic Posts, Dec. 1, 1975, NSA.

96. [MMCA], "Diario de las acciones combativas, Angola," entry of Dec. 11, 1975. For the number of SADF, see du Preez, *Avontuur*, p. 152.

97. Quotations from Breytenbach, *Sword*, p. 62; *Observer*, Dec. 7, 1975, p. 11; *Times*, Dec. 11, 1975, p. 7. See also du Preez, *Avontuur*, pp. 146-55, 173-85, and Spies, *Operasie*, pp. 192-218, 233-44.

98. For Botha, see H. H. Schwarz, Republic of South Africa, *House of Assembly Debates*, May 6, 1976, cols. 6223-24; for the SADF statement, see *Cape Times*, Feb. 4, 1977, p. 1.

99. Quotations from "Síntesis," pp. 29-30, and interview with Véliz. See also du Preez, *Avontuur*, pp. 154-73; MINFAR, "Parte operativo del puesto de mando especial," entries of Dec. 15, 19, 22, 1975; Spies, *Operasie*, pp. 203-18. Lieutenant Colonel Douglas Díaz de Dios, "El combate de `Catofe,'" n.d., gives Cuban casualties at twenty-eight between dead and missing.

100. Quotations from SecState to All American Republic Diplomatic Posts, Dec. 20, 1975, NSA, and Thom, "Angola's 1975-76 Civil War," p. 30.

101. See du Preez, *Avontuur*, pp. 186-201; Spies, *Operasie*, pp. 219-32; MINFAR, "Resumen operativo del puesto de mando especial," Dec. 13, 1975; MINFAR, "Parte operativo del puesto de mando especial," Dec. 17, 21, 27, 29, 30, 1975.

102. Bridgland, *Savimbi*, pp. 129-31, 137-43 (p. 142 quoted). See, for example, *WP*, Nov. 12, 1975, p. 1; *Times*, Nov. 15, 1975, p. 4; *Le Monde*, Nov. 16, 1975, p. 3; *Los Angeles Times*, Nov. 16, 1975, p. 1; *Time*, Nov. 17, 1975, p. 42; *Jornal Novo*, Nov. 22, 1975, p. 23.

103. *WP*, Nov. 23, 1975, p. 18. Actually, nine days earlier the *Guardian* had quoted Michael Nicholson, a British television journalist who had just returned from Angola, saying that South African regular troops were spearheading the advance on Luanda, but the paper failed to comment on the veracity of Nicholson's information and continued to describe the invaders as a "mercenary-supported FNLA-UNITA column." (*Guardian*. Nov. 14, 1975, p. 2; Nov. 15, p. 3; Nov. 17, p. 2 quoted. See also Nicholson, *Measure*, pp. 175-80.)

The *Observer* (Nov. 16, 1975, p. 6) published an intelligent article by Tony Hodges from Benguela that strongly suggested that the mysterious column included South African regular soldiers, but, like the *Guardian*, the paper let the matter drop.

104. Quotations from *NYT*, Dec. 9, 1975, p. 40 (ed.), and Dec. 12, p. 8; *Times*. Nov. 17, 1975, p. 1; Nov. 20, p. 6; Dec. 11, p. 7.

105. See, for example, *RDM*. Nov. 18, 26, 28, Dec. 2, 16, 17, 1975, all p. 1.

106. *Diário de Luanda*. Dec. 16, 1975, p. 2 quoted; Dec. 18, p. 1; Dec. 19, p. 1; *Daily Times* (Lagos), Dec. 19, 1975, p. 32. The four had been captured on December 13 near Catofe (du Preez, *Avontuur*, p. 170; Spies, *Operasie*, p. 214).

107. *RDM*, Dec. 20, 1975, p. 1. For the photograph, see *RDM*, Dec. 19, 1975, p. 1.

108. Quotations from *FBIS*, 8, Dec. 28, 1975, E3 (quoting Botha), and Steenkamp, *Border*, p. 55. In 1975, South Africa's army was 38,000 strong (7,000 regulars and 31,000 conscripts), its navy, 4,000 (including 1,400 conscripts), and its air force, 8,500 (including 3,000 conscripts) (Grundy, *Soldiers*, pp. 100-108).

109. *RDM*, Dec. 25, 1975, p. 6.

110. Quotations from Wilkowski to SecState, Lusaka, Oct. 29, 1975, NSA, and *Times*, Dec. 17, 1975, p. 1 (quoting the radio broadcast). See also ibid., Dec. 8, 1975, p. 7, and Dec. 10, p. 6; *Zambia Daily Mail*. Nov. 17, Dec. 8, 10, 12, 1975, all p. 1; *Elima*, Dec. 4, 1975, p. 7, and Dec. 20, p. 1; *World*, Dec. 1, 1975, p. 4, and Dec. 10, p. 3; *RDM*. Nov. 17, 1975, p. 1; Dec. 12, p. 17; Dec. 17, p. 1; *Cape Times*, Dec. 8, 1975, p. 2, and Dec. 10, p. 1.

111. *Cape Times*, Dec. 3, 1975, p. 1.

112. René Lefort, *Le Monde*, Dec. 24, 1975, p. 3.

113. "A head count from December 22 showed that the number was 2,994" (Spies, *Operasie*, p. 215).

U.S. intelligence estimated that by December 20 there were 5,000 to 6,000 Cubans in Angola (SecState to All American Republic Diplomatic Posts, Dec. 20, 1975, NSA). Cuban sources, however, indicate that the number hovered around 3,500 to 4,000 ("Informe," p. 11).

114. Risquet to Fidel Castro, Luanda, Dec. 30, 1975, ACC.

115. Calixto Rodriguez Proenza to Jefe del Frente Sur, "Informe de la situación desde las 0800 hasta las 1800 31-12-75," AIHC; Jesús Morejón Morales to Jefe Art. del Frente, "Parte diario," Jan. 2, 1976, AIHC; [MMCA], "Parte operativo," Jan. 2, 1976; MINFAR, "Resumen de los cables. Enero 1976," entries of Jan.

1 and 3, 1976; Lieutenant Rubén González Plana, report of Jan. 4, 1976; interview with Jesús Pérez, who participated in the battle.

116. *Le Monde*, Jan. 2, 1976, p. 16 (quoting the communiqué); Stockwell, *Search*, p. 194.

117. Quotations from *Zambia Daily Mail*, Nov. 22, 1975, p. 1 (which reprinted the full text of the release), and DIA, *Defense Intelligence Notice*, Nov. 22, 1975, NSA. See also DIA, *Defense Intelligence Notice*, Nov. 24, 1975, NSA; USIB, *National Intelligence Bulletin*, Nov. 24, 1975, p. 7, NSA; Stockwell, *Search*, p. 194; *NYT*, Jan. 18, 1976, p. 17.

118. Stockwell, *Search*, p. 195.

119. Hultslander, fax to Gleijeses, Dec. 22, 1998, p. 5.

120. Wilkowski to SecState, Nov. 17, 1975, p. 2, DOS MF 8705161/2.

121. *Newsweek*, Dec. 1, 1975, p. 57 quoted, and Dec. 29, p. 26.

122. *Daily News* (Dar-es-Salaam), Nov. 22, 1975, p. 1.

123. Foreign Minister Garba, *Daily Times*, Nov. 9, 1975, p. 1 (quoted), and Nov. 10, p. 32. See also the sharp editorial condemning the USSR in ibid., Nov. 11, 1975, p. 3.

124. Garba, *Diplomatic Soldiering*, p. 22 quoted. For useful overviews of Nigeria and the Angolan crisis, see ibid., pp. 15-35; Hinjari, "A Comparative Study," pp. 144-229; Sotumbi, *Nigeria's Recognition*.

125. See *Jornal de Angola*, Oct. 23, 1975, p. 1.

126. *Cape Times*, Aug. 2, 1975, p. 4; *Rhodesia Herald*, Aug. 2, 1975, p. 1; *RDM*, Aug. 2, 1975, p. 3; *Zambia Daily Mail*, Aug. 11, 1975, p. 4 quoted. The last South African police returned home on August 21 (the helicopters and their crews stayed behind). (*RDM*, Aug. 22, 1975, p. 1; Ian Smith, *Betrayal*, pp. 196, 212; David Martin and Johnson, *Struggle*, p. 143.)

127. *Fraternité-Matin* (Abidjan): Oct. 11, 1975, p. 22; Oct. 13, p. 20; Oct. 14, p. 18; Oct. 17, p. 15.

128. See chapter 13.

CHAPTER FIFTEEN

1. Quotations from INR, "Angola: Portuguese and African Efforts to Contain Violence," June 10, 1975, p. i, DOS MF 8802348, and interview with Mulcahy. Similarly NSSM 224 of May 26, 1975, which ordered a study of U.S. interests in Angola and created the Davis Task Force, asked the task force to examine "the extent of the involvement, past and future," of the Soviet Union and China in Angolan affairs but overlooked Cuba (NSSM 224, May 26, 1975, National Security Adviser, NSDM and NSSM, box 2, GRFL).

2. CIA, *National Intelligence Daily*, Oct. 11, 1975, p. 4, NSA. See also chapter 12.

3. CIA, *National Intelligence Daily*, Oct. 11, 1975, p. 4, NSA.

4. Quotations from USIB, *National Intelligence Bulletin*, Oct. 25, 1975, p. 7, NSA; Mulcahy and Rogers in Transcripts of Secretary of State Henry Kissinger's Staff Meetings, 1973-1977, Nov. 5, 1975, pp. 10, 12, box 9, NA (hereafter Transcripts, followed by date and box number); interview with Mulcahy; Kissinger, *Renewal*, p. 815.

5. Interview with O'Neill. In its overview of Communist activities in Africa, the administrative history of the State Department in the Johnson years did not mention Cuba ("The Department of State during the Administration of President Lyndon B. Johnson, November 1963-January 1969," vol. 1, ch. 5, "The Place of Africa in US Foreign Policy," unpaginated, Administrative History of the Department of State, LBJL).

6. Tel. interview with Hyland.

7. Quotations from tel. interview with Fugit; Mulcahy in Transcripts, Nov. 13, 1975, p. 29, box 9; CIA, *Intelligence Checklist*, Nov. 14, 1975, pp. A2-A5, NSA.

8. Steenkamp, *Border*, p. 50 quoted; Spies, *Operasie*, pp. 258-59; du Preez, *Avontuur*, p. 38.

9. Kissinger, *Renewal*, p. 818.

10. Stockwell, *Search*, pp. 206-7; Kissinger, *Renewal*, p. 826.

11. "GOP Leadership Meeting," Dec. 10, 1975, p. 1, Robert K. Wolthuis Files, box 2, GRFL.

12. Quotations from *Foreign Broadcast Information Service* (hereafter *FBIS*), 8, Oct. 31, 1975, C4-5, and DOS, briefing paper for Ford's December 1975 trip to China, n.d., pp. 2, 1, PPS, box 373. See also USIB, *National Intelligence Bulletin*, Nov. 5, 1975, p. 6, MF 00386, NSA; "Chinese Involvement in Angola," [late Nov. 1975], PPS, box 372; du Preez, *Avontuur*, p. 114.

13. Kissinger, *Renewal*, pp. 893-94.

14. See DOS, MemoConv (Mao Tse Tung, Ford, et al.), Beijing, Dec. 2, 1975, MF 00395, NSA.

15. Quotations from White House MemoConv (Teng Hsiao-p'ing, Ford, Kissinger, et al.), Beijing, Dec. 3, 1975, pp. 19, 21, MF 00398, NSA. See also Kissinger, "Talking Points on International Issues for Substantive Discussions with PRC Leaders," PPS, box 372; USIB, *National Intelligence Bulletin*, Dec. 11, 1975, p. 6, MF 00403, NSA; "Discussion of Substantive Policy Issues during Mr. Nixon's Visit to China, February 1976," PPS, box 378.

16. Biden, Feb. 4, 1976, in U.S. Senate, Committee on Foreign Relations, Subcommittee on African Affairs, *Angola*, p. 143 (hereafter U.S. Senate, *Angola*); Dick Clark, "Clark Amendment," June 1993, courtesy of Dick Clark.

17. See U.S. Senate, Committee on Foreign Relations, Subcommittee on African Affairs, *U.S. Policy toward Southern Africa*.

18. Interview with Mulcahy. See the list of members of Congress briefed in U.S. Senate, *Angola*, pp. 21-23.

19. Clark, *NYT*, Jan. 29, 1976, p. 33.

20. Interviews with Holt (quoted) and Clark; Biden, Jan. 29, 1976, in U.S. Senate, *Angola*, pp. 5, 30-31; Mulcahy, Jan. 26, 1976, in U.S. House, Committee on International Relations, *United States Policy on Angola*, pp. 25-26. The *Times* article is discussed later in this chapter.

21. *FBIS*, 8, Dec. 19, 1975, E5 (quoting Moynihan), and *Los Angeles Times*, Dec. 16, 1975, p. 1 (quoting Greener).

22. The vote was on an amendment to the defense appropriations bill for fiscal year 1976. The relevant phrase was: "none of which, nor any other funds appropriated in this act, may be used for any activities in Angola other than intelligence gathering." (For the debate on the vote, see *CR*, Senate, Dec. 15, 1975, pp. 40531-35; Dec. 16, pp. 40872-73, 40884-85; Dec. 17, pp. 41122-23, 41141-43, 41196-213; Dec. 18, pp. 41625-50; Dec. 19, pp. 42209-28.)

23. *WP*, Jan. 28, 1976, p. 1 quoted.

24. *WSJ*, Dec. 19, 1975, p. 14 (ed.); *NYT*, Jan. 28, 1976, p. 3; Solarz, Feb. 26, 1976, in U.S. House, Committee on International Relations, Subcommittee on International Resources, Food and Energy, *Disaster Assistance*, p. 43; Helms to Ford, Dec. 19, 1975, p. 1, WHCF, Subject File, box 22, GRFL.

25. Kissinger, Jan. 29, 1976, in U.S. Senate, *Angola*, pp. 10-11. See also Kissinger, *Renewal*, pp. 818-25.

26. Interview with Risquet.

27. Porter, *The USSR*, p. 173.

28. Valdés, "Revolutionary Solidarity," p. 102. "Cuba enviará tropas a Angola," *Diario de las Américas*, Mar. 5, 1976, p. 1, and "Castro's Barbados Connection," *Miami Herald*, Dec. 17, 1975, p. 20. Authors who take Porter's statement at face value include Garthoff, *Détente*, p. 571, and Shearman, *Soviet Union*, p. 42.

29. USIB, *National Intelligence Bulletin*, Dec. 15, 1975, p. 2, NSA.

30. SecState to All American Republic Diplomatic Posts, Dec. 16, 1975, p. 2, DOS MF 9001360; Amembassy Lisbon to SecState, Jan. 2, 1976, DOS MF 8904623; Kissinger to Amembassy Caracas, Jan. 8, 1976, ibid.

31. Acevedo to Columbié, Havana: Dec. 12, 19, 20, 22, 23, 1975; [MINFAR], "Buques empleados para el traslado de fuerzas y medios `Operación Carlota,'" n.d.

32. Kissinger, *Renewal*, pp. 822-25.

33. Tel. interview with Schaufele.

34. See Gleijeses, "Truth," esp. pp. 77-80.

35. Kissinger, *Renewal*, pp. 812, 813. The only authoritative account is Stockwell, *Search*, pp. 182-85, 216-26, 233-34, 244-48, 259.

36. Stockwell, *Search*, p. 183. Six American mercenaries eventually made it to Angola. For their stories, see Dempster and Tomkins, *Fire*, pp. 388-94; Mallin and Brown, *Merc*, pp. 122-55; Brown and Himber, "Story"; Acker, "Angolan Reflections."

37. Stockwell, *Search*, p. 184 quoted; Lunel, *Denard*, pp. 447-48; Weinberg, *Last*, p. 249; *WP*, Feb. 14, 1976, p. 19.

38. Stockwell, *Search*, pp. 217, 222-23, 244-45.

39. A list of 200 or so Britons who went to Angola to fight for the FNLA was drawn up by Scotland Yard (*Daily Telegraph*, Apr. 3, 1976, p. 15). The story of the British mercenaries can be followed in the *Daily Telegraph* and the *Times* from late January to late February 1976. Dempster and Tomkins, *Fire*, is an account by two of them. See also Valdés Vivó, *Angola*, Burchett and Roebuck, *Whores*.

40. Quotations from United Kingdom, *Parliamentary Debates*, 904:411; *Daily Telegraph*, Feb. 13, 1976, p. 16; *Jeune Afrique*, July 2, 1976, p. 36.

41. Dempster and Tomkins, *Fire*, p. 107.

42. Ibid., p. 119 quoted; *Le Soir* (Brussels): Jan. 30, 1976, p. 1; Jan. 31, p. 3; Feb. 12, p. 3; Amembassy Brussels to SecState, Jan. 30, 1976, DOS MF 8904623.

43. Amembassy London to SecState, Mar. 2, 1976, p. 2, DOS MF 8904623. According to some reports, Belgium also gave covert aid, including arms, to the FNLA (*Times*, Nov. 9, 1975, p. 10; *WP*, Jan. 6, 1976, p. 4; Klinghoffer, *Angola War*, p. 47). Belgian companies had significant investments in Angola, coming third after the Americans and the British (*Le Soir*, Mar. 18, 1975, p. 11; "L'enjeu," pp. 11-18).

44. Stockwell writes that the CIA was not involved (*Search*, pp. 223-24). For the opposite view, see Bloch and Fitzgerald, *British Intelligence*, pp. 194-95.

45. *NYT*, Jan. 28, 1976, p. 1.

46. Helms to Ford, Dec. 19, 1975, WHCF, Subject File, box 22, GRFL; DOS, MemoConv (Mao Tse Tung, Ford, et al.), Beijing, Dec. 2, 1975, p. 13, MF 00395, NSA.

47. White House MemoConv (Ford, Kissinger, Scowcroft), Apr. 15, 1975, p. 3, NSATPF, box A2, GRFL; DOS, MemoConv (Kissinger, Huang Chen, et al.), Washington, D.C., May 29, 1976, p. 5, MF 00409, NSA.

48. Risquet to Fidel Castro, Luanda, Jan. 3, 1976, ACC; [MINFAR], "Informe sobre las actividades ejecutadas por el Partido Comunista de Cuba y gobierno revolucionario para dar cumplimiento a la ayuda solicitada por el Movimiento Popular para la Liberación de Angola," n.d., p. 11 (hereafter "Informe"); [MINFAR], "Síntesis histórica de la ayuda internacionalista de Cuba a la R.P.A.," [1976], pp. 34-35.

49. Quotations from CIA, *National Intelligence Daily*, Jan. 8, 1976, p. 3, and *World* (Johannesburg), Jan. 13, 1976, p. 4. See also "Informe," pp. 12-13; MINFAR, "Resumen de los cables. Enero 76"; interviews with Xiyetu (the FAPLA's chief of staff), Ninth Brigade's officers Ngongo and Kianda, Risquet, Schueg, and Zayas (a senior Cuban officer who was assigned as adviser to the Ninth Brigade).

50. Risquet to Fidel Castro, Luanda, Jan. 7, 1976, pp. 1-3, ACC.

51. Brasemb Luanda, "Situação militar de Angola," Jan. 19, 1976, p. 1, NSA; *WP*, Feb. 19, 1976, p. 12; *NYT*, Jan. 30, 1976, p. 4.

52. Amembassy Kinshasa to SecState, Jan. 29, 1976, p. 2, DOS MF 8904623.

53. *Sunday Times* (London), Feb. 1, 1976, p. 6.

54. Quotations from *WP*, Feb. 24, 1976, p. 10, and *RDM*, Feb. 11, 1976, p. 1.

55. Quotations from *Newsweek*, Feb. 9, 1976, p. 31, and *Times*, Feb. 13, 1976, p. 6. See also *Times*, Jan. 30, 1976, p. 8; *World*, Jan. 30, 1976, p. 7; *RDM*, Jan. 13, 1976, p. 1; Feb. 3, p. 4; Feb. 5, p. 2.

56. *Salongo*, Feb. 4, 1976, p. 1, and Feb. 17, p. 3; *Daily Telegraph*, Feb. 13, 1976, p. 1 quoted; *WP*, Feb. 17, 1976, p. 16.

57. *Guardian* (Manchester), Feb. 18, 1976, p. 2.

58. "Vermerk über das Gespräch mit dem Präsidenten der VR Angola, Genossen Dr. Agostinho Neto, am 26.2.1976 in der Zeit von 19.40 bis 20.50

Uhr in dessen Amtssitz," p. 2, SED, DY30 IV 2/2.035/128 (hereafter "Vermerk").

59. *RDM*, Dec. 6, 1975, p. 5 quoted; *Jornal Novo*, Dec. 6, 1975, p. 24; *FBIS*, 8, Dec. 19, 1975, E1.

60. Quotations from *Le Monde*, Feb. 10, 1976, p. 3, and Marcum, *Angolan Revolution*, 2:276. See also *Los Angeles Times*, Jan. 11, 1976, p. 8; *Zambia Daily Mail*, Jan. 20, 1976, p. 1; *Times*, Jan. 28, 1976, p. 8; *WP*, Jan. 20, 1976, p. 7; *Jornal Novo*, Dec. 22, 1975, p. 23, and Dec. 27, p. 14; *Le Soir*, Jan. 29, 1976, p. 3; SecState to Amembassy Bangui et al., Jan. 29, 1976, NSA; Bridgland, *Savimbi*, pp. 151, 171; Spies, *Operasie*, pp. 252-55.

61. CIA, *National Intelligence Daily*, Jan. 8, 1976; "Informe," p. 14; MINFAR, "Resumen de los cables. Enero 76."

62. *Newsweek*, Feb. 23, 1976, p. 36 quoted; Spies, *Operasie*, p. 254.

63. *Le Monde*, Jan. 16, 1976, p. 4; *RDM*, Jan. 19, 1976, p. 1; *Times*, Jan. 15, 1976, p. 6 (quoting from *Agence France-Presse*).

64. Quotations from "Informe," pp. 13-14, and interview with Risquet.

65. Spies, *Operasie*, pp. 260-63; de Villiers and de Villiers, *PW*, pp. 266-69.

66. Quotations from Deon Geldenhuys, *Diplomacy*, p. 77; Hyland, *Rivals*, p. 146; *Elima*, Dec. 3, 1975, p. 1 (quoting Mobutu); *Cape Times*, Feb. 2, 1976, p. 8; G. W. Mills (United Party), Feb. 20, 1976, Republic of South Africa, *House of Assembly Debates*, cols. 1696-97.

67. Quotations from Admiral H. H. Biermann, *World*, Dec. 3, 1975, p. 1, and Thom, "Angola's 1975-76 Civil War," p. 31. See the pessimistic reports of Generals André van Deventer, Magnus Malan, and Viljoen in Spies, *Operasie*, pp. 259, 261, 264. "The operations in Angola had exposed certain deficiencies in the South African weaponry and equipment. . . . This was especially true of the SADF's artillery, which had been badly outranged by the Cubans' Soviet-supplied artillery and rocket systems" (Dorning, "A Concise History," p. 21).

68. Deon Geldenhuys, *Diplomacy*, p. 81 quoted. On Vorster, see also de Villiers and de Villiers, *PW*, pp. 263-73; Spies, *Operasie*, pp. 261-64, 268-69; du Preez, *Avontuur*, pp. 40-42, 208; *Cape Times*, Dec. 31, 1975, p. 1; Hallett, "The South African Intervention," p. 381.

On the OAU conference, see esp. the Jan. 11-14, 1976, issues of the *New York Times*, *Le Monde*, and the *Daily Times* (Lagos). On the role of the OAU during the Angolan crisis, see Klinghoffer, *Angolan War*, pp. 61-71, and Cervenka and Legum, "The Organization." The OAU recognized the PRA on Feb. 11, 1976.

69. *WP*, Feb. 4, 1976, p. 1.

70. *Sunday Times*, Feb. 15, 1976, p. 8.

71. Iko Carreira in "Vermerk," p. 3.

72. These were the only two countries, besides Cuba, that sent troops; the soldiers from Conakry arrived in early March 1976, too late to participate in the fighting. (Interviews with Xiyetu, Ndalu, Lúcio Lara, and Risquet; Darío to Osmany, Conakry, Dec. 1 and 9, 1975; Jefatura to Rogelio Acevedo, Mar. 15,

1976; Lúcio Lara, "A história do MPLA," n.d., p. 166; Paulo Jorge, "Resposta célere dos cubanos ao apelo de Agostinho Neto," *Jornal de Notícias* [Lisbon], Nov. 14, 1995, p. 14; *Nõ Pintcha*, Mar. 16, 1976, p. 1, and Mar. 20, p. 4; *Cape Times*, Feb. 12, 1976, p. 1; *Daily Times*, Feb. 9, 1976, p. 1.) There were false rumors about the presence of contingents from Mozambique, Algeria, and even from Czechoslovakia (see, for example, *Zambia Daily Mail*, Feb. 9, 1976, p. 1).

73. For the recognitions, see esp. *Le Monde*, *Times*, and *New York Times* for the last two weeks of February.

74. Marenches, *Evil*, pp. 77-83; Stockwell, *Search*, p. 233.

75. Quotations from Lunel, *Denard*, pp. 451-52, and Stockwell, *Search*, p. 243. See also Bridgland, *Savimbi*, p. 199, and du Preez, *Avontuur*, p. 222.

76. Quotations from "Informe evaluativo de la situación económica de la R.P. del Congo en el año 1975," p. 4, enclosed in Columbié to Carlos Rafael Rodríguez, Brazzaville, Jan. 9, 1976, MINREX; Risquet to Fidel Castro, Luanda, Dec. 30, 1975, ACC (emphasis in original); Schaufele, Transcripts, Apr. 2, 1976, p. 28, box 9.

77. Quotations from General Leopoldo Cintra Frías, in "Transcripción textual de los primeros contactos oficiales entre los representantes del gobierno sudafricano y la parte cubana, ocurrida el primero de abril de 1976," p. 9, and from Büttner, "Vermerk über ein Gespräch mit dem Mitglied des ZK der Kommunistischen Partei Kubas, Genossen Flavio Bravo am 27.2.1976 in der Zeit von 10.00 bis 11.30 Uhr," Luanda, p. 1, SED, DY30 IV 2/2.035/128. See also Major Carlos M. Pérez Pérez, "Informe de la visita realizada al frente sur del 4-12.3.76."

78. Castro had been in the Soviet Union attending the Congress of the CPSU and had then visited Rumania, Bulgaria, and Algeria.

79. Castro, Mar. 15, 1976, speech, *Granma*, Mar. 17, 1976, pp. 2-3.

80. Republic of South Africa, *House of Assembly Debates*, Mar. 25, 1976, cols. 3916-17.

81. Quotations from *Le Monde*, Mar. 30, 1976, p. 6, and from Brigadier (Ret.) J. G. Willers's letter to the editor, *Cape Times*, Apr. 28, 1976, p. 10.

82. NSC meeting, May 11, 1976, p. 6, NSAd, NSC Meeting Minutes, box 2, GRFL. For the debates and the vote, see UN Security Council, records of meetings no. 1900 (Mar. 26, 1976, 5 p.m.) through no. 1906 (Mar. 31, 1976, 3:30 p.m.). The quotations from the Chinese delegate are from meeting no. 1906, p. 137, and no. 1900, pp. 31-32.

83. Amembassy Cape Town to SecState, Apr. 21, 1976, FOIA.

84. "Vermerk," pp. 4-5.

85. Jannie Geldenhuys, *A General's Story*, pp. 58-59.

86. Quotations from *RDM*, Feb. 17, 1976, p. 10; Amembassy London to SecState, Mar. 2, 1976, p. 2, DOS MF 8904623; Republic of South Africa, *Report*, 1:579 (quoting the pamphlet).

87. Roger Sargent, *RDM*, Feb. 13, 1976, p. 13.

88. Quotations from *World*, Feb. 24, 1976, p. 4, and Gideon Jacobs (United Party), *RDM*, Feb. 28, 1976, p. 6.

89. *Observer*, June 20, 1976, p. 12.

90. *NYT*, Feb. 21, 1976, p. 3.

91. Ibid., quoted; Republic of South Africa, *Report*, 1:580; Timol and Mazibuko, *Soweto*, esp. p. 30.

CHAPTER SIXTEEN

1. Kissinger, Jan. 29, 1976, in U.S. Senate, Committee on Foreign Relations, Subcommittee on African Affairs, *Angola*, p. 9 (hereafter U.S. Senate, *Angola*); Schaufele, ibid., p. 193.

2. See chapters 11 and 12.

3. Legum, in Legum and Hodges, *After Angola*, pp. 19-20. Legum's source for the arms shipments the MPLA received after March is an article by a knowledgeable journalist, David Martin, which states, "In addition Russian planes have airlifted armaments to Brazzaville" ("The Fight for Angola," *Observer* [London], Aug. 24, 1975, p. 7).

4. Hodges, in Legum and Hodges, *After Angola*, p. 52. For Gelb's article, see "U.S., Soviet, China Reported Aiding Portugal, Angola," *NYT*, Sept. 25, 1975, p. 1.

5. Marcum, *Angolan Revolution*, 2:259, 435 nn. 148 and 151.

6. See Klinghoffer, *Angolan War*, pp. 22, 25; Garthoff, *Détente*, p. 561; Rodman, *Precious*, p. 169; Spikes, *Angola*, p. 144; Guimarães, *Origins*, p. 102.

7. Quotations from Heimer, *Entkolonisierungskonflikt*, p. 194 n. 537; Mabeko Tali, "Dissidences," p. 346; Kissinger, *Renewal*, p. 797; Ernesto Melo Antunes, quoted in Avillez, *Do Fundo*, p. 28.

8. Quotations from National Security Council Interdepartmental Group for Africa, "Response to NSSM 224: United States Policy toward Angola," June 13, 1975, pp. 3, 50, enclosed in Nathaniel Davis to the Assistant to the President for National Security Affairs, June 16, 1975, NSA (hereafter NSC, "Response"); Kissinger [to Ford], "Meeting of the National Security Council, Friday, June 27, 1975, 2:30 p.m.," p. 4, NSA; Sisco to Scowcroft, July 15, 1975, NSA.

9. Quotations from Lúcio Lara, "A história do MPLA," n.d., p. 161; interviews with Onambwe and Jorge; Díaz Argüelles to Raúl Castro, Havana, Aug. 11, 1975, pp. 1-2. Also interviews with Lúcio Lara, Rui de Matos, Xiyetu, and Ndalu; "Information des Mitglieds des Politbüros der Volksbefreiungsbewegung von Angola (MPLA), Iko Carreira, zur gegenwärtigen Lage in Angola," enclosed in "Vorlage für das Politbüro," Berlin, Sept. 3, 1975, SED, DY30 JIV 2/2A 1911.

On the *Postoyna*, see *Provincia de Angola*, May 6, 1975, p. 17; *O Comércio* (Luanda), May 1, 1975, p. 10; *RDM* (Johannesburg), May 2, 1975, p. 3.

10. CIA, "Staff Notes: Soviet Union and Eastern Europe," Aug. 20, 1975, p. 2, NSA.

11. "1975: Realisierung materielle Solidarität MPLA–VR Angola," Berlin, Jan. 22, 1976, SED, DY30 IV 2/2.035/128; "Realisierung materielle Solidarität

für die Volksbefreiungsbewegung der Volksrepublik Angola (MPLA)," Berlin, Feb. 19, 1976, ibid.

12. "Vorlage für das Politbüro," Berlin, Sept. 3, 1975, SED, DY30 JIV 2/2A 1911; "Protokoll Nr. 38/75 der Sitzung des Politbüros des Zentralkomitees vom 9. Sept. 1975," SED, DY30 JIV 2/2 1580; "Lieferung nichtziviler Güter 1975/76," n.d., SED, DY30 IV 2/2.035/128; "Realisierung materielle Solidarität für die Volksbefreiungsbewegung der Volksrepublik Angola (MPLA)," Berlin, Feb. 19, 1976, p. 2 quoted, ibid.

Nigeria, Guinea-Bissau, Mozambique, and a few other countries sent military aid, but only after independence.

13. "Information des Mitglieds des Politbüros der Volksbefreiungsbewegung von Angola (MPLA), Iko Carreira, zur gegenwärtigen Lage in Angola," p. 6, enclosed in "Vorlage für das Politbüro," Berlin, Sept. 3, 1975, SED, DY30 JIV 2/2A 1911. See also Heimer, *Entkolonisierungskonflikt*, p. 186.

14. "Informe de la entrevista sostenida con el Cro. Serre, Primer Consj. de la embajada de la URSS," Feb. 12, 1975, p. 2 quoted, enclosed in Columbié to Raúl Roa, Brazzaville, Feb. 13, 1975, MINREX. See also "Conversación con Pierre Nze, sostenida por Domingo García y Oscar Oramas (Febrero 27, 1975)," enclosed in García to Carlos Rafael Rodríguez, Havana, Feb. 28, 1975, MINREX; Anillo to Roa, Havana, July 22, 1975; Sardañas to Columbié, Brazzaville, Dec. 10, 1975 (reporting the complaints of the first secretary of the Soviet embassy), MINREX.

15. Westad, "Moscow," p. 25. By early October, when the Cuban ships arrived, the Portuguese had withdrawn from most of Angola and the only ports where they still had a military presence were Moçamedes and Luanda. The situation was, however, entirely different through the spring.

16. See chapter 12.

17. DOS, "Memorandum of Law," Feb. 20, 1976, pp. 2-3, FOIA (the memo received the very low classification level of "confidential," which indicates that the administration did not intend to keep it a jealously guarded secret); Schaufele, Jan. 26, 1976, in U.S. House, Committee on International Relations, *United States Policy on Angola*, p. 5.

18. Quotations from *NYT*, Jan. 20, 1976, p. 1, and Marcum, *Angolan Revolution*, 2:263. On the CIA undervaluing the weapons, see also *NYT*, Dec. 18, 1975, p. 14, and Jan. 27, 1976, p. 15, and *CIA: The Pike Report*, pp. 198, 200.

19. See chapter 13.

20. Garthoff, *Détente*, p. 567 n. 40 quoted; Westad, "Moscow," p. 26; Representação Especial [of Brazil] em Luanda to Foreign Ministry, Nov. 20, 1975, NSA; Columbié to Colomé, nos. 486 and 487, Oct. 29, 1975; Columbié to Carlos Rafael [Rodríguez], Nov. 17, 1975; Columbié to Osmany and Colomé, Nov. 25, 1975, no. 593. (All of Columbié's reports are from Brazzaville.) A former MPLA official claims that there were thirty Soviet military advisers in Angola in October 1975, but offers no proof. (See Guimarães, "Interviews," p. 27.) Given all the contrary evidence, this is not credible.

21. South African troops were already raiding southern Angola in late August and September, but their target was SWAPO.

22. See Marcum, *Angolan Revolution*, 2:260; Charles Mohr, *NYT*, Apr. 24, 1975, p. 2; Legum, "Letter," pp. 16-17; Heimer, *Entkolonisierungskonflikt*, p. 182. The Bakongo population increased by about 50 percent after the fall of Caetano with the return of about 200,000 Bakongo who had fled to Zaire in the early 1960s (see Heimer, "Décolonisation," p. 53 n. 13 and p. 69 n. 34).

23. Killoran to SecState, May 12, 1975, p. 4, DOS MF 8904623; tel. interview with Killoran.

24. Messiant, "Angola: The Challenge," p. 144 quoted; Messiant, "Angola, les voies," p. 1, pp. 167-69; Maria da Conceição Neto, "Entre" and "Contribuiçoes."

25. Quotations from tel. interview with Killoran; Robert Hultslander, fax to Piero Gleijeses, Dec. 22, 1998, pp. 1, 3; Dick Clark, "Clark Amendment," June 1993, courtesy of Dick Clark; Hultslander, fax to Gleijeses, Dec. 22, 1998, p. 5.

26. Quotations from Kissinger [to Ford], "Meeting of the National Security Council, Friday, June 27, 1975, 2:30 p.m.," p. 2, NSA, and Sisco to Scowcroft, July 15, 1975, NSA.

27. Quotations from Horan to Kissinger, June 18, 1975, NSA, and Davis, Hyland, and Lord to Kissinger, Apr. 4, 1975, p. 7, DOS MF 8802915/2. U.S. investment in Angola "is presently estimated at $400 million of which $300 million represents the Gulf Oil investment in Cabinda" (NSC, "Response," p. 61). On the limited strategic importance, see ibid., pp. 63-65; CIA, "Staff Notes: Soviet Union and Eastern Europe," Aug. 20, 1975, NSA; Deputy Secretary of Defense Ellsworth, Feb. 3, 1976, in U.S. Senate, *Angola*, p. 61; *NYT*, Dec. 17, 1975, p. 1.

28. DOS (prepared for the Senate Foreign Relations Committee), "United States Policy toward Angola," Dec. 16, 1975, p. 3, NSA (hereafter DOS, "U.S. Policy").

29. Colby and Kissinger, NSC meeting, Apr. 9, 1975, pp. 6-8, 15-16, NSAd, NSC Meeting Minutes, box 1, GRFL.

30. Gerald Ford, *Time*, p. 275; White House MemoConv (Ford, Kissinger, Scowcroft), Oct. 25, 1975, p. 2, FOIA 1997/1690.

31. Quotations from NSC, "Response," p. 82, and Kissinger [to Ford], "Meeting of the National Security Council, Friday, June 27, 1975, 2:30 p.m.," pp. 5-6, NSA.

According to Hyland, "The growing Portuguese crisis—July-August 1975—weighed heavily in the consideration in Washington of . . . Angola. . . . A powerful reason [for the decision to launch IAFEATURE] was the situation in Portugal. The interaction of the two crises—in Lisbon, where a Communist success appeared imminent, and in Angola, where the indigenous Communists also seemed about to prevail—was decisive" (Hyland, *Rivals*, p. 135). The declassified record, however, does not suggest any such linkage.

32. DOS, "U.S. Policy," p. 2.

33. Killoran to SecState, May 12, 1975, sec. 2, p. 2, DOS MF 8904623.

34. NSC, "Response," p. 55.

35. "Portuguese Policy and Objectives in Angola," June 24, 1975, p. 3 quoted, enclosed in Colby (DCI) to Senior Review Group, June 24, 1975, NSA; "Intelligence Brief–Angola–16 July 1975," NSA.

36. Quotations from Davis, Hyland, and Lord to Kissinger, Apr. 4, 1975, p. 3, DOS MF 8802915/2; interviews with Davis and Mulcahy; Kissinger, Transcripts of Secretary of State Henry Kissinger's Staff Meetings, 1973-1977, July 14, 1975, pp. 42-43, box 8, NA.

37. Pastor, *Condemned.*

38. Quotations from interviews with Davis, Y, and Sisco.

39. Quotations from interview with Davis; tel. interview with Killoran; Hultslander, fax to Gleijeses, Dec. 22, 1998, p. 3.

40. Handwritten note by the deputy undersecretary for management, n.d., NSA. See also Davis, "The Angola Decision," pp. 116-17; Sisco to Scowcroft, July 15, 1975, NSA. When Davis submitted his resignation, Eagleburger told him, on behalf of Kissinger, "if you resign from the service, there is no way we can keep the operation secret; your resignation would blow off the operation." Therefore Kissinger offered him the embassy in Bern and he accepted. (Interview with Davis. See also *WP*, Sept. 1, 1975, p. 1, and *NYT*, Dec. 14, 1975, p. 1.)

41. Kissinger, *Renewal*, pp. 798-805 (p. 801 quoted).

42. Davis to Sisco, July 12, 1975, p. 2, NSA.

43. Kissinger had shown how little he cared for African sensitivities during the 1973-74 Azores negotiations. His failure to oppose the Byrd amendment was another example.

44. Annex 4, enclosed in DOS, "United States Policy toward Angola," Dec. 16, 1975, DOS MF 8704129/2.

45. On Savimbi, see Bridgland, "Savimbi"; Radek Sikorski, "The Mystique of Savimbi," *National Review*, Aug. 18, 1989, pp. 34-36; *NYT*, Mar. 11, 1989, p. 1, and Mar. 12, p. 9; *WP*, Mar. 14, 1989, p. 20, and Sept. 30, 1990, D1.

46. Nathaniel Davis, Foreign Policy Lecture no. 14, May 24, 1978, p. 7, courtesy of Nathaniel Davis.

47. Tel. interview with Killoran.

48. Kissinger, Transcripts of Secretary of State Henry Kissinger's Staff Meetings, 1973-1977, Mar. 31, 1975, p. 43, box 6, NA.

49. Davis to Sisco, July 12, 1975, p. 5, NSA.

50. Quotations from DOS, "U.S. Policy," p. 3, and from Kissinger, Jan. 29, 1976, in U.S. Senate, *Angola*, pp. 8, 13.

51. Quotations from interview with Y and from Davis to Sisco, July 12, 1975, pp. 5, 2, NSA.

52. Interview with Sisco.

53. Hyland, *Rivals*, p. 139.

54. NSC, "Response," p. 5.

55. Quotations from Biden, Jan. 29, 1976, in U.S. Senate, *Angola*, p. 31, and Hyland, *Rivals*, p. 142. Interview with Diggs.

56. *NYT*, Feb. 11, 1976, p. 1 (quoting Ford); *WP*, Feb. 15, 1976, K6 (ed.); Lewis, *NYT*, Feb. 16, 1976, p. 19.

57. Kissinger, Jan. 29, 1976, in U.S. Senate, *Angola*, p. 12; Arthur Schlesinger, "The Troubles of Angola," *WSJ*, Feb. 9, 1976, p. 10.

58. Davis to Sisco, July 12, 1975, pp. 3-4, NSA.

59. *Zambia Daily Times*, Aug. 23, 1975, p. 1 quoted; *Expresso* (Lisbon), Aug. 30, 1975, p. 12; Representação Especial [of Brazil] em Luanda, "Situação politico militar de Angola," Aug. 22 and 25, 1975, NSA; *RDM*, Aug. 23, 1975, p. 5; *La Semaine* (Brazzaville), Sept. 7, 1975, p. 1.

60. *NYT*, Sept. 25, 1975, p. 1.

61. Davis, "The Angola Decision," p. 118.

62. *WP*, Sept. 27, 1975, p. 14 (ed.).

63. The first hint of U.S. involvement in Angola in the *Christian Science Monitor* is a sentence on October 24 (p. 12): "Although the United States officially is maintaining a hands-off policy toward the civil war in Angola, some officials clearly leave the impression that U.S. arms aid may be reaching two of the three factions fighting in the African colony." IAFEATURE was first mentioned in the *Chicago Tribune* on October 5 (p. 4); *Los Angeles Times* on November 11 (p. 25); *Newsweek* on November 17 (p. 61); *Time* on November 17 (p. 44); *Nation* on November 22 (p. 519); *Village Voice* on December 1 (p. 24); *New Republic* on December 6 (p. 8); *Wall Street Journal* on December 15 (p. 1). After its September 27 editorial, the *Post* did not mention the covert operation again until November 10 (p. 26, ed.).

64. *NYT*: Oct. 16, 1975, p. 2; Oct. 26, 4:4; Nov. 3, p. 34 (ed.).

65. *NYT*, Nov. 7, 1975, p. 3, and Nov. 9, 4:3 (emphasis added).

66. Quotations from *NYT*: Nov. 24, 1975, p. 3; Dec. 12, p. 1; Nov. 26, p. 28 (ed.). See also ibid.: Nov. 11, 1975, p. 30; Nov. 21, p. 6; Dec. 4, p. 40 (ed.); Dec. 9, p. 40 (ed.); Dec. 10, p. 12; Dec. 13, p. 8. The December 4 editorial noted that U.S. assistance, while less than the "massive" Soviet support of the MPLA, was "significant"; and the December 12 article, while expressing no criticism of U.S. policy, stated that U.S. aid to the FNLA and UNITA amounted to $25 million.

67. Quotations from *Chicago Tribune*, Oct. 5, 1975, p. 4, and *CSM*, Nov. 12, 1975, p. 27. The two instances of *Post* criticism in the period under consideration are the September 27 editorial already quoted and a November 10 editorial (p. 26).

68. Seymour Hersh, "Angola-Aid Issue Opening Rifts in State Department," *NYT*, Dec. 14, 1975, p. 1; Dec. 16, p. 38 (ed.) quoted.

69. *Pittsburgh Courier*, Dec. 27, 1975, p. 5 quoted. My sample includes the Baltimore *Afro-American*, the New York *Amsterdam News*, the *Chicago Defender*, the *Pittsburgh Courier*, *Muhammad Speaks*, and the *Crisis*. The *Afro American* (which from December 1975 had a correspondent in Luanda) provided the best and most extensive coverage. The *Crisis* printed no articles on Angola.

70. See, for example, the press release by the Black Caucus, in *Afro-American*, Dec. 27, 1975, p. 1.

71. Brigadier General Murtala Muhammed, "Foreign Interests and Africa's Fortune," Jan. 11, 1976, in Republic of Nigeria, *A Time for Action*, p. 47; Nyerere, *Daily News* (Dar-es-Salaam), Nov. 12, 1975, p. 1.

72. *NYT*, Jan. 7, 1976, p. 74, and Mar. 2, p. 3.

73. Kissinger, quoted in *NYT*, Feb. 5, 1976, p. 12; Ford, quoted in *NYT*, Feb. 11, 1976, p. 1.

74. Quotations from Garthoff, *Détente*, p. 578 (emphasis in original); *NYT*, Jan. 6, 1976, p. 3 (quoting Ford); *NYT*, Nov. 29, 1975, p. 3 (quoting Kissinger).

75. Clayton Fritchey, "Angola and U.S. Policy," *WP*, Jan. 3, 1976, p. 19.

76. Tel. interview with Hyland.

77. Quotations from Columbié to Carlos Rafael [Rodríguez], Nov. 17 and Dec. 18, 1975. Brazil recognized the People's Republic of Angola on November 11.

78. On Soviet policy, see Garthoff, *Détente*, pp. 582-93; Westad, "Moscow," pp. 21-32; Dobrynin, *In Confidence*, pp. 342-70; Klinghoffer, *Angolan War*, pp. 101-8; Burr, *Kissinger Transcripts*, pp. 426-75; Valenta, "Soviet"; Legum, "The Soviet Union."

79. My source is a conversation with Westad, based on his research in the Soviet archives (Washington, D.C., Dec. 14, 1999).

80. Kissinger, *Renewal*, p. 845.

81. Westad, "Moscow," pp. 26-27.

82. Quotations from NIE, "Soviet Military Policy in the Third World," Oct. 21, 1976, p. 26, MF 00500, NSA, and SecState to All American Republic Diplomatic Posts, Jan. 3, 1976, p. 2, FOIA (emphasis added). These figures are too high. For a lower U.S. estimate, a few days earlier, see chapter 14, n. 113.

83. SecState to All American Republic Diplomatic Posts, Dec. 20, 1975, NSA.

84. See "Informe sobre la visita realizada por el mayor Rodobaldo Díaz Padraga a Angola en los días del 16.11.75 al 26.11.75 (Frente sur)," n.d.; Lucas Molina to Colomé, "Informe del cumplimiento de la misión en Luanda entre los días 4-18.11.75," Havana, n.d., p. 1; Raúl Pérez Millares and Eliseo Matos Andreu (representatives of Cubana de Aviación in Barbados) to Olivio, Dec. 17, 1975.

85. Quotations from CIA, *Intelligence Checklist*, Nov. 14, 1975, p. A2, NSA; SecState to Amembassy Bogota et al., Dec. 1, 1975, p. 2, DOS MF 9001360; SecState to All American Republic Diplomatic Posts, Dec. 16, 1975, p. 2, ibid.; CIA, *Intelligence Checklist*, Dec. 18, 1975, NSA. For U.S. pressure on Barbados, see n. 87.

86. Quotations from *Economist*, Dec. 27, 1975, p. 26, and *Daily Telegraph*, Dec. 19, 1975, p. 4.

\-7287. Quotations from Juan Escalona, in Báez, *Secretos*, p. 443; Shlaudeman (U.S. ambassador, Caracas) to SecState, Jan. 26, 1976, p. 2 (quoting Pérez), DOS MF 8904623; Kissinger to Amembassy Caracas, Jan. 8 and 18, 1976, ibid. U.S. dispatches are very informative on the Cuban attempts to find airports and the U.S. campaign to close them. See Amembassy Bridgetown to SecState, Dec. 18, 1975, NSA; Kissinger to Amembassy Bridgetown, Dec. 18, 1975, NSA;

Amembassy Port of Spain to SecState, Dec. 19, 1975, and Jan. 12, 1976, NSA; SecState to All American Republic Diplomatic Posts, Dec. 20, 1975, NSA; Kissinger to Amembassy Georgetown, Dec. 20 and 24, 1975, NSA; Kissinger to Amembassy Paramaribo, Dec. 20, 1975, FOIA; Kissinger to Amembassy Lisbon, Dec. 22, 1975, and Jan. 8, 1976, NSA; SecState to All American Republic Diplomatic Posts, Dec. 24 and 31, 1975, and Jan. 3, 1976, DOS MF 9001360; CIA, *Intelligence Checklist*, Dec. 30, 1975, NSA; Amembassy Lisbon to SecState, Jan. 2 and 8, 1976, ibid.; Shlaudeman to SecState, Jan. 2, 1976, ibid. See also Ulises to Carlos Rafael, Guyana, Dec. 23, 1975, and Ulises to Roa, Guyana, Dec. 27, 1975.

88. Quotations from Jorge Risquet, note to Piero Gleijeses, Havana, Aug. 10, 1996, and [illegible], Ministerio de las Fuerzas Armadas Revolucionarias, "Conversación con el embajador soviético," [Havana, Jan. 6, 1976].

89. Gustavo Chui (deputy chief of the Puesto de Mando de Angola in the EMG) to Acevedo, Jan. 9, 1976.

90. SecState to All American Republic Diplomatic Posts, Jan. 13, 1976, p. 3, DOS MF 9001360 (emphasis added). Only one of the more than twenty U.S. cables on the Cuban airlift in my possession gives a slightly different version: "From late December to mid-January, Cubans used long-range IL-62 aircraft from the U.S.S.R. for airlifting men/materiel to Angola" (Kissinger to Amembassy Caracas, Jan. 31, 1976, DOS MF 8904623).

91. *CSM*, Jan. 22, 1976, p. 9.

92. Kissinger to Amembassy Caracas, Jan. 31, 1976, DOS MF 8904623.

93. Jorge Risquet, note to Piero Gleijeses, Havana, July 22, 1996, p. 1.

94. Raúl Castro to Severo Aguirre, handwritten, [Jan. 31, 1976]; Fidel [Castro] to Colomé and Acevedo, handwritten, Feb. 11, 1976.

95. "Convenio entre el Gobierno Revolucionario de la República de Cuba y el Gobierno de la Unión de Repúblicas Socialistas Soviéticas sobre la entrega de equipos especiales," Moscow, Jan. 16, 1976. The weapons to be delivered were listed in the appendix of the protocol.

96. Chui (deputy chief of the Puesto de Mando de Angola in the EMG) to Juanito (Cdte Juan Escalona, chief of the Puesto de Mando de Angola in the EMG), [early Feb. 1976].

97. Risquet to Fidel Castro, Luanda, Jan. 29, 1976, ACC.

98. Blight, Allyn, and Welch, *Cuba on the Brink*, p. 272; Castro interview in CNN, *Cold War*, pp. 10-11.

99. Dobrynin, *In Confidence*, p. 362.

100. Westad, "Moscow," p. 27.

101. Mabeko Tali, "Dissidences," p. 408 quoted; Westad, "Moscow," pp. 27-28.

102. The only in-depth discussion of the coup is Mabeko Tali, "Dissidences," pp. 392-438. See also Wolfers and Bergerol, *Angola*, pp. 85-99; Birmingham, "The Twenty-Seventh"; Bender, "Angola," pp. 23-26; Domínguez, *To Make*, pp. 158-59; Carreira (Neto's

defense minister), *O Pensamento*, pp. 147-56; Carreira, "A última batalla"; Garthoff, *Détente*, pp. 573-74; Kempton, *Soviet Strategy*, pp. 56-59.

For two Cuban reports that deal with the day of the revolt in Luanda and, in particular, the Cuban response, see Risquet to Castro, May 27, 1977, ACC, and Colonel Jesús Bermúdez Cutiño, "Síntesis sobre nuestra participación en los sucesos del 27.5.77 en la República Popular de Angola," May 31, 1977. Soviet involvement in the coup was confirmed by interviews with Lúcio Lara, Onambwe (one of the two deputy chiefs of the Angolan intelligence service), and Risquet.

103. Andrew Young, May 12, 1978, in U.S. Senate, Committee on Foreign Relations, Subcommittee on African Affairs, *U.S. Policy toward Africa*, p. 23. See also CIA, "Annex I: The Cuban-Soviet Presence in Africa," p. 4, enclosed in "Response, Presidential Review Memorandum–36: Soviet/Cuban Presence in Africa," Aug. 18, 1978, NSA.

104. "Respuesta de Raúl al Ministro de Defensa Soviético," [late May 1977].

CHAPTER SEVENTEEN

1. Denney (INR) to SecState, "Cuban Foreign Policy," Sept. 15, 1967, p. 7, Pol 1 Cuba, SNF, NA.

2. Quotations from "National Policy Paper–Cuba: United States Policy," draft, July 15, 1968, p. 16, FOIA 1996/3108, and DOS, "Soviet Intentions toward Cuba," Mar. 1965, p. 3, NSFCF, box 33/37.

3. White House MemoConv (Ford, President Leone, et al.), Sept. 25, 1974, p. 3 (quoting Leone), NSATPF, box A2, GRFL, and White House MemoConv (Ford, Foreign Minister Rumor, et al.), Sept. 23, 1975, p. 5 (quoting Rumor). See also Nuti, "Missiles or Socialists?"

4. CIA, Board of National Estimates, "Bolsheviks and Heroes: The USSR and Cuba," Nov. 21, 1967, p. 3, FOIA 1993/1807.

5. Quotations from Hughes (INR) to SecState, "Soviet Intentions toward Cuba," Mar. 12, 1965, pp. 1, i, 4, NSFCF, box 33/37, and CIA, Board of National Estimates, "Bolsheviks and Heroes: The USSR and Cuba," Nov. 21, 1967, pp. 5-7, FOIA 1993/1807.

6. DOS, "Political Currents in the Cuban Leadership," Mar. 1965, p. 3, NSFCF, box 33/37.

7. Quotations from CIA, *Current Intelligence Weekly*, "Castro's Cuba Today," Sept. 30, 1966, p. 16, NSFCF, box 19; CIA, DI, "Instability in the Western Hemisphere," Dec. 9, 1966, p. VIII-1, NSFCF, box 2; CIA, DI, "Political Trends in Cuba," Mar. 15, 1968, p. 1, NSFCF, box 19; Special NIE: Cuba: Castro's Problems and Prospects over the Next Year or Two," June 27, 1968, p. 1, NSF, NIE, box 8/9, LBJL.

8. Denney (INR) to SecState, "Cuban Foreign Policy," Sept. 15, 1967, pp. 4 and 5, Pol 1 Cuba, SNF, NA.

9. Sherman Kent to DCI, Sept. 4, 1963, NSC 145-10001-10126/205, JFKAC, RG 263, NA.

10. Special NIE, "Cuba: Castro's Problems and Prospects over the Next Year or Two," June 27, 1968, p. 3, NSF, NIE, box 8/9, LBJL.

11. CIA, DI, "Cuban Subversive Policy and the Bolivian Guerrilla Episode," May 1968, p. 3, NSFCF, box 19.

12. Special NIE, "The Situation in the Caribbean through 1959," June 30, 1959, p. 3, NSA.

13. NIE, "The Situation in Cuba," June 14, 1960, p. 9, NSA.

14. DOS, Policy Planning Council, "Caribbean: Cuba" (draft outline), Feb. 13, 1964, p. 6, NSFCF, box 26/29.

15. Quotations from "National Policy Paper–Cuba: United States Policy," draft, July 15, 1968, p. 17, FOIA 1996/3108, and Denney (INR) to SecState, "Cuban Foreign Policy," Sept. 15, 1967, p. 1, Pol 1 Cuba, SNF, NA.

16. DOS, "Soviet Intentions toward Cuba," Mar. 1965, p. 2, NSFCF, box 33/37.

17. CIA, OCI, "Cuban Subversion in Latin America," Apr. 23, 1965, p. 4, NSFCF, box 31/32.

18. CIA, OCI, "Survey of Latin America," Apr. 1, 1964, pp. 83-84, NSFCF, box 1.

19. Hughes (INR) to SecState, "Che Guevara's African Venture," Apr. 19, 1965, pp. 1-2, NSFCF, box 20.

20. Hughes (INR) to SecState, "The Cuban Revolution: Phase Two," Aug. 10, 1965, p. 16, NSFCF, box 18/19.

21. See Instituto de Historia del Movimiento Comunista y de la Revolución Socialista de Cuba, *Cuba y la defensa*, and Naranjo Orovio, *Cuba*, pp. 73-74.

22. Martí to Manuel Mercado, May 18, 1895, in Martí, *Epistolario*, 5:250.

23. Special NIE, "Communist Influence in Cuba," Mar. 22, 1960, p. 3, FOIA 1984/1513.

24. Hughes (INR) to SecState, "Cuba in 1964," Apr. 17, 1964, pp. 10-11, FOIA 1996/668.

25. Interview with Dreke.

26. "National Policy Paper–Cuba: United States Policy," draft, July 15, 1968, p. 15, FOIA 1996/3108.

27. Quotations from Special NIE, "Cuba: Castro's Problems and Prospects over the Next Year or Two," June 27, 1968, p. 3, NSF, NIE, box 8/9, LBJL, and CIA, ONE, "Castro, Model 1966," Mar. 24, 1966, p. 5, FOIA 1993/2415. The lack of Cuban aid was confirmed by Dominican rebel leaders I interviewed in 1969-71 for my *Dominican Crisis*.

28. Raúl Castro to Flavio Bravo and Jorge Serguera, Havana, Oct. 20, 1963, p. 4.

29. See chapter 8.

30. Interview with Turpin.

31. Hughes (INR) to SecState, "Cuba in 1964," Apr. 17, 1964, pp. 10-11, FOIA 1996/668.

32. Hughes (INR) to SecState, "The Cuban Revolution: Phase Two," Aug. 10, 1965, pp. 11-12, NSFCF, box 18/19.

33. Kissinger, *Renewal*, p. 785.

34. Annex 4, p. 2, enclosed in "Response, Presidential Review Memorandum–36: Soviet/Cuban Presence in Africa," Aug. 18, 1978, NSA (hereafter "Response").

35. *NYT*, Feb. 25, 1976, p. 8 quoted. On the execution of the Cuban prisoners, Defense Minister

Botha, Republic of South Africa, *House of Assembly Debates*, May 6, 1976, col. 6215; Bridgland, *Savimbi*, pp. 161 and 191.

36. *NYT*, Apr. 6, 1976, p. 2, and Apr. 13, p. 4; Ryan to Chapman, June 9, 1976, Richard D. Parsons Files, box 9, GRFL.

37. See *Paratus*: "Ons help Kubaanse krygsgevangenes," Nov. 1976, p. 27; "The Cuban POW's Are Alive and Well and Living in Pretoria," Jan. 1977, pp. 4-5; "Geen Klagtes Ne, Sé Kubane," Feb. 1978, p. 9; "POW Interlude in Angola," Oct. 1978, pp. 10-11.

38. Quotations from *WP*, Feb. 22, 1976, p. 18; "Response," pt. 1, p. 20; Pastor to Brzezinski and Aaron, June 8, 1978, FOIA 1999/3485.

39. Quotations from J. D. du P. Basson (United Party), Apr. 9, 1976, Republic of South Africa, *House of Assembly Debates*, col. 4934; LeoGrande, "Evolution," p. 43; Ramos Latour (Cuban ambassador, Dar-es-Salaam) to Roa, June 16, 1976, MINREX. On the shift in the Tanzanian government's policy, see its Dec. 5, 1975, communiqué, *Daily News* (Dar-es-Salaam), Dec. 6, 1975, p. 1, and Cuban embassy Dar-es-Salaam, "Informe sobre la Política exterior y la Política Interna de la Rep. Unida de Tanzania," Jan. 20, 1976, MINREX.

40. See Gonzalez, "Cuba," pp. 152-54; Domínguez, "The Cuban Operation"; Annex 4, enclosed in "Response."

41. Maxwell, *The Making*, p. 126.

42. *Jeune Afrique*, July 23, 1976, p. 28, and Peter Bourne, "Discussion with Delegates to the World Health Assembly," Geneva, May 1977, p. 1, Staff Offices: Special Assistant to President, Carter Library. See also Julián Álvarez, "Situación de la salud pública en la RPA," Jan. 29, 1976, enclosed in Risquet to Fidel Castro, Luanda, Jan. 29, 1976, ACC.

43. Raúl Castro, "Acerca de la necesidad de una masiva ayuda técnica (civil) a RPA," Luanda, Apr. 23, 1976, ACC; "Informe al Comité Central sobre la colaboración civil con Angola," 1978, pp. 45-49, 56, ACC; Notas del CECE (Angola).

44. The Bureau of African Affairs included only sub-Saharan Africa. Unless otherwise stated, the discussion in the pages that follow applies only to sub-Saharan Africa. North Africa–from Morocco to Egypt–was far more important to the United States.

45. Interview with Diggs (quoted). See also Metz, "The Anti-Apartheid Movement"; Challenor, "The Influence"; Krenn, *Black Diplomacy*, pp. 112-62; Staniland, *American Intellectuals*; Morris, "Black Americans." The African American press is particularly useful.

46. On Carmichael, see chapter 9; on the Black Panthers and Algeria, see Cleaver, "Back to Africa."

47. Dick Clark, "Clark Amendment," June 1993, courtesy of Dick Clark.

48. Davis, July 10, 1975, in U.S. Senate, Committee on Foreign Relations, Subcommittee on African Affairs, *U.S. Policy toward Southern Africa*, p. 179 quoted; Lake, *The "Tar Baby" Option*, pp. 198-285; DeRoche, "Strategic Minerals," pp. 217-310.

49. Quotations from *NYT*, Sept. 25, 1975, p. 42 (ed.), and *RDM*, Sept. 27, 1975, p. 3.

50. See DOS, "Policy Guidelines for Sub-Saharan Africa" (draft), enclosed in Davis and Lord to SecState, Apr. 3, 1975, PPS, box 351.

51. Rusk, OH, (IV, Mar. 8, 1970), pp. 33-34, LBJL.

52. CIA, DI, "The New Look in Chinese Communist Aid to Sub-Saharan Africa," Sept. 1968, FOIA 1998/2435.

53. Quotations from Hamilton to Rostow, Oct. 11, 1967, NSFCF, box 77; Morris to Rostow, Apr. 8, 1968, p. 1, FOIA 1999/0456; [Palmer], "Assistant Secretary Palmer's African Trip, May 30 to July 18, 1968," pp. 2-3, 8, NSFCF, box 77.

54. Spiro to Lord, Feb. 11, 1974, p. 1, enclosed in Lord to Brown, Feb. 11, 1974, PPS, box 345. On aid levels, see Newsom to SecState, Oct. 5, 1973, Pol Afr-US, SNF, NA.

55. Davis and Lord to SecState, "Your Meeting with the African Ambassadors April 8," Apr. 3, 1975, pp. 10-11, PPS, box 351.

56. Stremlau, *International Politics*; Shepard, *Nigeria*, pp. 34-49; Kissinger, *White House Years*, pp. 416-17. For useful insights by U.S. intelligence, see the following INR reports: "USSR-Nigeria: FMG Victory Hailed, but Moscow's Position May Be Weakened," Jan. 19, 1970, Pol Nigeria-USSR, SNF, NA; "USSR-Nigeria: Soviets Likely to Pursue Cautious Policy," Feb. 4, 1970, ibid.; "Nigeria and the United States: Implications of the New Nationalism," Apr. 16, 1970, Pol Nigeria-US, SNF, NA; "Nigeria/USSR: The Arms Supplier Earns Acceptability but Little Influence," May 13, 1970, Pol Nigeria-USSR, SNF, NA.

57. Quotations from Brubeck, memo for president, June 15, 1964, p. 1, NSFCF, box 81, and Denney (INR) to Harriman, "Chinese Communist Involvement in Congolese Insurrections," Aug. 11, 1964, p. 2, ibid.

58. NSC meeting, Aug. 11, 1964, p. 2, NSF, NSC Meetings File, box 1, LBJL.

59. Brubeck, memo for president, Aug. 6, 1964, NSFCF, box 81.

60. Congo Special Situation Report no. 10, Nov. 24, 1964, NSFCF, box 84; Hughes (INR) to SecState, "Dragon Rouge: Initial Observations and Projections," Nov. 24, 1964, ibid.; Godley to SecState, Nov. 26, 1964, ibid.; Odom, *Dragon Operations*, pp. 179-81.

61. Interview with Komer.

62. "Response," pt. 1, p. 1.

63. Minutes of cabinet meeting, Mar. 26, 1975, p. 1, Cabinet Meetings, box 2, GRFL. My discussion about détente through 1974 follows closely Garthoff's excellent *Détente*, pp. 360-520. See also Bowker and Williams, *Superpower Detente*; Isaacson, *Kissinger*, pp. 511-629; Schulzinger, *Henry Kissinger*, pp. 142-84; Cahn, *Killing Detente*.

64. Kissinger, *Renewal*, p. 299; Schlesinger, NSC meeting, Dec. 2, 1974, pp. 9, 11, NSAd, NSC Meeting Minutes, box 1, GRFL.

65. NSC meeting, Apr. 9, 1975, p. 26, NSAd, NSC Meeting Minutes, box 1, GRFL.

66. Ford, cabinet meeting, June 4, 1975, p. 2, Cabinet Meetings, box 2, GRFL.

67. Ford and Kissinger, NSC meeting, Mar. 28, 1975, pp. 2, 4, 6, 12, NSAd, NSC Meeting Minutes, box 1, GRFL. For shuttle diplomacy in 1975, see Quandt, *Peace Process*, ch. 9.

68. Kissinger, *Renewal*, p. 238 quoted. On the Panama Canal negotiations, see NSC meetings, May 15 and July 23, 1975, NSAd, NSC Meeting Minutes, box 2, GRFL.

69. Kissinger, NSC meeting, Sept. 17, 1975, p. 4, NSAd, NSC Meeting Minutes, box 2, GRFL. See also chapter 12, n. 59.

70. Kissinger, cabinet meeting, Mar. 26, 1975, pp. 2-3, Cabinet Meetings, box 2, GRFL; Ford, NSC meeting, Mar. 28, 1975, p. 9, NSAd, NSC Meeting Minutes, box 1, GRFL.

71. White House MemoConv (Cabinet Meeting), Aug. 8, 1975, p. 2, NSATPF, box A2, GRFL.

72. Kissinger, "Meet the Press," Oct. 12, 1975, DOS *Bulletin*, Nov. 10, 1975, p. 658. See also the following NSC meetings: July 25, 1975; Aug. 9, pp. 9-13; Sept. 17; Dec. 22; all NSAd, NSC Meeting Minutes, box 2, GRFL.

73. NSC meeting, Mar. 28, 1975, p. 7, NSAd, NSC Meeting Minutes, box 1, GRFL.

74. Kissinger, NSC meeting, Sept. 17, 1975, p. 4 quoted, NSAd, NSC Meeting Minutes, box 2, GRFL.

75. Quoted in Hershberg, "New East-Bloc Evidence," p. 1.

76. Quotations from Schaufele to SecState, Apr. 1, 1976, p. 1, DOS MF 8904623/1, and Lord to Kissinger, "Strategy for Southern Africa," Apr. 12, 1976, p. 2, PPS, box 357. On U.S. policy toward Rhodesia in 1976, see Horne, *Barrel*, esp. pp. 154-57. For memoirs by protagonists, see Kissinger, *Renewal*, pp. 903-1016; Ian Smith, *Betrayal*, pp. 183-222; Flower, *Serving*, pp. 164-79.

77. Quotations from Kissinger, NSC meeting, Apr. 7, 1976, p. 13, NSAd, NSC Meeting Minutes, box 2, GRFL; *Newsweek*, May 10, 1976, p. 51; Kissinger, NSC meeting, May 11, 1976, pp. 2, 4, NSAd, NSC Meeting Minutes, box 2, GRFL.

78. MemoConv, Risquet and the Soviet ambassador in Angola, Luanda, Nov. 28, 1978, p. 3 quoted. On the guerrilla school in Boma, see also MemoConv, Risquet and Nkomo, Luanda, Nov. 24, 1978; MemoConv, Risquet and Nkomo, Luanda, Nov. 27, 1978; Risquet to Castro, Luanda, Dec. 5, 1978; all ACC. For the best discussion of the Carter administration and Rhodesia, see Mitchell, "Pragmatic Moralist." See also Horne, *Barrel*, esp. pp. 157-67, and DeRoche, "Standing Firm."

79. Herbert Matthews, "Forward with Fidel Castro, Anywhere," *NYT*, Mar. 4, 1976, p. 31.

80. "Niederschrift über das Gespräch zwischen Genossen Erich Honecker und Genossen Fidel Castro am Sonntag, dem 3. April 1977, von 11.00 bis 13.30 Uhr und von 15.45 bis 18.00 Uhr, im Hause des ZK," Berlin, Apr. 3, 1977, p. 46, GDR, SED, JIV 2/201/1292.

81. Useful beginnings are Mesa-Lago and Belkin, *Cuba in Africa*; Wayne Smith, "The Cuban Role"; Gleijeses, "Truth"; Nazario, "Cuba's Relations"; López Blanch, *Cuban Blessing*, Bestard Pavón and Céspedes Carrillo, "La Colaboración"; Eckstein, "Structural and Ideological Bases"; Feinsilver, "Cuba"; Díaz-Briquets, *Cuban Internationalism*.

82. Quotations from Brzezinski, *Power*, p. 187; "Response," p. 15; Pastor to Brzezinski, Sept. 21, 1979, WHCF, box CO-21, Jimmy Carter Library.

83. Ball, *The Past*, p. 374.

84. "Convenio de Colaboración Científico-Técnica entre el Gobierno de la República de Cuba y el Gobierno de la República de Guinea-Bissau," Havana, Oct. 21, 1976, MIECE; "Protocolo de Colaboración Científico-Técnica entre el Gobierno de la República de Cuba y el Gobierno de la República de Guinea-Bissau," Apr. 4, 1978, MIECE; interviews with Drs. Rodríguez García and Morales, who headed the medical mission in 1977-78 and 1985-87 respectively; "Informe sobre la entrevista efectuada el 11.2.86 entre el comandante en jefe Fidel Castro Ruz y el presidente de Guinea Bissau, João Bernardo Vieira," Havana, Feb. 13, 1986, PCH; "Notas del CECE (Guinea-Bissau)," MIECE.

85. The rest of this paragraph is based on my personal observations in Bissau in May 1996, complemented by the "Notas del CECE (Guinea-Bissau)," MIECE.

86. See above, ch. 15.

87. Richard Cohen, "Mandela: A Mistake in Cuba," *WP*, July 30, 1991, p. 15; Mandela, quoted in *WP*, July 28, 1991, p. 32.

88. García Márquez, *Operación Carlota*.

89. See, for example, Ortíz, *Angola: un abril como Girón*, and Rius, *Angola*.

90. *Granma*, Jan. 24, 1977, p. 6, and Jan. 25, p. 1.

91. *Nõ Pintcha* (Bissau): Jan. 20, 1977, p. 1; Jan. 22, pp. 4-6 quoted; Jan. 27, p. 6; Feb. 1, p. 2.

92. Interview with Risquet.

BIBLIOGRAPHY

ARCHIVES

Belgium
Ministère des Affaires Etrangères, du Commerce Extérieur et de la Coopération au Développement [Ministry of Foreign Affairs, Trade, and Development], Brussels
14.732 Congo-Brazzaville
15.028 Congo-Brazzaville
15.337 Congo-Brazzaville
18.287 Congo-Léopoldville
18.288 Congo-Léopoldville
18.289 Congo-Léopoldville
18.292 Congo-Léopoldville
18.293 Congo-Léopoldville
18.518 Congo-Léopoldville
149.1 Politique Belge en Afrique [Belgian Policy in Africa]

Cuba
Centro de Información de la Defensa de las Fuerzas Armadas Revolucionarias [Center of Information of the Armed Forces], Havana
Comité Central del Partido Comunista de Cuba [Central Committee of the Communist Party of Cuba], Havana
Instituto de Historia de Cuba [Institute of Cuban History], Havana
Ministerio de Relaciones Exteriores [Ministry of Foreign Affairs], Havana
Ministerio de Salud Pública [Ministry of Public Health], Havana
Ministerio para la Inversión Extranjera y la Colaboración Económica [Ministry of Foreign Investment andEconomic Cooperation], Havana
Private collections, Havana. (Since these documents were given to me without official permission, I have maintained the anonymity of the donors.)

Although the Cuban documents I use in this book are still under lock and key in Havana, I have photocopies of all of them. I have deposited these photocopies in the library of the School of Advanced International Studies of the Johns Hopkins University in Washington, D.C., to enable scholars to verify that I have used them according to the most exacting standards of the historical profession.

Two documents will be withheld to protect the privacy of the Cubans who gave them to me. The first is a letter from a Cuban volunteer in Guinea-Bissau that includes very personal details. The second is Che Guevara's "Evaluación del personal a mis ordenes," which a Cuban who had it in his private archive allowed me to read in its entirety and to handcopy several paragraphs, but not to photocopy because it includes severe criticism of a number of members of the column he holds in high regard.

Federal Republic of Germany
Auswärtiges Amt [Foreign Ministry], Bonn
AA MF 00001 Algerien
AA MF 00004 Marokko
AA MF 000065 Algerien
AA 90.08 Kongo Leopoldville
AA 90.23 Kongo-Brazzaville
AA 90.47 Kongo-Brazzaville
AA 306 Kuba
AA 602 Angola
AA 628 Afrika
AA 664 Portug. Gebiete [Portuguese territories]
AA 692 Afrika Allg. [Africa general]
AA 714 Angola

German Democratic Republic
Auswärtiges Amt [Foreign Ministry], Berlin
A1154 Kongo Leopoldville
A1167 Kongo-Brazzaville
A1168 Kongo Leopoldville
A3177 Kuba
A3242 Kuba
A3363 Kuba
A14187 Kongo Leopoldville
A14593 Kongo Leopoldville
A16339 Kuba
A18130 Kuba
VVS Archiv (Tankanyika/Sansibar)
VVS Archiv (VR Kongo)
Stiftung Archiv der Parteien und Massenorganisationen der DDR im Bundesarchiv [Archive of the Political Parties and Mass Organizations of the German Democratic Republic in the Federal Archive], Berlin
Aussenpolitische Kommission [Foreign Policy Commission]
Büro [Office of] Her Axen
Büro [Office of] Gerhard Grüneberg
Büro [Office of] Honecker
Büro [Office of] Walter Ulbricht
Büro [Office of] Paul Verner
Internationale Verbindungen [International Relations]
Internationale Verbindungen–Bestandsergänzungen [International Relations–Supplement]
Politbüro
Sekretariat

United Kingdom
Public Record Office, Kew, Surrey
Foreign Office
A American Department
R Western Department
V North and East African Department
J West and Central African Department

United States
Jimmy Carter Library, Atlanta, Georgia
National Security Affairs, Brzezinski Material
Staff Offices: Special Assistant to President
White House Central File
Dwight D. Eisenhower Library, Abilene, Kansas

Eisenhower: Papers as President, 1953-1961 (Ann Whitman File)
Gordon Gray Papers
White House Office, Office of the Special Assistant for National Security Affairs
Gerald R. Ford Library, Ann Arbor, Michigan
Cabinet Meetings
Richard B. Cheney Files
James E. Connor Files
Max L. Friedersdorf Files
John Marsh Files
National Security Adviser
Ron Nessen Papers
Richard D. Parsons Files
President's Handwriting File
Michel Raoul-Duval Papers
Edward J. Savage Files
Paul Theis and Robert Orben Files
White House Central Files
Robert K. Wolthuis Files
Lyndon B. Johnson Library, Austin, Texas
Administrative History of the Department of State
George W. Ball Papers
Ramsey Clark Papers
Confidential File
Files of S. Douglas Carter
Handwriting File
Meeting Notes File
National Security: Defense
National Security File
Office Files of Bill Moyers
Office Files of the President
President's Appointment File
Vice-Presidential Security File
White House Central File
John F. Kennedy Library, Boston, Massachusetts
National Security Files
Adlai Stevenson Papers
White House Central Files
Library of Congress, Washington, D.C.
Averell Harriman Papers
National Archives, College Park, Maryland
Subject–Numeric Files: 1963-1973, RG 59
Central Decimal File: 1910-1963, RG 59
Lot Files, RG 59 (includes Mennen Williams Papers)
John F. Kennedy Assassination Collection, RG 263
Nixon Presidential Materials
Transcripts of Secretary of State Henry Kissinger's Staff Meetings, 1973-1977, RG 59
National Security Archive, Washington, D.C.
Documents in this superb archive, which is particularly rich for the 1970s and 1980s, are either on microfiche or in boxes that had not yet been labeled when I examined them (and are identified with only NSA).

PRESS

Unless otherwise stated, the newspapers listed below are dailies and the place of publication is the capital city. This is a list of those papers and magazines I have read systematically. Newspapers consulted for at least one month and weeklies for at least one year are listed. Monthlies and other magazines are listed only if they are particularly relevant and have been consulted for at least one year. However, I have also consulted these newspapers and magazines more broadly and less systematically and, on occasion, cite articles from them outside the mentioned dates.

Algeria
Alger Républicain: Oct. 1962-June 1963
La Dépêche d'Algérie: Feb.-June 1963
Le Peuple (called Al Chaab through Feb. 1963): Feb. 1963-June 1965
Révolution Africaine (weekly): 1963-66

Angola
A Província de Angola: Oct. 1974-June 1975
Diário de Luanda: 1975
Jornal de Angola (formerly A Província de Angola): July-Dec. 1975
Notícia (weekly): Aug. 1967-June 1968
O Comércio: Jan.-June 1975
O Planalto (Huambo, semiweekly, publication intermittent): July 1974-June 1975

Argentina
La Nación: Mar.-May 1964

Belgium
Le Soir: May 1964-Dec. 1965; Oct. 1968; Mar. 1975-Feb. 1976; Mar.-May 1977; May-June 1978

Cape Verde
Voz di Povo (weekly): 1988

Chile
El Mercurio: Feb. 1970

Congo
Dipanda (weekly): Apr. 1964-Oct. 1967
La Semaine (weekly; called La Semaine Africaine through 1964): 1963-68; 1974-75

Cuba
Bohemia (weekly): 1957-67; Nov. 1972-July 1982
Colaboración Internacional (quarterly): 1980-89
Granma: Oct. 1965-July 1978
Juventud Rebelde: Sept. 1967-Jan. 1968
El Oficial (monthly): 1982-90
Revolución: Oct. 1960-Oct. 1965
Vanguardia (Santa Clara; daily through 1990; 2-3 issues per week in 1991; weekly since 1992): 1989-95
Verde Olivo (weekly): 1961-65; 1975-76

Egypt
Egyptian Gazette: July 1964-June 1965

France
Afrique-Asie (weekly): 1974-78
Jeune Afrique (weekly): 1964-93
Le Figaro Littéraire (weekly): Sept. 1964-June 1965

Le Monde: Sept. 1960-Jan. 1961; Oct. 1962-Dec. 1963; June 1964-Feb. 1967; Mar.-Dec. 1968; Aug. 1969; Mar. 1970; Nov. 1970-Apr. 1971; May 1972; Apr. 1974-June 1978

Ghana
Evening News: Jan. 1965
Ghanaian Times: Jan. 1965

Guinea
Horoya: Sept.-Oct. 1961; Jan.-Feb. 1965; 1966; May-Aug. 1972

Guinea-Bissau
Nô Pintcha (three times a week when not shut down by power failures): Aug. 1975-Dec. 1983

Ivory Coast
Fraternité-Matin: Oct. 1975

Kenya
Daily Nation: July 1964-June 1965

Mali
L'Essor: Dec. 1964-Jan. 1965

Morocco
Le Petit Marocain (Casablanca): Oct. 1963-Jan. 1964; Jan. 1965

Mozambique
Notícias: Jan.-Feb. 1975

Nigeria
Daily Times: Aug. 1975-Feb. 1976; May-July 1978

Portugal
Diário da Manha: Jan.-Mar. 1967
Diário de Notícias: Feb. 1967; Mar.-Aug. 1968; Nov.-Dec. 1969; Mar.-Apr. 1971; Aug.-Sept. 1973; Apr. 1982
Expresso (weekly): 1974-77; 1988
Jornal do Comércio (Oporto): 1975
Jornal Novo: 1975

Senegal
Dakar-Matin: 1968

Sierra Leone
Daily Mail: 1972-73
People: June-Dec. 1972

South Africa
Cape Times (Capetown): July 1964-Dec. 1965; Jan. 1975-June 1978
Paratus (Pretoria, monthly): 1976-79
Post (Durban, weekly): 1976
Rand Daily Mail (Johannesburg): Jan. 1975-May 1976
World (Johannesburg): Nov. 1975-Aug. 1976

Sudan
Morning News: 1965

Tanzania
Daily News: July 1975-June 1976; Feb.-June 1978
Nationalist: Aug. 1964-Dec. 1965
Tanganyika Standard (in Nov. 1964, it became the *Standard*): 1964-65

United Kingdom
Daily Telegraph: Oct.-Nov. 1963; Mar. 1975-May 1976; Jan.-Feb. 1977
Economist (weekly): 1975
Guardian (Manchester): Mar. 1975-May 1976
Observer (weekly): 1965; 1975-76
Times: Sept.-Dec. 1963; 1970-71; 1975-78
West Africa (weekly): July 1964-Oct. 1965

United States
Africa Today (Denver, monthly): 1964-66
Afro-American (Baltimore, weekly): 1964-65; Sept. 1975-Apr. 1976
Amsterdam News (New York, weekly): 1964-65; Sept. 1975-Apr. 1976
Chicago Defender (Chicago, weekly): 1964-65; Sept. 1975-Apr. 1976
Chicago Tribune (Chicago): Aug. 1975-Apr. 1976
Christian Science Monitor (Boston): Oct.-Nov. 1962; Oct. 1963-Dec. 1965; 1975-76
Crisis (New York, monthly): 1962-77
Foreign Broadcast Information Service: Jan. 1975-Apr. 1976
Freedomways (New York, quarterly): 1964-66
Life (Chicago, weekly): Oct. 1962-Dec. 1965
Los Angeles Times (Los Angeles): Sept. 1975-Feb. 1976
Muhammad Speaks (Chicago; renamed *Bilalian News* on Nov. 1, 1975): 1964-65 (biweekly); Sept. 1975-Apr. 1976 (weekly)
Nation (New York, weekly): July 1964-Dec. 1965; Sept. 1975-Apr. 1976
New Republic (weekly): July 1964-Dec. 1965; Sept. 1975-Apr. 1976
Newsweek (New York, weekly): 1962-65; 1970; 1975-78
New York Times (New York): 1959-85
Pittsburgh Courier (Pittsburgh, weekly): July 1964-July 1965; Sept. 1975-Apr. 1976
Ramparts (Berkeley, monthly): Summer 1964-July 1965
Time (Chicago, weekly): 1962-65; 1975-76
U.S. News & World Report (weekly): 1964-65
Village Voice (New York, weekly): July 1964-June 1965; Sept. 1975-Apr. 1976
Wall Street Journal (New York): Jan.-Feb. 1964; July 1964-Dec. 1965; Sept. 1975-Apr. 1976
Washington Post: 1962-65; 1972-78

Zaire
Le Courrier d'Afrique: Aug. 1964-July 1967
Elima: Sept. 1974-June 1978
Le Progrès: 1964-65
Salongo: June-Aug. 1974; Dec. 1974; Jan.-Feb. 1976; Mar. 1977-June 1978

Zambia
Times of Zambia. 1975
Zambia Daily Mail. Jan. 1975-Apr. 1976

Zimbabwe
Rhodesia Herald. Aug.-Oct. 1964; July-Nov. 1965; Jan.-Mar. 1975; July-Oct. 1975

INTERVIEWS AMD CORRESPONDENCE
I list only the position[s] held by the interviewee that are relevant for this book.

Angola
Unless otherwise noted, the interviews were in Luanda. Many Angolans use their nom de guerre. In such cases, I include the real name in parenthesis.

Gato (Ciel da Conceição Cristovão). MPLA guerrilla officer. Jan. 13, 1997.
Jorge, Paulo. Senior MPLA official. Jan. 17, 1997.
Kianda (Salviano de Jesus Sequeira). MPLA guerrilla officer. Jan. 29, 1977.
Kiluanji (José César Augusto). MPLA guerrilla commander. Jan. 9, 1997.
Lara, Lúcio. MPLA leader. Jan. 9, 11, 15, and 29, 1997.
Lara, Paulo. MPLA guerrilla fighter. Jan. 15 and 29, 1997.
Ludy Kissassunda (Rodrigues João Lopes). MPLA guerrilla commander. Jan. 21, 1997.
Matos, Rui de. MPLA guerrilla commander. Jan. 22, 1997.
Ndalu (António dos Santos França). MPLA guerrilla commander. Washington, D.C., Nov. 13, 1996.
Ndunduma (Fernando Costa Andrade). MPLA official. Jan. 14, 17, and 22, 1997.
Neto, Maria da Conceição. Member of the MPLA militia, 1975. Jan. 27 and 29, 1997.
Ngongo (Roberto Leal Ramos Monteiro). MPLA guerrilla commander. Jan. 27, 1997.
Onambwe (Henrique Santos). MPLA guerrilla commander. Jan. 24, 25, and 28, 1997.
Tiro (João Antonio da Rosa). MPLA guerrilla officer. Jan. 14, 1997.
Xiyetu (João Luís Neto). MPLA guerrilla commander. Jan. 18 and 30, 1997.

Cuba
Unless otherwise noted, the interviews were in Havana.

Agramonte Sánchez, Manuel. Volunteer, the Congo, 1965-66; ambassador to the Congo, 1967-69; ambassador to Guinea, 1973-76. Dec. 17, 1993; July 2 and 5, 1994; Dec. 19, 1994.
Álvarez Blanco, Julián. Physician. The Congo, 1965-66; North Vietnam, 1968-69; Angola, 1975-76. Mar. 25, 1994.
Álvarez Cambras, Rodrigo. Physician. The Congo, 1965-66. Mar. 12, 1996.
Amaro Cano, María del Carmen. Nurse. Head of the Cuban nurses in Algeria, 1969-70. Mar. 16, 1994.
Ameijeiras Delgado, Efigenio. Commander, Cuban troop in Algeria, 1963-64. July 6, 1994.

Arsides Reyna, Tirso. Volunteer, the Congo, 1965-66. Mar. 5, 1996.
Batista Ramírez, Reynaldo. Volunteer, Guinea-Bissau, 1967-68; Angola, 1975-76. July 20, 1995.
Benítez y de Mendoza, Noemí. Deputy minister of the Ministerio para la Inversión y la Colaboración Económica, 1986- . July 20, 1995.
Burgos Coss, Luis. Volunteer, Guinea-Bissau, 1967-68; Angola, 1975-76. June 24, 1994.
Cadelo Serret, Carlos. Staffer for Angola and Mozambique, 1970-75, Communist party's Central Committee; Angola, 1975-76. July 7, 1995. Note to the author, July 15, 1995.
Camacho Duverger, Virgilio. Physician. Guinea-Bissau, 1966-67. Jan. 31, 1999.
Candebat Candebat, Raúl. Physician. Zaire, 1965; Guinea-Bissau, 1967-68. July 12, 1995.
Cárdenas Junquera, Osvaldo. Intelligence officer. Dec. 5 and 14, 1993.
Carretero Ibáñez, Juan. Senior intelligence officer. June 18, 1997. Note to the author, July 2, 1995.
Castellanos Villamar, Alberto. Member, Cuban-organized guerrilla group in Argentina, 1963-64. Dec. 14, 1994.
Cedeño Llovet, Manuel. Physician. Algeria, 1963-64 and 1969-70. Mar. 22, 1994.
Chaveco Núñez, Roberto. Volunteer, Zaire, 1965. Dec. 11, 1994.
Chivás González, Martín. Volunteer, Zaire, 1965. Santa Clara, Cuba, Jan. 25, 1999.
Dreke Cruz, Víctor. Deputy to Che Guevara, Zaire, 1965; head, military mission in Guinea and Guinea-Bissau, 1967-68; head, political office of the armed forces, 1968-70. Havana, Dec. 14, 1993; June 24, 26, and 27, 1994; July 7 and 11, 1994; Dec. 7, 1994. Conakry, Apr. 19 and 20, 1996; May 6, 1996. Havana, Jan. 10 and 30, 1999. Letter to the author, Oct. 20, 1994.
Duany Guillén, Rafael. Intelligence officer. The Congo, 1965-66. Mar. 12, 1996.
Eriksen, Tore Linné, ed. *Norway and National Liberation in Southern Africa.* Uppsala: Nordiska Afrikainstitutet, 2002
Escandón Carvajal, Tomás. Volunteer, Zaire, 1965. June 25, 1997.
Estrada Lescaille, Ulises. Senior intelligence officer. Dec. 20, 1993; Mar. 16, 1994; Dec. 7, 14, and 18, 1994; July 21, 1995.
Fernández Mell, Oscar. Volunteer, Zaire, 1965. Close friend of Che Guevara. June 26, July 2, and Dec. 17, 1994; July 6, 10, and 18, 1995.
Fernández Padilla, Oscar. Head intelligence task force, Cuban embassy in Tanzania, 1965-66. June 23, 27, and 30, 1994; July 12, 1994; June 24, 1997.
Ferrer Figueroa, Colman. Intelligence officer, Cuban embassy in Tanzania, 1965-67. Dec. 11, 13, and 15, 1993; Mar. 19, Apr. 2, June 27, and July 4, 1994; July 11, 1995.
Galarza, Armando. Volunteer, Guinea-Bissau, 1966-67; Sierra Leone, 1972. June 27,1995.
Galindo Santos, Fernando. Volunteer, the Congo, 1965-66. Mar. 12, 1996.

García Gutiérrez, Luis Carlos (Fisín). Intelligence officer. June 23, 1997.

Guerrero Pozo, José. Volunteer, Guinea-Bissau, 1972-73 and 1974-75; Angola, 1975-76. July 20, 1995.

Hechavarría Ferrera, Milton. Physician. Guinea-Bissau, 1967-68; head medical mission, 1970-71 and 1973-74; Angola, 1975-76. July 20, 1995.

Hernández Betancourt, Arcadio. Volunteer, Zaire, 1965; Guinea-Bissau, 1966-68. June 25 and Dec. 11, 1994.

Hernández Gattorno, René. Volunteer, the Congo, 1965-66; Guinea-Bissau, 1973-74; Angola, 1975-76. June 19, 1994.

Jacas Tornés, Manuel. Physician. The Congo, 1965-66. June 26, 1997.

Kindelán Blez, Rolando. Military commander, the Congo, 1965-66. Mar. 11, 1996.

Labrador Pino, Pedro. Chief political instructor, Cuban troop in Algeria, 1963-64. Jan. 16, 1999.

Lara Tuñón, José. Physician. Algeria, 1971-73. Mar. 28, 1994.

Lemus, Cándido. Volunteer, the Congo, 1965-67. Mar. 12, 1996.

Machado Ventura, José Ramón. Minister of Public Health, 1960-68. Note to the author, July 12, 1995.

Marín Valdivia, Julián. Volunteer, Zaire, 1965; Guinea-Bissau, 1967-68. Trinidad, Cuba, Jan. 23, 1999.

Martínez Vaillant, Melesio. Volunteer, Guinea, 1968-69; Sierra Leone, 1973. Dec. 20, 1994.

Medina, Manuel. Deputy commander, military mission in Guinea and Guinea-Bissau, 1973-74. Dec. 20, 1994.

Medina Savigne, Manuel. Volunteer, Zaire, 1965. Santa Clara, Cuba, Jan. 24, 1999.

Mesa Barrero, Cosme. Volunteer, Guinea-Bissau, 1966-68. June 25, 1994.

Monteagudo Rojas, Manuel Israel. Volunteer, Zaire, 1965. Trinidad, Cuba, Jan. 23, 1999.

Montero Lenzano, Enrique. Intelligence officer. Volunteer, Guinea-Bissau, 1967-70 (head of military mission in Guinea and Guinea-Bissau, 1969-70). Dec. 20, 1993; Mar. 16, Apr. 4, July 4, and Dec. 14, 1994.

Mora Secade, Lázaro. Ambassador to Zaire, 1974-77. June 24, 1995.

Moracén Limonta, Rafael. Volunteer, the Congo, 1965-67; Angola, 1975-77. Havana, June 21, 1994. Luanda, Jan. 12 and 30, 1997.

Morales Valera, Ana. Physician. Head, medical mission, Guinea-Bissau, 1985-87. June 27, 1994; Jan. 18, 1999.

Morejón Benítez, Angela. Physician. Algeria, 1963-64. July 2, 1995.

Morejón Estévez, Eduardo. Volunteer, South Yemen, 1973-74; chargé, Zambia, 1975-78. June 25, 1997.

Morejón Gibert, Julián. Volunteer, Zaire, 1965; Guinea-Bissau, 1967-68. Santa Clara, Cuba, Jan. 24, 1994.

Olachea de la Torre, Catalino. Volunteer, Zaire, 1965. Dec. 11, 1994.

Oramas Oliva, Oscar. Deputy chief of mission, 1964-65, and chargé, 1965-66, in Algeria; ambassador to Guinea, 1966-73; director, sub-Saharan Africa

bureau at the Foreign Ministry, 1973-75; ambassador to Angola, 1976-77. Dec. 12 and 15, 1994; June 30, 1995.

Padrón González, José Luis. Senior officer, Angola, 1975. Dec. 14, 1991.

Peraza Cabrera, Luis. Physician. Guinea-Bissau, 1966-68. July 5, 1994.

Perelló Perelló, Sara. Physician. Algeria, 1963-64. Dec. 17, 1994, and June 27, 1995.

Perera Limonta, Rafaela. Wife of MPLA commander Onambwe. Luanda, Jan. 21, 1997.

Pérez, Jesús. Volunteer, Angola, 1975-76. July 20, 1995.

Pérez Capdet, Pablo. Physician. Guinea-Bissau, 1968-71. Feb. 28, 1996.

Pérez de León, Rubén. Physician. Guinea-Bissau, 1967-69. Feb. 28, 1996.

Pérez Herrero, Tony. Head, Political Bureau of the Cuban armed forces, 1965. June 25, 1997.

Pina (Alfonso Pérez Morales). Volunteer, Guinea-Bissau, 1966-68, 1972-74. Feb. 28, 1996.

Puente Ferro, Rodolfo. Physician. The Congo, 1965-66; Angola, 1975-77. June 21, 1994.

Risquet Valdés, Jorge. Head of Cuban column, the Congo, 1965-66; labor minister, 1967-72; member of the Secretariat of the PCC, 1972-80; chief of mission, Angola, 1975-79. Dec. 20, 1993; Mar. 15, 18, and 22, 1994; June 20, 21, and 23, 1994; Dec. 10, 13, 15, and 21, 1994; June 22, 1995; July 4, 15, and 19, 1995; Feb. 14, 15, 16, and 28, 1996; June 19, 20, 23, and 24, 1997; Jan. 7 and 31, 1999; Nov. 30, 2000. Notes to the author: Aug. 1, 1995; July 22, 1996; Aug. 10, 1996.

Rivalta Pérez, Pablo. Ambassador to Tanzania, 1964-66. July 8, 1994.

Rodríguez García, Rolando. Physician. Mali, 1965-66; head, medical mission, Guinea-Bissau, 1977-78. Bissau, Apr. 30, 1996.

Romero Romeu, Enrique. Physician. Guinea-Bissau, 1973-74. Jan. 31, 1999.

Rumbau Hidalgo, Rómulo. Volunteer, Zaire, 1965. Dec. 14, 1993.

Salavarría Soriano, Heriberto. Volunteer, Guinea-Bissau, 1966-68. June 25, 1994.

Santamaría Cuadrado, Aldo. Senior officer, Cuban troop in Algeria, 1963. Jan. 12, 1999.

Saucedo Yero, Armando. Chief political instructor, Angola, 1975-76. June 13, 1997.

Schueg Colás, Víctor. Volunteer, Zaire, 1965; senior officer, Angola, 1975-76. Feb. 27, 1996.

Serguera Riverí, Jorge. Ambassador to Algeria, 1963-65; ambassador to the Congo, 1965-66. Dec. 18, 1993.

Suárez García-Calzadilla, Octavio. Volunteer, Angola, 1975-76. Dec. 6, 1991.

Torres Ferrer, Eduardo. Volunteer, Zaire, 1965; Guinea-Bissau, 1967, 1970-71. July 11, 1994.

Ulloa Cruz, Verena. Physician. Algeria, 1965-66. July 8, 1994.

Urra Torriente, Darío. Intelligence officer, Algeria, 1963-65; chargé, Brazzaville, 1965-67; volunteer, Guinea-Bissau, 1968-69, and Sierra Leone, 1973-74. Dec. 14, 17, and 18, 1994.

Vaillant Osmil, Rafael. Volunteer, Zaire, 1965; Guinea-Bissau, 1967-68. Jan. 30, 1999.

Veitía Fuentes, Osvaldo. Volunteer, the Congo, 1965-66; Guinea-Bissau, 1967-68. June 25, 1994.

Véliz Hernández, Félix. Volunteer, Guinea-Bissau, 1971-72; Angola, 1975-76. July 3, 1995.

Veranes Vedey, Augusto. Volunteer, Guinea, 1966-68. Mar. 12, 1996.

Vidiaux Robles, Erasmo. Volunteer, Zaire, 1965; Guinea-Bissau, 1967-69 (head of military mission in Guinea and Guinea-Bissau, 1968-69). July 1, 1994.

Zayas Ochoa, Luis Alfonso. Senior officer, Angola, 1975-76. June 17, 1997.

Zerquera Palacios, Rafael. Physician. Zaire, 1965. June 25, 1994.

Guinea

Unless otherwise noted, the interviews were in Conakry.

Ba, Safayo. Scholarship student in Cuba, 1972-79. Apr. 22, 1996.

Bangaly, Dabo. Scholarship student in Cuba, 1961-67; senior Foreign Ministry official, 1970-96. Apr. 18 and 20, 1996.

Beavogui, Moussa. Scholarship student in Cuba, 1973-79. Apr. 17, 1996.

Diallo, Mamoudou. Scholarship student in Cuba, 1973-79. Apr. 19, 1996.

Sadialiou Sow, Mohamed. Scholarship student in Cuba, 1974-81. Apr. 22, 1996.

Sidiki, Aboubacar. Scholarship student in Cuba, 1972-77. Apr. 20, 1996.

Sylla, Sékou. Scholarship student in Cuba, 1974-81. Washington, D.C., July 16, 1996.

Guinea-Bissau

All the interviews were in Bissau. Many Guineans use their nom de guerre. In such cases, I include the real name in parenthesis.

Alves, Paulo. Rebel physician's assistant. May 2, 1996.

Borges, António. Rebel commander. Apr. 26 and 30, 1996.

Cabral, Arlette. Rebel health official. Apr. 28, 1996.

Cabral, Fidelis. Rebel leader. Apr. 30, 1996.

Cabral, Vasco. Rebel leader. Apr. 29, 1996.

Duky (Leopoldo Alfama). Rebel commander. Apr. 25, 1996.

Furtado, Venancio. Rebel physician. May 1, 1996.

Lopes Moreira, Ernesto. Rebel physician's assistant. Apr. 29, 1996.

Mandjam Sambú, Félix. Scholarship student in Cuba, 1973-85. Apr. 26, 1996.

Mané, Arafam. Rebel commander. Apr. 28, 1996.

Medina, Paulo. Rebel physician. Apr. 29, 1996.

Monteiro Santos, Manuel. Rebel commander. May 1, 1996.

Nino (João Bernardo Vieira). Rebel commander; commander in chief, 1970-74; President of the Republic, 1980-98. May 1, 1996.

Pereira, Francisca. Rebel health official. Apr. 25, 1996.

Ramos, Armando. Rebel leader. Apr. 27, 1996.

Sousa Carvahlo, Gaudêncio de. Rebel dentist. May 2, 1996.

Turpin, Joseph. Rebel leader. Apr. 30, 1996.

United States

Unless otherwise noted, the interviews were in Washington D.C.

Arenales, Alfonso. Deputy director, Southern African Affairs, State Department, 1974-77. Mar. 5 and Oct. 10, 1991.

Ball, George. Under secretary of state, 1961-66. Tel. interview, May 18, 1992.

Blake, Robert. Deputy chief of mission in Zaire, 1964-67. May 21, 1992.

Briggs, Everett. Political officer, U.S. embassy Lisbon, 1963-67; Portugal desk officer and deputy director, Iberian Affairs, State Department, 1969-71; consul general, Luanda, 1972-74. Tel. interview, June 28, 1999.

Bundy, McGeorge. National security adviser, 1961-66. New York, Oct. 29, 1992.

Clark, Richard. Senator (D.-Iowa), 1973-79; chair of the Senate Foreign Relations Subcommittee on Africa, 1975-79. Apr. 20, 1995, and Oct. 10, 2000.

Cutler, Walter. Director, Central African affairs, State Department, 1974-75; ambassador to Zaire, 1975-79. Mar. 6, 1995.

Davis, Nathaniel. Assistant secretary of state for African affairs, 1975. Clarendon, Calif., Dec. 12, 1997.

DePorte, Anton. Policy Planning Staff, State Department, 1971-76. Tel. interview, June 5, 1999.

DePree, Willard. Policy Planning Staff, State Department, 1972-75. May 14, 1997, and Sept. 29, 1999.

Devlin, Lawrence. CIA station chief, Kinshasa, 1960-63; branch chief, East Africa, Directorate for Plans, 1963-65; CIA station chief, Zaire, 1965-67; division chief, Africa, Directorate for Plans, 1971-74. June 18, 1992, and May 18, 1999.

Diggs, Charles. Member of the U.S. House of Representatives (D.-Mich.), 1955-80; chair of the Subcommittee on African Affairs of the Foreign Affairs Committee, 1969-75. Prince George County, Md., Mar. 18, 1992.

Easum, Donald. Assistant secretary of state for African affairs, 1974-75. Oct. 30, 1996.

Fredericks, Wayne. Deputy assistant secretary of state for African affairs, 1961-67. Letter to the author, May 28, 1992.

Fugit, Edward. Vice consul, Luanda, 1973-75; Angola desk officer, State Department, 1975-77. Tel. interview, June 1, 1999.

Garrison, Lloyd. *NYT* correspondent in Zaire, 1964-65. Tel. interview, May 7, 1992.

Godley, McMurtrie. Ambassador to Zaire, 1964-66. Tel. interview, Oct. 27, 1992.

Halpern, Samuel. CIA, Directorate for Plans, executive assistant to director of Operation Mongoose, 1962; assistant to Chief Special Affairs Staff at CIA (the Cuba Task Force), 1963-65. St. Simons Island, Ga., June 1, 1996.

Haverkamp, Roy. Political officer, Brazzaville, 1964-65; DCM, Conakry, 1972-74; director, Southern African Affairs, State Department, 1975-76. Sept. 29, 2000.

Hawes, James. Navy Seal lieutenant in charge of the CIA naval patrol on Lake Tanganyika, 1965-66. May 3, 1999.

Helms, Richard. CIA, deputy director for plans, 1962-65. Apr. 6, 1993.

Hinton, Deane. Ambassador to Zaire, 1974-75. Letter to the author, July 24, 1999.

Holt, Pat. Staffer and then chief of staff, Senate Foreign Relations Committee. Bethesda, Md., Feb. 19, 1992.

Hultslander, Robert. CIA station chief, Luanda, 1975. Fax to the author, Dec. 22, 1998.

Hyland, William. Director, Intelligence and Research of the State Department, 1973-75; deputy assistant to the president for national security affairs, 1975-76. Tel. interview, Nov. 25, 1998.

Killoran, Tom. Consul General, Luanda, 1974-75. Tel. interviews, Apr. 7, 1998; Apr. 10, 1998; Sept. 14, 1998.

Komer, Robert. National Security Council staffer, 1961-66. Sept. 26, 1991.

McIlvaine, Robinson. Ambassador to Guinea, 1966-69. Feb. 5, 1996.

Mulcahy, Edward. Deputy assistant secretary of state for African affairs, 1974-76. Winchester, Va., Feb. 11, 1998.

Nelson, Harvey. Deputy chief of mission in Zambia, 1971-75. Great Falls, Va., Oct. 23, 1996.

O'Neill, Paul. Director, Southern African Affairs, State Department, 1973-75. Feb. 20, 1992.

Post, Richard. Consul general, Luanda, 1969-72; deputy chief of mission, Lisbon, 1972-75. Dec. 26, 1996.

Quintero, Rafael. Cuban exile leader working with the CIA. St. Simons Island, Ga., June 2, 1996.

Rogers, William. Assistant secretary of state for inter-American affairs, 1974-76. Tel. interview, Oct. 3, 2000.

Schaufele, William. Assistant secretary of state for African affairs, 1975-77. Tel. interview, May 24, 1999.

Sisco, Joseph. Under secretary of state for political affairs, 1974-76. Feb. 19, 1999.

Spiro, Herbert. Policy Planning Staff, State Department, 1970-75; nonresident ambassador to Equatorial Guinea, 1975-76. Tel. interview, Oct. 9, 1999.

Todman, Terence. Ambassador to Guinea, 1972-74. Oct. 28, 1999.

Walker, Lannon. Deputy chief of mission in Zaire, 1974-77. Bethesda, Md., June 25, 1999.

Wilkowski, Jean. Ambassador to Zambia, 1972-76. Oct. 16, 1996.

Other

Bajammal, Abdulkader. Party official, People's Democratic Republic of Yemen (1972-74). Washington, D.C., Nov. 29, 1998.

Dos Santos, Marcelino. Mozambican rebel leader. Havana, June 27, 1994.

Onguemby, Charles. Congolese scholarship student in Cuba, 1964-77. Havana, Dec. 14, 2000.

Tschamlesso, Godefroid. Zairean rebel official, 1964-65. Havana, June 30, 1994.

WORKS CITED

Abramson, Rudy. *Spanning the Century: The Life of W. Averell Harriman, 1891-1986.* New York: William Morrow, 1992.

Acker, Gary. "Angolan Reflections: A Mercenary's Road to Hell." *Soldier of Fortune,* February 1986, pp. 100-105, 130-33.

Adelman, Kenneth. "Report from Angola." *Foreign Affairs* 53 (April 1975): 558-74.

Albright, David. "Moscow's African Policy of the 1970s." In *Communism in Africa,* edited by David Albright, pp. 34-66. Bloomington: Indiana University Press, 1980.

Alle, Fritz. *Macht und Ohnmacht der Guerilla.* Munich: R. Piper, 1974.

Alsop, Joseph W., with Adam Platt. *"I've Seen the Best of It": Memoirs.* New York: Norton, 1992.

Amin, Samir, and Catherine Coquery-Vidrovitch. *Histoire économique du Congo, 1880-1968.* Paris: Anthropos, 1969.

Anderson, Jon Lee. *Che Guevara: A Revolutionary Life.* New York: Grove Press, 1997.

Anglin, Douglas, and Timothy Shaw. *Zambia's Foreign Policy: Studies in Diplomacy and Dependence.* Boulder, Colo.: Westview, 1979.

"Angola: La longue trahison de l'U.N.I.T.A." *Afrique-Asie* (Paris), July 8, 1974, pp. 8-17.

Ansprenger, Franz. *Die SWAPO: Profil einer afrikanischen Befreiungsbewegung.* Munich: Grunewald-Kaiser, 1984.

Anstee, Margaret. *Orphan of the Cold War: The Inside Story of the Collapse of the Angolan Peace Process, 1992-93.* New York: St. Martin's Press, 1996.

Antunes, Ernesto Melo. "A Descolonização portuguesa: mitos e realidades." In *História de Portugal dos tempos pré-históricos aos nossos dias,* edited by João Medina, 14:179-221. Amadora, Portugal: EDICLUBE, 1994.

Antunes, José Freire. *Cartas particulares a Marcello Caetano.* 2 vols. Lisbon: Dom Quixote, 1985.

———. *Os Americanos e Portugal.* Vol. 1: *Os anos de Richard Nixon (1969-1974).* Lisbon: Dom Quixote, 1986.

———. *Kennedy e Salazar: O leão e a raposa.* Lisbon: Difusão Cultural, 1991.

———. *Nixon e Caetano: promessas e abandono.* Lisbon: Difusão Cultural, 1992.

———. *A guerra de África (1961-1974).* 2 vols. Lisbon: Temas e Debates, 1996.

Aronson, James. *The Press and the Cold War.* Indianapolis: Bobbs-Merrill, 1970.

Associação 25 de abril. *Seminário 25 de abril: 10 anos depois.* Lisbon: Fundação Calouste Gulbenkian, 1984.

Attwood, William. *The Reds and the Blacks: A Personal Adventure.* New York: Harper and Row, 1967.

———. *The Twilight Struggle: Tales of the Cold War.* New York: Harper and Row, 1987.

Avillez, Maria João. *Do Fundo da Revolução*. Lisbon: Público, 1994.
——. *Soares: Ditadura e Revolução*. Lisbon: Público, 1996.
Ayers, Bradley. *The War That Never Was: An Insider's Account of C.I.A. Covert Operations against Cuba*. Indianapolis: Bobbs-Merrill, 1976.
Bach, Daniel. "La France en Afrique SubSaharienne." In *La politique extérieure de Valéry Giscard d'Estaing*, edited by Samy Cohen and Marie-Claude Smouts, pp. 284-310. Paris: Presses de la Fondation Nationale des Sciences Politiques, 1985.
"Back from the Brink: The Correspondence between President John F. Kennedy and Chairman Nikita S. Khrushchev on the Cuban Missile Crisis of Autumn 1962." *Problems of Communism* 41 (special issue, Spring 1992): entire issue.
Báez, Luis. *Secretos de generales. Desclasificado*. Havana: Editorial Si-Mar, 1996.
Bailey, Martin. *The Union of Tanganyika and Zanzibar: A Study in Political Integration*. Syracuse, N.Y.: Syracuse University, Maxwell School of Citizenship and Public Affairs, 1973.
Balfour, Sebastian. *Castro*. London: Longman, 1990.
Ball, George. *The Past Has Another Pattern: Memoirs*. New York: Norton, 1982.
Barnett, Don, ed. *The Making of a Middle Cadre: The Story of Rui de Pinto*. Richmond, British Columbia: Liberation Support Movement, 1973.
Barreto, Jesús. "Camarada Tato." *Moncada* (Havana), special issue, October 1987, pp. 92-97.
Barros, Maria da Luz Ferreira de. "Alguns aspectos da situação socioeconómica em Angola (1961-1974)." *Africana* (Oporto) 14 (September 1994): 41-62.
Bazenguissa-Ganga, Rémy. *Les voies du politique au Congo. Essai de sociologie historique*. Paris: Karthala, 1997.
Ben Bella, Ahmed. "Ben Bella parle de Che Guevara." In *Connaître Che Guevara*, edited by Ph. P-Ch, pp. 51-54. Cayenne, French Guyana: n.p., 1987.
——. "Ainsi était le ` Che.'" *Le Monde Diplomatique*, October 1997, p. 3.
Bender, Gerald. "Angola, the Cubans, and American Anxieties." *Foreign Policy* 31 (Summer 1978): 3-30.
——. *Angola under the Portuguese: The Myth and the Reality*. Berkeley: University of California Press, 1978.
——. "Kissinger in Angola: Anatomy of Failure." In *American Policy in Southern Africa: The Stakes and the Stance*, edited by René Lemarchand, pp. 63-143. Washington, D.C.: University Press of America, 1978.
Bender, Gerald, and Stanley Yoder. "Whites on the Eve of Independence: The Politics of Numbers." *Africa Today* 21 (Fall 1974): 23-37.
Benemelis, Juan. *Castro, subversión y terrorismo en Africa*. Madrid: Editorial San Martín, 1988.
Benigno [Dariel Alarcón Ramírez]. *Vie et mort de la révolution cubaine*. Paris: Fayard, 1996.
——. *Memorias de un soldado cubano: vida y muerte de la revolución*. Barcelona: Tusquets, 1997.

Benjamin, Jules. *The United States and the Origins of the Cuban Revolution: An Empire of Liberty in an Age of National Liberation*. Princeton: Princeton University Press, 1990.
Bennett, Andrew. *Condemned to Repetition? The Rise, Fall, and Reprise of Soviet-Russian Military Interventionism, 1973-1996*. Cambridge, Mass.: MIT Press, 1999.
Bennoune, Mahfoud. *The Making of Contemporary Algeria, 1830-1897*. New York: Cambridge University Press, 1988.
Bernardo, Manuel, ed. *Marcello e Spínola. A ruptura*. Lisbon: Edições Margem, 1994.
Berner, Wolfgang. "Kubaner-Interventionen in Afrika und Arabien." *Aussenpolitik* (Hamburg) 27 (July-September 1976): 325-31.
Bernstein, Victor, and Jesse Gordon. "The Press and the Bay of Pigs." *Columbia University Forum*, Fall 1967, pp. 5-13.
Berramdane, Abdelkhaleq. *Le Maroc et l'Occident (1800-1974)*. Paris: Karthala, 1987.
Beschloss, Michael. *The Crisis Years: Kennedy and Khrushchev, 1960-1963*. New York: HarperCollins, 1991.
——, ed. *Taking Charge: The Johnson White House Tapes, 1963-1964*. New York: Simon and Schuster, 1997.
Bestard Pavón, Elías, and Alicia Céspedes Carrillo. "La Colaboración de Cuba con los paises de Africa Subsahariana (1959-1988)." M.A. thesis, Instituto Superior de Relaciones Internacionales, Havana, 1989.
Birmingham, David. "The Twenty-Seventh of May: An Historical Note on the Abortive 1977 *Coup* in Angola." *African Affairs* (Oxford) 77 (October 1978): 554-64.
Bissell, Richard, with Jonathan Lewis and Francis Pudlo. *Reflections of a Cold Warrior: From Yalta to the Bay of Pigs*. New Haven: Yale University Press, 1996.
Blanco Muñoz, Agustín. *La lucha armada: hablan 5 jefes*. Caracas: Universidad Central de Venezuela, 1980.
——. *La lucha armada: hablan 6 comandantes*. Caracas: Universidad Central de Venezuela, 1981.
Blight, James, Bruce Allyn, and David Welch. *Cuba on the Brink: Castro, the Missile Crisis, and the Soviet Collapse*. New York: Pantheon Books, 1993.
Blight, James, and Peter Kornbluh, eds. *Politics of Illusion: The Bay of Pigs Invasion Reexamined*. Boulder, Colo.: Lynne Rienner, 1998.
Blight, James and Philip Brenner. *Sad and Luminous Days: Cuba's Struggle with the Superpowers after the Missile Crises*. Lanham: Rowman and Littlefield, 2002.
Bloch, Jonathan, and Patrick Fitzgerald. *British Intelligence and Covert Action: Africa, Middle East and Europe since 1945*. Dublin: Brandon, 1984.
Borge, Tomás. *La paciente impaciencia*. Mexico City: Editorial Diana, 1989.
Borstelmann, Thomas. *The Cold War and the Color Line: American Race Relations in the Global Arena*. Cambridge, Mass: Harvard University Press, 2001

Bourne, Peter. *Fidel: A Biography of Fidel Castro.* New York: Dodd, Mead, 1986.

Boutet, Rémy. *Les Trois Glorieuses ou la chute de Fulbert Youlou.* Dakar: éditions Chaka, 1990.

Bowker, Mike, and Phil Williams. *Superpower Detente: A Reappraisal.* London: Royal Institute of International Affairs, 1988.

Brache, Anselmo. *Constanza, Maimón y Estero Hondo.* Santo Domingo, D.R.: Editora Taller, 1985.

Braeckman, Colette. "La saga du Shaba." *La Revue Nouvelle* (Brussels), February 1979, pp. 141-50.

Bragança, Aquino de. "Independence without Decolonization: Mozambique, 1974-1975." In *Decolonization and African Independence: The Transfers of Power, 1960-1980,* edited by Prosser Gifford and Wm. Roger Louis, pp. 427-43. New Haven: Yale University Press, 1988.

Brassinne, Jacques, and Jean Kestergat. *Qui a tué Patrice Lumumba?* Louvain-la-Neuve: Duculot, 1991.

Breytenbach, Jan. *Forged in Battle.* Cape Town: Saayaman and Weber, 1986.

——. *They Live by the Sword.* Alberton, South Africa: Lemur, 1990.

——. *Buffalo Soldiers: The Story of South Africa's 32-Battalion 1975-1993.* Alberton, South Africa: Galago, 2002.

Bridgland, Fred. *Jonas Savimbi: A Key to Africa.* New York: Paragon House, 1987.

——. "The Future of Angola." *South Africa International* (Johannesburg) 19 (July 1988): 28-37.

——. *The War for Africa.* Gibraltar: Ashanti, 1990.

——. "Savimbi et l'exercice du pouvoir: un témoignage." *Politique Africaine* (Paris), no. 57 (March 1995): 94-102.

Brown, Robert. "Phantom Navy of the CIA." *Sea Classics,* May 1975, pp. 50-62.

Brown, Robert, and Robert Himber. "The Story of George Bacon: A Twentieth Century Crusader." *Soldier of Fortune,* Fall 1976, pp. 13-18, 76-77.

Brzezinski, Zbigniew. *Power and Principle: Memoirs of the National Security Adviser, 1977-1981.* New York: Farrar, Straus and Giroux, 1983.

Bumbacher, Beat. *Die USA und Nasser. Amerikanische Ägypten-Politik der Kennedy- und Johnson-Administration 1961-1967.* Stuttgart: Franz Steiner, 1987.

Bundy, William. *A Tangled Web: The Making of Foreign Policy in the Nixon Presidency.* New York: Hill and Wang, 1998.

Burchett, Wilfred, and Derek Roebuck. *The Whores of War: Mercenaries Today.* Middlesex: Penguin, 1977.

Burger, Frederik Johannes. "Teeninsurgensie in Namibië: Die Rol von die Polisie." M.A. thesis, Universiteit van Suid-Afrika, 1992.

Burr, William, ed. *The Kissinger Transcripts: The Top Secret Talks with Beijing and Moscow.* New York: New Press, 1998.

Buznego, Enrique, and Lázaro Cárdenas. "La batalla de Quifangondo." *El Oficial* (Havana), special issue, 1989, pp. 22-27.

Cabral, Amílcar. *Guinée "Portugaise": le pouvoir des armes.* Paris: Maspero, 1970.

Cabral, Luís. *Crónica da Libertação.* Lisbon: Edições O Jornal, 1984.

——. "A Guiné é o país da mentira." *Expresso* (Lisbon), July 2, 1994, pp. 48-58.

Caetano, Marcello. *Depoimento.* Rio de Janeiro: Distribudora Record, 1974.

Cahen, Michel. "Syndicalisme urbain, luttes ouvrières et questions éthniques à Luanda: 1974-1977/1981." In *"Vilas" et "cidades." Bourgs et villes en Afrique Lusophone,* edited by Michel Cahen, pp. 200-279. Paris: L'Harmattan, 1989.

Cahn, Anne Hessing. *Killing Detente: The Right Attacks the CIA.* University Park: Pennsylvania State University Press, 1998.

Calder, Bruce. *The Impact of Intervention: The Dominican Republic during the U.S. Occupation of 1916-1924.* Austin: University of Texas Press, 1984.

Calvão, Alpoim. *De Conakry ao M.D.L.P.: Dossier secreto.* Lisbon: Intervenção, 1976.

Camara, Sylvain Soriba. *La Guinée sans la France.* Paris: Presses de la Fondation Nationale des Sciences Politiques, 1976.

Cann, John. *Counterinsurgency in Africa: The Portuguese Way of War, 1961-1974.* Westport, Conn.: Greenwood, 1997.

Cardoso, Humberto. *O partido único em Cabo Verde.* Praia: Imprensa Nacional de Cabo Verde, 1993.

Carnoy, Martin, and Jorge Wertheim. "Cuba: Economic Change and Education Reform, 1955-1974." World Bank Staff Working Paper no. 317, January 1979. Washington, D.C.

Carrasco, Juana. "Tatu, un guerrillero africano." *Cuba Internacional* (Havana), no. 2 (1989): 32-36.

——. "Che in Africa." *Prisma* (Havana) 7 (May 1989): 45.

——. "El combate de Forces Bendera." *Verde Olivo* (Havana), June 1990, pp. 20-25.

Carreira, Iko. *O Pensamento estratégico de Agostinho Neto: Contribuição histórica.* Lisbon: Dom Quixote, 1996.

——. "A última batalha do general Iko Carreira." *Expresso* (Lisbon), October 19, 1996, pp. 39-60.

Carvalho, Otelo Saraiva de. *Alvorada em Abril.* Lisbon: Ulmeiro, 1984.

Castañeda, Jorge. *Compañero: The Life and Death of Che Guevara.* New York: Knopf, 1997.

Castanheira, José Pedro. *Quem mandou matar Amílcar Cabral?* Lisbon: Relógio D'Água, 1995.

Castro Hidalgo, Orlando. *Spy for Fidel.* Miami: E. A. Seemann, 1971.

Centre National de la Recherche Scientifique. *Annuaire de l'Afrique du Nord. II: 1963.* Paris: éditions du Centre National de la Recherche Scientifique, 1964.

Cervenka, Zdenek, and Colin Legum. "The Organization of African Unity." In *Africa Contemporary Record: Annual Survey and Documents, 1975-76,* edited by Colin Legum, pp. A66-A75. New York: Africana, 1976.

Chabal, Patrick. *Amílcar Cabral: Revolutionary Leadership and People's War*. Cambridge: Cambridge University Press, 1983.

——. "People's War, State Formation, and Revolution in Africa." *Journal of Commonwealth and Comparative Politics* (London) 21 (November 1983): 104-25.

Chaffard, Georges. *Les carnets secrets de la décolonisation*. 2 vols. Paris: Calmann-Lévy, 1967.

Chaliand, Gérard. *Lutte armée en Afrique*. Paris: Maspero, 1967.

Chaliand, Gérard, and Juliette Minces. *L'Algérie indépendante (Bilan d'une révolution nationale)*. Paris: Maspero, 1972.

Challenor, Herschelle Sullivan. "The Influence of Black Americans on U.S. Foreign Policy toward Africa." In *Ethnicity and U.S. Foreign Policy*, edited by Abdul Aziz Said, pp. 139-73. New York: Praeger, 1977.

Chang, Laurence, and Peter Kornbluh, eds. *The Cuban Missile Crisis, 1962: A National Security Archive Documents Reader*. New York: New Press, 1992.

Charles, Milene. *The Soviet Union and Africa: The History of the Involvement*. Lanham, Md.: University Press of America, 1980.

Chick, Slimane. "L'Algérie et l'Afrique (1954-1962)." *Revue algérienne des sciences juridiques, économiques et politiques* (Algiers) 5 (September 1968): 700-746.

Chilcote, Ronald. *Amílcar Cabral's Revolutionary Theory and Practice: A Critical Guide*. Boulder, Colo.: Lynne Rienner, 1991.

CIA: The Pike Report. With an introduction by Philip Agee. Nottingham: Spokesman Books, 1977.

Cilliers, J. K. *Counter-Insurgency in Rhodesia*. London: Croom Helm, 1985.

Clarke, John Henrik, ed. *Malcolm X: The Man and His Times*. Trenton, N.J.: Africa World Press, 1990.

Clarke, S. J. G. *The Congo Mercenary: A History and Analysis*. Braamfontein, Johannesburg: South African Institute of International Affairs, 1968.

Clayton, Anthony. *The Zanzibar Revolution and Its Aftermath*. Hamden, Conn.: Archon Books, 1981.

Cleaver, Kathleen Neal. "Back to Africa: The Evolution of the International Section of the Black Panther Party (1969-1972)." In *The Black Panther Party (Reconsidered)*, edited by Charles Jones, pp. 211-54. Baltimore: Black Classic Press, 1998.

Clerc, Jean-Pierre. *Fidel de Cuba*. Paris: éditions Ramsay, 1988.

——. *Les quatre saisons de Fidel Castro*. Paris: Seuil, 1996.

CNN. *Cold War*, script of episode 17: "Good Guys, Bad Guys," February 14, 1999 <http://www.cnn.com/specials/cold.war/episodes/17/script.html>.

Colby, William, with Peter Forbath. *Honorable Men: My Life in the CIA*. New York: Simon and Schuster, 1978.

Connell-Smith, Gordon. *The United States and Latin America: An Historical Analysis of Inter-American Relations*. London: Heinemann, 1974.

Coquery-Vidrovitch, Catherine, Alain Forest, and Herbert Weiss, eds. *Rébellions-Révolution au Zaïre 1963-1965*. 2 vols. Paris: L'Harmattan, 1987.

Cordero Michel, Emilio. "Las expediciones de junio de 1959." *Ecos* (Santo Domingo, D.R.), no. 7 (1999): 11-56.

Cormier, Jean, with Hilda Guevara and Alberto Granado. *Che Guevara*. Monaco: Éditions du Rocher, 1995.

Corn, David. *Blond Ghost: Ted Shackley and the CIA's Crusades*. New York: Simon and Schuster, 1994.

Correia, Pedro Pezarat. *Descolonização de Angola: a jóia da coroa do império português*. Lisbon: Inquérito, 1991.

——. "Portugal na hora da descolonização." In *Portugal contemporaneo*, vol. 6, edited by António Reis, pp. 117-70. Lisbon: Publicações Alfa, 1992.

Costa Gomes, Francisco da. *Sobre Portugal: Diálogos com Alexandre Manuel*. Lisbon: A Regra do Jogo, 1979.

——. "Costa Gomes conta tudo." *Expresso* (Lisbon), October 8, 1988, supplement, pp. 4-11.

Cowderoy, Dudley, and Roy Nesbit. *War in the Air: Rhodesian Air Force, 1935-1980*. Alberton, South Africa: Galago, 1987.

Crimi, Bruno. "Cabinda: Pour 400 millions de dollars." *Jeune Afrique* (Paris), October 5, 1974, pp. 36-39.

CRISP (Centre de Recherche et d'Information Socio-Politiques), ed. *Congo 1960*. 3 vols. Brussels: CRISP, 1961.

——. *Congo 1961*. Brussels: CRISP, 1962.

——. *Congo 1962*. Brussels: CRISP, 1963.

——. *Congo 1963*. Brussels: CRISP, 1964.

——. *Congo 1964*. Brussels: CRISP, 1966.

——. *Congo 1965*. Brussels: CRISP, 1967.

——. *Congo 1967*. Brussels: CRISP, 1969.

Crocker, Chester. *High Noon in Southern Africa: Making Peace in a Rough Neighborhood*. New York: Norton, 1992.

Cronjé, Suzanne, Margaret Ling, and Gillian Cronjé. *Lonrho: Portrait of a Multinational*. London: Julian Friedmann Books, 1976.

Cruz, Pompílio da. *Angola: Os Vivos e Os Mortos*. Lisbon: Editorial Intervenção, 1976.

[Cuban Government], Comisión de Historia de la Columna 19 "José Tey." *Columna 19 "José Tey."* Havana: Editorial de Ciencias Sociales, 1982.

——. *Peligros y principios: la Crisis de Octubre desde Cuba*. Havana: Editora Verde Olivo, 1992.

Cupull, Adys, and Froilán González. *Un hombre bravo*. Havana: Editorial Capitán San Luis, 1994.

Daniel, Jean. "Unofficial Envoy: An Historic Report from Two Capitals." *New Republic*, December 14, 1963, pp. 15-20.

Davezies, Robert. *Les Angolais*. Paris: Les Éditions de Minuit, 1965.

——. *La guerre d'Angola*. Bordeaux: Guy Ducros, 1968.

Davidson, Basil. *In the Eye of the Storm: Angola's People*. Harmondsworth: Penguin Books, 1974.

——. *No Fist Is Big Enough to Hide the Sky: The Liberation of Guiné and Cape Verde*. London: Zed Press, 1981.

Davis, Nathaniel. "The Angola Decision of 1975: A Personal Memoir." *Foreign Affairs* 57 (Fall 1978): 109-23.

Debray, Régis. *La critique des armes*. 2 vols. Paris: Seuil, 1974.

———. *Loués soient nos seigneurs. Une éducation politique*. Paris: Gallimard, 1996.

Decalo, Samuel. *Coups and Army Rule in Africa*. New Haven: Yale University Press, 1990.

Dempster, Chris, and Dave Tomkins. *Fire Power*. New York: St. Martin's Press, 1980.

DeRoche, Andrew. "Strategic Minerals and Multiracial Democracies: U.S. Relations with Zimbabwe, 1953-1980." Ph.D. diss., University of Colorado, 1997.

———. "Standing Firm for Principles: Jimmy Carter and Zimbabwe." *Diplomatic History* 23 (Fall 1999): 657-85.

Desjeux, Dominique. "Le Congo est-il situationniste? 20 ans d'histoire politique de la classe dirigeante congolaise." *Le Mois en Afrique* (Paris), nos. 178-79 (October 1980): 16-40.

Deutschmann, David, ed. *Changing the History of Africa: Angola and Namibia*. Melbourne: Ocean Press, 1989.

De Villiers, Dirk, and Johanna de Villiers. *PW—A Biography of South Africa's President PW Botha*. Cape Town: Tafelberg, 1984.

De Witte, Ludo. "De Lumumba à Mobutu: nouvelles clartés sur la crise congolaise." *Cahiers Marxistes* (Brussels), January-February 1998, pp. 9-49.

———. *L'assassinat de Lumumba*. Paris: Karthala, 2000.

Dhada, Mustafah. *Warriors at Work: How Guinea Was Really Set Free*. Niwot: University Press of Colorado, 1993.

———. "Guinea-Bissau's Diplomacy and Liberation Struggle." *Portuguese Studies Review* 4 (Spring-Summer 1995): 20-39.

Díaz-Briquets, Sergio, ed. *Cuban Internationalism in Sub-Saharan Africa*. Pittsburgh, Pa.: Duquesne University Press, 1989.

Diederich, Bernard, and Al Burt. *Papa Doc: Haiti and Its Dictator*. Rev. ed. Maplewood, N.J.: Waterfront Press, 1991.

Dippenaar, Marius de Witt. *The History of the South African Police, 1913-1988*. Silverton, South Africa: Promedia Publications, 1988.

Dobrynin, Anatoly. *In Confidence: Moscow's Ambassador to America's Six Cold War Presidents*. New York: Times Books, 1995.

Domínguez, Jorge. *Cuba: Order and Revolution*. Cambridge, Mass.: Harvard University Press, 1978.

———. "The Cuban Operation in Angola: Costs and Benefits for the Armed Forces." *Cuban Studies* 8 (January 1978): 10-21.

———. *To Make a World Safe for Revolution: Cuba's Foreign Policy*. Cambridge, Mass.: Harvard University Press, 1989.

Dorning, W. A. "A Concise History of the South African Defense Force (1912-1987)." *Militaria* (Pretoria) 17, no. 2 (1987): 1-23.

Dreke, Víctor. *De la sierra del Escambray al Congo: En la vorágine de la Revolución Cubana*. New York: Pathfinder, 2002.

Dudziak, Mary. *Cold War Civil Rights: Race and the Image of American Democracy*. Princeton: Princeton University Press, 2000.

Du Pisani, André. *SWA/Namibia: The Politics of Continuity and Change*. Johannesburg: Jonathan Ball Publishers, 1985.

Du Preez, Sophia. *Avontuur in Angola. Die verhaal van Suid-Afrika se soldate in Angola 1975-1976*. Pretoria: J. L. van Schaik, 1989.

Durch, William. "The Cuban Military in Africa and the Middle East: From Algeria to Angola." *Studies in Comparative Communism* 11 (Spring-Summer 1978): 34-74.

Ebinger, Charles. "External Intervention in Internal War: The Politics and Diplomacy of the Angolan Civil War." *Orbis* 20 (Fall 1976): 669-99.

Eckstein, Susan. "Structural and Ideological Bases of Cuba's Overseas Programs." *Politics and Society* 11, no. 1 (1982): 1-28.

Eliou, Marie. "La fuite en avant dans l'enseignement supérieur. Les boursiers congolais." *Tiers Monde* (Paris) 15, nos. 59-60 (1974): 567-82.

———. *La formation de la conscience nationale en République Populaire du Congo*. Paris: éditions Anthropos, 1977.

Ellert, Henrik. *The Rhodesian Front War: Counterinsurgency and Guerrilla Warfare, 1962-1980*. Gweru, Zimbabwe: Mambo Press, 1993.

Espinosa Martín, Ramón. *La batalla de Cabinda*. Havana: Ediciones Verde Olivo, 2000.

Eyinga, Abel. *L'U.P.C.: une révolution manquée?* Paris: éditions Chaka, 1991.

Fabião, Carlos. "A descolonização na Guiné-Bissau." In *Seminário 25 de abril: 10 anos depois*, edited by Associação 25 de abril, pp. 305-11. Lisbon: Fundação Calouste Gulbenkian, 1984.

Feinsilver, Julie. "Cuba as a 'World Medical Power': The Politics of Symbolism." *Latin American Research Review* 24 (Spring 1989): 1-34.

Fernández, Damián. *Cuba's Foreign Policy in the Middle East*. Boulder, Colo.: Westview, 1988.

Flower, Ken. *Serving Secretly: An Intelligence Chief on Record. Rhodesia into Zimbabwe, 1964 to 1981*. London: John Murray, 1987.

Foccart, Jacques. *Foccart parle. Entretiens avec Philippe Gaillard, 1*. Paris: Fayard/Jeune Afrique, 1995.

———. *Tous les soirs avec de Gaulle. Journal de l'Elysée—I, 1965-1967*. Paris: Fayard/Jeune Afrique, 1997.

Foner, Philip. *A History of Cuba and Its Relations with the United States*. 2 vols. New York: International Publishers, 1962 and 1963.

Ford, Gerald. *A Time to Heal: The Autobiography of Gerald R. Ford*. New York: Harper and Row, 1979.

Ford, Worthington, ed. *The Writings of John Quincy Adams*. Vol. 7. New York: Macmillan, 1917.

Fourie, Deon. "The Evolving Experience." In *Defense Policy Formation: Towards Comparative Analysis*, edited by James Roherty, pp. 87-106. Durham, N.C.: Carolina Academic Press, 1980.

Fournier, Nicolas, and Edmond Legrand. *Dossier E. . . comme Espionnage*. Paris: Editions Alain Moreau, 1978.

Fox, Renée, et al. "La deuxième indépendance. Etude d'un cas: La rébellion au Kwilu." *Etudes Congolaises* (Leopoldville), January-February 1965, 1-35.

Franqui, Carlos. *Cuba: el libro de los doce*. Mexico City: Ediciones Era, 1966.

—. *Diary of the Cuban Revolution*. New York: Viking, 1980.

—. *Vida, aventuras y desastres de un hombre llamado Castro*. Mexico City: Planeta, 1988.

Frappat, Stéphane. "Le choc de la décolonisation portugaise en Afrique centre-australe." In *La France et l'Afrique du Sud. Histoire, mythes et enjeux contemporains*, edited by Daniel Bach, pp. 215-31. Paris: Karthala, 1990.

Fursenko, Aleksandr, and Timothy Naftali. *"One Hell of a Gamble": Khrushchev, Castro and Kennedy, 1958-1964*. New York: Norton, 1997.

Gaddis, John Lewis. *We Now Know: Rethinking Cold War History*. New York: Oxford University Press, 1997.

Gaiduk, Ilya. *The Soviet Union and the Vietnam War*. Chicago: Ivan R. Dee, 1996.

Gaillard, Philippe. *Le Cameroun*. 2 vols. Paris: L'Harmattan, 1989.

Gálvez, William. *El sueño africano del Che ¿Qué sucedió en la guerrilla congolesa?* Havana: Casa de las Américas, 1997.

Garba, Joe. *Diplomatic Soldiering: Nigerian Foreign Policy, 1975-1979*. Ibadan: Spectrum Books, 1987.

García, René. "Operación Kamina." *Punto de Mira* (Miami) 1 (August 1989): 34-38.

García Blanco, Gisela. *La misión internacionalista de Cuba en Argelia (1963-1964)*. Havana: FAR, 1990.

—. "'El Che en el corazón de Africa.' La misión internacionalista en el Congo." *Historia Militar* (Havana), April 1992, pp. 43-53.

García Márquez, Gabriel. *Operación Carlota*. Lima: Mosca Azul Editores, 1977.

Garthoff, Raymond. *Reflections on the Cuban Missile Crisis*. Rev. ed. Washington, D.C.: Brookings, 1989.

—. *Détente and Confrontation: American-Soviet Relations from Nixon to Reagan*. Rev. ed. Washington, D.C.: Brookings, 1994.

Gates, Louis Henry. "After the Revolution: The Odyssey of Eldridge Cleaver." 1975. Unpublished manuscript.

Gauze, René. *The Politics of Congo-Brazzaville*. Stanford, Calif.: Hoover Institute Press, 1973.

Geldenhuys, Deon. *The Diplomacy of Isolation: South African Foreign Policy Making*. New York: St. Martin's Press, 1984.

Geldenhuys, Deon, and Hennie Kotzé. "P. W. Botha as Decision Maker: A Preliminary Study of Personality and Politics." *Politikon* (Pretoria) 12 (June 1985): 30-42.

Geldenhuys, Jannie. *A General's Story: From an Era of War and Peace*. Johannesburg: Jonathan Ball Publishers, 1995.

Gellman, Irwin. *Roosevelt and Batista: Good Neighbor Diplomacy in Cuba, 1933-1945*. Albuquerque: University of New Mexico Press, 1973.

Gérard-Libois, Jules. "L'aide extérieure à la République du Congo," (I and II). *Etudes Congolaises* (Leopoldville) 9 (May-June 1966): 1-36; 9 (July-August 1966): 1-20.

Germani, Hans. *Weisse Söldner im schwarzen Land*. Frankfurt am Main: Ullstein, 1966.

Geyer, Georgie Anne. *Guerrilla Prince: The Untold Story of Fidel Castro*. Boston: Little, Brown, 1991.

Gibbs, David. *The Political Economy of Third World Intervention: Mines, Money, and U.S. Policy in the Congo Crisis*. Chicago: University of Chicago Press, 1991.

Gleijeses, Piero. *The Dominican Crisis: The 1965 Constitutionalist Revolt and American Intervention*. Baltimore: Johns Hopkins University Press, 1978.

—. *Shattered Hope: The Guatemalan Revolution and the United States, 1944-1954*. Princeton: Princeton University Press, 1991.

—. "Ships in the Night: The CIA, the White House and the Bay of Pigs." *Journal of Latin American Studies* 27 (February 1995): 1-42.

—. "Truth or Credibility: Castro, Carter, and the Invasions of Shaba." *International History Review* 18 (February 1996): 70-103.

—. "The First Ambassadors: Cuba's Contribution to Guinea-Bissau's War of Independence." *Journal of Latin American Studies* 29 (February 1997): 45-88.

Goldenberg, Boris. *Kommunismus in Lateinamerika*. Stuttgart: Kohlhammer, 1971.

Gómez Ochoa, Delio. *Constanza, Maimón y Estero Hondo: La victoria de los caídos*. Santo Domingo, D.R.: Alfa y Omega, 1998.

Gonzalez, Edward. *Cuba under Castro: The Limits of Charisma*. Boston: Houghton Mifflin, 1974.

—. "Cuba, the Soviet Union, and Africa." In *Communism in Africa*, edited by David Albright, pp. 145-67. Bloomington: Indiana University Press, 1980.

Good, Robert. *U.D.I.: The International Politics of the Rhodesian Rebellion*. Princeton: Princeton University Press, 1973.

Gott, Richard. *Rural Guerrillas in Latin America*. Harmondsworth: Penguin, 1973.

Greig, Ian. *The Communist Challenge to Africa: An Analysis of Contemporary Soviet, Chinese and Cuban Politics*. Sandton City, South Africa: Southern African Freedom Foundation, 1977.

Gribkov, Anatoli, and William Smith. *Operation ANADYR: U.S. and Soviet Generals Recount the Cuban Missile Crisis*. Chicago: edition q, 1994.

Grimaud, Nicole. *La politique extérieure de l'Algérie*. Paris: Karthala, 1984.

Grundy, Kenneth. *Soldiers without Politics: Blacks in the South African Armed Forces*. Berkeley: University of California Press, 1983.

Guerra, Henrique. *Angola: Estrutura económica e classes sociais*. Luanda: União dos Escritores Angolanos, 1988.

Guerra, João Paulo. *Memória das Guerras Coloniais.* Oporto, Portugal: Afrontamento, 1994.

—. *Descolonização Portuguesa: o regresso das caravelas.* Lisbon: Publicações Dom Quixote, 1996.

Guevara, Ernesto Che. *Escritos y discursos.* 9 vols. Havana: Editorial de Ciencias Sociales, 1977.

—. *El diario del Che en Bolivia.* Edited by Adys Cupull and Froilán González. Havana: Editora Política, 1987.

—. *Pasajes de la guerra revolucionaria: Congo.* Edited by Aleyda March. Barcelona: Grijalbo, 1999.

Guimarães, Fernando Andresen. "Interviews with João Van Dunem." *Camões Center Quarterly* 5 (Winter 1993-94): 23-29.

—. *The Origins of the Angolan Civil War: Foreign Intervention and Domestic Political Conflict.* New York: St. Martin's Press, 1998.

Gunn, Gillian. "Cuba and Mozambique: A History of Cordial Disagreement." In *Cuban Internationalism in Sub-Saharan Africa,* edited by Sergio Díaz-Briquets, pp. 78-101. Pittsburgh, Pa.: Duquesne University Press, 1989.

Gup, Ted. *The Book of Honor: Covert Lives and Classified Deaths at the CIA.* New York: Doubleday, 2000.

Hall, David. "Naval Diplomacy in West African Waters." In *Diplomacy of Power: Soviet Armed Forces as a Political Instrument,* edited by Stephen Kaplan, pp. 519-69. Washington, D.C.: Brookings, 1981.

Hallett, Robin. "The South African Intervention in Angola, 1975-76." *African Affairs* (Oxford) 77 (July 1978): 347-86.

Halperin, Maurice. *The Rise and Decline of Fidel Castro: An Essay in Contemporary History.* Berkeley: University of California Press, 1972.

—. *The Taming of Fidel Castro.* Berkeley: University of California Press, 1981.

Harshe, Rajen. "Non-Alignement and Francophone Africa: A Case Study of Guinea." *Non-aligned World* (New Delhi), July-September 1983, pp. 371-85.

Heard, Tony. *The Cape of Storms: A Personal History of the Crisis in South Africa.* Johannesburg: Ravan Press, 1991.

Heikal, Mohamed Hassanein. *The Cairo Documents.* Garden City, N.Y.: Doubleday, 1973.

Heimer, Franz-Wilhelm. "Décolonisation et legitimité politique en Angola." *Revue française d'études politiques africaines* (Paris), June 1976, pp. 48-72.

—. *Der Entkolonisierungskonflikt in Angola.* Munich: Weltforum Verlag, 1979.

—. *The Decolonization Conflict in Angola, 1974-76: An Essay in Political Sociology.* Geneva: Institut Universitaire de Hautes Etudes Internationales, 1979.

Heinz, G., and H. Donnay. *Lumumba, Patrice: les cinquante derniers jours de sa vie.* Brussels: CRISP, 1966.

Heitman, Helmoed-Römer. *South African War Machine.* Novato, Calif.: Presidio, 1985.

Henriksen, Thomas. *Revolution and Counterrevolution: Mozambique's War of Inde-pendence, 1964-1974.* Westport, Conn.: Greenwood, 1983.

Hermann, Hamlet. *Caracoles: la guerrilla de Caamaño.* Santo Domingo, D.R.: Editorial Alfa y Omega, 1980.

—. *Francis Caamaño.* Santo Domingo, D.R.: Editorial Alfa y Omega, 1983.

Hernández de Zayas, Leonor del Carmen. "Sobre la vida de un revolucionario: el comandante Angelito." Museo Nacional de Lucha contra Bandidos, Trinidad (Cuba), n.d. Unpublished manuscript.

Hersh, Seymour. *The Price of Power: Kissinger in the Nixon White House.* New York: Summit Books, 1983.

—. *The Dark Side of Camelot.* Boston: Little, Brown, 1997.

Hershberg, James. "Before `The Missiles of October': Did Kennedy Plan a Military Strike against Cuba?" *Diplomatic History* 14 (Spring 1990): 163-98.

—. "New East-Bloc Evidence on the Cold War in the Third World and the Collapse of Détente in the 1970s." Cold War International History Project *Bulletin,* nos. 8-9 (Winter 1996-97): 1, 4.

—. "Their Men in Havana: Anglo-American Intelligence Exchanges and the Cuban Crises, 1961-62." In *American-British-Canadian Intelligence Relations, 1939-2000,* edited by David Stafford and Rhodri Jeffreys-Jones, pp. 121-76. London: Frank Cass, 2000.

—. "`The Best Laid Plans Go Awry': U.S.-(Cuban)-Brazilian Relations and the Cuban Crisis, 1960-1962." Unpublished manuscript.

Hinjari, Wilberforce. "A Comparative Study of Nigeria's Perception of the Soviet Union and the United States's Intervention in African States." Ph.D. diss., University of Pittsburgh, 1985.

Hoare, Mike. *Congo Mercenary.* London: Robert Hale, 1967.

—. "Congo Mercs' Masterpiece." *Soldier of Fortune,* June 1989, pp. 70-73, 79-80.

Holt, Pat. "Oral History." Washington, D.C.: U.S. Senate Historical Office, 1980.

Horne, Alistair. *Harold Macmillan.* Vol. 2: *1957-1986.* New York: Viking, 1989.

Horne, Gerald. *From the Barrel of a Gun: The United States and the War against Zimbabwe, 1965-1980.* Chapel Hill: University of North Carolina Press, 2001.

Howard, Lisa. "Castro's Overture." *War/Peace Report,* September 1963, pp. 3-5.

Hoyt, Michael. *Captive in the Congo: A Consul's Return to the Heart of Darkness.* Annapolis: Naval Institute Press, 2000.

Hyland, William. *Mortal Rivals: Superpower Relations from Nixon to Reagan.* New York: Random House, 1987.

Ibrahima, Bah. "Relaciones Guinea-Cuba." M.A. thesis, Instituto Superior de Relaciones Internacionales, Havana, 1991.

Institut für Zeitgeschichte, ed. (on behalf of the German Foreign Ministry). *Akten zur Auswärtigen*

Politik der Bundesrepublik Deutschland, 1963-65. Munich: R. Oldenbourg Verlag, 1994-96.

Instituto de Historia del Movimiento Comunista y de la Revolución Socialista de Cuba. *Cuba y la defensa de la República Española (1936-1939)*. Havana: Editora Política, 1981.

Isaacson, Walter. *Kissinger: A Biography*. New York: Simon and Schuster, 1992.

James, Martin. *A Political History of the Civil War in Angola, 1974-1990*. New Brunswick, N.J.: Transaction Publishers, 1992.

Jika [Gilberto Teixeira da Silva]. *Reflexões sobre a luta de libertação nacional*. Luanda: União dos escritores Angolanos, 1979.

Jiménez Rodríguez, Limbania. *Heroínas de Angola*. Havana: Editorial de Ciencias Sociales, 1985.

Johnson, Cecil. *Communist China and Latin America, 1959-1967*. New York: Columbia University Press, 1967.

Joseph, Richard. *Radical Nationalism in Cameroun: Social Origins of the U.P.C. Rebellion*. Oxford: Clarendon Press, 1977.

Júnior, Paulo. *Lembranças da vida*. Luanda: INALD, 1998.

Kahin, Audrey, and George Kahin. *Subversion as Foreign Policy: The Secret Eisenhower and Dulles Debacle in Indonesia*. New York: New Press, 1995.

Kalb, Madeleine. *The Congo Cables: The Cold War in Africa–from Eisenhower to Kennedy*. New York: Macmillan, 1982.

Kalflèche, Jean-Marc. *Jonas Savimbi: une autre voie pour l'Afrique*. Paris: Éditions Criterion, 1992.

Kalfon, Pierre. *Che: Ernesto Guevara, une légende du siècle*. Paris: Seuil, 1997.

Kapu<ac>sci<ac>nski, Ryszard. *Another Day of Life*. New York: Harcourt Brace Jovanovich, 1987.

Karol, K. S. *Guerrillas in Power: The Course of the Cuban Revolution*. New York: Hill and Wang, 1970.

Kelly, Sean. *America's Tyrant: The CIA and Mobutu of Zaire*. Washington, D.C.: American University Press, 1993.

Kempton, Daniel. *Soviet Strategy toward Southern Africa: The National Liberation Movement Connection*. New York: Praeger, 1989.

Kestergat, Jean. *Congo Congo*. Paris: La Table Ronde, 1965.

Kiluanji, César Augusto. *Trajectória da vida de um guerrilheiro*. Lisbon: Colecção Resistência, 1990.

Kirk, John, and Peter McKenna. *Canada-Cuba Relations: The Other Good Neighbor Policy*. Gainesville: University Press of Florida, 1997.

Kissinger, Henry. *White House Years*. Boston: Little, Brown, 1979.

—. *Years of Upheaval*. Boston: Little, Brown, 1982.

—. *Years of Renewal*. New York: Simon and Schuster, 1999.

Kissita, Achille. *Congo: trois décennies pour une démocratie introuvable*. Brazzaville: Les Editions S.E.D., 1993.

Klinghoffer, Arthur Jay. *The Angolan War: A Study in Soviet Policy in the Third World*. Boulder, Colo.: Westview, 1980.

Kornbluh, Peter. "JFK and Castro: The Secret Quest for Accommodation." *Cigar Aficionado*, September-October 1999, pp. 86-105.

—, ed. *Bay of Pigs Declassified: The Secret CIA Report on the Invasion of Cuba*. New York: New Press, 1988.

Kornbluh, Peter, and James Blight. "Dialogue with Castro: A Hidden History." *New York Review of Books*, October 6, 1994, pp. 45-49.

Krenn, Michael. *Black Diplomacy: African Americans and the State Department, 1945-1969*. Armonk, N.Y.: M. E. Sharpe. 1999.

Krop, Pascal. *Les secrets de l'espionnage français de 1870 à nos jours*. Paris: Jean Claude Lattès, 1993.

Lake, Anthony. *The "Tar Baby" Option: American Policy toward Southern Rhodesia*. New York: Columbia University Press, 1976.

Lamberg, Robert. *Die Guerilla in Lateinamerika: Theorie und Praxis eines revolutionären Modells*. Munich: Deutscher Taschenbuch Verlag, 1972.

Lambie, George. "Western Europe and Cuba in the 1970s: The Boom Years." In *The Fractured Blockade: West-European-Cuban Relations during the Revolution*, edited by Alistair Hennessy and George Lambie, pp. 276-311. London: Macmillan, 1993.

Lang, Nicolas. "Les Cubains en Afrique Noire." *Est et Ouest* (Paris), no. 385 (June 1, 1967): 21-24.

Lara, Jesús. *Guerrillero Inti*. La Paz: Los Amigos del Libro, 1971.

Lara, Lúcio, and Ruth Lara. *Um amplo movimento . . . Itinerário do MPLA através de documentos e anotações de Lúcio Lara. Vol. 1 (até fev. 1961)*. Luanda: private edition, 1998.

"La seule erreur de Ben Bella." *Jeune Afrique* (Paris), June 28, 1978, pp. 48-51.

Leacock, Ruth. *Requiem for Revolution: The United States and Brazil, 1961-1969*. Kent, Ohio: Kent State University Press, 1990.

Le Bailly, Jacques. *Une poignée de mercenaires*. Paris: Presses de la Cité, 1967.

Lechuga, Carlos. *En el ojo de la tormenta. F. Castro, N. Jruschov, J. F. Kennedy y la crisis de los misiles*. Havana: SI-MAR, 1995.

Ledda, Romano. *Una rivoluzione africana*. Bari: De Donato, 1970.

Legum, Colin. "A Letter on Angola to American Liberals." *New Republic*, January 31, 1976, pp. 15-19.

—. "The Soviet Union, China and the West in Southern Africa." *Foreign Affairs* 54 (July 1976): 745-62.

Legum, Colin, and Tony Hodges. *After Angola: The War over Southern Africa*. New York: Africana, 1976.

Leimgruber, Walter. *Kalter Krieg um Afrika: Die amerikanische Afrikapolitik unter Präsident Kennedy 1961-1963*. Stuttgart: Franz Steiner, 1990.

"L'enjeu économique international d'une décolonisation: le cas de l'Angola (II)." *Courrier hebdomadaire* (published by CRISP, Brussels), no. 671 (February 7, 1975): entire issue.

LeoGrande, William. *Cuba's Policy in Africa, 1959-1980*. Berkeley: Institute of International Studies, University of California, 1980.

—. "Evolution of the Nonaligned Movement." *Problems of Communism* 29 (January-February 1980): 35-52.

Lévesque, Jacques. *L'URSS et la révolution cubaine.* Montreal: Presses de l'Université de Montréal, 1976.

Liniger-Goumaz, Max. *La Guinée Équatoriale. Un pays méconnu.* Paris: L'Harmattan, 1980.

—. *Small Is Not Always Beautiful: The Story of Equatorial Guinea.* Totowa, N.J.: Barnes and Noble Books, 1989.

Lipinska, Suzanne. "Deux semaines dans les maquis de la Guinée Bissao." *Africasia* (Paris), May 25, 1970, pp. 10-14.

Lissouba, Pascal. *Congo: les fruits de la passion partagée.* Paris: Odilon Média, 1997.

Lofchie, Michael. "The Zanzibari Revolution: African Protest in a Racially Plural Society." In *Protest and Power in Black Africa,* edited by Robert Rotberg and Ali Mazrui, pp. 924-67. New York: Oxford University Press, 1970.

Loiseau, Yves, and Pierre-Guillaume de Roux. *Portrait d'un révolutionnaire en général: Jonas Savimbi.* Paris: La Table Ronde, 1987.

López, Andrea, et al., eds. *Mártires del MININT: semblanzas biográficas.* 2 vols. Havana: Editora Política, 1990.

López Blanch, Hedelberto. *Cuban Blessing in South-African Land: Medical Cooperation.* Havana: Editora Política, 1998.

Lunel, Pierre. *Bob Denard. Le roi de la fortune.* Paris: Édition 1, 1991.

Lynch, Grayston. *Decision for Disaster: Betrayal at the Bay of Pigs.* Dulles, Va.: Brassey's, 1998.

Mabeko Tali, Jean-Michel. "Le Congo et la question angolaise de 1963 à 1976." Institut d'Histoire, Université de Bordeaux III, 1987.

—. "Dissidences et pouvoir d'état: le MPLA face à lui-même (1962-1977)." Ph.D. diss., Université Paris VII, 1996.

—. *Dissidências e poder de estado: O MPLA perante si próprio (1962-1977).* 2 cols, Luanda: Nzila, 2001

MacQueen, Norrie. *The Decolonization of Portuguese Africa: Metropolitan Revolution and the Dissolution of Empire.* London: Longman, 1997.

Mann, James. *About Face: A History of America's Curious Relationship with China, from Nixon to Clinton.* New York: Knof, 1999

McCulloch, Jock. *In the Twilight of Revolution: The Political Theory of Amilcar Cabral.* London: Routledge and Kegan Paul, 1983.

McNamara, Robert, with Brian VanDeMark. *In Retrospect: The Tragedy and Lessons of Vietnam.* New York: Times Books, 1995.

Magalhães, José Calvet de. "Portugal e os Estados Unidos–relações no domínio da defesa." *Estratégia* (Lisbon), no. 3 (Spring 1987): 13-51.

Maganga-Boumba. *Le Congo et l'OUA.* Paris: L'Harmattan, 1989.

Mahoney, Richard. *JFK: Ordeal in Africa.* New York: Oxford University Press, 1983.

Maia, Salgueiro. *Capitão de abril. Histórias da guerra do ultramar e do 25 de Abril.* Lisbon: Editorial Notícias, 1994.

Malcolm X, with Alex Haley. *The Autobiography of Malcolm X.* New York: Ballantine, 1973.

Mallin, Jay, and Robert Brown. *Merc: American Soldier of Fortune.* New York: New American Library, 1979.

Mañon, Melvin. *Operación Estrella: con Caamaño, la Resistencia y la inteligencia cubana.* Santo Domingo, D.R.: Ediciones de Taller, 1989.

Marchetti, Victor, and John Marks. *The CIA and the Cult of Intelligence.* New York: Knopf, 1974.

Marcum, John. *The Angolan Revolution.* Vol. 1: *The Anatomy of an Explosion (1950-1962).* Cambridge, Mass.: MIT Press, 1969.

—. *The Angolan Revolution.* Vol. 2: *Exile Politics and Guerrilla Warfare (1962-1976).* Cambridge, Mass.: MIT Press, 1978.

Marenches, Alexandre de, with Christine Ockrent. *The Evil Empire: The Third World War Now.* London: Sidgwick and Jackson, 1988.

Marion, Pierre. *La Mission Impossible. A la tête des Services Secrets.* France: Calmann-Lévy, 1991.

Martens, Ludo. *Pierre Mulele ou la seconde vie de Lumumba.* Anvers: Editions EPO, 1985.

Martí, José. *Epistolario.* 5 vols. Havana: Editorial de Ciencias Sociales, 1993.

Martin, David, and Phyllis Johnson. *The Struggle for Zimbabwe: The Chimurenga War.* London: Faber and Faber, 1981.

Martin, Phyllis. "The Cabinda Connection: An Historical Perspective." *African Affairs* 76 (January 1977): 47-59.

Masetti, Jorge. *La loi des corsaires: itinéraire d'un enfant de la révolution cubaine.* Paris: Stock, 1993.

Masetti, Jorge Ricardo. *Los que luchan y los que lloran.* Buenos Aires: Editorial Freeland, 1958.

Maxwell, Kenneth. "The Legacy of Decolonization." edited by Richard Bloomfield, pp. 7-39. Algonac, Mich.: Reference Publications, 1988.

—. *The Making of Portuguese Democracy.* New York: Cambridge University Press, 1995.

—, ed. *The Press and the Rebirth of Iberian Democracy.* Westport, Conn.: Greenwood, 1983.

May, Ernest, and Philip Zelikow. *The Kennedy Tapes: Inside the White House during the Cuban Missile Crisis.* Cambridge, Mass.: Harvard University Press, 1997.

Melo, João de, ed. *Os Anos da Guerra 1961-75: Os Portugueses em África.* 2 vols. Lisbon: Dom Quixote, 1988.

Mendez, Guadalupe. "Fausto Gómez: Un hombre leyenda." *Punto de Mira* (Miami) 1 (August 1989): 46-47.

Menéndez Tomassevich, Raúl and Garciga Blanco, José Angel, *Escarmientos de pueblo.* "Patria Africana." Unpublished manuscript. Havana: Editorial de Ciencias Sociales, 2001.

Mercado, Rogger. *Las guerrillas del Perú. El MIR: De la prédica ideológica a la acción armada.* Lima: Fondo de Cultura Popular, 1967.

Mercier Vega, Luis. *Las guerrillas en América Latina: La técnica del contra-Estado.* Buenos Aires: Editorial Paidos, 1969.

Merle, Robert. *Ahmed Ben Bella.* Paris: Gallimard, 1965.

Mesa-Lago, Carmelo. *Cuba in the 1970s: Pragmatism and Institutionalization.* Rev. ed. Albuquerque: University of New Mexico Press, 1979.

———. *The Economy of Socialist Cuba: A Two-Decade Appraisal.* Albuquerque: University of New Mexico Press, 1981.

———, ed. *Revolutionary Change in Cuba.* Pittsburgh: University of Pittsburgh Press, 1971.

Mesa-Lago, Carmelo, and June Belkin, eds. *Cuba in Africa.* Pittsburgh: Center for Latin American Studies, University of Pittsburgh, 1982.

Messiant, Christine. "1961. L'Angola colonial, histoire et société. Les prémisses du mouvement nationaliste." Ph.D. diss., Ecole des Hautes Etudes en Sciences Sociales, Paris, 1983.

———. "Luanda (1945-1961): colonisés, société coloniale et engagement nationaliste." In *"Vilas" et "cidades." Bourgs et villes en Afrique Lusophone,* edited by Michel Cahen, pp. 125-99. Paris: L'Harmattan, 1989.

———. "Angola, les voies de l'ethnisation et de la décomposition," 2 parts. *Lusotopie* (Paris), nos. 1-2 (1994): 155-210; no. 3 (1995): 181-212.

———. "Angola: The Challenge of Statehood." In *History of Central Africa: The Contemporary Years since 1960,* edited by David Birmingham and Phyllis Martin, pp. 129-65. London: Longman, 1998.

———. "'Chez nous, même le passé est imprévisible.' L'expérience d'une recherche sur le nationalisme angolais, et particulièrement le MPLA: sources, critique, besoins actuels de la recherche." *Lusotopie* (Paris), 1998, pp. 157-97.

Metrowich, F. R. *South Africa's New Frontiers.* Sandton, South Africa: Valiant, 1977.

Metz, Steven. "The Anti-Apartheid Movement and the Formulation of American Policy toward South Africa, 1969-1981." Ph.D. diss., Johns Hopkins University, 1985.

Meyer, Cord. *Facing Reality: From World Federalism to the CIA.* Lanham, Md.: University Press of America, 1982.

Miller, Nicola. *Soviet Relations with Latin America, 1959-1987.* Cambridge: Cambridge University Press, 1989.

Minà, Gianni. *An Encounter with Fidel.* Melbourne: Ocean Press, 1991.

Minter, William, ed. *Operation Timber: Pages from the Savimbi Dossier.* Trenton, N.J.: Africa World Press, 1988.

Mitchell, Nancy. *The Danger of Dreams: German and American Imperialism in Latin America.* Chapel Hill: University of North Carolina Press, 1999.

———. "Pragmatic Moralist: Jimmy Carter and Rhodesia." Unpublished manuscript.

Mkandla, Strike. "The Thought of Amilcar Lopes Cabral of Guinea-Bissau: Revolution in an 'Underdeveloped' Country." Ph.D. diss., University of Kent at Canterbury, 1983.

Mockler, Anthony. *The Mercenaries.* New York: Macmillan, 1969.

Molina, Gabriel. *Jorge Ricardo Masetti, periodista y guerrillero.* Havana: n.p., 1968.

Mollin, Gerhard. *Die USA und der Kolonialismus: Amerika als Partner und Nachfolger der belgischen Macht in Afrika 1939-1965.* Berlin: Akademie Verlag, 1996.

Moniz Bandeira, Luiz Alberto. *De Martí a Fidel: A Revolução Cubana e a América Latina.* Rio de Janeiro: Civilização Brasileira, 1998.

Monnier, Laurent, comp. "L'Organisation de l'Unité Africaine. La conférence d'Accra." *Etudes Congolaises* (Leopoldville) 8 (November-December 1965): 57-84.

Montero, Enrique. "El legendario comandante Ramón." *Tricontinental* (Havana) 32 (July 1998): 59-60.

Moorcraft, Paul. *African Nemesis: War and Revolution in Southern Africa (1945-2010).* London: Brassey's, 1990.

Moore, Carlos. *Castro, the Blacks, and Africa.* Los Angeles: Center for Afro-American Studies, University of California, 1988.

Morley, Morris. *Imperial State and Revolution: The United States and Cuba, 1952-1986.* New York: Cambridge University Press, 1987.

Morris, Milton. "Black Americans and the Foreign Policy Process: The Case of Africa." *Western Political Quarterly* 25 (September 1972): 451-63.

Mortimer, Robert. "Foreign Policy and Its Role in Nation-Building in Algeria." Ph.D. diss., Columbia University, 1968.

Müller, Siegfried. *Les nouveaux mercenaires.* Paris: Editions France-Empire, 1965.

Namikas, Lise. "Battleground Africa: The Cold War and the Congo Crisis, 1960-1965." Ph.D. diss., University of Southern California, 2002.

Naranjo Orovio, Consuelo. *Cuba, otro escenario de lucha.* Madrid: Consejo Superior de Investigaciones Científicas, 1988.

Nazario, Olga. "Cuba's Relations with Africa in the Eighties: Scope and Limitations." In *Cuban Foreign Policy: The New Internationalism,* edited by Jaime Suchlicki and Damián Fernández, pp. 68-98. Miami: University of Miami, 1985.

Neto, Agostinho. *Sagrada esperança.* Lisbon: Sà da Costa, 1979.

Neto, Maria da Conceição. "Contribuições a um debate sobre 'as divisões étnicas' em Angola." *Cadernos do CODESRIA* (Luanda) 2 (1991): 16-34.

———. "Entre a tradição e a modernidade: os Ovimbundu do planalto central à luz da história." January 1994. Unpublished manuscript.

Ngouabi, Marien. *Vers la construction d'une société socialiste en Afrique. Ecrits et Discours.* Paris: Présence Africaine, 1974.

Niblock, Tim. "Aid and Foreign Policy in Tanzania, 1961-68." Ph.D. diss., University of Sussex, 1972.

Nicholson, Michael. *A Measure of Danger: Memoirs of a British War Correspondent.* New York: HarperCollins, 1991.

Nkouka-Menga, Jean-Marie. *Chronique politique congolaise. Du Mani-Kongo à la guerre civile.* Paris: L'Harmattan, 1997.

Noer, Thomas. *Cold War and Black Liberation: The United States and White Rule in Africa, 1948-1968.* Columbia: University of Missouri Press, 1985.

Nogueira, Franco. *Diálogos interditos.* 2 vols. Lisbon: Intervenção, 1979.

——. *História de Portugal: 1933-1974, II suplemento.* Oporto, Portugal: Civilização, 1981.

——. *Salazar: A Resistência (1958-1964).* Oporto, Portugal: Civilização, 1984.

——. *Salazar: O Último Combate (1964-1970).* Oporto, Portugal: Civilização, 1985.

——. *Um Político Confessa-se.* Oporto, Portugal: Civilização, 1986.

Nothomb, Patrick. *Dans Stanleyville.* Paris: Éditions Duculot, 1993.

Nuti, Leopoldo. "Missiles or Socialists? The Italian Policy of the Kennedy Administration." In *John F. Kennedy and Europe,* edited by Douglas Brinkley and Richard Griffiths, pp. 129-47. Baton Rouge: Louisiana State University Press, 1999.

O'Brien, Conor Cruise. *To Katanga and Back: A UN Case History.* New York: Simon and Schuster, 1962.

Odom, Thomas. *Dragon Operations: Hostage Rescues in the Congo, 1964-1965.* Fort Leavenworth: Combat Studies Institute, 1988.

"'Operação Madeira' tenta portugalizar a UNITA." *Expresso* (Lisbon), November 17, 1979, pp. 18-19; November 24, pp. 25-26; November 30, pp. 8-11.

Oramas Oliva, Oscar. *Amilcar Cabral: un précurseur de l'indépendance africaine.* Paris: Indigo, 1998.

Ortiz, Pepín. *Angola: un abril como Girón.* Havana: Ediciones Unión, 1983.

Ottaway, David, and Marina Ottaway. *Algeria: The Politics of a Socialist Revolution.* Berkeley: University of California Press, 1970.

Oudes, Bruce. "The Sacking of the Secretary." *Africa Report* 20 (January-February 1975): 17-19.

Ovalles, Alejandro. *Caamaño, el gobierno y las guerrillas.* Santo Domingo, D.R.: Taller de Impresiones, 1973.

Pabanel, Jean-Pierre. *Les coups d'état militaires en Afrique noire.* Paris: L'Harmattan, 1984.

Pachter, Elise. "Our Man in Kinshasa: U.S. Relations with Mobutu, 1970-1983." Ph.D. diss., Johns Hopkins University, 1987.

Parker, Phyllis. *Brazil and the Quiet Intervention, 1964.* Austin: University of Texas Press, 1979.

Pastor, Robert. *Condemned to Repetition: The United States and Nicaragua.* Princeton: Princeton University Press, 1987.

Paterson, Thomas. *Contesting Castro: The United States and the Triumph of the Cuban Revolution.* New York: Oxford University Press, 1994.

Pavlov, Yuri. *Soviet-Cuban Alliance: 1959-1991.* New Brunswick, N.J.: Transaction Publishers, 1994.

Péan, Pierre. *Affaires Africaines.* Paris: Fayard, 1983.

——. *L'homme de l'ombre: éléments d'enquête autour de Jacques Foccart.* Paris: Fayard, 1990.

"Pedro Peralta: a história de um processo." *Expresso* (Lisbon), September 14, 1974,pp. 5-6.

Pélissier, René. "Résistance et révoltes en Angola (1845-1961)." 3 vols. Ph.D. diss., Université de Paris I, 1975.

Pellicer de Brody, Olga. *México y la Revolución Cubana.* Mexico City: El Colegio de México, 1972.

Pepetela [Artur Pestana]. *Mayombe.* Luanda: União dos Escritores Angolanos, 1985.

Pérez, Louis. *Cuba and the United States: Ties of Singular Intimacy.* Athens: University of Georgia Press, 1990.

——. *The War of 1898: The United States and Cuba in History and Historiography.* Chapel Hill: University of North Carolina Press, 1998.

Perry, Bruce. *Malcolm: The Life of a Man Who Changed Black America.* Barrytown, N.Y.: Station Hill Press, 1991.

Pervillé, Guy. "L'insertion internationale du FLN algérien (1954-1962)." *Relations Internationales* (Paris), no. 31 (Fall 1982): 373-86.

Petterson, Don. *Revolution in Zanzibar: An American's Cold War Tale.* Boulder, Colo: Westview, 2002

"PIDE e SEDEC teriam elaborado as grandes linhas de acção." *Expresso* (Lisbon), January 24, 1976, pp. 14-15.

Piñeiro Losada, Manuel. "Mi modesto homenaje al Che." *Tricontinental* (Havana) 31 (July 1997): 14-23.

——. "Inmortalidad del Che." *Tricontinental* (Havana) 32, no. 38 (1997): 41-49.

——. *Barbarroja: Selección de testimonios y discursos del comandante Manuel Piñeiro Losada.* Edited by Luis Suárez Salazar. Havana: Editorial Tricontinental–Si-Mar, 1999.

Piñera, Arnaldo. *Utopía inconclusa del Che Guevara.* Buenos Aires: Cangrejal editores, 1997.

Pires, Pedro. "Os antigos chefes spinolistas mantiveram contactos com os conspiradores." *Expresso* (Lisbon), April 5, 1975, pp. 8-9.

Porra, Véronique. "L'Afrique du Che: Du mythe de Lumumba à la realité de la guérilla." In *Patrice Lumumba entre Dieu et diable: un héros africain dans ses images,* edited by Pierre Halen and János Riesz, pp. 277-94. Paris: L'Harmattan, 1997.

Porter, Bruce. *The USSR in Third World Conflicts: Soviet Arms and Diplomacy in Local Wars, 1945-1980.* New York: Cambridge University Press, 1984.

Portillo, Julio. *Venezuela-Cuba: 1902-1980.* Caracas: Portada Mateo, 1981.

[Portugal], Corpo das Tropas Pára-Quedistas. *História das Tropas Pára-Quedistas Portuguesas.* Vol. 4. Praia do Ribatejo: Corpo das Tropas Pára-Quedistas, 1987.

[Portugal], Estado-Maior do Exército. "O caso de Angola." *Cuadernos Militares* (Lisbon), no. 6 (1969): entire issue.

——. Comissão para o Estudo das Campanhas de África (1961-74). *Resenha Histórico-Militar das*

476 BIBLIOGRAPHY

Campanhas de Africa. Vol. 1. Lisbon: Estado-Maior do Exército, 1988.

Prieto, Alberto. *Guerrillas contemporáneas en América Latina.* Havana: Editorial de Ciencias Sociales, 1990.

Primer Congreso del Movimiento Popular de Liberación de Angola. Informe central: Agostinho Neto. Discursos: Raúl Castro. Havana: Editora Política, 1978.

Puren, Jerry, as told to Brian Pottinger. *Mercenary Commander.* Alberton, South Africa: Galago, 1986.

Quandt, William. *Revolution and Political Leadership: Algeria, 1954-1968.* Cambridge, Mass.: MIT Press, 1969.

——. *Peace Process: American Diplomacy and the Arab-Israeli Conflict since 1967.* Washington, D.C.: Brookings, 1993.

Quesada González, Pilar. *El MINFAR: Breves apuntes para su historia.* Havana: Centro de Estudios de Historia Militar, n.d.

Quirk, Robert. *Fidel Castro.* New York: Norton, 1993.

Rabe, Stephen. *Eisenhower and Latin America: The Foreign Policy of Anticommunism.* Chapel Hill: University of North Carolina Press, 1988.

——. *The Most Dangerous Area in the World: John F. Kennedy Confronts Communist Revolution in Latin America.* Chapel Hill: University of North Carolina Press, 1999.

Rahmani, Seghir. "Algerian-American Relations (1962-1985)." 2 vols. Ph.D. diss., Georgetown University, 1986.

Reed, David. *111 Days in Stanleyville.* New York: Harper and Row, 1965.

Rees, Mervyn, and Chris Day. *Muldergate.* Johannesburg: Macmillan, 1980.

Reitan, Ruth. *The Rise and Decline of an Alliance: Cuba and African American Leaders in the 1960s.* East Lansing: Michigan State University Press, 1999.

Republic of Nigeria. *A Time for Action.* Lagos: Federal Ministry of Information, 1976.

Republic of South Africa. *House of Assembly Debates,* January 23, 1976-June 16, 1978. Pretoria: Government Printer, 1976-78.

——. *Report of the Commission of Inquiry into the Riots at Soweto and Elsewhere from the 16th of June 1976 to the 28th of February 1977.* 2 vols. Pretoria: Government Printer, 1980.

Reyner, Anthony. "Morocco's International Boundaries: A Factual Background." *Journal of Modern African Studies* 1 (September 1963): 313-26.

Rikhye, Indar Jit. *Military Adviser to the Secretary-General: U.N. Peacekeeping and the Congo Crisis.* New York: St. Martin's Press, 1993.

Risquet Valdés, Jorge. *El segundo frente del Che en el Congo: Historia del batallón Patricio Lumumba.* Havana: Abril, 2000.

Rius, Hugo. *Angola: Crónicas de la esperanza y la victoria.* Havana: Editorial de Ciencias Sociales, 1982.

Rius, Hugo, and Ricardo Sáenz Padrón. *Caamaño.* Havana: Editorial de Ciencias Sociales, 1984.

Rivière, Claude. "La politique étrangère de la Guinée." *Revue française des études politiques africaines* (Paris), August 1971, pp. 37-68.

Robbins, Carla Anne. *The Cuban Threat.* New York: McGraw-Hill, 1983.

Rodman, Peter. *More Precious than Peace: The Cold War and the Struggle for the Third World.* New York: Scribner's, 1994.

Rodriguez, Felix, and John Weisman. *Shadow Warrior: The CIA Hero of a Hundred Unknown Battles.* New York: Simon and Schuster, 1989.

Rodríguez, Juan Carlos. *La Batalla inevitable: la más colosal operación de la CIA contra Fidel Castro.* Havana: Editorial Capitán San Luis, 1996.

Rodríguez Herrera, Mariano. *Ellos lucharon con el Che.* Havana: Editorial de Ciencias Sociales, 1982.

Roherty, James. *State Security in South Africa: Civil-Military Relations under PW Botha.* New York: Sharpe, 1992.

Roque, Fátima, et al. *Economia de Angola.* Venda Nova, Portugal: Bertrand Editora, 1991.

Rossi, Pierre-Pascal. *Pour une guerre oubliée.* Paris: Julliard, 1969.

Rowan, Carl. *Breaking Barriers: A Memoir.* Boston: Little, Brown, 1991.

Rudebeck, Lars. *Guinea-Bissau: A Study of Political Mobilization.* Uppsala: Scandinavian Institute of African Studies, 1974.

Rusk, Dean. "Oral History." Austin, Tex.: Lyndon B. Johnson Library, 1970.

Ryan, Henry. *The Fall of Che Guevara: A Story of Soldiers, Spies, and Diplomats.* New York: Oxford University Press, 1998.

Salisbury, Harrison. *Without Fear or Favor: The New York Times and Its Times.* New York: Ballantine, 1980.

Sánchez Cervelló, Josep. *A revolução portuguesa e a influência na transião espanhola (1961-1976).* Lisbon: Assírio and Alvim, 1993.

Savimbi, Jonas. *Angola: A resistência em busca de uma nova nação.* Lisbon: Edição da Agência Portuguesa de Revistas, 1979.

Scheman, Ronald, ed. *The Alliance for Progress: A Retrospective.* New York: Praeger, 1988.

Schlesinger, Arthur, Jr. *A Thousand Days: John F. Kennedy in the White House.* Boston: Houghton Mifflin, 1965.

——. *Robert Kennedy and His Times.* New York: Ballantine, 1979.

Schmidt, Hans. *The United States Occupation of Haiti, 1915-1934.* New Brunswick, N.J.: Rutgers University Press, 1971.

Schneidman, Witney. "American Foreign Policy and the Fall of the Portuguese Empire, 1961-1976." 2 vols. Ph.D. diss., University of Southern California, 1987.

Schoenbaum, Thomas. *Waging Peace and War: Dean Rusk in the Truman, Kennedy and Johnson Years.* New York: Simon and Schuster, 1988.

Schoultz, Lars. *Beneath the United States: A History of U.S. Policy toward Latin America.* Cambridge, Mass.: Harvard University Press, 1998.

Schramme, Jean. *Le Bataillon Léopard. Souvenirs d'un africain blanc.* Paris: Robert Laffont, 1969.

Schulzinger, Robert. *Henry Kissinger: Doctor of Diplomacy.* New York: Columbia University Press, 1989.

Schümer, Martin. *Die Wirtschaft Angolas 1973-1976: Ansätze einer Entwicklungsstrategie der MPLA-Regierung.* Hamburg: Institut für Afrika-Kunde, 1977.

Seegers, Annette. "Revolution in Africa: The Case of Zimbabwe (1965-1980)." Ph.D. diss., Loyola University of Chicago, 1983.

Sellström, Tor. *Sweden and National Liberation in Southern Africa.* 2 vols: *Formation of a Popular Opinion (1950-1970).* Uppsala: Nordiska Afrikainstitutet, 1999 and 2002.

——, ed. *Liberation in Southern Africa—Regional and Swedish Voices: Interviews from Angola, Mozambique, Namibia, South Africa, Zimbabwe, the Frontline and Sweden.* Uppsala: Nordiska Afrikainstitutet, 1999.

Serguera Riverí, Jorge. *Caminos del Che. Datos inéditos de su vida.* Mexico City: Plaza y Valdés, 1997.

Sesana, Renato. *Liberate il mio popolo. Diario di viaggio di un prete tra i guerriglieri della Guinea-Bissau.* Bologna: E.M.I., 1974.

Shearman, Peter. *The Soviet Union and Cuba.* London: Routledge and Kegan Paul, 1987.

Shepard, Robert. *Nigeria, Africa, and the United States: From Kennedy to Reagan.* Bloomington: Indiana University Press, 1991.

Shevchenko, Arkady. *Breaking with Moscow.* New York: Knopf, 1985.

Shore, Herbert. "Resistance and Revolution in the Life of Eduardo Mondlane." Preface in *The Struggle for Mozambique,* by Eduardo Mondlane, pp. xiii-xxxi. London: Zed Press, 1983.

Silva, António Duarte. *A independência da Guiné-Bissau e a descolonização portuguesa.* Oporto, Portugal: Afrontamento, 1997.

Silva Cunha, Joaquim Moreira da. *O Ultramar, a nação e o "25 de Abril."* Coimbra: Atlântida, 1977.

Sitkoff, Harvard. *The Struggle for Black Equality, 1954-1992.* Rev. ed. New York: Hill and Wang, 1993.

Sitte, Fritz. *Flug in die Angola-Hölle: der vergessene Krieg.* Graz: Verlag Styria, 1981.

Skinner, Elliott. "African, Afro-American, White American: A Case of Pride and Prejudice." *Freedomways* 5 (1965): 380-95.

Smith, Ian. *The Great Betrayal: The Memoirs of Ian Douglas Smith.* London: Blake, 1997.

Smith, Wayne. *The Closest of Enemies: A Personal and Diplomatic History of the Castro Years.* New York: Norton, 1987.

——. "The Cuban Role in Angola." In *Regional Conflict and U.S. Policy: Angola and Mozambique,* edited by Richard Bloomfield, pp. 120-34. Algonac, Mich.: Reference Publications, 1988.

Soggot, David. *Namibia: The Violent Heritage.* New York: St. Martin's Press, 1988.

Soremekun, Fola. *Angola: The Road to Independence.* Ibadan, Nigeria: University of Ife Press, 1983.

Soria Galvarro, Carlos, ed. *El Che en Bolivia: documentos y testimonios.* 3 vols. La Paz: CEDOIN, 1992-94.

Sotumbi, Abiodun Olufemi. *Nigeria's Recognition of the MPLA Government of Angola: A Case Study in Decision-Making and Implementation.* Lagos: Nigerian Institute of International Affairs, 1981.

Soudan, François. "Guerre secrète au Cabinda." *Jeune Afrique* (Paris), February 14, 1979, pp. 61-68.

Sousa, Valdemiro de. *Angola: A guerra e o crime.* Lisbon(?): Editorial Formação, 1976.

Spaak, Paul-Henri. *Combats Inachevés.* 2 vols. Paris: Fayard, 1969.

Spadafora, Hugo. *Experiencias y pensamiento de un médico guerrillero.* Panama City: Centro de Impresión Educativa, 1980.

Sparks, Allister. *The Mind of South Africa.* New York: Knopf, 1990.

Spies, F. J. du Toit. *Operasie Savannah. Angola 1975-1976.* Pretoria: S. A. Weermag, 1989.

Spikes, Daniel. *Angola and the Politics of Intervention: From Local Bush War to Chronic Crisis in Southern Africa.* Jefferson, N.C.: McFarland, 1993.

Spínola, António de. *País sem rumo. Contributo para a História de uma Revolução.* Lisbon: Scire, 1978.

Staniland, Martin. *American Intellectuals and African Nationalists, 1955-1970.* New Haven: Yale University Press, 1991.

Steenkamp, Willem. *South Africa's Border War, 1966-1989.* Gibraltar: Ashanti, 1989.

Stengers, Jean. "Precipitous Decolonization: The Case of the Belgian Congo." In *The Transfers of Power in Africa: Decolonization, 1940-1960,* edited by Prosser Gifford and Wm. Roger Louis, pp. 305-35. New Haven: Yale University Press, 1982.

Stiff, Peter. *The Silent War: South African Recce Operations 1969-1994.* Alberton, South Africa: Galago, 1999.

Stockwell, John. *In Search of Enemies: A CIA Story.* New York: Norton, 1978.

Stremlau, John. *The International Politics of the Nigerian Civil War, 1967-1970.* Princeton: Princeton University Press, 1977.

Szulc, Tad. "Lisbon and Washington: Behind the Portuguese Revolution." *Foreign Policy* 21 (Winter 1975-76): 3-62.

——. *Fidel: A Critical Portrait.* New York: Avon Books, 1987.

Taibo, Paco Ignacio, II. *El hombre de los lentes oscuros que mira el cielo se llama Domingos y se llama Raúl.* Havana: Editora Política, 1991.

——. *El año que estuvimos en ninguna parte.* Mexico City: Planeta, 1994.

——. *Ernesto Guevara, también conocido como el Che.* Mexico City: Planeta, 1996.

Tamarkin, M. *The Making of Zimbabwe: Decolonization in Regional and International Politics.* London: Frank Cass, 1990.

Theberge, James. *The Soviet Presence in Latin America.* New York: Crane, Russak, 1974.

Themido, João Hall. *Dez anos em Washington, 1971-1981: As verdades e os mitos nas relações luso-americanas.* Lisbon: Dom Quixote, 1995.

Thom, William. "Angola's 1975-76 Civil War." *Low Intensity Conflict and Law Enforcement* 7 (Autumn 1998): 1-44.

Thomas, Evan. *The Very Best Men: Four Who Dared.* New York: Simon and Schuster, 1995.

———. *Robert Kennedy: His Life.* New York: Simon and Schuster, 2000.

Thomas, Hugh. *Cuba: The Pursuit of Freedom.* New York: Harper and Row, 1971.

Timol, Razia, and Tutuzile Mazibuko. *Soweto: A People's Response.* Durban: Institute for Black Research, 1976.

Touval, Saadia. *The Boundary Politics of Independent Africa.* Cambridge, Mass.: Harvard University Press, 1972.

Trigo, Salvato, ed. *A voz igual: Ensaios sobre Agostinho Neto.* Oporto, Portugal: Fundação Eng. António de Almeida, 1989.

Trout, Frank. *Morocco's Saharan Frontiers.* Geneva: Droz, 1969.

Tutino, Saverio. *Guevara al tempo di Guevara.* Rome: Editori Riuniti, 1996.

Tyler, Patrick. *A Great Wall: Six Presidents and China.* New York: Public Affairs, 1999.

United Kingdom. *Parliamentary Debates, House of Commons.* 5th ser. Vols. 904-6. London, 1976.

Urquhart, Brian. *Ralph Bunche: An American Odyssey.* New York: Norton, 1993.

U.S. Congress. House. Committee on Foreign Affairs, Subcommittee on Africa. *Report on Portuguese Guinea and the Liberation Movement.* 91st Cong., 2d sess. Washington, D.C.: GPO, 1970.

———. *The Complex of United States-Portuguese Relations: Before and after the Coup.* 93d Cong., 2d sess. Washington, D.C.: GPO, 1974.

U.S. Congress. House. Committee on International Relations, Special Subcommittee on Investigations. *Mercenaries in Africa.* 94th Cong., 2d sess. Washington, D.C.: GPO, 1976.

U.S. Congress. House. Committee on International Relations, Subcommittee on International Resources, Food and Energy. *Disaster Assistance in Angola.* 94th Cong. Washington, D.C.: GPO, 1976.

U.S. Congress. House. Committee on International Relations. *United States Policy on Angola.* 94th Cong., 2d sess. Washington, D.C.: GPO, 1976.

U.S. Congress. House. Select Committee on Intelligence. *U.S. Intelligence Agencies and Activities: The Performance of the Intelligence Community.* Part 2. 94th Cong., 1st sess. Washington, D.C.: GPO, 1975.

U.S. Congress. Senate. Committee on Foreign Relations. *Executive Sessions of the Senate Foreign Relations Committee.* Historical Series, vol. 15. 88th Cong., 1st sess., 1963. Washington, D.C.: GPO, 1986.

———. *Cuba: A Staff Report.* 93d Cong., 2d sess. Washington, D.C.: GPO, 1974.

———. *Nomination of Nathaniel Davis to Be Assistant Secretary of State for African Affairs.* 94th Cong., 1st sess. Washington, D.C.: GPO, 1975.

U.S. Congress. Senate. Committee on Foreign Relations, Subcommittee on African Affairs. *Angola.* 94th Cong., 2d sess. Washington, D.C.: GPO, 1976.

———. *U.S. Policy toward Southern Africa.* 94th Cong., 1st sess. Washington, D.C.: GPO, 1975.

———. *U.S. Policy toward Africa.* 95th Cong., 2d sess. Washington, D.C.: GPO, 1978.

U.S. Congress. Senate. Committee on Foreign Relations, Subcommittee on African Affairs and Subcommittee on Foreign Assistance. *Security Supporting Assistance for Zaire.* 94th Cong., 1st sess. Washington, D.C.: GPO, 1975.

U.S. Congress. Senate. Select Committee to Study Governmental Operations with Respect to Intelligence Activities. *Alleged Assassination Plots Involving Foreign Leaders: An Interim Report.* 94th Cong., 1st sess. Washington, D.C.: GPO, 1975.

U.S. Congress. Senate. Staff Report of the Select Committee to Study Governmental Operations with Respect to Intelligence Activities. *Covert Action in Chile, 1963-1973.* Washington, D.C.: GPO, 1975.

U.S. Department of State. *Foreign Relations of the United States,* 1959-64. Washington, D.C.: GPO.

U.S. General Services Administration. *Public Papers of the Presidents of the United States: Dwight D. Eisenhower, 1953-1961.* 8 vols. Washington, D.C.: GPO, 1958-61.

———. *Public Papers of the Presidents of the United States: John F. Kennedy, 1961-1963.* 3 vols. Washington, D.C.: GPO, 1962-64.

Uys, Ian. *Bushman Soldiers: Their Alpha and Omega.* Germiston, South Africa: Fortress Publishers, 1993.

Valdés, Nelson. "Revolutionary Solidarity in Angola." In *Cuba in the World,* edited by Cole Blasier and Carmelo Mesa-Lago, pp. 87-117. Pittsburgh: University of Pittsburgh Press, 1979.

Valdés Vivó, Raúl. *Angola: fin del mito de los mercenarios.* Havana: Editorial de Ciencias Sociales, 1978.

Valdéz, Teresa. "Briones Montoto: Internacionalista." In *Varios Testimonios Policiales,* edited by Juan Carlos Fernández, pp. 144-56. Havana: Editorial Letras Cubanas, 1980.

Valenta, Jiri. "Soviet Decision-Making on the Intervention in Angola." In *Communism in Africa,* edited by David Albright, pp. 93-117. Bloomington: Indiana University Press, 1980.

Valimamad, E. D. "Nationalist Politics, War and Statehood: Guinea-Bissau, 1953-1973." Ph.D. diss., St. Catherine's College, Oxford, 1984.

Vandenbroucke, Lucien. *Perilous Options: Special Operations as an Instrument of U.S. Foreign Policy.* New York: Oxford University Press, 1993.

Van der Waals, Willem. "Angola 1961-1974: 'N Studie in Rewolusionêre Oorlog." Ph.D. diss., Oranje-Vrystaat, 1990.

———. *Portugal's War in Angola, 1961-1974.* Rivonia, South Africa: Ashanti, 1993.

Vandewalle, Frédéric. *L'Ommegang: Odyssée et Reconquête de Stanleyville 1964.* Brussels: F. Vandewalle–Le Livre Africain, 1970.

Vázquez-Viaña, Humberto, and Ramiro Aliaga Saravia. "Bolivia: ensayo de revolución continental." [Bolivia], 1970. Unpublished manuscript.

Venter, Al. *Portugal's Guerrilla War: The Campaign for Africa*. Cape Town: John Malherbe, 1973.

Verhaegen, Benoît. *Rébellions au Congo*. 2 vols. Brussels: CRISP, 1966 and 1969.

——. "L'Armée Nationale Congolaise." *Etudes Congolaises* (Leopoldville) 10 (September-October 1967): 1-29.

——. "La Première République (1960-1965)." In *Du Congo au Zaïre 1960-1980*, edited by Jacques Vanderlinden, pp. 111-37. Brussels: CRISP, 1984.

——. "Conditions politiques et participation sociale à la Rébellion dans l'Est du Zaïre." *Les Cahiers du CEDAF* (Brussels), nos. 7-8 (December 1986): 1-15.

——. "Les Simba au Soudan (1965-1970)." *Les Cahiers du CEDAF* (Brussels), nos. 7-8 (December 1986): 139-69.

Verhaegen, Benoît, and Jules Gérard-Libois. "Che Guevara dans les maquis de l'Est du Congo: Avril-Novembre 1965." Unpublished manuscript.

Vicente, Carmo. *Gadamael*. Lisbon: Edições Caso, 1985.

Vinicius, Marco, and Maria João Saldanha. *Jonas Savimbi: Um desafio à ditadura comunista em Angola*. Lisbon: Edições Armasilde, 1977.

Wagoner, Fred. *Dragon Rouge: The Rescue of Hostages in the Congo*. Washington, D.C.: National Defense University, 1980.

Washington, H. A., ed. *The Writings of Thomas Jefferson*. Vol. 5. Washington, D.C.: Taylor and Maury, 1853.

Wauthier, Claude. *Quatre présidents et l'Afrique. De Gaulle, Pompidou, Giscard d'Estaing, Mitterand*. Paris: Seuil, 1995.

Weinberg, Samantha. *Last of the Pirates: The Search for Bob Denard*. New York: Pantheon Books, 1994.

Weis, Michael. *Cold Warriors and Coups d'Etat: Brazilian-American Relations, 1945-1964*. Albuquerque: University of New Mexico, 1993.

Weiss, Herbert. "Pierre Mulele (1929-1968): La dernière victime des rébellions zairoises." In *Les Africains*, edited by Charles André Julien et al., pp. 161-89. Paris: Editions Jeune Afrique, 1977.

Weissman, Stephen. *American Foreign Policy in the Congo, 1960-1964*. Ithaca, N.Y.: Cornell University Press, 1974.

Welch, Richard. *Response to Revolution: The United States and the Cuban Revolution, 1959-1961*. Chapel Hill: University of North Carolina Press, 1985.

Westad, Odd Arne. "Moscow and the Angolan Crisis, 1974-1976: A New Pattern of Intervention." Cold War International History Project *Bulletin*, nos. 8-9 (Winter 1996-97): 21-37.

——, ed. "US-Soviet Relations and Soviet Foreign Policy toward the Middle East and Africa in the 1970s: Transcript from a Workshop at Lysebu, October 1-3, 1994." Oslo: Norwegian Nobel Institute, 1995.

Wettig, Gerhard. "Entspannungs-und Klassenpolitik. Das sowjetische Verhalten gegenüber Portugal."

Beiträge zur Konfliktforschung (Cologne), no. 1 (1976): 77-136.

Wheeler, Douglas, ed. *Historical Dictionary of Portugal*. Metuchen, N.J.: Scarecrow Press, 1993.

Wickham-Crowley, Timothy. *Guerrillas and Revolution in Latin America: A Comparative Study of Insurgents and Regimes since 1956*. Princeton: Princeton University Press, 1992.

Wild, Patricia Berko. "The Organization of African Unity and the Algerian-Moroccan Border Conflict." *International Organization* 20 (Winter 1966): 18-36.

Willame, Jean-Claude. *Patrice Lumumba. La crise congolaise revisitée*. Paris: Karthala, 1990.

Williams, Mennen. "Oral History." Boston, Mass.: John F. Kennedy Library, 1970.

Williams, Michael. "America and the First Congo Crisis, 1960-1963." Ph.D. diss., University of California at Irvine, 1991.

Wilson, Amrit. *United States Foreign Policy and the Creation of Tanzania*. London: Pluto Press, 1989.

Wolf, Markus. *Spionagechef in geheimen Krieg: Erinnerungen*. Munich: List Verlag, 1997.

Wolfers, Michael, and Jane Bergerol. *Angola in the Front Line*. London: Zed Press, 1983.

World Bank. *2001 World Development Indicators*. Washington, D.C.: World Bank, 2001.

Young, M. Crawford. "Rebellion and the Congo." In *Protest and Power in Black Africa*, edited by Robert I. Rotberg and Ali A. Mazrui, pp. 969-1011. New York: Oxford University Press, 1970.

Young, M. Crawford, and Thomas Turner. *The Rise and Decline of the Zairian State*. Madison: University of Wisconsin Press, 1985.

Zengo. *Tragédia "Bomboko."* Luanda: Execução Gráfica, 1998.

INDEX

Aaron, David, 356
Adams, John Quincy, 12-13
Adoula, Cyril, 62
Adzhubei, Alexei, 19
Afanasenko, Yevgeny, 270-71, 317-18, 366
Africa: decolonization of, 5-6. *See also* individual African countries
African Americans, 69, 131-32, 193, 364-65, 381-82
African National Congress (of South Africa), 346
Africa Today (Denver), 130
Afro-American (Baltimore), 132, 495 (n. 69)
Agate Island (Cuban ship), 333
Agramonte, Manuel, 89, 160
Aguirre, Severo, 369
Albert, Carl, 337
Alekseev, Aleksandr, 18, 54, 92, 155
Algeria, 30, 50-55, 92, 133, 349; and 1963 war with Morocco, 38-49. *See also* Ben Bella, Ahmed; Cuba
Allende, Salvador, 93, 221-22
Alliance for Progress, 16
Alsop, Joseph, 132
Álvarez, Julián, 166
Álvarez Cambras, Rodrigo, 166, 168, 170
Alvor agreement, 242, 263
Ameijeiras, Efigenio, 44-49, 410 (n. 82)
American Negro Leadership Conference on Africa, 129, 130
Amsterdam News (New York), 132
ANC (Zairean army), 62-64, 111, 124, 157-58
Anderson, Jon Lee, 102, 105
Andrés González Lines (Cuban ship), 44, 45, 409 (n. 72)
Angola, 233-36, 250-54, 257, 352. *See also* Cabinda; FNLA; MPLA; UNITA
Antunes, Ernesto Melo, 348, 349
Aracelio Iglesias (Cuban ship), 44, 45, 49
Aragonés, Emilio, 79, 104-5, 119, 120, 122, 139, 140, 143, 430 (n. 109)
Arbenz, Jacobo, 16
Argentina, 23, 28, 51, 93, 215, 221, 224, 225; and Operation Segundo Sombra, 52, 101
Artemio (Aurelio Ricard), 189-91
Asad, Hafez al-, 226
Assis, Mario Alberto de, 420 (n. 25)
Attwood, William, 23-25
Aurino (Francisco Torriente Acea), 436 (n. 24)
Azevedo, Luís de, 83
Azima (Jesús Ramón de Armas), 142
Azores, 195, 230-32, 368

Babu (Abdul Rahman Muhammad), 57
Badjoko, Charles, 64
Bakongo, 235, 238, 352, 492 (n. 22)
Bahía de Nipe (Cuban ship), 31
Bakhti, Nourredine, 51
Ball, George, 45, 60, 393; and Zaire, 63, 66-67, 74, 127, 129, 385n
Barbados, 307, 367-69

Barra do Dande, 349
Barroso Hipólito, Abel, 241
Batista, Fulgencio, 12
Batista, Reynaldo, 191
Bay of Pigs, 15
Bedeau, 46, 49
Belgium, 337, 488 (n. 43); and Zaire, 5-6, 61-63, 66-70, 75, 119, 127-28, 158
Ben Bella, Ahmed, 38-39, 41, 46-47, 52-53, 75, 85, 92, 134; and Cuba, 32-35, 41, 46, 50-52, 422 (n. 73)
Bendera, 115-16, 136
Benguela, 259, 303-4, 342
Benguela railroad, 237, 238
Benigno (Dariel Alarcón), 103, 144-47
Bergerol, Jane, 305
Bethencourt Rodrigues, José, 239
Biden, Joseph, 331-32, 361
Binder, David, 473 (n. 136)
Binh, 201
Bissell, Richard, 16
Black Muslims, 131
Blake, Robert, 134
Boende, 72
Boké, 201-3, 207
Bolivia, 93, 215-17, 220
Boma, 390
Bomboko, 182
Bonsal, Philip, 12
Bosque, 166
Botha, P. W., 298-99, 321, 324, 340-41, 345
Botha, Roelof (Pik), 299, 341
Botswana, 274
Boumedienne, Houari, 46, 48, 51, 53, 134
Bouteflika, Abdelaziz, 53
Bowdler, William, 299
Bravo, Flavio, 43, 46, 54, 254, 343, 409 (n. 62)
Brazil, 51, 93, 210-11, 334, 366, 495 (n. 77)
Breytenbach, Jan, 294-95, 300-304, 313-17, 320
Brezhnev, Leonid, 218, 225, 260, 307, 366, 371, 379
Bridgland, Fred, 235, 296-97, 321-22, 327
Briggs, Everett, 237, 278, 280, 281
Britain, 12, 30, 68, 133, 156, 210-11, 224, 230, 273, 373; and Angola, 293, 334-37, 343, 345, 478 (n. 102); and Zanzibar, 58-60
Brown, Dean, 191-92
Brzezinski, Zbigniew, 356, 392
Bulgaria, 203
Bukavu, 158
Bundy, McGeorge, 52, 58, 131, 140; and Cuba, 16, 17, 21, 24, 25
Burnham, Forbes, 368
Burundi, 133, 134
Byrd amendment, 277, 382, 390

Caamaño, Francisco, 221
Cabinda (enclave of), 175-78, 259, 261-64, 311-12, 320
Cabo San Braz, 268, 349
Cabral, Amílcar, 51, 185-86, 192-94, 201, 203, 210, 212, 213; and Cuba, 187-90, 196-99, 204, 208; and United States, 193-95
Cabral, Fidelis, 201
Cabral, Luís, 187, 189, 199-202, 210, 213, 393
Cadelo, Carlos, 245-49, 254-55, 257, 263

50; and decision to create military mission, 254-58; military instructors in, 259-61, 265-66, 269-72, 303, 349; and decision to send troops, 305-7; and battle of Quifangondo, 310-11; and battle of Cabinda, 311-12; and stopping South African invasion, 312-21, 324-25, 338-45; and airlift of troops, 333, 367-69; and impact of Cuban victory on southern Africa, 345-46, 390; and casualties, 380

—and Congo: and first contacts, 82, 84, 99; and 1965 dispatch of armed column, 160-63; and medical assistance and scholarships, 165-69, 442 (n. 28); and 1966 military uprising, 169-72; and decision to withdraw column, 172-74; and balance sheet of column's presence, 183-84; and relations during Angolan civil war, 264-65

—and Latin America, 93, 224-25; and armed struggle, 16, 21-23, 26, 28-29, 45, 50-52, 95, 99-100, 214-17, 220-22, 377, 403 (n. 27)

—and PAIGC: and decision to provide aid, 186-89; and military assistance, 190-91, 196-99, 210-11; and medical assistance, 199-203; balance sheet of Cuban presence in, 212-13

—and South Africa, 227, 390. *See also* Cuba—and Angola

—and United States, 12-14, 77-78, 95-99, 193, 219-20; and modus vivendi, 13-15, 21, 23-27, 224-25, 256, 378-79, 380

—and USSR, 265, 373-74, 391-93; early contacts between, 17-18; and Missile Crisis, 18-20; and relations in 1963-65, 28-29, 94-98; and relations in 1966-74, 217-20, 222-23, 225-26; on Africa, 79-80, 378; on Angola, 260, 307, 317-18, 333, 364-72, 379, 381; on Congo, 163, 168, 171, 174; on Guinea-Bissau, 212; on Zaire, 92-93, 121, 142, 155

—and volunteers, 228, 459 (n. 66); and Algeria, 35-38, 43-44, 48-50, 203, 206, 207; and Congo, 165-68, 203; and Guinea-Bissau, 189-90, 199-208, 212-13; and Zaire, 88-90, 108-9, 114-15, 119-20, 150-55, 203, 206

—and Zaire, 77-78, 83, 85-88, 98, 112, 122; and Cuban volunteers, 88-90, 108-9, 114-15, 119-20, 150-55, 203, 206; decision to send armed column, 90-99. *See also* Guevara, Ernesto

See also Castro, Fidel; Guevara, Ernesto

Cuban exiles, 15, 25; and Zaire, 63, 74, 97, 132, 134, 147, 158

Cunene dams, 342, 344. *See also* Calueque; Ruacana

Cutler, Walter, 288

Czechoslovakia, 165, 216, 220

Dahomey, 78

Daily Nation (Nairobi), 125n

Dangereux (Paulo da Silva Mungongo), 250, 466 (n. 22)

Daniel, Jean, 24-25

Dar-es-Salaam, 85, 107

Dash, Leon, 240-41

Davis, Nathaniel, 258, 268, 282, 284, 286, 353, 383; opposes covert operation in Angola, 290-92, 356-57, 359-63, 493 (n. 40)

De Borchgrave, Arnaud, 432 (n. 30)

Debray, Régis, 144, 216

De Gaulle, Charles, 5, 32, 81, 410 (n. 83)

Delfín, 438 (n. 51)

Delgado, Luis, 101

Del Valle, Sergio, 42

Dembos and Nambuangongo, 175, 178, 460 (n. 19)

Denard, Robert, 312, 334, 343

Deng Xiaoping, 331

Denmark, 212, 232, 343

DePree, Willard, 230-32

Devlin, Lawrence, 57, 126, 134-35, 136, 147, 157, 277

DGI (General Directorate of Intelligence), 23, 30, 45, 51, 99-100, 120, 216, 221, 406 (n. 7); and Guinea-Bissau, 190, 193, 203, 205-6; and Zaire, 89, 107, 109, 121, 155, 426 (n. 42)

Diário de Luanda, 300, 466 (n. 25)

Díaz Argüelles, Raúl: and creation of Cuban military mission in Angola, 248, 249, 254-57; heads military mission, 259-61, 264, 265-66, 269, 271, 303, 305, 314-17, 484 (n. 85)

Diggs, Charles, 131, 282, 361, 381, 432 (n. 39)

Dillon, Douglas, 69

Dobrynin, Anatoly, 260, 307, 330, 366, 371

Dominican Republic, 23, 28, 97, 221

Dondo, 314

Dorticós, Osvaldo, 50, 218

Dos Santos, Marcelino, 87, 227

Dreke, Víctor (Moya), 93, 430 (n. 109); and Guevara, 101, 105, 107-9, 123, 139, 143, 149; and Guinea-Bissau, 190-91, 194, 196-99, 204, 206; and Zaire, 88-90, 98, 111-12, 115, 117-18, 121, 136, 154

Dubcek, Alexander, 220

Dulac, René, 312

Dulles, Allen, 15

Dumois, Concepción (Conchita), 204, 206

Du Preez, Sophie, 276, 296, 300-302, 317, 321

Durch, William, 226

Eagleburger, Lawrence, 357, 493 (n. 40)

Easum, Donald, 231, 279, 280-82

Ebo, 316-17

Eduardo, Johnny, 257

Egypt, 30, 47, 49, 410 (n. 82); and Congo, 121, 133, 134, 142, 165, 172-73. *See also* Nasser, Gamal Abdel

Egyptian Gazette (Cairo), 125n

Eisenhower, Dwight, 6, 13-15, 16

Eisenhower administration, 12-15, 61. *See also* United States

Empson, Terry, 163

Entralgo, Armando, 160, 411 (n. 100)

Equatorial Guinea, 228

Eritrea, 227

Escalona, Juan, 368

Espinosa, Ramón, 261

Estrada, Ulises, 51, 52, 59, 99, 102, 122, 216, 438 (n. 51); and Guinea-Bissau, 190, 193, 204, 206

Ethiopia, 69, 238, 392

Expresso (Lisbon), 239, 466 (n. 25)

Fara, 438 (n. 65)

Felix Dzerzhinskii (Soviet ship), 163, 168

Fernández Mell, Oscar, 103, 149, 430 (n. 109); and Zaire, 119, 120, 121, 123, 139, 142, 143, 151, 438 (n. 68)

Fernández Padilla, Oscar, 121, 140-42, 149, 155-56, 438 (n. 51)

Ferrer, Colman, 87, 421 (n. 44); and Zaire, 91, 120, 122, 135-36, 148, 157, 437 (n. 33), 438 (n. 51)

Ferrer, Helenio, 168-69

Fizi-Baraka, 109-11

FLEC (Front for the Liberation of the Enclave of Cabinda), 262-64, 312

Flora (hurricane), 42

FNLA (National Front for the Liberation of Angola): and Angolan war of independence, 126, 175, 181, 235-39, 463 (n. 44); and civil war, 241-42, 250-54, 257-58, 262-63, 266-72, 301, 304, 308-11, 350-51; and defeat, 320, 338-40, 342; and South Africa, 275, 292, 295, 317

Foccart, Jacques, 163

Ford, Gerald: and Angola, 258, 282, 290, 293-94, 330, 337, 354; and China, 330-31; and 1976 elections, 362, 371, 390; and USSR, 365-66, 371

Ford administration: and détente, 387-90; and Rhodesia, 390

—and Angola, 258, 269, 281-85, 294, 330, 343, 350-51, 355, 356, 356; and U.S. Congress, 296, 330, 361-62; and decision to launch covert operation, 286-93; and mercenaries, 334-37; and Mobutu, 287-90, 312, 355, 479 (n. 109); and motivations and balance sheet, 353-62; and Portugal, 278, 283, 368; and response to arrival of Cuban troops, 329-38, 365, 367-69; and South Africa, 276, 291-92, 296-99, 304, 330, 337, 341, 345, 357-58; and USSR, 330, 361, 365-66, 371

Fourie, Brand, 297

Foxbat, 301, 316

France, 47, 188, 211, 224, 231, 373, 410 (n. 83), 453 (n. 126); and Angola, 293, 304, 312, 330, 334, 343, 345, 478 (n. 104); and Congo, 164-66, 172-73, 293; and Zaire, 67, 68, 133, 293

Franqui, Carlos, 102-3

Fredericks, Wayne, 58, 129, 385

Freedomways (New York), 433 (n. 433)

Frelimo, 85, 87, 119, 227, 233, 420 (n. 43)

Front de Force. *See* Bendera

Fugit, Edward, 236n, 278, 329

Fulbright, William, 382n

Gabela, 316

Gaddis, John Lewis, 20

Galarza, Armando, 189

Galindo, Fernando, 177, 183

Garba, Joe, 327

García, Calixto, 88

García, Guillermo, 123, 139

García Guitart, Luis, 411 (n. 100)

García Gutiérrez, Luis Carlos (Fisín), 216

García Márquez, Gabriel, 393

Garthoff, Raymond, 351, 365

Gato (Ciel da Conceição Cristóvão), 177, 182

Gelb, Leslie, 348, 363

Geldenhuys, Deon, 301, 341

German Democratic Republic, 60, 75, 164-65, 214, 219-20, 226, 349

Germany (Federal Republic of), 67, 164, 211, 230, 343, 373, 380, 422 (n. 77)

Ghana, 30, 92, 133, 134, 142

Giscard d'Estaing, Valéry, 333-34

Godley, McMurtrie, 63, 64, 66, 69, 76, 119, 125-26, 136, 157, 172; and mercenaries, 71-73, 124, 127-28

Goma, Silvain, 265

Gonçalves, Vasco, 261

Gonçalves Benedito, João, 182

González, Melquiades, 46

González, Roberto, 31

Goodwin, Richard, 15

Goulart, João, 93

Grafanil, 308

Greece, 211, 388

Greener, William, 332

Guatemala, 214, 217, 221

Guevara, Ernesto (Che), 24, 30, 37, 79, 87, 88, 91-92, 139, 227, 374; and armed struggle in Latin America, 22, 45, 51-52, 101-2, 118, 149, 214-17; and Fidel Castro, 18, 102-97, 122-23, 140, 215-17, 375, 455 (n. 13); and Nyerere, 108, 117, 156-57; and three-month trip in Africa, 77-88, 187, 212; and United States, 15, 77-78, 97; and USSR, 14, 17, 79-80, 102

—and Zaire, 77-78, 134-35; and decision to lead Cuban column, 85-88, 91-92, 101-7; and decision to enter Zaire incognito, 107-9; and Kabila, 88, 108, 112-15, 117-19, 156-57; and first weeks in Zaire, 109-16; at front of conflict, 118-19; and lack of communications with Havana, 120-22; and withdrawal, 137-44, 147-49; and Benigno, 144-47; and balance sheet, 149-55

Guiledje, 210-11

Guinea, 30, 99, 133, 134, 188, 208-9, 212; and Angola, 343, 344, 367

Guinea-Bissau, 185, 211, 343, 344, 367, 492 (n. 12). *See also* PAIGC

Gulf Oil, 262, 263, 312, 343, 483 (n. 61), 493 (n. 27)

Guyana, 368-69

Harper, Wally, 130

Harriman, Averell, 61, 63, 66-67, 69-70, 125, 127

Hassan II, 39-41, 47, 65

Hassi-Beida, 40-41

Hasslacher, Jakob, 164, 165, 172

Hawes, James, 134, 147

Hechavarría, Milton (Mariano Sixto), 202, 205, 207, 213

Heikal, Mohamed, 91-92

Heimer, Franz-Wilhelm, 251, 252, 253, 257, 272, 348

Heitman, Helmoed-Römer, 301

Helms, Jesse, 332, 337

Helms, Richard, 16

Henríquez, Miguel, 221

Hernández Angulo, Angel (Sitaini), 152, 425 (n. 30); 438 (nn. 43, 60)

Hernández Gattorno, René, 308, 316-17

Herter, Christian, 6

Hindi (Héctor Vera Acosta), 152-53

Hinton, Deane, 283, 287-89, 291

Hoare, Mike, 71, 73, 74n, 109-10, 128, 129, 339

Hodges, Tony, 251, 347-48

Hoffman, Sliman, 46

Holguín, 369